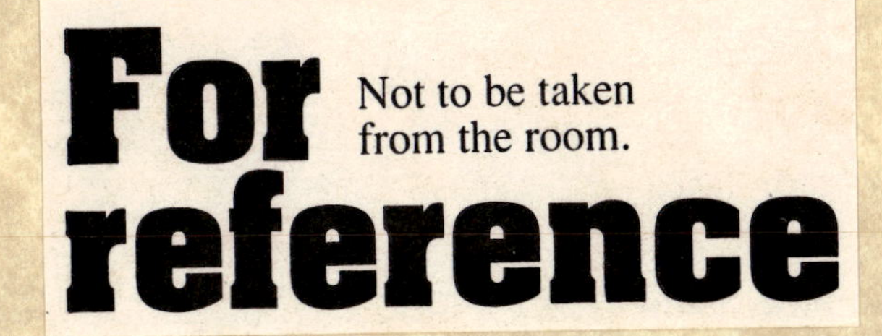
For
reference
Not to be taken
from the room.

D0212197

PS
Encycloped
American
literatu

ENCYCLOPEDIA OF AMERICAN LITERATURE

VOLUME II

THE AGE OF ROMANTICISM AND REALISM

1815–1914

ENCYCLOPEDIA OF AMERICAN LITERATURE

VOLUME II

THE AGE OF ROMANTICISM AND REALISM 1815–1914

Lisa Paddock

Facts On File, Inc.

Encyclopedia of American Literature, Volume II: The Age of Romanticism and Realism, 1815–1914

Facts On File, Inc.
132 West 31st Street
New York NY 10001

Library of Congress Cataloging-in-Publication Data

Encyclopedia of American literature.
p. cm.
Includes bibliographical references and indexes.
Contents: v. 1. The colonial and revolutionary era / Carol Ruth Berkin — v. 2. The age of romanticism and realism / Lisa Paddock — v. 3. The modern and post-modern period / Carl Rollyson.
ISBN 0-8160-4121-0 (set: acid-free paper)
1. American literature—Encyclopedias. I. Berkin, Carol. II. Paddock, Lisa Olson. III. Rollyson, Carl E. (Carl Edmund) IV. Facts on File, Inc.

PS21 .F33 2002
810'.3—dc21 2001040900

Facts On File books are available at special discounts when purchased in bulk quantities for businesses, associations, institutions, or sales promotions. Please call our Special Sales Department in New York at (212) 967-8800 or (800) 322-8755.

You can find Facts On File on the World Wide Web at http://www.factsonfile.com

Text design by Rachel L. Berlin
Cover illustration by Smart Graphics
Cover design by Cathy Rincon

Printed in the United States of America

VB FOF 10 9 8 7 6 5 4 3 2 1

This book is printed on acid-free paper.

Contents

Introduction

American literature from 1815 to 1914 divides fairly neatly in half, with the first half dominated by romanticism and the second by realism. Running down the middle of this 100-year period like a scar is the Civil War, the conflict that divided the nation. After four bloody years that killed more Americans than have died in all other American wars combined, the country was no longer young, and its optimism and idealism inevitably gave way to a darker mood. The period that followed ended with yet another war: World War I, also called the Great War and the War to End All Wars, and marks the point at which realism was replaced by the discontinuities of literary modernism.

Around the year 1815, at the close of America's second war with Britain, the War of 1812, American writers began to turn their attentions away from the external concerns of nationhood and train them inward—on the nation's psyche, as it were. The preoccupation of American literature during those years was discovering itself, discovering what was unique about this country and its people. In 1820 the English clergyman and critic Sydney Smith notoriously wrote, "In all the four quarters of the globe, who reads an American book?" Almost immediately, he had his answer. Washington Irving, in the East, would publish his hugely popular *The Sketch Book of Geoffrey Crayon* that same year, combining German romanticism and American folklore to create something altogether new. Three years later James Fenimore Cooper would publish *The Pioneers,* the first of his *Leather-Stocking Tales* series of novels and the first literary work to fire the world's imagination with the myth of the American frontier.

In the next generation of American writers, one novelist—writing about the other dominant novelist of the age—would be able to answer Smith's challenge with one of his own. In his fabled essay "Hawthorne and His Mosses" (1850), Herman Melville signaled both the achievement of his contemporary, Nathaniel Hawthorne, and the emergence of a new American literature with the remark, "The day will come when you shall say, who reads a book by an Englishman that is a modern?" The originality of these two fiction writers, Melville and Hawthorne, was also reflected in the works of the great poets of the time: Walt Whitman, with his self-referential and eternally renewed *Leaves of Grass* and Emily Dickinson, who transformed her quiet, circumscribed world into a stunningly individualistic vision of the whole of creation. Similarly, the two preeminent essayists of the day, Ralph Waldo Emerson and Henry David Thoreau, sought universal truths in the everyday particulars of their place and time.

Not all of these truths were happy ones, of course, and the grimmer aspects of American individualism are reflected nowhere more clearly than in the grotesque tales and menacingly mellifluous poetry of Edgar Allan Poe. Other, not unrelated explorations of the dark side of the American psyche were undertaken around this time by the anonymous authors of slave narratives. Frederick Douglass questioned the nature of freedom. Abolitionism became a national obsession—in no small part because of a novel, Harriet Beecher Stowe's *Uncle Tom's Cabin* (1852), the book that Abraham Lincoln half-jokingly claimed was responsible for the Civil War.

The most pronounced literary reaction to the carnage of the war and the economic exploitation that followed in its wake was the rise, around 1880, of the related literary movements that came to be known as realism and naturalism, both concerned with actualities rather than exceptions—a preoccupation naturalists amplified with their philosophy of determinism. It is not accidental that the first of these, realism, was largely a midwestern phenomenon, because the end of the Civil War coincided with the opening of the West to a flood of immigrants from the East. The de facto leader of this movement was the novelist and editor William Dean Howells, a native of Ohio who migrated to Boston and then to New York City but retained a midwesterner's suspicion of the kind of untrammeled capitalism practiced in the urban Northeast in the great age of industrialization. This period was dubbed the Gilded Age by Samuel Clemens (Mark Twain), himself the author of one of the undisputed masterpieces of American literary realism, *The Adventures of Huckleberry Finn* (1884–85), in which morality was seen to triumph over convention in a narrative that is partly a childhood idyl and partly a desperate search for individual liberty. It would be one of the last serious novels of the 19th century to consider the sunnier aspect of American life.

With its emphasis on slavery, *Huck Finn* is nonetheless a work written as a response to the Civil War. The next great novel to take the war as its subject would come from the pen of an author whose aim was to investigate war itself. Stephen Crane's *The Red Badge of Courage* (1895), with its ambiguous morality, is customarily considered one of the high-water marks of naturalism, but in fact it lacks the sense of inevitability that is a hallmark of the genre. The protagonists of works such as Frank Norris's *McTeague* (1899) and Theodore Dreiser's *Sister Carrie* (1900) lose control over their own fates and become victims of an uncaring, even brutal, society that is the product of industrialism and urbanization.

An optimistic, alternative vision of American life was still available to readers in escapist "dime novels" and the sentimental inspirations churned out by Horatio Alger. Owen Wister's best-selling western *The Virginian* (1902) managed to bridge the gap between determinism and heroism by recreating the myth of the frontier. For many, though, the gap between the old world of self-determination and the chaotic new one seemed unbridgeable. For them the pessimistic vision of the new century offered up in *The Education of Henry Adams* (1907) was unavoidable: In a world ruled by anarchy, history had no real meaning.

This volume provides entries devoted not only to individual authors and literary works but also to the historical events, persons, and places that put them in context. Readers will be able, for example, to investigate the post–Civil War period by looking to entries on the Gilded Age, Reconstruction, and Ulysses S. Grant, as well as others about the "carpetbagger" novelist Albion W. Tourgée; the author of the first novel published by an African American, Harriet E. Wilson; and the infamously racist novel *The Clansman* (1905). Because this volume covers an era in which many if not most creative writers were also journalists, a significant number of entries have been devoted to newspapers and other periodicals, from the highly influential *Atlantic Monthly* to the highly voguish gift book phenomenon. Entries on major characters such as Hester Prynne of *The Scarlet Letter* (1850) find counterparts in entries devoted to personages such as Davy Crockett, "characters" such as "Buffalo Bill" Cody, and legends such as Mike Fink. An extensive system of cross-referencing refers readers to related subjects, and definitions of literary movements, genres, and terms, as well as a chronology of the period, all provide a background for the century of literary history covered in this volume.

CHRONOLOGY 1815–1914

1815
Battle of New Orleans, final battle of the War of 1812

Philip Freneau, *Poems*
Richard Henry Dana Jr. (1815–82)
North American Review (1815–39) founded

1816
Second Bank of the United States founded

Parke Godwin (1816–1904)

1817
James Monroe administration (1817–25) begins
First Seminole War (1817–18)
University of Michigan founded

William Cullen Bryant, "Thanatopsis"
John Neal, *Keep Cool*
Henry David Thoreau (1817–62)

1818
49th Parallel established as northern boundary to Rocky Mountains
Lucy Stone (1818–93)
William Cullen Bryant, "To a Waterfowl"
John Howard Payne, *Brutus*

1819
The United States purchases Florida
University of Virginia founded

Washington Irving, *The Sketch Book* (1819–20)
Fitz-Greene Halleck, "Croaker Papers"
James Russell Lowell (1819–1891)
Herman Melville (1819–1891)
Walt Whitman (1819–1892)

1820
Missouri Compromise temporarily maintains balance between slaveholding and nonslaveholding states

Susan B. Anthony (1820–1906)
William Tecumseh Sherman, general (1820–1891)
James Fenimore Cooper, *Precaution*
Dion Boucicault (1820–90)

1821
Sante Fe Trail established
James Longstreet, Confederate general (1821–1904)
Mary Baker Eddy (1821–1910)
Jay Cooke, financier (1821–1905)
Clara Barton, founder of American Red Cross (1821–1912)

James Fenimore Cooper, *The Spy*
William Cullen Bryant, *Poems*
James Gates Percival, *Poems*
Frances Wright, *Views of Society and Manners in America*
Saturday Evening Post (1821–1969) founded

1822
Ulysses S. Grant (1822–85)
Rutherford B. Hayes, 19th U.S. president (1822–93)

Washington Irving, *Bracebridge Hall*
John Neal, *Logan*
Fitz-Greene Halleck, "Ainwick Castle"
E. E. Hale (1822–1909)

1823
Monroe Doctrine designates the Americas as U.S. sphere of influence

James Fenimore Cooper, *The Pioneers* and *The Pilot*
James Kirke Paulding, *Koningsmarke*
John Neal, *Seventy-Six*
New York Mirror (1823–60) founded
G. H. Boker (1823–90)

1824
"Stonewall" Jackson, Confederate general (1824–63)

Washington Irving, *Tales of a Traveller*
John Howard Payne, *Charles the Second*
John Neal, "American Writers" (1824–25)
Springfield Republican (1824–) founded
G. W. Curtis (1824–92)

1825
John Quincy Adams administration (1825–29) begins
Erie Canal opened
Rutgers College founded

Fitz-Greene Halleck, "Marco Bozzaris"
Daniel Webster, Bunker Hill oration
William Cullen Bryant, "A Forest"
R. H. Stoddard (1825–1903)
Bayard Taylor (1825–78)

1826
American Society for Promotion of Temperance founded
Stephen Foster, composer (1826–64)

James Fenimore Cooper, *Last of the Mohicans*
John Howard Payne, *Richelieu*
Timothy Flint, *Recollections of the Last Ten Years*
Graham's Magazine (1826–58) founded
J. W. De Forest (1826–1906)

1827
New York State abolishes slavery

Edgar Allan Poe, *Tamerlane and Other Poems*
James Fenimore Cooper, *The Prairie*
Catharine Maria Sedgwick, *Hope Leslie*
William Gilmore Simms (1806–70)

1828
President Adams signs "Tariff of Abominations," raising taxes on many imports
John C. Calhoun, *South Carolina Exposition and Protest,* argues that any state can nullify federal laws

Nathaniel Hawthorne, *Fanshawe*
Noah Webster, *American Dictionary of the English Language*
James Fenimore Cooper, *Red Rover*
Washington Irving, *Columbus*

1829
Andrew Jackson administration (1829–37) begins
David Walker's Appeal published, urging slaves to revolt
Roscoe Conkling, Republican politician (1829–88)
Carl Schurz (1829–1906)

Edgar Allan Poe, *Al Aaraaf*
Washington Irving, *Conquest of Granada*
James Fenimore Cooper, *Wept of Wish-ton-Wish*
Silas Weir Mitchell (1829–1914)
Charles Dudley Warner (1829–1900)

1830
James G. Blaine, Republican politician (1830–93)
Mormon Church founded

Oliver Wendell Holmes, "Ironsides"
James Kirke Paulding, *Lion of the West*
Book of Mormon
Joseph Emerson Worcester, *Dictionary*
Seba Smith, *Jack Downing Letters*
Sara Josepha Hale, "Mary Had a Little Lamb"
Godey's Lady's Book founded (1830–98)
Boston *Daily Evening Transcript* (1831–1941) founded
John Esten Cooke (1830–86)
Emily Dickinson (1830–86)
Paul Hamilton Hayne (1830–86)

1831
Nat Turner's Southampton, Virginia, slave revolt
New England Anti-Slavery Society founded

Edgar Allan Poe, *Poems*
Robert Montgomery Bird, *The Gladiator*
John Greenleaf Whittier, *Legends of New England*
James Kirke Paulding, *Dutchman's Fireside*
Liberator (1831–65) founded
Rebecca Harding Davis (1831–1910)

1832
President Jackson vetoes bill renewing charter of the Bank of the United States
South Carolina state convention declares tariffs of 1818 and 1832 nullified
President Jackson vows to collect national tariffs by force if necessary

William Cullen Bryant, *Poems*
John Pendleton Kennedy, *Swallow Barn*
Robert Montgomery Bird, *Oralloossa*
Washington Irving, *The Alhambra*
Fanny Trollope, *Domestic Manners of the Americans*
Nathaniel Hawthorne, "Roger Malvin's Burial"
Louisa May Alcott (1832–88)
H. H. Bancroft (1832–1918)

1833
American Anti-Slavery Society founded
Haverford College founded
Oberlin College founded
Benjamin Harrison (1833–1901)
R. G. Ingersoll, orator and lecturer (1833–99)
J. E. B. Stuart, Confederate cavalry commander (1833–64)

Henry Wadsworth Longfellow, *Outre-Mer*
William Gilmore Simms, *Martin Faber*
John Neal, *The Down-Easters*
Edgar Allan Poe, "MS. Found in a Bottle"
Knickerbocker Magazine (1833–65) founded
New York *Sun* (1833–1966) founded
Parley's Magazine (1833–41) founded

1834
Whig Party established
McCormick reaper invented
James McNeil Whistler, painter (1834–1903)
James Fisk, financier (1834–72)

Life of David Crockett
William Gilmore Simms, *Guy Rivers*
George Bancroft, *History of the United States* (1834–76)
Southern Literary Messenger (1834–64) founded
Frank Stockton (1834–1902)
Horatio Alger (1834–99)

1835
Second Seminole War (1835–42)
Andrew Carnegie, industrialist and philanthropist (1835–1919)
John La Farge, painter (1835–1910)

Augustus Baldwin Longstreet, *Georgia Scenes*
William Gilmore Simms, *The Yemassee* and *The Partisan*
Nathaniel Hawthorne, "Young Goodman Brown"
Washington Irving, *Tour on the Prairies*
Edgar Allan Poe, "Berenice" and "Morella"
Robert Montgomery Bird, *The Hawks of Hawk-Hollow*
John Pendleton Kennedy, *Horse-shoe Robinson*
The Crockett Almanacs, an anonymous series, enlarges the myth of Davy Crockett before and after his death (1835–56)
New York *Herald* (1835–1966) founded
Western Messenger (1835–41) founded
Samuel Langhorne Clemens (Mark Twain) (1835–1910)

1836
Texas established as a republic (1836–45)
Battle of the Alamo marks the turning point of Texas's revolt against Mexican colonization
Colt revolver manufactured
Mount Holyoke Seminary (first U.S. women's college) founded
Jay Gould, speculator (1836–1892)
Winslow Homer, painter (1836–1910)

Ralph Waldo Emerson, *Nature*
Oliver Wendell Holmes, *Poems*
William Holmes McGuffey, *Eclectic Readers* (1836–57)
Transcendental Club (1836–44) founded
Thomas Bailey Aldrich (1836–1907)
Bret Harte (1836–1902)

1837
Martin Van Buren administration (1837–41) begins
First great U.S. depression
Grover Cleveland (1837–1908)
Mark Hanna, capitalist and politician (1837–1904)
J. P. Morgan, financier (1837–1913)
Joaquin Miller (1841–1913)

Nathaniel Hawthorne, *Twice-Told Tales*
Ralph Waldo Emerson, *The American Scholar*
Henry Charles Carey, *Principles of Political Economy*
Nathaniel Parker Willis, *Bianca Visconti*
Robert Montgomery Bird, *Nick of the Woods*
William Hickling Prescott, *Ferdinand and Isabella*
James Fenimore Cooper, *Gleanings in Europe* (1837–38)
Baltimore *Sun* (1837–) founded
New Orleans Picayune (1837–) founded
United States Magazine and Democratic Review (1837–49) founded
Burton's Gentleman's Magazine (1837–40) founded
John Burroughs (1837–1921)
William Dean Howells (1837–1920)
Edward Eggleston (1837–1902)

1838
Underground Railroad established
Joshua Giddings (1795–1864), first abolitionist seated in Congress

Ralph Waldo Emerson, "Divinity School Address"
James Fenimore Cooper, *American Democrat*
John Pendleton Kennedy, *Rob of the Bowl*
John Greenleaf Whittier, *Ballads and Anti-Slavery Poems*
Harriet Martineau, *Retrospect of Western Travel*
John Neal, *Charcoal Sketches*
Alexis de Tocqueville, *Democracy in America*
Edgar Allan Poe, "Silence" and "Ligeia" and *Narrative of Arthur Gordon Pym*
Henry Adams (1838–1918)
John Hay (1838–1905)
John Muir (1838–1914)
Francis Hopkinson Smith (1838–1915)
Albion Tourgée (1838–1905)

1839
Slave revolt on the *Amistad*
John D. Rockefeller, petroleum magnate and philanthropist (1839–1937)

Henry Wadsworth Longfellow, *Hyperion* and *Voices of the Night*
Jones Very, *Essays and Poems*
Nathaniel Parker Willis, *Tortesa*
Caroline Kirkland, *A New Home*
Edgar Allan Poe, *Tales of the Grotesque and Arabesque*
Mortimer Neal Thompson, *The Green Mountain Boys*
Henry George (1839–1897)

1840
Thomas Nast (1840–1902)

Richard Henry Dana, *Two Years Before the Mast*
James Fenimore Cooper, *The Pathfinder*
Bronson Alcott, "Orphic Sayings"
William Gilmore Simms, *Border Beagles*
The Dial (1840–44)

1841
William Henry Harrison administration (1841) begins
John Tyler administration (1841–45) begins
Brook Farm (1841–47) founded

Ralph Waldo Emerson, *Essays, First Series*
James Fenimore Cooper, *The Deerslayer*
James Russell Lowell, *A Year's Life*
Thomas Bangs Thorpe, "Big Bear of Arkansas"
Edgar Allan Poe, "The Murders in the Rue Morgue"
Henry Wadsworth Longfellow, *Ballads and Other Poems*
New-York Tribune (1841–1966) founded

1842
Amana Community founded
Fruitlands (1842–43) founded
Hopedale (1842–56) founded
Barnum's American Museum established

Nathaniel Hawthorne, *Twice-Told Tales* (expanded)
William Gilmore Simms, *Beauchampe*
Charles Dickens, *American Notes*
John Greenleaf Whittier, "Massachusetts to Virginia"
James Fenimore Cooper, *Wing-and-Wing*
Edgar Allan Poe, "Eleonora" and "Masque of the Red Death"
Sidney Lanier (1842–81)
William James (1842–1910)
Bronson Howard (1842–1908)
Ambrose Bierce (1842–1914?)

1843
William McKinley (1843–1901)

William Hickling Prescott, *Conquest of Mexico*
Daniel Webster, Second Bunker Hill oration
Mortimer Neal Thompson, *Major Jones's Courtship*
Edgar Allan Poe, "The Gold Bug" and "The Black Cat"
Henry James (1843–1916)

1844
Samuel Morse exhibits telegraph
Bethel Community (1844–80) founded
Thomas Eakins, painter and photographer (1844–1916)
Anthony Comstock, morality crusader (1844–1915)

Ralph Waldo Emerson, *Essays, Second Series*
James Fenimore Cooper, *Afloat and Ashore*
John Greenleaf Whittier, *Voices of Freedom*
Richard Penn Smith, *The Drunkard*
Charles Dickens, *Martin Chuzzlewit*
Littell's Living Age (1844–1941) founded
Orestes Brownson's *Quarterly Review* (1844–75) founded
George Washington Cable (1844–1925)

1845
James K. Polk administration (1845–49) begins
Texas annexed to United States
U.S. Naval Academy founded
Elihu Root, politician and diplomat (1845–1937)

Edgar Allan Poe, *The Raven and Other Poems* and "The Literati"
Anna Cora Mowatt, *Fashion*
Life of Frederick Douglass
Margaret Fuller, *Woman in the Nineteenth Century*
James Fenimore Cooper, *Satanstoe*
Broadway Journal (1845–46) founded
Harbinger (1845–49) founded

1846
U.S.-Mexican War (1846–48)
United States acquires Oregon
Wilmot Proviso, contentious "Free Soil" congressional proposal attempting to bar slavery from any U.S. territory acquired during the Mexican War
Donner Party, snowbound wagon train remembered for its resort to cannibalism
Smithsonian Institution established
Carry Nation (1846–1911), temperance crusader
W. F. "Buffalo Bill" Cody (1846–1917)

Herman Melville, *Typee*
Nathaniel Hawthorne, *Mosses from an Old Manse*
Oliver Wendell Holmes, *Poems*
Ralph Waldo Emerson, *Poems*
Edgar Allan Poe, "The Cask of Amontillado" and "The Philosophy of Composition"

1847
Free Soil Party (1847–54) founded
Mormons settle in Utah

Thomas Edison, inventor (1847–1931)
Jesse James (1847–82)
Alexander Graham Bell, inventor (1847–1922)

Henry Wadsworth Longfellow, *Evangeline*
Herman Melville, *Omoo*
William Hickling Prescott, *Conquest of Peru*
James Kirke Paulding, *The Bucktails*
Union Magazine (1847–52) founded

1848

Oneida Community (1848–79) founded
College of the City of New York founded
University of Wisconsin founded
Seneca Falls woman suffrage convention

James Russell Lowell, *Biglow Papers* and *Fable for Critics* and *Vision of Sir Launfal*
Edgar Allan Poe, *Eureka*
The Independent (1848–1928) founded
H. H. Boyesen (1848–95)
Joel Chandler Harris (1848–1908)

1849

Zachary Taylor administration (1849–50) begins
California gold rush begins
Astor Place Riot, deadly brawl between theater patrons seen as a dispute between democracy and Anglomania
Luther Burbank, botanist (1849–1926)

Francis Parkman, *Oregon Trail*
Herman Melville, *Mardi* and *Redburn*
Henry Wadsworth Longfellow, *Kavanagh*
Henry David Thoreau, *A Week on the Concord and Merrimack* and "Civil Disobedience"
John Greenleaf Whittier, *Margaret Smith's Journal*
James Kirke Paulding, *The Puritan and His Daughter*
Edgar Allan Poe, "Annabel Lee," "The Bells," and "Eldorado"
Sarah Orne Jewett (1849–1909)
James Lane Allen (1849–1925)
James Whitcomb Riley (1849–1916)

1850

Millard Fillmore administration (1850–53) begins
Fugitive Slave Law authorizes seizure of escaped slaves in northern states
Compromise of 1850 allows new states to decide their own status regarding slavery
Samuel Gompers (1850–1924), labor leader
Henry Cabot Lodge (1850–1924), long-term senator

Nathaniel Hawthorne, *The Scarlet Letter*
Bayard Taylor, *Eldorado*
S. Weir Mitchell, *Reveries of a Bachelor*
Herman Melville, *White-Jacket*
Ralph Waldo Emerson, *Representative Men*
John Greenleaf Whittier, "Ichabod," *Songs of Labor*
John Calhoun, "Fourth of March" speech
Daniel Webster, "Seventh of March" speech
Edward Bellamy (1850–98)
Eugene Field (1850–1902)
Lafcadio Hearn (1850–1904)

1851

Northwestern University founded
Maine passes Prohibition law

Herman Melville, *Moby-Dick*
Francis Parkman, *Conspiracy of Pontiac*
William Gilmore Simms, *Katharine Walton*
Nathaniel Hawthorne, *The Snow-Image* and *The House of the Seven Gables*
S. Weir Mitchell, *Dream Life*
Stephen Foster, "Old Folks at Home"
Lewis Henry Morgan, *League of the Ho-dé-no-sau-nee*
Henry Rowe Schoolcraft, first volume of *Indian Tribes* (1851–57)
Kate Chopin (1851–1904)

1852

American Women's Education Association founded

Harriet Beecher Stowe, *Uncle Tom's Cabin*
Nathaniel Hawthorne, *The Blithedale Romance*
Herman Melville, *Pierre*
Mary Wilkins Freeman (1852–1930)

1853

Franklin Pierce administration (1853–57) begins
Gadsden Purchase of land from Mexico for southern transcontinental railroad
Commodore Matthew Perry's voyage to Japan
Railroad between New York and Chicago established
Antioch College founded

Joseph Glover Baldwin, *Flush Times in Alabama and Mississippi*
George William Curtis, *Potiphar Papers*
William Gilmore Simms, *The Sword and the Distaff*
Putnam's Monthly Magazine (1853–1910) founded
E. W. Howe (1853–1937)
Thomas Nelson Page (1853–1922)

1854

Trade treaty with Japan
Ostend Manifesto proposes U.S. acquisition of Cuba by force
Kansas-Nebraska Act divides western Indian lands into slave- and nonslave-holding territories

Henry David Thoreau, *Walden*
Philip Pendleton Cooke, *Leather Stocking and Silk* and *The Virginia Comedians*

Herman Melville, "The Encantadas"
T. B. Thorpe, *Hive of the Bee Hunter*
Francis Marion Crawford (1854–1909)

1855

Massachusetts ends racial segregation in schools
Proslavery legislature elected in Kansas territory
Eugene Debs (1855–1926), socialist leader
Robert La Follette (1855–1925), political reformer

Walt Whitman, *Leaves of Grass*
Henry Wadsworth Longfellow, *Hiawatha*
Herman Melville, "Benito Cereno"
William Gilmore Simms, *The Forayers*
John Bartlett, *Familiar Quotations*
George Henry Boker, *Francesca da Rimini*
Mortimer Neal Thomson, *Doesticks*
Evert Duyckinck, *Cyclopaedia of American Literature*
Washington Irving, *Life of Washington* (1855–59)
Saturday Club of Boston (1855–) founded
New York Ledger (1855–1903) founded
David Belasco (1855?–1931)
H. C. Bunner (1855–96)
Josiah Royce (1855–1916)
Edgar Saltus (1855?–1921)
George Woodberry (1855–1930)

1856

Know-Nothing movement established
Republican Party organized
Woodrow Wilson (1856–1924)
Louis Brandeis (1856–1941), jurist
John Singer Sargent (1856–1925), painter
Louis H. Sullivan (1856–1924), architect

Harriet Beecher Stowe, *Dred*
John Lothrop Motley, *Rise of the Dutch Republic*
William Gilmore Simms, *Eutaw*
Ralph Waldo Emerson, *English Traits*
George William Curtis, *Prue and I*
Mortimer Neal Thomson, *Pluribus-tah*
Sabin's Dictionary
First U.S. copyright law passed

1857

James Buchanan administration (1857–61) begins
Dred Scott decision declares slaves are not citizens
First Otis elevator
Clarence Darrow (1857–1938)
William Howard Taft (1857–1930)

Dion Boucicault, *The Poor of New York*
Atlantic Monthly (1857–) founded
Harper's Weekly (1857–1916) founded
Gertrude Atherton (1857–1948)
H. B. Fuller (1857–1929)
Thorstein Veblen (1857–1919)

1858

Lincoln-Douglas debates
First transatlantic cable
Theodore Roosevelt (1858–1919)

Henry Wadsworth Longfellow, *Courtship of Miles Standish*
Oliver Wendell Holmes, *Autocrat of the Breakfast Table*
Bayard Taylor, *Our American Authors* (1858–71)
Charles Waddell Chesnutt (1858–1932)

1859

John Brown's raid on Harpers Ferry
First commercial production of oil
Cooper Union (New York City) founded

Harriet Beecher Stowe, *The Minister's Wooing*
Dion Boucicault, *The Octoroon*
William Gilmore Simms, *The Cassique of Kiawah*
"Dixie"
Vanity Fair (1859–63) founded
John Dewey (1859–1952)

1860

Pony Express established (1860–61)
South Carolina secedes from the Union
William Jennings Bryan (1860–1925)
John Pershing (1860–1948)

Nathaniel Hawthorne, *The Marble Faun*
Oliver Wendell Holmes, *Professor at the Breakfast-Table*
Henry Timrod, *Poems*
Ralph Waldo Emerson, *Conduct of Life*
Dion Boucicault, *The Colleen Bawn*
John Greenleaf Whittier, *Home Ballads*
Frederick Goddard Tuckerman, *Poems*
Hamlin Garland (1860–1940)

1861

Abraham Lincoln administration (1861–65) begins
Mississippi, Florida, Alabama, Georgia, Louisiana, Texas, Virginia, Tennessee, Arkansas, and North Carolina secede from the Union
Jefferson Davis becomes president of the Confederate States of America
Confederates attack Fort Sumter
First Battle of Bull Run
Gatling machine gun invented
Vassar College founded

Oliver Wendell Holmes, *Elsie Venner*
Henry Timrod, "Ethnogenesis"
Henry Wadsworth Longfellow, "Paul Revere's Ride"

1862

Robert E. Lee is put in command of the Confederate army
Monitor vs. *Merrimac,* first engagement of ironclad ships

Battles of Shiloh, Antietam, second Bull Run, siege of Vicksburg (1862–63)
Homestead Act transfers ownership of public lands to private individuals
Charles Evans Hughes (1862–1948), jurist and politician

Julia Ward Howe, "Battle Hymn of the Republic"
Rebecca Harding Davis, *Margaret Howth*
Harriet Beecher Stowe, *The Pearl of Orr's Island*
Edith Wharton (1862–1937)
William Sidney Porter ("O. Henry") (1862–1910)

1863

Battles of Chancellorsville, Gettysburg, and Chattanooga
Emancipation Proclamation
Henry Ford (1863–1947), automotive pioneer
William Randolph Hearst (1863–1951)
George Santayana (1863–1952), philosopher

Henry Wadsworth Longfellow, *Tales of a Wayside Inn*
Abraham Lincoln, "Gettysburg Address"
Henry David Thoreau, *Excursions*
Nathaniel Hawthorne, *Our Old Home*
Edward Everett Hale, "The Man Without a Country"

1864

Maximilian governs in Mexico (1864–67)
Ulysses S. Grant takes command of Union army
Sherman marches to the sea
Battle of the Wilderness, Spotsylvania, and Mobile Bay
First Pullman car
Alfred Stieglitz (1864–1946), photographer

George Henry Boker, *Poems of the War*
David Ross Locke, *The Nasby Papers*
Richard H. Davis (1864–1910)
Richard Hovey (1864–1900)
Paul Elmer More (1864–1937)

1865

Robert E. Lee surrenders at Appomattox and ends Civil War
Abraham Lincoln assassinated
Andrew Johnson administration (1865–69) begins
Thirteenth Amendment outlaws slavery
Molly Maguires organized (1865–67)
Ku Klux Klan first organized
Cornell University founded
Warren Harding (1865–1923)

Walt Whitman, *Drum-Taps*
Samuel Clemens (Mark Twain), "The Celebrated Jumping Frog of Calaveras County"
Henry David Thoreau, *Cape Cod*
Francis Parkman, *Pioneers of France in the New World*
The Nation (1865–) founded
Irving Babbitt (1865–1933)

1866

Congress passes Civil Rights Act
Second trans-Atlantic cable
Massachusetts elects the first two African Americans to serve in a legislative assembly

John Greenleaf Whittier, *Snow-Bound*
William Dean Howells, *Venetian Life*
New York World (1866–1931) founded
The Galaxy (1866–78) founded
George Ade (1866–1944)
Lincoln Steffens (1866–1936)

1867

National Ku Klux Klan organized
Reconstruction Act passed by Congress
United States purchases Alaska
Granger movement pits farmers against railroads
Howard University founded
J. P. Morgan Jr. (1867–1943)

Bret Harte, *Condensed Novels*
George Washington Harris, *Sut Lovingood Yarns*
John William De Forest, *Miss Ravenel's Conversion*
Henry Wadsworth Longfellow, translation of the *Divine Comedy*
Francis Parkman, *The Jesuits in North America*
Henry Timrod, "Ode"
John Greenleaf Whittier, *The Tent on the Beach*
James Russell Lowell, *Biglow Papers* (second series)
Ralph Waldo Emerson, *May-Day and Other Poems*
Radical Club (1867–75) founded
David Graham Phillips (1867–1911)

1868

Andrew Johnson impeached and acquitted
President Johnson grants amnesty to Confederates
Fourteenth Amendment grants citizenship to former slaves

Bret Harte, "The Luck of Roaring Camp"
Elizabeth Ward, *The Gates Ajar*
Oliver Wendell Holmes, *The Guardian Angel*
Bronson Alcott, *Tablets*
Louisa May Alcott, *Little Women* (1868–69)
Lippincott's Magazine (1868–1916) founded
Overland Monthly (1868–1933) founded
Vanity Fair (1868–1936) founded
Mary Austin (1868–1934)
W. E. B. Du Bois (1868–1963)
Robert Herrick (1868–1938)
William Allen White (1868–1944)
Edgar Lee Masters (1868–1950)

1869

Ulysses S. Grant administration (1869–1877) begins

Fifteenth Amendment guarantees the right to vote
Knights of Labor organized
Prohibition Party organized
Union Pacific Railroad completed
Frank Lloyd Wright (1869–1959), architect

Samuel Clemens (Mark Twain), *Innocents Abroad*
Harriet Beecher Stowe, *Oldtown Folks*
Bret Harte, "Tennessee's Partner" and "Outcasts of Poker Flat"
Francis Parkman, *La Salle*
Thomas Bailey Aldrich, *Story of a Bad Boy*
James Russell Lowell, "The Cathedral"
Appleton's Journal (1869–81) founded
William Vaughn Moody (1869–1910)
Edwin Arlington Robinson (1869–1935)
George Sterling (1869–1926)
Booth Tarkington (1869–1946)

1870

Standard Oil Company established
Benjamin Cardozo (1870–1938), jurist

Bret Harte, "Plain Language from Truthful James"
Ralph Waldo Emerson, *Society and Solitude*
Bronson Howard, *Saratoga*
William Cullen Bryant, translation of the *Iliad*
Scribner's Monthly (1870–81) founded
Frank Norris (1870–1902)

1871

Chicago fire
Smith College founded
P. T. Barnum opens circus

Henry James, "A Passionate Pilgrim"
John Burroughs, *Wake-Robin*
Bret Harte, *East and West Poems*
Edward Eggleston, *Hoosier Schoolmaster*
James Russell Lowell, *My Study Windows*
Joaquin Miller, *Songs of the Sierras*
William Dean Howells, *Their Wedding Journey*
Walt Whitman, *Democratic Vistas* and *Passage to India*
William Cullen Bryant, translation of the *Odyssey* (1871–72)
Winston Churchill (1871–1947)
Stephen Crane (1871–1900)
Theodore Dreiser (1871–1945)

1872

Yellowstone National Park, first national park, is created
Calvin Coolidge (1872–1933)

Samuel Clemens (Mark Twain), *Roughing It*
Paul Hamilton Hayne, *Legends and Lyrics*
Stanley, Sir Herbert Morton, *How I Found Livingstone*
Clarence King, *Mountaineering in the Sierra Nevada*
Oliver Wendell Holmes, *Poet at the Breakfast Table*
Paul Laurence Dunbar (1872–1906)

1873

Financial panic
Nevada silver rush
Alfred E. Smith (1873–1944), politician

William Dean Howells, *A Chance Acquaintance*
Samuel Clemens and Charles Dudley Warner, *The Gilded Age*
Thomas Bailey Aldrich, "Marjorie Daw"
Henry Timrod, *The Cotton Boll*
The Delineator (1873–1937) founded
St. Nicholas (1873–1940) founded
Woman's Home Companion (1873–1957) founded
Anne D. Sedgwick (1873–1935)
Willa Cather (1873–1947)

1874

Women's Christian Temperance Union
Political cartoonist Thomas Nast first uses elephant to depict Republican Party
Herbert Hoover (1874–1964)

Edward Eggleston, *The Circuit Rider*
John Fiske, *Outlines of Cosmic Philosophy*
Ellen Glasgow (1874–1945)
Charles Beard (1874–1948)
Owen Davis (1874–1956)
Clarence Day (1874–1935)
Zona Gale (1874–1938)
Amy Lowell (1874–1925)
Gertrude Stein (1874–1946)
Robert Frost (1874–1963)

1875

Greenback Party organized
Brigham Young University founded
Arbor Day founded

Mary Baker Eddy, *Science and Health*
William Dean Howells, *A Foregone Conclusion*
Chicago Daily News (1875–1978) founded
Lambs Club (1875–) founded

1876

Bell Telephone founded
Barbed wire invented
Battle of Little Bighorn
Centennial Exposition in Philadelphia
Johns Hopkins University founded
University of Texas founded
Socialist-Labor Party organized
Samuel Tilden and Rutherford B. Hayes dispute presidential election

Samuel Clemens (Mark Twain), *Tom Sawyer*
Henry James, *Roderick Hudson*
Walt Whitman, *Leaves of Grass* (centennial edition)
Julia A. Moore, *Sweet Singer of Michigan*

Herman Melville, *Clarel*
Frank Leslie's Popular Monthly (1876–1906) founded
Sherwood Anderson (1876–1941)
Jack London (1876–1916)
Ole Rolvaag (1876–1931)

1877

Hayes administration (1877–1881) begins
End of Reconstruction
Chief Joseph's revolt
Railroad and coal strikes
Thomas Edison invents phonograph

Sarah Orne Jewett, *Deephaven*
Henry James, *The American*
Sydney Lanier, *Poems*
Lewis Henry Morgan, *Ancient Society*
John Burroughs, *Birds and Poets*
Francis Parkman, *Count Frontenac and New France under Louis XIV*
Puck (1877–1918) founded

1878

American Bar Association established
Arc light invented
Isadora Duncan (1878–1927)

Henry James, *Daisy Miller* and *The Europeans*
Edward Eggleston, *Roxy*
Sydney Lanier, "The Marshes of Glynn"
Upton Sinclair (1878–1968)
Carl Sandburg (1878–1967)

1879

Thomas Edison invents light bulb
First Madison Square Garden built
Chicago Art Institute founded
U.S. Supreme Court allows female attorneys to argue cases

Henry George, *Progress and Poverty*
George Washington Cable, *Old Creole Days*
Albion W. Tourgée, *A Fool's Errand*
John Burroughs, *Locusts and Wild Honey*
Frank R. Stockton, *Rudder Grange*
William Dean Howells, *Lady of the Aroostook*
James Branch Cabell (1879–1955)
Vachel Lindsay (1879–1931)
Dorothy Canfield Fisher (1879–1958)
Wallace Stevens (1879–1955)

1880

Bryn Mawr College founded

Henry Adams, *Democracy*
George Washington Cable, *The Grandissimes*
Thomas Bailey Aldrich, *Stillwater Tragedy*
Albion W. Tourgée, *Bricks Without Straw*
Samuel Clemens (Mark Twain), *A Tramp Abroad*
Percy MacKaye, *Hazel Kirke*
The Dial (1880–1929) founded

1881

James Garfield administration (1881) begins
President Garfield assassinated
Chester A. Arthur administration (1881–85) begins
American Federation of Labor established
Tuskegee Institute founded

Henry James, *Washington Square* and *The Portrait of a Lady*
Joel Chandler Harris, *Uncle Remus*
Century Association (1881–1930) established

1882

U.S. Exclusion Act bars Chinese immigration for 10 years
Knights of Columbus founded
Jesse James shot to death
Franklin Delano Roosevelt (1882–1945)
Felix Frankfurter (1882–1965), jurist

Samuel Clemens (Mark Twain), *Prince and the Pauper*
Frances Marion Crawford, *Mr. Isaacs*
Frank R. Stockton, "The Lady or the Tiger?"
Bronson Howard, *Young Mrs. Winthrop*
Walt Whitman, *Specimen Days and Collect*
William Dean Howells, *A Modern Instance*

1883

Civil Service Reform Act
Brooklyn Bridge completed
Maxim machine gun invented
Joseph Pulitzer buys the New York *World*
Metropolitan Opera founded in New York City

Samuel Clemens (Mark Twain), *Life on the Mississippi*
E. W. Howe, *Story of a Country Town*
James Whitcomb Riley, *Old Swimmin'-Hole*
Edward Eggleston, *Hoosier Schoolboy*
Ladies' Home Journal (1883–) founded
Life magazine (1883–1936) founded

1884

National Bureau of Labor
Iowa prohibits sale of alcohol
U.S. Naval War College established
Cornerstone laid for Statue of Liberty

Samuel Clemens (Mark Twain), *Huckleberry Finn*
Mary Murfee, *In the Tennessee Mountains*
Francis Parkman, *Montcalm and Wolfe*
Helen Hunt Jackson, *Ramona*
Sarah Orne Jewett, *A Country Doctor*
James Russell Lowell, "On Democracy"
Sara Teasdale (1884–1933)

1885

Grover Cleveland administration (1885–89) begins

Statue of Liberty erected
Stanford University founded

William Dean Howells, *Rise of Silas Lapham*
Josiah Royce, *Religious Aspect of Philosophy*
Ulysses S. Grant, *Personal Memoirs* (1885–86)

1886

Haymarket Riot erupts in Chicago over demand for eight-hour work day
Geronimo is captured in last major Indian war
Sears Roebuck founded
Coca-Cola marketed

Henry James, *The Bostonians* and *The Princess Casamassima*
Sarah Orne Jewett, *A White Heron*
Francis Hodgson Burnett, *Little Lord Fauntleroy*
William Dean Howells, *Indian Summer*
Cosmopolitan (1886–) founded
Forum (1886–1950) founded

1887

Interstate Commerce Act
First electric streetcar
First U.S. social register

Thomas Nelson Page, *In Ole Virginia*
Bronson Howard, *The Henrietta*
Caroline Kirkland, *Zury*
Mary Wilkins Freeman, *A Humble Romance*
Frances Marion Crawford, *Saracinesca*
Harold Frederic, *Seth's Brother's Wife*
Scribner's Magazine (1887–1939) founded

1888

Department of Labor established
National Geographic founded
Labor Day first observed as legal holiday in New York State

Walt Whitman, *November Boughs*
Edward Bellamy, *Looking Backward*
Bronson Howard, *Shenandoah*
James Russell Lowell, *Political Essays*
Henry James, *Aspern Papers*
Walt Whitman, *Complete Poems and Prose*
Collier's (1888–1957) founded
American Folklore Society founded (1888–)

1889

Benjamin Harrison administration (1889–93) begins
Department of Agriculture established
Barnard College founded
Oklahoma opened for settlement
Johnstown flood takes 2,200 lives when dam bursts in Pennsylvania
First Pan-American Congress

William Dean Howells, *Annie Kilburn*
Eugene Field, *A Little Book of Western Verse*
Samuel Clemens (Mark Twain), *A Connecticut Yankee*
Lafcadio Hearn, *Chita*
Henry Adams, *History of the United States* (1889–91)
Theodore Roosevelt, *Winning of the West* (1889–96)

1890

Sherman Anti-Trust and Silver Purchase Acts
Daughters of the American Revolution organized
New Madison Square Garden built
Idaho becomes 43rd State
Sitting Bull killed
Indian massacre at Wounded Knee, South Dakota

Emily Dickinson, *Poems*
William James, *Principles of Psychology*
Jacob Riis, *How the Other Half Lives*
William Dean Howells, *A Hazard of New Fortunes*
Henry James, *The Tragic Muse*
George Woodberry, *Poems*
Literary Digest (1890–1938) founded
Smart Set (1890–1930) founded

1891

Forest Reserve Act (beginning of Conservation movement)
Populist Party
Basketball invented
International copyright law

Ambrose Bierce, *Tales of Soldiers and Civilians*
Hamlin Garland, *Main-Travelled Roads*
William Dean Howells, *Criticism and Fiction*
Mary Wilkins Freeman, *A New England Nun*
Emily Dickinson, *Poems: Second Series*
Review of Reviews (1891–1937) founded

1892

Homestead Strike of steelworkers broken, weakening labor movement
Ellis Island established as immigrant station
University of Chicago founded

Sewanee Review (1892–) founded

1893

Grover Cleveland administration (1893–97) begins
Gold Panic
Chicago World Fair
Anti-Saloon League founded

Henry Blake Fuller, *The Cliff-Dwellers*
Stephen Crane, *Maggie*
Frederick Jackson Turner, "Significance of the Frontier"
McClure's Magazine (1893–1929) founded
Outlook (1893–1915) founded

1894

Pullman, coal, and American Railway Union strikes

First U.S. Open golf tournament
Bureau of Immigration established

Richard Hovey, *Songs from Vagabondia*
John Muir, *Mountains of California*
Samuel Clemens (Mark Twain), *Pudd'nhead Wilson*
George Santayana, *Sonnets*
Kate Chopin, *Bayou Folk*
William Dean Howells, *A Traveler from Altruria*
Chap Book (1894–98) founded

1895
Cuban rebellion
New York Public Library founded

Stephen Crane, *The Red Badge of Courage* and *Black Riders*
S. Weir Mitchell, *Amos Judd*
Hamlin Garland, *Rose of Dutcher's Coolly*
Bookman (1895–1933) founded
William Allen White's *Emporia Gazette* (1895–) founded
Collier's Weekly (1895–) founded

1896
Klondike gold rush
William Jennings Bryan's "Cross of Gold" speech
Rural free delivery instituted
Thomas Edison invents motion picture camera
College of New Jersey renamed Princeton University

Samuel Clemens (Mark Twain), *Joan of Arc*
Emily Dickinson, *Poems: Third Series*
Sarah Orne Jewett, *Country of the Pointed Firs*
Edwin Arlington Robinson, *Torrent and the Night Before*
George Santayana, *The Sense of Beauty*
John Kendrick Bangs, *Houseboat on the Styx*
Harold Frederic, *Damnation of Theron Ware*

1897
William McKinley administration (1897–1901) begins
John Phillip Sousa, "The Stars and Stripes Forever"
Library of Congress building completed

Henry James, *What Maisie Knew* and *The Spoils of Poynton*
S. Weir Mitchell, *Hugh Wynne*
Mary Eleanor Wilkins Freeman, *Jerome*
Edwin Arlington Robinson, *The Children of the Night*
William James, *The Will to Believe*
Survey Graphic (1897–1944) founded

1898
Spanish-American War
United States annexes Hawaii

Finley Peter Dunne, *Mr. Dooley in Peace and War*
Stephen Crane, *The Open Boat*
S. Weir Mitchell, *Adventure of Francois*
Henry James, "The Turn of the Screw"

1899
Philippine insurrection (1899–1902)
"Open Door" policy in China adopted
United Mine Workers organized
Carnegie Steel Corporation established

Stephen Crane, *The Monster* and *War Is Kind*
George Ade, *Fables in Slang*
Edwin Markham, "The Man with the Hoe"
Elbert Hubbard, *Message to Garcia*
Frank Norris, *McTeague*
Winston Churchill, *Richard Carvel*
Thorstein Veblen, *Theory of the Leisure Class*
Paul Leicester Ford, *Janice Meredith*
Henry James, *The Awkward Age*
Charles W. Chesnutt, *The Conjure Woman*
Booth Tarkington, *Gentleman from Indiana*
Everybody's (1899–1928) founded

1900
Galveston tornado kills thousands, leaving Texas city in ruins
Socialist Party founded
Carnegie Institute of Technology founded
First U.S. national automobile show

Jack London, *Son of the Wolf*
Theodore Roosevelt, *The Strenuous Life*
Stephen Crane, *Whilomville Stories*
Thedore Dreiser, *Sister Carrie*
Booth Tarkington, *Monsieur Beaucaire*
William Dean Howells, *Literary Friends and Acquaintances*
L. Frank Baum, *Wonderful World of Oz*
Josiah Royce, *The World and the Individual*

1901
Theodore Roosevelt administration (1901–09) begins
Panama Canal Treaty
First transatlantic radio
Consolidation of U.S. Steel Corporation and of Union, Central, and Southern Pacific railroads

Frank Norris, *The Octopus*
William Vaughn Moody, *Poems*
Winston Churchill, *The Crisis*
Jacob Riis, *The Making of an American*
Henry James, *Sacred Fount*
Booker T. Washington, *Up from Slavery*
John Muir, *Our National Parks*

1902
Anthracite coal strike by United Mine Workers settled without union recognition
Maryland enacts first state workmen's compensation law

Oregon adopts first state initiative and referendum laws

William James, *Varieties of Religious Experience*
Jacob Riis, *The Battle with the Slum*
Owen Wister, *The Virginian*
Henry James, *Wings of the Dove*
Ellen Glasgow, *The Battleground*
Edith Wharton, *The Valley of Decision*
South Atlantic Quarterly (1902–) founded

1903

Department of Commerce established
Wisconsin enacts first state primary law
United States recognizes Panama's independence
Wright brothers airplane
Rhodes scholarships established

Jack London, *Call of the Wild*
Frank Norris, *The Pit*
W. E. B. Du Bois, *The Souls of Black Folk*
Henry James, *The Ambassadors*

1904

Pacific cable completed
United States begins construction of Panama Canal
Chicago meat packers strike

Henry James, *The Golden Bowl*
Jack London, *The Sea Wolf*
James Branch Cabell, *The Eagle's Shadow*
Ida M. Tarbell, *History of the Standard Oil Company*
William Sydney Porter (O. Henry), *Cabbages and Kings*
Lincoln Steffens, *Shame of the Cities*
Ellen Glasgow, *Deliverance*
Winston Churchill, *The Crossing*
William Dean Howells, *Son of Royal Langbrith*
Paul Elmer More, *Shelburne Essays* (1904–35)
Henry Adams, *Mont-Saint-Michel and Chartres*
American Academy of Arts and Letters founded (1904–)

1905

Rotary Clubs founded
I.W.W. (International Workers of the World), also known as the Wobblies, organized
Chicago Defender published

Jack London, *War of the Classes*
Thomas Dixon, *The Clansman*
Edith Wharton, *The House of Mirth*
George Santayana, *The Life of Reason* (1905–06)
Variety (1905–) founded

1906

San Francisco earthquake and fire
Pure Food and Drug Act
Meat Inspection Act
President Theodore Roosevelt wins Nobel Peace Prize for mediating end of Russo-Japanese War

Mary Austin, *The Flock*
William Sydney Porter (O. Henry), *The Four Million*
Upton Sinclair, *The Jungle*
Winston Churchill, *Coniston*

1907

Georgia and Alabama adopt Prohibition
First Ziegfeld Follies
Oklahoma becomes the 46th state
President Roosevelt's "Great White Fleet" sails the world

William Graham Sumner, *Folkways*
Henry James, *The American Scene*
William James, *Pragmatism*
William Sydney Porter (O. Henry), *The Trimmed Lamp*

1908

Henry Ford introduces Model T
Sullivan Ordinance in New York City forbids women to smoke in public

Robert Herrick, *Together* and *Master of the Inn*
Josiah Royce, *Philosophy of Loyalty*
Zona Gale, *Friendship Village*
Percy MacKaye, *The Scarecrow*
Jack London, *The Iron Heel*

1909

William Howard Taft administration (1909–13) begins
Robert Peary's last North Pole expedition
Rise of the Progressive movement
Model T is mass-produced
National Association for the Advancement of Colored People (NAACP) founded

Gertrude Stein, *Three Lives*
Jane Cunningham Croly, *The Promise of American Life*
Andrew D. White, *A Certain Rich Man*
William Sydney Porter (O. Henry), *Roads of Destiny*
Jack London, *Martin Eden*
William Vaughn Moody, *Great Divide* and *Faith Healer*
Ezra Pound, *Personae*

1910

First long-distance airline flight, from Albany to New York City
Boy Scouts of America chartered
Victor L. Berger (1860–1929), first Socialist elected to Congress

Edwin Arlington Robinson, *Town Down the River*
Jane Addams, *Twenty Years at Hull-House*

1911

La Follette organizes National Republic Progressive League
Standard Oil and American Tobacco Trusts broken up
First airline flight across United States
Triangle Building Fire in New York City kills 146 garment workers, mostly young women

Theodore Dreiser, *Jennie Gerhardt*
Edith Wharton, *Ethan Frome*
Ambrose Bierce, *Devil's Dictionary*
Masses, later *New Masses,* founded
Amy Lowell, *A Dome of Many-Coloured Glass*
Poetry: A Magazine of Verse (1912–) founded

1912

Progressive Party (1912–46) formed
Massachusetts establishes first minimum wage for women and children
New Mexico becomes 47th state
Arizona becomes 48th state
The *Titanic* strikes an iceberg and sinks; 1,502 drown

James Weldon Johnson, *Autobiography of an Ex-Colored Man*
Theodore Dreiser, *The Financier*
Zane Grey, *Riders of the Purple Sage*
Edna St. Vincent Millay, "Renascence"
Jack London, *Smoke Bellew*

1913

Woodrow Wilson administration (1913–21), begins
Sixteenth Amendment authorizes an income tax
Seventeenth Amendment provides for direct election of senators
Federal Reserve Bank Act establishes central banking system
Parcel Post System established
Department of Labor established
Ludlow strike of Colorado coal miners commences; Upton Sinclair would turn this violent incident into his novel *King Coal* (1917)

Willa Cather, *O Pioneers!*
Robert Frost, *A Boy's Will*
Ellen Glasgow, *Virginia*
Jack London, *Valley of the Moon*
Vachel Lindsay, *General William Booth Enters into Heaven*
Winston Churchill, *Inside of the Cup*
Robert Herrick, *One Woman's Life*
Henry James, *A Small Boy and Others*

1914

Panama Canal opened
Federal Trade Commission created
Kiwanis Clubs founded
World War I begins

Robert Frost, *North of Boston*
Amy Lowell, *Sword Blades and Poppy Seed*
Booth Tarkington, *Penrod*
Vachel Lindsay, *The Congo*
Robert Herrick, *Clark's Field*
New Republic (1914–) founded
Little Review (1914–29) founded

Abbott, Jacob (1803–1879) *educator*

Born in Hallowell, Maine, Jacob Abbott was a Congregational clergyman and educator who founded the Mount Vernon School for Girls in Boston in 1832. He was also the author of hundreds of books for children, many of them written in collaboration with his brother, John S. C. Abbott (1805–77). The first of Jacob Abbott's books, *The Young Christian,* appeared in 1832. He is perhaps best remembered for the sequence of instructional novels known—for their protagonist—as the Rollo series, the first of which appeared in 1835.

Sources

Weber, Carl Jefferson. *A Bibliography of Jacob Abbott.* Waterville, Me.: Colby College Press, 1948.

Abbott, Lyman (1835–1922) *theological writer*

A clergyman and philosopher, Lyman Abbott was born in Roxbury, Massachusetts, the son of the educator and Congregational clergyman Jacob ABBOTT. Ordained as a minister in 1860, Lyman Abbott succeeded Henry Ward BEECHER—whose biography he would publish in 1903—to the pulpit of the important Plymouth Congregational Church in BROOKLYN, New York in 1888. In 1876 Abbott began editing a periodical called *The Christian Union* with Beecher. Abbott would eventually take over the editorship of the journal, changing its name to *The Outlook* in 1893. A leader of the rationalist approach to religion, Abbott attempted to reconcile Christianity with Darwinism. In addition to his biography of Beecher, Abbott published *Christianity and Social Problems* (1896), *The Theology of the Evolutionist* (1897), *Reminiscences* (1915), and *What Christianity Means to Me* (1921).

Sources

Brown, Ira V. *Lyman Abbott, Christian Evolutionist: A Study in Religious Liberalism.* Cambridge: Harvard University Press, 1953.

abolitionism *movement*

This term applied to the movement advocating the abolition of slavery. Active agitation against slavery and the slave trade began in the late 18th century. By 1807 the British Parliament had outlawed the slave trade in the British Empire. A year later the U.S. Congress also put a stop to traffic in slaves. Such prohibitions did not prevent the illegal business of buying and selling slaves, and tensions within the United States increased as slave states declared their interest in spreading slavery to new territories acquired in the country's expansion across the continent.

By the 1830s slavery had been outlawed in the northern states, although the northern economy still depended heavily on the South's cotton industry, which thrived on the use of slave labor. This reliance on slavery bothered the conscience of certain northerners, and a campaign against the very idea of slavery began in earnest in 1831 with the formation of the New England Anti-Slavery Society. One of its chief organizers, William Lloyd GARRISON, also established *The LIBERATOR,* a militant periodical, which demanded the immediate and outright emancipation of all slaves.

By 1833 the American Anti-Slavery Society had formed along with several local organizations devoted to freeing the slaves. Garrison and other abolitionists orchestrated demonstrations and protests that aroused public sentiment both for and against slavery in the North. Such writers as Ralph Waldo EMERSON, Henry David THOREAU, James Russell LOWELL, and John Greenleaf WHITTIER supported the abolitionists' efforts. Northern mobs attacked abolitionists and showed little sympathy for the plight of slaves. An outraged Garrison staged a public burning of the U.S. Constitution because he believed the government had degraded itself by condoning slavery. His opponents argued that radical abolitionism was itself tearing the union apart and posed a threat to the peace of the nation.

Certainly the response in the South to abolitionism was a hardening of the rationale for a slave society. Southern apologists for slavery attacked northern hypocrisy, pointing out the misery of "wage slavery" in the factories. To southern patriots, abolitionism became just one more sign that the North wished to dominate the Union by excluding the spread of slavery to the territories. The abolitionist effort to shame southerners into realizing the evil of their "peculiar institution"—as it was often called—had the opposite effect: many southerners tended to take even more exaggerated pride in their slave owning tradition. Others simply saw the agitation over slavery as a northern excuse for restricting the South's power.

Congress tried many different ways of reconciling North and South while never addressing directly the issue of abolishing slavery. The Fugitive Slave Act of 1854 required northerners to return escaped slaves to their owners, thus infuriating the abolitionists and redoubling their efforts. The South felt stymied because in Kansas and Nebraska they had to fight abolitionists like John BROWN, who gathered followers in order to stop, by physical force, the entry of slaveholders into the territories. When Brown's gang actually murdered slaveholders, and when Brown attempted a raid on Harper's Ferry in order to incite a slave uprising, many in the South believed that the consequences of abolitionist agitation had led directly to the South's secession from the Union.

In literary terms, the cause of abolitionism was furthered by the powerful testimony of an escaped slave, Frederick DOUGLASS. His autobiography, first published in 1845, not only detailed the degradation of slavery in vivid, dramatic scenes, it also demonstrated the dignity and power that the ex-slave could attain by virtue of the strength of his own desire to be free and to become educated. What Douglass did to fortify the abolitionists—he was also a commanding platform speaker—was enhanced by the enormous success of UNCLE TOM'S CABIN (1852), Harriet Beecher STOWE's novel about the horrors of slavery and its long-suffering Christian victim, Uncle Tom. The virtue of Stowe's book was that it told the appalling story of slavery in sentimental and melodramatic terms that were easily transferrable to the stage, so that the injustices of slavery could be dramatized for hundreds of thousands of Americans who could not read or were not previously moved by the abolitionist cause.

Sources

Bracey, John H., Jr., August Meier, and Elliott Rudwick, eds. *Blacks in the Abolitionist Movement.* Belmont, Calif.: Wadsworth, 1971.

Cain, William E., ed. *William Lloyd Garrison and the Fight Against Slavery: Selections from The Liberator.* New York: St. Martin's Press, 1995.

Finkelman, Paul, ed. *Antislavery.* New York: Garland, 1989.

Matthews, Donald G., ed. *Agitation for Freedom: The Abolitionist Movement.* New York: Wiley, 1972.

Mayer, Henry. *All on Fire: William Lloyd Garrison and the Abolition of Slavery.* New York: St. Martin's Press, 1998.

Adams, Andy (1859–1935) *novelist, short story writer*

Andy Adams is one of only a handful of cowboy writers (see COWBOY WRITING) to have gained recognition for their literary achievements. Born in Indiana, he moved to Texas specifically to become a cowboy, later moving on to Colorado to work as a miner. It was in Colorado that he took up writing, publishing his semiautobiographical account of a Texas cattle drive, *The Log of a Cowboy,* in 1903. While *Log* dealt primarily with the adventure of this western phenomenon, *The Outlet* (1905) considered the cattle drive as a business proposition, exploring the forces behind the movement of livestock to the railhead by providing enduring portraits of venal congressional lobbyists and greedy railroad operators. Adams also published a collection of stories about frontier life, *Cattle Brands* (1906); and a novel about a Texas cattle rancher he called *Reed Anthony, Cowman: An Autobiography* (1907).

Sources

Hudson, Wilson Mathis. *Andy Adams: Storyteller and Novelist of the Great Plains.* Austin, Tex.: Steck-Vaughn Co., 1967.

Adams, Brooks (1848–1927) *historian*

Born in Quincy, Massachusetts, Brooks Adams was a member of an illustrious American family that included two presidents: his great-grandfather John Adams (1735–1826), second president of the United States; and his grandfather John Quincy ADAMS (1767–1848), sixth president of the United States. His father was the diplomat Charles Francis Adams (1807–86), and his brothers the writer and businessman Charles Francis ADAMS Jr. and the historian Henry ADAMS.

Brooks Adams was himself a historian. After graduating from Harvard College in 1870 and spending a year at Harvard Law School, he served as his father's secretary while the elder Adams arbitrated U.S. claims against Great Britain resulting from British collusion with the Confederacy during the CIVIL WAR.

Adams began his writing career even while practicing law and lecturing at the Boston University law school. After publishing a study of the religious and political prejudices of the American colonists in *The Emancipation of Massachusetts* (1895), he began exploring his hypothesis about the cyclical nature of human history with *The Law of Civilization and Decay* (1896) and his *Theory of Social Revolutions* (1913). A long essay concerning the Adams family's intellectual tradition first appeared in his brother Henry's "Letter to American Teachers of History" (1910) and was subsequently reprinted in Brooks Adams's *The Degradation of the Democratic Dogma* (1919). An ardent racist and nativist, Adams came to view America's generous immigration policies as its doom.

Sources

Adams, James Truslow. *The Adams Family.* Boston: Little, Brown, 1930.

Beringause, Arthur F. *Brooks Adams: A Biography.* New York: Alfred A. Knopf, 1955.

Donovan, Timothy Paul. *Henry Adams and Brooks Adams: The Education of Two American Historians.* Norman: University of Oklahoma Press, 1961.

Adams, Charles Francis, Jr. (1835–1915)
historian, biographer

Charles Francis Adams Jr. was a member of an illustrious American family that included two presidents: his great-grandfather John Adams (1735–1826), second president of the United States; and his grandfather John Quincy ADAMS (1767–1848), sixth president of the United States. His father was the diplomat Charles Francis Adams (1807–86), and his brothers the historians Brooks ADAMS and Henry ADAMS. The younger Charles Francis Adams was an eclectic writer, but his *Railroads: Their Origin and Problems* (1878) was clearly linked to his later position as president of the Union Pacific Railroad (1884–90). He wrote two biographies, one of the Massachusetts man of letters Richard Henry DANA Jr., which was published in 1890; and one of his own father, which appeared a decade later. In 1892, like his brother Brooks, he published a history of Massachusetts; and in 1916, like his brother Henry, he published an autobiography.

Sources

Adams, James Truslow. *The Adams Family.* Boston: Little, Brown, 1930.

Ford, Worthington Chauncey, ed. *A Cycle of Adams Letters, 1861–1865.* Boston: Houghton Mifflin, 1920.

Adams, Henry Brooks (1838–1918) *historian, novelist, memoirist*

Born in BOSTON, Henry Adams was the grandson of President John Quincy Adams (1767–1848) and the son of statesman Charles Francis Adams (1807–86). Although a member of one of America's most distinguished families, Adams demonstrated early on that he would not take the same course as his ancestors. Rather than lead the nation forward, he preferred to think and write about the greater world. With typical irony and modesty, he would later write, "So far as [I] had a function in life, it was as a stable-companion to statesmen." Accompanying his father to England, where Charles Adams served as minister during the CIVIL WAR, Henry Adams served as a secretary in the ministry, but he also worked as a foreign correspondent for the Boston *Courier* and the *New York Times.* After he returned from England in 1867 he became editor of the NORTH AMERICAN REVIEW, as well as an assistant professor of history. For seven years, from 1870 to 1877, Adams taught medieval, European, and American history, subjects he would later transform into an original philosophy of history.

In 1872 Adams married fellow Bostonian Marian Hooper, who would commit suicide in 1885. Other than the fact that he published two novels, *Democracy* (1880) and *Esther* (1884), while he was married, little is known about Adams's life during this 13-year period, for he omits it from his autobiographical writing. He also omits any mention of his wife, although her death clearly affected him profoundly. He commissioned the sculptor Augustus Saint-Gaudens (1848–1907) to create a symbolic sculpture, *The Peace of God,* for her grave in Washington, D.C., where they had been living, and then he left the country.

Adams traveled first through Asia, returning to Washington to complete his monumental study of the politics and diplomacy of the early republic, the nine-volume *History of the United States of America During the Administrations of Thomas Jefferson and James Madison* (1889–91). He then made several trips to France. At the Paris Exposition of 1900 he saw the enormous dynamo that would serve in his autobiography as a symbol for the mechanical power and multiplicity of the 20th-century as well as a counterpart for the Virgin Mary. The latter, "the ideal of human perfection," represented for Adams the unity of medieval Europe, the subject of his *Mont-Saint-Michel and Chartres* (1904), in which Adams began to enunciate a theory of history. This book's complement, THE EDUCATION OF HENRY ADAMS (1918), elaborates Adams's dynamic theory of history, coupling it with an autobiographical evaluation of the failures and poor education of a kind of everyman figure who bears his name.

Sources

Byrnes, Joseph F. *The Virgin of Chartres: An Intellectual and Psychological History of the Work of Henry Adams.* Rutherford, N.J.: Fairleigh Dickinson University Press, 1981.

Decker, William M. *The Literary Vocation of Henry Adams.* Chapel Hill: University of North Carolina Press, 1990.

Wasserstrom, William. *The Ironies of Progress: Henry Adams and the American Dream.* Carbondale: Southern Illinois University Press, 1984.

Adams, John Quincy (1767–1848) *sixth president of the United States, diarist*

Born in Braintree (later Quincy), Massachusetts, to John Adams, the second U.S. president, and his wife Abigail, John Quincy Adams was a precocious child whose introduction to statesmanship began early, when he accompanied his father on diplomatic missions to Europe. After studying in Paris and at the University of Leiden in Holland, Adams graduated from Harvard in 1787 and began practicing law.

Adams did not work long as a lawyer, however. In 1791 his response to Thomas Paine's *Rights of Man*—a series of articles in which Adams defended the Federalist position and signed himself "Publicola"—brought him to the attention of President George Washington (1732–99), who in 1794 appointed Adams U.S. minister to Holland.

Adams went on to serve as minister to Portugal and Prussia before returning to the United States in 1801. He continued his political career by winning a seat in the U.S. Senate in 1803, a position he resigned in 1808 after his independent voting record caused him to break with the Federalist Party. Diplomatic postings in Russia and England followed, and in 1817 Adams was called back to serve as secretary of state in the administration (1817–25) of President James Monroe (1758–1831). In this position Adams became the primary author of the Monroe Doctrine, which unilaterally declared that the continents of the western hemisphere were no longer "to be considered as subjects for future colonization by any European power."

Adams ran as the Republican candidate for president in the election of 1824. Although his rival, Andrew Jackson (1767–1845), received more popular votes, neither candidate held a majority of electoral votes, and the election was decided in the House of Representatives. There the support of Speaker of the House Henry Clay (1777–1852) decided the outcome in Adams's favor. When Adams named Clay as secretary of state, Jackson cried foul, splitting the Republican Party and defeating Adams in the next election.

In 1830 Adams was elected to the U.S. House of Representatives, where he served for the next 17 years without any true party affiliation. His independence permitted him to oppose slavery by fighting for the petitions of abolitionists (see ABOLITIONISM) and against the admission of Texas to the Union as a slaveholding state.

Adams's nonconformity is reflected in his 12-volume set of *Memoirs,* written with what one editor called "malice towards all" and published between 1874 and 1877. Covering more than 60 years of American political history, they provide a significant chronicle of the life and times of the nation as well as the author. Adams's other notable works include his classic treatise *On Weights and Measures* (1821) and his *Harvard Lectures on Rhetoric and Oratory* (1810), delivered in 1806 during his tenure as professor of rhetoric and belles lettres.

Sources

Allen, David Grayson, et al., eds. *Diary of John Quincy Adams.* Cambridge, Mass.: Harvard University Press, 1981– .

Parsons, Lynn H. *John Quincy Adams.* Madison, Wis.: Madison House, 1998.

Shepherd, Jack. *The Adams Chronicles: Four Generations of Greatness.* Boston: Little, Brown, 1975.

Adams, Mary

See WARD, ELIZABETH STUART PHELPS.

Adams, William Taylor (Oliver Optic) (1822–1897) *educator*

William Taylor Adams was a Boston schoolteacher who, under the pen name Oliver Optic, began in the 1850s to publish books and magazine stories aimed at young readers and modeled on the extremely popular works of Horatio ALGER. Adams, too, succeeded with such works, and in 1865 he left the teaching profession to devote himself full-time to the literary world. In addition to publishing more than 100 novels (most of them in sequences with titles like the "Starry Flag Series," or the "Onward and Upward Series") and more than 1,000 stories, he edited a number of periodicals for youngsters, including his own *Oliver Optic's Magazine for Boys and Girls* (1867–75).

Sources

Jones, Dolores Blythe, comp. *An "Oliver Optic" Checklist: An Annotated Catalog-Index to the Series, Nonseries Stories, and Magazine Publications of William Taylor Adams.* Westport, Conn.: Greenwood Press, 1985.

Addams, Jane (1860–1935) *social reformer*

Jane Addams's landmark autobiography, *Twenty Years at Hull House* (1910), details many of the experiences that made her life so extraordinary. One of the most significant social reformers of the 19th century, Addams founded Hull-House in Chicago in 1889. At this meeting place for political and civic groups and neighborhood gathering place, Addams lectured about and lobbied for social reform through "settlement," whereby social workers literally took up residence among the urban poor in order to serve these communities' needs. Addams also worked for international peace, publishing such works as *Democracy and Social Ethics* (1902) and *Peace and Bread in Time of War* (1922). Her activism earned her a label as a radical and also, in 1931, a Nobel Peace Prize (as corecipient).

Sources

Stinson, Peggy. "Jane Addams." In *American Women Writers,* Vol. 1, edited by Lina Mainiero. New York: Ungar, 1979, pp. 20–23.

Trolander, Judith Ann. "Settlement House Movement." In *Women's Studies Encyclopedia,* Vol 3, edited by Helen Tierney. New York: Greenwood Press, 1991, pp. 405–407.

Agassiz, Louis (Jean Louis Rodolphe Agassiz) (1807–1873) *naturalist, essayist*

Born in Switzerland, Louis Agassiz was educated in medicine in his own country, but in 1831 he went to Paris. There, under the influence of the German botanist Alexander von Humboldt (1769–1859) and the French comparative anatomist George Cuvier (1769–1832), he became interested in the natural sciences. Agassiz had already made a name for himself as an expert on glaciers and on fossil fishes when he came to the United States in 1846 on a lecture tour. Two years later he accepted a professorship at Harvard, where he began work on the collections that became the Harvard Museum of Comparative Zoology.

Although he remained at Harvard until his death, Agassiz was also associated with the Charleston Medical College, Cornell University, and the Smithsonian Institution. Agassiz's enormous energies also helped him found the Marine Biological Laboratory at Wood's Hole, Massachusetts, in 1872, and lead extensive research expeditions to Brazil (1865–66) and along the Atlantic and Pacific coasts of the Americas (1871–72).

Agassiz's emphasis on direct observation of nature proved enormously influential, as did his *Contributions to the Natural History of the United States* (1857–62). The latter includes his famous "Essay on Classification," elaborating his views on geology and paleontology and his opposition to the evolutionary theories of British scientist Charles Darwin (1808–82). Agassiz's second wife, Elizabeth Cary Agassiz (1822–1907), was both his biographer and the founder and first president of Radcliffe College.

Sources

Bolles, Edmund Blair. *The Ice Finders: How a Poet, a Professor, and a Politician Discovered the Ice Age.* Washington, D.C.: Counterpoint, 1999.

Lurie, Edward. *Louis Agassiz: A Life in Science.* Chicago: University of Chicago Press, 1960.

Tharp, Louise Hall. *Adventurous Alliance: The Story of the Agassiz Family of Boston.* Boston: Little, Brown, 1959.

Ahab, Captain *character*

Herman MELVILLE created one of the most memorable characters in American fiction in Captain Ahab, the monomaniacal captain of the whale ship *Pequod* in MOBY-DICK; OR, THE WHALE (1851). When Ishmael, the narrator of the novel, meets Ahab, the captain has lost a leg to the great white whale, and he is consumed by a desire for revenge. This meeting does not, however, occur until the *Pequod* is well out to sea, as Ahab remains below decks in his cabin. When he finally does address his crew, both his appearance and his speech are singular. A white scar runs down middle of his face and neck and, as rumor would have it, down the length of his body, as if he had been struck by lightning that left him permanently divided. With great passion and wonderful oratorical skill, Ahab enlists his crew in the hunt for the whale Moby-Dick, nailing a gold doubloon to the mast as an incentive. Some, however, remain skeptical, including Ishmael, who describes how Ahab lost his leg and hints at the import of the captain's scar: After he lost his leg to the whale, Ahab's "torn body and gashed soul bled into one another; and so interfusing, made him mad."

The extent of Ahab's obsession begins to come clear as soon as the *Pequod* sights the white whale. Five men who have been hidden below suddenly appear on deck; this is Ahab's own whaleboat crew. The crew leader, Fedallah, is a malevolent fire worshiper who seems to have some mysterious hold on Ahab. Fedallah is contrasted with the *Pequod*'s righteous first mate, Starbuck, who brings out what remains of Ahab's humanity—as does the cabin boy, Pip, who fills a role similar to King Lear's Fool.

Once Moby-Dick is sighted, however, Ahab loses all vestiges of sanity. After three grueling days of chasing the whale, Ahab manages to land his harpoon in the leviathan, only to become fouled in his line. Tied to the white whale, Ahab drowns as Moby-Dick destroys the *Pequod* and all aboard except Ishmael, who lives to tell the tale.

Sources

Bloom, Harold, ed. *Ahab.* New York: Chelsea House, 1991.

Levin, Harry. *The Power of Blackness.* New York: Alfred A. Knopf, 1958.

Thompson, Lawrance. *Melville's Quarrel with God.* Princeton, N.J.: Princeton University Press, 1952.

Aiken, George L. (1830–1876) *playwright*

Born in Boston, actor and playwright George L. Aiken made his stage debut in an 1848 production of *Six Degrees of Crime* in Providence, Rhode Island. Although he was not a star, he played many important roles, and his own play, *Helos the Helot* (1852), won a prize intended to encourage American play-writing. He is best remembered, however, for his stage adaptation of Harriet Beecher STOWE'S UNCLE TOM'S CABIN, which Aiken supposedly completed in one week. The play premiered in Troy, New York, on September 27, 1852, and was an instant success. Aiken appeared in the premiere performance, and the play continued to run another 99 nights, after which it went to New York City, where it played for a record 300 performances.

Sources

Aiken, George L. *Leaves From an Actor's Life; or, Recollections of Plays and Players.* Boston, 188?.

Aimard, Gustave

See GLOUX, OLIVER.

Alamo *historic site*

Known as "the cradle of Texas liberty," the Alamo was a chapel added in 1744 to the mission of San Fernando de Valero, founded by Franciscan friars in 1718 in what is now San Antonio. Later converted into a fortress, the Alamo was taken over in December 1835 by Texas revolutionaries fighting for independence from Mexico. The following March the Alamo was the site of a desperate battle between 150 revolutionaries and 4,000 Mexican troops led by General Santa Anna, who had besieged the fortress for 10 days. All of the defenders were killed, including such celebrated folk heroes as Davy CROCKETT and James Bowie (1790?–1836). The defeat proved to be a turning point in the Texas revolution, however. Rallied by cries of "Remember the Alamo!" Texan troops decisively defeated the Mexicans six weeks later at San Jacinto.

Purchased by the state of Texas in 1883, the site was enlarged and restored in the 1930s. In 1960 the Alamo was declared a National Historic Landmark. A number of novels have featured the battle for the Alamo, including Augusta Evans's *Inez* (1855) and Herbert Gorman's *The Wine of San Lorenzo* (1945).

Sources

Adair, A. G., and M. H. Crockett, eds. *Heroes of the Alamo.* New York: Exposition Press, 2d ed. 1957.

Alcott, Amos Bronson (1799–1888) *educator, social theorist*

Born in Connecticut, Bronson Alcott supported himself as a teacher in New England and Pennsylvania between 1822 and 1833. Later in Boston (1834–1839) and much later in Concord, Massachusetts (after 1859), Alcott advocated a program of progressive education that included promoting a concept of the whole student—one who was fit physically and mentally and had an aesthetic and moral sensibility. A committed transcendentalist (see TRANSCENDENTALISM), Alcott believed that individuals carried within them the spirit of the universe and an affinity for a central Mind, which he equated with the idea of God. This core belief has much in common with ROMANTICISM in that the child, as the English poet William Wordsworth (1770–1850) put it, is father to the man; in other words, the individual had an inborn sense of truth, an intuition of knowledge that education could draw out.

Alcott set forth his philosophy in several books, including *Record of a School, Exemplifying the General Principles of Spiritual Culture* (1835); and the two-volume *Conversations with Children on the Gospels* (1836–37). Although Alcott's ideas were rejected in Boston, where Alcott was considered an extremist, they later were affirmed by other transcendentalists in Concord, most notably Ralph Waldo EMERSON and William Ellery CHANNING (2).

After 1840, Alcott tried farming and failed. He traveled to England to discuss his ideas with thinkers like Thomas Carlyle (1795–1881) and then returned to the United States to participate in the ill-fated utopian community of FRUITLANDS. Thereafter Alcott took to giving public lectures, though he was supported, in the main, by his wife and his daughter Louisa May ALCOTT.

In 1859 Bronson Alcott became Concord's superintendent of schools and introduced singing, dancing, and reading aloud as well as the study of physiology into the curriculum. He believed that education should be a kind of recreation and that students should understand both their bodies and their minds. Alcott extended his influence on American education by establishing the Concord School of Philosophy (1879–88), an expression of what Emerson called a "pure intellect." Alcott believed the cerebral and emotional aspects of life ought to blend, as they did in his own household, which many observers deemed serene if also unworldly.

Rather like Plato, who was an important influence on the transcendentalists, Alcott spread his ideas through public dialogue. His conversations were memorable and served to entice followers who spread the word of his philosophy. Alcott's writing did not, however, capture the charm of the man. His books are a repository of his ideas, but they do not convey the charm of his person.

Alcott's other noteworthy titles include *Observations on the Principles and Methods of Infant Instruction* (1830) and *The Doctrine and Discipline of Human Culture* (1836). *Concord Days* (1872) contains excerpts from his journals. Other editions of his journals have been published, as have his efforts at autobiography, including *Table Talk* (1877) and *New Connecticut* (1887). *The Letters of A. Bronson Alcott* appeared in 1969.

Sources

Dahlstrand, Frederick C. *Amos Bronson Alcott: An Intellectual Biography.* Rutherford, N.J.: Fairleigh Dickinson University Press, 1982.

Sanborn, F.B. and William T. Harris. *A. Bronson Alcott: His Life and Philosophy.* New York: Biblo & Tannen, 1965.

Shepard, Odell. *Pedlar's Progress: The Life of Bronson Alcott.* Boston: Little, Brown, 1937.

Stoehr, Taylor. *Nay-saying in Concord: Emerson, Alcott, and Thoreau.* Hamden, Conn.: Archon Books, 1979.

Alcott, Louisa May (1832–1888) *novelist*

Born in Pennsylvania, Louisa May Alcott was the daughter of Bronson ALCOTT, a prominent transcendentalist (see TRANSCENDENTALISM). She spent her early years in Boston, where her father taught school. He instructed her at home, where she also learned from the visits of Ralph Waldo EMERSON, Henry David THOREAU, and Theodore PARKER. At a very early age she turned to writing, producing at 16 a book, a collection of fairy tales called *Flower Fables* (1854). Like her mother, she helped to support the family; her father was not steadily employed from 1840 until 1859, when he became Concord's superintendent of schools.

Louisa wanted to become an actress and wrote several unpublished melodramas for the stage. She also wrote short stories and poetry, some of which were published in THE ATLANTIC MONTHLY. During the CIVIL WAR she worked as a nurse, and *Hospital Sketches* reflect this experience. *Moods* (1865) was her first novel, but she spent much of her time writing anonymous gothic (see GOTHICISM) romances, later identified and published as *Behind a Mask* (1975), *Plots and Counterplots* (1976), *A Double Life: Newly Discovered Thrillers of Louisa May Alcott* (1988), *Freaks of Genius: Unknown Thrillers of Louisa May Alcott* (1991), and *From Jo March's Attic: Stories of Intrigue and Suspense* (1993).

In 1867 Alcott became the editor of *Merry's Museum*, a magazine for young readers. There she published her most enduring work, LITTLE WOMEN, the story of a spirited young woman, Jo MARCH, and her sisters Amy, Beth, and Meg. The novel was based on Alcott's own family life and was so popular that it brought the whole family financial security.

Little Women's continuing appeal is clear not only from the countless editions of the book but also from its three film adaptations. Alcott's later novels include *An Old-Fashioned Girl* (1870), *Little Men* (1871), and *Work* (1873)—the last having been described as Alcott's most feminist book (see FEMINISM). This side of Alcott is ably represented in Madeleine Stern's edition of *The Feminist Alcott: Stories of a Woman's Power* (1996).

Alcott wrote many other books for children in her later years, although none to match *Little Women.* Her collections of stories include *Proverb Stories* (1882) and *Spinning-Wheel Stories* (1884). Although Alcott's fiction is often heavily moralistic, it is also one of the finest examples of domestic fiction, in which the joys of home and family are evoked with tenderness and enthusiasm. *Silver Pitchers and Independence* (1876) includes the short story "Transcendental Wild Oats," a fictionalized account of her father's utopian experiment, FRUITLANDS.

Alcott's *Selected Letters* were published in 1987, her *Journals* in 1989, and her *Girlhood Diary* in 1993. A newly discovered manuscript of a novel, *A Long Fatal Love Chase,* was published in 1995. *The Early Stories of Louisa May Alcott, 1852–1860* appeared in 2000.

Sources

Alberghene, Janice M. and Beverly Lyon Clark, eds. *Little Women and the Feminist Imagination: Criticism, Controversy, Personal Essays.* New York: Garland, 1999.

Keyser, Elizabeth Lennox. *Whispers in the Dark: The Fiction of Louisa May Alcott.* Knoxville: University of Tennessee Press, 1993.

Saxton, Martha. *A Modern Biography of Louisa May Alcott.* Boston: Houghton, Mifflin, 1977.

Stern, Madeleine B., ed. *Critical Essays on Louisa May Alcott.* Boston: G. K. Hall, 1984.

———. *Louisa May Alcott.* New York: Random House, 1996.

Alden, Henry Mills (1836–1919) *editor, nonfiction writer*

Born in Mt. Tabor, Vermont, Henry Mills Alden was known as the "dean of American magazine editors," serving from 1869 until his death in 1919 as the editor of HARPER'S MONTHLY. A highly religious man, he attempted to make *Harper's* into wholesome fare suitable for the whole family. His books include *God in His World* (1890), *A Study of Death* (1895), and *Magazine Writing and the New Literature* (1908).

Aldine, The (1868–1879) *periodical*

Named for a typeface, *The Aldine* was originally an in-house publication of a New York printer and publisher. R. H. Stoddard, who served as general editor from 1871 to 1875, transformed *The Aldine* into a general circulation periodical known for its fine graphics and typography. After 1875 *The Aldine* stopped publishing literature for lay readers and began to publish only every other month. It finally ceased publication altogether in 1879.

Aldrich, Thomas Bailey (1836–1907) *editor, journalist, poet, novelist, short story writer, dramatist, essayist*

Born in Portsmouth, New Hampshire, Thomas Aldrich was obliged by his father's early death to enter business at 16. At the same time, however, Aldrich began to write poetry, publishing his first collection, *The Bells,* in 1855 while performing a variety of editorial duties at a New York magazine. With the coming of the CIVIL WAR, he became a correspondent for the *Tribune,* and from 1862 to 1865 he also served as managing editor of the *Illustrated News.* After the war, Aldrich settled in Boston, where he edited *Every Saturday* from 1866 to 1874 and in 1881 succeeded William Dean HOWELLS as editor of the ATLANTIC MONTHLY.

In 1890 Aldrich retired to devote more time to writing. He was already an accomplished writer, known for such works as "Marjorie Daw" (1873), an ingenious tale about an epistolary hoax; and *The Story of a Bad Boy* (1869), an autobiographical novel set in Portsmouth. In 1880 he published *The Stillwater Tragedy,* a successful detective mystery, and broadened his range by dramatizing a number of his poems, most notably "Mercedes" in 1894. Aldrich also published essays and travel sketches. His prolific output was collected and published first in eight volumes in 1897, with nine more volumes appearing in 1907.

Sources

Samuels, Charles E. *Thomas Bailey Aldrich.* New York: Twayne, 1965.

Alger, Horatio, Jr. (1832–1899) *writer of children's literature*

The son of a Massachusetts Unitarian minister (see UNITARIANISM), Horatio Alger Jr. graduated from Harvard College and Harvard Divinity School but then rebelled against his upbringing and ran away to Paris, where he took up a bohemian lifestyle. In 1864, however, Alger returned to the United States, where he took a position as a Unitarian minister after suffering some sort of breakdown. Ten years later he moved to New York, where he became chaplain at the Newsboys' Lodging House and began his literary career. Over the next three decades Alger wrote almost 130 books for boys, all of them following the premise that pluck and hard work would save their heroes from poverty. Among his more popular works were the RAGGED DICK series (1867ff.), the *Luck and Pluck* series (1869ff.), and the *Tattered Tom* series (1871ff.). Alger also wrote biographies of famous men for his young audience. Altogether some 20 million copies of his books have been printed, and in his lifetime Alger became a wealthy man. Most of his time and money, however, were given over to the Newsboys' House, which remained his first priority.

Sources

Hoyt, Edwin P. *Horatio's Boys: The Life and Works of Horatio Alger, Jr.* Radnor, Penn.: Chilton Book Co., 1983.
Mayes, Herbert R. *Alger: A Biography Without a Hero.* 1928. Reprint, Des Plaines, Ill.: G. K. Westgard II, 1978.

Allen, Elizabeth Anne Chase Akers (Florence Percy) (1832–1911) *journalist, poet*

A poet who was also the literary editor of the Portland, Maine, *Daily Advertiser,* Elizabeth Allen wrote a great deal of highly popular verse. The only one of her poems that has endured, however, is "Rock Me to Sleep," which first appeared in the June 9, 1860, issue of the SATURDAY EVENING POST under the pseudonym Florence Percy. The poem includes two lines—"Backward, turn backward, O Time, in your flight, / Make me a child again just for tonight"—that were later incorporated into more than 30 different musical compositions.

Sources

Allen, Elizabeth Akers. *Poems.* Boston: Ticknor & Fields, 1866.

Allen, James Lane (1849–1925) *essayist, poet, short story writer, novelist*

A native of Kentucky, James Lane Allen taught school there until 1880, when he took up a literary career. In addition to essays, he published short stories, such as the LOCAL COLOR sketches that appeared in HARPER'S MAGAZINE in the 1880s, later collected and published as *The Blue-Grass Region of Kentucky* (1892); and the romantic (see ROMANTICISM) stories that constitute the collection *Flute and Violin* (1891). The relationship of man and nature is the theme of his best-known works, the novels *The Kentucky Cardinal* (1894), its sequels, *Aftermath* (1896), and *The Choir Invisible* (1897). Later in his career he wrote realistic novels about farm life, such as the realistic novel *A Summer in Arcady* (1896); a prose poem about the new ice age, *The Last Christmas Tree* (1914); and the CIVIL WAR novella *The Sword of Youth* (1915).

Sources

Bottorff, William K. *James Lane Allen.* New York: Twayne, 1964.

Allibone, Samuel Austin (1816–1889) *bibliographer*

Born in Philadelphia, S. Austin Allibone was a bibliographer who compiled the important three-volume reference work *A Critical Dictionary of English Literature and British and American Authors,* which was published between 1858 and 1871. In 1879 he became the head of the Lenox Library, established in New York City by the philanthropist James Lenox (1800–80) to house his collection of early printed works, Bibles, and bibliographical studies. The Lenox Library was later incorporated into the New York Public Library.

Altgeld, John Peter (1847–1902) *public figure*

Born in Germany, John Peter Altgeld immigrated to the United States with his parents while he was a child; the family settled in Ohio. Although he received little formal education, he succeeded in reading law and becoming first an attorney and, in 1886, a judge of the Superior Court of Cook County, Illinois. His election to this position probably owed something to his publication in 1884 of *Our Penal Machinery and Its Many Victims,* in which he argued that American criminal justice discriminates against the poor.

In 1892 Altgeld was elected governor of Illinois, and during his four-year term he pardoned three anarchists convicted for their part in the HAYMARKET SQUARE RIOT of 1886. This act, together with opposition to the use of federal troops during the Pullman strike of 1894 and his support for populist politician William Jennings BRYAN, earned Altgeld a reputation as a radical and cost him reelection. For some writers, however, Altgeld would remain a hero. Vachel Lindsay (1879–1931) made Altgeld the subject of his poem "The Eagle That Is Forgotten" (1913), and novelist Howard Fast (1914–) based the protagonist of his novel *The American* (1946) on Altgeld.

Sources

Ginger, Ray. *Altgeld's America: The Lincoln Ideal Versus Changing Realities.* New York: Funk & Wagnalls, 1958.

Ambassadors, The *Henry James* (1903) *novel*

In this novel Henry JAMES explores his customary theme: the interactions of America and Europe. Lambert Strether, an upright American editor, is one of a succession of ambassadors sent by the wealthy and widowed Mrs. Newsome to retrieve her son Chad from Paris. Strether, who is engaged to marry Mrs. Newsome, stands to gain from the successful completion of his mission, but instead he too falls under France's spell and comes to believe that Chad's relationship with the attractive Mme. de Vionnet is strictly platonic. Mrs. Newsome then sends another ambassador, her daughter Sarah, to force Chad to come home and to tell Strether that her mother has called off their engagement. Even after Strether discovers that Chad and Mme. de Vionnet are indeed lovers, he feels that Chad's exposure to the sophisticated, civilizing influence of the Old World has changed Chad for the better, and he supports the younger man's decision to stay. Memorably, Strether implores, "Live all you can; it's a mistake not to." In the end Strether himself does go back to America, although in doing so he is obliged to give up his attachment to Maria Gostrey, an American expatriate living in Paris.

James considered *The Ambassadors,* his last completed novel but one, to be his best book. Later critics have praised it for its graceful structure and its insight into the limited but not insensitive mind of Strether.

Sources

Beidler, Paul G. *Frames in James: The Tragic Muse, The Turn of the Screw, What Maisie Knew, and The Ambassadors.* Victoria, B.C.: University of Victoria, 1993.

Johnson, Courtney. *Henry James and the Evolution of Consciousness: A Study of The Ambassadors.* East Lansing: Michigan State University Press, 1987.

American Commonwealth, The (1888, 1910) *history*

English historian and politician James Bryce (1838–1922) visited the United States five times and did extensive research into U.S. history before undertaking this monumental survey of American politics and society. Published in two volumes in 1888, the study presented Bryce's vision of what he considered "the nation of the future" in six sections: (1) the Constitution, the structure of federal government, and the relationship between federal and state government; (2) state and local governments; (3) political parties; (4) how public opinion influences government policy; (5) a discussion of the "strengths and weaknesses of democratic government" in the United States; and (6) the social, intellectual, and spiritual life of the nation. Bryce's evaluation was largely positive, and *The American Commonwealth* was republished in a supplemented and revised version in 1910 while Bryce was serving as British ambassador to the United States (1907–13). *The American Commonwealth* was the most influential study of the nation to appear since Alexis de Tocqueville's *Democracy in America* (1840).

Sources

Ions, Edmund. *James Bryce and American Democracy, 1870–1922.* London: Macmillan, 1968.

American Folklore Society *organization*

Founded in 1888 and based in Arlington, Virginia, this organization is devoted to the study of all aspects of American folk life, from family traditions to ethnic conflicts. It publishes the quarterly *Journal of American Folklore* and encompasses a number of branch groups, some of which have documented valuable information about American Indians and African Americans. The society has worked for more than a century to study and conserve American folklore as well as to promote public policies that advance cultural diversity.

Sources

The American Folklore Newsletter. El Paso, Tex.: Published at the University of Texas at El Paso for the American Folklore Society, 1972–82.

American Geographical Society *organization*

Established in New York City in 1851, the American Geographical Society is the oldest geographical organization in the United States, linking business with the scholarly and professional spheres in an attempt to encourage exploration and disseminate geographical knowledge. It publishes two periodicals, the *Geographical Review* (formerly the *Bulletin*) and *Focus* magazine, and houses its collection of reference and research materials—the largest in the

Western hemisphere—at the University of Wisconsin in Milwaukee.

Sources

Wright, John Kirtland. *Geography in the Making: The American Geographical Society, 1851–1951.* New York: Published by the Society, 1952.

American Historical Association *organization*

Established in Saratoga, New York, in 1884 and incorporated by Congress in 1889, the American Historical Association promotes historical studies by academics, independent scholars, museum curators, archivists, librarians, and others. Now headquartered in Washington, D.C., it is the largest historical society in the country and has been responsible for classifying official documents, preserving historical artifacts, and disseminating historical research through such publications as the *American Historical Review* (1895–).

Sources

Norton, Mary Beth, ed. *The American Historical Association's Guide to Historical Literature.* New York: Oxford University Press, 1995.

American Monthly Magazine, The *periodicals*

Several significant magazines have borne this title or variations on it.

The American Magazine, or, A Monthly View of the Political State of the British Colonies (1741) was the first magazine published in the colonies. Published in Philadelphia, it lasted for only three issues, with most of its pages devoted to proceedings of colonial assemblies.

Noah WEBSTER also edited an *American Magazine* that was New York City's first monthly. This magazine lasted for 12 issues. Webster, a staunch Federalist, used its pages to print articles supporting the newly drafted Constitution. He also published articles supporting education, another of his pronounced interests.

Nathaniel Parker WILLIS published an *American Monthly Magazine* in Boston from 1829 to 1831. Modeled on London's *New Monthly Magazine,* this periodical was devoted to entertainment and published stories, reviews, and humorous essays contributed by such writers as Park BENJAMIN and Lydia SIGOURNEY. The satirical tone of the magazine offended some proper Bostonians, and in 1831 Willis joined the *New York Mirror* as associate editor, taking his *American Monthly* subscription list with him.

Henry William Herbert (1807–1858) started his *American Monthly Magazine* in New York in 1833 as a competitor of the newly founded *Knickerbocker Magazine* (see KNICKERBOCKER SCHOOL). Charles Fenno HOFFMAN joined Herbert in the second year and together the two wrote much of the magazine's contents. In 1835 Park BENJAMIN took over from Herbert, but the former's attempt to publish the magazine in Boston and Philadelphia as well as New York failed. In its last few years, what had been a variety magazine gradually turned into a political review, with pieces supporting the Whig party contributed by Horace GREELEY. In 1838 it ceased publication altogether.

Frank Leslie's Popular Monthly—which would later bear the title *American Magazine*—was founded in New York in 1876. Priced at $2.50 per year, it was meant as competition for the monthly variety magazines, which averaged $4.00 at the time. Until Frank Leslie's death in 1880, his magazine did well, publishing contributions by writers like Brander MATTHEWS, Joaquin MILLER, and Amelia E. BARR. His widow, however, began leasing the magazine to others in 1895, and circulation went into decline. After three years she resumed control, changing the format and lowering the price of each issue to just ten cents. By 1904 the periodical—then known as *Leslie's Magazine*—began to focus on public affairs and to publish writers such as Stephen CRANE and Frank STOCKTON. In 1906 the magazine was purchased by a group of former MCCLURE'S writers—including Ida TARBELL, Lincoln STEFFENS, and Finley Peter DUNNE— who renamed it the *American Magazine* and concentrated on muckraking. In 1915 the magazine changed hands again when it was purchased by the Crowell-Collier group, which parlayed a concentration of success stories and detective fiction into a circulation that reached 2.5 million in the 1920s. From that peak, however, the general circulation of *American Magazine* declined until it was discontinued in 1956.

Sources

Huntzicker, William. *The Popular Press, 1833–1865.* Westport, Conn.: Greenwood Press, 1999.

American Review, The

See AMERICAN WHIG REVIEW.

American Scholar, The *Ralph Waldo Emerson (1837) address*

Ralph Waldo EMERSON first delivered this lecture to the Phi Beta Kappa Society of Harvard on August 31, 1837. It was published separately in 1837, and in 1849 it was collected with other Emerson works in *Nature, Addresses, and Lectures* (1849). In what Oliver Wendell HOLMES called "our intellectual Declaration of Independence," Emerson exhorted his audience of native intellectuals to rouse and lead American society into mental independence and self-reliance. The scholar is, he says, the "delegated intellect . . . he is *Man Thinking.*" It is the scholar's job as the finest product of American society to lead his people out of their bondage to old cultures, the "popular cry" of received wisdom, and everyday modes of thought. The address itself proved to be immensely popular, and it firmly established Emerson as a leader of the intellectual foment then brewing in New England. In its idealistic call for indigenous leaders, it remains a classic piece of American rhetoric and reason.

Sources

Sealts, Merton M. *Emerson on the Scholar.* Columbia: University of Missouri Press, 1992.

American Whig Review *periodical*

This political magazine was founded in 1845 primarily to promote the presidential aspirations of Henry Clay (1777–1852). The Whig party was a coalition of various political factions allied by their common opposition to President Andrew Jackson (1767–1845); it arose in the early 1830s. Their first successful presidential candidate was William Henry Harrison (1773–1841), but he died after only a month in office, and his vice presidential successor, John Tyler (1790–1862), was eventually ousted from the party. Attention shifted to Clay, whose 1844 presidential bid was defeated by Democrat James K. Polk (1795–1849) and his expansionist policies. A final run for the nomination in 1848 proved unsuccessful when the Whigs nominated the military hero Zachary Taylor (1784–1850).

From 1845 to 1852 the magazine was known simply as *The American Review.* Over time it was transformed from a campaign piece to a mainstream political and literary journal, publishing such works as Edgar Allan POE's "The Raven" as well as contributions from journalist Horace GREELEY and South Carolina statesman John C. Calhoun (1782–1850). The defeat of Whig candidate Winfield Scott (1786–1866) in the election of 1852, however, spelled the end of both the party and the *American Whig Review.*

Sources

Holt, Michael F. *The Rise and Fall of the American Whig Party: Jacksonian Politics and the Onset of the Civil War.* New York: Oxford University Press, 1999.

Andrews, Stephen Pearl (1812–1886) *linguist, political writer*

A religious and political free thinker, Stephen Pearl Andrews was also a brilliant linguist. In his book *The Science of Society* (1851) Andrews developed a social theory he labeled "Pantarchy," a method of organizing society using anarchic principles. He also developed his own universal language, which he called "Alwato," a kind of early Esperanto. He was instrumental in helping the feminist Victoria WOODHULL and her sister Tennessee Celeste Claflin (1846–1923) establish their radical periodical, *Woodhull and Claflin's Weekly,* in 1870. In addition to such ambitious pursuits, Andrews also published several instructional texts about shorthand.

Sources

Stern, Madeleine B. *The Pantarch: A Biography of Stephen Pearl Andrews.* Austin: University of Texas Press, 1968.

Anthony, Susan Brownell (1820–1906) *feminist reformer, historian*

Born into a Massachusetts Quaker family, Susan B. Anthony was exposed from birth to ideas of human equality and to the Quaker commitment to ABOLITIONISM. When financial reverses forced her to leave her teaching position and return to the family farm in Rochester, New York, her family responded by supporting her interest in working for social reform.

Anthony initially joined the TEMPERANCE MOVEMENT to ban intoxicating drink, but after she was denied permission to speak at a temperance convention because she was a woman, in 1852 she turned to the abolitionist cause. After passage of the Emancipation Proclamation in 1863, she adopted women's issues such as suffrage, equal pay, improved working conditions, and equitable marriage laws.

Anthony pursued her goals largely through public speaking. She was a commanding rhetorician, and for 50 years she traveled around the country lecturing audiences on the need for equal rights. In partnership with Elizabeth Cady STANTON, Anthony also founded the National Woman Suffrage Association and joined with Stanton and Matilda Gage (1826–1898) in writing the first three volumes of the *History of Woman Suffrage* (1881–86). She also contributed to volume four of this six-volume series, which was completed by Ida Husted Harper (1851–1931) between 1900 and 1922. Anthony died before seeing her goals fulfilled, but as Gertrude Stein portrayed her in the 1947 opera Stein wrote with composer Virgil Thompson, Anthony was *The Mother of Us All.*

Sources

Anthony, Susan B. *Failure Is Impossible: Susan B. Anthony in Her Own Words.* Edited by Lynn Sherr. New York: Times Books, 1995.

Barry, Kathleen. *Susan B. Anthony: A Biography of a Singular Feminist.* New York: New York University Press, 1988.

Dubois, Ellen Carol, ed. *Elizabeth Cady Stanton, Susan B. Anthony: Correspondence, Writings, Speeches.* New York: Schocken Books, 1981.

Anti-Rent War (1839–1854) *historical event*

When Stephen Van Rensselaer, a Hudson River landholder, died in 1839, his heirs attempted to collect back rent from tenants on his estate. The tenants forcibly resisted, turning back a sheriff's posse that had been sent to evict them. The revolt against the system of "patroonship"—perpetual leases dating from the time of Dutch and English rule—spread quickly as Anti-Rent Associations were formed throughout north central New York state. The level of violence also escalated as tenants dressed as Indians harassed landlords and their agents. When a deputy sheriff was killed in Delaware County, New York, in 1845, Governor William H. Seward (1801–1872) declared a state of emergency and called on the militia. The rent resisters then turned to the political process to redress their grievances, helping to elect a Whig governor, John Young, and pressuring the legislature to pass a law prohibiting long-term leases. The movement continued until 1845, forcing the breakup of large estates as worried landowners sold off their holdings. James Fenimore COOPER used the Anti-Rent Wars as a backdrop for his Littlepage Manuscripts trilogy: *Satanstoe* (1846), *The Chainbearer* (1846), and *The Redskins* (1846).

Sources

Christman, Henry. *Tin Horns and Calico.* Cornwallville, N.Y.: Hope Farm Press, 1975.

Ellis, D. M. *Landlords and Farmers in the Hudson-Mohawk Region, 1790–1850.* 1946. Reprint, Ithaca, N.Y.: Cornell University Press, 1967.

Appleseed, Johnny

See CHAPMAN, JOHN.

Appleton's Journal periodical

Originally a weekly magazine devoted to literature and current events, after 1872 *Appleton's Journal* began, under the editorship of O. B. Bunch (1828–1890), to commission illustrations by prominent artists to accompany its publication of original fiction by writers such as Thomas Bangs THORPE. Other contributors included Julian HAWTHORNE, Rebecca Harding DAVIS, John BURROUGHS, and Brander MATHEWS. Beginning in 1876, the magazine became a monthly, and in its last three years it primarily reprinted pieces taken from foreign periodicals.

Arena, The (1889–1901) periodical

This Boston monthly was edited by Benjamin O. Flower (1858–1918) and was concerned with issues of social and economic reform. Like many other general circulation periodicals of the time, it combined a socio-political agenda with literature; appropriately, *The Arena* chose to publish works by such realists (see REALISM) as Hamlin GARLAND.

Sources

Riley, Sam G., ed. *American Magazine Journalists, 1850–1900.* Detroit: Gale Research, 1989.

Armory Show (1913) *historical event*

This is the common name of a seminal event in the art world, the International Exhibition of painting and sculpture held at the 69th Regiment Armory in New York City. This event marked the introduction of modern art to America, with a display of some 1,600 art works representing then-current European avant-garde movements such as cubism, futurism, fauvism, and expressionism. Perhaps the most controversial piece in the show was Marcel Duchamp's cubist-futurist canvas, *Nude Descending a Staircase,* which depicts a continuous action through a series of overlapping images. Singled out at the time by critics as a prime example of all that was decadent and insane about the European art scene, this painting attracted enormous public attention, which in turn helped pave the way for public acceptance of new American art inspired by the exhibit. The influence of the Armory Show would extend beyond painting and sculpture to American literature, where aspects of expressionism can be seen in the psychological orientation of such 20th-century works as the poetry of T. S. Eliot and the plays of Eugene O'Neill.

Sources

Brown, Milton. *The Story of the Armory Show.* New York: Abbeville Press, 1988.

Arnold, George (1834–1865) *poet*

A member of the group of self-styled bohemians that frequently met at the PFAFF'S CELLAR watering hole in New York City, George Arnold was a poet and humorist who specialized in burlesquing others. He published under many pseudonyms—often in magazines—and it was only after his early death that his poems were collected and edited by the drama critic William Winter (1836–1917) as *Drift: A Sea-Shore Idyll and Other Poems* (1866) and *Poems, Grave and Gay* (1867). The two volumes were later combined when Arnold's work was reissued in 1870.

Sources

The Poems of George Arnold. Boston: J. R. Osgood and Co., 1880.

Arp, Bill

See SMITH, CHARLES H.

Arthur, Timothy Shay (1809–1885) *propagandist, novelist*

The TEMPERANCE MOVEMENT to ban alcoholic beverages reached its zenith in the 1850s, and T. S. Arthur was one of its most prolific and successful propagandists. He wrote approximately 100 tracts, over a million copies of which were circulated. He edited several magazines devoted to the abolition of alcohol, and his novel *Ten Nights in a Barroom and*

What I Saw There (1854) was adapted for the stage in 1858 with great success by William W. Pratt.

Sources

Epstein, Barbara. *The Politics of Domesticity: Women, Evangelism, and Temperance in Nineteenth-Century America.* Middletown, Conn.: Wesleyan University Press, 1981.

Atherton, Gertrude Franklin (1857–1948)

novelist, short story writer, historian

Born in San Francisco, Gertrude Atherton embarked on a literary career in the 1890s after the death of her husband, when she moved to New York to begin a new life. Her novels, which began to appear in the 1880s, initially received more attention abroad than in her own country. *The Doomswoman* (1892) began her chronicle of California which, unlike the work of her contemporaries Bret HARTE and Ambrose BIERCE, focused on city life in the Golden State, to which she returned permanently in 1932. Toward the end of her life she published two memoir/biographies of San Francisco, *Golden Gate Country* (1945) and *My San Francisco* (1947), that complemented her earlier work, *California: An Intimate Portrait* (1914). Atherton was, however, more than a strictly California writer, producing among other works a biographical novel about Alexander Hamilton, *The Conqueror* (1902); a novel set in ancient Greece, *The Immortal Marriage* (1927); and a sensational best-seller, *Black Oxen* (1923). Atherton's range was wide, but she is perhaps best remembered for her insights into the psychosocial elements influencing the lives of urban dwellers and her creation of unconventional heroines.

Sources

Leider, Emily. *California's Daughter: Gertrude Atherton and Her Times.* Stanford, Calif.: Stanford University Press, 1991.

McClure, Charlotte S. *Gertrude Atherton.* Boston: Twayne, 1979.

Atlantic Monthly, The periodical

Founded in BOSTON in 1857 by the publisher Moses Dresser Phillips and several prominent writers, the *Atlantic Monthly* was from the outset a product of the New England literary elite. Its very name was bestowed by Oliver Wendell HOLMES, who also contributed his *AUTOCRAT OF THE BREAKFAST TABLE* series over many years. James Russell LOWELL was another early contributor who also served as editor during the magazine's first four years, despite its sale in 1859 to the publisher Ticknor & Fields. Lowell got the magazine off to an excellent start by soliciting work from such literary lights as Ralph Waldo EMERSON, Henry Wadsworth LONGFELLOW, John Greenleaf WHITTIER, and Harriet Beecher STOWE. The magazine's focus was trained squarely on New England during this period, and it was only when James T. FIELDS took over as editor that *The Atlantic Monthly* turned its attention elsewhere. Fields served as editor for the next decade, which saw the beginning and end of the great national trauma of the CIVIL WAR, which Fields addressed through contributions on contemporary matters by William Graham SUMNER and Carl SCHURZ. William Dean HOWELLS assumed the editor's chair in 1871 and widened the magazine's field of vision by publishing regional authors from all over the country: Mark Twain (see CLEMENS, Samuel), Bret HARTE, Mary N. MURFREE, and Paul Hamilton HAYNE were only some of his contributors. Howells also added new departments devoted to science, music, and education, and he introduced book reviews to the magazine's pages.

The Atlantic Monthly remained largely a literary periodical, however, until Ellery Sedgwick, the magazine's eighth editor, took over in 1909, emphasizing economic, political, social, and scientific aspects of the American scene, thereby greatly increasing circulation. The magazine has nonetheless maintained its original identity, continuing into the 21st century as one of the sole surviving literary periodicals.

Sources

Sedgwick, Ellery. *The Atlantic Monthly, 1857–1909: Yankee Humanism at High Tide and Ebb.* Amherst: University of Massachusetts Press, 1994.

Audubon, John James (1785–1851) *naturalist artist, writer*

Born in Santo Domingo (now Haiti), John James Audubon was the son of a French naval officer and a Creole woman. After studying art in France with the great historical painter and portraitist Jacques-Louis David (1748–1825), in 1804 Audubon went to live at his father's estate, Mill Grove, near Philadelphia. It was there that he began to observe birds and conduct the first bird-banding experiments in America in order to track ornithological behavior.

In 1808 Audubon married Lucy Bakewell and moved to Kentucky, which he used as a base from which to travel to the American frontier. There he began the series of avian portraits that would culminate in his masterwork, *The Birds of America* (1827–38). In the interim Audubon depended greatly on the financial support of his wife, who ran a private school in Louisiana, where the family had moved in 1820. It proved difficult for him to find a publisher in the United States, but a trip to England in 1826 resulted in publication of *Birds of America* in elephant-folio size (approximately 14 by 23 inches), with accompanying text written by Audubon and the Scottish naturalist William McGillivray (1764?–1825).

Audubon was also a keen observer of American frontier life. *Delineations of American Scenery and Character* (1926) and *Audubon's America* (1940) contain extracts from his journals that reveal a vivid style and a gift for narrative. His portraits of birds however, remain his main contribution to American intellectual history.

Sources

Alexander, Pamela. *Commonwealth of Wings: An Ornithological Biography Based on the Life of John James Audubon.* Hanover, N.H.: University Press of New England, 1991.

Proby, Kathryn Hall. *Audubon in Florida. With Selections from the Writings of John James Audubon.* Coral Gables, Fla.: University of Miami Press, 1974.

Austin, Mary Hunter (1868–1934) *novelist, poet, short story writer, playwright, essayist*

Born in Carlinville, Ohio, Mary Hunter's affinity for the natural world began, she said, at the age of five when she talked to God beneath a walnut tree in her back yard. In 1888 she moved with her family to California, where she and her mother and siblings (her father had died in 1878) homesteaded in the southern San Joaquin Valley. Her record of the journey from Los Angeles to the homestead, *One Hundred Miles on Horseback,* was published in 1889.

In 1891 Mary Hunter married a fellow homesteader, Stafford Austin. When their attempt at grape growing failed, they moved in 1892 to San Francisco, where Mary Austin published her first story, "The Mother of Felipe," in the *OVERLAND MONTHLY* that same year. Around the same time the Austins' marriage began to fail. They moved together to the desert Owens Valley, where their only child, a mentally retarded daughter named Ruth, was born. This sojourn in the Mojave Desert inspired Austin to write *The Land of Little Rain,* a collection of nature essays serialized in the *ATLANTIC MONTHLY* in 1903.

The Land of Little Rain launched Austin's literary career. After she and her husband separated in 1905 (they would divorce nine years later, and Ruth would die, institutionalized, in 1918), Austin moved to Carmel, California, where she became associated with Jack LONDON and George STERLING. A few years later, believing herself ill with cancer, Austin traveled to Italy, where she undertook a variety of mystical exercises. Restored to health, she returned to New York in 1920 for the production of what would be her most popular play, *The Arrow Maker,* the story of a female shaman. For the next 14 years she divided her time between New York and Carmel, lecturing widely on American aboriginal life. She was profoundly interested in the women's movement and wrote an autobiographical novel, *A Woman of Genius* (1912), about a woman who attempts to escape her restricted existence by immersing herself in the theater. She also wrote a more overtly feminist novel, *No. 26 Jayne Street* (1920), set in New York.

In 1924 Austin moved permanently to Santa Fe, New Mexico, where she became deeply involved in the struggle for aboriginal rights and the preservation of Indian and Spanish folk art. New Mexico also inspired some of her most lasting works, including the nature studies of *The Land of Journey's Ending* (1924) and her final novel, *Starry Adventure* (1931), in which the New Mexican landscape serves as the main character.

Sources

Fink, Augusta. *I-Mary: A Biography of Mary Austin.* Tucson: University of Arizona Press, 1983.

Graulich, Melody and Elizabeth Klimasmith, eds. *Exploring Lost Borders: Critical Essays on Mary Austin.* Reno: University of Nevada Press, 1999.

Lanigan, Esther F. *Mary Austin: Song of a Maverick.* New Haven, Conn.: Yale University Press, 1989.

Authors League of America *organization*

Founded in 1912 in the aftermath of the adoption of the 1909 Copyright Act, the Authors League had as its mission the protection of authors' rights in their creative products. These rights were somewhat enlarged by the new statute, but they were still not entirely safeguarded. The types of members admitted to the organization have changed over the years, and in 1964 the League formed alliances with the Authors Guild and the Dramatists' Guild, with which the League has overlapping but not identical interests.

Sources

Middleton, George. *The Dramatists' Guild, What It Is and Does, How It Happened and Why.* New York: Dramatists' Guild, 1966.

Autocrat of the Breakfast Table, The Oliver Wendell Holmes (1858) *essays*

This series of discursive essays by Oliver Wendell HOLMES grew out of two works by the same name which Holmes published in 1831–32 in *THE NEW-ENGLAND MAGAZINE.* The later series takes the form of a continuing conversation among a stock set of characters (such as the Schoolmistress, the Divinity Student, and the Poor Relation) around the breakfast table of an imaginary boarding house. This loose format allowed Holmes to expatiate amusingly on a wide range of topics, even permitting him to interject poems, some of which—"The Deacon's Masterpiece" and "The Chambered Nautilus," for example—gained recognition independently for their artistry.

Sources

Broaddus, Dorothy C. *Genteel Rhetoric: Writing High Culture in Nineteenth-Century Boston.* Columbia: University of South Carolina Press, 1999.

Hoyt, Edwin Palmer. *The Improper Bostonian: Dr. Oliver Wendell Holmes.* New York: Morrow, 1979.

Small, Miriam Rossiter. *Oliver Wendell Holmes.* New York: Twayne, 1963.

Awakening, The *Kate Chopin* (1899) *novel*

Set in Louisiana, Kate CHOPIN's second novel features a young wife, Edna Pontellier, coming to terms with her awakening sexuality. Born and raised in Kentucky, Edna has spent the first six years of her marriage to a respectable businessman in the traditional fashion, taking care of her family and paying calls on respectable neighbors. Then one summer, while on a visit to Grand Isle, near New Orleans, she makes friends with several people who are more interested in her than in her husband's family ties. Edna forms an especially close attachment with a young Creole man, Robert Lebrun, who teaches her how to swim. At first afraid of the water, Edna soon learns to love the sense of solitude it gives her, venturing farther and farther from the shore until a vision of death frightens her.

At the end of the summer Robert leaves for Mexico and Edna and her family return to New Orleans, but Edna finds that she cannot settle back into her old routine. Openly expressing to her husband her distaste for her old life, Edna keeps up her relationship with two of the women she got to know on Grand Isle. She also corresponds with Robert—who confesses his love for her—while awaiting his return.

Edna's distraction alienates her husband, who spends more and more time away from home and finally suggests that their boys be sent to stay with their grandmother in the country. Seeking diversion, Edna goes alone to the racetrack, where she meets another attractive Creole man, Alcée Arobin, with whom she begins an affair. While her husband is away on an extended business trip, she then moves into a cottage, where she lives alone and entertains Arobin. One day Robert returns, only to leave abruptly again, saying that he cannot reconcile his love with her status as a married woman. The next day Edna goes to Grand Isle, where she rents a room. That evening she walks down to the water, where she takes off her clothes and swims out to her death.

Not surprisingly, *The Awakening* was condemned by male reviewers as "unwholesome." After its publication Chopin wrote only a few short stories before dying in 1904 of a cerebral hemorrhage. She was almost completely forgotten until the 1960s, when the burgeoning women's movement rediscovered her, transforming *The Awakening* into not only a popular book but also a classic of American literature.

Sources

Koloski, Bernard J. *Approaches to Teaching Kate Chopin's "The Awakening."* New York: Modern Language Association of America, 1988.

Toth, Emily. *Kate Chopin.* New York: Morrow, 1990.

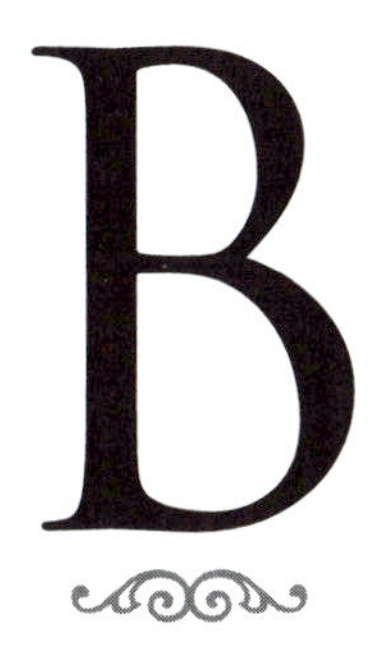

Bacheller, Irving Addison (1859–1950) *journalist, novelist*
Born in Pierpont, New York, Irving Bacheller graduated from St. Lawrence University in 1882 and founded the first newspaper syndicate in the nation in 1884. In addition to a number of autobiographical works, he published *A Man for the Ages* (1919), a tale about Abraham LINCOLN, and a number of novels concerning early American life. The most famous of his works is *Eben Holden* (1900), the story of a homely hired man that proved to be wildly popular. It placed Bacheller in the so-called B'Gosh School of novelists such as E. N. Westcott (1846–1898) who developed memorable characters of the folk philosopher type.

Sources

Hanna, Alfred Jackson. *A Bibliography of the Writings of Irving Bacheller.* Winter Park, Fla.: Rollins College, 1939.

Bagby, George William (1828–1883) *journalist, humorist*
A Virginia journalist, George William Bagby edited the *SOUTHERN LITERARY MESSENGER* from 1860 to 1864, but he is best remembered for the "Mozis Addums" letters, a series of humorous newspaper pieces in which Bagby posed as an unlettered common man, dating from 1859. In that year Bagby half-humorously committed himself to "The Unkind but Complete Destruction" of John Esten COOKE, the author of highly romanticized tales about antebellum Virginia, the "Old Dominion." But the regime of the unlettered, uncouth Mozis Addums did not last, as even Bagby gave way to nostalgia in the wake of the CIVIL WAR. His sketch "The Old Virginia Gentleman" (1877) presented as sentimental and idealized a picture of antebellum life in his native state as Cooke ever had been guilty of conjuring up.

Sources

King, Joseph Leonard. *Dr. George William Bagby: A Study of Virginian Literature, 1850–1880.* New York: Columbia University Press, 1927.

Bailey, James Montgomery (1841–1894) *journalist, humorist*
Known as the "Danbury News Man," James Montgomery Bailey was a Civil War journalist widely considered to be the father of the humorous newspaper column. The local Danbury, Connecticut, newspaper published a series of his articles that dealt with current events in a light-handed—if not lighthearted—fashion. The articles were later reprinted in highly popular collections.

Sources

Riley, Sam G. *The American Newspaper Columnist.* Westport, Conn.: Praeger, 1998.

Ballou, Adin (1803–1890) *journalist, theologian*
Born in Cumberland, Rhode Island, Adin Ballou was a Universalist clergyman (see UNIVERSALISM) who was also the publisher of a magazine called the *Independent Messenger* from 1831 to 1839. During that same period he was a powerful voice in the movement that resulted in the Massachusetts Association of Universal Restorationists, which

espoused the belief that all men would be restored to a happy state in the afterlife. In 1841 Ballou became one of the principal founders of the Hopedale Community near Milford, Massachusetts. Hopedale was one of the many Utopian communities that flourished under religious auspices during that period. After it disbanded in 1856, Ballou wrote the *History of the Hopedale Community* (1857). Other works include the Universalist *Practical Christian Socialism* (1854) and *Primitive Christianity and Its Corruptions* (1870).

Sources

Memoir of Adin Augustus Ballou. Hopedale: Community Press, 1853.

Spann, Edward K. *Hopedale: From Commune to Company Town.* Columbus: Ohio University Press, 1992.

Ballou, Maturin Murray (Lieutenant Murray) (1820–1895) *editor, novelist*

The son of Hosea Ballou (1771–1852), the leading exponent of the Universalist religious doctrine (see UNIVERSALISM) and a distant relative of Adin Ballou, Maturin Ballou was a Boston publisher and editor who made his name as the author of numerous works of popular fiction—many published under the pseudonym Lieutenant Murray. Ballou was among the first to write using a specific formula, and as an editor he insisted that others adhere to prescribed structures and plotting. A busy man, he was responsible at various times for the journals *Flag of Our Country, Gleason's Pictorial Drawing Room Companion, Ballou's Dollar Monthly,* and the *Boston Globe.*

Baltimore *Sun* *periodical*

Founded in 1837 as a nonpartisan penny daily, this newspaper came to national attention when, during the MEXICAN WAR, it scooped the federal government by reporting news of the U.S. victory at Veracruz before the War Department could make an official announcement. During the CIVIL WAR, the paper—like Maryland itself—looked toward the South but opposed secession. In 1910 the paper began to publish a separate edition called *The Evening Sun,* and in 1918–19 it issued an overseas edition for American troops serving in World War I. Perhaps the most celebrated writer to have been connected with the *Sun* was H. L. Mencken, who was a member of the staff from 1906 to 1916 and then again from 1918 to 1941.

Bancroft, George (1800–1891) *historian, poet*

Born in Worcester, Massachusetts, George Bancroft began life as a scholar, studying divinity at Harvard and history at Göttingen in Germany. After lecturing in Greek at Harvard for a time, he established his own school following an advanced European model. A second career as a statesman included his appointment as secretary of the navy under James K. Polk (1795–1849) from 1845 to 1846—during which time Bancroft helped to establish the U.S. Naval Academy—as well as service as U.S. minister to Britain (1846–49) and Germany (1867–74). A poet as well as an accomplished writer of prose, Bancroft's most important work was his monumental 10-volume *History of the United States,* published between 1834 and 1876 and revised and expanded between 1883 and 1885.

Sources

Handlin, Lilian. *George Bancroft, the Intellectual as Democrat.* New York: Harper & Row, 1984.

Vitzthum, Richard C. *The American Compromise: Theme and Method in the Histories of Bancroft, Parkman, and Adams.* Norman: University of Oklahoma Press, 1974.

Bancroft, Hubert Howe (1832–1918) *historian*

Born in Granville, Ohio, Hubert Howe Bancroft migrated west to California in 1852 in search of gold. Once there, he opened a bookstore and publishing firm in San Francisco. Bancroft was soon the leading bookseller in the West, and he amassed a fortune which, in 1859, he began to spend on acquisition of regional source materials. This collection provided Bancroft with materials for his five-volume history of the *Native Races* (1874–75), his 34-volume *History of the Pacific States* (1882–90), and his seven-volume *Chronicles of the Builders* (1891–92). These works made Bancroft the first prominent historian of the American West—although it is now widely accepted that he depended heavily on contributions from others in writing them. Bancroft also wrote books about Spanish California and the Gold Rush for general readers as well as two autobiographical works: *Literary Industries* (1890) and *Retrospection, Political and Personal* (1910). In 1905 Bancroft sold his collection—then comprising some 60,000 volumes and known as The Bancroft Library—to the University of California.

Sources

Caughey, John Walton. *Hubert Howe Bancroft, Historian of the West.* Berkeley: University of California Press, 1946.

Bandelier, Adolph Francis Alphonse (1840–1914) *archaeologist, novelist*

Born in Berne, Switzerland, in 1848, Adolph Bandelier was brought to the United States, where he became a pioneering archaeologist and anthropologist who focused on the pre-Columbian cultures of the Southwest. This work gave rise to many scholarly writings as well as to popular books such as *The Delight Makers* (1890), concerning the prehistoric Pueblo Indians of New Mexico, and *The Gilded Man* (1893), a story about the search for El Dorado, the mythical lost City of Gold. Between 1892 and 1903, Bandelier continued his archaeological work in Peru and Bolivia, returning to the United States to take up museum and teaching positions in New York and Washington, D.C. The Bandelier National Monument, a collection of prehistoric Indian ruins near Santa Fe, New Mexico, was established in his honor in 1913.

Sources

Lange, Charles H. *Bandelier: The Life and Adventures of Adolph Bandelier.* Salt Lake City: University of Utah Press, 1996.

Bangs, John Kendrick (1862–1922) *humorist*

Born in Yonkers, New York, and educated at Columbia University, John Kendrick Bangs was the editor of the American humor magazine *Puck* from 1904 to 1905. In addition to editing a series of other magazines, he published more than 30 books of poetry, stories, and plays covering a wide range of subjects. He is best remembered for his collections of extravagantly humorous tales such as *Tiddlywink Tales* (1891), *The Idiot* (1895), and *A Houseboat on the Styx* (1896).

Sources

Bangs, Francis Hyde. *John Kendrick Bangs, Humorist of the Nineties: The Story of an American Editor–Author–Lecturer and His Associations.* New York: Alfred A. Knopf, 1941.

Bannister, Nathaniel Harrington (1813–1847) *playwright*

A Baltimore-based actor and prolific author of historical melodramas, Nathaniel Bannister wrote only one successful work: *Putnam, the Iron Son of '76* (1844). Heavily laced with humor, the basic story concerns the hero's escape from the British and his rescue of an Indian child. After it premiered at the BOWERY THEATRE in New York, the play ran for 78 performances and was regularly revived there and elsewhere in subsequent years. Bannister's other plays, like *England's Iron Days* (1837), concerning the Norman Conquest, proved to be far less popular.

Barnes, Charlotte Mary Sanford (1818–1863) *playwright, novelist*

The daughter of English emigré actors John (1761–1841) and Mary (1780?–1864) Barnes, Charlotte Barnes made her acting debut at age four on the stage of the PARK THEATRE in New York, where her parents were a part of the company for decades. She continued her stage career, appearing in classical and contemporary roles at theaters in New York, Boston, and London, as well as at Philadelphia's Arch Street Theatre when it was managed by her husband, Edmond S. Connor. Barnes also translated several French melodramas and wrote plays based on popular novels and legends. Notable works in the latter category are *Octavia Bragaldi* (1837), a blank verse play set in 15th-century Milan and based on the KENTUCKY TRAGEDY; and *The Forest Princess* (1848), concerning the adventures of Pocahontas.

Sources

Barnes, Charlotte Mary Sanford. *Plays, Prose and Poetry.* Philadelphia: E. H. Butler & Co., 1848.

Barnum, Phineas Taylor (1810–1891) *showman, memoirist*

Born in Connecticut, P. T. Barnum worked a variety of jobs (salesman, boarding house manager) before discovering his true metier. In 1835, he bought and exhibited the octogenarian Joice Heth, a slave who claimed that she was 161 years old and had been George Washington's nurse. In 1842 he opened his American Museum in New York City, where he exhibited such curiosities as the "Fiji mermaid" (created by joining the upper half of a monkey with the stuffed lower half of a fish), the three-foot-tall man he called "General Tom Thumb," and the Siamese twins Chang and Eng. The museum also hosted sideshows and stage entertainment, becoming famous for its extravagant publicity. In 1844 Barnum began to build an international reputation as a showman when he toured with Tom Thumb; this reputation was enhanced when he managed the American tour of the "Swedish nightingale," the singer Jenny Lind.

So great was Barnum's fame that in 1855 he retired from show business and took up politics, serving as mayor of Bridgeport, Connecticut, as well as in the state legislature. He was no politician, however, and ill-advised business ventures drove him back into show business. He reopened his museum, and in 1871 he organized a circus, which he advertised as "the greatest show on earth." In 1881 Barnum's circus merged with that of his arch competitor, James A. Bailey. The Barnum & Bailey Circus—with its star attraction, the 6 ½-ton African elephant, Jumbo—continued for a generation after Barnum's death. After Jumbo's death, the elephant was stuffed and placed on exhibit at the Barnum Museum of Natural History, founded in 1883 at Tufts University, where Barnum had served as a trustee.

Barnum first published his *Life of P.T. Barnum, Written by Himself* in 1855; it was frequently revised and reprinted. He also wrote *The Humbugs of the World* (1865), *Struggles and Triumphs* (1869), and *Money Getting* (1883). The inventor of modern American show business, Barnum was extremely popular—even influential—in his day, and appeared in works of fiction, including Herman MELVILLE's *Mardi* (1849).

Sources

Harris, Neal. *Humbug: The Art of P.T. Barnum.* Boston: Little, Brown, 1973.

Tompert, Ann. *The Greatest Showman on Earth: A Biography of P.T. Barnum.* Minneapolis, Minn.: Dillon Press, 1987.

Barr, Amelia Edith Huddleston (1831–1919) *novelist*

Born in Lancashire, England, Amelia Edith Barr came to the United States in 1853 with her husband. The couple spent several years in Texas during its days as a republic. In 1868, after her husband's death, Barr moved with her three daughters to New York City, where she began writing for newspapers and started a career as a novelist. She specialized in historical fiction aimed at the general reader. Among the best known of her more than 60 volumes of fiction are *Jan Vedder's Wife* (1885), set in the Shetland Islands; and *The Bow of Orange Ribbon* (1886), set in New York before the Revolutionary War. An autobiography, *All the Days of My Life,* appeared in 1913.

"Bartleby, the Scrivener" *Herman Melville* (1853) *short story*

One of the most celebrated pieces of short fiction written by Herman MELVILLE, "Bartleby" concerns a scribe who is hired by the narrator, a Wall Street lawyer. Bartleby, whose job is that of a human copying machine, goes about his work in a thorough, precise way until one day, when asked to help proofread a document, he replies, "I would prefer not to." Over time Bartleby refuses to do more and more work, instead spending his days staring out a window at a blank wall. Eventually the lawyer, who has not treated Bartleby unkindly—so he believes—is obliged to fire the scrivener, but Bartleby refuses to leave, even at night.

Bartleby's passive resistance and haunting presence begin to affect the morale of the other employees and to threaten the lawyer's professional reputation. Since he cannot dislodge Bartleby, the lawyer decides to move his office. But the new tenant tells the lawyer that Bartleby still haunts the place, and out of charity, responsibility, or fear for his own prestige, the lawyer seeks out his former employee. When Bartleby again declines to bend to his will, the lawyer calls the police, who take Bartleby off to jail.

When the lawyer visits Bartleby in the Tombs, he finds that the one-time scrivener has refused to eat the special meals his former employer has provided for him, instead spending his days staring catatonically at a blank prison wall. In the end, one day when the lawyer stops in to see Bartleby, he finds the emaciated prisoner dead, lying next to the wall. Afterward, the lawyer hears a rumor that Bartleby had once worked as a clerk in the Dead Letter Office.

"Bartleby" has been interpreted variously as a barely veiled autobiographical account of Melville's own failed literary career and subsequent job as a civil servant at the Custom-House near Wall Street, as an allegory about the fundamental loneliness of existence, and as a narrative of insanity (Bartleby) or self-satisfied obtuseness (the lawyer)—or both. The story—and in particular its evocative ending, "Ah Bartleby! Ah, humanity!"—add to the paradoxically rich but elusive quality of this story named for a character who is both something more and something less than a human cipher.

Sources

Inge, M. Thomas, ed. *Bartleby the Inscrutable: A Collection of Commentary on Herman Melville's Tale "Bartleby the Scrivener."* Hamden, Conn.: Archon Books, 1979.

Bartlett, John (1820–1905) *editor*

Born in Plymouth, Massachusetts, John Bartlett went on to own the University Book Store in Cambridge, Massachusetts, a popular gathering place for Harvard faculty and students. His book of *Familiar Quotations,* first published in 1855, was compiled while he was still working at his store. In 1863 Bartlett joined the Boston publisher Little, Brown & Company, and in 1878 he became the firm's senior partner. His book of quotations went through nine editions during his lifetime and since his death has been revised and enlarged several more times. A Shakespeare concordance he published in 1894 is still considered a standard reference work.

Sources

Morgan, M. H. *John Bartlett.* Boston: n.p., 1908.
Morley, Christopher. *Preface to "Bartlett."* Boston: Little, Brown, 1937.

Bassett, John Spencer (1867–1928) *historian*

Born in Tarboro, North Carolina, John Spencer Bassett was a history professor at Trinity College (now Duke University) from 1893 to 1906. He served a similar role at Smith College from 1906 to 1928. In 1902 he founded the important literary journal *SOUTH ATLANTIC QUARTERLY*. In addition to editing *The Writings of "Colonel William Byrd . . ."* (1901) and the seven-volume *Correspondence of Andrew Jackson* (1926–35), Bassett published several important historical works, including *The Federalist System, 1789–1801* (1906) and a *Life of Andrew Jackson* (1911).

Baum, Lyman Frank (1856–1919) *writer of children's literature, playwright, journalist*

Born in Chittenango, New York, and educated at Peekskill Military Academy, L. Frank Baum first worked as a poultry farmer. This experience would serve him well when writing his first book, *Father Goose: His Book* (1899), which he completed while working as a newspaperman in South Dakota. *Father Goose* was an immediate success, and a year later Baum sealed his reputation as a master of children's literature when he published *The Wonderful Wizard of Oz,* which he would turn into a play that was produced in 1901. Baum would write 14 more books set in Oz. In addition, under the pen names Captain Hugh Fitzgerald and Floyd Akers he wrote books for boys and used the name Mrs. Edith Van Dyne when writing for girls. He adopted yet another pseudonym, Schuyler Stanton, for three of his adventure tales. Altogether his output reached some 60 volumes.

Sources

Hearn, M. P., ed. *The Annotated Wizard of Oz.* New York: Clarkson Potter, 1973.

Moore, Raylyn. *Wonderful Wizard, Marvelous Land.* Bowling Green, Ohio: Bowling Green University Popular Press, 1974.

Beadle, Erastus (1821–1894) *novelist*

This master marketer is widely remembered as the father of the DIME NOVEL. Beadle began his career publishing song books and game manuals that cost 10 cents. In 1860 he found his true métier when he advertised Ann S. Stephens's *Malaeska, the Indian Wife of the White Hunter,* as "a dollar book for a dime." Reportedly the book sold 300,000 copies the first year after publication. Hundreds of novels concerning frontier adventures penned by the likes of "Buffalo Bill" CODY and Fred Whittaker followed. After 1880, when Beadle turned to books about train robbers and detectives, the dime novel lost much of its luster, instead acquiring a reputation for cheap sensationalism.

Sources

Denning, Michael. *Mechanic Accents: Dime Novels and Working-Class Culture in America.* New York: Verso, 1987.

Sullivan, Larry E., and Lydia Cushman Schurman, eds. *Pioneers, Passionate Ladies, and Private Eyes: Dime Novels, Series Books, and Paperbacks.* New York: Haworth Press, 1996.

Beecher, Catharine Esther (1800–1878) *essayist*

Born in East Hampton, New York, the daughter of the prominent clergyman Lyman BEECHER and the older sister of the future novelist Harriet Beecher STOWE, Catharine Beecher became an educator. After teaching in New London, Connecticut, for two years, in 1823 she opened a girls' school with her sister Harriet that would later become Hartford Female Seminary. In 1831 she opened the Western Female Academy in Cincinnati, Ohio, and subsequently, similar institutions in Quincy, Illinois, Milwaukee, Wisconsin, and Burlington, Iowa. The founder of the American Women's Educational Association in 1852, Beecher was a proponent of liberal education for women but an opponent of female suffrage. An ardent abolitionist (see ABOLITIONISM), in 1837 she published *An Essay on Slavery and Abolitionism.* She is also famous for the housewives' handbooks she wrote with her sister, most importantly, *The American Woman's Home* (1869) and the *New Housekeeper's Manual* (1873).

Sources

Sklar, Kathryn Kish. *Catharine Beecher: A Study in American Domesticity.* New Haven, Conn.: Yale University Press, 1973.

Beecher, Henry Ward (1813–1887) *theologian, writer, editor*

Born in Litchfield, Connecticut, Henry Ward Beecher was the son of Lyman BEECHER and the brother of Catharine BEECHER and Harriet Beecher STOWE. After graduating from Amherst College and attending Lane Theological Seminary, he began his clerical career in Indiana before taking the pulpit of the important Plymouth Congregational Church in BROOKLYN, New York, in 1847. A celebrated orator and lecturer, he was prominent in the antislavery and women's suffrage movements and was an exponent of the doctrine of evolution. In addition to editing the *Independent* and the *Christian Union,* he published a life of Jesus (1871); *Evolution and Religion* (1885); and a sentimental novel, *Norwood; or, Village Life in New England* (1867). His sermons were also published and widely distributed. A lawsuit brought against him by Theodore Tilton in 1874 accused Beecher of adultery, and although the jury could not agree on a verdict, the scandal tarnished Beecher's reputation.

Sources

Ryan, Halford Ross. *Henry Ward Beecher: Peripatetic Preacher.* New York: Greenwood Press, 1990.

Beecher, Lyman (1775–1863) *theologian, essayist*

Born in New Haven, Connecticut, and educated at Yale University, Lyman Beecher became a famous Congregationalist minister known for his campaign against liquor and his strong anti-Catholic sentiments. In 1816 he helped found the American Bible Society, and from 1832 to 1852 he served as president of Lane Theological Seminary in Cincinnati, Ohio. While there, Beecher was a defendant in a heresy trial, which resulted in his acquittal. His sermons and essays were published as part of his *Collected Works* in 1852, and his *Autobiography* appeared in 1864. He was the father of 13 children, among them Henry Ward BEECHER, Catharine BEECHER, and Harriet Beecher STOWE.

Sources

Fraser, James W. *Pedagogue for God's Kingdom: Lyman Beecher and the Second Great Awakening.* Lanham, Md.: University Press of America, 1985.

Beer, Thomas (1888–1940) *novelist, short story writer, biographer*

Born in Iowa, Thomas Beer graduated from Yale University in 1911 and served in World War I before taking up a writing career. He wrote three novels: *The Fair Rewards* (1922), concerning a New York theater impresario; *Sandoval* (1924), which he called "a romance of bad manners" and which is set in the New York of the 1870s; and *The Road to Heaven* (1928), a romance about rural life. Beer was also known for his humorous short stories, collected in *Mrs. Egg and Other Barbarians* (1933) and the posthumously published *The Agreeable Finish* (1941). His biography *Stephen Crane* (1923) helped establish CRANE's reputation—perhaps based on details Beer manufactured. Another biography, *Hanna* (1929), concerns the businessman and Republican kingmaker Mark Hanna (1837–1904), who is believed to have engineered the 1896 and 1900 presidential victories of William McKinley (1843–1901). Beer's interest in turn-of-the-century American life is also reflected in his literary and historical survey, *The Mauve Decade* (1926), which provided the 1890s with a memorable moniker.

Belasco, David (1859–1931) *playwright*

Born in San Francisco, David Belasco came from a Portuguese-Jewish family whose name was originally Velasco. While he was still a child, Belasco came under the influence of a Father McGuire; he later claimed that his affectation of wearing a clerical collar was meant as an homage to his early mentor.

Belasco's introduction to theater came early, and he may have made his theatrical debut as early as 1864, playing the Duke of York opposite the celebrated actor Charles Kean in Shakespeare's *Richard III.* Belasco wrote his first play, *Jim Black; or, The Regulator's Revenge* when he was a mere 12 years old. While still a teenager, he shared the stage with such leading actors of the day as John McCullogh and Edwin Booth at the Metropolitan Theatre in San Francisco. In Virginia City, Nevada, he was associated with the playwright Dion BOUCICAULT, from whom he learned stagecraft as well as much about acting and playwriting. Back in San Francisco, Belasco—then 19 years old—was appointed stage manager of the Baldwin Theatre, which mounted several of his early productions. In 1880 he toured the country with the play *Hearts of Oak,* which he and James A. Hearne adapted from an old melodrama.

In 1882, under the auspices of the theater impresario David Frohman, Belasco came to New York, where he managed the Madison Square Theatre for two years. After returning to San Francisco for two years, Belasco came back to New York to take up a position as stage manager at Frohman's Lyceum. While there Belasco wrote a number of plays, but he did not make a name for himself until he became an independent producer with *The Heart of Maryland* (1895), a CIVIL WAR romance which he also wrote and directed. Many hits followed, including the East-meets-West romance *Madame Butterfly* (1900) and the Western romance *The Girl of the Golden West* (1905). Some of these were plays that Belasco wrote himself or in collaboration, some were adaptations, and some he simply produced.

Belasco was known for the realism he brought to the stage and for his innovations in stage lighting. He was also a starmaker, fostering the careers of such actors as Mrs. Leslie Carter, Blanche Bates, Ina Claire, and David Warfield. In 1906 he built his own theater, which he first called the Stuyvesant but later rechristened with his own name. His collection of theatrical materials, associated with the more than 400 plays he produced, is held at the New York Public Library.

Sources

Marker, Lise-Lone. *David Belasco: Naturalism in the American Theatre.* Princeton, N.J.: Princeton University Press, 1975.

Timberlake, Craig. *The Life & Work of David Belasco, the Bishop of Broadway.* New York: Library Publishers, 1954.

Bellamy, Edward (1850–1898) *novelist*

Born in Massachusetts, Edward Bellamy came from a long line of New England ministers. He himself eschewed theology, choosing instead to study law, although he never practiced. After a period working as a journalist, Bellamy began writing fiction: first short stories that appeared in magazines and then a novel based on Shays's Rebellion, *The Duke of Stockbridge,* which was published serially in 1879. In 1878 he published *One: A Nantucket Idyl* (1878), which had grown out of a trip to Hawaii the previous year. *Dr. Heidenhoff's Process* (1880) and *Miss Ludington's Sister* (1884) reflected Bellamy's interest in psychic phenomena as well as the influence of Nathaniel HAWTHORNE.

Fame came in 1888 with the publication of *Looking Backward: 2000–1887,* a Utopian romance that depicted a future society under a system of state socialism. The novel proved to be immensely popular, selling nearly a million copies over the next 10 years. It was imitated by others and led to the founding of the Nationalist Party, which was based on principles enunciated in the novel. Bellamy did not capitalize on his success commercially, opting instead to campaign for social reform. In 1891 he founded the weekly *New Nation,* which he edited. He also lectured widely and wrote *Equality* (1897), which is less a sequel to *Looking Backward* than a theoretical tract outlining the principles espoused in the earlier novel. While writing this last work, Bellamy succumbed to tuberculosis.

Sources

Bowman, Sylvia E. *Edward Bellamy.* Boston: Twayne, 1986.

Patai, Deborah, ed. *Looking Backward: 1988–1888: Essays on Edward Bellamy.* Amherst: University of Massachusetts Press, 1988.

"Benito Cereno" *Herman Melville* (1856) *short story*
This story opens with Delano, captain of the seal ship *Bachelor's Delight,* spotting a ship in trouble in a desolate area off the southern coast of Chile. In an attempt to offer help, he and a small crew of his men row over to the *San Dominick,* a ship with a cargo of Senegalese slaves captained by the Spaniard Don Benito Cereno. Seeing the sad state of affairs aboard the slaver, Delano sends his men back to the *Bachelor's Delight* for additional supplies. Delano himself stays aboard the *San Dominick,* where the dispirited and seemingly disoriented Don Benito, accompanied by his attentive black body servant, Babo, explains that the slaver, buffeted by storms and disease, has lost all of its Spanish officers. As a result, the ship and its human cargo are in a pronounced state of disorder.

Delano, who can see this much for himself, nevertheless cannot make sense of the whole picture aboard the *San Dominick.* He finds Don Benito's demeanor especially incomprehensible. When one of the slaves stabs a white sailor, the Spanish captain shrugs off the incident. Don Benito seems similarly indifferent when a magisterial slave, Atufal, is brought before him in chains but refuses to beg Benito's pardon for the offense that caused him to be manacled. Other slaves, engaged in polishing hatchets, make threatening gestures that Benito ignores. And when Don Benito sullenly refuses Delano's offer of hospitality aboard the *Bachelor's Delight,* the American is almost convinced that the Spaniard is not what he seems. Babo, Delano concludes, is both more polite and more commanding.

It is only at the end of this very long tale that the accuracy of Delano's perceptions becomes the focus of the narrative. As he takes his leave of Don Benito, the Spaniard suddenly leaps into Delano's boat, followed by Babo, who clearly aims to kill his captain. Suddenly Amasa Delano experiences a revelation. As he casts his eyes towards the *San Dominick,* where armed slaves pursue the few remaining Spaniards, he understands that the former have been in control all along. As the appended deposition makes clear, the *San Dominick* had been the scene of a bloody slave revolt led by Babo, who also masterminded the masquerade of subservience played out for Delano's benefit.

A coda to the story, however, gives rise to still more ambiguity. As the two captains sail together toward Lima, Don Benito is unable to shake free from his melancholy. When Amasa Delano inquires, "[W]hat has cast such a shadow upon you?" Benito Cereno replies, "The negro." The master, having been violently forced into the role of a slave, finds himself unable to come to terms with the experience.

Published in the bloody, contentious period leading up to the CIVIL WAR, "Benito Cereno" provided commentary on what Melville called "the power of blackness," the power that derives from human depravity and original sin.

Sources

Burkholder, Robert E., ed. *Critical Essays on Herman Melville's "Benito Cereno."* New York: G. K. Hall, 1992.

Benjamin, Park (1809–1864) *journalist*
Born in British Guiana, Park Benjamin was first the owner and editor of *The* NEW-ENGLAND MAGAZINE. In 1835 this was merged with *AMERICAN MONTHLY MAGAZINE,* where Benjamin became associate editor. He is best known, however, for the magazine he founded in 1839, *New World.* Because of the near absence of international copyright laws, this weekly, which lasted until 1845, reprinted works by British authors without paying them or their estates. Benjamin himself was notorious for his journalistic excesses, which eventually landed him among those whom James Fenimore COOPER successfully sued for libel. Benjamin is less well known for his own verse, which was frequently reprinted during his lifetime.

Sources

Hoover, Merle Montgomery. *Park Benjamin, Poet & Editor.* New York: Columbia University Press, 1948.

Benton, Thomas Hart (1782–1858) *journalist*
Born in Hillsboro, North Carolina, Thomas Hart Benton eventually settled in St. Louis, Missouri, where he edited a newspaper and went into politics. A U.S. senator from the time of Missouri's 1821 admission to the Union until 1850, he was known for his oratory and edited a 16-volume *Abridgment of the Debates of Congress from 1789 to 1856* (1857–61). An ardent supporter of President Andrew Jackson (1767–1845), Benton was also known for his opposition to the Bank of the United States and was called "Old Bullion" because of his advocacy of the gold standard. Benton also favored development of the West and was instrumental in obtaining federal support for the explorations of his son-in-law, John C. Frémont (1813–90). In 1854–56 he published a two-volume autobiography, *Thirty Years' View.*

Sources

Smith, Elbert B. *Magnificent Missourian: The Life of Thomas Hart Benton.* Philadelphia: Lippincott, 1958.

Berenson, Bernard (Bernhard Berenson)
(1865–1959) *art historian, critic*
Born in Lithuania and raised in Boston, Bernard Berenson graduated from Harvard in 1887. Afterward, he resided first in England, where he was associated with the art dealer Lord Duveen, then in Italy. In 1900 he settled with his wife in Settignano, near Florence, where in a villa he called I Tatti he built a world-renowned collection of art and books.

Berenson's speciality was Italian Renaissance painting, about which he wrote numerous monographs. Works such as *Venetian Painters of the Renaissance* (1894) and *Florentine Painters of the Renaissance* (1896) were for many generations standard texts in the study of art history. Known for his brilliant conversation as well as his elegant style, Berenson was both an art advisor to wealthy collectors like Isabella Stewart Gardner and a host to such literary luminaries as Ernest Hemingway. After his death I Tatti was willed to Harvard University.

Sources

Berenson, Bernard. *Sunset and Twilight . . . Diaries 1947–1958.* Edited by Nicky Mariano. London: H. Hamilton, 1964.

Mariano, Nicky. *Forty Years with Berenson.* London: H. Hamilton, 1966.

Bernard, William Bayle (1807–1875) *playwright*

In the 1830s William Bayle Bernard was one of the most popular playwrights in America, responsible for more than 100 theatrical successes. He is notable for having popularized the stage type of the rural eccentric in plays such as *The Dumb Bell* (1831) and *The Kentuckian; or, A Trip to New York* (1831). In 1832 he became one of the first to adapt Washington IRVING's "RIP VAN WINKLE" for the stage.

best-sellers

In 1895 *THE BOOKMAN* began publishing a list of "Books in Demand" at selected bookstores in major metropolitan areas. "Books in Demand" was changed in 1903 to "The Six Best Sellers," and this categorization was quickly adopted by other literary periodicals, giving rise to a marketing phenomenon. Best-sellers had of course existed earlier in the United States, as exemplified by the always brisk sales of the Bible. Other early religious works, such as Michael Wigglesworth's poem *The Day of Doom* (1662), and those associated with MORMONISM and CHRISTIAN SCIENCE, also sold well, as did certain political works, like Thomas Paine's *Common Sense* (1776) and Parson Weems's short life of George Washington (c. 1800).

During the 19th century, educational works such as William MCGUFFEY's Readers and Noah WEBSTER's dictionaries enjoyed great popularity, as did poetry such as Henry Wadsworth LONGFELLOW's *Song of Hiawatha* (1855) and a wide variety of almanacs and GIFT BOOKS. By mid-century the majority of American readers had turned their attention to fiction, however, making best-sellers of a whole new genre, the DIME NOVEL; and of particular works of long fiction, such as Harriet Beecher STOWE's *UNCLE TOM'S CABIN,* a literary sensation that focused the nation on the issue of slavery and probably hastened the CIVIL WAR.

Sources

Elson, Ruth Miller. *Myths and Mores in American Best Sellers, 1865–1965.* New York: Garland, 1985.

Reep, Diana C. *The Rescue and Romance: Popular Novels Before World War I.* Bowling Green, Ohio: Bowling Green State University Popular Press, 1982.

Ruttenburg, Nancy. *Democratic Personality: Popular Voice and the Trial of American Authorship.* Stanford, Calif.: Stanford University Press, 1998.

Biblical Repertory *periodical*

From its founding in 1825 until 1878, the *Biblical Repertory* was the most important periodical put out by the Presbyterian Church. In that year its name was changed to *The Princeton Review,* and its focus shifted to secular matters in hopes of competing with *THE NORTH AMERICAN REVIEW,* which—although affiliated with Harvard University and UNITARIANISM and inherently scholarly—was aimed at a national audience. *The Princeton Review* did not achieve its goals. In 1884 it ceased publication, only to reappear two years later as *The New Princeton Review,* a literary magazine which over the next two years published works by Theodore ROOSEVELT and Charles Eliot NORTON, among others.

Bibliographical Society of America *organization*

The Bibliographical Society of America was originally an outgrowth of the Bibliographical Society of Chicago (1899–1904). Founded in 1904 and incorporated in 1927, the society has as its mission the promotion of bibliographical research with an emphasis on American materials. Membership is open both to institutions and individuals. It meets every January in New York City and publishes a journal, *The Papers of the Bibliographical Society of America,* and, through Oak Knoll Press, monographs on bibliographical subjects.

Bidwell, John (1819–1900) *memoirist*

Born in Chautauqua County, New York, John Bidwell was living in Missouri in 1841 when he joined the first wagon train out of Independence bound for California in 1841. He would later describe this experience in two memoirs, *A Journey to California* (1842) and *Echoes of the Past* (1900). Bidwell played an important role in California's fight to separate from Mexico, drawing up the new republic's resolution of independence in 1846 in the wake of the Bear Flag Revolt staged by American settlers. After California was admitted to the Union in 1850, Bidwell played a prominent role in state politics, but his 1867 gubernatorial bid was unsuccessful, as were his two attempts to reach the presidency: in 1875 as an antimonopolist independent and in 1892 as the candidate of the Prohibition Party.

Sources

Hunt, Rockwell D. *John Bidwell, Prince of California Pioneers.* Caldwell, Idaho: The Caxton Printers, Ltd., 1942.

Bierce, Ambrose Gwinnett (1842–1914?)
journalist, short story writer, poet

Born in Ohio, Ambrose Bierce served in the CIVIL WAR, the subject of some of his tales and sketches. He had a savage wit and collected his bitter, ironic short pieces in volumes such as *The Fiend's Delight* (1873), *Nuggets and Dust Panned Out in California* (1873), and *Cobwebs from an Empty Shell* (1874). Much of this work was written during a stay in England (1872–75), where he had gone after working as a journalist in San Francisco.

Bierce returned to San Francisco in 1875, where he became one of the most influential writers on the West Coast. His most important book during this period was *Tales of Soldiers and Civilians* (1891), a collection that has been said to share Edgar Allan POE's macabre sensibility. On the one hand, Bierce outfitted his prose with surprise endings and strange twists; on the other, his descriptions of characters and scenes profited from the realism he had employed in his journalism. *Can Such Things Be* (1893) continues the mood of *Tales of Soldiers* in that Bierce once again alternates between riveting, authentic California and Civil War scenes and phantasmagoric and horrifying episodes, lacing both with a kind of black humor more often found in 20th-century American literature.

In 1897 Bierce moved to Washington, D.C., to work for the HEARST newspapers. There he issued two books, *The Cynic's Word Book* (1906) and *The Devil's Dictionary* (1911), that suggested how far removed his sensibility was from his moralistic, genteel contemporaries. Like Mark Twain (see Samuel CLEMENS), Bierce was a fierce critic of his times, expressing his pessimism in fables and sardonic essays collected in *Fantastic Fables* (1899) and *Shadow on the Dial* (1909).

Bierce was also a deft poet, producing satirical volumes of verse, including *Black Beetles in Amber* (1892) and *Shapes of Clay* (1903).

From 1909 to 1912 Bierce put together a 12-volume edition of his best work. But because he had grown weary of the United States, he moved to Mexico, preferring the commotion of the Mexican Revolution to a stultifying status quo. How and exactly when Bierce died has never been ascertained. He disappeared in circumstances and in a mood that is as mysterious and disturbing as his own best fiction.

Several posthumous collections of Bierce's work have appeared, including *The Letters of Ambrose Bierce* (1922); *Ambrose Bierce's Civil War* (1956); *The Enlarged Devil's Dictionary* (1967); *Skepticism and Dissent: Selected Journalism, 1898–1901 by Ambrose Bierce* (1986); and *A Sole Survivor: Bits of Autobiography: Ambrose Bierce* (1998).

Sources

Davidson, Cathy, ed. *Critical Essays on Ambrose Bierce.* Boston: G. K. Hall, 1982.

Morris, Roy, Jr., *Ambrose Bierce: Alone in Bad Company.* New York: Crown, 1995.

Lindley, Daniel. *Ambrose Bierce Takes on the Railroad: The Journalist as Muckraker and Cynic.* Westport, Conn.: Praeger, 1999.

Schaefer, Michael W. *Just What War Is: The Civil War Writings of De Forest and Bierce.* Knoxville: University of Tennessee Press, 1997.

Woodruff, Stuart C. *The Short Stories of Ambrose Bierce: A Study in Polarity.* Pittsburgh: University of Pittsburgh Press, 1964.

"Big Bear of Arkansas, The" *Thomas Bangs Thorpe* (1841) *short story*

This story, written by Thomas Bangs THORPE, a humorist of the OLD SOUTHWEST, is considered a classic of the TALL TALE genre. A story within a story, "The Big Bear of Arkansas" is told by a storyteller to a group of passengers aboard a Mississippi steamboat. The storyteller, who claims he is the best bear hunter in Arkansas, tells a drawn-out tale about his numerous futile attempts to kill an apparently "unhuntable bear" until, on his third try, he finally succeeds in shooting the animal. The story, which first appeared in the journal *SPIRIT OF THE TIMES*, was later reprinted in Thorpe's collection *The Hive of the Bee Hunter* (1854). It would prove to be a long-lived and influential piece of work, and it probably played a part in William Faulkner's writing of his own ursine hunting story, "The Bear."

Sources

Rickels, Milton. *Thomas Bangs Thorpe, Humorist of the Old Southwest.* Baton Rouge: Louisiana State University Press, 1962.

Bigelow, John (1817–1911) *historian, biographer, journalist, diplomat*

Born in Malden, New York, John Bigelow was admitted to the New York bar before joining with William Cullen BRYANT in owning and editing the New York *Evening Post* from 1848 to 1861. On the *Evening Post* Bigelow maintained a free-soil and free-trade editorial stance, and in 1856 he published a campaign biography for Free Soil Party presidential candidate John C. Frémont. His own political career began in earnest in 1861, when he was appointed consul general in Paris. After serving in that role for four years, Bigelow was appointed U.S. minister to France, a position he used to help influence the French government not to support the Confederacy during the CIVIL WAR.

While in Paris, he found the original manuscript of Benjamin Franklin's *Autobiography,* which Bigelow edited for publication in 1868. Three other monographs—*Beaumarchais the Merchant* (1870), *France and Hereditary Monarchy* (1871), and *France and the Confederate Navy* (1888)—grew out of his experiences as a foreign diplomat. When Samuel J. Tilden (1814–86) was elected governor of New York in 1874, Bigelow served as his secretary of state. Later he would serve as Tilden's biographer, publishing *Samuel L. Tilden* in 1895. In 1893 Bigelow published another biography of one of his political associates and former editorial colleague, William Cullen Bryant. Bigelow's own autobiography, *Retrospections of an Active Life,* would appear in five volumes between 1909 and 1913.

Sources

Clapp, Margaret. *Forgotten First Citizen, John Bigelow.* Boston: Little, Brown, 1947.

Billings, Josh

See SHAW, HENRY WHEELER.

Billy Budd *Herman Melville* (1924) *novella*

This posthumously published work was the last of Herman MELVILLE's prose fiction, a piece that he had worked on for many years before his death in 1891. Perhaps inspired by the infamous *Somers* mutiny, in which three sailors were hanged without a proper court martial, it grew out of a poem, "Billy in the Darbies," which Melville appended to his novella. Pressed into service aboard *The Indomitable,* Billy Budd is taken from a merchant ship called *The Rights of Man.* An illiterate orphan, Billy has a sweet voice and an even sweeter temperament. But this "upright barbarian," as the narrator calls him, also has a fatal flaw: he is nearly inarticulate and stutters when distressed.

Billy's beauty and sweetness soon attracts the jealousy of the ship's master-at-arms, John Claggart, who is his polar opposite. Where Billy is light, Claggart is dark; where Billy is good, Claggart is evil. Billy, in his simplicity, cannot comprehend why anyone should hate him. Despite Billy's impeccable work record, Claggart finds minor infractions to carp about. One day Billy accidentally spills soup in Claggart's path. Claggart takes it as an insult and later reports to Captain Vere that the newly impressed sailor is a "dangerous character" trying to foment mutiny. When the captain interviews Billy in Claggart's presence, Billy is dumbfounded by the charges and, choked with emotion, lashes out at Claggart, striking him dead.

Vere then blurts out: "Struck dead by an angel of God! Yet the angel must hang!" Mindful of the rumors of mutiny that poison the air, Vere quickly convenes a drumhead court—instead of simply imprisoning Billy and waiting for a full court martial—and pressures the other officers to find Billy guilty. As Billy is hanged, his last words, "God bless Captain Vere!," hang in the air. For the crew that has assembled to watch his execution, the spar from which he has been hanged becomes like a piece of the true cross, and the handsome sailor's myth is perpetuated in the poem "Billy in the Darbies," with which Melville ends his tale.

Often interpreted as allegory, *Billy Budd* is Melville's final literary attempt to reconcile good and evil. His conclusion—that extremes of both are doomed—seemed not to rest easily with him, however: despite years of effort, this last work was left unfinished.

Sources

Critical Essays on Melville's Billy Budd, Sailor. Introduction by Robert Milder. Boston: G. K. Hall, 1989.

Parker, Hershel. *Reading Billy Budd.* Evanston, Ill.: Northwestern University Press, 1990.

Billy the Kid

See BONNEY, WILLIAM H.

Bird, Robert Montgomery (1806–1854)

playwright, novelist

Born in Delaware and educated at the University of Pennsylvania, where he received his M.D. in 1827, Robert Montgomery Bird supposedly gave up his medical practice owing to a reluctance to charge his patients fees. He did teach at the Pennsylvania Medical College from 1841 to 1843, but most of his adult life was devoted to writing. Starting out as a dramatist, he wrote a number of tragedies and comedies about Philadelphia before penning several prize-winning verse dramas for his friend, the actor Edwin Forrest. These included *The Gladiator* (1831), Bird's most popular play; and *The Broker of Bogota* (1834), considered to be his best. The two friends later had a falling out, and because Forrest, who had purchased and produced several of Bird's plays, refused to relinquish his copyright claims, Bird turned to novel writing.

Bird's training as a dramatist helped make his novels—many of them historical romances—both popular and remunerative. *Calavar* (1834) and its sequel, *The Infidel* (1835), concern the Spanish conquest of Mexico, and *The Hawks of Hawk Hollow* (1835) is set during the Revolutionary War. Bird set what is considered his best novel, *Nick of the Woods* (1837), in the aftermath of the American Revolution and created in it a memorable hero with a split personality. In this book Bird also, in contrast with his contemporary James Fenimore COOPER, portrayed Indians not as noble savages but simply as savages.

Ill health eventually forced Bird to give up writing, but in 1847 he came out of retirement to work as literary editor of the Philadelphia *North American,* a position he held until his death.

Sources

Dahl, Curtis. *Robert Montgomery Bird.* New York: Twayne, 1963.

Foust, Clement E. *Life and Dramatic Works of Robert Montgomery Bird.* New York: Knickerbocker Press, 1919.

Black Hawk (1767–1838) *memoirist*

An American Indian leader of the Fox and Sac (or Sauk) tribes, Black Hawk was born in a Sac village near what is now Rock Island, Illinois. During the war of 1812 he fought on the side of the British and denounced the Treaty of 1804, which provided that the Fox and Sac should give up their lands and be removed west of the Mississippi. Black Hawk actively resisted removal and in 1832 returned to Illinois with 400 of his men. He made peaceful overtures to the federal government, but when one of his emissaries was shot in cold blood, Black Hawk made war on a variety of frontier settlements in what has come to be known as the Black Hawk War (1832). Defeated in battle at the Bad Axe River, Black Hawk surrendered, was briefly imprisoned, and was allowed to return to the remnants of his tribe that remained in Iowa. In his 1833 *Autobiography,* he defended his actions and parsed the illegality of the Treaty of 1804. A colossal statue executed by Lorado Taft in 1911 and located near Oregon, Illinois, is known as the Black Hawk Monument.

Sources

Cole, Cyrenus. *I Am a Man: The Indian Black Hawk.* Iowa City: The State Historical Society of Iowa, 1938.

Blavatsky, Helena Petrovna Hahn (Madame Blavatsky) (1831–1891) *spiritualist*

A world traveler born in Russia and with vague connections to the Russian aristocracy, Madame Blavatsky came to the United States in 1873 bearing, she said, occult secrets she had learned during a seven-year sojourn in Tibet. In the aftermath of the CIVIL WAR, during which most families had lost loved ones, SPIRITUALISM was embraced by many, and Madame Blavatsky capitalized on the vogue. In 1875, however, Blavatsky founded the mystical Theosophical Society and denounced spiritualism two years later in a plagiarized book on the occult, *Isis Unveiled.* Schisms within the association forced her in 1878 to move her headquarters to India. From there she continued to propound her theosophical doctrine—an occult philosophy incorporating aspects of Buddhism—with some success and gained many followers through demonstrations of supernatural phenomena. Fraud charges leveled against her in the 1880s and 1890s undermined her reputation and forced her to flee to Europe. But Blavatsky managed to keep her enterprise going, in 1888 publishing her two-volume summation of theosophy, *The Secret Doctrine.* After suffering from various severe illnesses, she died venerated by her followers as a saint and martyr. The day of her death, May 8, continued to be celebrated by Theosophists as "White Lotus Day."

Sources

Meade, Marion. *Madame Blavatsky: The Woman Behind the Myth.* New York: Putnam, 1980.

Washington, Peter. *Madame Blavatsky's Baboon: Theosophy and the Emergence of the Western Guru.* London: Secker & Warburg, 1993.

Blood, Benjamin Paul (1822–1919) *poet*

Benjamin Paul Blood was a poet and mystic who subscribed to the philosophy of *pluralism,* the belief that the universe is explicable in terms of numerous, often conflicting concepts. He came to this belief through the use of anesthetics, an experience he described in *The Anaesthetic Revelation and the Gist of Philosophy* (1874). Publication of this work started an extended correspondence with the philosopher William JAMES, another exponent of pluralism. Blood's other works include the long poem in Spenserian stanzas, *The Bride of the Iconoclast* (1854); and two unorthodox analyses of Christianity, *The Philosophy of Justice* (1851) and *Optimism* (1860).

Bloomer, Amelia Jenks (1818–1894) *journalist*

Born in Homer, New York, Amelia Bloomer was a reformer dedicated to the frequently aligned causes of SUFFRAGISM and the TEMPERANCE MOVEMENT. From 1848 to 1854 she edited *The Lily,* a journal published in Seneca Falls, New York, and devoted to these causes. In 1851 she recommended—and adopted—a costume consisting of a short skirt and long trousers. These "Bloomers," as they became known, were introduced to the public through advertisements in *The Lily* and through Bloomer's lectures, to which she wore her invention. The phenomenon gave rise in 1904 to a musical called "Bloomer Girl."

Sources

Gattey, Charles Neilson. *The Bloomer Girls.* London: Femina Books, 1967.

Bly, Nellie

See SEAMAN, ELIZABETH COCHRAN.

Boker, George Henry (1823–1890) *playwright, poet*

Born in Philadelphia and educated at Princeton University, George Henry Boker originally intended to practice law. Instead he chose to travel abroad and to write. After publishing a volume of poetry, he took up playwriting. He wrote numerous romantic and heroic tragedies, many of them in verse in the style of the Elizabethans. Only one play, *Francesca da Rimini* (1856), was a genuine success. Based on the story of Paolo and Francesca in Dante's *Inferno,* the play was first produced in 1855 but later was revived numerous times. Boker's last produced play appeared in 1855, and he did not take up playwriting again until *Francesca* was first revived to critical acclaim in 1882. In the interim he continued to write poetry and also served with distinction as minister to Turkey (1871–75) and to Russia (1875–78).

Sources

Bradley, Edward S. *George Henry Boker: Poet and Patriot.* 1927. Reprint, Philadelphia: University of Pennsylvania Press, 1972.

Evans, Oliver H. *George Henry Boker.* Boston: Twayne, 1984.

Bonney, William H. (Billy the Kid) (Henry McCarty) (1859–1881) *outlaw*

Born in New York City, this outlaw's real name was probably Henry McCarty. When he was still a child, his family moved to Kansas and then to New Mexico, where in 1878 the teenager led a gang in the Lincoln County cattle war, killing two deputies and stealing cattle. Having begun his career in murder, he went on to combine it with large-scale cattle rustling. In 1880 local cattlemen elected a sheriff whose primary job was to capture the errant Billy the Kid. Bonney was in fact captured, tried, and sentenced to death, but he escaped before he could be executed. Finally he was trapped and shot by Sheriff Pat F. Garrett (1850–1908).

Billy the Kid gained immortality as the subject of countless DIME NOVELS as well as serious works such as Aaron Copland's ballet score "Billy the Kid" (1938) and Michael Ondaatje's *The Collected Works of Billy the Kid: Left-Handed Poems* (1970).

Sources

Tatum, Stephen. *Inventing Billy the Kid: Visions of the Outlaw in America, 1881–1981.* Albuquerque: University of New Mexico Press, 1982.

Tuska, Jon. *Billy the Kid, His Life and Legend.* Westport, Conn.: Greenwood Press, 1994.

Bookman, The (1895–1933) *periodical*

Originally edited by Harry Thurston Peck (1856–1914), a Columbia University Latin professor, this monthly magazine was modeled along the lines of its English counterpart of the same name. The magazine's mission was to provide modern American writers with a forum, although English authors were frequent contributors. In 1902 editorship passed from Peck to a series of equally conservative individuals until, in 1927–28, the post was held by Burton Rascoe (1892–1957). Perhaps following the spirit of the times, Rascoe published such politically radical works as Upton Sinclair's *Boston* (1928). When *The Bookman* folded in 1933, its last editor, Seward Collins, founded *The American Review.*

Sources

Rascoe, Burton. *A Bookman's Daybook.* New York: Liveright, 1929.

Boone, Daniel (1734–1820) *frontiersman*

Born in Pennsylvania to English Quakers, Boone moved as a child to North Carolina, where he learned survival skills such as hunting and marksmanship. He made his name, however, in the wilderness lands that would later become Tennessee and Kentucky, which he explored in the 1760s. Boone's first attempt to settle there in 1763 was foiled by Indian attacks, but two years later he and an armed band of 30 men managed to blaze the Wilderness Road through to the Kentucky River, where Boonesboro was established. The next year, when Kentucky was made a county of Virginia, Boone was elected captain of the local militia. During the Revolutionary War he was captured in 1778 by Shawnee Indians, who took him to a British military post in Detroit, where he was briefly imprisoned. Learning that Boonesboro was about to be attacked, he escaped in time to ward off an Indian assault.

Boone would leave Boonesboro for good in 1779, founding a new settlement, Boone's Station, near what is now Athens, Kentucky. Over the next 20 years he served several terms in the Virginia legislature, but his failure to properly register title to several large tracts of land led to their loss and Boone's permanent removal from Kentucky. He and his wife, Rebecca Bryan, moved to Spanish territory near St. Louis, Missouri, where Boone was granted a large tract of land and where he served as a district magistrate. After the Louisiana Purchase (1803), Boone again lost title to his lands, but in consideration of his service to the federal government and the American people, Congress interceded and restored his property in 1814. Boone died there in 1820, the patriarch of a dynasty that by that time included five generations.

Boone's legend as a frontiersman and as the discoverer of Kentucky was enhanced by an autobiographical account published in John Filson's (c. 1747–88) *The Discovery, Settlement, and Present State of Kentucke* in 1784, as well as laudatory verses in the English poet Lord Byron's *Don Juan* (1823). James Fenimore COOPER used Boone's legend as a prototype for his own fictitious frontiersman, Natty BUMPPO. John James AUDUBON, who met Boone in Missouri, would also publish a flattering account of some of Boone's adventures in his *Ornithological Biography* (1831–39). Many of the contemporary accounts of Boone's prowess and exploits were later shown to be exaggerated, but his biography continued to be a source of inspiration for American writers such as Winston CHURCHILL, who featured Boone in his romance *The Crossing* (1904), and Elizabeth Madox Roberts (1886–1941), who did the same in her historical novel *The Great Meadow* (1930).

Sources

Faragher, John M. *Daniel Boone: The Life and Legend of an American Pioneer.* New York: Holt, 1992.

Borden, Lizzie Andrew (1860–1927) *public figure*

Born in Fall River, Massachusetts, Lizzie Borden came to the attention of the public in 1892, when she was accused of hacking her father and stepmother to death. Her murder trial, which proved to be a national sensation and obsession, ended in an acquittal. Subsequently, Lizzie became the subject of folk songs, novels, John Colton's play *Nine Pine Street* (1948), Agnes de Mille's ballet *Fall River Legend* (1948), and an opera, *Lizzie Borden* (1965), by Jack Beeson.

Sources

Sullivan, Robert. *Goodbye Lizzie Borden.* New York: Viking Penguin, 1974.

Boston, Massachusetts *geographical location*

The principal seaport of New England and the capital of Massachusetts, Boston was the most important cultural center throughout the colonial period and much of the 19th century. Once the seat of Puritan learning and political power, the city evolved in the 19th century into an industrial hub and liberal bulwark for abolitionists, transcendentalists, feminists, and other individuals and groups dedicated to a more democratic and progressive country.

Various utopian communities sprang up near Boston, including BROOK FARM and FRUITLANDS; Bronson ALCOTT founded the Temple School in the city. Boston became a center of publishing with the establishment of magazines such as the *ATLANTIC MONTHLY* and *THE NORTH AMERICAN REVIEW* and publishing firms such as Ticknor & Fields, Houghton Mifflin, and Little, Brown. These firms and others published Boston-based writers Francis PARKMAN, William Hickley PRESCOTT, Henry JAMES Sr., William Dean HOWELLS, and Julia Ward HOWE. Also part of the Boston orbit were writers living nearby in Concord and Cambridge, including Henry Wadsworth LONGFELLOW, James Russell LOWELL, Nathaniel HAWTHORNE, Richard Henry DANA (Jr. and Sr.), and Thomas Wentworth HIGGINSON.

After the CIVIL WAR, Boston became less Protestant and Puritan as groups of immigrant workers, especially the Irish and Italians, began to find employment and to participate in the political system. Harvard University still produced its share of writers and thinkers, and the old families retained political control, but the newcomers gradually established their own power enclaves and began to express themselves—a process that Howells explores in *THE RISE OF SILAS LAPHAM* (1885).

Near the end of the 19th-century, Boston had lost much of its literary energy—a fact signaled by Howell's own move from Boston to New York, for the latter was overtaking the former in both financial and literary terms. Henry JAMES's novels charted this decline in Boston, and Henry Adams regretted his own family's declining importance in *THE EDUCATION OF HENRY ADAMS* (1918).

Sources

O'Connell, Shaun. *Imagining Boston: A Literary Landscape.* Boston: Beacon Press, 1990.

Roman, Judith A. *Annie Adams Fields: The Spirit of Charles Street.* Bloomington: Indiana University Press, 1990.

Swift, Lindsay. *Literary Landmarks of Boston: A Visitor's Guide to Points of Literary Interest in and about Boston.* Boston: Houghton Mifflin, 1903.

Winship, Michael. *Ticknor and Fields: The Business of Literary Publishing in the United States of the Nineteenth Century.* Chapel Hill: Hanes Foundation, Rare Book Collection/University Library, University of North Carolina at Chapel Hill, 1992.

Boston Daily Advertiser *periodical*

Founded in 1813, the *Boston Daily Advertiser* was the first successful daily newspaper in New England, and by the mid-19th century it was one of the most prominent newspapers in the country. Criticized for its elitist editorial policies and bias toward the Boston upper class (Henry ADAMS was for a time the paper's Washington correspondent), in 1917 it was taken over by William Randolph HEARST, who in 1921 made the venerable newspaper into an illustrated tabloid.

Sources

Dicken Garcia, Hazel. *Journalistic Standards in Nineteenth-Century America.* Madison: University of Wisconsin Press, 1989.

Boston Daily Evening Transcript *periodical*

Known for its reporting of cultural events in Boston and around the nation, this newspaper, founded in 1830, had a conservative bent that inspired T. S. Eliot (1888–1965) to use the paper, in a poem of the same name (1917), as a symbol of dullness and weary routine.

Boston Quarterly Review, The *periodical*

Founded and edited by Orestes BROWNSON in 1838, this magazine served mainly as an outlet for Brownson's own thought and work. Its editorial stance reflected his frequent changes of orientation: from Presbyterian to Universalist to

Unitarian, from Democratic to Workingman's Party to Christian Socialism. Brownson did publish contributions from other writers, however, including Margaret FULLER, Elizabeth PEABODY, and Bronson ALCOTT. In 1842 Brownson merged his magazine with the *Democratic Review.* After this periodical declined to print any more of Brownson's opinion pieces, however, he founded *BROWNSON'S QUARTERLY REVIEW* in 1843.

Boucicault, Dion (Dionysius Lardner Boursiquot) (1820?–1890) *playwright*

Born Dionysius Lardner Boursiquot in Dublin, Boucicault (as he later christened himself) was educated in London, where he began acting and writing plays. He made his London debut in 1839 using the name Lee Moreton, but by 1841, when his comedy *London Assurance* played successfully at Covent Garden, he had changed his name to Dion Boucicault. After his first wife died under mysterious circumstances in the 1840s in France, Boucicault married the actress Agnes Robertson, who was the adopted daughter of the actor Charles Kean. Together they came to America in 1853, and Boucicault continued to act and to write plays.

Boucicault's first significant production in the United States was *Grimaldi, or The Life of an Actress,* in which he and his wife both appeared. His first stay in this country lasted until 1860, when he returned to work on the English stage, but he returned to the United States a decade later and stayed until his death. Altogether Boucicault wrote or adapted over 300 farces, comedies, and melodramas. Many were marked by sensational stage business, such as a rescue from a burning building in *The Poor of New York* (1857), a burning ship in *The Octoroon* (1859), and an underwater rescue in *The Colleen Bawn* (1860). Over time he began to specialize in plays with Irish settings, such as *Arrah-na-Pogue* (1864), which instituted the use in his native land of the shamrock as a patriotic symbol.

Boucicault was the most popular playwright of his day, and also one of the most energetic. He continued to act throughout his career, and he inaugurated the use of a touring company for a single play. He was also instrumental in working for change in the copyright law, lobbying Congress assiduously until it passed the Copyright Law of 1850. Late in life his reputation was tarnished, however, when he repudiated his marriage to Agnes Robertson in order to marry again. Boucicault's final years were spent as an acting teacher at a drama school founded by the New York theater impresario A. M. Palmer (1838–1905).

Sources

Molin, Sven Eric, and Robin Goodfellow, eds. *Dion Boucicault, the Shaughraun: A Documentary Life, Letters and Selected Works.* Newark, Del.: Proscenium Press, 1979.

Hogan, Robert G. *Dion Boucicault.* New York: Twayne, 1969.

Bowery, the *geographical location*

This area of Lower Manhattan known for its down-and-out denizens is named for an old street that originally ran through Peter Stuyvesant's farm, or *bouwerij,* as it was called by New York's Dutch settlers. By the 19th century the Bowery had become notorious for its dance halls, beer gardens, cheap theaters, and dives, as well as for its lower-class inhabitants, who were said to have a dialect all their own.

A stage type, the "Bowery boy," was first introduced in 1848 in Benjamin A. Baker's play *A Glance at New York.* The Bowery's unsavory reputation was featured on stage again in 1891 in Charles Hoyt's farce *A Trip to Chinatown.* Stephen CRANE featured the Bowery in two works of fiction: *Maggie, A Girl of the Streets* (1893) and *George's Mother* (1893), republished together in 1900 as *Bowery Tales.* Crane's friend Edward W. Townsend (1855–1942) also made use of the district in a series of stories that first appeared in the *NEW YORK SUN* at the turn of the century and were later collected in *Chimmie Fadden, Major Max, and Other Stories* (1895) and *Chimmie Fadden Explains* (1895). By the early 20th century legitimate theater had relocated elsewhere in Manhattan, and the Bowery was left with a large homeless population that only contributed to its unsavory reputation.

Sources

Bendiner, Elmer. *The Bowery Man.* New York: Nelson, 1961.

Slotkin, Alan Robert. *The Language of Stephen Crane's Bowery Tales: Developing Mastery of Character Diction.* New York: Garland, 1993.

Bowery Theatre (1826–1929)

Built on the site of a former tavern in New York City, this theater was originally called the Bull's Head Theatre, a name that changed by opening day to the New York Theatre. The name did not stick, however, and the playhouse was always known as the BOWERY Theatre, owing to its location in the lower Manhattan district of the same name.

The New York home stage of the famed tragedian Edwin Forrest (1806–72), the Bowery was for a time the principal competitor of the PARK THEATRE. The Bowery burned to the ground for the first time in 1828. It was immediately rebuilt and, under new management, began featuring new plays, principally popular melodramas. Two more devastating fires, one in 1836 and another two years later, added to the Bowery's declining fortunes, precipitated in part by the uptown movement of the theater district.

Although the theater was rebuilt after both fires, its productions moved to exaggerated melodrama, then pantomime. It was during this period that the Bowery became legendary for its rambunctious clientele. The last major playhouse to retain an audience pit—with the audience situated below the stage, as in Shakespeare's day—the Bowery's layout encouraged participation from the rough crowd that hurled abuse, together with trash, onto unlucky performers. Those actors who pleased the crowd did so by engaging its members in impromptu dialogue. By 1879 the Bowery was surrounded by immigrant tenements and staged theatrical fare in German and Yiddish. When it burned to the ground again in 1929, it was not rebuilt.

Sources

Fields, Armond. *From the Bowery to Broadway: Lew Fields and the Roots of American Popular Theatre.* New York: Oxford University Press, 1993.

Boyesen, Hjalmar Hjorth (1848–1895) *novelist, philologist*

Born in Norway and educated at the universities of Leipzig in Germany and Christiania in Norway, Hjalmar Hjorth Boyesen came to the United States in 1869, intending only to visit. Instead he stayed, becoming editor of the Norwegian weekly *Fremad,* published in Chicago, and later a professor of German at Cornell and Columbia Universities.

Although Boyesen published scholarly works on German and Scandinavian literature, he is remembered primarily as a novelist. His first success as a writer of fiction came with a romance about Norwegian life, *Gunnar* (1874), which first appeared in serial form in the *ATLANTIC MONTHLY,* whose editor, William Dean HOWELLS, encouraged him to write more. Howells's dedication to REALISM also influenced Boyesen, who turned his back on the romanticism of *Gunnar* to write *The Mammon of Unrighteousness* (1891), a realistic urban novel about the conflict between two brothers, one an amoral politician and the other a social idealist. *The Golden Calf* (1892) concerns the loss of innocence to money, and *The Social Strugglers* (1893), the last of the four novels on which Boyesen's reputation rests, is likewise a critique of society—albeit one outlined with a lighter touch. Boyesen also wrote several popular works intended for juvenile readers, such as *Boyhood in Norway* (1892).

Sources

Eckstein, Neil Truman. *The Marginal Man as Novelist: The Norwegian-American Writers, H. H. Boyesen and O. E. Rølvaag, as Critics of American Institutions.* New York: Garland, 1990.

Fredrickson, Robert S. *Hjalmar Hjorth Boyesen.* Boston: Twayne, 1980.

Brady, Mathew B. (c. 1823–1896) *photographer*

Born in Warren County, New York, Mathew Brady learned the art and science of the daguerreotype process from Samuel F. B. Morse (1791–1872). In 1844 Brady opened his own photographic studio in New York City and quickly became a sensation. In 1850 he published his *Galley of Illustrious Americans,* and in 1860 he began photographing President Abraham LINCOLN. When the CIVIL WAR began, Brady was commissioned to photograph the Union armies. His efforts led to the vast *National Photographic Collection of War Views* (1869), a virtually complete record of the war in all its aspects. In 1875 the federal government purchased part of this collection, but the remainder was acquired by private individuals after Brady experienced financial failure.

Sources

Horan, James David. *Mathew Brady, Historian with a Camera.* New York: Crown Publishers, 1955.

Brann, William Cowper (1855–1898) *journalist*

William Brann made his mark as a newspaperman, first at the St. Louis, Missouri, *Globe-Democrat,* and later in Texas. He was known for his vituperative attacks on anything he considered fraudulent, and his outspokenness cost him dearly. After being fired for his violent editorials in the Houston *Post,* in 1891 Brann launched his own monthly magazine, which he called *The Iconoclast.* Three years later he sold the monthly to W. S. Porter; then he bought back his press and resumed publishing *The Iconoclast* in Waco, Texas, where his attitudes and unpopularity led to his murder. During his lifetime he published his *Speeches and Lectures* (1895?) and *Brann's Scrap-Book* (1898). *Brann, the Iconoclast,* a collection of his writings, was published posthumously in 1898.

Sources

Carver, Charles. *Brann and the Iconoclast.* Austin: University of Texas Press, 1957.

Bread and Cheese Club *organization*

This informal social club was formed around 1822 by James Fenimore COOPER and his circle of friends, including the inventor Samuel F. B. Morse (1791–1872) and the banker and poet Fitz-Greene HALLECK. Membership was limited to 35, and the club met variously at Washington Hall and the City Hotel, both located in Manhattan. In 1827 some members seceded and formed the Literary Club and the Sketch Club, which later became the CENTURY ASSOCIATION.

Breitmann, Hans

See LELAND, CHARLES GODFREY.

Briggs, Charles Frederick (1804–1877) *novelist, editor*

Charles Frederick Briggs published at least two autobiographical novels: *The Adventures of Harry Franco* (1839), based on the experience of a Wall Street financial panic; and *Working a Passage* (1844), which grew out of his adventures at sea. In 1845 he founded the *BROADWAY JOURNAL*, which was eventually taken over by Edgar Allan POE. Briggs went on to do editorial work at *Putnam's Magazine*, the *NEW YORK TIMES*, and the Brooklyn *Union. The Trippings of Tom Pepper: The Results of Romancing. An Autobiography by Harry Franco* (1847–50) may also be Briggs's work.

Brisbane, Albert (1809–1890) *social theorist*

Born in Batavia, New York, Albert Brisbane studied with the French social philosopher Charles Fourier (1772–1837) in Paris, returning to the United States to form cooperative Fourierist groups, or "phalanxes," in Philadelphia and New York. Brisbane popularized FOURIERISM through his column in the *NEW YORK TIMES* and through his book *The Social Destiny of Mankind* (1840), which mixed translations from Fourier in with Brisbane's own commentary. Brisbane's most famous convert was the newspaperman Horace GREELEY, but more than 8,000 Americans invested themselves in more than 40 Fourierist communities around the country. The most famous of these communes was BROOK FARM, which Nathaniel HAWTHORNE fictionalized—along with Brisbane—in his novel *The Blithedale Romance* (1852). All but one of these experiments in communal living failed, and Brisbane faded into obscurity. In 1876 he published a defense of his philosophy in his *General Introduction to Social Sciences.*

Sources

Carlson, Oliver. *Brisbane: A Candid Biography.* New York: Stackpole Sons, 1937.

Broadway *geographical location*

Broadway is the name of both a street that runs the length of Manhattan and Manhattan's theater district. First laid out by Dutch settlers early in the 17th century, Broadway was the main street of what was known then as New Amsterdam. Although originally a residential street, by the 19th century Broadway was New York City's principal commercial thoroughfare. The street's name began to evolve into a synonym for New York theater as early as 1735, when a map of the city included a reference to a "Playhouse on Broadway." Broadway's nickname "The Great White Way"—a reference to the bright lights of its many theater marquees—supposedly derives from a play by the same name written by Albert Bigelow Paine and published in 1901. Today the New York theater district is largely located on the side streets around Broadway, between Times Square and 53rd Street. After World War II, experimental theater, often staged far away from Broadway itself, came to be known as "off-Broadway," and toward the end of the 20th century, truly fringe theater was still named, with reference to The Great White Way, "off-off Broadway."

Sources

Bloom, Ken. *Broadway: An Encyclopedic Guide to the History, People, and Places of Times Square.* New York: Facts On File, 1991.

Dunlap, David W. *On Broadway: A Journey Uptown over Time.* New York: Rizzoli, 1990.

Broadway Journal *periodical*

This literary periodical was founded by Charles Frederick BRIGGS and Edgar Allan POE in 1845. Within 10 months Poe was the sole owner and editor, and he used his journal as a venue for airing his dispute with the transcendentalists (see TRANSCENDENTALISM) and with Henry Wadsworth LONGFELLOW, whom Poe accused of plagiarism. Poe also used the journal as a ready outlet for reprints of his short stories and poetry, although he did publish the story "The Premature Burial" here for the first time. The *Broadway Journal* was also ostensibly dedicated to theater criticism, but here, too, Poe tended to go overboard, in the end robbing his periodical of reputability and consigning it to an early death in 1846.

Brook Farm *utopian community*

This experimental farm in Roxbury, Massachusetts, grew out of the ideals of the TRANSCENDENTAL CLUB, which began the farm in an attempt to put their social theories to work. Founded by the Unitarian minister George RIPLEY in 1841, the farm was financed initially by a joint stock company holding 24 shares, each valued at $500. Under the name Brook Farm Institute of Agriculture and Education, the goal of this experiment in communal living was to attain self-sufficiency through manual labor while promoting the higher aspects of human culture through moral and intellectual education.

The Brook Farm school was in fact its most successful venture, but the agricultural inexperience of such members as Nathaniel HAWTHORNE, Charles A. DANA, and Isaac Hecker (1819–88), later a Roman Catholic priest and journalist, meant that farming at Brook Farm failed miserably. In 1843 the community came under the influence of Albert BRISBANE and FOURIERISM, with the result that in 1844 the farm was changed to a phalanx (a Fourierist economic unit). As a center of TRANSCENDENTALISM, Brook Farm was visited by many of the day's leading intellectuals, such as Ralph Waldo EMERSON and Margaret FULLER. As a center of Fourierism, Brook Farm issued the journals *The Phalanx* (1843–45) and *Harbinger* (1845). When the uncompleted and uninsured central building of the farm burned down in 1846, the community disbanded, but many of its members and visitors were disenchanted with it long before that time. Hawthorne's novel *The Blithedale Romance* (1852) revealed the hypocrisy he found at the heart of such utopian living arrangements, and Emerson referred to Brook Farm as "the Age of Reason in a patty-pan," bringing it back down to earth by comparing it to a lowly squash.

Sources

Curtis, Edith R. *A Season in Utopia: The Story of Brook Farm.* New York: Nelson, 1961.

Francis, Richard. *Transcendental Utopias: Individual and Community at Brook Farm, Fruitlands, and Walden.* Ithaca, N.Y.: Cornell University Press, 1997.

Brooklyn, New York *geographical location*

One of New York City's five boroughs, Brooklyn occupies the southwestern end of Long Island. Settled by Dutch farmers in the early 17th century, by the time of the Revolutionary War Brooklyn was already an important city in its own right, and it remained so until 1898, when it became part of metropolitan New York.

The first ferry connected Brooklyn with Manhattan in 1642, and the journey across the East River was immortalized by Walt WHITMAN's poem "Crossing Brooklyn Ferry" (1856). Whitman, who from 1846 to 1848 edited the daily *Brooklyn Eagle,* is perhaps the most significant 19th-century literary figure to be associated with what was then the third-largest city in the United States. Henry Ward BEECHER also made his name in Brooklyn. In the 20th century, novelists like Joseph Heller (1923–99) and Norman Mailer (1923–) have written about their origins in Brooklyn, while Hart Crane's (1899–1932) masterpiece, the poem *The Bridge* (1930), uses as its organizing symbol architect J. A. Roebling's (1806–69) masterpiece, the Brooklyn Bridge, begun in 1869 and completed in 1883.

Sources

Kazin, Alfred. *A Walker in the City.* New York: Harcourt, Brace, 1951.

Robbins, Michael W., ed. *Brooklyn: A State of Mind.* New York: Workman, 2001.

Weld, Ralph Foster. *Brooklyn Village, 1816–1834.* New York: Columbia University Press, 1938.

Brooklyn Eagle *newspaper*

Founded by Henry C. Murphy (1810–1882) in 1841, this decidedly Democrat daily was edited by Walt WHITMAN from March 1846 to January 1848. Other literary notables who served on its staff were journalist and memoirist Edward W. Bok (1863–1930) and journalist and broadcaster H. V. Kaltenborn (1878–1965). With the exception of a brief suspension in 1861 owing to the paper's proslavery editorial posture, *The Brooklyn Eagle* published continuously until 1955.

Sources

Schroth, Raymond A. *The Eagle and Brooklyn: A Community Newspaper, 1841–1955.* Westport, Conn.: Greenwood Press, 1974.

Brown, John (1800–1859) *abolitionist leader*

Born in Torrington, Connecticut, John Brown's life until the 1850s consisted largely of a series of business failures in a number of different states. He was, however, an ardent abolitionist, and when he moved to Ossawatomie, Kansas, in 1855, these beliefs began to shape his life—and his death. Brown had come to the territory with five of his sons specifically to aid what would come to be known as "bleeding Kansas" in its quest for admission to the Union, and to ensure that it would be a free rather than slaveholding state. Confident that he was God's instrument, Brown led four of his sons and two other men in the slaughter of five proslavery men living along the banks of the Pottawatamie River. This exploit, as well as his former role as a conductor on the Underground Railroad shepherding slaves north to freedom while still living in Pennsylvania, made Brown into a national celebrity. He used his fame to recruit men for an effort to liberate slaves through armed intervention. Eventually this effort took the form of a raid on the federal arsenal at Harper's Ferry, West Virginia.

On October 16, 1859, Brown and his 21-man army succeeded in their goal. The expected slave uprising failed to materialize, however. Instead, the following night a company of U.S. Marines, led by Colonel Robert E. Lee, attacked the arsenal, killing 10 members of Brown's "army" and wounding Brown himself. Brown and the other survivors were arrested. During his treason trial, Brown conducted himself with great dignity, as he did when he was swiftly convicted and then hanged on December 2, 1859. Both his conduct and his conviction made Brown a martyr for many. Immortalized in the Union marching song "John Brown's Body Lies A-Mouldering in the Grave," Brown was also celebrated in such works as a Henry David THOREAU lecture series published as *The Last Days of John Brown* (1860) and "The Portent" (1866), a startling poem by Herman MELVILLE that opens his collection of CIVIL WAR poems, *Battle-Pieces* (1866).

Sources

Boyer, Richard Owen. *The Legend of John Brown: A Biography and a History.* New York: Alfred A. Knopf, 1973.

Finkelman, Paul, ed. *His Soul Goes Marching On: Responses to John Brown and the Harpers Ferry Raid.* Charlottesville: University of Virginia Press, 1995.

Oates, Stephen B. *To Purge This Land with Blood: A Biography of John Brown.* New York: Harper & Row, 1970.

Brown, William Wells (1816–1884) *novelist*

Born into slavery in Kentucky, William Wells Brown worked for the abolitionist printer Elijah Lovejoy (1802–37) in St. Louis, Missouri. Eventually Brown moved to Ohio, where he gained his freedom and worked with the Underground Railroad. His autobiographical *Narrative* (1847), published just two years after Frederick DOUGLASS's appeared, propelled Brown to prominence in the abolitionist movement. In 1856 Brown successfully dramatized his autobiographical narrative and produced a successor volume, *Experience; or How to Give a Northern Man a Backbone.* His novel *Clotel; or, The President's Daughter* (1853), was first published in England and is believed to be the first novel written by an African American. The story it purports to tell is of Thomas Jefferson's daughter, a mulatto born of one of the president's slaves. Seemingly, it was more truth than fiction, and when it was published in the United States, it appeared as *Clotel; A Tale of the Southern States* (1864). Brown also published a book of poetry, a play, and a homage, *The Black Man: His Antecedents, His Genius, and His Achievements* (1863), later expanded and republished as *The Rising Sun* (1874).

Sources

Whelchel, L. H. *My Chains Fell Off: William Wells Brown, Fugitive Abolitionist.* Lanham, Md.: University Press of America, 1985.

Browne, Charles Farrar (Artemus Ward) (1834–1867) *journalist, lecturer*

Born in Waterford, Maine, Charles Farrar Browne began his journalistic career at age 13 when, after his father's death, he became a printer. After working on a number of New England newspapers, Browne settled in Ohio, where his writing for the Toledo *Commercial* attracted the attention of the editors of the Cleveland *Plain Dealer,* who invited Browne to write a humor column for their paper. Browne responded in 1858 by submitting the first of a series of "Artemus Ward Letters," supposedly written in Yankee dialect by a savvy but nearly illiterate showman. The bad grammar and wild misspellings of this Down East character made Browne's reputation, and by the time he resigned from the *Plain Dealer* (he had eventually risen to the position of city editor), his name was synonymous with his character's. Thereafter Browne was known as Artemus Ward.

Browne went from Cleveland to New York City, where he joined the staff of VANITY FAIR. In 1861 he made his debut as a lecturer with a humorous address titled "Babes in the Woods." Browne proved to be a popular lecturer, traveling around the United States and in 1866 landing in London, where he became an editor for the English humor magazine *Punch.* Less than a year later he died prematurely of tuberculosis.

Sources

Austin, James C. *Artemus Ward.* New York: Twayne, 1964.

Nock, Albert J., ed. *Selected Works of Artemus Ward.* New York: A&C Boni, 1924.

Brownson, Orestes Augustus (1803–1876) *theologian, editor, novelist*

Born in Stockbridge, Vermont, Orestes Brownson was a self-educated theological thinker who was raised a Puritan, joined the Presbyterian Church, left to become a Universalist (see UNIVERSALISM), and in 1836 founded his own church, the Society for Christian Union and Progress. In truth, Brownson's views were so extreme and so eccentric that he seemed unable to adhere to any code. After converting to Roman Catholicism in 1844, he was branded a heretic for attempting to organize an American Catholic Church.

For many years an ardent supporter of socialistic schemes such as the short-lived Workingmen's Party and Brook Farm, Brownson eventually joined the Democratic Party and helped to establish the *Democratic Review* (1842–44), only to renounce democracy in favor of an extremely conservative republicanism. The *Democratic Review* was only one of the magazines Brownson founded as a mouthpiece for his views. In 1838 he had established the *BOSTON QUARTERLY REVIEW,* which merged with the *Democratic Review* upon its creation. When the editorial board of the *Democratic Review* grew weary of the Brownson's tirades, he started up *BROWNSON'S QUARTERLY REVIEW,* which lasted from 1844 to 1865 and was briefly revived from 1872 to 1875. Brownson also published numerous books, including autobiographical and novelistic treatments of his various religious conversions, as well as *The Spirit-Rapper* (1854), an attack on SPIRITUALISM, and such polemics as *The American Republic* (1865). His *Complete Works* were published in 20 volumes between 1882 and 1887.

Sources

Gilhooley, Leonard, ed. *No Divided Allegiance: Essays in Brownson's Thought.* New York: Fordham Univerity Press, 1980.

Lapati, Americo D. *Orestes A. Brownson.* New York: Twayne, 1965.

Brownson's Quarterly Review (1844–1875) *periodical*

An outgrowth of Orestes BROWNSON's *BOSTON QUARTERLY REVIEW* and its successor, the *United States Quarterly Review, Brownson's Quarterly Review* functioned as a mouthpiece for its founder's views on Roman Catholicism, to which he had recently converted. Critical of orthodox Catholicism, Brownson freely gave vent to his disagreements with the "radicalism and despotism" of the church. In 1864 he switched the magazine's orientation toward a chauvinistic appreciation of

American civilization, but that approach failed the following year, and the *Review* was not revived until 1872, when Brownson's editorial policy shifted back toward Catholicism.

Sources

Lapati, Americo D. *Orestes A. Brownson.* New York: Twayne, 1965.

Bryan, William Jennings (1860–1925) *orator, editor, politician*

Born in Salem, Illinois, William Jennings Bryan practiced law in Illinois before moving to Lincoln, Nebraska, in 1887. In 1890 his Nebraska district elected him as a representative to the U.S. Congress; he was reelected in 1892. Defeated in his bid for a third term, Bryan worked for the next two years as editor in chief of the Omaha *World-Herald,* in 1896 making a political comeback by delivering an electrifying speech to the Democratic Presidential Convention in Chicago. What became known as the "Cross of Gold" speech identified Bryan with the Populist Party's "free silver" platform (advocating unlimited coinage of silver as a means of alleviating the economic woes of farmers and industrial workers) and guaranteed his place as the Democratic presidential nominee. However, Bryan was defeated, as he was again in 1900 and in 1908. At the 1912 Democratic Convention, Bryan threw his support to Woodrow Wilson, who after the election made him secretary of state. Bryan resigned the position in 1915 in protest over Wilson's increasingly warlike posture toward Germany.

Bryan's populism earned him the honorific "the Great Commoner," and in 1901 he founded a magazine, *The Commoner,* as a platform for his ideas. He also gained a platform on the CHAUTAUQUA circuit, which allowed him to deliver his talk on "The Prince of Peace" in every state in the union. Known for his defense of Christian fundamentalism, Bryan sided with legislators who opposed the teaching of evolution in the public schools. When the issue was put to the test in the infamous "Scopes-Monkey trial" in 1925, Bryan served as the prosecutor for the state of Tennessee. Then, defying good sense and accepted legal procedure, he agreed to a defense request that he testify as an expert witness on the Bible. Lead defense counsel Clarence Darrow (1857–1938) succeeded in making a fool of Bryan, who died in his sleep five days after the trial ended. After his death he was both hailed in works like Vachel Lindsay's (1879–1931) *Bryan, Bryan, Bryan, Bryan: The Campaign of 1896, as Viewed at the Time by a 16-Year Old* (1919) and reviled by H. L. Mencken (1880–1956) in *In Memoriam: W.J.B.* (1926) and John Dos Passos (1896–1970), who featured Bryan in his *U.S.A.* trilogy (1938).

Sources

Koenig, Louis W. *Bryan: A Political Biography of William Jennings Bryan.* New York: Putnam, 1971.

Springen, Donald K. *William Jennings Bryan: Orator of Small-Town America.* New York: Greenwood Press, 1991.

Bryant, William Cullen (1794–1878) *poet, journalist*

Born in Cummington, Massachusetts, the precocious William Cullen Bryant was educated at Williams College. At the age of 14 he published *The Embargo* (1808), an attack on Thomas Jefferson's administration. He was writing poetry at an early age as well, producing in 1817 his most well-known poems, "THANATOPSIS" and "To A Waterfowl," but postponing their publication while he pursued a legal career, which he abandoned in 1825.

Bryant's emergence as a major poet began in 1821 with the publication of *Poems.* By 1825 he had solidified his reputation with such poems as "A Forest Hymn," "Monument Mountain," and "An Indian at the Burial Place of His Fathers." Bryant's poetry fused a feeling for nature and the past with a firm moral message that his readers found uplifting. He continued to write poetry until the mid-1830s, publishing a new collection of *Poems* in 1832, but his output waned and none of his later work matches the fresh diction and descriptions of his earlier work. His later collections include *The Fountain* (1842), *A Forest Hymn* (1860), *Among the Trees* (1874), and *The Flood of Years* (1878).

Bryant's best work is in the romantic tradition (see ROMANTICISM). He was heavily influenced by William Wordsworth's (1770–1850) depictions of nature, although Bryant took a very American tack in explicitly invoking God and avoiding the charges of pantheism and paganism that dogged the English Romantics. It was this conventional and rather conformist side of Bryant that eventually dulled his verse and made him incapable of extending his poetic range. At his best, though, he expresses a sturdy melancholy over the fleeting nature of life and the human effort to comprehend existence. His work has been praised for its elegant simplicity and dignity, which has been deemed "Doric restraint."

Bryant had a successful career as a newspaper editor and public opinion shaper. He became coeditor of the *New York Review and Athenaeum Magazine* in 1825. By 1829 he was editor of the New York *Evening Post.* Although a force in the Democratic Party, he eventually turned to Abraham LINCOLN and the Republicans because of their opposition to slavery.

Some of Bryant's best prose is collected in *Letters of a Traveller* (1850 and 1859) and *Orations and Addresses* (1873). *The Letters of William Cullen Bryant* appeared in six volumes between 1975 and 1992.

Sources

Brodwin, Stanley and Michael D'Innocenzo, edss. *William Cullen Bryant and his America: Centennial Conference Proceedings, 1878–1978.* New York: AMS Press, 1983.

Brown, Charles H. *William Cullen Bryant.* New York: Scribner's, 1971.

Krapf, Norman, ed. *Under Open Sky: Poets on William Cullen Bryant.* New York: Fordham University Press, 1986.
McLean, Albert F. *William Cullen Bryant.* Boston: Twayne, 1989.

Buffalo Bill

See CODY, WILLIAM FREDERICK.

Bumppo, Nathaniel (Natty Bumppo) *character*

The hero of James Fenimore COOPER's *LEATHER-STOCKING TALES* is a woodsman whose rugged individualism and commitment to wilderness and the American frontier owe something to a leatherstockinged hunter named Shipman, whom Cooper had known as a boy in upstate New York, and to that archetypal American hero Daniel BOONE (1734–1820). Natty Bumppo—who goes by many names, including "Leather-Stocking," "Hawkeye," "Deerslayer," and "la Longue Carbine"—is presented in numerous ways. Sometimes, for instance, Cooper has his hero speak a crude vernacular, while other times Bumppo employs poetic diction. This variety only contributes to the sense that Natty Bumppo is meant to personify America in the early decades of its foundation and development. Like the speaker in Walt WHITMAN's *LEAVES OF GRASS,* Bumppo contains multitudes, embodying the spirit that occupied a continent. When last seen, in *THE PRAIRIE,* Bumppo has reached the end of a long life. Even while mourning the death of wilderness, he turns westward and utters his dying word: "Here!"

Sources

Dennis, Ian. *Nationalism and Desire in Early Historical Fiction.* New York: St. Martin's Press, 1997.
Franklin, Wayne. *The New World of James Fenimore Cooper.* Chicago: University of Chicago Press, 1982.
Rans, Geoffrey. *Cooper's Leather-Stocking Novels: A Secular Reading.* Chapel Hill: University of North Carolina Press, 1991.

Bunner, Henry Cuyler (1855–1896) *editor, short story writer*

Born in Oswego, New York, H. C. Bunner became editor of the American humor magazine *PUCK* one year after its establishment in 1877, and he remained on the staff of the magazine until he died. *Puck* arguably shaped the remainder of Bunner's literary career, which resulted mostly in the production of short stories and the anecdotal tale, a genre he almost singlehandedly established in the United States. The most famous of his productions is *Short Sixes: Stories to be Read While the Candle Burns* (1891).

Sources

Jensen, Gerard Edward. *The Life and Letters of Henry Cuyler Bunner.* Durham, N.C.: Duke University Press, 1939.

Buntline, Ned

See JUDSON, EDWARD ZANE CARROLL.

Bunyan, Paul *folk hero*

The model for this legendary character may have been a French Canadian called "Bon Jean," but the tales of his exploits that were popular in the timber country of North America from Michigan westward quickly metamorphosed into the fantastic. Like JOHN HENRY and other folk heroes of prodigious strength, Paul Bunyan was capable of performing Herculean tasks—in Bunyan's case, creating the Grand Canyon and Puget Sound. But unlike the mythological heroes of the ancient world—unlike, in fact, John Henry—Paul Bunyan is a comic figure, created by storytellers and writers competing against one another to see who could tell the tallest tale. So, for example, Paul Bunyan's prize possession is presented as a blue ox named Babe, who measures 42 ax handles high and has a plug of Star tobacco between the eyes. Bunyan is said to have invented a griddle so huge that it was greased by underlings who strapped slabs of bacon to their feet and skated over its surface.

Paul Bunyan first appeared in print in 1914 in the advertising pamphlet *Paul Bunyan and His Big Blue Ox,* published by the Red River Lumber Company of Minnesota. The same year, Douglas Malloch (1877–1938) published a poem about Paul Bunyan, "The Round River Drive," in *The American Lumberman.* In the 20th century Bunyan was treated poetically by Robert Frost (1874–1963) ("Paul's Wife" in *New Hampshire* [1923]); Carl Sandburg (1878–1967) ("Who Made Paul Bunyan?" in *The People, Yes* [1936]); and Louis Untermeyer (1885–1977), one of many who collected Paul Bunyan tales (*The Wonderful Adventures of Paul Bunyan* [1945]). Paul Bunyan has also been the subject of an operetta of the same name written by W. H. Auden (1907–73) and Benjamin Britten (1913–76) and produced in 1941.

Sources

Hoffman, Daniel. *Paul Bunyan: Last of the Frontier Demigods.* New York: Temple University Publications; distributed by Columbia University Press, 1966.

Burnett, Frances Eliza Hodgson (1849–1924) *writer of children's literature*

English by birth, Frances Hodgson Burnett came to the United States in 1865 and settled in Tennessee with her parents. She began writing at the age of 17 and had her first literary success in 1877 with *That Lass o' Lowrie's,* an adult novel set in the Lancashire coal-mining region. She is chiefly remembered, however, for her children's books, two of which have become perennial favorites: *Little Lord Fauntleroy* (1886) and *The Secret Garden* (1911). The first of these proved to be a great success when she adapted it for the stage in 1888; it also made copyright history in England when she successfully stopped an unauthorized stage version. During her long career, Burnett published over 50 books and wrote or collaborated on a dozen plays.

Sources

Bixler, Phyllis. *Frances Hodgson Burnett.* Boston: Twayne, 1984.
Thwaite, Ann. *Waiting for the Party: The Life of Frances Hodgson Burnett, 1849–1924.* London: Secker & Warburg, 1974.

Burroughs, John (1837–1921) *naturalist, essayist, poet, critic*

Born in Roxbury, New York, the son of a farmer, John Burroughs worked at a variety of professions before settling on a farm near Esopus, New York, in 1874. By this time he was already an accomplished writer. In 1860, greatly influenced by Ralph Waldo EMERSON, Burroughs published his first contribution to the *ATLANTIC MONTHLY.* While working as a clerk in the Treasury Department in Washington, D.C., he also became friends with Walt WHITMAN; his *Notes on Walt Whitman as Poet and Person* (1867) was the first biographical study of the great American bard.

Burroughs had already begun, with *Wake-Robin* (1871), to produce the kind of simple, poetic essays about nature that would make his own reputation. After moving to Riverby, his farm on the Hudson River, Burroughs wrote numerous other works of natural history, such as *Locusts and Wild Honey* (1879) and *Squirrels and Other Fur-Bearers* (1900). Such works of scientific inquiry yielded, in Burroughs's later years, to a growing interest in philosophy, which he expressed in works like *The Breath of Life* (1915) and *Accepting the Universe* (1920).

Burroughs was by this time a national figure known as "The Sage of Slabsides" (named for the rustic cabin he had built himself at Riverby) and a friend of such luminaries as John MUIR, Thomas Edison (1847–1931), Henry Ford (1863–1947), and Theodore ROOSEVELT. In 1916 Burroughs received a gold medal from the National Academy of Arts and Letters. Eventually a medal was named in his honor: the John Burroughs Medal is awarded to those writers who have distinguished themselves in the field of natural history.

Sources

Burroughs, John. *Birch Browsings: A John Burroughs Reader.* Edited by Bill McKibben. New York: Penguin Books, 1992.
Renehan, Edward. *John Burroughs: An American Naturalist.* Post Mills, Vt.: Chelsea Green Pub. Co., 1992.

Burton's Gentleman's Magazine

See GENTLEMAN'S MAGAZINE.

Cable, George Washington (1844–1925)

short story writer, novelist, historian

Born in New Orleans, George Washington Cable joined the Confederate army in 1862 and served until the end of the CIVIL WAR, garnering experiences that he would later put to use in his novel *The Cavalier* (1901). After the war, Cable worked first as a cotton wholesaler and then as a surveyor for an engineering expedition. In this last position he contracted malaria and was obliged to quit working for the next two years. He put this time to good use, however, publishing a weekly column of humor sketches in the *New Orleans Picayune* under the pen name "Drop Shot."

After leaving the newspaper, Cable immersed himself in New Orleans history and culture and began publishing a series of stories about his home town in *SCRIBNER'S MONTHLY*. Seven of these tales were collected and published as *Old Creole Days* in 1879, his first real literary success. A year later Cable published his first novel, *The Grandissimes,* a study of 19th-century Creole life, which demonstrated his mastery of Creole and slave dialects and helped to solidify his reputation as a local colorist (see LOCAL COLOR). Other novels and stories of the antebellum South followed, as did a history, *The Creoles of Louisiana* (1884), and *The Silent South* (1885), a collection of essays arguing for prison reform and the abolition of slavery. Both of the last works made Cable so unpopular in his native South that he moved to Massachusetts, where he continued to work for reform and to write about social problems in such works as *The Negro Question* (1888) and *The Southern Struggle for Pure Government* (1890).

Sources

Cleman, John. *George Washington Cable Revisited.* New York: Twayne, 1996.

Rubin, Louis D. *George W. Cable: The Life and Times of a Southern Heretic.* New York: Pegasus, 1969.

Call of the Wild, The Jack London (1903) *novel*

This was the work that made Jack LONDON famous around the world. Its protagonist is Buck, a half-St. Bernard, half-Scottish shepherd dog that goes wild, eventually joining a wolf pack. Raised on a California estate, Buck is stolen and shipped to the Klondike, where he becomes a sled dog. Buck's allegiance to his new owner, John Thornton, is absolute, but after Thornton is killed, grief prompts Buck to heed the call of the wild. London is said to have been influenced by Egerton R. Young's (1840–1909) memoir *My Dogs in the Northland* (1902). Although *The Call of the Wild* is at times sentimental, it is shaped by London's burgeoning ideas about the necessity of environmental adaptation and the influence of heredity, ideas he would later explore in depth.

Sources

Tavernier-Coubin, Jacqueline. *The Call of the Wild: A Naturalistic Romance.* New York: Twayne, 1994.

Carey, Henry Charles (1793–1879) *essayist*

Born in Philadelphia, Henry Charles Carey was the son of the publisher Mathew Carey (1760–1839), in whose firm the younger Carey worked until 1835, when he retired and took up economics. That year he published his *Essay on the Rate of Wages,* which adhered to a laissez-faire belief that the market, not government, should control economic life. His *Principles of Political Economy* (1837–40) and *Principles of Social Science* (1858–59) were the first truly important American works in their fields. His *Harmony of Interests, Agricultural, Manufacturing, and Commercial* (1851) promoted the protective tariff to foster U.S. goods and influenced the U.S. Tariff Act of 1861.

Sources

Green, Arnold Wilfred. *Henry Charles Carey, Nineteenth-Century Sociologist.* Philadelphia: University of Pennsylvania Press, 1951.

Carman, William Bliss (1861–1929) *poet*

Born in Fredericton, New Brunswick, Bliss Carman first came to the United States when he was a student at Harvard, where he met Richard HOVEY, with whom he later collaborated. After 1888 Carman made his home in Connecticut and New York, but an 1892 trip to Nova Scotia and New Brunswick with Hovey resulted in three collections of verses marked by a spirit as blithe as their titles: *Songs from Vagabondia* (1894), *More Songs from Vagabondia* (1896), and *Last Songs from Vagabondia* (1901). The poems in these volumes, as well as others Carman wrote alone and published in collections—such as *Low Tide on Grand Pré* (1893), the *Pipes of Pan* five-volume series (1902–05), and *April Airs* (1916)—are marked by spontaneity, sensuous imagery, and profound musicality.

While he continued to produce poetry prolifically, Carman served on the editorial staff of *The Independent* and other magazines and lectured on Canadian literature. He made frequent visits to his home country, where he was regarded as the unofficial poet laureate. His *Talks on Poetry and Life,* concerning Canadian literature, was published in 1926.

Sources

Bliss Carman's Poems. New York: Dodd, Mead, 1931.

Lynch, Gerald, ed. *Bliss Carman: A Reappraisal.* Ottawa: University of Ottawa Press, 1990.

Miller, Muriel. *Bliss Carman: Quest & Revolt.* St. John's, Newfoundland: Jesperson Press, 1985.

Carpet-Bag, The *periodical*

Founded in 1851, this humorous weekly was published in Boston and edited by Benjamin Shillaber, who contributed sketches about the fictitious "Mrs. Partington," who became famous for her misuse of English, to the magazine. The first published work by Mark Twain (Samuel CLEMENS), Artemus Ward (Charles Farrar BROWNE), and the occasional wit, "John Phoenix" (G. H. Derby) (1823–61), all appeared in the May 1, 1852, issue.

Carson, Christopher (Kit Carson) (1809–1868) *frontiersman*

Born in Kentucky, Kit Carson moved with his family while he was still a young child to the Missouri frontier. After his father died, Carson was apprenticed to a saddle maker, but in 1826 he ran away, joining a caravan that took him to Santa Fe and Taos in what is now New Mexico. Taos became the base from which, for the next 14 years, he served as a guide to parties traveling the Santa Fe Trail. From 1829 to 1831 he accompanied one of the first overland journeys to California. In 1842 Carson became the guide for John C. Frémont's (1813–90) Western expeditions and was instrumental in seizing California from Mexican control during the Mexican War. Frémont's reports of his skill and courage helped make Carson's reputation, but the former mountain man added to his growing fame by becoming an accomplished Indian fighter. Appointed U.S. Indian agent in the Southwest in 1853, Carson served in that role until the commencement of the CIVIL WAR, when he helped organize the First New Mexican Volunteers. He rose to the rank of brigadier general and commanded Fort Garland, Colorado, from 1866 to 1867.

Carson was featured as the hero of countless DIME NOVELS, but he is also the subject of Joaquin MILLER's poem *Kit Carson's Ride* (1871). In the 20th century, Carson figured in Willa Cather's (1873–1947) novel *Death Comes for the Archbishop* (1927), Harvey Fergusson's (1890–1971) *Wolf Song* (1927), and several works by Stanley Vestal.

Sources

Guild, Thelma S. *Kit Carson: A Pattern for Heroes.* Lincoln: University of Nebraska Press, 1984.

Century Association *organization*

This New York social club for writers and artists was founded in 1847 as an offshoot of the Sketch Club, itself an outgrowth of the BREAD AND CHEESE CLUB. Originally the club had one hundred members—hence the name—but that number has long since been surpassed. Past presidents include historian and politician George BANCROFT, poet William Cullen BRYANT, and the statesman Elihu Root (1845–1937).

Century Illustrated Monthly Magazine, The *periodical*

In 1881 management difficulties led to a change of the ownership and name of what had been *SCRIBNER'S MONTHLY.* Like its predecessor, however, *The Century Illustrated Magazine* was meant to be "An Illustrated Magazine for the People," which would compete with *Harper's New Monthly* (see

Harper's Monthly Magazine). Under the editorship of R. W. Gilder, who held that position from 1881 to 1909, the magazine increased its emphasis on public affairs—featuring, for example, a long series on the CIVIL WAR that included contributions from George McClellan (1826–85), Ulysses S. GRANT, and other military heroes. The magazine also ran important literary serials of such novels as William Dean HOWELLS's *THE RISE OF SILAS LAPHAM* and Henry JAMES's *The Bostonians.* The magazine reached its highest circulation in 1890, and in 1930 it merged with *THE FORUM.*

Channing, William Ellery (1) (1780–1842) *theologian*

Born in Newport, Rhode Island, William Ellery Channing was ordained at age 23 as the minister of the Federal Street Congregationalist Church in Boston, a position he held for the rest of his life. He rebelled, however, against Calvinism, and the sermon on the subject that he preached at the 1819 ordination of Jared Sparks made Channing's reputation as the "apostle" of UNITARIANISM. His dedication to the promotion of humanitarianism and tolerance helped pave the way for TRANSCENDENTALISM as well. In 1821 Channing founded and coedited a Unitarian magazine, *The Christian Register,* and he advocated against slavery in such works as *Slavery* (1835), *The Abolitionist* (1836), *Emancipation* (1840), and *The Duty of the Free States* (1842). His *Remarks on American Literature* (1830) calls for a literary Declaration of Independence, an objection to the influence of English writers on Americans.

Sources

Mendelsohn, Jack. *Channing, the Reluctant Radical: A Biography.* Boston: Little, Brown, 1971.

Channing, William Ellery (2) (1818–1901) *essayist, poet*

The nephew of the Unitarian minister of the same name, William Ellery Channing was born in Boston. After three months at Harvard he left for the West, where he tried farming in Illinois and journalism in Cincinnati before returning to Massachusetts and settling in Concord, near the home of Ralph Waldo EMERSON. Married to Ellen Fuller, the sister of the writer Margaret FULLER, Channing was intimate with a coterie of Concord writers and transcendentalists (see TRANSCENDENTALISM). He was especially close to Henry David THOREAU and in 1873 published the first biography of Thoreau. Channing wrote for magazines and newspapers and also published a great deal of poetry that was widely criticized for its lack of polish. Thoreau memorably referred to Channing's style as "sublimoslipshod," alluding to Channing's transcendentalist bias toward "natural" expression.

Sources

McGill, Frederick T. *Channing of Concord: A Life of William Ellery Channing II.* New Brunswick, N.J.: Rutgers University Press, 1967.

Channing, William Henry (1810–1884) *editor*

Born in Boston, William Henry Channing was the nephew of the elder William Ellery CHANNING (1). A member of the TRANSCENDENTAL CLUB and a leading Unitarian, Channing also edited the socioreligious magazines *THE WESTERN MESSENGER, The Present,* and *THE SPIRIT OF THE AGE.* He spent time at BROOK FARM and converted to FOURIERISM. In addition to his religious writings, he also published (with Ralph Waldo EMERSON and Unitarian minister J. F. Clarke [1810–88]) Margaret FULLER's *Memoirs* (1852) and a biography of his famous uncle *A Memoir of William Ellery Channing* (1848).

Chap Book, The *periodical*

Founded in 1893 in Cambridge, Massachusetts, as the house organ of the publisher Stone and Kimball, this LITTLE MAGAZINE moved the next year with the publishing house to Chicago. There it emerged as an independent literary magazine of superior quality, publishing works by such American contributors as Henry JAMES and foreign authors like H. G. Wells (1866–1946) and William Butler Yeats (1865–1939). In style it resembled the handsome, lavishly illustrated English periodical *The Yellow Book,* and in turn it influenced other American magazines like *The Lark.* In 1898 it merged with the transcendentalist journal, *THE DIAL.*

Chapman, John (Johnny Appleseed) (Jonathan Chapman) (1774–1845) *orchardist*

Born in Springfield, Massachusetts, John Chapman migrated westward as a young man. In Pennsylvania he gave apple seeds and saplings to families migrating further west. Then, around 1800, he followed them to Ohio, sowing apple seeds as he went. In Ohio Chapman became an orchardist and a follower of the Swedish mystical philosopher Emanuel Swedenborg (1688–1772), who advocated direct communication with the spirit world. For more than 40 years Chapman wandered through Ohio, Illinois, and western Pennsylvania, caring for his trees and helping settlers plant more. His eccentric appearance and mystical beliefs made Chapman a legend in his own time, and after his death he became the subject of FOLKLORE and countless TALL TALES. The poet Vachel Lindsay (1879–1931) wrote many verses about him, including the long work *In Praise of Johnny Appleseed* (1923).

Sources

Price, Robert. *Johnny Appleseed: Man and Myth.* Bloomington: Indiana University Press, 1954.

Chautauqua *movement*

An outgrowth of the LYCEUM MOVEMENT in education, Chautauqua was conceived in 1873 by the Methodist bishop John Heyl Vincent (1832–1920) at a Sunday school institute he was attending at Chautauqua, New York. Vincent proposed to integrate secular with religious training at the summer institute, and this ambitious program—now called the Sunday-School Teachers' Assembly—was begun the following summer at a defunct camp site on Lake Chautauqua. This summer program, initially attended by 40 students, eventually grew into a worldwide adult education program offering not only on-site lectures, recreation, and entertainment, but also correspondence courses and a book club (the first in America). Other communities around the country were inspired to imitate the institute's success, with the result that "Chautauqua" became a generic term for traveling bands of lecturers and entertainers who performed in rural settings. At the peak of its popularity, the Chautauqua movement was a powerful cultural force for disseminating not just the arts but also information on such diverse topics as women's suffrage and soil conservation. After 1924, however, the movement began to decline.

Sources

Gould, Joseph E. *The Chautauqua Movement: An Episode in the Continuing American Revolution.* New York: State University of New York, 1961.

Chesnut, Mary Boykin Miller (1823–1886) *diarist*

The daughter of a U.S. senator from South Carolina and the wife of an important South Carolina planter and state senator who was an ardent supporter of the Confederacy, Mary Boykin Chesnut was 37 years old when she began her journal chronicling the CIVIL WAR. Witness to such pivotal events as the siege of Fort Sumter (1861) and General William Tecumseh Sherman's (1820–91) march to the sea (1864), she recorded her observations in a diary that was at least 400,000 words long. After the war she began to revise her journal, highlighting daily life during the conflict. In 1905 her *A Diary from Dixie* was published posthumously in a bowdlerized edition. The complete text, edited by historian C. Van Woodward (1908–99), was published as *Mary Chesnut's Civil War* in 1982, when it won a Pulitzer Prize.

Sources

Muhlenfeld, Elisabeth. *Mary Boykin Chesnut: a Biography.* Baton Rouge: Louisiana State University Press, 1981.

Chesnutt, Charles Waddell (1858–1932) *short story writer*

Born in Cleveland, Ohio, and raised in Fayetteville, North Carolina, Charles W. Chesnutt is widely regarded as the most influential African-American fiction writer of the late 19th and early 20th centuries. He is best known for his short-story collection *The Conjure Woman,* published in 1899 and comprising dialect tales told by a character named Uncle Julius McAdoo. That same year he published a biography of Frederick DOUGLASS. Chesnutt was outspoken about the oppression endured by African Americans, but he was also adept at presenting complex black lives to the white majority. The title story of *The Wife of His Youth and Other Stories of the Color Line* (1899) explores the conflicting loyalties of a freed black man who is torn between the wife he married in slavery and the more sophisticated woman he has met in his new life.

Chesnutt's literary career tapered off during his last 25 years, but in 1928 the NAACP awarded him the Springarn Medal for his "pioneer work as a literary artist depicting the life and struggles of Americans of Negro descent."

Sources

Keller, Frances Richardson. *An American Crusade: The Life of Charles Waddell Chesnutt.* Provo, Utah: Brigham Young University Press, 1978.

Render, Sylvia Lyons. *Charles W. Chesnutt.* Boston: Twayne, 1980.

Chicago Daily News *periodical*

In 1876, when it was less than a year old, the Chicago *Daily News* beat out every other local newspaper in announcing that Rutherford B. Hayes (1822–93) would be the Republican candidate for president. The subsequent history of the *Daily News* included many other scoops—often sensational ones—but the paper also ran some excellent literary contributions, including a column, "Sharps and Flats," written between 1883 and 1895 by Eugene FIELD. In 1931 the paper became a Republican mouthpiece, but in 1944 it resumed its politically independent editorial policy. In 1961 Marshall Field Jr. took over as publisher and editor.

Chicago Times *periodical*

Both before and during the CIVIL WAR, the *Times,* founded in 1854, was considered a "Copperhead" newspaper, because its denunciations of Abraham LINCOLN were indicative of northern sympathy with the Confederacy. In the antebellum period, however, it was read for its superior foreign news coverage. In 1891 the paper changed hands and became radically Democratic. In 1895 it merged with the Chicago *Herald* to become the *Times-Herald,* and in 1918 it was finally purchased by William Randolph HEARST, who folded it into his existing *Examiner.*

Chicago Tribune *periodical*

Founded in 1847, this daily newspaper rose to prominence between 1855 and 1899, when it was edited by Joseph Medill

(1823–99). Medill was one of the founders of the newly reorganized Republican Party, and the *Tribune* reflected his views in its pronounced Republican editorial policy, which promoted both ABOLITIONISM and Abraham LINCOLN. Medill's descendants continued to control the paper through the middle of the 20th century. Under the control of the journalist and World War I veteran Robert Rutherford McCormick (1880–1955), the paper took on a decidedly conservative tone, opposing labor unions and the presidency (1932–45) of Franklin D. Roosevelt (1882–1945). After McCormick's death the *Tribune*'s political stance moved back toward the center, and it became the dominant newspaper in the Midwest.

Sources

Smith, Richard Norton. *The Colonel: The Life and Legend of Robert R. McCormick.* Boston: Houghton Mifflin, 1997.

Wendt, Lloyd. *Chicago Tribune: The Rise of a Great American Newspaper.* Chicago: Rand McNally, 1979.

Child, Lydia Maria Francis (1802–1880) *essayist, poet*

Born in Medford, Massachusetts, Lydia Maria Child founded the first monthly magazine for children, the *Juvenile Miscellany,* in 1826. An ardent abolitionist, her early antislavery monograph, *Appeal in Favor of That Class of Americans Called Africans* (1833), and the later publication of her *Correspondence* (1860) with the governor of Virginia, won many converts to the cause. She was also among the first to write formally about household economy in *The Frugal Housewife* (1829) and *The Mother's Handbook* (1831). A pioneering advocate of women's suffrage and sex education, she wrote *A History of the Condition of Women in Various Ages and Nations* (1835). Her fiction tended toward the didactic, as in *Hobomok* (1824), a romance set in colonial Massachusetts that lauds Indians as "noble savages." She also wrote verse and is perhaps best remembered for her poem *Thanksgiving Day* (1857), which begins: "Over the river and through the wood, / To grandfather's house we'll go."

Sources

Clifford, Deborah Pickman. *Crusader for Freedom: A Life of Lydia Maria Child.* Boston: Beacon Press, 1992.

Chingachgook *character*

Chingachgook is the Indian chieftain in James Fenimore COOPER's *LEATHER-STOCKING TALES,* consisting of *The Pioneers* (1823), *The Pathfinder* (1826), *The Last of the Mohicans* (1827), *The Prairie* (1840), and *The Deerslayer* (1841). Also known as "le Gros Serpent," "Indian John," "the Sagamore," and "John Mohegan," Chingachgook is the embodiment of the "noble savage" and has the singular distinction of being the last of the Mohicans.

Born early in the 18th century, Chingachgook is a member of the Delaware tribe, which allies itself with the British in the French and Indian Wars of 1689–1763. He first tastes battle in the company of the white American woodsman Natty BUMPPO, his boon companion. Bumppo has arranged to accompany Chingachgook in an attempt to rescue the latter's betrothed, Wah-ta!-Wah, who has been kidnapped by the French-allied Iroquois. After a series of battles and narrow escapes, Chingachgook and Natty Bumppo rescue the Indian maiden, who survives only long enough to bear Chingachgook a son, Uncas. Uncas grows to manhood alongside his father and the white Leatherstocking, fighting the Iroquois until 1757, when the three are enlisted to protect the daughters of a British officer, an adventure that ends in Uncas's death.

Alone again and the last of his kind, Chingachgook stays by Leatherstocking's side, steadily growing more silent and self-sacrificing. For a time the pair settles near Otsego, New York, but the chieftain is unable to come to terms with white civilization and notions of property. Finally, in 1793 Chingachgook dies in the middle of a forest fire, one of his arms pointing westward.

Sources

Barker, Martin. *The Lasting of the Mohicans: History of an American Myth.* Jackson: University Press of Mississippi, 1995.

Rans, Geoffrey. *Cooper's Leather-Stocking Novels: A Secular Reading.* Chapel Hill: University of North Carolina Press, 1991.

Chivers, Thomas Holley (1809–1858) *poet*

A native of Georgia, Thomas Holley Chivers was trained as a physician but gave up that career in order to devote himself to poetry. Among his better-known works, *The Path of Sorrow* (1832) chronicled his unhappy first marriage; *Conrad and Eudora* (1834) was one of many works created during the period out of materials supplied by the KENTUCKY TRAGEDY. Chivers is remembered for his connection with Edgar Allan POE during the 1840s. Poe accused him of plagiarism in the latter's *Eonchs of Ruby* (1851), a charge Chivers countered with accusations of his own. In fact, many believe that Chivers's poem "Isadore," among other poems, greatly influenced Poe's later verses "The Raven" and "Ulalume." After the death of his children, Chivers became increasingly interested in mysticism, an interest reflected in his *Search After Truth; or, A New Revelation of the Psycho-Physiological Nature of Man* (1848).

Sources

Watts, Charles Henry. *Thomas Holley Chivers, His Literary Career and His Poetry.* Athens: University of Georgia Press, 1956.

Chopin, Katherine O'Flaherty (1851–1904)

novelist, short story writer

Born in St. Louis, Missouri, Kate Chopin lost her father to a railroad accident when she was five years old. Raised in a wealthy household by her widowed mother (who never remarried), grandmother, and great-grandmother (both of them also widowed), Kate was well educated, graduating from the St. Louis Academy of the Sacred Heart in 1868. Two years later she married Oscar Chopin, the son of a Louisiana cotton planter, and moved with him to New Orleans.

During the nine years the Chopins lived in the Crescent City, Kate bore five sons and grew increasingly familiar with the Creole and Cajun cultures. In 1879, after Oscar Chopin's cotton-trading business failed, the family moved to Cloutierville, a tiny village in north Louisiana, where Oscar ran a general store and Kate had the last of her children, a girl. Oscar died of malaria in 1882, leaving Kate deeply in debt. After making an attempt to continue her husband's business, Chopin returned in 1884 to St. Louis with her six children.

Back in her hometown, Chopin began writing stories about Louisiana, the first of which appeared in 1889. Her first novel, *At Fault,* appeared in 1890, but she became a force in the LOCAL COLOR movement when her stories were collected and published as *Bayou Folk* (1890) and *A Night in Acadie* (1897). Her second novel, *THE AWAKENING,* the tale of a married woman's sexual rebirth, shocked critics and ended her literary career. After Chopin's death in 1904 of a cerebral hemorrhage, she was forgotten until the 1960s when, buoyed by the women's movement, her work received into the mainstream of American literature.

Sources

Boren, Lydia S., and Sara deSaussure Davis, eds. *Kate Chopin Reconsidered: Beyond the Bayou.* Baton Rouge: Louisiana State University Press, 1992.

Toth, Emily. *Unveiling Kate Chopin.* Jackson: University Press of Mississippi, 1999.

Christian Disciple, The periodical

This Unitarian magazine was founded in 1813 in Boston by the elder William Ellery CHANNING (1) and was first a monthly. It became a bimonthly publication in 1819, and in 1823 its name was changed to *The Christian Examiner.* The leading religious review of its day, it took a more secular turn in 1857, embracing TRANSCENDENTALISM. In 1866, however, it moved to New York and embraced religious conservatism; thereafter its influence waned.

Christian Science *religious movement*

Established as the Church of Christ, Scientist, in 1879 by Mary Baker EDDY, Christian Science grew out of principles of divine healing that Eddy discovered in the New Testament. In 1866, after a prolonged period of illness, Eddy recovered her health immediately after reading an account of one of Jesus's healings. In 1875 she published *Science and Health* (later published as *Science and Health, with Key to the Scriptures*), which would become the official statement of her movement, based on a conviction that the power of what she called the "Eternal Mind" could help believers overcome what she saw as the illusions of sickness, sin, and even death.

The "mother church" of Christian Science was founded in Boston in 1892 and soon had branch churches around the world. Despite attacks by writers such as Mark Twain (Samuel Langhorne CLEMENS), who in 1907 published a book debunking the faith, the religion grew steadily during the first third of the 20th century, reaching a peak of 250,000 members in the United States in 1936. Since about 1950, the number of branch churches and affiliated societies has decreased, but many of the publications associated with the church, particularly *The Christian Science Monitor,* a newspaper Eddy founded in 1908, continue to be vigorous.

Sources

Gill, Gillian. *Mary Baker Eddy.* Reading, Mass.: Perseus Books, 1998.

Knee, Stuart E. *Christian Science in the Age of Mary Baker Eddy.* Westport, Conn.: Greenwood Press, 1994.

Churchill, Winston (1871–1947) *novelist*

A native of St. Louis, Churchill graduated from the Naval Academy at Annapolis in 1894, although he never served in the navy. Instead, he moved to New Hampshire, where he launched his literary career with the novel *The Celebrity* (1898), said to have been intended as a satire of the colorful Richard Harding DAVIS. Churchill turned next to American history as subject matter. *Richard Carvel* (1899), a romance set during the Revolutionary War, proved to be a best-seller, as did *The Crisis* (1901), a novel about politics and society during the CIVIL WAR, and *The Crossing* (1904), a romance concerning the settlement of Kentucky.

Churchill turned next to more contemporary subject matter in *Coniston* (1906), portraying a mid-19th-century New Hampshire politician's ethical conflicts. *Mr. Crewe's Career* (1908) is the story of a railroad's attempt to control state government. *A Far Country* (1915) tells the tale of conflicting private and public interests in a midwestern city. Churchill's literary focus mirrored his biographical one: his service in the New Hampshire legislature led, in 1913, to an unsuccessful bid for the governorship as the candidate of Theodore ROOSEVELT's Progressive Party.

Throughout the first two decades of the new century, Churchill continued to write novels concerning contemporary social problems, as well as a play, *Dr. Jonathan* (1919), tracing the spread of industrialization in the wake of World

War I. After 1919 his only publication was the declaration of Christian belief, *The Uncharted Way: The Psychology of the Gospel Doctrine* (1940).

Sources

Schneider, Robert W. *Novelist to a Generation: The Life and Thought of Winston Churchill.* Bowling Green, Ohio: Bowling Green University Popular Press, 1976.

Titus, Warren I. *Winston Churchill.* New York: Twayne, 1963.

Cisco Kid *character*

This stock character originated with the story "The Caballero's Way" by O. Henry (William Sydney PORTER) in *Heart of the West* (1907). Appearing repeatedly in countless WESTERNS and television series, the Cisco Kid became a romantic Latin cowboy who filled the role of a Robin Hood in the Southwest, robbing from the rich so as to give to the poor.

Sources

Nevins, Francis M. *The Films of the Cisco Kid.* Waynesville, N.C.: World of Yesterday, 1998.

"Civil Disobedience" *Henry David Thoreau* (1849) *essay*

Henry David THOREAU spent the night of January 26, 1848, in the Concord, Massachusetts, jail after refusing to pay a poll tax as a gesture of his opposition to the MEXICAN WAR. The experience resulted in this essay, first delivered as the lecture "The Relation of the Individual to the State" and then published in May 1849 under the title "Resistance to Civil Government" in Elizabeth Palmer PEABODY's periodical *Aesthetic Papers.* After Thoreau's death in 1862, the essay was reprinted on numerous occasions under the title "Civil Disobedience."

Thoreau took his notions of civil disobedience performed in the service of individual liberty from his readings of such founding fathers as Thomas Jefferson (1743–1826) and Thomas Paine (1737–1809). Although Thoreau's essay slipped into obscurity after his death, in the 20th century it proved highly influential with such pioneers of civil rights as the Reverend Martin Luther King Jr. (1929–68) in the United States and Mahatma Gandhi (1869–1948) in India. Such notions as "That government is best which governs least" and "We must be men first and subjects afterwards" have made their way into the American consciousness, contributing to the not uncommon belief that individuals have a right—even a duty—to resist unjust government actions.

Sources

Bridgman, Richard. *Dark Thoreau.* Lincoln: University of Nebraska Press, 1982.

Salt, Henry. *Life of Henry David Thoreau.* Urbana: University of Illinois Press, 1993.

Thoreau, Henry David. *Walden and Civil Disobedience: Authoritative Texts, Background, Reviews, and Essays in Criticism.* Edited by Owen Thomas. New York: W. W. Norton, 1966.

Civil War (1861–1865) *historical event*

The Civil War was the result of tensions between North and South over the development of the nation, the status of slavery, the role of the federal government, the conduct of international commerce, and the setting of tariffs. Historians have debated whether the war was inevitable because of the conflicting interests of the two regions or could have been prevented with the aid of better political leadership. The different terminology used by the two regions suggests that preventing war was probably beyond even the best diplomatic efforts.

The term *Civil War* is now used because the North won the war and, by force of arms, the argument that the Union was one and indivisible. Yet to southerners there was no Civil War but instead a War between the States, a phrase that articulates the South's view that each state was sovereign and had the right to secede from the Union. South Carolina senator John C. Calhoun (1782–1850) developed the doctrine of *nullification,* which posited that states had the right to nullify federal laws.

The South hearkened back to the principles of Thomas Jefferson, emphasizing a weak central government. The North relied more on federal power in developing the infrastructure of the country (aiding railroad companies, for example), and to principles derived from Alexander Hamilton (1755–1804) that led to the creation of a national bank and a strong federal judiciary, especially a Supreme Court, which—to Jefferson's dismay—would become the arbiter of the Constitution. Thus southerners saw the actions of the federal government as interference with their internal affairs, whereas northerners saw the federal government's action in the light of creating a "more perfect union."

Abraham LINCOLN's election in 1860 brought the different sectional views of the nation to a crisis point because Lincoln refused to allow the South free access to the new territories. Although he emphatically stated that he would not take any action to end slavery in the South, southerners believed that without the ability to expand their economies westward, slavery and their way of life was doomed.

In spite of an active abolitionist movement (see ABOLITIONISM), slavery per se was not the precipitating cause of the Civil War. Lincoln worried that too strong a stand on slavery would alienate border states such as Kentucky, Tennessee, Maryland, and parts of Delaware. Yet the radical wing of his Republican party was determined to make slavery a major issue of the war, and Lincoln gradually adopted aspects of the Radical Republican program, beginning with his

Emancipation Proclamation in January 1863. Limited in scope—it freed only those slaves in the states that had seceded—the proclamation nevertheless shifted the emphasis from a war about secession and states' rights to a war about slavery and freedom.

In the early years of the war, until Ulysses S. GRANT was given full command of the Union armies in 1864, the North was outgeneraled and outfought in most of the major battles. The courage of the Southern fighting man against great odds, the Southern victories against better-equipped Northern armies often twice as large as Confederate forces, the ingenuity of Southern naval commanders, and the courage of the Southern people whose homes and livelihoods were destroyed made the story of the war in the South profoundly moving, capturing the public imagination and after the war making the South a region saturated in the romantic mystique of the lost cause.

In terms of public fascination with the war, the South, in a sense, won. The North simply did not produce dashing and daring figures such as the cavalier Confederate military commanders Jeb Stuart (1833–64) and Nathan Bedford Forrest (1821–77). Even Grant did not have the soldierly, aristocratic bearing of the distinguished Robert E. Lee (1807–70). Northern generals such as William Tecumseh Sherman (1820–91) and Philip H. Sheridan (1831–88) were no match for the aura of Stonewall Jackson (1824–63), who had the virtue of dying a martyr to the cause—as did Stuart, who reportedly exclaimed on his deathbed that he would rather die than live in a South that had lost the war.

The irony is that much of the 19th-century literature about the legendary figures of the Civil War–era South is not very good, because it sentimentalizes and simplifies both the nature of the soldiers and the cause for which they fought. Henry TIMROD and William Gilmore SIMMS, for example, never came to grips with the reasons the South lost. Not until the 20th century did great Southern writers such as William Faulkner (1897–1962), Shelby Foote (1916–), and Alan Tate (1899–1979) deal with the war in tragic and comic terms that did justice to the moral complexity of the war.

In the North the war's hero was Abraham Lincoln. He emerged as a great figure, particularly in the poetry of Walt WHITMAN. On the war itself, no southern writer came near to matching the supple style and profound explorations of the conflict and its major figures that Whitman demonstrated in *Drum-Taps* (1865) and Herman MELVILLE achieved in *Battle-Pieces* (1866). The diary of Mary Boykin CHESNUT provides the best 19th-century southern account of the war. Other important 19th-century novels and stories about the Civil War have been produced by William DE FOREST, Stephen CRANE, and Ambrose BIERCE.

Sources

Aaron, Daniel. *The Unwritten War: American Writers and the Civil War.* New York: Alfred A. Knopf, 1973.

Cullen, Jim. *The Civil War in Popular Culture: A Reusable Past.* Washington, D.C.: Smithsonian Institution Press, 1995.

Lively, Robert Alexander. *Fiction Fights the Civil War: An Unfinished Chapter in the Literary History of the American People.* Chapel Hill: University of North Carolina Press, 1957.

Madden, David and Peggy Bach, ed. *Classics of Civil War Fiction.* Jackson: University Press of Mississippi, 1991.

Wilson, Edmund. *Patriot Gore: Studies in the Literature of the Civil War.* New York: Oxford University Press, 1962.

Clansman, The *Thomas Dixon* (1905) *novel*

This novel by Thomas DIXON is the second of a trilogy of novels (the others are *The Leopard's Spots* [1902] and *The Traitor* [1907]) set in the South during RECONSTRUCTION. The trilogy is melodramatic, offering up a virulently racist view of blacks and an apology for the vigilante Ku Klux Klan. The book was popular in its day, and Dixon did well with his dramatization of it, which toured in 1905–06. In 1915 the legendary silent film director D. W. Griffith (1880–1948) adapted *The Clansman* for the screen as *The Birth of a Nation.*

Sources

Cook, Raymond Allen. *Thomas Dixon.* New York: Twayne, 1974.

Clapp, Henry (1814–1875) *journalist, novelist*

Henry Clapp was a New York journalist who founded the *SATURDAY PRESS* in 1858. Often writing under the pen name "Figaro," he championed such avant-garde works as Walt WHITMAN's *Leaves of Grass* and earned the sobriquet "The King of Bohemia." He also translated the works of Charles Fourier (see FOURIERISM) and wrote novels including *The Pioneer; or, Leaves from an Editor's Portfolio* (1846). He was a regular at the Manhattan literary watering hole PFAFF'S CELLAR.

Clarke, James Freeman (1810–1888) *editor, biographer*

Born in Hanover, New Hampshire, James Freeman Clarke became one of the more militant leaders of the transcendentalist movement (see TRANSCENDENTALISM). After graduating from Harvard Divinity School and ordination as a Unitarian minister, Clarke assumed the pulpit of a church in Louisville, Kentucky, where he also helped to establish and edit the Unitarian periodical *THE WESTERN MESSENGER*. Returning to Boston in 1841, he helped found the Church of the Disciples and served as a professor at his alma mater. Clarke became a member of the TRANSCENDENTAL CLUB and collaborated with Ralph Waldo EMERSON and William Henry CHANNING (2) in a memoir of Margaret FULLER. A committed activist on behalf of ABOLITIONISM and SUFFRAGISM, Clarke also wrote a number of texts that were highly influential in their day, including *Ten Great Religions* (1871–83), *Essentials and Non-Essentials in Religion* (1878), and *Self-Culture* (1880).

Sources

Bolster, Arthur S. *James Freeman Clarke: Disciple to Advancing Truth.* Boston: Beacon Press, 1954.

Clavers, Mary

See KIRKLAND, CAROLINE.

Clemens, Samuel Langhorne (Mark Twain)

(1835–1910) *novelist, journalist*

Samuel Clemens was born in Florida, Missouri, and raised by a father who believed in frontier values and the American Dream of striking it rich. A land speculator always looking for a big profit, this restless man settled in Hannibal, Missouri, where Samuel grew up in surroundings similar to those he created in his American classics *Tom Sawyer* and *Huckleberry Finn.* From an early age Clemens worked in publishing, first as a printer's apprentice and then as a journeyman printer at various newspapers in the East and Middle West. By the mid-1850s he was a Mississippi River boat pilot, an experience he wrote about memorably in *Life on the Mississippi* (1883).

The CIVIL WAR stopped traffic on the Mississippi, and Clemens and his brother headed west to make their fortune, an adventure Twain describes in *Roughing It* (1872). Not until 1862, when he began working for the *Territorial Enterprise* newspaper in Virginia City, Nevada, did Clemens adopt his pen name of Mark Twain. His first pieces were a familiar species of frontier humor, later collected in *Mark Twain of the Enterprise* (1957).

By the early 1860s Twain had made friends with writers such as Artemus Ward (Charles Farrar BROWNE) and Bret HARTE and made his own reputation with the publication of *The Celebrated Jumping Frog of Calaveras County and Other Sketches* (1867). He also turned his travels to the Sandwich Islands, the Mediterranean, and the Holy Land into popular lectures and then a book, *The Innocents Abroad* (1869).

In 1870 Twain married and settled in Hartford, Connecticut. This move into genteel society did not inhibit his robust frontier sensibility, although his darker vision of politics and of human nature began to develop in this period. With C. D. WARNER he produced *The Gilded Age* (1873), a satire on the post–Civil War period that portrayed a country corrupted by the enormous sums spent and invested during the war. *Tom Sawyer* (1876) and *Huckleberry Finn* (1883), on the other hand, dealt exuberantly with the pre-Civil War period and drew heavily on Twain's memories of his own frontier childhood. These highly nostalgic looks at a lost past—in fact, a lost innocence—were overlaid with a complex consciousness of the brewing danger inherent in a country that practiced slavery and suffered from enormous inequalities in economic standards, not to mention the tensions inherent in a society that prided itself on its anarchic frontier values and at the same time pursued the quest for civilization and even gentility.

Twain's consciousness of the tremendous disparity between the rich and poor is evident in his fantasy novel *The Prince and the Pauper* (1882). His growing concern about what it meant to be civilized is reflected in *A Connecticut Yankee in King Arthur's Court* (1889). In the latter work he burlesqued the very idea of civilization, pointing out the ridiculousness not only of medieval values but of the equally absurd principles of his provincial Yankee.

Poor financial investments forced Twain back on to the lecture circuit in the 1890s. Out of this renewed period of travel he produced *Following the Equator* (1897), which lacked the ebullience of his earlier travel narratives and marked the emergence of a more troubled sensibility. Twain's creative energy in this period seemed to diminish as he turned out lame sequels to his greatest work in such books as *Tom Sawyer Abroad* (1894) and *Tom Sawyer, Detective* (1896). *The Tragedy of Pudd'nhead Wilson* (1864) and especially *Personal Recollections of Joan of Arc* (1896) are more worthy of Twain's talent and do justice to his brooding, maturing explorations of the fate of civilization.

After 1898, when Twain had finally achieved financial stability, his pessimism and his art coalesced in three brilliant works: *The Man That Corrupted Hadleyburg* (1900), *What is Man?* (1906), and *The Mysterious Stranger* (1916). Indeed, the last book was so bitter and grim that Twain deliberately set it aside for posthumous publication.

Twain's last years were spent organizing his legacy in the form of his memoirs and an authorized biography. Albert Bigelow Paine's authorized biography appeared in three volumes in 1912, Twain's *Letters* in 1917, and his *Autobiography* in 1924. In 1910 William Dean HOWELLS issued *My Mark Twain: Reminiscences and Criticisms,* the first and still one of the most valuable accounts of Twain's career and his significance. Other Twain scholars issued collections such as *The Love Letters of Mark* Twain (1949), *Mark Twain-Howells Letters* (two volumes, 1960), and *Letters from the Earth* (1963).

Twain's greatness as a novelist is still debated. While his humor, style, and gift for characterization are undisputed, certain critics have suggested that Twain's sense of form was inadequate. This school sees the comic sketch as his natural medium. But other critics laud his comic genius, the epic sweep of books like *Life on the Mississippi,* his penetrating and shrewd explorations of human character, and his evocation of the American mythos. His fierce criticism of American imperialism has also appealed to many critics on the political left. Liberals have praised his handling of race, yet some African-American critics have charged him with racism. Twain's legacy may be mixed, but his persona and his work are indelible.

Sources

Bloom, Harold, ed. *Mark Twain.* New York: Chelsea House, 1986.

Hoffman, Andrew. *Inventing Mark Twain: The Lives of Samuel Langhorne Clemens.* New York: Morrow, 1997.

Quirk, Tom. *Mark Twain: A Study of the Short Fiction.* New York: Twayne, 1997.

Rasmussen, R. Kent. *Mark Twain A to Z: The Essential Reference to His Life and Writings.* New York: Facts On File, 1995.

Robinson, Forrest G., ed. *The Cambridge Companion to Mark Twain.* New York: Cambridge University Press, 1995.

Cody, William Frederick (Buffalo Bill) (1846–1917) *performer*

A popular performer and hero of many 19th-century DIME NOVELS, William Cody was born near Davenport, Iowa, and reared in Kansas. At the age of 10 Cody became his family's sole support when his father died. He worked first for the railroads and then migrated west to the Colorado gold mines in 1859. In 1860 he rode briefly for the Pony Express until he took a job as a hunter of horse thieves and hostile Indians. By the time he joined the Union army during the CIVIL WAR, Cody was an accomplished horseman and marksman, skills he subsequently honed as a Western scout for the army and a railroad company bison hunter. In 1872 Cody came into his own when Edward JUDSON ("Ned Buntline") wrote several dime novels about him and convinced Cody to appear as himself on stage in the drama *The Scout of the Plains* (1872). This was the beginning of Cody's theatrical career. In 1883 he organized a group of hunters and roughriders and featured them in what he billed as "Buffalo Bill's Wild West Show." For the next 20 years the wildly popular show toured the United States and Europe, featuring such celebrities as the sharpshooter Annie Oakley (1860–1926). In the end, Cody's financial recklessness ruined him; he lost control of his show and ended his days in poverty in Denver, Colorado. Still, he lived on in more than 200 dime novels and in the town of Cody, Wyoming, named in his honor.

Sources

Blackstone, Sarah J. *Buckskins, Bullets, and Business: A History of Buffalo Bill's Wild West.* Westport, Conn.: Greenwood Press, 1986.

Collier's *periodical*

Founded in 1888 as a weekly by the bookseller Peter F. Collier (1849–1909), this magazine was originally intended to be a marketing tool for Collier's installment book-buying plan. Within a few years, however, *Collier's* had been converted into an illustrated literary journal. Edited by Norman Hapgood (1868–1937) from 1903 to 1912, the magazine exhibited a decidedly left-leaning editorial policy, publishing muckraking journalism (see MUCKRAKING MOVEMENT). The magazine's orientation then changed into a general circulation magazine that combined literary fiction and articles on current affairs with coverage of sports and celebrities. This winning formula increased circulation to a high-water mark of roughly 2.5 million subscribers. In the mid-20th century, however, *Collier's* fell on hard times, in 1953 publishing only every two weeks until it was eventually bought out by *Look* magazine.

Cooke, John Esten (1830–1886) *novelist, biographer, historian*

The younger brother of the literary critic Philip Pendleton COOKE, John Esten Cooke was likewise a scion of the Old South and a member of the elite group known as First Families of Virginia. Fittingly, Cooke made his name as the author of romances set in colonial Virginia and inspired largely by the novels of James Fenimore COOPER; *Leather Stocking and Silk* (1854), concerning a Virginia frontiersman, is the most obvious of these.

Related by marriage to the Confederate general J. E. B. Stuart, Cooke also served with the army of the Confederacy during the CIVIL WAR. While not actively involved in military campaigns, he used this period to write a *Life of Stonewall Jackson* (1863). Earlier he had published a biography of Thomas Jefferson (1854), and he would continue his career as a biographer with lives of Robert E. Lee (1871) and Samuel J. Tilden (1876). The strong strain of sentimentality in Cooke's fiction made him highly popular in his day. In later times, his *Virginia: A History of the People* (1883) has been regarded his most successful work.

Sources

Beaty, John Owen. *John Esten Cooke, Virginian.* New York: Columbia University Press, 1922.

Cooke, Philip Pendleton (1816–1850) *critic*

Like his younger brother John Esten COOKE, Philip Pendleton Cooke was a writer, although his vocation was literary criticism, written for the *The SOUTHERN LITERARY MESSENGER.* He died young of tuberculosis, and his literary output was slim. His only book, *Froissart's Ballads* (1847), consists of translations from a French writer that Cooke adapted to verse. He also wrote several prose romances that were published in *The Southern Literary Messenger.* He was, however, long remembered for his sentimental piece, "Florence Vane," which appeared in *Burton's GENTLEMAN'S MAGAZINE* in 1840 and long remained a favorite of American Victorians.

Sources

Allen, John Daniel. *Philip Pendleton Cooke.* Chapel Hill: University of North Carolina, 1942.

Cooper, James Fenimore (1789–1851) *novelist*

Renowned frontier author James Fenimore Cooper was born in Burlington, New Jersey. His father William subsequently moved the family to Cooperstown, New York, west of Albany. James was educated in local schools and then sent to Yale, from which he was expelled in 1806. After five years at sea he married, settling first in Cooperstown (1814) and then on a farm in Scarsdale (1817).

Cooper's literary career did not begin until 1820, when he published his first novel, *Precaution,* written after he claimed he could write a better novel of manners than what he was reading at the time. This novel is quite conventional, but Cooper did in fact do it better than others by relying on his own experience. His 1821 novel, *The Spy,* drew in part on his seagoing adventures and on his grasp of the American scene. He returned to this material in *The Pilot* (1823), again seeking to show that he could write better fiction than his British contemporaries, and particularly Sir Walter's Scott *The Pirate* (1822).

Cooper's enormous literary reputation was founded with *The Pioneers* (1823), the first of his LEATHER-STOCKING TALES, featuring the adventures of Natty BUMPPO. In *THE LAST OF THE MOHICANS* (1826), *THE PRAIRIE* (1827), *The Pathfinder* (1840), and *The Deerslayer* (1841), Cooper elaborated the myth of the Western hero, scornful of Eastern effeteness and contemptuous of settlers who spoil the land and defile nature. Cooper drew on his childhood memories of Cooperstown and on his father, a leading citizen who came into conflict with the pioneer stock who resented the destruction of the wilderness and the values of independence and discipline it represented. Cooper's view of the Indians in these novels reflects the myths of the noble savage and of the primitive, violent society that white civilization was eradicating. Part nostalgia, part a realistic evocation of the frontier, Cooper's novels remain an enduring portrait of a world in transition and of the ambivalent feelings that change stimulates.

By the mid-1820s Cooper had established himself as the outstanding American novelist of his day. Although Washington IRVING had become the first American author to be widely read in Europe, Cooper was the first to concentrate almost exclusively on the American landscape and its history, vying with Sir Walter Scott (1771–1832) and other European novelists for preeminence in the English-speaking world.

Although Cooper had planned to write a series of novels about the American past—beginning with *Lionel Lincoln* (1825), set in Boston during the Revolutionary War—he returned instead to material that grew out of his sea experiences: *The Red Rover* (1827), *The Wept of Wish-ton-Wish* (1829), and *The Water-Witch* (1830). A stout proponent of democracy, he published a trilogy of novels—*The Bravo* (1832), *The Heidenmauer* (1832), and *The Headsman* (1833)—disparaging the cult of the middle ages that Scott and other Romantics (see ROMANTICISM) had popularized.

Now a public figure who often traveled abroad (he was away from the United States for most of the period between 1826 and 1833), Cooper wrote as a representative American, defending the country's values in books such as *Notions of the Americans* (1828) and *A Letter to General Lafayette* (1831). These works argued for the superiority of republican government over the monarchies of the past.

On his return home in 1833, Cooper found that much had changed. He reacted violently against a culture that he thought had become greedier and coarser. Public life seemed corrupt and without manners. He emerged in a series of books as a rather bitter conservative, a satirist, and an alarmist who believed that democracy was degenerating into mob rule. During this contentious decade of the 1830s he devoted himself almost exclusively to nonfiction, producing *A Letter to His Countrymen* (1834), *Gleanings in Europe* (four volumes published in 1837 and 1838), and *The American Democrat* (1838). Toward the end of the decade he returned to fiction that reinforced his elitist views, including *Homeward Bound* (1838) and *Home as Found* (1838).

Often attacked in the press, Cooper launched several successful lawsuits, winning judgments for libel. Even so, his literary activity did not slow. In 1839 he published *History of the Navy;* continued his Leather-Stocking series; and wrote histories of Christopher Columbus, *Mercedes of Castile* (1840), and of the British navy, *The Two Admirals* (1842).

In the mid-1840s Cooper returned to the setting of upstate New York that he knew so well, producing several novels, the best of which are *Satanstoe* (1845), *The Chainbearer* (1845), and *The Redskins* (1846). In these works he dramatized the conflicts over land ownership and the growing divide between those who owned and those who worked the land.

By the late 1840s Cooper had returned to the historical romance, publishing *Jack Tier* (1848), *The Oak Openings* (1848), and *The Sea Lions* (1848). These later novels retained his strong gift for narrative and for the authentic details of life at sea. His last novel, *The Ways of the Hour* (1850), has often been cited as foreshadowing the modern mystery novel. *The Letters and Journals of James Fenimore Cooper* was published in six volumes from 1960 to 1968.

Cooper was a prolific if uneven writer. He had a gift for narrative and for inventing stirring dramatic incidents. His descriptive powers, especially the landscapes of *The Pioneers* and *The Prairie,* evinced a profound engagement with nature and the human connection to it. The positive and negative aspects of land development—indeed of civilization itself—are treated in Cooper's fiction and nonfiction with superb clarity and suggestiveness. His evocation of the American myth of progress and its attendant periods of corruption pointed out a cycle repeated in the works of many 20th-century American authors, such as William Faulkner (1897–1962) and Norman Mailer (1923–).

Cooper's faults as a novelist are also grave. Mark Twain (Samuel CLEMENS) wrote a famous article lampooning some of Cooper's awkward and redundant phrasing. Cooper's characters often seem one-dimensional, and he resorts too often to melodrama. He remains a towering figure, however, for the broad range of his work and the example he set as both a writer and a public figure.

Sources

McWilliams, John P., Jr. *Political Justice in a Republic: James Fenimore Cooper's America.* Berkeley: University of California Press, 1972.

Dekker, George and John P. McWilliams, eds. *Fenimore Cooper—The Critical Heritage.* Boston: Routledge & Kegan Paul, 1973.

Rans, Geoffrey. *Cooper's Leather-Stocking Novels: A Secular Reading.* Chapel Hill: University of North Carolina Press, 1991.

Verhoeven, W. M., ed. *James Fenimore Cooper: New Historical and Literary Contexts.* Atlanta: Rodopi, 1993.

Cosmopolitan *periodical*

Cosmopolitan was founded in 1886 in Rochester, New York, by Joseph N. Hallock as a conservative magazine for the whole family. In 1887, however, the magazine's editorial offices were moved to New York City, where *Cosmopolitan* was purchased by John B. Walker in 1889. Under Walker's editorship, which lasted until 1905, *Cosmopolitan* became one of the most successful periodicals of the day, publishing works by such distinguished contributors as Samuel CLEMENS, Rudyard Kipling (1865–1936), Henry JAMES, and Alfred Conan Doyle (1859–1930). The magazine's many articles devoted to education led to the 1897 founding of Cosmopolitan University, a correspondence school. *Cosmopolitan* also acted for a time as a book publisher. In 1900 the magazine joined the MUCKRAKING MOVEMENT, but by 1905, when it was sold to William Randolph HEARST, *Cosmopolitan* consisted largely of popular fiction and celebrity profiles. Hearst maintained this editorial policy, even after he merged *Cosmopolitan* with *Hearst's International* in 1925. In 1965 the high-profile Helen Gurley Brown (1922–), author of the popular nonfiction book *Sex and the Single Girl* (1962), took over the magazine's editorship, turning it into a periodical aimed squarely at single working women, an emerging market.

cowboy writing *genre*

Whereas the WESTERN was largely the creation of easterners like Owen WISTER and Bret HARTE, authentic cowboy writers also plied their trade during the 19th century. Among the best of these was Andy ADAMS, whose novel *The Log of a Cowboy* (1903) was a synthesized account of the many cattle drives from Texas to Montana in which he had participated. Straightforward and almost devoid of romanticism, Adams's work—together with the classic *A Texas Cowboy, or, 15 Years on the Hurricane Deck of the Spanish Cow Pony* (1885) by Charles A. Siringo (1855–1928)—stands in rather stark contrast to the yarns spun out in Alfred Henry LEWIS's Wolfville novels, which began appearing in 1897. Such romanticizing of the West and the cowboy experience originated with the enormously popular DIME NOVELS that entertained a weary public in the wake of the CIVIL WAR. The romance was counteracted not only by Wister's stoic hero in *THE VIRGINIAN* but also by the realism that inhabits the work of the former cowboy, government scout, and cult figure E. M. Rhodes (1869–1934), many of whose stories—the best known is "The Little Eohippus" (1912)—appeared in such popular outlets as the *SATURDAY EVENING POST.*

Sources

Davis, Robert M. *Playing Cowboys: Low Culture and High Art in the Western.* Norman: University of Oklahoma Press, 1992.

Walle, Alf H. *The Cowboy Hero and Its Audience: Popular Culture as Market Derived Art.* Bowling Green, Ohio: Bowling Green State University Popular Press, 2000.

Wallmann, Jeffrey M. *The Western: Parables of the American Dream.* Lubbock: Texas Tech University Press, 1999.

crackerbarrel humor *genre*

Named for the cracker barrel customarily found in New England general stores that served as gathering places for locals to exchange gossip and witticisms, this rural brand of humor was originally associated with Yankee cunning and idiomatic speech. Literary practitioners of the genre include the Nova Scotia native Thomas Chandler Haliburton (1796–1865), whose creation Sam Slick, a Yankee peddler, embodied the energy and wisdom that came to be associated with the genre. The satiric verses published in James Russell LOWELL's *The Biglow Papers* (1846, 1867), although dedicated to such serious topics as the MEXICAN WAR and slavery, were written largely in Yankee dialect and helped introduce the American reading public to nonstandard English. Riddled with solecisms and malapropisms, crackerbarrel humor was nevertheless down-to-earth, homely, and wise. Ultimately the term would be applied to rustic, commonsense humor delivered in any regional idiom.

Sources

Blair, Walter. *Native American Humor.* San Francisco: Chandler, 1960.

McGlinchee, Claire. *James Russell Lowell.* New York: Twayne, 1967.

Rourke, Constance. *American Humor: A Study of the National Character.* New York: Harcourt Brace Jovanovich, 1959.

Craddock, Charles Egbert

See MURFREE, MARY NOAILLES.

Crane, Ichabod *character*

Ichabod Crane, an awkward schoolmaster, is the protagonist of Washington IRVING's story "The Legend of Sleepy Hollow," published in 1820 as part of Irving's volume *The Sketch Book.* In Irving's tale, Sleepy Hollow is an old Dutch outpost up the Hudson River where ghost stories fill the air. The most notorious of these concerns a Hessian trooper who periodically rides through the area in search of the head he lost during the Revolutionary War. The schoolmaster, a devotee of Puritan leader Cotton Mather's (1663–1728) book on witchcraft, *Magnalia Christi Americana* (1702) seems particularly susceptible to the local legends.

Ichabod Crane is also susceptible to the charms of a local beauty, Katrina Van Tassel. One would think that Crane, whom Irving describes as a "scarecrow eloped from a cornfield," would be unattractive to the ladies, but in fact Crane's wit makes him popular with the local girls—all but Katrina, that is. Crane's rival for her hand is the strapping, handsome Brom Van Brunt, but the avaricious Ichabod is determined to beat him. One night during a party at the Van Tassel house he makes his move, only to be spurned by the object of his love. The party breaks up after a long night of dancing and storytelling, featuring Brom "Bones" Van Brunt's story of how he once almost bested the Headless Horseman in a race.

Astride his pitiful mount, the stricken Ichabod sets out for home along the very path said to be frequented by the Headless Horseman. Before long Crane hears someone following him, and as he turns to look at his pursuer, a seemingly headless horseman hurls his head—actually a pumpkin—at the schoolmaster before disappearing into the darkness.

When Ichabod fails to turn up at school the next day, the old Dutch wives conclude that he has been carried away by the Hessian rider. In fact the schoolmaster, motivated both by fear of the horseman and fear of failure with Katrina, has moved on to study law and become a judge. Katrina, as expected, settles into domestic tranquility with Brom, who is heard to laugh knowingly whenever the story of the horseman and the schoolmaster is recalled.

Sources

Aderman, Ralph M., ed. *Critical Essays on Washington Irving.* Boston: G. K. Hall, 1990.

Tuttleton, James W., ed. *Washington Irving: The Critical Reaction.* New York: AMS Press, 1993.

Crane, Stephen (1871–1900) *short story writer, novelist, journalist, poet*

Stephen Crane was born in New Jersey but grew up in upstate New York and attended Lafayette College and Syracuse University. He obtained work as a journalist in New York City, where he not only reported on events and people but also began to write sketches of city life and dramatic vignettes that presaged much of the grim, naturalistic fiction that writers such as Frank NORRIS and Theodore DREISER would pursue (see NATURALISM).

Crane's first major work, MAGGIE: A GIRL OF THE STREETS (1893), was considered so explicit about the sordidness of the urban poor that he was forced to have it printed privately. He achieved overnight success, however, with the novel *The Red Badge of Courage* (1895), a stunning account of a CIVIL WAR battle and the impact of war on the common soldier. The vividness of Crane's reportorial style and the spare use of description and symbolism made the work seem like nonfiction even though Crane had had no direct experience of war. Like his city sketches, the novel foreshadows the understated style of such 20th-century writers as Ernest Hemingway (1899–1961).

The success of Crane's novel made possible the printing of earlier works and the reissue of *Maggie.* He followed up with a collection of naturalistic Civil War stories, *The Little Regiment* (1896); and another masterpiece, *George's Mother* (1896), a short, evocative novel about a young man and his mother.

Even as Crane achieved popular success, the literary elite recognized him as a young writer with a new kind of sensibility, evident especially in his despairing poetry. *The Black Riders* (1895) presented a bleak view of the universe, but the poetry itself was so compact and unsentimental that it marked a great departure from the rather fulsome rhetoric of Crane's contemporaries.

At the beginning of the SPANISH-AMERICAN WAR Crane became a war correspondent, reporting first from the Southwest and in Mexico and then from Cuba. When the ship he was on sank, he wrote the story "THE OPEN BOAT," which, like his poetry, probes the plight of man alone in a hostile or indifferent world.

Crane then went off to Greece to cover another war, although an illness forced him to recover in England, where he was lionized by writers such as Joseph Conrad (1857–1924) and H. G. Wells (1866–1946). During this period Crane published *Wounds in the Rain* (1900), a collection of his journalistic dispatches; and *Active Service* (1899), a satire about the life of a war correspondent.

Crane's health was by this time deteriorating, and he was living with a common-law wife. Rumors spread that he was a drunk, a drug addict, and a degenerate. He continued to write fresh and provocative prose, however, publishing *The Open Boat* (1898) and *The Monster* (1899), both collections of stories; *War is Kind* (1899), another collection of his laconic free verse; and *Whilomville Stories* (1900), set in the upstate New York milieu of his youth. These works combine elements of the grotesque with an unflinching REALISM that is reminiscent of Crane's great contemporary Ambrose BIERCE.

While roaming Europe in search of a cure for his tuberculosis, Crane died in Germany, still at the peak of his literary power. His intense suffering certainly contributed to the unevenness of his final poetry and prose.

Many collections of Crane's work have been published since his death, including *The Collected Poems of Stephen Crane* (1932), *The Sullivan County Sketches of Stephen Crane* (1949), *The Complete Stories and Sketches of Stephen Crane* (1963), *The New York City Sketches of Stephen Crane, and Related Pieces* (1966), *Complete Novels* (1967), *The Poems of Stephen Crane: A Critical Edition* (1972), and *The Correspondence of Stephen Crane* (1988).

Sources

Basson, Maurice, ed. *Stephen Crane: A Collection of Critical Essays.* Englewood Cliffs, N.J.: Prentice Hall, 1967.

Benfy, Christopher. *The Double Life of Stephen Crane.* New York: Alfred A. Knopf, 1992.

Robertson, Michael. *Stephen Crane, Journalism, and the Making of Modern American Literature.* New York: Columbia University Press, 1997.

Schaefer, Michael. *A Reader's Guide to the Short Stories of Stephen Crane.* New York: G. K. Hall, 1996.

Weatherford, Richard M., ed. *Stephen Crane: The Critical Heritage.* Boston: Routledge & Kegan Paul, 1973.

Crawford, Francis Marion (1854–1909) *novelist, short story writer, dramatist*

The son of noted sculptor Thomas Crawford (1813–57) and the nephew of Julia Ward HOWE, F. Marion Crawford was the most popular—and one of the most prolific—novelists of his day. Born in Tuscany, Italy, Crawford was educated in Rome; Cambridge, England; Heidelberg, Germany; and at Harvard University. A world traveler, he is said to have been conversant in 16 languages. His first novel, *Mr. Isaacs: A Tale of Modern India* (1882), was based on the life story of a diamond merchant Crawford met while living in India. The book won him immediate fame, and it was followed by more than 40 others, many also based on true stories and nearly all set in the various countries in which he lived. Crawford also wrote historical romances—such as his highly touted story of Philip II's Spain, *In the Palace of the King* (1900)—and popular histories of Italy. He adapted several of his novels for the stage and wrote one original play, *Francesca Da Rimini* (1902), a vehicle for French actress Sarah Bernhardt (1844–1923). Most of his short stories dealt with the supernatural and bore titles like *Wandering Ghosts* (1911). In *The Novel What It Is* (1901), Crawford outlined his notions about the form as popular entertainment. In 1885 Crawford moved to Sorrento, Italy, where he spent the remainder of his life.

Sources

Moran, John Charles. *An F. Marion Crawford Companion.* Westport, Conn.: Greenwood Press, 1981.

Pilkington, John. *Francis Marion Crawford.* New York: Twayne, 1964.

Crockett, David (1786–1836) *frontiersman, public official, soldier, autobiographer*

Born in Tennessee, Davy Crockett married at age 18 and then moved with his bride to a new settlement on the Elk River. Here, according to Crockett, "I began to distinguish myself as a hunter and to lay the foundation for all my future greatness." The personal mythmaking for which he has become known had already begun. After the Creek War (1813–14), in which he garnered the commendation of General Andrew Jackson (1767–1845), Crockett went into politics, first as a magistrate, then as a state legislator, and finally as a U.S. congressman, in which capacity he served two terms, 1827–31 and 1833–35.

In 1829 Crockett's longstanding admiration for Andrew Jackson—by now the president—changed to opprobrium. The opposition Whig party immediately seized on the "coonskin Congressman" as a representative of the common man's anti-Jacksonian sentiment. In reaction, the Jacksonian press turned Crockett into a villain. In order to set the record straight, Crockett wrote—almost certainly with considerable assistance—his *Narrative of the Life of David Crockett* (1834), followed by the 1835 *Account of Col. Crockett's Tour to the North and Down East,* which may have been ghostwritten from Crockett's notes.

Crockett clearly enjoyed his newfound fame and contributed readily to the Whig campaign to make him a folk hero. His deviation from Democratic principles, however, ultimately cost him his congressional seat, and he left Tennessee to help the Texans fight for their independence from Mexico. After he died a hero's death defending the Alamo, his star rose even higher, as Crockett was transformed into a larger-than-life character who fit right in with such legends as Mike FINK and Daniel BOONE, who were featured in the folkloric *Crockett Almanacs* that were released between 1835 and 1859 by a variety of publishers.

Sources

Derr, Mark. *The Frontiersman: The Real Life and Many Legends of Davy Crockett.* New York: William Morrow, 1993.

Lofaro, Michael A., and Joe Cummings, eds. *Crockett at Two Hundred: New Perspectives on the Man and the Myth.* Knoxville: University of Tennessee Press, 1989.

Croly, Jane Cunningham (Jennie June) (1829–1901) *journalist*

Born in England, Jane Cunningham came to the United States when she was 12 years old. In 1857 she married the author and editor David Goodman Croly (1829–89). She was one of the first female journalists in America and one of the first to syndicate her articles, writing for various New York newspapers under the pseudonym "Jennie June." From 1860 to 1887 she edited *Demorest's Quarterly Mirror of Fashion* and later became part owner of GODEY'S LADY'S BOOK. In 1856 Croly convened the first women's congress; in 1868 she founded Sorosis, the first professional women's club; and in 1889 she founded the New York Women's Press Club. Croly wrote *For Better or Worse: A Book for Some Men and All Women* (1875) and *The History of the Women's Club Movement in America* (1898).

Sources

Woman's Press Club of New York City. *Memories of Jane Cunningham Croly, "Jenny June."* New York: G. P. Putnam's Sons, 1904.

Curtis, George William (1824–1892) *journalist, essayist*

Born in Rhode Island, George William Curtis spent two years of his youth at BROOK FARM, where he came under the influence of the transcendentalists (see TRANSCENDENTALISM). This influence would not be reflected in his writing until later in his life. He began his writing career as a Middle Eastern correspondent for the NEW-YORK TRIBUNE, an experience that resulted in the travel sketches published as *Nile Notes of a Howadji* (1851) and *The Howadji in Syria* (1852). *Lotus-Eating* (1852) is a collection of letters Curtis sent back to the paper during trips to various spas. Two collections of New York sketches, *The Potiphar Papers* (1853) and *Prue and I* (1856), were followed by his novel *Trumps* (1861), which was set in New York City and Washington, D.C. From 1863 until his death, Curtis edited *HARPER'S WEEKLY*, for which he also wrote a regular column called the "Editor's Easy Chair."

In middle age Curtis also became well known as a reformer and orator. His speech "The Duty of the American Scholar to Politics and the Times" (1856) marked a turning point in his life. Thereafter he lectured widely on the lyceum circuit (see LYCEUM MOVEMENT) on such topics as ABOLITIONISM, women's rights, and industrial reform. He also served as president of the National Civil Service Reform League from the time of its founding in 1881 until his death more than a decade later.

Sources

Milne, Gordon. *George William Curtis and the Genteel Tradition.* Bloomington: Indiana University Press, 1956.

Daisy Miller: A Study Henry James (1878) novella

In what is perhaps James's most accessible and certainly one of his most widely read works, the author addresses one of his perennial themes: the interplay of Old World and New. Frederick Winterbourne, an American expatriate visiting Vevey, Switzerland, becomes fascinated with Daisy Miller from Schenectady, New York. The bold and naive Daisy and her family blunder about in the sophisticated European environment. When Daisy is unwisely left to her own resources, Winterbourne is astonished to find himself alone with her on a trip to the Castle of Chillon. Later he meets Daisy and her family in Rome. She is now regarded with suspicion and disgust by resident Americans who think she is flouting the proper code of conduct for a young lady, especially when she allows herself to be escorted by Giovanelli, an Italian opportunist. One night Winterbourne finds Daisy with Giovanelli in the Colosseum. Daisy insists she is not engaged to the Italian, and when Winterbourne tells Giovanelli that he should not expose Daisy to the malarial atmosphere, the Italian laconically replies, "But when was the Signorina ever prudent?" Daisy dies with shocking suddenness a few days later. At her funeral Giovanelli sincerely praises Daisy's purity and affirms that she would never have consented to marry him.

Much of the power of James's story derives from the shock of Daisy's death. Although she has been reckless and ignorant, Winterbourne admires her independence and her lack of concern for what others think of her. Her premature death therefore seems a tragic end to a spirited young woman who might have made more of herself than her more conventional contemporaries supposed.

Daisy Miller preceded James's more complex portraits of women, which include Isabel Archer in *THE PORTRAIT OF A LADY* (1884) and Maisie Farange in *What Maisie Knew* (1897).

Sources

Bender, Todd K. *A Concordance to Daisy Miller.* New York: Garland, 1987.

Hoffman, Charles G. *The Short Novels of Henry James.* New York: Bookman, 1957.

Pollak, Vivian R., ed. *New Essays on Daisy Miller and The Turn of the Screw.* New York: Cambridge University Press, 1993.

Dana, Charles Anderson (1819–1897) journalist

Born in Hinsdale, New Hampshire, Charles A. Dana began his career as a reformer, spending five years at BROOK FARM. When that experiment in Utopian communal living failed, Dana became a newspaperman, working first for the Boston *Daily Chronotype.* He then spent 15 years (1847–62) at the *NEW-YORK TRIBUNE,* where he held positions as city editor and managing editor. He lost his job at the *Tribune* when he disagreed with editor Horace GREELEY's views about the prosecution of the CIVIL WAR. Dana worked for a time for the federal War Department as a western special investigator, and in 1864 he was named assistant secretary of war. When the Civil War ended, Dana became editor and part owner of the NEW YORK SUN, turning it into the most influential newspaper in the nation. In those years his politics grew increasingly conservative, and the paper's editorials reflected his views, although he was also extremely critical of the corruption that haunted President Ulysses S. GRANT's administration. Dana laid out his journalistic philosophy in *The Art of Newspaper Making* (1895).

Sources

Steele, Janet E. *The Sun Shines for All: Journalism and Ideology in the Life of Charles A. Dana.* Syracuse, N.Y.: Syracuse University Press, 1993.

Dana, Richard Henry, Jr. (1815–1882) *novelist*

Born in Cambridge, Massachusetts, the younger Richard Henry Dana spent two years at sea (1834–36) before completing his Harvard degree in 1837. He attended law school (1837–40) and was admitted to the bar in 1840. Dana was an outspoken political activist, and he defended fugitive slaves in the early 1850s when a federal law required their return to their southern masters. He served as U.S. district attorney for Massachusetts from 1861 to 1866. His autobiographical novel, *TWO YEARS BEFORE THE MAST* (1840), heavily influenced Herman MELVILLE. Melville's *White-Jacket* and *MOBY-DICK* both profit from Dana's vivid narratives and efforts at authenticity.

Sources

Gale, Robert L. *Richard Henry Dana, Jr.* New York: Twayne, 1969.

Shapiro, Samuel. *Richard Henry Dana, Jr.* East Lansing: Michigan State University Press, 1961.

Dana, Richard Henry, Sr. (1787–1879) *editor, poet*

Born in Cambridge, Massachusetts, the elder Richard Dana was trained as a lawyer but preferred to devote his time to writing. He was one of the founders of *THE NORTH AMERICAN REVIEW*, and when his brand of literary criticism proved unpopular with the magazine's readers, he began another journal in New York, *The Idle Man*, which lasted only a year. Dana's best-known poem, "The Buccaneer," appeared in 1827, and his collected *Poems and Prose Writings* was published in 1833. He remained a popular lecturer, but in his later years he was overshadowed by his more famous son, Richard Henry DANA Jr.

Sources

Hunter, Doreen M. *Richard Henry Dana, Sr.* Boston: Twayne, 1987.

Davis, Andrew Jackson (1826–1910) *spiritualist, lecturer*

Born in Blooming Grove, New York, Andrew Jackson Davis became known as the "Poughkeepsie Seer" after he fell under the spell of a mesmerist in 1843. In 1845, together with his own hypnotist and his own reporter, he began to deliver a series of highly popular public lectures on mysticism and the occult—all while supposedly in a trance state. These lectures were collected in *Principle of Nature, Her Divine Revelations, and a Voice to Mankind* (1847), a work said to have influenced Edgar Allan POE's *EUREKA: A PROSE POEM* (1848) and Thomas Holley CHIVERS's *Search After Truth* (1848). Davis's interest later switched to SPIRITUALISM, as detailed in his book *The Great Harmonium* (1850).

Sources

Goldfarb, Russell M. *Spiritualism and Nineteenth-Century Letters.* Rutherford, N.J.: Fairleigh Dickinson University Press, 1978.

Davis, Rebecca Blaine Harding (1831–1910) *novelist, short story writer*

Born in Alabama and educated at a Pennsylvania seminary, Rebecca Harding Davis grew up in the town of Wheeling in what is now West Virginia. Based on personal observations of her own town, her novella *Life in the Iron Mills,* which appeared in *THE ATLANTIC MONTHLY* in 1861, established her as an early proponent of REALISM. Her purpose, Davis told readers, was to "dig into this commonplace, this vulgar American life, and see what is in it." This credo was announced in Davis's milltown novel *Margaret Howth* (1862), which showed signs of the sentimentality that marred much of her writing. Her output was prodigious: She published 10 novels and more than 100 short stories, together with essays, miscellaneous journalism, and literature written for children. Later works include *Waiting for the Verdict* (1868), a novel about the treatment of African Americans after Emancipation; *Earthen Pitchers* (1873–74), a novel focused on the newly won self-sufficiency of professional women; and *John Andoss* (1874), one of the first novels to take as its subject American political corruption.

Throughout her career, Davis lived a conventional middle-class existence. In 1863 she married a Philadelphia journalist, with whom she had three children. One of her offspring grew up to be the celebrated journalist Richard Harding DAVIS, whose fame eclipsed her own. By the time she published her memoir, *Bits of Gossip,* in 1904, Davis had become largely forgotten. It was only in the 1970s that Davis's work was rescued from obscurity by the feminist writer Tillie Olsen (1913–).

Sources

Harris, Sharon M. *Rebecca Harding Davis and American Realism.* Philadelphia: University of Pennsylvania Press, 1991.

Pfaelzer, Jean. *Parlor Radical: Rebecca Harding Davis and the Origins of American Social Realism.* Pittsburgh, Pa.: University of Pittsburgh Press, 1996.

Rose, Jane Atteridge. *Rebecca Harding Davis.* New York: Twayne, 1993.

Davis, Richard Harding (1864–1916) *journalist*

The son of novelist Rebecca Harding DAVIS, Richard Harding Davis would become the leading journalist of his day. As a reporter for the NEW YORK SUN and other newspapers, he served as a war correspondent during the Spanish war in Cuba (1895–96), the Greco-Turkish War (1897), the SPANISH-AMERICAN WAR (1898), the Boer War (1899–1902), the Russo-Japanese War (1904–05), and World War I (1914–18). His dispatches from various fronts were vivid and accurate, in part because of his own enthusiasm for the conflicts he covered. Although such conduct was forbidden to journalists by the rules of war, during the Spanish-American War Davis joined the ranks of Theodore Roosevelt's Rough Riders during the Battle of San Juan Hill. In his rush to get to the front lines in World War I, Davis was almost shot as a spy by the Germans. He exhibited similar involvement with even minor events that he covered—for example, serving as a yachtsman while covering yacht club races and turning his own engagement into a news event by sending his fiancée's ring 8,000 treacherous miles via a messenger; he tracked the ring's progress with daily press bulletins.

After becoming managing editor of *HARPER'S WEEKLY* in 1890, Davis collected a great deal of his reports and republished them in a number of volumes. He also published numerous collections of short fiction. Many of his stories were set in the exotic locales he covered as a reporter, but he also wrote stories about a New York socialite, Courtlandt Van Bibber, whose courage and nobility helped shape the popular conception of the ideal fin-de-siècle American male, such as those in Thomas BEER's *The Mauve Decade* (1926). Another of Davis's fictional alter egos is a cub reporter who is the eponymous hero of *Gallegher and Other Stories* (1891). The energetic Davis also wrote a number of novels and some 25 plays, many of them based on his own stories. Davis's fast-paced fiction, immensely popular in his own time, has proven no more lasting than his idealized hero; neither managed to survive long into a more cynical 20th century.

Sources

Langford, Gerald. *The Richard Harding Davis Years: A Biography of Mother and Son.* New York: Holt, Rinehart and Winston, 1961.

Osborn, Scott Compton. *Richard Harding Davis.* Boston: Twayne, 1978.

De Forest, John William (1826–1906) *novelist*

Born in Connecticut, John William De Forest was the son of a small-town manufacturer who gave him a strong work ethic. Chronic illness began to bedevil De Forest in early manhood, making it impossible for him to attend college. Instead he attempted to broaden his horizons and improve his health by traveling for some years in the Near East and Europe. This experience provided him with material he used in two of his earliest works, the travel books *Oriental Acquaintance* (1856) and *European Acquaintance* (1858). Neither his life nor his writing came into focus, however, until he had served three years with the Union army during the CIVIL WAR. After his discharge, De Forest worked with the Veteran Reserve Corps in Washington, D.C., and with the Freedmen's Bureau in South Carolina before returning to Connecticut in 1869.

While still engaged in RECONSTRUCTION work, De Forest published the novel on which his reputation rests: *Miss Ravenal's Conversion from Secession to Loyalty* (1867), considered by many to be the first realistic novel about the war and a precursor to Stephen CRANE's *The Red Badge of Courage* (1895). For the next decade De Forest scratched out a living as a professional writer, turning out a series of realist novels reflecting his disillusionment with the GILDED AGE, such as *Kate Beaumont* (1872), a study of South Carolina manners and morals; and *Honest John Vane* (1875) and *Playing the Mischief* (1875), political novels set during the corrupt administration of Ulysses S. GRANT.

The reading public failed to respond to De Forest's best efforts, and after the death of his wife in 1878 he confined his artistic efforts to largely private reminiscences, two of which—a war memoir titled *A Volunteer's Adventures* (1946) and its sequel, *A Union Officer in the Reconstruction* (1948)—were published posthumously. Later William Dean HOWELLS would follow De Forest's realist path, extolling his predecessor as a major novelist whose work was ahead of its time.

Sources

Gargano, James W., ed. *Critical Essays on John William De Forest.* Boston: G. K. Hall, 1981.

Hijiya, James A. *John De Forest and the Rise of American Gentility.* Hanover, N.H.: University Press of New England, 1988.

Light, James F. *John William De Forest.* New York: Twayne, 1965.

Delineator, The *periodical*

Founded in Massachusetts in 1873 by the tailor Ebenezer Butterick (1826–1903), *The Delineator* was a monthly magazine devoted to women's fashion. A year later it moved to New York, where it began publishing paper patterns and fashion plates as well as fiction. At its peak it had a circulation of two million and put out four foreign editions. From 1907 to 1910 it was edited by Theodore DREISER, under whose leadership the magazine began to promote women's suffrage (see SUFFRAGISM) and improved housing for the poor. Honoré Willsie Morrow edited the magazine from 1914 to 1920, focusing on postwar morality and radicalism. In 1937 *The Delineator* merged with the *Pictorial Review.*

detective fiction *genre*

Edgar Allan POE is widely believed to have invented the modern detective story with "The Murders in the Rue Morgue," published in 1841 in GRAHAM'S MAGAZINE. The story featured a French detective, C. Auguste DUPIN, and a formula that has endured. Detective fiction customarily follows Poe in reversing the usual narrative time frame, opening with a calamity—usually a murder—which the sleuth then investigates by following up on clues and lining up suspects. The reader is left in suspense until the end of the tale, when the detective, after detailing the motives and methods of the crime, reveals the culprit with a flourish. Dupin would appear in only two more stories—"The Mystery of Marie Rogêt" (1842–43), a sequel to "The Murders in the Rue Morgue," and "The Purloined Letter" (1845)—but he was the prototype of other intellectual sleuths who followed, including Sherlock Holmes, introduced to the reading public in 1887 by the English writer Arthur Conan Doyle (1859–1930).

Although DIME NOVELists sometimes featured detective heroes, full-length detective novels did not become popular in the United States until British writers such as Conan Doyle and Wilkie Collins (1824–89) began to publish their mysteries there. Sherlock Holmes inspired many imitations, but the first truly American detective hero was a private eye named Race Williams, introduced by Carroll John Daly in 1923 in the pulp magazine *Black Mask.* Daly's hard-boiled detective was followed shortly thereafter—again in *Black Mask*—by a similarly unintellectual and rough-edged character, the "Continental Op," created by Dashiell Hammett (1894–1961). Yet another *Black Mask* writer, Raymond Chandler (1888–1959), would extrapolate on Hammett's realism, elevating the detective story into an art form and inspiring a legion of imitators and followers who helped make the genre exceedingly popular in the later decades of the 20th century.

Sources

Carlson, Eric W., ed. *A Companion to Poe Studies.* Westport, Conn.: Greenwood Press, 1996.

Geherin, David. *The American Private Eye: The Image in Fiction.* New York: F. Ungar, 1985.

Penzler, Otto, ed. *The Great Detectives.* Boston: Little, Brown, 1978.

Dewey, John (1859–1952) *philosopher, educator*

Born in Vermont, John Dewey earned his B.A. degree at the University of Vermont and received his Ph.D. from Johns Hopkins in 1884. He taught at several universities, including Minnesota, Michigan, Chicago, and Columbia. He is best known for his theories of progressive education as propounded in *Psychology* (1887), *The School and Society* (1899), *The Child and the Curriculum* (1902), *Moral Principles in Education* (1909), and *Interest and Effort in Education* (1913). These early works reflected Dewey's pragmatism, an approach to philosophy and education pioneered by William JAMES. Dewey believed that modern education had to take into account a changing industrial society, the findings of science, and the tenets of democracies. But education also had to infuse students with the practical applications of what it taught; thus, for Dewey, education became not merely a way of acquiring wisdom but also of transforming the world. Dewey advocated education for good citizenship and for the common man whose ideas had to be rooted in experience.

Dewey developed his own concept of "instrumentalism," arguing that truth and knowledge grew out of a changing reality. Education therefore had to be dynamic and the curriculum subject to constant revision. Through constant observation, as in the natural sciences, a democratic society would prosper. Dewey expanded on this approach in *Studies in Logical Theory* (1903); *How We Think* (1909); *The Influence of Darwin on Philosophy* (1910); *Democracy and Education* (1916); *Reconstruction in Philosophy* (1920); *Experience and Nature* (1925); *Individualism, Old and New* (1930); *Art as Experience* (1934); *Liberalism and Social Action* (1935); and *Freedom and Culture* (1939).

Dewey's stature as a public intellectual was extraordinary. Although he was not a political activist, his work was certainly regarded as one of the pillars of liberal civilization and Dewey himself a man of outstanding integrity. When Joseph Stalin (1879–1953) carried on his famous purge trials in 1935, Dewey headed a commission to determine whether the defendants were getting a fair hearing. His findings that the trials were, in fact, bogus turned many liberal thinkers away from the notion that the Soviet Union could serve as a model of the socially responsible welfare state.

Dewey's philosophy and political stance was clarified in later works such as *The Public Schools and Spiritual Values* (1944) and *Problems of Men* (1946), a collection of essays.

Sources

Archambault, Reginald D., ed. *Dewey on Education: Appraisals.* New York: Random House, 1966.

Caspary, William R. *Dewey on Democracy.* Ithaca, N.Y.: Cornell University Press, 2000.

Haskins, Casey and David I. Seiple, eds. *Dewey Reconfigured: Essays on Deweyan Pragmatism.* Albany: State University of New York Press, 1999.

Ryan, Alan, *John Dewey and the High Tide of American Liberalism.* New York: W. W. Norton, 1995.

Shook, John R. *Dewey's Empirical Theory of Knowledge and Reality.* Nashville: Vanderbilt University Press, 2000.

Dial, The *periodical*

Four different periodicals have borne this name. Originally an organ of the transcendentalist movement (see TRANSCEN-

DENTALISM), the first *Dial* was founded in 1840 by Theodore PARKER, Bronson ALCOTT, Orestes BROWNSON, Margaret FULLER, James Freeman CLARKE, and Ralph Waldo EMERSON; it was published in BOSTON. Fuller served as editor until 1844, when Emerson briefly took over the post. This version of the magazine, although savagely attacked in the press for its obscurity, still managed to influence the public greatly through the publication of works by such influential thinkers as Henry David THOREAU.

When *The Dial* was revived in 1860 by UNITARIAN clergyman Moncure Conway (1832–1907) in Cincinnati, it served once again as a transcendentalist mouthpiece. Conway, a Congregationalist minister who championed causes such as ABOLITIONISM, published writing by Emerson, Alcott, and William Dean HOWELLS, among others.

In its third incarnation *The Dial* was a conservative literary journal that was harshly critical of works such as Stephen CRANE's *The Red Badge of Courage* (1895) and Walt WHITMAN's *Leaves of Grass* (1855). Founded in Chicago in 1880, the magazine kept this stance until it moved to New York City in 1916. There, under the guidance of such contributing editors as Conrad Aiken (1889–1973), Randolph Bourne (1886–1918), and Van Wyck Brooks (1886–1963), *The Dial* was transformed into a journal of radical opinion that published works by such thinkers as Thomas DEWEY and Thorstein VEBLEN. In 1919 Scofield Thayer (1889–1982) took over the editor's chair and transformed the magazine once again, making it one of the foremost literary magazines in the country and a promoter of such distinguished new voices as T.S. Eliot (1888–1965), Sherwood Anderson (1876–1971), and E. A. Robinson (1869–1935). After 1926 the poet Marianne Moore (1887–1972) assumed the editorship until the magazine ceased publication in 1929.

A Fourth *Dial* appeared in New York from 1959 to 1962. This literary quarterly published the work of writers like Bernard Wolfe (1915–1985) and Herbert Gold (1924–).

Sources

Joost, Nicholas. *Scofield Thayer and The Dial: An Illustrated History.* Carbondale: Southern Illinois University Press, 1964.

Myerson, Joel. *The New England Transcendentalists and the Dial: A History of the Magazine and Its Contributors.* Rutherford, N.J.: Fairleigh Dickinson University Press, 1980.

Wasserstrom, William. *The Time of the Dial.* Syracuse, N.Y.: Syracuse University Press, 1963.

Dickinson, Emily Elizabeth (1830–1886) *poet*

Born in Amherst, Massachusetts, a daughter of the distinguished lawyer Edward Dickinson, Emily Dickinson went to the Amherst Academy and attended Mount Holoyke Female Seminary for a year. The rest of her life was spent at home among a few close friends; her only other contacts were correspondents. Although she never married, Dickinson formed close friendships with several men, including Benjamin F. Newton, a law student with whom she could share her interest in reading and in poetry; the Reverend Charles Wadsworth of Philadelphia, who met her in 1854 and became a confidant and inspiration for some of her poetry; and Thomas Wentworth HIGGINSON, who took an interest in her poetry and who visited her.

Although Dickinson led a quiet life away from the world, her poetry and letters testify to an active mind very much engaged with her surroundings and the world outside Amherst. She took an active interest in life but she shared her poetry with very few people. Some, like Higginson, mistakenly thought her limited by her circumstances and did not realize that her creativity and her knowledge of poetry far outdistanced virtually all of her contemporaries.

Dickinson's dedication to the craft and art of poetry is apparent in her work on poems that number well over 1,000. Her poems can be about a moment's revelation, observations of nature, sexual stirrings, and commentaries on the meaning of life and death. A descendant of New England Puritans, Dickinson looked for signs of a spiritual significance in the creatures and objects of this world. She had a New England wit and gift for understatement that foreshadowed the work of the 20th-century poets Edwin Arlington Robinson (1869–1935) and Robert Frost (1874–1963).

Dickinson excelled in her development of metaphors and in gnomic, metaphysical statements such as her description of a hummingbird as "A Route of Evanescence." Her eccentric punctuation, especially her use of the dash, still intrigues scholars of her work and has led to much debate about her intentions. She tended to work in short forms with simple meters.

Only a handful of Dickinson's poems were published during her lifetime, and no one then had the evidence to conclude that she was the greatest American poet of the 19th century; her only rival was Walt WHITMAN. After her death, friends began to sort through the jumbled manuscripts, some in bundles, others on scraps of paper. Several editions of her work, edited by Mabel Loomis TODD and Thomas Wentworth Higginson, began to appear in the 1890s. However, these early editions are unreliable, since liberties were taken with the arrangement of the poems and their punctuation. Other poems were suppressed or severely edited. The first completely reliable edition of Dickinson's poems did not appear until 1955 in three volumes edited by the scholar Thomas H. Johnson. Dickinson's letters in three volumes were also published with great care by Johnson in 1958. *The Manuscript Notebooks of Emily Dickinson* appeared in 1982.

Dickinson could write with great simplicity—sometimes deceptive simplicity—a trait she shares with Robert Frost. Yet many poems are quite mysterious and have been subject to many different interpretations. In part, Dickinson's elusiveness has to do with her metaphysical bent—her suggestion that life itself was elusive and its import ambiguous, so that interpretations are by definition provisional.

Sources

Bloom, Harold, ed. *Emily Dickinson.* New York: Chelsea House, 1985.

Crumbley, Paul. *Inflections of the Pen: Dash and Voice in Emily Dickinson.* Lexington: University Press of Kentucky, 1997.

Johnson, Tamara, ed. *Readings on Emily Dickinson.* San Diego, Calif.: Greenhaven Press, 1997.

Sewall, Richard, ed. *Emily Dickinson: A Collection of Critical Essays.* Englewood Cliffs, N.J.: Prentice Hall, 1963.

Wolff, Cynthia Griffin. *Emily Dickinson.* New York: Alfred A. Knopf, 1986.

dime novel *genre*

Edward Z. C. JUDSON ("Ned Buntline") laid the ground for these cheap thrillers with his WESTERNS, which he began publishing in the 1840s. Although Judson is sometimes referred to as the father of the dime novel, the genre came into its own thanks to Erastus BEADLE, who had experienced great success with a *Dime Song Book* he published in Buffalo, New York. In 1858 Beadle moved to New York City and—first with his brother Irwin, then with partner Robert Adams—began publishing a string of yellow-backed novels dealing with frontier life, the American Revolution, and the Indian fighting. These so-called dime novels—which were distantly related to the sensational English "penny dreadfuls" and often, in fact, cost only five cents—received a tremendous boost from the CIVIL WAR, which increased their audience numbers exponentially as soldiers sought cheap, easy diversions from the rigors of battle. By mid-1865 the firm of Beadle & Adams had sold more than 4 million books; some titles sold as many as 80,000 copies. Among the best-sellers were Ann S. Stephens's *Malaeska: The Indian Wife of the White Hunter* (1860) and *Seth Jones, or The Captive of the Frontier* (1860).

Beadle & Adams published numerous series of dime novels simultaneously in order to exploit the dime novel's popularity. Most of these were based on original stories, but as competition for readers increased, publishers turned to cheap reprints of foreign novels, which at the time were not covered by U.S. copyright laws. By the end of the century the genre had run its course, losing its audience to pulp magazines and other series with different emphases, such as the Rover Boys and Tom Swift series.

Sources

Denning, Michael. *Mechanic Accents: Dime Novels and Working-Class Culture in America.* New York: Verso, 1998.

Johannsen, Albert. *The House of Beadle and Adams and its Dime and Nickel Novels: The Story of a Vanished Literature.* Norman: University of Oklahoma Press, 1950.

Jones, Daryl. *The Dime Novel Western.* Bowling Green, Ohio: Popular Press, Bowling Green State University, 1978.

Dix, Dorothea Lynde (1802–1887) *reformer*

Born in Hampden, Maine, Dorothea Dix began her professional career as an educator, running a school in Boston. A visit to a prison in East Cambridge, Massachusetts, in 1841 shocked her because of the deplorable conditions the prisoners had to endure—especially the mixing of the insane with the sane. Other prison inspections followed, resulting in Dix's famous *Memorial to the Legislature of Massachusetts* (1843), a work so comprehensive and so persuasive that it prompted the foundation of state hospitals for the insane not only in Massachusetts, but also across the nation and in Europe. Dix was also a notable penologist, and during the CIVIL WAR she acted as superintendent of female nurses.

Sources

Brown, Thomas J. *Dorothea Dix: New England Reformer.* Cambridge, Mass.: Harvard University Press, 1998.

Dix, Dorothy

See GILMER, ELIZABETH MERIWETHER.

Dixon, Thomas (1864–1946) *novelist*

Born in North Carolina, Thomas Dixon was a southerner who referred to himself as a "reactionary individualist." Before making a name for himself as a writer, Dixon made his living as a Baptist minister, lawyer, legislator, and lyceum lecturer (see LYCEUM MOVEMENT). He wrote more than 20 novels, but his biggest success came with a trilogy set in the South during RECONSTRUCTION: *The Leopard's Spots* (1902), THE CLANSMAN (1905), and *The Traitor* (1907). Of these, the middle volume proved to be the most successful. After Hollywood director D. W. Griffith adapted it for the screen, it became the first "million-dollar movie" and proved to be so influential that it led to a revival of the Ku Klux Klan. All of Dixon's novels were vehicles for his social theories, and all of them were highly conservative. After Griffith had made Dixon's name a household word, Dixon himself moved to southern California, where he wrote dramas and screenplays and adapted his own novels for the movies, five of which he produced at his Los Angeles studio.

Sources

Cook, Raymond Allen. *Fire From the Flint: The Amazing Careers of Thomas Dixon.* Winston-Salem, N.C.: J. F. Blair, 1968.

———. *Thomas Dixon.* New York: Twayne, 1974.

Dodge, Mary Elizabeth Mapes (1831–1905) *Children's book author*

Born in New York City, Mary Mapes Dodge made her name as an author of children's books, the most famous of which is

Hans Brinker; or, The Silver Skates (1865). She also edited ST. NICHOLAS, a magazine for children, from 1873 until her death. In this position she became the most influential individual of the day in the field of children's literature, and she was able to attract such popular contributors to the magazine as Rudyard Kipling (1865–1936) and Mark Twain (Samuel CLEMENS).

Sources

Gannon, Susan R., and Ruth Anne Thompson. *Mary Mapes Dodge.* New York: Twayne, 1992.

Doesticks, Q. K. Philander

See THOMSON, MORTIMER NEAL.

Donnelly, Ignatius (1831–1901) *politician, editor, novelist, historian*

Born in Philadelphia, Ignatius Donnelly trained to be a lawyer and in 1856 moved to Minnesota to found a utopian community called Nininger City. When Nininger failed, Donnelly became active in state politics, serving as lieutenant governor, congressman, and state senator. A leader in the agrarian reform movement to improve conditions for farmers, he was also one of the founders of the Populist Party. He used his weekly magazine, the *Anti-Monopolist* (1874–79), to disseminate his views, which also informed his novels. In addition to publishing novels like *Caesar's Column* (1891), which depicts a future that is technologically advanced for the rich but oppressive for the poor, he wrote *Atlantis: The Antediluvian World* (1882), a book that argued for the lost continent as the cradle of civilization; and *Ragnarok* (1883), an attempt to explain earth's geology in terms of a collision with a giant comet. Later in life Donnelly took up the theory that the English philosopher Francis Bacon (1561–1626) was responsible not only for the plays of William Shakespeare (1564–1616), but also for Christopher Marlowe's (1564–93) plays, Robert Burton's (1577–1640) *Anatomy of Melancholy* (1621), and the essays of Michel de Montaigne (1533–92). *The Great Cryptogram* (1888) and *The Cypher in the Plays and on the Tombstone* (1899) were both attempts to prove Bacon's authorship of Shakespeare's plays.

Sources

Anderson, David D. *Ignatius Donnelly.* Boston: Twayne, 1980.

Douglass, Frederick (1818–1895) *journalist, autobiographer*

Born into slavery in Maryland in 1818, Douglass escaped to freedom in the North, where he first settled in Massachusetts. There his eloquence soon became apparent, and he was hired by the Massachusetts Anti-Slavery Society to travel throughout the northern states lecturing on ABOLITIONISM. Douglass was a powerful and successful orator, and in 1845 he took his talents abroad, embarking on a 21-month lecture tour of England, Ireland, and Scotland to advertise the first of his three autobiographical narratives, the *Narrative of the Life of Frederick Douglass, An American Slave: Written by Himself* (1845). This work proved to be the most popular of the extant slave narratives, selling 11,000 copies in the United States during its first three years in print, plus substantial sales abroad.

On the strength of his newfound success, Douglass returned to the United States in 1847 to start up his own newspaper, THE NORTH STAR. He not only served as editor but also wrote most of the paper's contents. On the strength of his writing, he managed to keep it and its successor newspapers, *Frederick Douglass's Paper* and *Frederick Douglass's Monthly,* going until 1863.

Douglass's rupture with his one-time mentor William Lloyd GARRISON over methods of promoting abolitionism led, in 1855, to the publication of the second of Douglass's autobiographies, *My Bondage and My Freedom,* which clarified his political approach to abolitionism. Declining John BROWN's invitation to participate in the raid on Harper's Ferry, Douglass instead organized two regiments of his fellow African-American Massachusetts residents to fight in the CIVIL WAR. After the war ended, he petitioned President Andrew Johnson (1808–75) for a national voting rights act giving African Americans the franchise in all of the states in the union. His loyalty to the Republican Party eventually won Douglass a series of political appointments: federal marshal and recorder of deeds for the District of Columbia, president of the Freedman's Bureau Bank, consul to Haiti, and chargé d'affaires to the Dominican Republic.

The income from such positions and from shrewd real estate investments permitted Douglass and his family to live comfortably in Uniontown, just outside Washington, D.C. Until the end, Douglass maintained an active life as a public man, working on behalf of women's suffrage, lecturing, and writing. The third of his autobiographies, *Life and Times of Frederick Douglass,* first appeared in 1881 and was expanded in 1892.

Sources

Andrews, William L., ed. *Critical Essays on Frederick Douglass.* Boston: G. K. Hall, 1991.

McFeely, William S. *Frederick Douglass.* New York: Norton, 1991.

Marin, Waldo E. *The Mind of Frederick Douglass.* Chapel Hill: University of North Carolina Press, 1984.

Sundquist, Eric, ed. *Frederick Douglass: New Literary and Historical Essays.* New York: Cambridge University Press, 1990.

drama *genre*

American drama in the 19th century remained firmly rooted in the colonial tradition; that is, although the United States produced its own playwrights, the overwhelming number of productions were based on the classics, especially Shakespeare, whose work continued to be popular with all classes of Americans—as can be seen, for example, in Mark Twain's (see Samuel CLEMENS) use of a Shakespearian medley in the theatrical productions of the reprobate Duke and Dauphin in HUCKLEBERRY FINN. Plays written and produced by Americans dealt with such American subjects as American Indians, the frontier, farm and rural life, New England and the Yankee sensibility, temperance plays, minstrel shows, and various kinds of burlesques and melodramas. These works did not achieve a high level of art; indeed, American drama did not emerge as a worthy complement to world literature until the 20th century. In the 19th century, American drama was noteworthy for promoting a sense of national history and for confronting current events and issues.

American heroes emerged in plays about the frontier and western expansion. The rustic, the woodsman, the farmer, the soldier, the frontiersman—these types of characters dominated plays such as James Nelson Barker's (1784–1858) *She Would Be a Soldier; or, The Plains of Chippewa* (1819) and Samuel Woodworth's (1785–1842) *The Forest Rose; or, American Farmers* (1825).

The American settler's encounter with the Indian became a staple of the stage beginning with John Augustus Stone's (1800–34) *Metamore; or, The Last of the Wampanoags* (1829). Such plays reflected the American consciousness that the drive westward was changing the face of a continent and obliterating the lives of its indigenous peoples. In this context, surviving Indians became the last of a noble race—as they are in James Fenimore COOPER's novels. Famous episodes such as John Smith's encounter with Pocahontas were also dramatized, as in George Washington Parke Custis's *Pocahontas; or, The Settlers of Virginia* (1830).

Along with the settling of America came moral crusades to uplift and reform rowdy frontier manners and urban dissipations. The drama became part of these campaigns to ban alcohol and to enforce Christian values. William Henry Smith's (1806–72) *The Drunkard; or, The Fallen Saved* (1843), for example, combined the popular form of the melodrama—a villain, a secret will, a forgery, and last minute rescues—with a meticulous realistic account of the protagonist's alcoholism.

Quite a different tradition—the comedy of manners—came to America with Anna Cora MOWATT's *Fashion; or, Life in New York* (1854). On the one hand, Mowatt satirized the pretensions of newly minted rich Americans who clumsily imitated European fashions; on the other hand, she exulted in the American strain of forthrightness and independence.

Very few women, let alone African Americans, had the opportunity or the resources to pursue careers in playwriting. A notable exception, William Wells BROWN, produced *The Escape; or, A Leap to Freedom* (1856), which has been compared in style and subject matter to Harriet Beecher STOWE's UNCLE TOM'S CABIN (1852). Both the play adapted from Stowe's novel and Brown's play initiate the tradition of American protest drama.

After the CIVIL WAR, the issues of slavery and the degradation of African Americans were deflected by the minstrel shows, which sentimentalized plantation life and transformed African Americans into grinning, simple-minded servants and entertainers. Whatever the limitations of this form of theater, by the end of the century it had produced African-American playwrights including Bob Cole (*A Trip to Coontown*, 1898); Marian Cook and Paul Laurence DUNBAR (*Clorindy, the Original of the Cake Walk*, 1898); and Jese A. Shipp (*Senegamia Carnival*, 1898). A notable exception to the tradition of minstrelsy appeared in William Easton's verse drama *Dessalines, a Dramatic Tale; a Single Chapter from Haiti's History*, which was produced in Chicago in 1893.

In the period between the Civil War and the end of the century, plays about American heroes and the settling of the continent continued to be produced—notably *Rip Van Winkle* (1865), the work of several authors; and *Davy Crockett; or, Be Sure You're Right, Then Go Ahead* (1872). But as in novels of the time, there was a call for stage productions that were more realistic and less melodramatic. James A. Herne was the first playwright to fashion dialogue and plots that reflected everyday life and the problems that tore families apart. *Margaret Fleming* (1890) dramatized the plight of a woman who chose to rear her husband's illegitimate child. Although such themes were beginning to be explored in American novels, to present them on stage was unheard of. Herne had trouble convincing theater managers to book his play, which, in the end, was performed only sporadically and for brief periods.

Herne had more success with *Shore Acres* (1892), the story of a hard-hearted father and his efforts to thwart his daughter's elopement. Although Herne made concessions to the popular desire for melodrama and sentimentality, his dialogue and characters moved American drama closer to a frank exploration of domestic life.

At the end of the 19th century, two playwrights, William Vaughn MOODY and Clyde Fitch (1865–1909), moved American theater toward a greater complexity and high art. In *The Great Divide* (1906), Moody dramatized the conflicting sensibilities of the American East and West, the drive for freedom, and the desire to civilize and domesticate the continent. The play avoided simplistic moralizing and melodrama and demonstrated a subtle use of symbolism. Even more impressive is Clyde Fitch's *The City* (1909), with characters who speak in coarse epithets; the play's naturalistic style and theme approached the candor evinced in novels such as Theodore DREISER's SISTER CARRIE (1900). The play includes a character who commits incest and another who attempts suicide. This darker side of American domestic life would not again be fully explored until the emergence of Eugene O'Neill (1888–1953) and 20th-century American drama.

Sources

Bank, Rosemarie K. *Theatre Culture in America, 1825–1860.* New York: Cambridge University Press, 1997.

Engle, Ron and Tice L. Miller, eds. *The American Stage: Social and Economic Issues from the Colonial Period to the Present.* New York: Cambridge University Press, 1993.

Gassner, John, ed. *Best Plays of the Early American Theatre, 1787–1911.* Mineola, N.Y.: Dover Publications, 2000.

McConachie, Bruce A. *Melodramatic Formations: American Theatre and Society, 1820–1870.* Iowa City: University of Iowa Press, 1992.

Dreiser, Theodore (1871–1945) *novelist*

Theodore Dreiser was born in Terre Haute, Indiana, and spent much of his early life in that city and in other Indiana towns. While his brother Paul succeeded as a songwriter, Theodore struggled at various menial jobs and quit Indiana University in Bloomington after a year of frustration. He moved to Chicago, where he wrote for newspapers. Other journalistic jobs took Dreiser to midwestern cities and then to New York, where he achieved some success as a magazine editor.

SISTER CARRIE (1900), Dreiser's first novel, established his prowess in the naturalistic school of American fiction (see NATURALISM). Dreiser wrote his story of a young woman without using sentimentality. He did not moralize, and he did not strive to achieve a happy ending. Consequently, his brutal vision of how a young woman could achieve success in turn-of-the-century America outraged the reading public and the publishing industry. Dreiser's belief that human beings often acted on impulse and on a raw biological drive seemed to challenge the rules of society and mock conventional religious beliefs. At the same time, discerning readers were exhilarated with Dreiser's frankness about the role of sex in human relationships and the power a woman like Carrie could wield because of her physical appeal. Dreiser showed extraordinary compassion for characters who had to contend with the overwhelming forces of America's commercial culture and industrial might. Carrie Meeber begins by working at menial jobs, but she suppresses all feelings that do not contribute to her overwhelming desire to be a success. Carrie crassly uses any man who crosses her path—the slick Drouet, for example, and the stylish Hurstwood. Her life is a triumph and a flouting of every genteel virtue that late 19th-century America professed to uphold. That she prevails by using her sexuality is a condemnation of society, not a judgment of her.

Jennie Gerhardt (1911) extends Dreiser's merciless analysis of a corrupt and grasping culture, but he presents a heroine with a softer, more compassionate nature than Carrie's, even though the women come from similar backgrounds. Jennie is the fallen woman of 19th-century fiction, but the fact that she ends up living with a man who is not her husband proves to be not a sign of her sinful nature but instead an expression of her loyal and loving temperament. Dreiser treats the seduction of Jennie by Senator Brander Matthews with a sensitive, even loving attitude. When the senator dies, Jennie is not to be pitied, because her second lover, Lester Kane, another seducer, calls into question conventional religion and morality. Kane cherishes Jennie and sets up a clandestine life with her. Although he ultimately proves to be something less than a great man, and he exposes Jennie to much sorrow and hardship, she survives largely because of her own generous interpretation of human nature and society. The novel demonstrates how certain individuals triumph even in a society that marks them for destruction.

Dreiser then embarked on a major exposé of American business culture in his trilogy *The Financier* (1912), *The Titan* (1914), and *The Stoic* (published posthumously in 1947). All three novels center on tycoon Frank Cowperwood, who was modeled after Chicago businessman Charles T. Yerkes. Dreiser's exploration of an American economy that values profit over individuals is heavily influenced by his reading of Arthur Schopenhauer, Friedrich Nietzsche, Karl Marx, Herbert Spencer, and others. In this grim social Darwinist world there is still room for magnificent individuals like Frank Cowperwood, although even his character is in part driven by what Dreiser calls his "chemisms," the biological imperatives that make human society a contest, a survival of the fittest. None of these novels equals the raw power of *Sister Carrie,* but they do keep vigorous faith with Dreiser's uncompromising vision of the battle between individuals and a coercive society.

Dreiser surpassed the achievement of *Sister Carrie* in *An American Tragedy* (1925), a massive novel about the pursuit of the American dream of success. He based his work on the story of Chester Gillette, who had murdered a young working-class woman. The sensational trial that ensued became the basis for Dreiser's story and its meticulous documentary feel, especially in the final pages, which are set on death row.

Dreiser's Clyde Griffiths is the quintessential American dreamer. Coming from a family of religious fanatics, he sets off on his own to seek his fortune. After a disappointing beginning, he finds a promising niche at a rich relative's factory. There he meets a working-class woman, Roberta Alden, whom he falls in love with and impregnates. Roberta becomes a burden when Clyde is introduced to Sondra Finchley, a beautiful society girl whom he adores. The climactic scene of the novel takes place in a boat, with Clyde wavering between his compassion for Roberta and his determination to get rid of her. He knows she cannot swim, and he has already contrived a situation that ensures her drowning. But does he actually rock the boat? Uncertain, he remains paralyzed as she falls into the water and he remains seated, unable (apparently) to save her.

The focus of this novel is as much on Clyde's society as on Clyde himself. What kind of a world is it, Dreiser asks, in which success can seem so all-important, when Clyde (as he later realizes) violates his own humanity by not coming to Roberta's rescue? Dreiser's long experience in journalism and his profound meditation on American culture make *An American Tragedy* a masterpiece.

Dreiser wrote a great many works of journalism, philosophy, and autobiography, including *A Traveler at Forty* (1913); *A Hoosier Holiday* (1916); *Hey, Rub-a-Dub-Dub!* (1920); *A Book about Myself* (1922); The *Color of a Great City* (1923); and *Tragic America* (1931). The *Letters of Theodore Dreiser* was published in 1959; *American Diaries, 1902–1926* in 1982; and the *Selected Magazine Articles of Theodore Dreiser* in 1985. His short fiction is included in *Free and Other Stories* (1918), *Chains: Lesser Novels and Stories* (1927), *Fine Furniture* (1930), and *The Best Stories of Theodore Dreiser* (1947). Dreiser wrote several plays published in *Plays of the Natural and Supernatural* (1916) and *The Hand of the Potter: A Tragedy in Four Acts* (1919). His poetry appears in *Moods: Cadenced and Declaimed* (1926), *The Aspirant* (1929), and *Epitaph: A Poem* (1929).

However, it is for his novels that Dreiser is best remembered. Although he has often been criticized for his clumsy style and crude philosophizing, Dreiser's creation of vibrant human beings and compelling dramatic scenes has ensured his place in the canon of American literature.

Sources

Gerber, Philip. *Theodore Dreiser Revisited.* New York: Twayne, 1992.

Lingemann, Richard. *Theodore Dreiser: At the Gates of the City 1871–1907.* New York: Putnam's, 1986.

———. *Theodore Dreiser: An American Journey 1908–1945.* New York: Putnam's, 1990.

Orlov, Paul A. *An American Tragedy: Perils of the Self Seeking "Success."* Lewisburg, Ohio: Bucknell University Press, 1998.

Pizer, Donald, *Critical Essays on Theodore Dreiser.* Boston: G. K. Hall, 1981.

Du Bois, William Edward Burghardt

(1868–1963) *historian, biographer, journalist, critic, editor, novelist*

Born in Great Barrington, Massachusetts, W. E. B. Du Bois grew up within a community of African Americans who had settled there during the American Revolution. Although his father deserted his mother after he was born, Du Bois was raised in a traditional and conventional environment that included membership in the Congregational Church.

A formidable intellect, Du Bois showed early promise as a scholar. However, his studies at Fisk University in Nashville, Tennessee, exposed him for the first time to the barbaric nature of what he later called the "color line," the absolute separation of whites and blacks. From Fisk Du Bois went to Harvard to study history under such famous figures as William JAMES and George Santayana (1863–1952). He went on to the University of Berlin to study sociology. By 1894 Du Bois was back in "nigger-hating America" and found it difficult to get a job in spite of his holding a Ph.D. Eventually he found positions at Wilberforce University in Ohio and then at the University of Pennsylvania and Atlanta University. Du Bois's dissertation, *The Suppression of the African Slave-Trade to the United States, 1638–1870,* was published in 1896. This brilliant work of history was followed by the groundbreaking sociological study *The Philadelphia Negro* (1899).

Du Bois's development as a writer took a great leap forward with his collection of essays entitled *THE SOULS OF BLACK FOLK* (1903), a powerful affirmation of African-American identity and an attack on Booker T. WASHINGTON's accommodationist position towards the larger white society that Du Bois believed deprived African Americans of their dignity and their own cultural heritage. His book remains a classic of American literature and a source of inspiration to generations of African American writers.

From 1905 to 1909, Du Bois suspended his work as a scholar to edit the magazines *Moon* and *Horizon* in the belief that he had to reach a broader audience and advocate more radical positions than African-American leaders of the time espoused. He also wrote a biography, *John Brown* (1909), which emphasized the virtues of extremism. In 1910 he resigned his professorship at Atlanta University and became the publicity director for the National Association for the Advancement of Colored People (NAACP) as well as the founder and editor of the organization's magazine, *Crisis.*

In these years Du Bois forecast a resurgence of African-American creativity and published a novel, *The Quest of the Silver Fleece* (1911). Set in rural Alabama and concentrating on young African-American protagonists, Du Bois exposed the evils of the plantation system in a style that has been compared to 20th-century naturalists such as Frank NORRIS (1870–1902) and Upton Sinclair (1878–1968). At the same time, he believed that the plight of African Americans had to be seen in a more global and specifically Pan-Africanist perspective taking into account the black African diaspora occasioned by slavery, which he explored in *The Negro* (1915).

Although Du Bois welcomed a new generation of writers, especially the poets Langston Hughes (1902–67) and Countee Cullen (1903–46), he also attacked them in "The Negro in Art" (1926) for being insufficiently radical. His second novel, *The Dark Princess* (1928), is an explicitly propagandist work in which the darker nations rise up and rid themselves of white domination.

By 1934 Du Bois had so radicalized himself that he broke with the NAACP because he considered it too moderate. He resumed teaching at Atlanta University, publishing in 1935 *Black Reconstruction in America,* which took a Marxist view of the conditions that had led to strict segregation of blacks in American society. He explained the evolution of his own thinking in an autobiography, *Dusk of Dawn: An Essay Toward an Autobiography of a Race Concept* (1940).

Although Du Bois rejoined the NAACP in 1944, his tenure there was short, and he gravitated toward communist affiliations and anticolonialist organizations. In 1950 he ran for the U.S. Senate as a member of the Labor Party. In 1951 he was indicted as the agent of a foreign power owing to his chairmanship of the group Peace Information Center, but a judge threw the case out of court; Du Bois published an account of this experience in *In Battle For Peace: The Story of My Eighty-third Birthday* (1952).

By the 1950s Du Bois was largely ignored by both white and black readers, although he published *The Ordeal of Mansart* (1957), *Mansart Builds a School* (1959), and *Worlds of Color* (1961)—a trilogy of novels that presented his view of African-American and world history. In 1959 he moved to Ghana and began work on the *Encyclopedia Africana,* which he left uncompleted at his death.

Du Bois is an inimitable figure in African-American history, a renaissance man in every sense of the word and the founder of the ideas of the black intellectual and a black aesthetic. Unlike the trajectory of many American intellectuals, black or white, he grew more radical in his later years, sometimes preferring propaganda over art. But his lasting legacy and example are undeniable, and he remains one of the few figures in American history who has been able to be both activist and intellectual, artist and historian—combining roles, in other words, that have become separated in contemporary culture.

Sources

Andrews, William, L., ed. *Critical Essays on W. E. B. Du Bois.* Boston: G. K. Hall, 1985.

Lewis, David Levering, *W. E. B. Du Bois: Biography of a Race, 1868–1919.* New York: Holt, 1993.

———. *W. E. B. Du Bois: The Fight for Equality and the American Century 1919–1963.* New York: Henry Holt, 2000.

Rampersad, Arnold. *The Art and Imagination of W. E. B. Du Bois.* Cambridge: Harvard University Press, 1976.

Du Chaillu, Paul Belloni (c. 1831–1903) *explorer, travel writer*

Paul Du Chaillu's early years are shrouded in mystery, but he is believed to have been born in Paris and to have spent his youth along the west coast of Africa, where his father worked as a trader. Du Chaillu came to the United States, probably in 1852, with the intention of securing financing for his own African explorations. He became a citizen of the United States and in 1856 gained the support of the Philadelphia Academy of Sciences for an expedition to Gabon. He returned four years later with the first gorilla ever to be seen in America, along with stories about great apes that were thought so fantastic that he was deemed a fraud. Nonetheless, Du Chaillu published his findings in 1861 as *Explorations and Adventures in Equatorial Africa* and returned to Africa in 1863 to gain further proof of the accuracy of his account.

Just as his earlier report had upset notions about the geography of Africa, *Journey to Ashangoland* (1867), *Stories of the Gorilla Country* (1868), *Life under the Equator* (1869), *Lost in the Jungle* (1869), *My Apingi Kingdom* (1870), and *The Country of the Dwarfs* (1871) were thought to be fabrications—particularly the last work, which confirmed the existence of Pygmies. Later explorers, however, validated many of Du Chaillu's findings. Later he traveled to Scandinavia, where he gleaned material for two other books, *Land of the Midnight Sun* (1881) and *The Viking Age* (1889). He died in Russia while gathering material for a book about that country.

Sources

Vaucaire, Michel. *Paul Du Chaillu, Gorilla Hunter: Being the Extraordinary Life and Adventures of Paul Du Chaillu.* New York: Harper, 1930.

Dunbar, Paul Laurence (1872–1906) *poet, novelist*

Born in Dayton, Ohio, to former slaves, Paul Laurence Dunbar was taught to read by his mother, who inculcated in him a powerful sense of the oral tradition of pre-CIVIL WAR African-American culture. At Dayton Central High School, Dunbar was the only black student. He nevertheless excelled and had begun writing poetry by the time he graduated. Afterward, forced by racial discrimination to work at menial jobs, he nevertheless managed to maintain his poetic vision. Working as an elevator operator at a Dayton hotel, he used his slack hours to write, and in 1893 he self-published his book of lyrics, *Oak and Ivy.* That year he attended the World's Columbian Exposition in Chicago, where he hawked his book and captured the attention of Frederick DOUGLASS. When his second collection of poetry, *Majors and Minors* (1895), was enthusiastically reviewed by William Dean HOWELLS, Dunbar was finally established as a literary star.

Dunbar's next volume, *Lyrics of Lowly Life* (1896), reprinted some of his earlier work and was brought out by a major publisher. Dunbar began reading poetry on the lecture circuit. He took a job at the Library of Congress and, under the influence of the Scottish poet Robert Burns (1759–96) and the American dialect poet James Whitcomb RILEY, he began using folk materials taken from plantation life to create dialect poetry of his own. At the time the only practitioners of African-American dialect poetry and prose were white men like Joel Chandler HARRIS and Thomas Nelson PAGE. In volumes like *Lyrics of the Hearthside* (1899) and *Lyrics of Love and Laughter* (1899), Dunbar was able to bring a degree of authenticity to the form that was inaccessible to his predecessors. The contemporary vogue for LOCAL COLOR helped make Dunbar's dialect verse popular with black and white readers alike.

Still, there were problems with Dunbar's work. In his dialect poems he wrote at one remove from the source of his inspiration which, as an Ohioan born after emancipation, he never knew firsthand. Dunbar himself felt that his writing in the genre was flawed, and he regretted the neglect of his earlier work. After his premature death from tuberculosis and the aftereffects of alcohol abuse, many black critics found his dialect poems derivative and even racist. Dunbar's reputation was restored, however, with the revival of interest in African-American culture in the second half of the 20th century. A new edition of his work appeared after the celebration in 1972 of the centenary of his birth.

Sources

Dunbar, Paul Laurence. *The Paul Laurence Dunbar Reader: A Selection of the Best of Paul Laurence Dunbar's Poetry and Prose, Including Writings Never Before Available in Book Form.* Edited by Jay Martin and Gossie H. Hudson. New York: Dodd, Mead, 1975.

Gayle, Addison. *Oak and Ivy: A Biography of Paul Laurence Dunbar.* Garden City, N.Y.: Doubleday, 1971.

Martin, Jay, ed. *A Singer in the Dawn: Reinterpretations of Paul Laurence Dunbar.* New York: Dodd, Mead, 1975.

Dunne, Finley Peter (1867–1936) *journalist*

Born in Chicago, Finley Peter Dunne was the editor of COLLIER'S magazine from 1918 to 1919. He is best known for his creation of the character "Mr. Dooley," an Irish saloon keeper whose witty commentary on contemporary events proved to be exceedingly popular. The character first appeared in the Chicago *Post.* Dunne wrote more than 700 Mr. Dooley pieces, which were collected in various volumes. The first of these, *Mr. Dooley in Peace and in War,* appeared in 1898; the last of the series, *Mr. Dooley on Making a Will,* was published in 1919.

Sources

Eckley, Grace. *Finley Peter Dunne.* Boston: Twayne, 1981.

Dupin, C. Auguste *character*

Edgar Allan POE featured this intellectual French sleuth in three stories that mark the beginning of DETECTIVE FICTION in the United States: "The Murders in the Rue Morgue" (1841), "The Mystery of Marie Rogêt" (1842–43), and "The Purloined Letter" (1845). In these stories Dupin is the child of a wealthy Parisian family that has mysteriously lost its money, and as a consequence he is obliged to live by his wits, indulging in few luxuries aside from books. In the course of prowling through bookstores, Dupin meets a fellow book lover with whom he rents a Gothic Parisian mansion and who becomes his companion in crime solving. This pairing of a brilliant eccentric with a somewhat dimmer but unfailingly loyal companion provided a formula that would be followed by many subsequent mystery writers, including Arthur Conan Doyle (1859–1930) in his Sherlock Holmes and Dr. Watson tales and Agatha Christie (1890–1976) in her mysteries featuring the Belgian detective Hercule Poirot and his sidekick Captain Hastings.

Sources

Eco, Umberto, and Thomas A. Sebeok, eds. *The Sign of Three: Dupin, Holmes, Peirce.* Bloomington: Indiana University Press, 1983.

Merivale, Patricia, and Susan E. Sweeney, eds. *Detecting Texts: The Metaphysical Detective Story from Poe to Postmodernism.* Philadelphia: University of Pennsylvania Press, 1999.

Walsh, John E. *Poe the Detective: The Curious Circumstances Behind the Mystery of Marie Roget.* New Brunswick, N.J.: Rutgers University Press, 1968.

Duyckinck, Evert Augustus (1816–1878) *editor, literary historian*

Together with his brother George (1823–63), Evert Augustus Duyckinck was at the center of New York literary life in the middle of the 19th century. From 1847 to 1853 they edited the influential literary weekly the New York *Literary World,* and in 1855 they published their collaborative effort, the *Cyclopedia of American Literature.* This 1,470-page tome was the most comprehensive work of literary scholarship of its time. It included lengthy discussions of many of the writers the Duyckincks had themselves befriended and published, including Nathaniel HAWTHORNE, William Cullen BRYANT, Washington IRVING, William Gilmore SIMMS, and, most prominently, Herman MELVILLE.

Together with Cornelius Mathews, the elder Duyckinck also founded the literary journal *Arcturus,* which Duyckinck edited from 1840 to 1842. When he died he left his large and important library—which had been an invaluable resource for his friend Melville—to the New York Public Library.

Dwight, Theodore (1764–1846) *political writer, poet*

Born in Northampton, Massachusetts, Theodore Dwight was the grandson of the theologian Jonathan Edwards (1703–58) and the brother of the poet Timothy Dwight (1752–1817). One of the younger Connecticut Wits, an 18th-century group of American poets, Dwight often put his ample satiric prowess to work for the Federalist cause, which was dear to his heart. He served in Congress (1806–07), in the Connecticut state council (1809–15), and as secretary to the Hartford Convention (1815). He wrote about this last service in his *History of the Hartford Convention* (1833), in which he harshly criticized the Antifederalists, as he did again in *The Character of Thomas Jefferson* (1839). Dwight also wrote verse, sketches, and a history of his state, and he worked as an editor, first on the *Albany Daily Advertiser* (1796–1866), and thereafter the *New York Daily Advertiser.*

Eclectic Magazine, The (1819–1907) *periodical*

Founded in 1819, until 1844 The *Eclectic* was known variously as the *Philadelphia Register and National Recorder, The National Recorder, The Saturday Magazine, The Museum of Foreign Literature,* and finally, *The Eclectic Museum.* All of these journals had common elements: They were edited by Eliakim Littell (1797–1870), and they reprinted materials from American newspapers or British literary magazines. Littell left in 1844 and went on to found a rival periodical called *Living Age.*

Eddy, Mary Morse Baker Glover Patterson (1821–1910) *religious leader, philosophical writer*

Born in New Hampshire, Mary Baker Eddy was married three times although she was in poor health until she was a middle-aged woman. In 1862 she first consulted Phineas P. Quimby, a Portland, Maine, physician who treated her through the unorthodox methodology of suggestion. Eddy improved under Quimby's care, and when she suffered a crippling fall four years later, she employed some of his techniques while consulting the New Testament in search of relief. After experiencing a miraculous recovery, Eddy went on to codify her belief in the healing power of Christ into the faith that became known as CHRISTIAN SCIENCE.

In 1875 Eddy published *Science and Health with Key to the Scriptures,* which reflected the influence of Quimby as well as transcendentalists (see TRANSCENDENTALISM) like Ralph Waldo EMERSON, who had once admonished, "Never name sickness." The book won her a large number of followers, and the next year Eddy founded the Christian Scientists' Association. Three years later she founded the religion's first Church of Christ, Scientist, in Boston; in 1881 the Massachusetts Metaphysical College was begun in the same city. To keep her religion growing, Eddy spread the word through mass media, founding the *Christian Science Journal* in 1898, the *Christian Science Sentinel* in 1898, and the *Christian Science Monitor* newspaper in 1908. When she died in 1910, the religion Eddy had founded claimed some 100,000 members.

Sources

Gill, Gillian. *Mary Baker Eddy.* Reading, Mass.: Perseus Books, 1998.

Peel, Robert. *Mary Baker Eddy: The Years of Authority.* New York: Holt, Rinehart and Winston, 1977.

———. *Mary Baker Eddy: The Years of Discovery.* New York: Holt, Rinehart and Winston, 1966.

———. *Mary Baker Eddy: The Years of Trial.* New York: Holt, Rinehart and Winston, 1971.

Education of Henry Adams, The *Henry Adams* (1918) *autobiography*

Historian Henry ADAMS's most important work is less a personal history (famously, he mentions his wife's suicide only in passing) than a history of the times. In this book Adams refers to himself in the third person, using his own name "for purpose of model, to become a mannikin on which the toilet of education is to be draped in order to show the fit or misfit of the clothes." Subtitled a *Study of Twentieth-Century Multiplicity,* the book was meant to complement *Mont-Saint-Michel and Chartres* (1904), in which Adams declared Europe in the 13th century to be "the point of history when man held the highest idea of himself as a unit in a unified universe."

Adams's own century, by contrast, is bewilderingly complex. As a result, he declares, his own education—and, by extension, everyone else's—is a failure. In a remarkable chapter titled "The Virgin and the Dynamo," he contrasts the symbol of the Virgin Mary, the worship of whom had unified medieval Europe, with the modern mechanical dynamo and finds that electrical energy makes a poor substitute for faith. The far-sighted *Education* predicted that modern society's production of power and the ever accelerating development of technology would end in chaos if man did not learn to control it. Toward the end of this, his last book, Adams elaborates a dynamic theory of history and proposes the development of a new class of leaders educated by scientific means.

Sources

Chalfant, Edward. *Better in Darkness: A Biography of Henry Adams, His Second Life, 1862–1891.* Hamden, Conn.: Archon Books, 1994.

———. *Both Sides of the Ocean: A Biography of Henry Adams, His First Life, 1838–1862.* Hamden, Conn.: Archon Books, 1982.

Rowe, John Carlos, ed. *New Essays on The Education of Henry Adams.* New York: Cambridge University Press, 1996.

Eggleston, Edward (1837–1902) *novelist*

Born in Indiana, Edward Eggleston was, for the first half of his life, a strict Methodist. He worked as a Bible seller, a circuit-riding minister, a local pastor, and a writer and editor of Sunday school materials and literature for the juvenile market. In 1874 he abandoned Methodism and founded his own "creedless" Church of Christian Endeavor in BROOKLYN, New York. He never stopped being a Hoosier, however. In 1879 he retired from his duties as pastor of his Brooklyn church and devoted himself full-time to his writing.

At the time Eggleston was already a well-known writer, most famous for his *The Hoosier Schoolmaster* (1871), a realistic tale of life in the Indiana backwoods that drew heavily on the experiences of his younger brother George Eggleston (1839–1911), a teacher in a country school there. Edward Eggleston's other novels to that date included *The End of the World* (1872), an Indiana love story featuring the Millerite (see MILLERITES) version of the apocalypse; *The Circuit Rider* (1874), a novel about a Methodist preacher's adventures in the lawless Ohio country in the early 19th century; and *Roxy* (1878), a story of Indiana poor whites. After his retirement, Eggleston added to his reputation as a regionalist with *The Hoosier Schoolboy* (1883), with its underlying message of the need for school reform; *The Graysons* (1888), a historical romance featuring Abe LINCOLN as lawyer; and *The Faith Doctor* (1891), a send-up of well-to-do Christian Scientists (see CHRISTIAN SCIENCE). After his death, two volumes of Eggleston's ambitious history of the United States appeared.

Sources

Randel, William Peirce. *Edward Eggleston.* New York: Twayne, 1963.

Emerson, Ralph Waldo (1803–1882) *essayist, poet*

Ralph Waldo Emerson was born in Boston, the son of a Unitarian minister descended from an old Puritan family. After his father's early death, Emerson was reared by his mother with help from an aunt, Mary Moody Emerson, whose sharp mind guided Emerson's own brand of thinking. He began writing early, keeping journals at Harvard University that would become the basis of his most famous essays and poems. After teaching at a school for young women for two years, he entered Harvard's divinity school. An undisciplined student, he nevertheless completed his studies, married, and became a popular preacher at Boston's Second Church.

Emerson's wife died in 1832, and the following year he resigned from his position in the church, no longer a believer in its doctrines and yearning for another kind of faith. He toured Europe in 1832 and 1833 and met the English Romantic writers Thomas Carlyle (1795–1881); William Wordsworth (1770–1850); and Samuel Taylor Coleridge (1772–1834), who turned Emerson's attention to German idealism and Plato. Emerson broadened his education to include European masters of rational thought such as Montaigne, mystics like Emmanuel Swedenborg, and British thinkers and empiricists—notably George Berkeley, David Hume, and John Locke.

Emerson returned to Boston and put his considerable speaking skills to good use on the lecture circuit. His addresses, drawn from his journals, were titled "The Philosophy of History," "Human Culture," "Human Life," and "The Present Age." He would eventually refine these talks into the classic essays "SELF-RELIANCE," "The Over-Soul," "Compensation," "Spiritual Laws," "Love," and "Friendship." Emerson wrote in circular fashion, announcing a thought and then gradually expanding its range of reference to other matters. He was not concerned with the essay's classical form of introduction, body, and conclusion. Instead, each sentence seemed to be enlarged by the next until he had covered the circumference of his subject.

Emerson remarried in 1835 and made his home in Concord, Massachusetts, where he befriended other writers such as Henry David THOREAU, Bronson ALCOTT, Jones VERY, Margaret FULLER, Orestes BROWNSON, and others who became known as transcendentalists. Emerson's essay "Nature" became a key text in TRANSCENDENTALISM: It expressed his conviction that the individual in contact with nature could comprehend the great and universal truths of the universe. He solidified his argument in "THE AMERICAN SCHOLAR" (1837), which called on Americans to have faith in their own creativity and not to rely so much on the age-old learning of Europe. Emerson's bracing creed helped to further the development of a distinctly American literature. His position grew even more radical in his "Divinity School Address" (1838) at Harvard, in which he rejected traditional religion and advocated the kind of intuitive spiritual experience that had led critics to attack the Romantics in England as atheists. Harvard, still very much a conservative institution, did not invite Emerson to speak again for another three decades.

Emerson spread his ideas not only through essay writing and public lecturing but also through his own magazine, *THE DIAL*, which became the home publication for many transcendentalists. He gradually extended the interests of transcendentalists to include direct engagement with public affairs and politics, endorsing strong abolitionist statements, for example (see ABOLITIONISM). By the early 1840s, Emerson had earned both a national and an international reputation. He published his first volume of verse, *Poems*, in 1847. "Brahma" is his most famous poem, for it states most clearly the transcendentalist creed—a universalist vision incorporating the cyclical view of the universe influenced greatly by Eastern thought and religion. Like Emily DICKINSON, Emerson's poetry is rather gnomic and metaphysical, although he lacks Dickinson's gift for original metaphors and her incisive observations of nature. His poetry tends toward the abstract in works like "Threnody," "Compensation," and "Each and All." Nevertheless, his deep probing of nature had a profound influence on 20th-century poets, especially Robert Frost (1874–1963).

Emerson's engagement with more worldly subjects is evident in *Representative Men* (1850), a study of history's heroes somewhat reminiscent of *Heroes and Hero Worship* by Thomas Carlyle, one of Emerson's friends and correspondents. Out of this friendship and his travels to England, Emerson published *English Traits* (1856). This period also marked Emerson's growing concern with ethical behavior in such books as *The Conduct of Life* (1860) and *Society and Solitude* (1870).

Emerson continued to lecture and to publish books in the 1870s, but his major contribution to American letters was over. *Letters and Social Aims* (1876) and *Natural History of Intellect* (1893) collect his last lectures. Various editions of his journals, letters, notebooks, and complete works have been published, including a scholarly edition that began appearing in 1972.

Sources

Bloom, Harold, ed. *Ralph Waldo Emerson.* New York: Chelsea House, 1985.

Buell, Lawrence, ed. *Ralph Waldo Emerson: A Collection of Critical Essays.* Englewood Cliffs, N.J.: Prentice Hall, 1993.

Porte, Joel, and Saundra Morris, eds. *The Cambridge Companion to Ralph Waldo Emerson.* New York: Cambridge University Press, 1999.

Richardson, Robert D., Jr., *Emerson: The Mind on Fire: A Biography.* Berkeley: University of California Press, 1995.

Ethan Frome Edith Wharton (1911) novel

In this brief, ironic tale about imprisonment in a loveless marriage, Edith WHARTON's eponymous protagonist is a Massachusetts farmer who barely manages to make a living out of his hardscrabble land. His is a family farm, and he manages to escape it only once when, as a youth, he briefly studies science before his parents' illness calls him back. Left alone by their deaths, he marries a distant cousin, Zeena, who had nursed his mother. When Zeena herself becomes neurasthenic, Ethan turns to Zeena's impoverished cousin Mattie, who nurses Zeena and helps her with the housework.

Ethan finds himself drawn to Mattie, a young woman who shares his love of the stark New England landscape. His fascination is not lost on Zeena who, increasingly jealous of her cousin, announces that Mattie must leave to make way for someone better qualified to nurse Zeena's ills. Heartbroken, Ethan decides to leave with Mattie, but his sense of duty and his impoverishment prevent him from doing so. As he escorts Mattie to the train station, however, he realizes that he does have one way out of his dilemma. Convincing Mattie to go sledding with him, he first kisses her ardently and then steers their sled into a giant elm.

Instead of being killed, however, Ethan and Mattie are injured—Mattie horribly so. She is brought back to the house, where Zeena begins to nurse the woman who once nursed her. As Zeena's health and vigor return, Mattie assumes the place formerly occupied by her cousin, becoming the crabbed hypochondriac Zeena once was.

Ethan Frome—stark, economical, and ironic—is often cited as Wharton's best work. Although she imbued the novel with autobiographical elements—in particular her sense of suffocation in an unworkable marriage—Wharton herself did not regard her work in this light, choosing instead to see it as an allegory.

Sources

Ethan Frome: *Authoritative Text, Backgrounds and Contexts, Criticism.* Edited by Kristin O. Lauer and Cynthia Griffin Wolff. New York: Norton, 1995.

Springer, Marlene. Ethan Frome: *A Nightmare of Need.* New York: Twayne, 1993.

Eureka: A Prose Poem Edgar Allan Poe (1848) essay

This lengthy metaphysical piece, which its author Edgar Allan POE called "an essay on the material and spiritual universe," is a meditation both on science and on philosophy—

and an attempt to reconcile the two. For the French poet Paul Valéry (1871—1945), whom the essay greatly influenced, *Eureka* was "the intuitive progenitor of Einstein's theory [of relativity]." In Poe's vision of the universe, atomic particles radiate outward from a divine unity to form an infinite multiplicity of matter, governed by the countervailing forces of attraction and repulsion. According to Poe, all things, including literature, are explicable in terms of this harmonious, ordered existence. And just as all elements in a well-ordered plot are interdependent, so are good and evil. The essay is a literary philosopher's attempt to justify the ways of God to men: "God—the material *and* spiritual God—*now* exists solely in the diffused Matter and Spirit of the Universe." By reuniting this diffused matter, God, "the *purely* Spiritual and individual God," can be recreated. Such concepts as "Inexorable Fate" are thus rendered comprehensible as burdens man has imposed upon himself.

Sources

Halliburton, David. *Edgar Allan Poe: A Phenomenological View.* Princeton, N.J.: Princeton University Press, 1973.

McCaslin, Susan. *Eureka, Poe's Cosmogonic Poem.* Salzburg, Austria: Institut für Anglistik und Amerikanistik, Universität Salzburg, 1981.

Swirski, Peter. *Between Literature and Science: Poe and Lem.* Montreal: McGill-Queen's University Press, 2000.

Evans, George Henry (1805–1856) *editor, polemicist*

Born in England, George Henry Evans immigrated to the United States in 1820. In New York City he worked as a newspaper editor for, among others, the *Workingman's Advocate.* The leader of various working men's parties from 1827 to 1837, Evans published his *History of the . . . Working Men's Party* in 1840. Known for his opposition to FOURIERISM, he agitated for agrarian reform and the right of "free homesteads" for all.

Everett, Alexander Hill (1790–1847) *diplomat, editor, essayist*

Born in Boston, Alexander Everett served as a U.S. diplomat in Russia; the Netherlands; and Spain, where he appointed Washington IRVING as attaché to the Madrid legation. Everett's experiences abroad provided him with material for his books *Europe* (1822) and *America* (1827). Between 1830 and 1835 he served as editor of *THE NORTH AMERICAN REVIEW,* to which he contributed translations from classical, European, and Asian literature that helped shape the transcendentalist movement (see TRANSCENDENTALISM). Some of the essays he published in the review were later collected in his *Essays, Critical and Miscellaneous* (1845–46).

Everett, Edward (1794–1865) *editor, orator*

Born in Dorchester, Massachusetts, Edward Everett was the brother of Alexander EVERETT. Starting out as a Unitarian minister, he went on to become a professor of Greek at Harvard. He also edited *THE NORTH AMERICAN REVIEW* from 1820 to 1823, and he served in the U.S. Congress as a representative for Massachusetts from 1825 to 1835. Thereafter he was governor of Massachusetts (1836–39), minister to England (1841–45), president of Harvard University (1846–49), and U.S. secretary of state (1852–53). Elected to the U.S. Senate in 1852, Everett served only the first year of his term, resigning because his Whig orientation called for compromise on the slavery issue. During the CIVIL WAR he traveled the country widely, delivering florid, highly popular speeches in defense of the Union; one such speech was delivered at Gettysburg just prior to Abraham LINCOLN's address there in 1863.

Sources

Reid, Ronald F. *Edward Everett: Unionist Orator.* New York: Greenwood Press, 1990.

Everybody's *periodical*

Founded in 1899 as an internal publication of Wanamaker's department store in Philadelphia, the magazine became independent in 1903 and almost immediately plunged into the MUCKRAKING MOVEMENT, publishing articles by such writers as Upton Sinclair (1878–1968) and Lincoln STEFFENS. As the movement waned, in 1910 *Everybody's* became an outlet for popular fiction and features. Eventually it was absorbed into the journal *Romance;* it had ceased to exist by 1920.

feminism *movement*

American feminism begins, in a literary sense, with Emma Willard's (1787–1870) *Plan for Improving Female Education* (1819). As the title suggests, however, Willard's concern fell somewhat short of a complete feminist program, which would include the reform of society itself to ensure that women were treated equally with men in both the social and political realms. Feminism requires that women have the same rights as men, and it pursues an independence of thought that characterized writers and activists such as Margaret FULLER, author of *Woman in the Nineteenth Century* (1845); and Elizabeth Cady STANTON and Lucy STONE, who began in the 1840s to spearhead the drive for women's suffrage (see SUFFRAGISM).

These leaders broke away from the American tradition in which questions of women's rights were subsumed in the drive for the abolition of slavery (see ABOLITIONISM) and the enforcement of TEMPERANCE, the term used for anti-alcohol campaigns. Not only was the "woman question" subordinated to other reform movements, but the women in these movements were often relegated to the sidelines and not permitted to take leadership roles.

In July 1848—with the support of clergymen such as Henry Ward BEECHER and Wendall Phillips (1811–84) as well as writers like Ralph Waldo EMERSON—Stanton, Stone, Lucretia Mott (1793–1880), and others held the first women's rights convention at Seneca Falls, New York. They resolved to work for the right to vote and issued a declaration of sentiment based on the American Declaration of Independence.

Abolitionist leaders William Lloyd GARRISON and Horace GREELEY supported this new movement, but many others—including many male reformers—objected to the idea of full, equal rights for women. Outside the reform movement, various newspapers and critics ridiculed feminists and branded the suffrage movement "unfeminine." Feminist meetings were often attacked and disrupted by male thugs, and feminists themselves were portrayed in literature as fanatics. The character Olive Chancellor in Henry JAMES's novel *The Bostonians* is a good example of a feminist portrayed as neurotic and rabid.

Feminism also posed a problem for abolitionists who wanted to address one inequality at a time, in effect. To focus on women's rights, these abolitionists feared, would only delay the day when slaves would be released from bondage. After the CIVIL WAR these concerns only increased, since abolitionists now feared the drive for women's suffrage would weaken agitation on behalf of suffrage for freed male slaves.

In May 1869 the National Woman Suffrage Association was established to advocate for a constitutional amendment giving all women the right to vote. A rival organization, the American Suffrage Association, took a state-by-state approach toward suffrage.

The two organizations merged in 1890 and, working at the state and federal levels, achieved suffrage for women in Colorado (1893), Utah and Idaho (1896), and Washington (1910). Other states followed suit, although a constitutional amendment spelling out women's right to vote was not ratified until August 18, 1920.

Sources

Kraditor, Aileen S., ed. *Up from the Pedestal: Selected Writings in the History of American Feminism.* Chicago: Quadrangle Books, 1968.

Whittier, Nancy. *Feminist Generations: The Persistence of the Radical Women's Movement.* Philadelphia: Temple University Press, 1995.

Fern, Fannie

See PARTON, SARA PAYSON WILLIS.

Field, Eugene (1850–1895) *journalist, poet*

Born in St. Louis, Eugene Field worked for newspapers in St. Joseph and Kansas City, Missouri, as well as the Denver *Tribune,* before settling in 1883 in Chicago, where, writing for the Chicago *Daily News,* he became one of the first featured columnists in American newspapers. Over the next 12 years he filled his column, "Sharps and Flats," with humor and verse that had enormous popular appeal. Field reused much of his material in his numerous books, such as the parody *Tribune Primer* (1882), *A Little Book of Western Verse* (1889), and *A Little Book of Profitable Tales* (1889). Some of his best-known work was poetry written by and for children, such as "Little Boy Blue" and the "Dutch Lullaby" (better known as "Wynken, Blynken, and Nod"). His *Love Affairs of a Bibliomaniac* (1896) addressed a more mature concern, his love of book collecting.

Sources

Conrow, Robert. *Field Days: The Life, Times, & Reputation of Eugene Field.* New York: Scribner, 1974.

Fields, James Thomas (1817–1881) *editor, poet*

Born in Portsmouth, New Hampshire, James T. Fields migrated to Boston, where he became one of the nation's most influential publishers. In addition to being the junior partner to W. D. TICKNOR in the firm of Ticknor & Fields and in the ownership of the popular Old Corner Bookstore, Fields edited the *ATLANTIC MONTHLY* and was himself an active poet. Some of his verse proved to be highly popular—for example, "The Ballad of the Tempest" (1858), which includes the memorable lines: "'We are lost!' the captain shouted, as he staggered down the stairs." Fields published several volumes of poetry as well as memoirs, including *Yesterdays with Authors* (1872).

Sources

Tryon, Warren Stenson. *Parnassus Corner: A Life of James T. Fields, Publisher to the Victorians.* Boston: Houghton Mifflin, 1963.

Fink, Mike (1770?–1823?) *folk hero*

Mike Fink's legend has become so elaborate with time that the true facts of his existence are difficult to discover. He was probably born in Pittsburgh, then an outpost on the frontier; fought Indians in Ohio; then became a keelboatman on the Ohio and Mississippi Rivers. Before long he was known as the "King of the Keelboatmen" and "The Snapping Turtle of Ohio." He was renowned for his marksmanship and, later, for his skills as a trapper. He was an accomplished teller of TALL TALES and a masterful humorist—albeit one said to have had a sadistic streak. Accounts of his death are so various that they are hard to untangle, but Fink was probably killed in a shooting incident somewhere near the mouth of the Yellowstone River while he was part of an expedition up the Missouri River.

The first accounts of Mike Fink's prowess appeared in 1829 in Morgan Neville's *Western Souvenir.* One account of Fink's death is told by Joseph M. Field (1810–56) in *The Drama in Pokerville* (1847). Thomas Bangs THORPE enhanced the Mike Fink legend in *The Mysteries of the Backwoods* (1846), as did Emerson Bennett in *Mike Fink* (1848), and John G. Neihardt in *The River and I* (1910).

Sources

Blair, Walter, ed. *Half Horse, Half Alligator: The Growth of the Mike Fink Legend.* Chicago: University of Chicago Press, 1956.

Fiske, John (1842–1901) *historian, philosopher*

Born in Connecticut, John Fiske worked as a philosophy lecturer at Harvard before becoming a professor of American history at Washington University in St. Louis. Early in his career he was a follower of the French positivist philosopher Auguste Comte (1798–1857) and the British Darwinian sociologist Herbert Spencer (1820–1903), whose works he helped popularize in the United States through lectures and through such works as *The Outline of Cosmic Philosophy* (1874), *Darwinism and Other Essays* (1879), and *The Destiny of Man Viewed in the Light of His Origin* (1884). He went on to apply Comte's "positive," supposedly scientific ideas about the evolution of society to American history in works like *The Critical Period of American History, 1783–1789* (1888) and *The Beginnings of New England* (1889). Fiske also served as one of the editors of *Appleton's Cyclopædia of American Biography* (1887–89) and went on to write histories of New England, the American Revolution, and the CIVIL WAR.

Sources

Berman, Milton. *John Fiske: The Evolution of a Popularizer.* Cambridge, Mass.: Harvard University Press, 1961.
Winston, George P. *John Fiske.* New York: Twayne, 1972.

Flint, Timothy (1780–1840) *novelist, editor*

Born in North Reading, Massachusetts, Timothy Flint graduated from Harvard in 1800 and entered the ministry, eventually becoming a missionary in Arkansas and Missouri. He recounted his experiences there in *Recollections of the Last Ten Years* (1826) and used them as background material for a number of novels about the frontier. From 1827 to 1830 he also published *The Western Monthly Review,* a literary journal. He edited and probably largely wrote the *Personal Narrative of James Ohio Pattie* (1831) and a *Memoir of Daniel Boone* (1833).

Sources

Folsom, James K. *Timothy Flint.* New York: Twayne, 1965.

folklore *genre*

Washington IRVING was the first American author to capitalize on the rich resources of American folklore, an amalgam of legends, beliefs, and practices originating with common people. In "RIP VAN WINKLE," for example, he crafted the story of a man who falls asleep as a colonial subject of King George III and wakes up 20 years later as an American citizen during the administration of George Washington. Irving uses the frame of the folk tale and its indulgence in fantasy and whimsy to make certain political points and social observations, such as that one George has been substituted for another and that although history is subject to major change, it is also marked by continuities of thought and action.

Irving's other famous tale, "The Legend of Sleepy Hollow" (see CRANE, ICHABOD) not only draws on the folktale's fascination with the supernatural but also creates an enduring American stereotype: the ineffectual teacher, absurd, eccentric, and removed from reality. The tale sets up a dichotomy between reality and fantasy, between the intellectual world and the practical world, that has become a long-running thread in American literature.

Other myths, tall tales, and outsized characters grew out of the folklore of westward expansion as well as the CIVIL WAR and its aftermath: Daniel Boone, whose opening of the wilderness is recounted in *Biographical Memoir of Daniel Boone* (1833); Davy CROCKETT, the bear-fighting pioneer; Mike FINK, the rowdy boatman; Billy the Kid (see BONNEY, WILLIAM H.); and Jesse JAMES. In these American heroes the romance of the outlaw and the hero fuse. In the epic battles of the American West, Indians such as Crazy Horse and Sitting Bull become legendary figures as well. William CODY, as "Buffalo Bill," seized on this American obsession with frontier heroes and the noble Indians they fought in his shows that toured the U.S. and Europe. His showmanship blended history and folklore.

At the same time, scholars such as Henry Rowe SCHOOLCRAFT began to make the study of folklore a science, taking special care to collect and preserve the stories and traditions of Native Americans. In a fictional vein, Joel Chandler HARRIS memorialized African American folklore in his "Uncle Remus" stories. Other writers who draw on the rich stock of American folklore include Bret HARTE and Mark Twain (Samuel Langhorne CLEMENS).

Sources

Brown, Carolyn S. *The Tall Tale in American Folklore and Literature.* Knoxville: University of Tennessee Press, 1987.
Dorson, Richard M. *America in Legend: Folklore from the Colonial Period to the Present.* New York: Pantheon, 1973.
———. *Buying the Wind: Regional Folklore in the United States.* Chicago: University of Chicago Press, 1964.
Brown, Carolyn S., ed. *American Negro Folk Tales.* Greenwich, Conn.: Fawcett, 1967.

Force, Peter (1790–1868) *publisher, historian*

Born near Paterson, New Jersey, Peter Force served in the War of 1812, then became a printer in Washington, D.C. From 1823 to 1831 he published the *National Journal,* a Whig newspaper, and became involved in local politics. He served as president of both the city council and the board of aldermen, and between 1836 and 1840 he served as mayor of the city. He is best remembered for his historical works, such as the *National Calendar and Annals of the United States* (1820–24, 1828–30), a yearbook of historical and statistical events; and his *Tracts and Other Papers, Relating Principally to the Origin, Settlement, and Progress of Colonies in North America* (1837–53). He published only nine of a planned 36 volumes of his *American Archives* (1837–53), a supplementary collection of rare documentary material. When the U.S. secretary of state refused to sanction further volumes, Force was obliged to sell his collection of 22,000 books and 40,000 pamphlets to the Library of Congress. One of Force's works demonstrated the spuriousness of the so-called Mecklenburg County Resolutions, supposedly dating from 1775, which apparently annulled any royal proclamations or appointments made in North Carolina; the original was never found.

Sources

McGirr, Newman F. *Bio-bibliography of Peter Force, 1790–1868.* Hattiesburg, Miss.: The Book Farm, 1941.

Ford, Paul Leicester (1865–1902) *bibliographer, historian, novelist*

When Paul Ford was born in BROOKLYN, New York, his father owned what was probably the finest collection of Americana in the nation. With his father, Gordon Lester Ford, and his brother, Worthington Ford, Paul Ford issued the bibliographies *Winnowings in American History* (1890–91) and made available scholarly editions of such historically important works as *The Writings of Thomas Jefferson* (1892–94); *The True George Washington* (1896), a candid portrait of the nation's first president; and *The Many-Sided Franklin* (1899). Ford also used his intimate knowledge of American history to write two highly popular novels: *Honorable Peter Stirling and What People Thought of Him* (1894), generally taken to be a portrait of Grover Cleveland; and *Janice Meredith: A Story of the American Revolution* (1899).

Sources

DuBois, Paul Z. *Paul Leicester Ford: An American Man of Letters, 1865–1902.* New York: B. Franklin, 1977.

Forum, The *periodical*

Founded in 1886, this magazine of current affairs was edited from 1891 to 1895 by the eminent journalist and later statesman, Walter Hines Page (1855–1918). In 1923 when H. G. Leach became the editor, the magazine began to debate current world controversies. In 1930 it merged with *The Century* and was called *Forum and Century* until 1940, when it merged with *Current History* and became *Current History and Forum.*

Sources

Cooper, John Milton. *Walter Hines Page: The Southerner as American, 1855–1918.* Chapel Hill: University of North Carolina Press, 1977.

Fourierism *movement*

Based on the theories of French sociologist Charles Fourier (1772–1837), Fourierism was a popular social movement in the United States during the 1840s and 1850s. Fourier advocated a communistic reorganization of society into "phalasteries," or units of approximately 1,600 individuals of different but complementary talents who would live together as one family, each contributing his or her skills to the general support of the community.

Fourierism was introduced to the United States by the radical reformer Albert BRISBANE, whose *Social Destiny* (1840) discussed its philosophy. But Fourier's first important American disciple was Parke GODWIN, a journalist who published *A Popular View of the Doctrines of Charles Fourier* in 1844. Fourierist colonies sprang up around the country, including the NORTH AMERICAN PHALANX in Red Bank, New Jersey; FRUITLANDS, a Bronson ALCOTT endeavor in Cambridge, Massachusetts; an outpost in Texas founded by Fourier's lieutenant, Victor Considérant; and, most famously, BROOK FARM in West Roxbury, Massachusetts. Under Brisbane's leadership the Brook Farm collective, which was associated with such literary figures as Nathaniel HAWTHORNE and Margaret FULLER, published the Fourierist journals *The Phalanx* and *The Harbinger.*

As a social experiment, Fourierism was short-lived; the phalanxes all failed, and toward the end of the 1850s what had been a popular movement faded from the public consciousness.

Sources

Guarneri, Carl. *The Utopian Alternative: Fourierism in Nineteenth-Century America.* Ithaca, N.Y.: Cornell University Press, 1991.

Kessous, Naaman. *Two French Precursors of Marxism: Rousseau and Fourier.* Brookfield, Vt.: Ashgate Pub. Co., 1996.

Spencer, M. C. *Charles Fourier.* Boston: Twayne, 1979.

Frederic, Harold (1856–1898) *novelist, short story writer*

Born and educated in Utica, New York, Harold Frederic began his professional career first as a photographer's assistant, then as a reporter for his hometown newspaper, the *Utica Observer,* where he was eventually promoted to editor. He went on to become editor of the *Albany Evening Journal* and London correspondent for the NEW YORK TIMES. Although he remained in journalism his whole life, he was able to parlay the skills of observation acquired in that world into a distinguished career as a writer of realist fiction (see REALISM).

Frederic published contemporary novels set in his native Mohawk Valley, beginning with *Seth's Brother's Wife* (1887) and its sequel, *The Lawton Girl* (1890). After publishing *In the Valley* (1890), a romance set during the Revolutionary War, he began to produce his most distinguished realist works, novels set during the CIVIL WAR and told from a civilian's point of view: *The Copperhead* (1893), *Marsena* (1894), and *In the Sixties* (1897). His most popular and best-known novel is *The Damnation of Theron Ware* (1896), the story of a Methodist minister's fall from grace after his exposure to the Higher Criticism of the Bible, the New Science, with its emphasis on sensory perception and contemporary aestheticism.

Sources

Briggs, Austin. *The Novels of Harold Frederic.* Ithaca, N.Y.: Cornell University Press, 1969.

Garner, Stanton. *Harold Frederic.* Minneapolis: University of Minnesota Press, 1969.

Myers, Robert M. *Reluctant Expatriate: The Life of Harold Frederic.* Westport, Conn.: Greenwood Press, 1995.

Freeman, Mary Eleanor Wilkins (1852–1930) *short story writer, novelist*

Born in Randolph, Massachusetts, Mary E. Wilkins Freeman was educated at Mount Holyoke College and the Glenwood Seminary in West Brattleboro, Vermont. She had moved to Brattleboro with her parents, with whom she lived until their deaths. In 1884 she returned to Randolph, where she lived with a childhood friend, Mary Wales, for almost two decades. In 1902, after a decade-long courtship, she married Dr. Charles M. Freeman and moved to

Metuchen, New Jersey, which remained her home for the remainder of her life.

Freeman's best work was published before her marriage and drew heavily on the rural New England life she knew so well. Although she published more than 30 volumes, she is best known for her first two books: *A Humble Romance and Other Stories* (1887) and *A New England Nun and Other Stories* (1891). A keen observer of human psychology, Freeman made a powerful contribution to the LOCAL COLOR movement with her portrayals of repressed people trapped in the decaying Puritanism of the New England of her day. Many of her early stories focus on the struggles of aging, unmarried New England village women for self-determination. In attempting to give these women a voice Freeman differed from other local colorists, who wrote primarily to amuse.

In the 1890s Freeman turned to the novel, producing such works as *Pembroke* (1894), a story about a broken engagement that was her most popular work of long fiction. She also wrote historical and social novels, a drama about the Salem witchcraft trials, and a volume of stories of the supernatural. Late in life she turned back to her original métier, producing *Edgewater People* (1918), a collection of stories whose strength rivals that of her earliest literary productions.

Sources

Glasser, Leah Blatt. *In a Closet Hidden: The Life and Work of Mary E. Wilkins Freeman.* Amherst: University of Massachusetts Press, 1996.

Marchalonis, Shirley, ed. *Critical Essays on Mary Wilkins Freeman.* Boston, Mass.: G.K. Hall, 1991.

Westbrook, Perry D. *Mary Wilkins Freeman.* Boston: Twayne, 1988.

Free Religious Association *organization*

This nonsectarian, almost secular association had no church or creed. Instead, it was meant to be a spiritual society for thinking individuals. Founded in 1865, it was supported by such luminaries as Bronson ALCOTT, Ralph Waldo EMERSON, and Thomas Wentworth HIGGINSON. *The Index,* a socioreligious weekly promoting free thinking, was affiliated with the group.

Sources

Persons, Stow. *Free Religion: An American Faith.* New Haven, Conn.: Yale University Press, 1947.

frontier fiction *genre of mostly long fiction set in and concerning the American "frontier," an ever-changing location and concept.*

The notion of a frontier in American literature stems from the earliest settlement period, when the continent seemed a vast wilderness. European settlers took it as their mission to civilize this world, which was populated by indigenous peoples whom the settlers considered primitive and savage—or noble in their closeness to nature and individual dignity. These contradictory attitudes toward Native Americans suggest a conflicted idea of civilization and progress in the minds of American pioneers. On the one hand, the pioneer brought civilization to the wilderness. On the other hand, in this "new world" the pioneer, as that French observer of early American life, Hector de Crèvecoeur (1731–1813), argued, was a "new man" spurning the corruption of Europe and seeking to reestablish a romantic bond with nature, which the Indians already had. This aspect of the romance of the frontier coincided with the writing of European romantics such as Jean-Jacques Rousseau (1712–78) and William Wordsworth (1770–1850), who wrote about "natural piety," the idea that man was good by virtue of his proximity to nature, not to religious doctrine or to the state. Yet to the Puritans the frontier seemed lawless; they saw the untamed forest and wilderness as promising ground for the machinations of the devil and of the ungodly.

These contradictory attitudes toward the frontier appear in the work of James Fenimore COOPER and Nathaniel HAWTHORNE. Cooper's Natty BUMPPO consorts with the Indians and regards the steady encroachment of white civilization as a corruption of the pristine lands on which he has roamed and hunted. The civilization of the town constricts Natty's freedom of movement, and he bitterly resents the officious and tyrannous methods of settlers—particular in *The Pioneers* (1823), the first novel in the Leather-stocking saga. Hawthorne, on the other hand, probes 17th-century Massachusetts, the time of his Puritan ancestors, and suggests in *THE SCARLET LETTER* (1850) that the harshness of the Puritans is in part understandable as a way of disciplining anarchic individualism—passions that romanticism justifies as having their own sanction and dignity but that also threaten the idea of community. When Hester Prynne enters the wilderness in *The Scarlet Letter,* she may be expressing her dynamic individualism, but she is also isolating herself from the community; she is in danger of exulting in passions that lead to mere self-indulgence. Hawthorne does not attempt to resolve this conflict but instead maintains the tension between civilization and wilderness and between the romantic and Puritan strains in his characters.

Outside of New England and upstate New York, where Hawthorne and Cooper set their fiction and where their sensibilities were shaped, writers in the South, Southwest, and West developed a different sense of the frontier. Writers like William Gilmore SIMMS presented vivid LOCAL COLOR portrayals of the South, unburdened by Puritan moralizing. The land offered wealth and the prospect of an agrarian economy that would produce a leisured aristocratic class. Exploring the frontier, then, was equated with progress, although

Simms and other writers certainly acknowledged the violence at the heart of a slave-owning and Indian-fighting society.

In the Southwest and West, writers such as Bret HARTE and Mark Twain (Samuel CLEMENS) provided a robust and rollicking version of frontier life. This was the land of FOLKLORE and TALL TALE heroes like Davy CROCKETT, Daniel BOONE, and later Paul BUNYAN. After the CIVIL WAR, the frontier story in the West became the story of the Western, the lawman's confrontation with the outlaw. Figures such as Wild Bill HICKOK (lawman) and Billy the Kid (outlaw; see BONNEY, William H.) represented not so much conflicting tensions in frontier fiction and folklore as aspects of the same drive to reconcile the centrifugal energies of unbridled individualism.

Mark Twain's HUCKLEBERRY FINN is perhaps the definitive statement about the frontier in American literature. Huck finds civilization confining, and he heads out for the territory. Yet the novel shows that slavery and the conflict between individual and society would not be resolved by simply pushing the frontier farther west as a means of escape.

At the end of the 19th century, the American historian Frederick Jackson Turner (1861–1932) declared that the frontier had disappeared. He elaborated what came to be known as the Turner thesis, encapsulated in this formulation: "The existence of an area of free land, its continuous recessions, and the advance of American settlement westward, explain American development." Turner attributed the hardiness of American individualism to its confrontation with the wilderness. Out of the grappling with the nature came the American dedication to freedom. His powerful explanation of the role of the frontier has been challenged many times as simplistic, chauvinistic, and even fanciful. Critics have pointed out that the frontier was a harsh and often undemocratic environment, producing a violence that is the antithesis of democracy and majority rule. Yet as a description of American literature and of the myth of the frontier, Turner's thesis remains viable and worth constant reevaluation as the country confronts what he saw as its greatest challenge: the disappearance of new land in which the American character can be tested.

Sources

Jacobs, Wilbur, R. *On Turner's Trail: 100 Years of Writing Western History.* Lawrence: University Press of Kansas, 1994.

Miller, David Harry, ed. *The Frontier: Comparative Studies.* Norman: University of Oklahoma Press, 1977.

Nobles, Gregory H. *American Frontiers: Cultural Encounters and Continental Conquest.* New York: Hill & Wang, 1997.

Slotkin, Richard. *The Fatal Environment: The Myth of the Frontier in the Age of Industrialization, 1800–1890.* Norman: University of Oklahoma Press, 1998.

Smith, Henry Nash. *Virgin Land: The American West as Symbol and Myth.* Cambridge, Mass.: Harvard University Press, 1950.

Fruitlands *Utopian community*

This Utopian cooperative community was founded in Harvard, Massachusetts, in 1844 by Bronson ALCOTT. Originally Alcott planned a rural location where members would live off the land as vegetarians and, through education and labor, achieve "the harmonic development of their physical, intellectual, and moral natures." Like most of the other 19th-century experiments in communal living, this one was short-lived: Fruitlands lasted only seven months. Louisa May ALCOTT would later poke fun at the extreme idealism of the place in "Transcendental Wild Oats," a sketch that appeared in 1876.

Sources

Francis, Richard. *Transcendental Utopias: Individual and Community at Brook Farm, Fruitlands, and Walden.* Ithaca, N.Y.: Cornell University Press, 1997.

Fuller, Henry Blake (Stanton Page) (1857–1929) *novelist, poet, critic*

A Chicago native, Henry B. Fuller's name became synonymous with the city after publication of his best known work, *The Cliff-Dwellers* (1893). Focused on the lives of office workers in one high-rise building, the book became known as the first important American novel of the city and a forerunner of literary NATURALISM.

Fuller was a well-traveled book critic whose first novel, *The Chevalier of Pensieri-Vani* (1890), published under the pen name Stanton Page, was an altogether different story about the differences between European and American culture. Fuller continued to alternate between continental refinement and gritty American REALISM throughout his novel-writing career. He also published two collections of verse, *The New Flag* (1899) and *Lines Long and Short* (1917), and was active in Chicago literary circles, particularly the group that kept the influential magazine *Poetry* vital.

Sources

Pilkington, John. *Henry Blake Fuller.* New York: Twayne, 1970.

Scambray, Kenneth. *A Varied Harvest: The Life and Works of Henry Blake Fuller.* Pittsburgh, Pa.: University of Pittsburgh Press, 1987.

Fuller, Sarah Margaret (Marchesa Ossoli) (1810–1850) *editor, poet, critic, polemicist*

Born into the BOSTON Brahmin class, Margaret Fuller was educated by her father, and by the age of six the precocious girl could recite Latin translations. She had a gift for languages and great literary aspirations which, when they threatened to set her too far apart from her contemporaries, resulted in her parents sending her to a girls' school in Groton, Connecticut, where she became socialized as a young lady.

When Fuller was 25 her father died, plunging her into a crisis that forced her to come to terms with her financial powerlessness as a woman. She first made her way in the world as a schoolteacher but soon found a better outlet for her talents in the seminar-style "conversations" for women held every Saturday afternoon at Elizabeth PEABODY's home in Boston. These sessions, held from 1839 to 1844, provided Fuller with the material for her most significant work, *Woman in the Nineteenth Century* (1845), the first serious American consideration of feminism.

The seminars also brought Fuller to the attention of Boston's male intellectual elite, starting with Ralph Waldo EMERSON. Later she was chosen by the members of the TRANSCENDENTAL CLUB as editor of their journal *THE DIAL*. Her book *Summer on the Lakes in 1843* (1844), recording her observations about life in the West gleaned during a visit to Chicago, attracted the attention of Horace GREELEY, who invited Fuller to become literary critic for his newspaper, the *NEW-YORK TRIBUNE*. Her negative valuations of such writers as Henry Wadsworth LONGFELLOW and James Russell LOWELL put her in bad standing with some members of the Boston literati, but her work for the newspaper was held in such high esteem that she was able to continue writing for it as a foreign correspondent when, in 1846, she fulfilled a lifelong desire to go to Europe.

Fuller stayed in Europe for nearly five years, meeting the leading authors of the day and finally settling in Italy, where she met the Italian nobleman Giovanni Angelo, marchese Ossoli. Ossoli, 10 years Fuller's junior, became her lover; together they had a son, then married. Ossoli became involved in the Italian revolutionary cause, and Fuller began to write a book about its leader, Giuseppe Mazzini (1805–72). When the revolution faltered, the Ossolis boarded a ship bound for the United States that sank off the New York coastline during a storm. Only the child's body was found; Fuller's Mazzini manuscript was not recovered.

Almost inevitably, Fuller's extraordinary intellect and ambition, combined with her dramatic personality, polarized those who knew her. Lowell, still stinging from her humiliating remarks about him, featured her in his *Fable for Critics* (1848), emphasizing her egotism and malevolence. Nathaniel HAWTHORNE based many aspects of the histrionic heroine of his BROOK FARM novel, *The Blithedale Romance* (1852), on Fuller. Ralph Waldo Emerson both admired and feared her. The literary scholar Vernon Parrington (1871–1929) accurately but condescendingly said of Fuller: "Her tragic life, despite its lack of solid accomplishment, was an epitome of the great revolt of the New England mind against Puritan asceticism and Yankee materialism." For the feminists who came after her, however, Fuller was nothing less than an inspiration.

Sources

Ellison, Julie K. *Delicate Subjects: Romanticism, Gender, and the Ethics of Understanding.* Ithaca, N.Y.: Cornell University Press, 1990.

Urbanski, Marie Mitchell Olesen. *Margaret Fuller's Woman in the Nineteenth Century: A Literary Study of Form and Content, of Sources and Influence.* Westport, Conn.: Greenwood Press, 1980.

Von Mehren, Joan. *Minerva and the Muse: A Life of Margaret Fuller.* Amherst: University of Massachusetts Press, 1994.

Galaxy, The (1866–1878) *periodical*

This New York literary monthly was intended as a sophisticated antidote to the "provincialism" of the *ATLANTIC MONTHLY,* the nation's leading literary magazine. In addition to publishing fiction by writers such as Henry JAMES and Rebecca Harding DAVIS, it featured literary criticism, historical and political pieces, and science articles. Mark Twain (Samuel Langhorne CLEMENS) served as an assistant editor and published humorous sketches in a "Memoranda" section. In the end, *The Galaxy* could not achieve its goal and was obliged to sell its subscription list to its one-time rival, the *Atlantic Monthly.*

Gallatin, Abraham Alphonse Albert (1761–1849) *diplomat, nonfiction writer*

Born in Geneva, Switzerland, Albert Gallatin came to the United States in 1780, eventually settling in western Pennsylvania. Active in politics and a Republican, in 1793 he was elected to the U.S. Senate but was disqualified two months later owing to what the Federalist majority claimed was the inadequate duration of his citizenship. Returning to Pennsylvania, he played a prominent role in quieting the Whiskey Rebellion against government excise taxes (1794). He returned to Washington in 1795 as a leading Republican Congressman, serving three terms in the House of Representatives. Afterward he served as Thomas Jefferson's (1743–1826) secretary of the Treasury, helping to reduce the national debt substantially despite the Louisiana Purchase (1803). Gallatin was blamed for America's military unpreparedness in the War of 1812, but he was also largely responsible for the Treaty of Ghent that ended the war in 1814. Later he served as minister to France and Britain. Gallatin was keenly interested in Native Americans, founding the American Ethnological Society in 1842. He considered his most important work to be his *Synopsis of the Indian Tribes . . . of North America* (1846), which won him the title of "father of American ethnology."

Sources

Kuppenheimer, L. B. *Albert Gallatin's Vision of Democratic Stability: An Interpretive Profile.* Westport, Conn.: Praeger, 1996.

Garland, Hannibal Hamlin (1860–1940) *short story writer, novelist*

Born in western Wisconsin, Hamlin Garland moved with his family to Iowa in 1869. In 1881, when his family moved again to a homestead in what was then the Dakota territory, Garland worked in Illinois and Wisconsin before working his own South Dakota homestead for a year in 1883. The experience of farming in the harsh conditions afforded by frontier homesteads in the upper Midwest would become the subject matter of his writing.

After his 1884 graduation from Cedar Valley Seminary in Osage, Iowa, Garland went east to teach at the Boston School of Oratory. In Boston he came under the dual influences of Henry GEORGE's social theories and William Dean HOWELLS's literary REALISM. Returning home to what had become known as the Middle Border region, Garland combined these influences with his own experience to produce the six stories published as *Main-Travelled Roads* in 1891. The collection went through a number of editions and variations until the *Main-Travelled Roads* stories totalled 30. Characterized by closely observed detail and a passionate dedication to regional values—a combination Garland labeled *veritism* in his 1894 critical work, *Crumbling Idols*—these stories constitute his most enduring work.

Garland went on to write a number of novels burdened by political import, such as the 1892 *Jason Edwards: An Average Man,* with its endorsement of Henry George's theory of taxation. But when he returned to the material and landscape he knew best, Garland was capable of writing memorable long fiction. *Rose of Dutcher's Cooley* (1895), for example, tells the compelling story of a Wisconsin farm girl's attempt to break free of her circumstances and become a writer in Chicago. Some of Garland's later work was more straightforwardly autobiographical, as in *A Son of the Middle Border* (1917), a narrative about his family that stops with the author's 33rd year; and that book's Pulitzer Prize-winning sequel, *A Daughter of the Middle Border* (1921).

Sources

McCullough, Joseph B. *Hamlin Garland.* Boston: Twayne, 1978.

Nagel, James, ed. *Critical Essays on Hamlin Garland.* Boston: G.K. Hall, 1982.

Pizer, Donald. *Hamlin Garland's Early Work and Career.* New York: Russell & Russell, 1969.

Garrison, William Lloyd (1805–1879) *editor, essayist*

Born into poverty in Newburyport, Massachusetts, William Lloyd Garrison grew up to be a radical reformer. ABOLITIONISM became the primary focus of his considerable energies. Garrison began his career in 1829 editing *The Genius of Universal Emancipation* in Baltimore with antislavery pioneer and editor Benjamin Lundy (1789–1839), but after he was imprisoned for libel the following year, he returned home to pursue even more radical activities. On January 1, 1831, he published the first issue of a weekly he called *THE LIBERATOR,* proclaiming on its masthead, "I will be heard!" He would continue to publish *The Liberator* for the next 34 years, until official emancipation made it redundant.

Despite its relatively small circulation, *The Liberator* was enormously influential. Garrison also drew attention to his views by organizing an Anti-Slavery Society that drew in a number of important writers and orators. But he refused to modify his passionate beliefs, even after a mob dragged him through the streets of Boston in 1835. Eventually his extreme views—which included the heterodox (for northerners) endorsement of secession—led to the breakup of the Anti-Slavery Society.

After Congress passed the 13th Amendment outlawing slavery in 1865, Garrison took up the causes of women's suffrage, temperance, and world peace. His works include *Thoughts on African Colonization* (1832), *Sonnets* (1832), and *Selections* (1852), which includes speeches as well as polemical writings. Garrison himself served as a subject for numerous literary works, including a poem by one of *The Liberator's* major contributors, John Greenleaf WHITTIER.

Sources

Mayer, Henry. *All on Fire: William Lloyd Garrison and the Abolition of Slavery.* New York: St. Martin's Press, 1998.

Merrill, Walter McIntosh. *Against Wind and Tide: A Biography of William Lloyd Garrison.* Cambridge, Mass.: Harvard University Press, 1963.

Gentlemen's Magazine, The *periodical*

Later known as *Burton's Gentleman's Magazine,* this monthly journal of literature and the arts—which seems to have included sports—was founded in 1837 in Philadelphia by English emigré W. E. Burton (1802–60). From July 1839 to June 1840, Edgar Allan POE served as editor, also contributing such works as "William Wilson" and "The Fall of the House of Usher." Poe and Burton had severe editorial disagreements, however, and in the end Burton gave up the enterprise, selling his magazine to George R. Graham, who merged it with *Atkinson's Casket* to create a third entity, *Graham's Magazine.*

George, Henry (1839–1897) *economist, editor*

Born into a middle-class Episcopalian home in Philadelphia, Henry George departed at the age of 16 for a voyage to Calcutta. Serving as a lowly foremast boy, he saw firsthand the degrading conditions that not only citizens of the Indian subcontinent but also common sailors endured. After his return to the United States, in 1857 he went to San Francisco, where he struggled for nearly a decade, barely making a living in a printer's office, in gold mining, and as a freelance editor and writer.

In 1868 the *OVERLAND MONTHLY* printed George's article "What the Railroad Will Bring Us," which anticipated the ramifications of completion of the Transcontinental Railroad and his later economic theory of how social progress promotes unequal distribution of wealth. This was an idea he would expand in his greatest work, *Progress and Poverty* (1879), written while George was working as editor of the newly established Democratic newspaper, the *Oakland Transcript.* In *Progress and Poverty,* George argues that poverty is the result of private ownership of land, because the person who works the land loses part of the value of his or her labor to rent. Furthermore, in heavily populated areas the increasing value of land can be attributed to the community, not to the landholder, who thus robs both the tenant and the community by charging rent. The solution, George proposed, was a single tax on the land that would relieve a burden from labor and industry while at the same time providing government with the funds it needed to continue functioning.

Initially printed at the author's own expense, *Progress and Poverty* went through more than 100 editions and proved highly influential among the populace at large and with some writers, particularly William Dean HOWELLS and Hamlin GARLAND. George elaborated the book's thesis in six other books as well as in his own weekly, *The Standard* (1886–92), and he used the popularity it won him with labor unions to stage two unsuccessful campaigns, in 1886 and 1897 for the New York mayor's office. Already ill before he undertook the second campaign, George died before the election.

George's ideas have been kept alive in the United States by the Henry George schools of social science located in New York and around the country. During his lifetime, George had lectured extensively at home and abroad, influencing such important world figures as the Chinese National leader Sun Yat-Sen (1867–1925), the British Labour Party leader Ramsay MacDonald (1866–1937), the Russian novelist Leo Tolstoy (1828–1910), and the British intellectuals who formed the socialist Fabian Society. His work contributed to the introduction in Germany and Austria of incremental taxation, and as late as 1947 a party calling itself the Georgists and espousing George's economic theories won several seats in the Danish parliament.

Sources

An Anthology of Henry George's Thought. Edited by Kenneth C. Wenzer. Rochester, N.Y.: University of Rochester Press, 1997.

Hellman, Rhoda. *Henry George Reconsidered.* New York: Carlton Press, 1987.

Rose, Edward J. *Henry George.* New York: Twayne, 1968.

Gettysburg Address (1863) *speech*

On November 19, 1863, President Abraham LINCOLN delivered this address at the dedication of a national cemetery on a former battlefield in Pennsylvania that was the site, on July 1–3, 1863, of what many regarded as the turning point of the CIVIL WAR. Gettysburg was one of the bloodiest battles in this bloodiest of all American wars. Lincoln's stated purpose was to deliver a "few remarks," and when he delivered the scant three paragraphs he had written—in the wake of a two-hour oration delivered by Edward EVERETT—they were thought to be of little significance. The audience seemed barely to have heard Lincoln's speech, and Lincoln himself felt he had botched the job.

In retrospect it is clear, however, that Lincoln had written one of the most eloquent and compelling arguments in favor of nationhood ever created. Many phrases from his speech have been incorporated into the lexicon of hallowed American political speech, from "a new birth of freedom" to "four score and seven years ago."

Six versions of the address exist. The first, written at the White House, was revised on the way to the ceremony. The speech Lincoln delivered was yet another variation on what he had written. At Everett's request he wrote still another version, copies of which were sold at a fair with the proceeds benefitting Union army veterans. Two more versions were written for similar purposes.

Sources

Nevins, Allan, ed. *Lincoln and the Gettysburg Address: Commemorative Papers.* Urbana: University of Illinois Press, 1964.

Petersen, Svend. *The Gettysburg Addresses: The Story of Two Orations.* New York: Ungar, 1963.

Wills, Garry. *Lincoln at Gettysburg: The Words That Remade America.* Thorndike, Me.: G. K. Hall, 1992.

Gibson, Charles Dana (1867–1944) *illustrator, editor*

Born in Roxbury, Massachusetts, Charles Dana Gibson had prodigious talents that were evident from the time he was a youth. A regular contributor to *LIFE*, which he edited for a time, as well as to other magazines, Gibson also illustrated numerous books, including those of Richard Harding DAVIS. He also published his own books, consisting of collections of his drawings, as well as travel observations. His most lasting creation, however, was the "Gibson Girl," a stylish but refined version of the ideal American woman whose dress, hairstyle, and manner were widely imitated. Modeled on the artist's wife, the Gibson Girl was featured in Gibson's series *The Education of Mr. Pipp* (1899), which spawned a popular play of the same name written by Augustus Thomas (1857–1934) and produced in 1905.

Sources

The Best of Charles Dana Gibson. Edited by Woody Gelman. New York: Bounty Books, 1970.

gift books *literary form*

Highly popular in the mid-1800s (from roughly 1825 to 1865), gift books were annual miscellanies that collected poetry, essays, and stories—customarily those of a didactic nature—between hard covers that also contained lavish illustrations. Patterned after the European literary almanacs that flourished in France, Germany, and England, the first American gift book was *Le Souvenir, or Picturesque Pocket Diary; containing an Almanac, Ruled Pages for Memoranda, Literary Selections, and a Variety of Useful Information for 1825,* which appeared in Philadelphia in 1824. A second volume appeared the next year, as did a competitor, the *Philadelphia Souvenir; A Collection of Fugitive Pieces from the Philadelphia Press, With Biographical and Explanatory Notes, By J.E. Hall.*

The first truly literary American gift book was *The Atlantic Souvenir,* which was published annually in Philadelphia from 1826 to 1832, and afterward in Boston, where it was combined with a competing publication and appeared as *The Token and Atlantic Souvenir* from 1833 to 1842. Other East

Coast gift books included New York's *The Talisman,* and the formula took hold elsewhere in the country with, for example, Cincinnati's *The Western Souvenir,* Detroit's *The Souvenir of the Lakes, The Charleston Book,* and *The New-Orleans Book.* In all, more than a thousand different gift books were produced—some annually, others only once—during their heyday. Beautifully bound—sometimes in tooled leather or varnished papier-mâché or inlaid mother-of-pearl—these books, often presented as special Christmas or New Year gifts, could also serve as table decorations.

Some of the leading literary lights of the day contributed work to gift books, including such writers as William Gilmore SIMMS, Lydia SIGOURNEY, Sarah Josepha HALE, and Harriet Beecher STOWE. Even the august Ralph Waldo EMERSON first appeared in print—anonymously—in a gift book, *The Offering, for 1829.* By 1845, when the gift-book vogue was at its high-water mark, among the established writers of the era probably only Herman MELVILLE, Henry David THOREAU, and Walt WHITMAN had resisted the temptation to sell work to such collections. In fact, gift books bucked the trend toward reprinting pirated English works, instead offering a paying venue for American writers.

Gift books performed other services as well, printing polemical works in favor of ABOLITIONISM and TEMPERANCE and, during the CIVIL WAR, serving as an outlet for Union propaganda. By the end of the war, however, the publication of gift books declined as monthly magazines increased in number and circulation.

Sources

Thompson, Ralph. *American Literary Annuals & Gift Books, 1825–1865.* Hamden, Conn.: Archon Books, 1967.

Gilded Age (1873; c. 1865–1873) *era*

An 1873 novel written by Mark Twain (Samuel CLEMENS) and Charles Dudley WARNER, *The Gilded Age,* subtitled "A Tale of To-day," gave its name to an entire era. The plot of the book revolves around a Colonel Beriah Sellers, a perpetual optimist who constantly involves himself and others in get-rich-quick schemes that inevitably fail. Sellers convinces his friend Squire Hawkins to speculate in Missouri real estate, an "investment" that costs Hawkins several fortunes. After his death, his adopted daughter Laura is seduced and betrayed by a philanderer she eventually murders. Acquitted after a sensational trial, Laura succumbs to a heart attack when she fails to make her way as a lecturer. To add to the giddy mix, the authors throw in some political corruption involving Sellers and Laura and a love-struck U.S. senator.

The novel was a success, in part because of the comic turn provided by Colonel Sellers. Dramatized by G. S. Densmore in 1874, the theatrical version was revised that same year by Twain, who later changed Sellers's name to Mulberry in a sequel to the novel titled *The American Claimant* (1892).

The same elements that made the original novel so popular were present in the post-CIVIL WAR years, when the economy boomed, fueled by wild speculation, greed, and amorality. The political corruption represented by opportunistic "carpetbaggers" who went South both to oversee RECONSTRUCTION and to rake in money on the side came to a head with the election of Ulysses S. GRANT as president in 1868. Grant was a reluctant politician, and his two administrations were marred by scandals generated by his chosen subordinates. The party that was the Gilded Age came to an abrupt end when the depression of 1873, hastened in part by the drain on social services occasioned by the emancipation of slaves, burst the bubble of northern optimism.

Sources

Cashman, Sean Dennis. *America in the Gilded Age: From the Death of Lincoln to the Rise of Theodore Roosevelt.* New York: New York University Press, 1984.

Clark, Judith Freeman. *America's Gilded Age: An Eyewitness History.* New York: Facts On File, 1992.

French, Bryant M. *Mark Twain and The Gilded Age: The Book That Named an Era.* Dallas: Southern Methodist University Press, 1965.

Gilder, Jeanette Leonard (1849–1916) *critic*

Born in Flushing, New York, Jeanette Gilder was the sister of the editor and poet Richard GILDER. With him she worked as an assistant editor at *SCRIBNER'S MONTHLY.* She also wrote drama and music criticism for a variety of newspapers; one of her other contributions was "Chats About Books," the first literary gossip column in the country. With her other brother, Joseph, she founded and coedited *The Critic* from 1881 to 1885, after which she served as the sole editor until 1906. She and Joseph also collaborated on *Essays from "The Critic"* (1883) and *Authors at Home* (1888). Continuing in this vein, Jeanette Gilder published *The Autobiography of a Tomboy* (1900) and *The Tomboy at Work* (1904), in which she humorously described her encounters with the literati.

Gilder, Richard Watson (1844–1909) *editor, poet*

Born in Bordentown, New Jersey, Richard Watson Gilder was a poet who made his living as an editor, first of a newspaper in Newark, New Jersey, then of *SCRIBNER'S MONTHLY* (1870–81) and its successor, *THE CENTURY ILLUSTRATED MAGAZINE* (1881–1909) in New York City. He and his wife, the artist Helena de Kaye, made their home into a literary salon which was the site where the Authors' Club, a literary society that included the likes of Brander MATTHEWS and Edward EGGLESTON, was founded in 1882. Gilder himself published 16 volumes of poetry, including *The New Day* (1876), as well as books about Presidents Abraham LINCOLN (1909) and Grover Cleveland (1910).

Sources

John, Arthur. *The Best Years of the Century: Richard Watson Gilder, Scribner's Monthly, and the Century Magazine, 1870–1909.* Urbana: University of Illinois Press, 1981.

Gilman, Caroline Howard (1794–1888) *memoirist, poet*

Born and reared in Boston, Caroline Howard married a Unitarian minister, Samuel Gilman, in 1819, and moved with him to Charleston, South Carolina. There, in 1832, she began a journal for youth—one of the first in the nation—called *Rose Bud* (later *Southern Rose*), which featured sketches Gilman later collected in her first domestic narrative, *Recollections of a New England Bride* (1834). She followed that with *Recollections of a Southern Matron* (1837), another domestic narrative, this time reflecting her affection for her newfound home—and, not incidentally, including a justification of slavery. She also published several volumes of poetry, including her autobiographical *The Poetry of Traveling in the United States* (1838).

Sources

Saint-Amand, Mary Scott. *A Balcony in Charleston.* Richmond, Va.: Garrett and Massie, 1941.

Gilman, Charlotte Perkins Stetson (1860–1935) *novelist, short story writer, reformer*

Born in Hartford, Connecticut, Charlotte Perkins Gilman was related through her father, the editor and biographer Frederick Beecher Perkins (1828–99), to Lyman BEECHER, Henry Ward BEECHER, and Harriet Beecher STOWE. Frederick Perkins deserted the family shortly after his only daughter's birth, and Charlotte suffered throughout her childhood from his continuing rejection and her mother's constant need to move in search of work or to aid relatives. After a brief period at the Rhode Island School of Design, Charlotte Perkins taught art and designed greeting cards. In 1883, the same year she married the artist Charles Stetson, she published her first poem which began, "In duty bound, a life hemmed in. . . ."

In 1885, following the birth of a daughter, Perkins sought treatment for postpartum depression from the neurologist and writer S. Weir MITCHELL. The experience, including his prescription for total bed rest without intellectual stimulation and a rededication to domestic life, led Perkins to what she said was the brink of "utter mental ruin" and later provided the inspiration for her masterwork, the story "The Yellow Wallpaper" (1892). The story is a fictional indictment of the sexual status quo in which a woman is driven to madness by the well-meaning but destructive care administered by her physician husband.

Perkins's story was also influenced by her separation from her husband. After she moved with her daughter to California in 1887, Perkins and Stetson divorced, with Perkins relinquishing custody of their daughter to her ex-husband and his new wife. Perkins was publically condemned for her actions, but she nevertheless managed to get a job editing the *Pacific Monthly* from 1889 to 1891. During the 1890s Perkins toured the United States, lecturing on behalf of women's rights. She also wrote a number of celebrated books on the subject, including *Women and Economics* (1898), which concluded that women's economic dependence on men harmed all of humanity.

In 1900 Perkins remarried, and her union with her cousin George Houghton Gilman lasted until his death one year before her own. She continued to lecture and publish prolifically, from 1909 to 1916 producing a monthly magazine called *The Forerunner.* Her literary output was equally prodigious, including poetry, some 200 short stories, and three Utopian novels, including the feminist classic *Herland* (1915), concerning an all-female society.

Charlotte Perkins Gilman committed suicide in 1935, suffering from terminal breast cancer and all but forgotten by a society that had moved on to newer notions of female emancipation through personal fulfillment and sexual liberation. All of her books were out of print. It would be another three decades before her writing would be revived by a new women's liberation movement.

Sources

Golden, Catherine J., and Joanna Schneider Zangrando, eds. *The Mixed Legacy of Charlotte Perkins Gilman.* Newark: University of Delaware Press, 2000.

Karpinski, Joanne B., ed. *Critical Essays on Charlotte Perkins Gilman.* New York: G. K. Hall, 1992.

Lane, Ann J. *To Herland and Beyond: The Life and Work of Charlotte Perkins Gilman.* New York: Pantheon Books, 1990.

Gilmer, Elizabeth Meriwether (Dorothy Dix) (1861–1951) *journalist*

Born in Montgomery County, Tennessee, Elizabeth Meriwether married George O. Gilmer in 1882. Two years later he suffered a nervous breakdown from which he never recovered. His wife would support him financially for the remainder of his life.

Suffering from the strain occasioned by her husband's first hospitalization, Gilmer went to Mississippi to recuperate. There she took up writing as a distraction from her worries; she also met Eliza Holbrook-Nicholson, the owner-publisher of the *New Orleans Daily Picayune* (see *NEW ORLEANS PICAYUNE*), who helped Gilmer get a job with the paper in 1894.

The next year Gilmer began writing a weekly column under the pen name Dorothy Dix. Her advice to the lovelorn proved to be highly popular, and in 1901 she went to work for the *New York Journal,* taking her column with her. The column appeared three times per week, but Gilmer also managed to exercise her reportorial skills, covering such events as murder trials involving women. In 1917 Gilmer and her column went back to the *Picayune,* where "Dorothy Dix Talks" was published for the next 33 years, becoming the longest-running column in the world and ending only with her death. The column also generated two books: *Every-day Help for Every-day People* (1926) and *How to Win and Hold a Husband* (1939).

Sources

Kane, Harnett T. *Dear Dorothy Dix: The Story of a Compassionate Woman.* Garden City, N.Y.: Doubleday, 1952.

Gloux, Oliver (Gustave Aimard) (1818–1883) *novelist*

Born in Paris, Oliver Gloux originally traveled to the United States as a cabin boy. For 10 years he lived in Arkansas and other parts of the OLD SOUTHWEST, where he was supposedly adopted by an Indian tribe. Later travels took him to Spain, Turkey, and the Caucasus, but he returned to America to garner more material for romances like *The Indian Chief* (1861) and *The Prairie Flower* (1861). He wrote more than 25 such novels, a production that earned him the sobriquets "The Dumas of the Indians" and "The French James Fenimore COOPER."

Godey's Lady's Book *periodical*

Founded in 1830 in Philadelphia by Louis A. Godey (1804–78), *Godey's Lady's Book* was the most successful serial publication of its day. Edited from 1837 to 1877 by Sarah J. HALE, the magazine, with its hand-colored fashion plates and engraved art reproductions, came to be regarded as a trendsetter and guardian of taste. It also published leading American writers such as Edgar Allan POE, Nathaniel HAWTHORNE, and Harriet Beecher STOWE. After Hale retired in 1877 and Godey died in 1878, the magazine fell out of favor. In 1892 it moved to New York and was eventually taken over by the *Puritan.*

Godkin, Edwin Lawrence (1831–1902) *journalist*

Born in Ireland, E. L. Godkin worked on the staffs of several British newspapers before immigrating to the United States in 1856. Once in America he became a lawyer, but with the advent of the CIVIL WAR he went back to the newspaper business, working as a correspondent for the London *Daily News.* In 1865, after the war ended, he served as the first editor of *The Nation,* a liberal-leaning weekly devoted to the arts and public affairs which he helped found. After 1881, when *The Nation* merged with the New York *Post,* Godkin served as the newspaper's associate editor, then editor, until 1900, when he returned to England.

Godkin was both fearless and articulate, helping to make *The Nation* and *Post* influential throughout the country. A strong supporter of the Union cause, he became one of the GILDED AGE's harshest critics after the war, attacking the corruption of Ulysses S. GRANT's administration as well as Grover Cleveland's (1837–1908) jingoism (although he supported Cleveland's presidency). A prescient social critic, he claimed that American democracy "owed much of its force and violence" to the influence of the frontier, a theory he explored at length in *Problems of Democracy* (1896) and *Unforeseen Tendencies of Democracy* (1898). A gifted book reviewer, he also reprinted some of his journalistic work in *Reflections and Comments, 1865–95* (1895).

Sources

Armstrong, William M. *E. L. Godkin: A Biography.* Albany: State University of New York Press, 1978.

Godwin, Parke (1816–1904) *journalist, editor, biographer*

Born in Paterson, New Jersey, Parke Godwin graduated from Princeton University and then took a job with the New York *Post,* where he worked for the editor William Cullen BRYANT, who would later become his father-in-law. Godwin was at heart a transcendentalist (see TRANSCENDENTALISM) and a reformer, and he used the *Post,* and later the Fourierist (see FOURIERISM) journal *THE HARBINGER,* as outlets for his views. He also published a variety of polemical pamphlets and monographs, including *Democracy, Constructive and Pacific* (1844), and *A Popular View of the Doctrines of Charles Fourier* (1844). Between 1846 and 1847, Godwin also published a translation of the autobiography of the German romantic writer Johan Wolfgang von Goethe (1749–1832) and, in 1866, a biography of Bryant, whom he had succeeded as the *Post*'s editor in chief in 1876. In 1881 Godwin left the *Post* to become editor of the *Commercial Advertiser.*

Goodrich, Samuel Griswold (Peter Parley) (1793–1860) *writer of children's literature, editor*

Born in Connecticut, Samuel Griswold Goodrich made his mark in Boston as the publisher of the annual GIFT BOOK *The Token* (1828–42), which introduced Nathaniel HAWTHORNE to the reading public as the author of *TWICE-TOLD TALES,* some of which were printed in *The Token* for the first time. As "Peter Parley," Goodrich initiated juvenile literature into the mainstream, publishing more than 100 instructional and moralistic tales, beginning with *The Tales of Peter Parley About America* in 1827. He also published volumes of verse, prose sketches, advice to parents, and a periodical, *Parley's Magazine* (1833–44). His *Recollections of a Lifetime* (1856) describes his relationships with other writers, including Hawthorne, whom he had hired to help write the "Peter Parley" books.

Sources

Roselle, Daniel. *Samuel Griswold Goodrich, Creator of Peter Parley: A Study of His Life and Work.* Albany: State University of New York Press, 1968.

gothicism

Gothicism is a literary style prominent during the late 18th and early 19th centuries that emphasizes the grotesque, the mysterious, and the supernatural. The gothic strain in American literature stems from the English gothic novel, which often featured an intense, romantic hero with a fatal flaw, a doomed family, or a haunted house set in a atmosphere of evil and corruption. Edgar Allan *POE*'s "The Fall of the House of Usher" is a masterpiece of the genre in America. Roderick Usher and his sister Madeleine live in a crumbling mansion that symbolizes the decay often associated with the gothic tradition, which originated in England with novels such as Horace Walpole's (1717–97) *Castle of Otranto* (1764). Gothicism suggests the idea of a curse, often a family crime, that must be expiated. The protagonist of Nathaniel HAWTHORNE's *THE HOUSE OF THE SEVEN GABLES* (1851) labors under just such a Puritan curse.

Sources

Fiedler, Leslie. *Love and Death in the American Novel.* Rev. ed. New York: Anchor Books, 1992.

MacAndrew, Elizabeth. *The Gothic Tradition in Fiction.* New York: Columbia University Press, 1979.

Graham's Magazine periodical

What was to become one of the nation's foremost monthlies started out in 1826 as an unambitious, fairly eclectic Philadelphia magazine named the *Casket.* In 1839, however, it was taken over by George Rex Graham (1813–94), who quickly merged it with *Burton's GENTLEMAN'S MAGAZINE* and solicited contributions from prominent authors. From 1841 to 1842 Edgar Allan POE acted as the magazine's literary editor, increasing circulation from 5,000 to 37,000 with such contributions as "The Murders in the Rue Morgue" and "The Masque of the Red Death." After Poe was succeeded by Rufus W. Griswold (1815–57) and other editors, *Graham's* continued to publish serious work by the likes of James Russell LOWELL, William Cullen BRYANT, Henry Wadsworth LONGFELLOW, and James Fenimore COOPER. *Graham's* paid well, and it was also known for its colored fashion plates and engravings. After 1850, however, circulation began to drop as more competitors—in particular, *Harper's New Monthly Magazine* (see *HARPER'S MONTHLY MAGAZINE*)—appeared on the scene.

Grant, Ulysses Simpson (1822–1885) *eighteenth president of the United States, memoirist*

Born in rural Ohio, Ulysses S. Grant attended the U.S. Military Academy at West Point, where his indifferent academic performance nonetheless resulted in an officer's commission. But Grant disliked military life, and after serving in the MEXICAN WAR he retired to pursue a variety of failed careers in business. With the advent of the CIVIL WAR he entered the Union army, where he was given the rank of brigadier general and assigned to the western theater of combat. After a successful campaign in western Kentucky, he rose to the rank of major general. Several more victories brought him the nickname "Unconditional Surrender" Grant and the attention of President Abraham LINCOLN, who appointed Grant commander in chief of the Union forces in March 1864. Grant's campaign of attrition finally wore down the Confederate forces, and on April 9, 1865, he accepted General Robert E. Lee's (1807–70) surrender at Appomattox Courthouse, Virginia, ending the war.

Grant's unrivaled postwar popularity, together with his opposition to the highly unpopular administration of President Andrew Johnson (1808–75), made him the inevitable Republican nominee in the election of 1868. Grant was reelected in 1872, but both of his administrations were marred by cronyism and corruption. The Northern postwar period known as the GILDED AGE came to an abrupt end with the economic depression of 1873, further darkening Grant's reputation.

Grant himself lost virtually all his wealth in a speculative investment scheme. Samuel CLEMENS (Mark Twain), then the head of a successful publishing house, suggested Grant could recoup his losses by writing his memoirs. Suffering from throat cancer, Grant completed his two-volume *Personal Memoirs* (1885–86), which were published after his death. Generally acknowledged as one of the greatest autobiographies ever written, the work won praise from the critics for its candor and yielded enormous royalties for his widow.

Sources

Memoirs and Selected Letters: Personal Memoirs of U.S. Grant, Selected Letters 1839–1865. New York: Library of America, 1990.

Simpson, Brooks D. *Ulysses S. Grant: Triumph Over Adversity, 1822–1865.* Boston: Houghton Mifflin, 2000.

Ulysses S. Grant: Essays and Documents. Edited by David L. Wilson and John Y. Simon. Carbondale: Southern Illinois University Press, 1981.

Greeley, Horace (1811–1872) *journalist, reformer*

Born in Amherst, New Hampshire, Horace Greeley served an early newspaper apprenticeship in his home state before traveling to NEW YORK CITY, where he worked for a time as a printer before founding his own weekly, *The New Yorker,* in

1834. Greeley also edited two periodicals for the conservative Whig Party, and in 1841 he combined one of then, *Log Cabin,* with the *New Yorker* to found the *NEW-YORK TRIBUNE,* the newspaper he edited for the next 30 years.

The success of the *Tribune* owed much to Greeley's editorials, which proved highly influential in the northern and western parts of the country. In his column Greeley advocated for organized labor and against monopolies and boosted the cause of a homestead law with his memorable phrase, "Go West, Young Man!" A reformer, Greeley favored temperance, women's suffrage (see SUFFRAGISM), and the protective tariff meant to foster domestic production of goods. A committed Fourierist (see FOURIERISM), he helped found the NORTH AMERICAN PHALANX. Although he opposed many of Abraham LINCOLN's policies, Greeley was instrumental in securing Lincoln's presidential nomination. Greeley was also an ardent abolitionist (see ABOLITIONISM), yet he opposed the stringent measures imposed on the South after the CIVIL WAR by the Radical Republicans who controlled Congress.

In 1872 Greeley was nominated for the presidency by the Liberal Republican and Democratic parties, but he was defeated by Ulysses S. GRANT. His disappointment over his loss of the election, coupled with his wife's death, is said to have driven him insane.

Greeley published several nonfiction works, among them a two-volume history of abolitionism and the Civil War, *The American Conflict* (1864–66); and a memoir, *Recollections of a Busy Life* (1868). He himself appears as a character in Irving BACHELLER's novel, *Eben Holden* (1900).

Sources

Cross, Coy F. *Go West, Young Man!: Horace Greeley's Vision for America.* Albuquerque: University of New Mexico Press, 1995.

Lunde, Erik S. *Horace Greeley.* Boston: Twayne, 1981.

Schulze, Suzanne. *Horace Greeley: A Bio-Bibliography.* New York: Greenwood Press, 1992.

Greene, Sarah Pratt McLean

See MCLEAN, SARAH PRATT.

Grey, Zane (1875–1939) *novelist*

Born in Zanesville, Ohio, and an 1896 graduate of the University of Pennsylvania, Zane Grey intended to be a dentist before having a change of heart in 1904, when he took up writing. An inheritor of the DIME NOVEL tradition, he wrote about outdoor life but made his mark as a writer of WESTERNS. His first popular success, *Riders of the Purple Sage* (1912), was his best-selling work, but he wrote more than 60 books, some of them published posthumously and many adapted for motion pictures.

Sources

Jackson, Carlton. *Zane Grey.* Boston: Twayne, 1989.

Kimball, Arthur G. *Ace of Hearts: The Westerns of Zane Grey.* Fort Worth: Texas Christian University Press, 1993.

Grimké, Angelina Emily

See GRIMKÉ, SARAH MOORE.

Grimké, Sarah Moore (1792–1873) and Angelina Emily Grimké (1805–1879) *pamphleteers*

Born into a family of wealthy South Carolina planters, the sisters Sarah and Angelina Grimké displayed a penchant for the unconventional. Although they received no formal education, Sarah taught herself law and was enraged when she was denied an opportunity to practice her chosen profession. Both sisters were devoted to the cause of ABOLITIONISM, and in 1836 Angelina published her *Appeal to the Christian Women of the South,* beseeching her peers to work for the abolition of slavery.

While in their 20s, the Grimkés renounced their parents' values and moved to Philadelphia, where they became Quakers and feminist antislavery leaders. They were exceptionally bold and effective orators and prolific pamphleteers. In 1837 Angelina also published an *Appeal to the Women of the Nominally Free States* and, when attacked in print by the educator Catharine BEECHER for her unwomanly outspokenness, responded with a pamphlet entitled *Letters to Catharine Beecher in Reply to an Essay on Slavery and Abolitionism Addressed to A.E. Grimké.*

In fact, although both Grimkés equated slavery with sexism, Sarah was more dedicated than her sister to the cause of women's rights. It was she who wrote the first women's rights pamphlet to appear in the United States, *Letters on the Equality of the Sexes and the Condition of Women* (1838). Sarah never married, and when Angelina did, in 1838, Sarah moved in with her sister and new brother-in-law, the antislavery orator Theodore Weld. Retired from public life, the Grimkés kept up an active commitment to FEMINISM: At the ages of 75 and 68, respectively, they led a band of suffragists on a march through a snowstorm.

Sources

Lerner, Gerda. *The Grimké Sisters from South Carolina: Rebels against Slavery.* Boston: Houghton Mifflin, 1967.

The Public Years of Sarah and Angelina Grimké: Selected Writings, 1835–1839. Edited by Larry Ceplair. New York: Columbia University Press, 1989.

Yellin, Jean Fagan. *Women and Sisters: The Antislavery Feminists in American Culture.* New Haven, Conn.: Yale University Press, 1989.

Hale, Edward Everett (1822–1909) *short story writer, memoirist*

Born in Boston, Edward Everett Hale graduated from Harvard in 1839 and became a Unitarian minister who at the end of his life served as chaplain of the United States Senate. In between, he wrote prolifically for magazines. His output included literary criticism (he was the first to write warmly about Walt WHITMAN's *LEAVES OF GRASS*) and short stories, the most famous of which, "The Man Without a Country," first appeared anonymously in the *ATLANTIC MONTHLY* in 1863. The protagonist of the tale, Philip Nolan, a naval officer who makes a wish never to see America again, was Hale's invention, but he quickly became a national myth—partly because of the realism of Hale's storytelling and partly because of the intensity of patriotic feeling during the CIVIL WAR. Hale also published novels, memoirs, and scholarly works, the most significant of which was *Franklin in France* (1887–88).

Sources

Adams, John R. *Edward Everett Hale.* Boston: Twayne, 1977.

Hale, Lucretia Peabody (1820–1900) *writer of children's literature, novelist*

Born in Boston, Lucretia Hale was Edward Everett HALE's sister, and like the rest of her family, she was a Unitarian (see UNITARIANISM). Educated at Elizabeth PEABODY's progressive school, Hale quickly grew interested in FEMINISM, social work, and education. Her career, however, was as a writer. Initially she wrote for the *ATLANTIC MONTHLY*, and then collaborated with her brother Edward on two novels. But it was only when she published *The Peterkin Papers* (1880), a series of absurdist sketches for children, that she made a name for herself. These stories have proven to be so popular that they have never gone out of print.

Hale, Sarah Josepha Buell (1788–1879) *editor, polemical writer*

Born near Newport, New Hampshire, Sarah J. Hale ran a private school from 1806 until 1813, when she married. Her husband died nine years later, leaving her with five children and no means of support. She turned to writing domestic poetry—including "Mary Had a Little Lamb"—and prose, winning an award for her novel *Northwood* (1827). Then, in 1828, she began a long career as an editor, working at the *Ladies' Magazine* (later *GODEY'S LADY'S BOOK*) until 1877. Owing to the popularity of the magazine, Hale gained enormous influence, and she used it to promote education reforms for women and female property ownership. She wrote or edited more than 50 books, perhaps the most important of which was the 1854 *Women's Record*, an encyclopedia of "distinguished women" from "the creation to A.D. 1854."

Sources

Okker, Patricia. *Our Sister Editors: Sarah J. Hale and the Tradition of Nineteenth-Century American Women Editors.* Athens: University of Georgia Press, 1995.

Tonkovich, Nicole. *Domesticity with a Difference: The Nonfiction of Catharine Beecher, Sarah J. Hale, Fanny Fern, and Margaret Fuller.* Jackson: University Press of Mississippi, 1997.

Halleck, Fitz-Greene (1790–1867) *poet*

Born in Guilford, Connecticut, Fitz-Greene Halleck was a banker and secretary to the tycoon John Jacob Astor (1763–1848). He was also a literary man by avocation and a leading member of the KNICKERBOCKER SCHOOL. With Joseph Rodman Drake (1795–1820) he coauthored the "Croaker Papers" (1819), a series of comic verses that appeared in the New York *Evening Post* and made his reputation. Drake's death in 1830 occasioned one of Halleck's best known verses, an elegy that begins: "Green be the turf above thee, friend of my better days." Two other long poems, *Fanny* (1819), and *Marco Bozzaris* (1825)—the first a burlesque of Lord Byron and the second an admiring imitation—are among Halleck's best work.

Sources

Hallock, John W. *The American Byron.* Madison: University of Wisconsin Press, 2000.

Harbinger, The (1845–1849) *periodical*

This weekly journal, edited by George RIPLEY, was for the first two years of its existence the official publication of BROOK FARM. Fourierist in orientation (see FOURIERISM), *The Harbinger* was dedicated to "the examination and discussion of the great questions in social science, politics, literature, and the arts, which command the attention of all believers in the progress and elevation of humanity." It published writers like James Russell LOWELL; John Greenleaf WHITTIER; Horace GREELEY; and John S. Dwight (1813–93), whose music criticism made *The Harbinger* the leading outlet in the nation for this branch of journalism. After the Brook Farm experiment ended, Ripley and Parke GODWIN edited the journal in New York City, where it became connected with the American Union of Associationists, another group of like-minded idealists.

Sources

Delano, Sterling F. *The Harbinger and New England Transcendentalism: A Portrait of Associationism in America.* Rutherford, N.J.: Fairleigh Dickinson University Press, 1983.

Harland, Henry (Sidney Luska) (1861–1905) *editor, novelist, short story writer*

Some sources indicate that Henry Harland was born in Russia of American parents and educated at Harvard University. Others indicate that this background was the invention of Harland himself, a native New Yorker who attended City College. Whichever is true, he began his literary career using the pen name Sidney Luska, under which he produced several rather artificial, easily dismissed novels of Jewish immigrant life with such titles as *The Yoke of the Torah* (1887) and *My Uncle Florimond* (1888).

In 1889 Harland moved to Paris where, under his own name, he published in quick succession a collection of short stories and four novels. In 1890 he moved to England and came into his own as a man of letters. Associating himself with the fin-de-siècle aesthetic movement, he helped found and was the original editor of the highly influential *The Yellow Book* (1894–97), a journal of arts and letters that was a primary outlet for the productions of art-for-art's-sake adherents such as the caricaturist Max Beerbohm (1872–1956) and the art nouveau artist Aubrey Beardsley (1872–98). During his years in England Harland also produced a number of frothy romances, the best known of which is *The Cardinal's Snuff Box* (1900), about the love affair of an English novelist and an Italian duchess.

Sources

Beckson, Karl E. *Henry Harland, His Life and Work.* London: The Eighteen Nineties Society, 1978.

Harper's Bazar *periodical*

This magazine, founded in 1867 by the New York publishing house of Harper & Brothers, began as a weekly for women. Meant as a complement to *HARPER'S WEEKLY*, the periodical at first published articles by some of the country's leading thinkers and writers. In 1901 it became a monthly publication, and in 1913 it was published by William Randolph HEARST, who transformed it into a magazine concentrating on women's fashion. In 1920 the spelling of the magazine's name was changed to *Harper's Bazaar.*

Sources

Blum, Stella Cimp. *Victorian Fashions and Costumes from Harper's Bazar, 1867–1898.* New York: Dover Publications, 1974.

Harper's Monthly Magazine *periodical*

Like *HARPER'S WEEKLY*, this magazine was founded by Fletcher Harper of the New York publishing firm Harper & Brothers. It began in 1850 by reprinting serial British fiction—initially pirated—by such luminaries as Charles Dickens and Anthony Trollope. In a decade *Harper's* circulation had grown to 200,000, an unprecedentedly large number for an expensive magazine (a year's subscription cost $3). Gradually the magazine introduced material written by American authors—originally in its internal "departments" such as "The Easy Chair," which commented on the arts and public affairs. In 1869, after Henry M. Mills became its editor and the magazine was challenged by *SCRIBNER'S MONTHLY*, *Harper's* published an increasing amount of American literature by such diverse authors as Herman MELVILLE, Sarah Orne JEWETT, and Mark Twain (Samuel CLEMENS). In 1885, after William Dean HOWELLS occupied the "Editor's Study" department, the magazine endorsed realistic fiction (see REALISM). Although Howells left the department in 1894, by century's end *Harper's* had made a commitment to addressing contemporary problems, publishing contributions by Woodrow WILSON and Theodore ROOSEVELT in a magazine that had also taken on a new moniker: *Harper's New Monthly Magazine* (a name that would last for a quarter of a century).

After World War I the magazine took on a markedly more liberal tone, but its quality began to slide. In the 1960s the periodical—then called simply *Harper's Magazine*—became the property of the *Minneapolis Tribune.* By the early 1980s it was nearly defunct, but it was saved by the MacArthur Foundation, which purchased *Harper's* and turned it into a not-for-profit endeavor.

Harper's Weekly *periodical*

Fletcher Harper, of the New York publishing firm Harper & Brothers, was responsible for founding what he thought of as this "Journal of Civilization" in 1857. Although, like the older *HARPER'S MONTHLY,* it carried serialized fiction, *Harper's Weekly* was primarily a journal of opinion intent on influencing national politics. It was known for its finely executed illustrations—first woodcuts, then halftones. Drawings by Thomas NAST helped bring the CIVIL WAR into the homes of average Americans, and Nast's 1871 campaign against the New York politician Boss Tweed and his corrupt circle, known as the Tweed Ring, marked a high point in American political cartooning. Charles Dana GIBSON's drawings of the idealized "Gibson Girl' also appeared here. The magazine was never profitable, and in 1914 it was sold to the McClure organization, which two years later sold it in turn. In 1916 *Harper's Weekly* was merged with *THE INDEPENDENT.*

Sources

Konwenhoven, John A. *Adventures of America 1857–1900; A Pictorial Record from Harper's Weekly.* New York: Harper, 1938.

Harris, Frank (1856–1931) *biographer, journalist*

Born in Ireland, Frank Harris came to the United States in 1870. He worked a variety of odd jobs, including that of cowboy, an adventure he would later describe in his memoir *My Reminiscence As a Cowboy* (1930). Harris attended the University of Kansas and gained admission to the Kansas state bar, but he found the practice of law uninspiring and returned to Europe. In England he served as editor of several magazines and became friendly with Oscar Wilde (1854–1900), George Bernard Shaw (1856–1950), and Max Beerbohm (1872–1956). He also wrote some short stories and novels as well as a play, *Mr. and Mrs. Daventry* (1900), which some claim to be Wilde's work.

Back in America Harris continued his journalism, but his pro-German stance during World War I caused his departure from *Pearson's Magazine* and from the United States. Taking up residence in France, Harris published a notorious biography of his friend Oscar Wilde; a series of inaccurate sketches of other acquaintances, *Contemporary Portraits* (1915–27); and then his own three-volume scandalous (and probably exaggerated) "autobiography," *My Life and Loves* (1923–27). Sexually explicit material in this last work caused it to be banned in the United States and England for decades, but it is the work for which he is remembered, despite other, more serious literary endeavors.

Sources

Bain, Linda Morgan. *Evergreen Adventurer: The Real Frank Harris.* London: Research Publishing Co., 1975.

Brome, Vincent. *Frank Harris: The Life and Loves of a Scoundrel.* New York: T. Yoseloff, 1960.

Pearsall, Robert B. *Frank Harris.* New York: Twayne, 1970.

Pullar, Philippa. *Frank Harris: A Biography.* London: Hamilton, 1975.

Harris, George Washington (Sut Lovingood) (1814–1869) *humorist*

Born in Pennsylvania, Harris held jobs as, variously, a jeweler, a Tennessee River steamboat pilot, and a railroad superintendent before he found his niche as a political writer and dialect humorist. He is best known for the newspaper and magazine pieces collected as *Sut Lovingood: Yarns Spun by a "Nat'ral Born Durn'd Fool"* (1867). This collection of TALL TALES and humorous OLD SOUTHWEST pieces became immensely popular and was reprinted many times.

Sources

Caron, James E., and M. Thomas Inge, eds. *Sut Lovingood's Nat'ral Born Yarnspinner: Essays on George Washington Harris.* Tuscaloosa: University of Alabama Press, 1996.

Harris, Joel Chandler (1848–1908) *short story writer, novelist, journalist*

Joel Chandler Harris was born in Georgia, and at the age of 13 he was apprenticed to the printer of a weekly called *The Countryman,* which was published at Turnwold, a Georgia plantation. At Turnwold, Harris received some formal education from the publisher's son and even published some of his own work anonymously in the newspaper. He left Turnwold when he was 15 and worked first for newspapers in Macon, New Orleans, and Savannah. In 1876 he joined the staff of the Atlanta *Constitution,* with which he would remain associated for the next 30 years.

Harris began his career at the *Constitution* writing humorous short pieces that featured African Americans and African-American dialect, with which he had become familiar at Turnwold. Three years later, inspired by an article about African-American FOLKLORE, Harris invented the character who would make him famous: Uncle Remus, who made his debut in the story "Negro Folklore. The Story of Mr. Rabbit and Mr. Fox, as Told by Uncle Remus." This story first appeared in the *Constitution* on July 20, 1879; it would later form the introduction to Harris's first collection of stories, *Uncle Remus, His Songs and His Sayings* (1880).

Harris's Uncle Remus stories were among the first and best in the school of black folk literature. Harris's ear for the spoken word and his sophisticated use of Uncle Remus as a narrator turned what had been a simple folk tale into art. Uncle Remus won immediate popularity, and Harris capitalized on it by publishing the classic "Brer Rabbit, Brer Fox, and the Tar Baby" in the *Constitution* on November 16, 1879. Numerous tales featuring Uncle Remus—some written for a juvenile audience—followed, eventually giving rise to more than seven collections. In 1907 Harris and his son Julian founded *Uncle Remus's Magazine*, which was later merged with *Home Magazine*.

Harris also published numerous other stories, novellas, and two novels that feature Georgia settings but not Uncle Remus. Perhaps the best of these is *Mingo and Other Sketches in Black and White* (1884), in which Harris explored the relationship between whites and blacks and the disparity between the Southern aristocracy and its middle class. Together with his folk tales, they help make Harris one of the primary practitioners in the LOCAL COLOR movement. In later times, however, he fell out of favor with some readers and critics who found his broad characterization of African Americans racist.

Sources

Bickley, Bruce R., ed. *Critical Essays on Joel Chandler Harris.* Boston: G. K. Hall, 1981.

———. *Joel Chandler Harris.* Boston: Twayne, 1978.

Brasch, Walter M. *Brer Rabbit, Uncle Remus, and the "Cornfield Journalist": The Tale of Joel Chandler Harris.* Macon, Ga.: Mercer University Press, 2000.

Cousins, Paul M. *Joel Chandler Harris: A Biography.* Baton Rouge: Louisiana State University Press, 1968.

Harte, Francis Brett (1836–1902) *editor, short story writer, novelist*

Born in Albany, New York, Francis Harte was largely self-educated but still managed to publish his first literary work, a poem, in *The Sunday Morning Atlas* when he was just 11 years old. In 1854 he and his sister sailed to San Francisco to join their mother. In California, Harte followed a number of pursuits—teaching, working an unsuccessful gold mining claim, perhaps even serving as a guard for the Pony Express—before finding his true métier. He entered the field of journalism with a piece entitled "The Valentine," which appeared in *The Golden Era* in March 1857 under the name Bret Harte—his first use of that moniker.

Harte published steadily—first humorous sketches, then poetry, and finally the short stories that would make him famous. Together with the newspaperman Charles H. Webb (1834–1905), Harte started *The Californian* in 1864, where many of his pieces would appear, and in 1868 he became editor of the *OVERLAND MONTHLY*. Harte stayed in that post for the next two years, using the magazine as an outlet for some of his most celebrated LOCAL COLOR stories, including "The Luck of Roaring Camp" (1868), a story about the spiritual transformation of a frontier gold-mining settlement under the spell of an orphaned child (probably the first true piece of local color literature); and "The Outcasts of Poker Flat" (1869), a heady mix of Wild West humor and 19th-century sentimentalism featuring a group of ne'er-do-wells and a naive young couple. When his story collection, *The Luck of Roaring Camp and Other Sketches*, was published in 1870, Harte became famous nationwide.

In 1871 Harte moved back east after accepting a handsome offer from the *ATLANTIC MONTHLY*, which gave him $10,000 per year for his contributions. Unfortunately, Harte proved incapable of further invention, and when the magazine grew weary of his sentimentality and what it called Harte's "unmoral treatment of immoral subjects," the *Atlantic Monthly* did not renew his contract. Soon Harte was in dire financial straits from which neither a lecture tour nor publication of a novel, *Gabriel Conroy* (1875–76), could save him. Like some other writers who failed to make a living from their craft—including Nathaniel HAWTHORNE and Herman MELVILLE—Harte sought a government appointment, and in 1878 he served as U.S. consul at Crefeld in Prussia, then as consul in Glasgow, Scotland, from 1880 to 1885. He lived the remainder of his life in London, where he worked more or less as a hack writer, recirculating ideas from his earlier work about California and producing nothing of lasting merit. Still, he is remembered as the original practitioner of the local color movement, for having made San Francisco a literary capital, and for serving as the leader of a group of Western writers that included his friend and sometime-collaborator Mark Twain (Samuel CLEMENS).

Sources

Nissen, Axel. *Bret Harte: Prince and Pauper.* Jackson: University Press of Mississippi, 2000.

O'Connor, Richard. *Bret Harte: A Biography.* Boston: Little, Brown, 1966.

Scharnhorst, Gary. *Bret Harte: Opening the American Literary West.* Norman: University of Oklahoma Press, 2000.

Hawthorne, Julian (1846–1934) *novelist, historian, biographer*

The son of Nathaniel HAWTHORNE, Julian Hawthorne was born in Boston but spent much of his early life abroad when his father was engaged in foreign service. In addition to writing books about his famous family, such as *Nathaniel Hawthorne and His Wife* (1884) and *Hawthorne and His Circle* (1903), Julian Hawthorne was an author in his own right. His first popular fiction was the melodramatic novel *Bressant* (1873), which was followed by many other works of fiction, as well as an autobiography and a memoir.

Sources

Bassan, Maurice. *Hawthorne's Son: The Life and Literary Career of Julian Hawthorne.* Columbus: Ohio State University Press, 1970.

Hawthorne, Nathaniel (1804–1864) *short story writer, novelist*

Born in Salem, Massachusetts, Nathaniel Hawthorne descended from a distinguished Puritan family, including a judge who had presided at the Salem witchcraft trials. After his father died in 1808, Nathaniel's mother brought up her son in virtual seclusion, marking him with a lifelong solitary streak and brooding temperament. An imaginative child, Hawthorne immersed himself in romances and poetry. He graduated from Bowdoin College in 1825 and returned to Salem to write his first tales, many of them symbolic and allegorical and set in colonial New England.

Hawthorne's first significant work was *TWICE-TOLD TALES*, first published in 1837 and expanded in 1842. Many of his most important stories appeared in this volume, including "The Maypole of Merrymount," "Endicott and the Red Cross," "The Minister's Black Veil," "Dr. Heidegger's Experiment," "The Gray Champion," and "The Ambitious Guest." In these early works, as in his mature novels, there is always some hint of the supernatural, an evocation of incidents that challenge the rationality of the modern mind. Hawthorne was much impressed by the Puritan religious consciousness and its belief that human reason was fallible and even misguided. Although he also revealed the narrow-mindedness and antidemocratic tendencies of Puritanism, his work is always informed by a tension between past and present values. Compared to Puritan convictions, the beliefs of 19th-century characters seem somewhat shallow. Hawthorne recognizes the value of science, for example, but he also sees in science's claims a human pride that would defeat itself.

The publication of *Twice-Told Tales* initiated a new phase in Hawthorne's life, taking him out of his isolation of the late 1820s and early 1830s. He edited and wrote for such publications as *American Magazine of Useful and Entertaining Knowledge* (1836); and he wrote books for children, including *Grandfather's Chair* (1841), *Famous Old People* (1841), *Liberty Tree* (1841), and *Biographical Stories for Children* (1842). His work in the Boston Custom House (1839–41) was explored in the introduction to his masterpiece, *THE SCARLET LETTER*. Indeed, this government job made him acutely conscious of the common run of humanity that he had largely ignored in his earlier reclusive period.

Hawthorne's other great change was to attempt a life at BROOK FARM, the Utopian community set up by several transcendentalists (see TRANSCENDENTALISM). Altogether he spent about six months there, but he found life in a commune incompatible with his aloof temperament. Indeed, the idea of establishing an ideal community later struck him as rather absurd, if well-meaning, and he dealt shrewdly with this passion to build model communities in *The Blithedale Romance* (1852).

After he left Brook Farm Hawthorne married Sophia Peabody, who successfully encouraged him to be more outgoing. He also produced some of his greatest short stories, such as "Young Goodman Brown," "The Celestial Railroad," "Rappaccini's Daughter," "The Artist of the Beautiful," "The Birthmark," and "Roger Malvin's Burial"—all of which were collected in *Mosses from an Old Manse* (1846). It was this volume that inspired Herman MELVILLE to rank Hawthorne as a genius comparable to Shakespeare. Melville spoke of Hawthorne's power of blackness, for he saw in Hawthorne a willingness to confront the dark depths of human nature in a way that no other American writer had ventured.

Hawthorne confirmed Melville's hopes with the publication of *The Scarlet Letter,* a work of surpassing beauty and moral depth. Hawthorne created a great romantic heroine in Hester PRYNNE, and yet the novel also provides one of the greatest critiques of romanticism. Toward Puritanism—always his main subject—Hawthorne is both highly critical and admiring. The very strictness of the Puritans, which strikes at the heart of individual exuberance and creativity, is also portrayed as a spiritual discipline lacking in those who would deny the claims and obligations of religion.

Hawthorne never equaled, let alone surpassed, the achievement of *The Scarlet Letter,* although *THE HOUSE OF THE SEVEN GABLES* (1852) and *The Blithedale Romance* are considerable achievements that demonstrate his capacity to make exquisite moral discriminations. He also continued to produce classic short fiction like "Ethan Brand" in *The Snow-Image and Other Twice-Told Tales* (1851). He wrote another charming book for children, *Tanglewood Tales* (1852).

In the 1850s, Hawthorne became involved in politics and in 1852 even wrote a campaign biography for his friend Franklin Pierce (1804–69). When Pierce was elected president, Hawthorne was given a diplomatic post in Liverpool. He would spend much of the 1850s in Europe, publishing his last complete novel, *The Marble Faun,* in 1860. Some critics see in this novel a decline in Hawthorne's creative powers, since much of it was reworked from travel journals. Nevertheless, in many ways the novel anticipates the international theme that Henry JAMES would brilliantly develop in his novels.

After he returned home in 1860, Hawthorne worked on a collection of essays, *Our Old Home* (1863), which is full of penetrating observations about his European experience. He was no longer able to complete any longer works of fiction, but fragments of his efforts have been published as *Septimus Felton* (1872), *The Dolliver Romance* (1876), *Dr. Grimshawe's Secret* (1883), and *The Ancestral Footstep* (1883).

Hawthorne's perceptive nonfiction has been collected in *Passages from the American Notebooks* (1868), *Passages from the English Notebooks* (1870), *Passages from the French and Italian Notebooks* (1871), and *The English Notebooks* (new edition in 1942).

Along with Edgar Allan POE, Hawthorne is credited with creating the first mature, fully realized American short stories. Poe seemed intent on portraying states of mind and what might be called an ontological dread; Hawthorne instead sought the moral underpinnings of society. His work can be read as the decay of Puritanism into ROMANTICISM, except that Hawthorne himself cannot be put clearly in either tradition: he had an affinity for both and could see both Puritanism and romanticism as incomplete in themselves. His work appeals to the modern skeptical mind because he is willing to face squarely the nature of human doubt. At the same time, he treats the human quest for perfection with enormous sympathy and expresses regret at the discovery that no heaven on earth is possible.

Sources

Baym, Nina. *The Shape of Hawthorne's Career.* Ithaca, N.Y.: Cornell University Press, 1977.

Bloom, Harold, ed. *Nathaniel Hawthorne.* New York: Chelsea House, 1986.

Miller, Edward Haviland. *Salem Is My Dwelling Place: A Life of Nathaniel Hawthorne.* Iowa City: University of Iowa Press, 1991.

Newman, Lea Bertani Vozar. *A Reader's Guide to the Short Stories of Nathaniel Hawthorne.* Boston: G. K. Hall, 1979.

Von Frank, Albert J., ed. *Critical Essays on Hawthorne's Short Stories.* Boston: G. K. Hall, 1991.

Haymarket Square Riot *historical event*

On May 4, 1886, a demonstration in support of the eight-hour working day, staged by a small group of anarchists in Haymarket Square in Chicago, swelled to a crowd of 1,500. When police attempted to disperse the demonstrators, a bomb exploded, causing the crowd to riot. Seven policemen were killed and 68 others wounded. Subsequently, eight anarchist leaders were tried and found guilty. Four of these individuals were hanged. The others were sent to prison, where one committed suicide. The trial aroused controversy, for there was no evidence that any of the eight had been involved with the bombing. Public pressure on Governor John Peter Altgeld (1847–1942) ultimately forced him to pardon the three remaining prisoners in 1893.

The Haymarket Riot was often used to discredit organized labor, but the anarchists had their defenders, among them Frank HARRIS, whose novel *The Bomb* (1908) presents a sympathetic picture of them. The riot would figure in other works of American literature, including Robert HERRICK's *The Memoirs of an American Citizen* (1905).

Sources

Avrich, Paul. *The Haymarket Tragedy.* Princeton, N.J.: Princeton University Press, 1984.

Hayne, Paul Hamilton (1830–1886) *poet, editor, biographer*

Born in Charleston, South Carolina, and educated at Charleston College, Paul Hamilton Hayne was a distinctly Southern poet considered the "last of the literary cavaliers." Prior to the CIVIL WAR, Hayne was known for his nature poetry. He contributed to the *SOUTHERN LITERARY MESSENGER* and worked on the staff of the *Southern Literary Gazette.* In 1857 he founded *Russell's Magazine,* named for the RUSSELL'S BOOKSTORE GROUP in Charleston. With Confederate secession, however, Hayne's magazine and literary orientation changed. During the war, poor health prevented Hayne from seeing more than limited service, but his powerful feelings about his native South were expressed in ardently patriotic verses. During General William Tecumseh Sherman's (1820–91) march to the sea in 1864, Hayne's home was destroyed. Retreating to a small estate amid the Georgia pines, Hayne continued to support his impoverished family with his writings, including such works as *Legends and Lyrics* (1872), *Lives of Robert Young Hayne and Hugh Swinton Legaré* (1878), and an edition of his friend Henry TIMROD's poems.

Sources

Moore, Rayburn S. *Paul Hamilton Hayne.* New York: Twayne, 1972.

Hearn, Lafcadio (Patricio Lafcadio Tessima Carlos Hearn) (1850–1904) *journalist, novelist, travel writer*

Born on the Greek island of Santa Maura, Lafcadio Hearn was the son of a British army surgeon and a local Greek woman; he was raised by relatives in Dublin, Ireland, and educated in England and France. In 1869 Hearn immigrated to the United States, where he lived for the next 18 years. From 1875 to 1878 he worked as a reporter for the *Cincinnati Commercial,* but he lost his job there over a scandal occasioned by his living with—and probably marrying—a mulatto woman. He subsequently moved to New Orleans, where he worked for the *New Orleans Item* (1878–81) and for the *New Orleans Times-Democrat* (1881–87) before leaving for the island of Martinique, where he wrote for *Harper's New Monthly Magazine.*

During these years Hearn published his first book, *One of Cleopatra's Nights* (1882), a translation of stories by the French writer Théophile Gautier (1811–72); *Stray Leaves from Strange Literature* (1884), a reconstruction of stories taken from exotic sources; *Gombo Zhêbes* (1885), a collection of Creole proverbs; and *Some Chinese Ghosts* (1887), a collection of Chinese legends. His travels to Grand Isle in Louisiana resulted in the novel *Chita: A Memory of Last Island* (1889). His residence in Martinique gave him material for *Two Years in the French West Indies* (1890) as well as a novel, *Yourma* (1890), a novel set during the island slave rebellion of 1848.

Also in 1890, Hearn did some hack work in New York City to raise money for a trip to Japan, where he would spend the remainder of his life. Marrying into a samurai family, Hearn took the name Koizumi Yakumo and became a Japanese citizen in 1895. He continued to write prolifically, but thereafter all his publications in one way or another concerned his adopted country. A year spent teaching in the small town of Matsue allowed him to observe closely the feudal customs he relates in *Glimpses of Unfamiliar Japan* (1894). During the decade he held the chair in English literature at the Imperial University of Tokyo, he published a dozen books detailing the look, smell, and feel of Japan. His collections of stories, such as *Out of the East* (1895), were often written in the form of essays. In *Japan: An Attempt at Interpretation* (1904), Hearn summarized his observations and feelings about the people with whom he finally found a home.

Sources

Hirakawa, Sukehiro, ed. *Rediscovering Lafcadio Hearn: Japanese Legends, Life & Culture.* Folkestone, Kent, England: Global Oriental, 1997.

Murray, Paul. *A Fantastic Journey: The Life and Literature of Lafcadio Hearn.* Folkestone, Kent, England: Japan Library, 1993.

Stevenson, Elizabeth. *The Grass Lark: A Study of Lafcadio Hearn.* New Brunswick, N.J.: Transaction Publishers, 1999.

Hearst, William Randolph (1863–1951) *journalist*

Born in San Francisco, William Randolp Hearst was the son of a mine operator and U.S. senator who also owned the San Francisco *Examiner.* In 1887 the younger Hearst took control of his father's newspaper, making such a success of the endeavor that he was able in 1895 to buy the New York *Morning Journal.* This was the start of what was to become one of the greatest newspaper chains the country has ever known.

Hearst's fiercest competitor was Joseph PULITZER, owner of the NEW YORK *WORLD*. In an effort to best Pulitzer, Hearst's newspapers developed a sensationalistic slant that came to be known as "yellow journalism." Yellow journalism was blamed for inciting war with Spain in 1898, but it helped Hearst succeed in his quest for a congressional seat from New York, which he held from 1903 to 1907. Later efforts to achieve public office failed: his 1905 and 1907 New York City mayoral campaigns floundered, as did a 1906 New York gubernatorial bid and an attempt, while serving in Congress, to obtain the Democratic presidential nomination.

Hearst's public life was equally colorful. His media empire—which eventually included motion picture studios, radio stations, popular magazines such as *COSMOPOLITAN* and *Good Housekeeping,* and some 30 newspapers—gave him the wealth to build an extravagant mansion, San Simeon, on a hilltop overlooking the Pacific Ocean in California. At San Simeon he housed his mistress, the actress Marion Davies, and played host to countless celebrities. When Hearst died in 1951 San Simeon was still unfinished, but its grandeur, together with its creator's controversial career as a public figure, had helped to inspire one of the most celebrated films of all time, Orson Welles's *Citizen Kane* (1940).

Sources

Mugridge, Ian. *The View from Xanadu: William Randolph Hearst and United States Foreign Policy.* Montreal: McGill-Queen's University Press, 1995.

Nasaw, David. *The Chief: The Life of William Randolph Hearst.* Boston: Houghton Mifflin, 2000.

Swanberg, W. A. *Citizen Hearst: A Biography of William Randolph Hearst.* New York: Scribner, 1961.

Hearth and Home *periodical*

This New York-based weekly began in 1868 as a source of agricultural information and literary entertainment for rural audiences. Its early editors included Harriet Beecher STOWE, Mary Mapes DODGE, and Frank R. STOCKTON. The magazine went into a decline until it was rescued by Edward EGGLESTON, who not only took over as literary editor but also contributed his novel *The Prairie Schoolmaster* (1870–71) as a serial publication. The work proved to be highly popular and saved *Hearth and Home,* which went on to publish work by Rebecca Harding DAVIS, Louisa May ALCOTT, and Edward Everett HALE. The magazine folded in 1875.

Helicon Home Colony (Helicon Hall) *location*

This experiment in communal living was founded in 1906 near Englewood, New Jersey, by Upton Sinclair (1878–1968) with royalties from his muckraking novel *The Jungle* (1906). Residents were mostly young, married, unknown writers; Sinclair Lewis (1885–1951), having enjoyed much public attention, was an exception. Notables such as one-time anarchist Emma Goldman (1869–1940), William JAMES, and John DEWEY visited. Journalists visited, too, but came away with reports that Helicon was little more than a "free-love nest." A suspicious fire destroyed the main building in 1907, after which the colony was abandoned.

Sources

Harris, Leon. *Upton Sinclair, American Rebel.* New York: Crowell, 1975.

Henry, John

See JOHN HENRY.

Henry, O.

See PORTER, WILLIAM SYDNEY.

Herrick, Robert (1868–1938) *novelist, short story writer*

Born in Cambridge, Massachusetts, and educated at Harvard, Robert Herrick taught in the English department at the University of Chicago for 30 years (1893–1923). During his years in academia and afterward, Herrick published a steady stream of novels and stories that analyzed the dilemma of man in modern, industrialized society and, in particular, the corrupting effects of materialism.

Herrick's first published work, a story entitled "The Man Who Wins" (1897), concerns a scientist caught in a dilemma between his sense of personal integrity and financial pressures. Similar themes would inform his subsequent work: In *The Common Lot* (1904), the protagonist is an architect who gives in to greed when he designs a shoddy tenement that goes up in flames, destroying its inhabitants. His most widely read book, *The Master of the Inn* (1908), showcases the dire effects of modern urban life; and in *Chimes* (1926), Herrick attacks the business methods employed at the University of Chicago. In numerous other novels and stories he pursued similar themes, informing his work with a generosity and humanity that helped offset his stern idealism. Remembered primarily for its REALISM, Herrick's work has often been criticized for technical faults, resulting in novels that fail for want of structural unity.

Sources

Budd, Louis J. *Robert Herrick.* New York: Twayne, 1971.

Nevius, Blake. *Robert Herrick: The Development of a Novelist.* Berkeley: University of California Press, 1962.

Hickok, James Butler (Wild Bill Hickok) (1837–1876) *scout, U.S. marshal*

Born in Troy Grove, Illinois, James Hickok participated in the pro- and antislavery battle over "Bleeding Kansas" that preceded the CIVIL WAR. He also worked as a stagecoach driver in this period. During the war itself, he served as a Union scout. After the war, Hickok fought Indians under Generals William Armstrong Custer (1839–76) and Philip Sheridan (1831–88). He subsequently became a Kansas marshal, gaining a reputation as a gunfighter for his many successful encounters with frontier desperadoes. During 1872–73 he toured the East with Buffalo Bill's Wild West Show (see CODY, WILLIAM FREDERICK). He later returned to Deadwood, South Dakota, where he was shot to death in a saloon during a poker game. Hickok's life became the stuff of legend, and many books were written about him, including Frank J. Wilstach's *Wild Bill Hickok, the Prince of the Pistoleers* (1926); William E. Connelley's *Wild Bill and His Era* (1933); Mary Sandoz's *The Buffalo Hunters* (1954); and Joseph Ross's *They Called Him Wild Bill* (1964).

Sources

Rosa, Joseph G. *Wild Bill Hickok: The Man and His Myth.* Lawrence: University Press of Kansas, 1996.

Higginson, Thomas Wentworth (1823–1911) *editor, essayist*

Although Thomas Wentworth Higginson was an accomplished man of letters in his own right, he is best remembered for the editorial service he provided to another writer, the poet Emily DICKINSON. Born in Cambridge, Massachusetts, Higginson became a Unitarian minister (see UNITARIANISM) and ardent abolitionist (see ABOLITIONISM). During the CIVIL WAR he served as the colonel of the first regiment of African-American soldiers, an experience he would later describe in *Army Life in a Black Regiment* (1870). After the war he devoted himself to writing and to social reform, particularly in the areas of equal rights for African Americans and women's suffrage (see SUFFRAGISM).

Higginson came to know most of the major literary lights of his day, whom he would later recall in the autobiographical *Cheerful Yesterdays* (1898) and in biographies of Margaret FULLER (1884), John Greenleaf WHITTIER (1902), and Henry Wadsworth LONGFELLOW (1902). In 1862, after publishing an essay in *THE ATLANTIC MONTHLY* that urged writers to seek an audience for their work, he received an unsolicited letter from Dickinson, who wanted to know "if my Verse is alive?" Higginson encouraged her, and the two kept up a correspondence for many years. After her death Higginson and Dickinson's friend Mabel Loomis TODD edited two volumes of Dickinson's poetry. Celebrated for bringing such an original talent to the world's attention, Higginson has also been heavily criticized for amending Dickinson's eccentric style, which he considered "spasmodic."

Sources

Broaddus, Dorothy C. *Genteel Rhetoric: Writing High Culture in Nineteenth-Century Boston.* Columbia: University of South Carolina Press, 1999.

Edelstein, Tilden G. *Strange Enthusiasm: A Life of Thomas Wentworth Higginson.* New Haven, Conn.: Yale University Press, 1968.

Tuttleton, James W. *Thomas Wentworth Higginson.* Boston: Twayne, 1978.

historical novel *genre*

The American historical novel—primarily long fiction based on actual historical events—was born with the 19th century. Although arguably not a novel in the formal sense, Washington IRVING's *History of New York* (1809), which was begun as a burlesque of historical methods, developed into a more serious work that helped give the American people—perhaps for the first time—a sense of their own past. "Before the appearance of my work," Irving wrote, "the popular traditions of our city were unrecorded; the peculiar and racy customs and usages derived from our Dutch progenitors were unnoticed or regarded with indifference, or adverted to with a sneer." James Fenimore COOPER took up where Irving left off, transporting the ROMANTICISM of the Scottish novelist Sir Walter Scott (1771–1832) to American soil, where the rugged individualist Natty BUMPPO became the embodiment of the frontier spirit in the *LEATHER-STOCKING TALES.*

The historical novel in mid-century was dominated by two figures: Nathaniel HAWTHORNE and Herman MELVILLE. Hawthorne turned back to the nation's—and his own family's—past in order to produce two classics of American literature. *THE SCARLET LETTER* (1850) and *THE HOUSE OF THE SEVEN GABLES* (1851) both take as their subject the consequences of Puritan intolerance. In the famous "Custom House" essay that acts as a preface for *The Scarlet Letter,* Hawthorne spells out his own connection, through a direct forebear, to the Salem witchcraft trials that serve as a muted backdrop to his masterpiece. While Melville often looked beyond America's shores for subject matter, in *Israel Potter: His Fifty Years of Exile* (1855), he employed the modernist technique of basing a fictional narrative on the life of an historical figure, the eponymous Revolutionary War soldier. In South Carolina, around the same time, William Gilmore SIMMS was revisiting the colonial and Revolutionary periods in his Border Romances and Revolutionary Romances series, portraying these periods from a Southern perspective.

The CIVIL WAR gave Americans a sense of history—with a vengeance—and it was followed, almost inevitably, by the age of literary REALISM. But the war also gave rise to a surfeit of historical novels concerning the war. Perhaps the most notable of these works is Stephen CRANE's *The Red Badge of Courage* (1895), a naturalistic (see NATURALISM) account of daily life on the front lines written by a young man who had yet to see a day of battle. In contrast, the "carpetbagger" Albion W. TOURGÉE wrote about some of the evils of RECONSTRUCTION from firsthand experience in *A Fool's Errand* (1879) and *Bricks Without Straw* (1880). Most notoriously, perhaps, Reconstruction gave rise to Thomas DIXON's extremist Southern perspective, expressed in the trilogy that includes *The Leopard's Spots* (1902), *THE CLANSMAN* (1905), and *The Traitor* (1907).

As the postwar period itself faded into history, American literature began to fracture into regionalism, giving rise to the LOCAL COLOR movement, with its emphasis on what was close at hand. It would take another great war before great novels once again focused on the broad canvas of history.

Sources

Clark, Robert. *History and Myth in American Fiction, 1823–52.* New York: St. Martin's Press, 1984.

Gould, Philip. *Covenant and Republic: Historical Romance and the Politics of Puritanism.* New York: Cambridge University Press, 1996.

Kennedy, J. Gerald, and Daniel Mark, eds. *American Letters and the Historical Consciousness: Essays in Honor of Lewis P. Simpson.* Baton Rouge: Louisiana State University Press, 1987.

Hoffman, Charles Fenno (1806–1884) *editor, novelist, poet*

Born in New York City, Charles Fenno Hoffman was trained as a lawyer, but he quickly abandoned the law for literature. In addition to his contributions to such periodicals as *AMERICAN MONTHLY MAGAZINE, Knickerbocker Magazine,* and the NEW-YORK MIRROR—for all of which he served at various times as an editor—in 1835 Hoffman published an account of his journey across the Alleghenies and the prairies, *A Winter in the West.* He also wrote fiction, most notably *Greyslaer* (1840), an account of the KENTUCKY TRAGEDY, which was successfully adapted for the stage. Hoffman was also well known for his poetry, which was collected in the 1873 volume entitled simply *Poems.* Tragically, in 1849 Hoffman lost his mental bearings and was committed the following year to an institution; he was never to publish again.

Sources

Barnes, Homer F. *Charles Fenno Hoffman.* New York: Columbia University Press, 1930.

Holm, Saxe

See JACKSON, HELEN MARIA FISKE HUNT.

Holmes, Oliver Wendell (1809–1894) *poet, essayist, novelist, biographer*

A member of the Boston Brahmin class, Oliver Wendell Holmes was the son of the famed Cambridge, Massachusetts, Congregational clergyman Abiel Holmes (1763–1837) and a direct descendant of the Puritan poet Anne Bradstreet (c. 1612–72). Holmes himself first studied law before turning to medicine, receiving his medical degree from Harvard in 1836.

He had, however, already begun another career as a man of letters, publishing a series of reunion poems about his Harvard undergraduate class of 1829 as well as the poem "Old Ironsides" (1830), which proved to be a successful protest against the proposed destruction of the War of 1812 ironclad ship, the *Constitution.* In *THE NEW ENGLAND MAGAZINE* in 1831–32, Holmes published two pieces entitled "THE AUTOCRAT OF THE BREAKFAST TABLE," which were precursors of the famous essay series he published between 1858 and 1881 in *THE ATLANTIC MONTHLY.* However, after the 1836 publication of *Poems,* Holmes turned his attention to medicine.

Holmes was a professor of anatomy at Dartmouth College from 1838 to 1840, after which he published two important medical books. From 1847 until his retirement in 1882, he was Parkman Professor of Anatomy and Physiology at Harvard, where he also served for six years as dean of the medical school. It was not long, however, before his superior skills as a lecturer brought him before the general public on the lyceum circuit (see LYCEUM MOVEMENT). A staple of Boston society and club life, he was a noted conversationalist and composer of occasional verse, especially when it came to Harvard occasions; at least 108 of his 408 poems deal in some way with his alma mater. Holmes was also a humanitarian reformer and a militant Unitarian (see UNITARIANISM) who attacked the Calvinist faith of his fathers in his works, perhaps most notably in his poem "The Deacon's Masterpiece" (1858) and in his novel *Elsie Venner: A Romance of Destiny* (1861), an allegorical work meant "to test the doctrine of 'original sin' and human responsibility."

Like most of his later work, *Elsie Venner* first appeared in the *Atlantic Monthly.* After this magazine was founded in 1857—with a name bestowed on it by Holmes himself—Holmes's identity was primarily that of a man of letters. In addition to his verse and fiction, Holmes poured forth a seemingly endless series of essays, addresses, and lectures, as well as two biographies, one of Ralph Waldo EMERSON and another of John Lothrop MOTLEY. But it is for the *Autocrat* series—his own admixture of verse and narrative, conversation and soliloquy, anecdote and essay—that Holmes is best remembered.

Sources

Broaddus, Dorothy C. *Genteel Rhetoric: Writing High Culture in Nineteenth-Century Boston.* Columbia, S.C.: University of South Carolina Press, 1999.

Hoyt, Edwin P. *The Improper Bostonian: Dr. Oliver Wendell Holmes.* New York: Morrow, 1979.

Small, Miriam R. *Oliver Wendell Holmes.* New York: Twayne, 1963.

House of Mirth, The *Edith Wharton* (1905) *novel*

Edith Wharton was a member of the New York high society she mocked in this classic novel. Her heroine, Lily Bart, has beauty and charm but only a trace of the proper lineage. Literally a poor relation of those with whom she socializes, the 29-year-old Lily's only hope of survival in this refined atmosphere is to land a rich husband. Two of her most ardent suitors, however, prove unsuitable: Simon Rosedale is rich but vulgar and, even worse for Lily's prospects, Jewish; and Lawrence Selden, the man Lily truly loves, does not have enough money. Gambling rather desperately one night at a house party, Lily loses her head and her money to Gus Trenor, who nevertheless holds out some hope to her with his offer to invest the remainder of her modest capital. The returns she receives in fact comes out of his own pocket, but Lily does not realize this until it is too late. When Trenor suggests that she repay him with sexual favors, Lily runs away, vowing to return his money. But on yet another outing with the rich and powerful, Lily—through no fault of her own—is forced to give up her contest for social position, which had always been weighted against her. After she is falsely accused of an adulterous affair, she loses her last hope when her aunt and protector dies.

Forced to work for a living, Lily becomes a milliner, a job she quickly loses because of her incompetence. Poor and desperate, she briefly considers blackmail but discards the notion when she impulsively declares her love to Lawrence Selden. When Selden reacts rather cooly, having heard rumors about Lily's sexual involvement with Gus Trenor, Lily returns alone to her pathetic boardinghouse room and takes an overdose of the sedative to which she has become addicted. When Selden arrives later with the intention of asking Lily to marry him, he finds her already gone, her last act having been to sign over her aunt's entire bequest to Gus Trenor.

Widely admired for its portrayal of the late 19th-century New York high society that was Wharton's milieu, *The House of Mirth* has become a staple of American literature.

Sources

Ammons, Elizabeth, ed. *The House of Mirth: Authoritative Text, Backgrounds, and Contexts Criticism.* New York: Norton, 1990.

Goodman, Susan. Edith Wharton's Women: Friends & Rivals. Hanover, N.H.: University Press of New England, 1990.

Stange, Margit. *Personal Property: Wives, White Slaves, and the Market in Women.* Baltimore: Johns Hopkins University Press, 1998.

House of the Seven Gables, The *Nathaniel Hawthorne* (1851) *novel*

In this dark romance, Nathaniel HAWTHORNE drew upon his own background—more particularly, on an incident involving his great-grandfather, who acted as one of the judges at the Salem witchcraft trials—to explore the debilitating effects of the past upon the present. The efforts of Hawthorne's ancestor, Judge John Hathorne (Hawthorne had himself added a "w" to his surname, perhaps to differentiate himself from those who had gone before), had notoriously engendered a curse on the entire Hathorne family.

The House of the Seven Gables is itself cursed, blighting the lives of its inhabitants, the Pyncheons. When the novel opens, the house is already two centuries old, built on land fraudulently obtained by an ancestral Pyncheon from Wizard Maule, whom the former had helped to condemn to death for witchcraft. With his dying breath, Maule had issued a curse on the Pyncheons that continues to exert its influence over the family generations later. The current inhabitants of the house are the destitute spinster Hepzibah Pyncheon and her unmarried brother Clifford, who has just been released from prison after serving a 30-year term for the supposed murder of his rich uncle. The pair do not actually own House of the Seven Gables; it is the property of their hypocritical cousin, Judge Jaffrey Pyncheon, who was responsible for having Clifford wrongly imprisoned in order to cheat his cousin out of his inheritance. When Jaffrey suddenly dies, Holgrave, Clifford and Hepzibah's boarder, reveals that he is a descendant of the Wizard Maule and that both Jaffrey and the rich uncle were victims of Maule's curse, which has expired with the former's death. Clifford and Hepzibah are named as Jaffrey's heirs, and Holgrave, redeemed by his love for Phoebe, a Pyncheon country cousin, hands the deeds to the House of the Seven Gables over to its rightful owners.

Together with *The Scarlet Letter, The House of the Seven Gables* functions as a masterful portrayal of Hawthorne's—and New England's—spiritual history.

Sources

Robinson, Enders A. *Salem Witchcraft and Hawthorne's House of the Seven Gables.* Bowie, Md.: Heritage Books, 1992.

Rosenthal, Bernard, ed. *Critical Essays on Hawthorne's The House of the Seven Gables.* New York: G. K. Hall, 1995.

Hovey, Richard (1864–1900) *poet, playwright*

Born in Illinois, Richard Hovey was a precocious poet who published his first volume of verse at age 16. His first venture into drama came in 1891, when he published *Launcelot and Guinevere: A Poem in Dramas.* That same year he left for Europe, where he came under the influence of the French Symbolist poets and translated eight plays written by the Belgian dramatist Maurice Maeterlinck (1862–1949). Returning to the United States in 1892, he left for Nova Scotia and New Brunswick with his friend, the Canadian poet BLISS CARMAN. Inspired by the Canadian Maritimes, the two collaborated on three volumes of poetry that extolled the idea of the open road and the camaraderie of youth: *Songs from Vagabondia* (1894), *More Songs from Vagabondia* (1896), and *Last Songs from Vagabondia* (1901, published after Hovey's death).

The outbreak of the SPANISH-AMERICAN WAR in 1898 brought out a streak of American nationalism in Hovey, who published such poems as "Unmanifest Destiny" and "The Word of the Lord from Havana," which extolled American virtues, in the collection *Along the Trail* (1898). During this period he also renewed his interest in Arthurian legend, laboring over what was to be a three-volume cycle of poetic dramas inspired by Sir Thomas Malory's *Morte d'Arthur* (1485). Hovey's early death left all but a few fragments of this project—posthumously published as *The Holy Grail* (1907)—unfinished.

Sources

Linneman, William R. *Richard Hovey.* Boston: Twayne, 1976.

Macdonald, Allan H. *Richard Hovey: Man and Craftsman.* Durham, N.C.: Duke University Press, 1957.

Howard, Bronson Crocker (1842–1908) *journalist, playwright*

Born in Detroit, Bronson Howard came to New York in 1865. He worked as a newspaper reporter even after the success of his play *Saratoga* (1870), a pioneering farce. After *The Banker's Daughter* became a hit in 1878, Howard finally quit his day job, becoming the first American dramatist to earn a living entirely from play-writing. His most popular work was *Shenandoah* (1888), a CIVIL WAR drama. Howard himself was unconcerned about fame, but he took great pride in his craft, in 1891 organizing the American Dramatists' Club (later the Society of American Dramatists and Composers). He also worked actively to secure international copyright protection for American writers. Howard's *The Autobiography of a Play* (1914), a history of his hit play *The Banker's Daughter,* provides insight into both his craft and his character.

Sources

Howard, Bronson. *The Autobiography of a Play.* New York: Printed for the Dramatic Museum of Columbia University, 1914.

Howe, Edgar Watson (1853–1937) *journalist, novelist*

Born near Wabash, Indiana, E. W. Howe was primarily a small-town Midwestern journalist. From 1877 to 1911 he was the owner and editor of the Atchison, Kansas, *Daily Globe,* and in 1911 he founded *E. W. Howe's Monthly,* which lasted until his death. Nicknamed the "Sage of Potato Hill," Howe was famous during his lifetime for his pithy editorials, which were collected in such volumes as *Lay Sermons* (1911), *Ventures in Common Sense* (1919), and *The Indignations of E. W. Howe* (1933). But Howe was also a novelist, his best work being *The Story of a Country Town* (1883), a pioneering work of naturalistic fiction (see NATURALISM).

Sources

Bucco, Martin. *E. W. Howe.* Boise, Idaho: Boise State University Press, 1977.

Howe, Julia Ward (1819–1910) *poet, editor*

In 1843 New York City native Julia Ward married Samuel Gridley Howe, a prominent humanitarian and teacher of the blind, with whom she edited the Boston *Commonwealth,* an abolitionist paper (see ABOLITIONISM). After her husband's death, Howe continued her work on behalf of the abolitionist cause, also taking up women's suffrage, prison reform, and international peace. She was a prodigious worker, lecturing around the country and writing prolifically, turning out several volumes of verse as well as works such as *Sex and Education* (1874) and a life of Margaret FULLER (1883). Howe is best remembered, however, for "The Battle Hymn of the Republic," which she wrote after watching Union soldiers march off to the CIVIL WAR in November 1861. The song has retained a central position in the canon of American patriotic music.

Sources

Clifford, Deborah Pickman. *Mine Eyes Have Seen the Glory: A Biography of Julia Ward Howe.* Boston: Little, Brown, 1979.

Williams, Gary. *Hungry Heart: The Literary Emergence of Julia Ward Howe.* Amherst: University of Massachusetts Press, 1999.

Howells, William Dean (1837–1920) *novelist*

The Ohio-born William Dean Howells worked in his father's printing office and got most of his education by reading the books there. One of his first publications was a campaign biography for Abraham Lincoln, published in 1860. The work led him to a job in the consulate in Venice, Italy, and provided material for two books: *Venetian Life* (1866) and *Modern Italian Poets* (1867). Much later he would demonstrate his learning in Italian literature in *Modern Italian Poets* (1887).

Howells returned to the United States in 1865, worked briefly at *THE NATION,* and then became an editor at *THE ATLANTIC MONTHLY,* serving a editor in chief from 1871 to 1881. His base was now BOSTON, and he became one of the important figures in the city's literary life. He rapidly produced several novels that compared American and Italian manners: *A Chance Acquaintance* (1873), *A Foregone Conclusion* (1875), *The Lady of Aroostook* (1879), and *A Fearful Responsibility* (1881).

Howells then embarked on his mature period as a novelist, producing *A Modern Instance* (1882) and *THE RISE OF SILAS LAPHAM* (1885), two novels that embodied his desire to portray American characters in realistic settings confronting problems of everyday and business life. The former has some vestiges of the melodrama and simplistic characterization that Howells would soon jettison, but the latter is a careful, critical, yet affectionate portrait of an American businessman.

In the late 1880s Howells moved to New York, a decision that signaled the growing importance of that city and the eclipse of Boston as a literary center. He reported on current events for *Harper's Magazine* and wrote one of his finest novels, *A Hazard of New Fortunes* (1890), which presents a picture of daily life in New York that still resonates today.

The social and political problems Howells wrote about in his nonfiction also became the subject of novels such as *A Traveler From Altruria* (1894) and *Through the Eye of the Needle* (1907). In *Criticism and Fiction* (1891), *My Literary Passions* (1895), and *Literature and Life* (1902), Howells wrote extensively about fiction and REALISM, establishing himself as the preeminent man of letters of his day. He traveled widely throughout the United States and abroad and helped to advance the careers of such writers as Stephen CRANE and Frank NORRIS.

Howells believed that literature should accurately reflect the way ordinary Americans actually lived and spoke and worked. This adherence to realism, however, was somewhat contradicted by his aversion to the seamy side of life and his observance of Victorian conventions in his fiction. The naturalists (see NATURALISM) would overturn his doctrine, as they dealt more candidly with the violent, criminal, and corrupt aspects of American civilization and abandoned his belief that fiction should teach sound morality.

Howells wrote many fine memoirs of both his youth and later years: *A Boy's Town* (1890), *My Year in a Log Cabin* (1893), *Impressions and Experiences* (1896), *Literary Friends and Acquaintances* (1900), and *Years of My Youth* (1916). *Mark Twain–Howells Letters: The Correspondence of Samuel L. Clemens and William D. Howells, 1872–1910* appeared in 1960; *John Hay–Howells Letters: The Correspondence of John Milton Hay and William Dean Howells, 1861–1905* was published in 1980.

Sources

Eble, Kenneth, ed. *Howells: A Century of Criticism.* Dallas: Southern Methodist University Press, 1962.

Eschholz, Paul A., ed. *Critics on William Dean Howells: Readings in Literary Criticism.* Coral Gables: University of Miami Press, 1975.

Peyser, Thomas. *Utopia & Cosmopolis: Globalization in the Era of American Literary Realism.* Durham, N.C.: Duke University Press, 1998.

Hubbard, Elbert Green (1856–1915) *publisher, editor, essayist*

Born in Bloomington, Indiana, Elbert Hubbard began his professional life as a soap salesman. He made a great deal of money in this line of work, but, hungering for intellectual and spiritual fulfillment, he gave it up to emulate the English designer, printer, artisan, and writer William Morris (1834–96). An admirer of the finely crafted books turned out by Morris's Kelmscott Press, Hubbard founded the Roycroft Press in East Aurora, New York, which turned out cheap imitations of Morris's works.

Hubbard specialized in writing biography, and he produced two pretentiously arty but successful magazines, *The Philistine* (1895–1915) and *The Fra* (1908–17). His best-known work is the narrative essay *A Message to Garcia* (1899), an inspirational account of an event that took place during the SPANISH-AMERICAN WAR. *A Message from Garcia* proved to be so popular with American business magnates that they distributed copies to their employees, hoping to encourage greater loyalty and productivity. Hubbard died on board the *Lusitania,* a ship sunk by a German submarine in the period leading up to America's entry into World War I.

Sources

Hamilton, Charles Franklin. *As Bees in Honey Drown: Elbert Hubbard and the Roycrofters.* South Brunswick, N.J.: A. S. Barnes, 1973.

White, Bruce A. *Elbert Hubbard's The Philistine, A Periodical of Protest (1895–1915): A Major American "Little Magazine."* Lanham, Md.: University Press of America, 1989.

Huckleberry Finn, The Adventures of *Mark Twain* (1884) *novel*

A sequel to *The Adventures of Tom Sawyer, Huckleberry Finn* is considered a greater work of literature for its entertaining, picaresque style and for Mark Twain's (Samuel Langhorne CLEMENS) more complex exploration of social and political issues such as slavery and the frontier experience.

Huck tells his own story. Abandoned by his derelict father, Pap, Huck lives with the Widow Douglas and her sister, Miss Watson. Used to living on his own, setting his own hours and enjoying his own activities, he chafes under the women's regimen of good manners and schooling. Huck is then kidnapped by his father but escapes to Jackson's Island, where he encounters JIM, Miss Watson's runaway slave. Huck and Jim decide to travel together on a raft down the Mississippi River. When their raft collides with a steamboat, they are separated. Huck swims ashore, taking refuge with the Grangerfords, who are consumed by a feud with the Shepardsons. Here Huck experiences the bloody, anarchic side of frontier life.

When Huck and Jim reunite, they set off again but soon encounter two con-men posing as the Duke and the Dauphin. These two "royals" make money by giving lectures, acting, and generally bilking earnest people by preying on their desire to be uplifted. Along the way Huck witnesses a murder, a near-lynching, and then learns the Duke and Dauphin have sold Jim into slavery again, this time to Tom Sawyer's uncle. Huck enlists his friend Tom in a plan to liberate Jim, but Tom, full of his reading of romance literature, puts Jim and Huck through unnecessary contortions so that Jim's liberation will conform to the plot of an adventure novel. To compound the absurdity, Tom eventually tells Huck that Miss Watson has died and set Jim free in her will. Tom's cruelty—really a kind of madness—becomes clear to Huck when Tom says he wanted to rescue Jim for the "*adventure* of it." Disgusted with the absurd preconceptions of so-called civilized life, Huck announces that he is going to "light out for the territory."

The ending of the novel reflects Twain's ambivalence about the frontier. On the one hand, it is the refuge of the lawless; on the other, it still represents a free space where the individual can pursue his dreams of freedom.

Sources

Bloom, Harold, ed. *Mark Twain: The Adventures of Huckleberry Finn.* New York: Chelsea House, 1986.

Champion, Laurie, ed. *The Critical Response to Mark Twain's Huckleberry Finn.* New York: Greenwood Press, 1991.

Colley, Thomas, ed. *Adventures of Huckleberry Finn: An Authoritative Text, Contexts and Sources, Criticism.* New York: W. W. Norton, 1999.

Hutchinson, Stuart, ed. *Mark Twain: Tom Sawyer and Huckleberry Finn.* New York: Columbia University Press, 1999.

Johnson, Claudia Durst. *Understanding Adventures of Huckleberry Finn: A Student Casebook to Issues, Sources, and Historical Documents.* Westport, Conn.: Greenwood Press, 1996.

humorists of the Southwest *literary school*

In the early part of the 19th century, the southern frontier—later known as the OLD SOUTHWEST—consisted of Georgia, Alabama, Louisiana, Mississippi, Arkansas, Kansas, and Tennessee. Early settlers in this area, sometimes pejoratively called "crackers," developed a distinctive form of humor that employed tall tales and eccentric characters whose adventures were often related in an exaggerated dialect. Later, these stories were recorded and expanded by writers, many of whom chose the New York sporting journal *SPIRIT OF THE TIMES* as their outlet. This group, consisting largely of nonprofessional writers, included such now-familiar names as Augustus LONGSTREET, Thomas Bangs THORPE, and George Washington HARRIS. Other southwestern humorists included the Alabama lawyer and newspaperman Johnson Jones Hooper (1815–62), who wrote about the backwoods gambler Captain Simon Suggs; the actor Joseph M. Field (1810–56), who wrote about Mike FINK; and the Alabama and Mississippi jurist Joseph Glover Baldwin (1815–64), author of *Flush Times in Alabama and Mississippi* (1853). Related to this group is the frontiersman Davy CROCKETT, whose ghost-written autobiography and almanacs are filled with the kind of comic exaggeration and mythmaking characteristic of the Old Southwest school of humor.

Perhaps the most accomplished practitioner of the genre was George Washington Harris, whose metaphoric use of southern dialect in the "Sut Lovingood" yarns would influence such inheritors of the tradition as Mark Twain (Samuel CLEMENS) and William Faulkner.

Sources

Inge, M. Thomas, ed. *The Frontier Humorists: Critical Views.* Hamden, Conn.: Archon Books, 1975.

Lynn, Kenneth S. *Mark Twain and Southwestern Humor.* Boston: Little, Brown, 1960.

Miles, Elton. *Southwest Humorists.* Austin, Tex.: Steck-Vaughn Co., 1969.

Illinois Monthly Magazine, The (1830–1837) *periodical*

Founded in Vandalia, Illinois, this was the first literary periodical to be published west of Ohio. James Hall (1793–1868), the founder and editor, wrote most of the magazine's contents, which consisted of stories, poems, criticism, historical pieces, and literary gossip. In 1832 Hall moved to Cincinnati, taking his magazine—which he rechristened *The Western Monthly Magazine*—with him. Hall made one more move, to Louisville, before he ceased publishing the magazine in 1836.

Sources

Randall, Randolph C. *James Hall: Spokesman of the New West.* Columbus: Ohio State University Press, 1964.

imagism *literary movement*

Grounded in the philosophy of English poet and aesthetician T. E. Hulme (1881–1917), who advocated adherence to the "hard dry image," imagism was born as a reaction to romanticism. Hulme's philosophy initially attracted a group of poets living in London, including the American Ezra Pound (1885–1972), who coined the term "School of Imagism" and soon became the unofficial leader of the group. For Pound, imagism embraced three basic principles: (1) "direct treatment of 'the thing,' whether subjective or objective"; (2) the prescription to "use absolutely no word that does not contribute to the presentation"; and (3) composition "in the sequence of the musical phrase, not in the sequence of a metronome." Pound looked to Chinese and Japanese poetry for exemplars of the type of poetry he espoused, and eventually his theory evolved into another literary school called vorticism.

Between 1915 and 1917, the imagist movement was led by the American poet Amy LOWELL, who published three poetry anthologies, all titled *Some Imagist Poets,* between 1915 and 1917. The works these books collected adhered to T. E. Hulme's belief that poetry should employ the language of everyday speech while at the same time recalling the purity of the classics. The imagist poets were also represented in the United States in the "little magazine" *Poetry: A Magazine of Verse,* published in Chicago by Harriet Monroe. Monroe published the work of such American imagists as Pound, H. D. (1886–1961), John Gould Fletcher (1886–1950), and Lowell, as well as that of the English poets F. S. Flint (1885–1960), Richard Aldington (1892–1962), and D. H. Lawrence (1885–1930).

By the time imagism per se disappeared from the literary scene, around 1917, this short-lived movement had made a profound impact on a younger generation of poets. The imagists' insistence on spareness and their concentration on an image, which Pound defined in 1913 as "that which presents an intellectual and emotional complex in an instant of time," can be seen in the poetry of T. S. Eliot (1888–1965), William Carlos Williams (1883–1963), Wallace Stevens (1879–1955), and Marianne Moore (1887–1972).

Sources

Gage, John T. *In the Arresting Eye: The Rhetoric of Imagism.* Baton Rouge: Louisiana State University Press, 1981.

Harmer, J. B. *Victory in Limbo: Imagism 1908–1917.* London: Secker & Warburg, 1975.

Kermode, Frank. *Romantic Image.* London: Routledge and Paul, 1957.

Independent, The *periodical*

Founded in 1848 in New York City as a Congregationalist periodical, over time *The Independent* became increasingly secular. In 1863, when Henry Ward BEECHER was succeeded as editor by Theodore Tilton, the focus of the magazine shifted toward social reform, emphasizing such matters as women's suffrage. Contributions came in from such distinguished writers as John Greenleaf WHITTIER, Harriet Beecher STOWE, and James Russell LOWELL. After Tilton's tenure ended in 1870, subsequent editors turned *The Independent* into an interdenominational religious and literary magazine, then one devoted largely to politics. In 1916 it took over *HARPER'S WEEKLY* and carried a multitude of illustrations from the European war. In 1923 the magazine moved to Boston, and five years later it merged with *The Outlook,* another originally Christian periodical.

Irving, Washington (1783–1859) *short story writer, humorist, nonfiction writer*

Born in New York City, the gifted Washington Irving was educated at private schools and studied law. However, he was soon drawn to a writing career, and under the name "Jonathan Oldstyle, Gent," he contributed articles to New York newspapers that poked fun at New York society. He continued this vein of writing with *Salmagundi; or, The Whim-Whams and Opinions of Launcelot Langstaff, Esq. and Others* (1807–08). Becoming famous as a wit, he created yet another persona, "Diedrich Knickerbocker," who produced a burlesque *History of New York* (1809), often called the first great book of American humor. Irving, a conservative in politics, used this ruse of an account of the Dutch settlement of New York to attack what he considered the radical absurdities of Jeffersonian Democrats.

Irving did not have another great success until *The Sketch Book* (1819), which contains the classic tales "RIP VAN WINKLE" and "The Legend of Sleepy, Hollow" (see CRANE, ICHABOD), both derived from European FOLKLORE but transferred to American settings. The enormous success of his book made Irving the first internationally successful American author. *Bracebridge Hall* (1822), another book of sketches, was equally successful, although it is not considered the best of Irving's work.

As his literary creativity flagged, Irving turned to works of history, publishing *History of the Life and Voyages of Christopher Columbus* (1828) and *A Chronicle of the Conquest of Granada.* He returned to short, comic writing in *The Alhambra.*

By the late 1820s Irving had taken up a diplomatic career in Spain and London, where he continued to produce historical and travel works while his literary reputation spread in Europe and increased in America. When he returned home in 1832, he was received as a great American author. He embarked on an ambitious trip to the West, producing *A Tour of the Prairies* (1835) and *Astoria* (1836), an account of John Jacob Astor's fur-trading empire. Irving's *Western Journals* were not published until 1844.

Irving's final years were taken up with biography. In 1840 he published a biography of Oliver Goldsmith (1728–74), one of his literary models. From 1855 to 1859 he published his monumental *Life of Washington* in five volumes. These works marked Irving's retreat to the past and his reluctance to respond to an America that had changed radically from the early days of his literary apprenticeship.

Sources

Aderman, Ralph M., ed. *Critical Essays on Washington Irving.* Boston: G. K. Hall, 1990.

Roth, Martin. *Comedy and America: The Lost World of Washington Irving.* Port Washington, N.Y.: Kennikat Press, 1976.

Tuttleton, James, ed. *Washington Irving: The Critical Reaction.* New York: AMS Press, 1993.

Ishmael *character*

Ishmael is narrator of *MOBY-DICK* by Herman MELVILLE. In the Bible, Ishmael is the son of Abraham by the slave Hagar; he is also an Old Testament wanderer, sent into the forest because Sarah, Abraham's wife, favors her own son, Isaac. An angel prophesies that Ishmael will become the ancestor of a great nation but also be subjected to conflict and violence: "And he will be a wild man; his hand will be against every man, and every man's hand against him" (*Genesis* 16:1; 17:18–25; 21:6–21; 25:9–17). In *Moby-Dick,* Melville emphasizes his character's restiveness and isolation as well as his willingness to seek out situations in which the Biblical prophecy is likely to occur. Ishmael is an observer of his fellow crew members, who fall under AHAB's spell even as they fear their captain's monomania. Like his biblical namesake, Ishmael is both an outcast and a survivor. The first-person narrator of this prototypically modern novel, he is also the progenitor of the observer/participant narrators who are a hallmark of modern fiction.

Sources

Higgins, Brian, and Hershel Parker, eds. *Critical Essays on Herman Melville's Moby-Dick.* New York: G. K. Hall, 1992.

Hayes, Kevin J., ed. *The Critical Response to Herman Melville's Moby Dick.* Westport, Conn.: Greenwood Press, 1994.

Jackson, Helen Maria Fiske Hunt (Saxe Holm) (1830–1885) *novelist, poet, essayist*

Born in Amherst, Massachusetts, and educated at boarding schools, Helen Hunt Jackson began writing poetry after the death of her husband in 1863. Her earliest works, *Verses by H.H.* (1870) and *Sonnets and Lyrics* (1886), were well received critically, and her travelogue *Bits of Travel* (1872) won her a sizeable popular audience. A number of stories, published under the pseudonym Saxe Holm, followed. The most notable of these is the last, "Esther Wynn's Love Letters" (1874), thought to be based loosely on her friend, the Amherst poet Emily DICKINSON, who probably also provided the model for a Helen Hunt Jackson novel, *Mercy Philbrick's Choice* (1876).

After Jackson married for a second time in 1875, she made her home in Colorado Springs, Colorado, where she became sympathetic to the plight of the local Native Americans. Her attendance at an 1879 lecture given by Ponca tribal leader Standing Bear, during which he protested the removal of the Poncas from their tribal lands, converted Hunt to the cause of Indian policy reform. Her commitment resulted in the tract *A Century of Dishonor* (1881), which excoriated government abuse of Native Americans, and in her appointment to a special federal commission investigating the predicament of the Mission Indians. In 1884 Jackson produced a popular romance, *Ramona,* which she hoped would perform the same service for Indians that *UNCLE TOM'S CABIN* had for African-American slaves. Although her ambitions for the book were not fully realized, in 1891 it did result in legislation that helped the few surviving Mission Indians in California.

Sources

Mathes, Valerie Sherer. *Helen Hunt Jackson and Her Indian Reform Legacy.* Austin: University of Texas Press, 1990.

May, Antoinette. *Helen Hunt Jackson: A Lonely Voice of Conscience.* San Francisco: Chronicle Books, 1987.

Whitaker, Rosemary. *Helen Hunt Jackson.* Boise, Idaho: Boise State University, 1987.

Jacobs, Harriet Ann (c. 1813–1897) *memoirist*

Born into slavery in Edenton, North Carolina, Harriet Jacobs was taught to sew and to read by her owner, Margaret Hornblow. After Hornblow's death in 1825, Jacobs became the property of Hornblow's three-year-old niece, Mary Norcom, whose father, Dr. James Norcom, repeatedly tried to force Jacobs into sexual slavery. To put him off, Jacobs began a consensual sexual relationship with a white attorney, Samuel Treadwell Sawyer, with whom she had a son and a daughter. Norcom retaliated by sending Jacobs to work under brutal conditions at his son's plantation. When Norcom threatened to sell her children, Jacobs escaped. After hiding in her grandmother's attic for almost seven years, Jacobs fled to the North in 1842, sending for her children afterward. In 1852 the abolitionist Cornelia Grinnell Willis (1825–1904) raised funds to purchase Jacobs's freedom.

At the suggestion of the feminist abolitionist Amy Post (1802–89), in 1853 Jacobs began to write her memoir, entitled *Incidents in the Life of a Slave Girl, Written by Herself.* Jacobs resisted Harriet Beecher STOWE's suggestion that her story be integrated into *UNCLE TOM'S CABIN* (1851) as fiction, and with the editorial help of the abolitionist writer Lydia Maria CHILD, she published her autobiography in 1861 under the pseudonym Linda Brent. One of the first SLAVE NARRATIVES to be written by a woman, *Incidents* was not taken up by scholars until a new edition, edited by Jean Fagin Yellin, appeared in 1987.

Sources

Andrew, William L. *To Tell a Free Story: The First Century of Afro-American Autobiography, 1760–1865.* Urbana: University of Illinois Press, 1986.

Johnson, Yvonne. *The Voices of African American Women: The Use of Narrative and Authorial Voice in the Works of Harriet Jacobs, Zora Neale Hurston, and Alice Walker.* New York: Peter Lang, 1998.

Sánchez-Eppler, Karen. *Touching Liberty: Abolition, Feminism, and the Politics of the Body.* Berkeley: University of California Press, 1993.

James, Alice (1848–1892) *diarist*

Born in New York City, Alice James was the fifth child and only daughter of Mary Robertson Walsh and Henry JAMES Sr. The sister of novelist Henry JAMES and philosopher William JAMES, she was long overshadowed by her more famous family members. Although plainly brilliant and politically radical, she was denied the education granted her siblings and discouraged from pursuing any sort of profession. As her brother Henry once remarked, "in our family group girls seem scarcely to have had a chance." Perhaps not surprisingly, from about the age of 19 onward, Alice James suffered from repeated mental breakdowns and depression.

She was not without resources, however. In 1889 she started a diary that spoke in plain and vivid terms about her interior life and about the great world around her—a task she undertook with the apparent intention that it be published. She was also an avid correspondent, and her letters are among the most memorable written during her time. In 1873 Alice James met another single woman, Katherine Loring, with whom she formed an intense bond of the sort referred to at the time as a "Boston marriage." Succumbing in early middle age to breast cancer, James became in the late 20th century a kind of feminist icon, the subject of such works as Susan Sontag's play *Alice in Bed* (1992).

Sources

The Diary of Alice James. Edited by Leon Edel. New York: Penguin Books, 1964.

Lewis, R. W. B. *The Jameses: A Family Narrative.* New York: Farrar, Straus, and Giroux, 1991.

Strouse, Jean. *Alice James: A Biography.* London: Jonathan Cape, 1980.

Yeazell, Ruth Bernard, ed. *The Death and Letters of Alice James: Selected Correspondence.* Berkeley: University of California Press, 1981.

James, Henry, Jr. (1843–1916) *short story writer, novelist, critic*

Henry James was one of four children fathered by Henry James Sr., a prominent writer on religion and philosophy. Born in New York City, Henry Jr. grew up abroad. He was greatly influenced by his father's cosmopolitan outlook and exposed at an early age to his father's intellectual friends. He also had the example of his older brother William JAMES, who became a distinguished philosopher and psychologist. Educated by tutors, Henry spent his time in Newport, Rhode Island, and in Europe. In 1862 he entered Harvard Law School, but he soon concluded that writing was his métier and that America was unlikely to foster his talent. To James, Americans seemed too intent on commerce and lacked the sophisticated social structures and manners that he found so enticing in Europe.

James began his literary career by writing articles, stories, and reviews. He did not find his major theme until writing "A Passionate Pilgrim" (1871), which contains the kernel of his "international theme," the confrontation between Americans and European culture. By 1875 James had settled permanently in Europe and published *Transatlantic Sketches* (1875). *Roderick Hudson* (1876) is his first novel to squarely deal with the international theme in the story of an American sculptor who cannot adjust to Rome. Similarly, *The American* (1877) focuses on American Christopher Newman's struggle to negotiate the intricacies of French life and to fathom standards of conduct so different from his American values. *The Europeans* (1878) reverses James's angle by importing Europeans into a New England setting.

Of the novels and stories of this early period, the finest is *DAISY MILLER* (1879), the story of a young, naive American woman who pays with her life for her ignorance of the European milieu, but whose life is also an affecting rebuke to European corruption. For the first time, James finds a kind of nobility in innocence and a value in not being spoiled by so much culture. To be sure, Daisy is not presented as superior to her European contemporaries, and yet her death condemns a jaded world that would kill a creature too fresh and unseasoned for it.

An International Episode (1879) presents Americans in England as well as Englishmen in American for a simultaneous exploration of aristocratic and democratic values. James returned twice more to American settings for his international stories: *WASHINGTON SQUARE* (1881) and *The Bostonians* (1886). Both novels show that he had become increasingly distanced from the American scene, which he would return to later only in his nonfiction.

THE PORTRAIT OF A LADY (1881) marks the major phase of James's creativity. Certainly it is his first prolonged exploration of the American mind in Europe—in this case a sensitive portrayal of a young woman, Isabel ARCHER, who mistakes European sophistication for moral sensitivity. She makes a horrendous mistake in her choice of husband precisely because the man's affectation of disinterest and his polish misleads her into thinking he also possesses scruples of a finer tone than her brash American suitor. For all his fascination with European culture, James reveals in this novel a depth of hypocrisy among his European characters that is deeply disconcerting. Isabel Archer's error is tragic because she must live with an awareness not available to the innocent Daisy Miller.

The novel *The Princess Casamassima* (1886) was a departure for James because it dealt so directly with politics. Although his treatment of radicals in London is more a study than a full-blown dramatic account, he anticipated the political novels of Joseph Conrad in portraying the futility and absurdity of fanatics who believe they can change their world with their narrow but fervent ideas. More typical of James's work is *The Aspern Papers* (1888), a novella that deals with a biographer's efforts to obtain the papers of a notable poet, Jeffrey Aspern, and the reluctance of his beloved to yield them. Set in Venice, this story wonderfully evokes the conflict in points of view that made James in his last phase one of the world's great psychological novelists.

During the 1880s and 1890s, James wrote many of his classic short stories, collected in volumes such as *A London Life* (1889), *The Real Thing and Other Tales* (1893), *The Private Life* (1893), and *The Wheel of Time* (1923). The four plays he wrote during this period were such failures that he abandoned the stage. He could not write convincing dialogue, and his dramatic works have never been revived.

By the late 1890s James had not only returned to the novel but also produced his greatest works: *What Maisie Knew* (1897), "THE TURN OF THE SCREW" (1898), *The Wings of the Dove* (1902), *THE AMBASSADORS* (1903), and *The Golden Bowl* (1904). In these novels James is elusive, sometimes convoluted, but also acute on the subject of human relationships and cultural settings. The works distill and elaborate on a lifetime of observation of the old and new worlds, of America and Europe. Lambert Strether in *The Ambassadors* is James's quintessential narrator. The novel is told from Strether's point of view but not in his voice, as if the author is looking through the lens of Strether's sensibility. He is the finest example of a James narrator who is an observer but only a partial participant in life. In James's Strether are the seeds of 20th-century narrators such as Nick Carraway in F. Scott Fitzgerald's *The Great Gatsby* and Ike McCaslin in William Faulkner's "The Bear."

James continued to write after this golden period (1897–1904), but his novels *The Ivory Tower* (1917) and *The Sense of the Past* (1917) were never finished. He did, however, manage to complete two superb volumes of short stories, *The Altar of the Dead* (1909) and *The Finer Grain* (1910).

James brought to American fiction a degree of sophistication not seen before. In theme and technique—his exquisite studies of European and American societies and his experimentation with point of view and exploration of states of mind—brought American literature into the world arena. He influenced poets as well as novelists. The early work of Ezra Pound (1885–1972) and T. S. Eliot (1888–1965) show James's influence, particularly in dramatic monologues like Eliot's "Portrait of a Lady."

James also made an incalculable contribution to the criticism of American fiction and to the American writer's sense of himself as pursuing a disciplined craft. James advanced the art of the novel not only through the brilliant prefaces to his novels, collected as *The Art of the Novel: Critical Prefaces* (1934), but also in works of literary criticism, including *French Poets and Novelists* (1878), *Hawthorne* (1879), *The Art of Fiction* (1884), *Partial Portraits* (1888), *Essays in London and Elsewhere* (1893), *The Lesson of Balzac* (1905), *Notes on Novelists* (1914), *Within the Rim and Other Essays* (1918), and *Notes and Reviews* (1921).

James is also an important figure in the history of American travel writing. His works in this genre include *Portraits of Places* (1883), *A Little Tour in France* (1885), *English Hours* (1905), *The American Scene* (1907), and *Italian Hours* (1909).

James wrote several volumes of autobiography: *A Small Boy and Others* (1913), *Notes of a Son and Brother* (1914), and *The Middle Years* (1917). *The Complete Tales of Henry James* appeared in 12 volumes between 1962 and 1965. *The Complete Plays of Henry James* was published in 1949, and *The Complete Notebooks* appeared in 1987. *Henry James: Letters* was issued in five volumes between 1974 and 1984.

Sources

Bloom, Harold, ed. *Henry James.* New York: Chelsea House, 1987.

Edel, Leon. *Henry James: A Life.* Rev. ed. New York: Harper & Row, 1985.

Gargano, James W., ed. *Critical Essays on Henry James: The Early Novels.* Boston: G. K. Hall, 1987.

———, ed. *Critical Essays on Henry James: The Late Novels.* Boston: G. K. Hall, 1987.

Kaplan, Fred. *Henry James: The Imagination of Genius.* New York: Morrow, 1992.

James, Henry, Sr. (1811–1882) *essayist*

Father of Henry, William, and Alice JAMES, Henry James Sr. was an extraordinary man in his own right. Born into a wealthy and sternly Calvinist family in Albany, New York, James rebelled against the strictures of orthodoxy. An accident in childhood cost him a leg and turned him to intellectual pursuits, helped by an early display of independence of mind. After two years at the Princeton Theological Seminary, he withdrew in 1835, finding religious orthodoxy incompatible with his beliefs. Two years later, during a trip to England, he encountered the works of Robert Sandeman (1718–1771), a Scottish rebel against Calvinism whose ideas James adopted and one of whose books he edited in 1838. Two years later, however, James was introduced to the philosophy of Swedish theologian Emanuel Swedenborg (1688–1772), whose mystical approach to Christianity had a profound affect on him, as it had on a number of other 19th-century idealists.

Independently wealthy, James spent much of his life traveling and accumulating experiences and friends, among them some of the most influential thinkers of the day. An intimate of Albert BRISBANE and George RIPLEY, James came to embrace many of the doctrines of FOURIERISM. Most of his writings, however, were devoted to religious philosophy and an exploration of the Swedenborgian-based concept of "divine-natural humanity," or "the immanence of God in the unity of mankind." Among James's most important works are *Christianity, the Logic of Creation* (1857); *Substance and Shadow; or Morality and Religion in Their Relation to Life* (1863); *The Secret of Swedenborg* (1869); and *Society, the Redeemed Form of Man* (1879). Henry James Sr. had a profound impact on his namesake, who likewise entertained the thoughts of Swedenborg and who wrote about his father in the works *A Small Boy and Others* (1913) and *Notes of a Son and Brother* (1914).

Sources

Bell, F. A., ed. *Henry James: Fiction as History.* Totowa, N.J.: Barnes & Noble, 1984.

Habegger, Alfred. *The Father: A Life of Henry James, Sr.* New York: Farrar, Straus, and Giroux, 1994.

Margolis, Anne Throne. *Henry James and the Problem of Audience: An International Act.* Ann Arbor, Mich.: UMI Press, 1985.

James, Jesse Woodson (1847–1882) *outlaw*

Jesse James was born in Clay County, Missouri, and raised on a farm. During the CIVIL WAR he joined the guerrilla band led by William Quantrill (1837–65) and joined in the fighting that amounted to a separate civil war in neighboring Kansas. In 1866 Jesse and his brother Frank (1843–1915) formed a gang and ranged through the Midwest, robbing banks and trains and murdering numerous people as they went. Declared an outlaw, James nonetheless became a popular hero, a kind of Robin Hood. A $10,000 bounty was placed on his head, however, and he was ultimately shot in the back by a member of his own band. Almost immediately James became a legend, his death the subject of an anonymous ballad. He was the hero of countless DIME NOVELS and of more serious works, including a poem by William Rose Benét (1886–1950), a musical pantomime by Douglas Moore (1893–1969), and the play *Missouri Legend* (1938).

Sources

Bruns, Roger. *The Bandit Kings: From Jesse James to Pretty Boy Floyd.* New York: Crown, 1995.

James, William (1842–1910) *philosopher, psychologist*

William James was born in New York City, but he lived abroad a good deal of the time with his brother Henry and the rest of the JAMES family, headed by Henry JAMES Sr., a writer on religious, social, and literary topics. Although interested in art, especially painting, William studied medicine at Harvard and obtained an M.D. in 1869. In poor health and apparently suffering from doubts about his abilities, James became interested in psychology as a discipline that might liberate the mind.

James began teaching at Harvard in 1872, drawing on the thought of both Charles Darwin (1809–82) and the philosopher Herbert Spencer (1820–1903) and offering a course entitled "The Philosophy of Evolution." He shifted from medicine to philosophy and established the first laboratory for psychological studies. His first important published work, *Principles of Psychology,* appeared in 1890. The landmark work relied on James's understanding of physiology, which he had taught at Harvard, to explore the nexus between human emotions and bodily functions.

James traveled widely in Europe, meeting with philosophers and psychologists and participating in the Society for Psychical Research. The result of this experience is evident in *The Will to Believe* (1897), in which James showed considerable sympathy for the way science and faith might collaborate in better understanding the human personality. Although he never abandoned his belief in empiricism, he wished to vigorously investigate the claims of spiritualists and the practices of Christian Scientists. This extraordinary desire to reconcile the ideas of science and religion culminated in his masterpiece, *VARIETIES OF RELIGIOUS EXPERIENCE* (1902), which explored the psychological and practical bases of religious experience without denigrating the idea of faith itself.

James's great contribution to American philosophy is the concept of PRAGMATISM, a term first used by the philosopher C. S. Peirce (1839–1914) and developed by James in *Pragmatism* (1907). This book advanced the argument that ideas have significance only insofar as they have an impact on the world of experience. Pragmatism has often been cited as the only original contribution to philosophy made by an American. The concept has been discussed as an example of the American devotion to practicality: that is, no idea is important if it is not useful.

James also wrote classic essays, most notably "The Moral Equivalent of War" (1910), which has become an important part of the American literature canon. This piece reflects James's liberalism, his dedicated search to find alternatives to the inhumanity of war, and his belief that the mind could be disciplined to avoid violence.

Several collections of James's writing appeared after his death, including *Some Problems of Philosophy: A Beginning of an Introduction to Philosophy* (1911), *Memories and Studies* (1911), *Essays in Radical Empiricism* (1912), *Collected Essays and Reviews* (1920), and *Selected Letters* (1961). His brother Henry published a memoir, *Notes of a Son and Brother,* in 1914. *William and Henry James: Selected Letters* appeared in 1997. Beginning in 1992, the University Press of Virginia began publishing *The Correspondence of William James* in several volumes.

Sources

Gale, Richard M. *The Divided Self of William James.* New York: Cambridge University Press, 1999.

Oliver, Phil. *William James's "Springs of Delight": The Return to Life.* Nashville: Vanderbilt University Press, 2001.

Putnam, Ruth Anna, ed. *The Cambridge Companion to William James.* New York: Cambridge University Press, 1997.

Simon, Linda. *Genuine Reality: A Life of William James.* New York: Harcourt Brace, 1998.

Jewett, Theodora Sarah Orne (1849–1909) *short story writer, novelist*

Sarah Orne Jewett was born in South Berwick, Maine, where she spent much of her life and which she used as the setting (renamed Deephaven) for her fiction. She came from a distinguished New England family and was especially close in childhood to her father, a physician. Jewett's first novel, *The Country Doctor* (1884), is a fictionalized account of their relationship. Dr. Jewett introduced his daughter to literature and fostered her keen perception of the rocky, unproductive farms and abandoned harbors of her native region, which she used in creating her first mature literary sketches.

Jewett began by writing children's stories in 1868, but that same year her first sketch was accepted for publication by the prestigious *ATLANTIC MONTHLY.* In 1873 the magazine published "The Shore House," the first of a series of LOCAL COLOR sketches later collected as *Deephaven* (1877), itself a rehearsal for Jewett's most accomplished work, *The Country of the Pointed Firs* (1877), a series of loosely connected stories revolving around the interplay between a decaying Maine seaport and its summer tourists.

The novels and stories Jewett published between 1885 and 1896 made her one of the most important writers of the local color movement. Through use of such narrative techniques as the implied narrator, who observes and comments on events without entering into them directly, she was able to imbue her stories with a gentle, meditative irony, which she combined with keen observations about both the local landscape and domestic interiors. Her most characteristic tone is one of nostalgia, specifically for the time when New England was home to thriving shipbuilders, fleets of ships, and prosperous merchants. What makes her work so effective, however, is its contrast of this past with the present, which offers up a landscape peopled largely with aging widows and spinsters left behind by industrialization, urbanization, and the movement westward.

Jewett's was a formula that seduced readers from the outset, and she enjoyed critical and popular success throughout her career. She found an influential mentor early in William Dean HOWELLS, who helped her publish with the *Atlantic Monthly.* Her patrician background provided an entrée to Boston literary circles, where she met Annie Adams Fields, wife of the publisher James T. FIELDS. After Jewett's husband's death in 1881, Annie Fields became her closest companion, and the two women wintered together in Boston and summered in Manchester, Massachusetts. Together they developed a literary salon and traveled to Europe, where they were entertained by a wide array of literary celebrities. When she was home in South Berwick, Jewett continued to live with her sister and her widowed mother, who died in 1891.

Even after her most productive period had passed, Jewett continued to turn out fiction of high caliber, such as "The Queen's Twin." In 1902, however, her career was cut short by a carriage accident that injured her spine. Jewett's mastery of local-color writing provides a link between the New England regionalist stories of her literary forebear, Harriet Beecher STOWE, and the romanticized realism of Willa Cather (1873–1947), who found in Jewett's work a "perfection that endures."

Sources

Kilcup, Karen L., and Thomas S. Edwards, eds. *Jewett and Her Contemporaries: Reshaping the Canon.* Gainesville: University Press of Florida, 1999.

Sherman, Sarah Way. *Sarah Orne Jewett, An American Persephone.* Hanover, N.H.: University Press of New England, 1989.

Silverthorne, Elizabeth. *Sarah Orne Jewett: A Writer's Life.* Woodstock, N.Y.: Overlook Press, 1993.

Jim *character*

The companion of Huckleberry Finn in Mark Twain's (see CLEMENS, Samuel Langhorne) 1885 novel of the same name (see HUCKLEBERRY FINN, THE ADVENTURES OF), Jim is a grown man and a fugitive slave who at first appears slow, superstitious, and childish but is revealed to be both tender and wise. Jim, fearing that he is about to be sold down the river to a slave master, takes advantage of the confusion surrounding Huck's faked death, staged to allow the boy to run away from home, to escape. Huck and Jim are in fact escaping from a pair of elderly sisters, Jim's owner and Huck's guardian, respectively, who represent a kind of "civilization" both find oppressive, albeit for different reasons.

On board the raft they build to navigate the Mississippi, there is tension between Jim's profound need to escape and Huck's simple desire for adventure—although the boy does have powerful motivation to get away from his abusive, degenerate father. However, after Huck and Jim are separated for hours in a dense fog, the balance rights itself. When Huck finally gets back to the raft, he finds the exhausted Jim asleep. Waking him, Huck manages to convince Jim temporarily that their separation was all a dream, but when Jim realizes the trick Huck has played on him, his sense of hurt and betrayal indicate both the power the young white boy has over him and Huck's own immaturity in not realizing its life-threatening implications. When a moment does arrive that Huck can—and, following both contemporary mores and the law, should—turn Jim over to slave catchers, the boy demonstrates that he has become a man. Declaring that he would rather go to hell himself than turn Jim in, Huck chooses what is truly morally right.

After Huck gets back ashore, however, his moral compass goes awry under the influence of a couple of white con men, the Duke and the Dauphin, and the romantic scheming of his more socialized friend, Tom Sawyer. As a result, Jim is jailed and then victimized by an elaborate escape plan, only to discover that he has already been freed.

Twain's portrayal of Jim represented a breakthrough in American literature. A black man, with a heart as pure as a child's, is revealed as the embodiment of moral consciousness—an achievement realized largely because Jim is permitted to speak for himself in a voice that rings with authenticity.

Sources

Chadwick-Joshua, Jocelyn. *The Jim Dilemma: Reading Race in Huckleberry Finn.* Jackson: University Press of Mississippi, 1998.

Fishkin, Shelley Fisher. *Was Huck Black?: Mark Twain and African-American Voices.* New York: Oxford University Press, 1993.

Leonard, James S., Thomas A. Tenney, and Thadious M. Davis, eds. *Satire or Evasion?: Black Perspectives on Huckleberry Finn.* Durham, N.C.: Duke University Press, 1992.

John Henry *folk hero*

This legendary African-American hero of folk tales and popular ballads was said to have been born in "Black River Country" and employed as either a roustabout on steamboats or a steel driver on a railroad construction gang. In the most popular version of his story, he once took on a steam drill, vowing to best it with only a hammer and steel and his own enormous strength. He succeeds, but the effort kills him. The legend of John Henry apparently arose circa 1870 among miners working on the Big Bend Tunnel of the Chesapeake & Ohio Railway in West Virginia and may or may not have been based on a real person. Originally only an oral tradition, the legend of John Henry was first published in 1909 in the *Journal of American Folklore.* A collection of the various ballads about the hero was published by Guy B. Johnson in 1931 as *John Henry: Tracking Down a Negro Legend.*

Sources

Williams, Brett. *John Henry, a Bio-Bibliography.* Westport, Conn.: Greenwood Press, 1983.

Judson, Edward Zane Carroll (Ned Buntline) (1823–1886) *novelist*

Born in Stamford, New York, Edward Judson lived a life worthy of the 400 DIME NOVELS he would write under the pseudonym Ned Buntline. After serving in the navy and gaining a reputation as a duelist, he fought a duel in Nashville with his mistress's husband. Judson killed the husband, but was then himself lynched by a mob—only to be cut down secretly on the point of death and released. In 1849 he led the Astor Place Riot, a revolt of theatergoers in New York that resulted in 22 deaths, and was sent to prison for a year. A fervent anti-Papist, he founded the xenophobic Know-Nothing Party in the 1850s. During the CIVIL WAR Judson was thrown out of the Union army for drunkenness, but he later bestowed upon himself with the rank of colonel and proclaimed that he had been the chief scout for the Army of the Potomac.

Judson is credited with having been one of the inventors of the dime novel and also with having christened W. F. CODY "Buffalo Bill"—then writing a play and a series of dime novels about him. Judson wrote hymns and, despite his own history, lectured about the virtues of temperance. He also published a journal, *Ned Buntline's Own,* and is said to have written a 600-page novel in 62 hours.

Sources

Monaghan, Jay. *The Great Rascal: The Life and Adventures of Ned Buntline.* Boston: Little, Brown, 1952.

June, Jennie

See CROLY, JANE CUNNINGHAM.

Keckley, Elizabeth (c. 1818–1907) *memoirist*

Elizabeth Keckley was born into slavery in Dinwiddie Court House, Virginia. She proved to be such a skilled seamstress, however, that she was able to purchase her own and her son's freedom and move to Washington, D.C. Serving first as dressmaker to the wife of then-Senator Jefferson Davis (1808–89), Keckley eventually became the dressmaker of First Lady Mary Todd Lincoln (1818–82) during Abraham LINCOLN's first term as president. In 1868 Keckley published *Behind the Scenes, or Thirty Years a Slave and Four Years in the White House,* which placed her at the center of a controversy. Because of revelations about Mary Todd Lincoln—particularly her attempts to raise money after her husband's assassination—and inclusion of some of Mrs. Lincoln's letters, Keckley's publisher was pressured into withdrawing the book.

Sources

Braxton, Joanne M. *Black Women Writing Autobiography: A Tradition within a Tradition.* Philadelphia: Temple University Press, 1989.

Kemble, Frances Anne (1809–1893) *diarist*

Born into a stage family in London, England, Fanny Kemble followed her forebears and made her acting debut at the age of 13. In 1832, while on a two-year acting tour of the United States with her father, she began her writing career, keeping a journal she would publish in 1835 as *Journal of an American Residence.* Kemble subsequently did not return to England with her father but instead consented in 1834 to marry a Georgia planter, Pierce Butler, who had fallen in love with her stage presence. In 1838 she visited her husband's ancestral home and gradually became aware not only that he was a slaveholder, but also that his slaves were mistreated. Kemble was particularly incensed by the practice of forcing slave women back into the fields a mere three weeks after they had given birth, an atrocity she recorded in a journal she kept for a friend. Although she agreed to her husband's desire that she not publish the journal in 1842 to support the abolitionist cause (see ABOLITIONISM), her outspoken opposition to slavery caused the Butler family to ban her from the plantation. Kemble and her husband were finally divorced in 1848, and in 1863, hoping to influence British public opinion against the Confederacy, she finally published her *Journal of a Residence on a Georgia Plantation, 1838–1839.*

Kemble supported herself in the United States and Britain primarily through public readings, although she continued to write plays, poetry, criticism, an autobiography, and a novel, *Far Away and Long Ago* (1889), set in the Berkshire Mountains, where she lived. Ever attractive and controversial, she is said to have supplied some of the inspiration for Nathaniel HAWTHORNE's character Zenobia in *The Blithedale Romance* (1852) and was the inspiration for Henrietta Buckmaster's 1948 historical novel *Fire in the Heart.*

Sources

Clinton, Catherine. *Fanny Kemble's Civil Wars.* New York: Simon & Schuster, 2000.

Furnas, J. C. *Fanny Kemble: Leading Lady of the Nineteenth-Century Stage: A Biography.* New York: Dial Press, 1982.

Ransome, Eleanor, ed. *The Terrific Kemble: A Victorian Self-Portrait from the Writings of Fanny Kemble.* London: Hamish Hamilton, 1978.

Scott, John A. *Fanny Kemble's America.* New York: Crowell, 1973.

Kennedy, John Pendleton (Mark Littleton) (1795–1870) *novelist*

Born in Baltimore, John Pendleton Kennedy was a lawyer by profession and a writer by avocation. Disliking the practice of law, he entered politics, serving in the U.S. Congress as a representative and as Speaker of the House. He also worked in the administrative branch as Millard Fillmore's secretary of the Navy. In the latter position he was instrumental in Commodore Matthew Perry's 1853 expedition to Japan and Elisha Kent Kane's second Arctic expedition (1853–55). An educational activist, Kennedy also lent his services to the University of Maryland and the Peabody Institute.

Literature, however, was Kennedy's abiding interest. His first important work, a series of sketches titled *Swallow Barn* (1832), is the first significant fictional treatment of Virginia plantation life. Kennedy published this work and others under the pen name Mark Littleton. He often wrote about politics, often satirically, as in the satire *Quodlibet* (1840), which concerns Jacksonian democracy. Many critics consider his best work to be *Rob of the Bowl* (1838), a historical novel set in St. Mary's City, Maryland's first capital, in 1681. Kennedy's last important literary endeavor was an 1849 two-volume biography of William Wirt, one of Andrew Jackson's political opponents.

In addition to his political affiliations, Kennedy was connected with such literary personages as Edgar Allan POE, whose career Kennedy boosted by awarding first prize in a short-story contest to Poe's "Ms. Found in a Bottle" (1833), and the Englishman William Makepeace Thackeray (1811–63), who in his novel *The Virginians* (1857–58) made good use of information supplied by Kennedy.

Sources

Bohner, Charles H. *John Pendleton Kennedy, Gentleman from Baltimore.* Baltimore: Johns Hopkins University Press, 1961.
Ridgely, J. V. *John Pendleton Kennedy.* New York: Twayne, 1966.

Kentucky Tragedy (1825) *historical event*

This sensational crime—also known as the Beauchamp case—supplied the material for numerous works of literature. A Kentucky girl named Anna Cook was seduced by Colonel Solomon P. Sharpe, the solicitor general of Kentucky. Afterward, in 1824, she married another attorney, Jeroboam O. Beauchamp, and forced him to take an oath to kill her seducer. After several unsuccessful attempts to fulfill his promise (Sharp, when confronted, refused to fight), Beauchamp disguised himself and fatally stabbed Sharp on November 5, 1825. On trial for murder, Beauchamp declared himself innocent but was nevertheless found guilty. Denied a pardon, he was joined on the night before his execution by his wife, and both took a potentially fatal dose of laudanum. When this method of suicide failed, they stabbed themselves. Although Anna died, her husband survived, only to be hanged the next day.

Beauchamp's own *Confession,* accompanied by some verse written by his wife, was published in 1826. The Kentucky Tragedy has been dramatized several times by others: Thomas Holley CHIVERS's verse drama, *Conrad and Eudora,* appeared in 1834; sections of Edgar Allan POE's unfinished blank verse drama, *Politan,* were published in 1835 and 1836; and the same form was also used in Charlotte Mary BARNES's *Octavia Bragaldi; or, The Confession* (1837) and Mary E. McMichael's *The Kentucky Tragedy* (1838). A novel by William Gilmore SIMMS titled *Beauchampe, or, The Kentucky Tragedy* was published in 1842; and in 1856 Simms expanded the first part of this book into a new novel, *Charlemont, or, The Pride of the Village, A Tale of Kentucky.* Other novelists who have made use of the material include Charles Fenno HOFFMAN (*Greyslaer* [1849]) and Robert Penn Warren (1905–89) (*World Enough and Time* [1950]).

Sources

Clark, Robert. *History and Myth in American Fiction, 1823–52.* New York: St. Martin's Press, 1984.

Kilmer, Alfred Joyce (1886–1918) *poet, essayist, critic, editor*

Born in New Brunswick, New Jersey, Joyce Kilmer began his professional life as a high school teacher and then adopted the literary life, working as a poet, essayist, book reviewer, and editor. He attracted little attention until his highly accessible poem "Trees" was published in 1913, making him a national celebrity. He published two volumes of poetry before enlisting in the army during World War I. He was killed at the second Battle of the Marne and was transformed into a symbol of poetic idealism struck down by war.

Sources

Conell, John E. *Joyce Kilmer: A Literary Biography.* Brunswick, Ga.: Write-Fit Communications, 2000.

King, Clarence (1842–1901) *science writer*

Born in Newport, Rhode Island, and educated at Yale, King rode horseback across the country to work in the mines of the Comstock Lode in Nevada and in California. From 1866 to 1877 he worked as federal geological surveyor of an area stretching from eastern Colorado to California. This work resulted in a seven-volume report (1870–80) that was praised for its detail and exactitude. During this period King also wrote his most popular work, a series of sketches collected as *Mountaineering in the Sierra Nevada* (1872). In 1871 King met Henry ADAMS in Colorado, and their friendship is said to have influenced Adams's subsequent emphasis on scientific thinking and his novel *Democracy* (1880). From 1878 to 1881 King headed the U.S. Geological Survey, after which he continued to turn out both scientific and scientifically accurate popular works.

Sources

Wilkins, Thurman. *Clarence King: A Biography.* Albuquerque: University of New Mexico Press, 1988.

Kirkland, Caroline Matilda Stansbury (Mrs. Mary Clavers) (1801–1864) *short story writer, essayist, editor*

The granddaughter of the poet Joseph Stansbury (1742–1809), Caroline Stansbury was born in New York City, where she received a classical education. In 1828 she married William Kirkland, an educator with whom she established a girls' school in Utica, New York. In 1835 the couple moved to Detroit, where Samuel headed a girls' seminary before the Kirklands moved again, two years later, to Pinckney, Michigan, where they were among the earliest settlers. Caroline Kirkland found her new surroundings culturally bare but sociologically interesting, and she offered up her observations in satirical letters sent to her friends back east. These letters later formed the backbone for the series of humorous sketches about frontier life she published in 1839 under the title *A New Home—Who'll Follow?* using the pen name Mrs. Mary Clavers. Her later works about frontier life, a series of essays published as *Forest Life* (1842) and a story collection called *Western Clearings* (1845), lacked the wit and the biting edge of her first publication.

In 1843 the Kirklands returned to New York, where William's death in 1846 left Caroline the sole supporter of their five children. She went to work as a literary professional, editing the *Union Magazine* in 1847 and then producing a steady stream of essays about such diverse issues as prison reform and women writers. However, although illustrative of her versatility and descriptive powers, these essays never matched the humorous originality of her first work.

Sources

Kolodny, Annette. *The Land Before Her: Fantasy and Experience of the American Frontiers, 1630–1860.* Chapel Hill: University of North Carolina Press, 1984.

Osborne, William S. *Caroline M. Kirkland.* New York: Twayne, 1972.

Klondike Gold Rush (1896) *historical event*

When George Washington Carmack struck a large vein of gold in the Klondike region of the Yukon Territory in northwestern Canada, the find caused a stampede of gold miners to rush to the area. The gold rush reached its apex in 1898 and continued for several years. By 1900 roughly $22,000 worth of gold had been taken out of the ground. During this period the settlement of Dawson became a boom town peopled with a broad spectrum of humanity that provided material for many writers, among them the poet Robert Service (1874–1958) and the journalist Joaquin MILLER. Perhaps the best literary use of the hardships associated with traveling along the Yukon River and mining the frozen ground was made by Jack LONDON in such works as *THE CALL OF THE WILD* (1903) and *White Fang* (1912).

Sources

Berton, Pierre. *The Golden Trail: The Story of the Klondike Rush.* Toronto: Macmillan of Canada, 1974.

Wharton, David. *The Alaska Gold Rush.* Bloomington: Indiana University Press, 1972.

Knickerbocker School *organization*

In honor of Washington IRVING's *Knickerbocker History of New York* (1809), this name was bestowed on a loosely organized association of writers who lived and worked in New York City in the first half of the 19th century. Among the group's members were Irving himself, James Fenimore COOPER, William Cullen BRYANT, Lydia Maria CHILD, and Fitz-Greene HALLECK. Their association helped to increase the importance of New York as a literary center, as its members attempted to foster a national literature. Often, however, they were criticized for their superficial sophistication, as in Edgar Allan POE's essay "The Literati of New York City" (1846). They often published in *The Knickerbocker Magazine* (1833–65).

Ladies' Home Journal, The *periodical*

In December 1883 the publisher Cyrus H. K. Curtis spun off the women's section of his Philadelphia *Tribune and Farmer* as a separate monthly edited by "Mrs. Louisa Knapp"—his wife, Louisa Knapp Curtis. The Curtises were able to attract well-known contributors almost from the start. The magazine paid attention to public affairs early on, becoming a leader of the campaign that led to enactment of the Food and Drug Act in 1938. In 1903 *The Ladies' Home Journal* became the first upscale monthly to attract 1 million subscribers. The magazine's popularity greatly increased under the editorship (1889–1920) of Edward W. Bok (1863–1930), who developed its intimate, casual style while continuing to publish fiction and poetry by such writers as William Dean HOWELLS and Sarah Orne JEWETT and articles by such distinguished personages as Franklin D. Roosevelt (1882–1945).

The Ladies' Home Journal was one of the first magazines to adopt four-color illustrations, publishing work by such artists as Charles Dana GIBSON. In 1935 the well-known editing team of Bruce and Beatrice Gould took over, increasing the magazine's attention to national and international affairs and publishing nonfiction pieces by such important contributors as Dorothy Thompson (1894–1961) and First Lady Eleanor Roosevelt (1884–1962). As late as 1990, the magazine still attracted more than 5 million subscribers for its blend of domestic and personal advice and public-affairs reporting.

Sources

Hershey, Lenore. *Between the Covers: The Lady's Own Journal.* New York: Coward-McCann, 1983.

Scanlon, Jennifer. *Inarticulate Longings: The Ladies' Home Journal, Gender, and the Promises of Consumer Culture.* New York: Routledge, 1995.

Steinberg, Salme H. *Reformer in the Marketplace: Edward W. Bok and the Ladies' Home Journal.* Baton Rouge: Louisiana State University Press, 1979.

Langstaff, Launcelot

See PAULDING, JAMES KIRKE.

Lanier, Sydney (1842–1881) *poet, critic*

Born in Macon, Georgia, Sydney Lanier was headed for a career in music when his plans were cut short by the CIVIL WAR. A Confederate volunteer, he was captured by Union forces and imprisoned at Point Lookout, Maryland, for four months in 1864. The experience broke his health, and he emerged infected with the tuberculosis that would eventually take his life.

After the war Lanier pursued his musical and literary interests simultaneously, playing flute for the Peabody Symphony Orchestra in Baltimore and publishing a Civil War novel, *Tiger-Lilies* (1867). His novel was not a success, but he had the good fortune to meet the journalist and novelist Bayard TAYLOR, through whom he gained an outlet for his poetry in *LIPPINCOTT'S MAGAZINE*, which published "Corn" in 1875. Lanier continued to produce important poems for the remainder of his life: *The Symphony* in 1875, *The Song of the Chattahoochee* in 1877, *The Marshes of Glynn* in 1878, and *The Revenge of Hamish* in 1878. In such works Lanier succeeded in bringing his poetic theory to fruition, deliberately manipulating elements of prosody to mimic the poem's content. Lanier's poetic theory greatly resembles Edgar Allan POE's, and like Poe, Lanier consistently made his poetry reproduce musical effects.

In 1879 Lanier was appointed to a lectureship in English at Johns Hopkins University, and during his time there he produced three important works of literary criticism. *The Science of English Verse* (1880) explicated his poetic methods. In 1883 a much different work of criticism was published posthumously: *The English Novel*, which bears the explanatory subtitle *From Aeschylus to George Eliot: The Development of Personality*. A third work, *Shakespeare and His Forerunners*, is a collection of public lectures that was not published until 1902. Lanier's complete *Poems* were also published posthumously, in 1884.

Sources

DeBellis, Jack. *Sidney Lanier*. New York: Twayne, 1972.

Gabin, Jane S. *A Living Minstrelsy: The Poetry and Music of Sidney Lanier*. Macon, Georgia: Mercer University Press, 1985.

Parks, Edd W. *Sidney Lanier: The Man, the Poet, the Critic*. Athens: University of Georgia Press, 1968.

Larcom, Lucy (1824–1893) *poet, editor*

Born in Beverly, Massachusetts, Lucy Larcom began writing poetry when she was only seven. By age 11, owing to her father's early death, she was working in the Lowell, Massachusetts, textile mills, where she spent the next 10 years. In 1846 she left for the Illinois prairie, where she taught school and attended Monticello Seminary in Godfrey, Illinois, before returning to Massachusetts in 1854 to teach at Wheaton Seminary (now Wheaton College) in Norton. She then became the editor of a children's magazine, *Our Young Folks* (1865–73), and published her own poetry. She also published a book of criticism, *Landscape of American Poetry* (1879), and an autobiography, *A New England Girlhood* (1889).

Sources

Marchalonis, Shirley. *The Worlds of Lucy Larcom, 1824–1893*. Athens: University of Georgia Press, 1989.

Selden, Bernice. *The Mill Girls: Lucy Larcom, Harriet Hanson Robinson, Sarah G. Bagley*. New York: Atheneum, 1983.

Last of the Mohicans, The *James Fenimore Cooper* (1826) *novel*

The second of five novels in James Fenimore COOPER's series *LEATHER-STOCKING TALES*, *The Last of the Mohicans* opens in 1757 during the French and Indian War. Cora and Alice Munro, daughters of the British commander, are attempting to reach their father at Fort William Henry near Lake Champlain. They are accompanied by two official escorts: Major Duncan Heyward, who is Alice's fiancé; and David Gamut, a voice teacher. Magua, a treacherous Huron who is secretly in league with the French, serves as their guide. Magua's initial plan to betray the party to his Iroquois allies is foiled by Hawkeye, the Leatherstocking frontiersman also known as Natty BUMPPO; Hawkeye's friend, the old chief CHINGACHGOOK; and Chingachgook's son Uncas, "the last of the Mohicans."

Magua escapes, only to return with Iroquois reinforcements in order to capture the sisters. The mixed nature of Magua's motives becomes clear when he offers to release the party of whites if Cora agrees to become his squaw. She refuses, but then the sisters and their escorts are once again saved by Hawkeye and company. The party reaches Fort William Henry, but after the British surrender to the French, the group must set off again. Even though they leave under a grant of safe passage, they are set upon by Indians. The fair Alice is taken to a Huron camp with Uncas, while her darker sister is imprisoned by the Delaware. Heywood manages to rescue Alice and Uncas, and the three set off to save Cora. In the Delaware camp, however, they receive a cordial welcome, with old chief Tamenund hailing Uncas as his true successor. Nevertheless, Magua claims Cora as his property. Uncas, his noble counterpart, also loves Cora, but with a pure and passionate heart, the last of the Mohicans leads his English allies in an assault against the Hurons—and against Magua.

In the battle that follows, Uncas and Cora are killed, leaving Hawkeye to shoot the evil Magua. The survivors then return to civilization—all, that is, but Hawkeye and the grieving Chingachgook.

With its clear depictions of noble white and red men, its dark and light beauties, its contrasting stories of pure and impure motives and loves, of civilization and untainted nature, *The Last of the Mohicans* set patterns that would influence generations of American novelists. The clear outlines of Cooper's depictions of manly honor and courage would be appropriated wholeheartedly—and often artlessly—by most writers of the type of popular fiction that came to be classed together as WESTERNS.

Sources

Barker, Martin, and Roger Sabin. *The Lasting of the Mohicans: History of an American Myth*. Jackson: University Press of Mississippi, 1995.

McWilliams, John P. *The Last of the Mohicans: Civil Savagery and Savage Civility*. New York: Twayne, 1995.

Peck, Daniel H., ed. *New Essays on The Last of the Mohicans*. New York: Cambridge University Press, 1992.

Lazarus, Emma (1849–1925) *poet*

Born in New York City in privileged circumstances, Emma Lazarus is best remembered for her sonnet "The New Colossus" (1883), which is inscribed on the pedestal of the Statue of Liberty. Her best work, however, is considered to be the poetic drama *The Dance to Death,* published in the volume *Songs of a Semite* (1882). This work—indeed the entire collection—was inspired by the Russian pogroms of 1882, in which thousands of her fellow Jews were persecuted. Whereas Lazarus's early work, collections like *Admetus and Other Poems* (1872) and a novel, *Alide: An Episode in Goethe's Life* (1874), have been judged flowery and sentimental by modern standards, by the time Lazarus published *By the Waters of Babylon* in *Century* magazine (see *CENTURY ILLUSTRATED MONTHLY MAGAZINE*) in 1887, her poetry had begun to take on echoes of Walt WHITMAN. Lazarus also published a translation of ballads and poems by the German writer Heinrich Heine (1797–1856) in 1881.

Sources

Vogel, Dan. *Emma Lazarus.* Boston: Twayne, 1980.
Young, Bette Roth. *Emma Lazarus in Her World: Life and Letters.* Philadelphia: Jewish Publication Society, 1995.

Lea, Henry Charles (1825–1909) *publisher, historian*

Born in Philadelphia into a publishing dynasty, Henry Charles Lea began to work in the firm Carey & Lea (later Blanchard & Lea) in 1843, becoming a partner in 1851. His avocation was history, and his first book, *Superstition and Force* (1866), a history of jurisprudence, led him to a lifelong study of the Roman Catholic Church and its influence on the medieval world. His three most important works all dealt with the Inquisition: *A History of the Inquisition of the Middle Ages* (1888), *A History of the Inquisition of Spain* (1906–1907), and *The Inquisition of the Spanish Dependencies* (1908).

Sources

Bradley, Sculley. *Henry Charles Lea, a Biography.* Philadelphia: University of Pennsylvania Press, 1931.

Leather-Stocking Tales *James Fenimore Cooper* (1823–1841) *series of novels*

James Fenimore COOPER focused this series of works on his idealized frontiersman, Nathaniel ("Natty") BUMPPO, whose nickname "Leatherstocking" stems from his preference for deerskin leggings. Bumppo would carry other nicknames as well—"Deerslayer," "Hawkeye," "Pathfinder," "Longue Carabine," and finally, simply "the trapper"—in the five novels that make up the series: *The Pioneers* (1823), *THE LAST OF THE MOHICANS* (1826), *THE PRAIRIE* (1827), *The Pathfinder* (1840), and *The Deerslayer* (1841). The novels follow, although not in chronological order, the progress of Leatherstocking's career from youth to old age, and his personality remains remarkably consistent throughout. Reverent of nature and discomforted by civilization, he is the perfect counterpart for his Indian companion, CHINGACHGOOK. Together with his dog Hector and his rifle Killdeer, Leatherstocking follows the American frontier as it advances westward. When he is last seen, in *The Prairie,* he is more than 80 years old, surrounded by Pawnee on the Midwestern prairie. With this area threatened by settlement, Bumppo turns his eyes westward and gives voice to his dying word: "Here!"

In creating Bumppo, Cooper probably drew upon his memories of a leatherstockinged hunter named Shipman whom he had known as a boy and also upon tales of the legendary frontiersman Daniel BOONE. Bumppo is born on the East Coast, where he is raised by the rapidly disappearing Delaware nation. His mettle is first tested during the French and Indian War (1754–63), during which he is forced to shed human blood and distance himself from romantic entanglements. He does, in fact, eventually fall in love, but his suit ends in disappointment, and he returns to his beloved woods. Finally, after he loses even his boon companion Chingachgook, he heads west, walking all the way to the Pacific. Back on the prairie, Bumppo finally expires. Cooper's series encourages readers to see his hero's death in emblematic terms: Something wild yet gentle, solitary and yet humane disappears with the death of the frontiersman and the wilderness he has represented.

Sources

Rans, Geoffrey. *Cooper's Leather-stocking Novels: A Secular Reading.* Chapel Hill: University of North Carolina Press, 1991.

Leaves of Grass *Walt Whitman* (1855) *poetry collection*

In 1855 Walt WHITMAN published the first edition of this collection, together with a famous "Preface," which he later deleted, but he continued to revise and add to the collection for the remainder of his life. The first edition appeared anonymously and contained only 12 untitled poems, including the seminal one later called "SONG OF MYSELF." The volume did include a picture of the poet, with rolled shirtsleeves and a casual stance, that conformed to the statement of poetic principles in his preface: Whitman declared that the poet must be a complete lover of nature and the embodiment of the common man. This was something altogether new to a nation accustomed to formal verses drafted by the so-called Schoolroom poets with elaborate names like John Greenleaf WHITTIER, Henry Wadsworth LONGFELLOW, and William Cullen BRYANT. *Leaves of Grass* was a collection of poems at once small and unassuming and ambitious and all-embracing. "The United States themselves," the preface announced, "are essentially the greatest poem," and the poet (Whitman himself, naturally) incarnated the life of the country. Few of the 800 copies in the first printing sold.

The following year, Whitman published a revised and expanded version of *Leaves of Grass,* substituting for the

"Preface" an open letter to Ralph Waldo EMERSON, whom he addressed as "Master." This second edition included the important poem that would come to be known as "Crossing Brooklyn Ferry" (then more prosaically titled "Sun-Down Poem"), but it is the third edition, which appeared in 1860, that critics have come to regard as crucial to Whitman's poetic development. Not only did the third edition include many new poems, it was also arranged in a symbolic order, opening with "Starting from Paumanok" and closing with "So Long!" It also contained two groups of poems celebrating human sexuality, causing much controversy among Whitman's readers.

Six more editions of *Leaves of Grass* followed, some annexing other collections, as in the 1867 edition's addition of the CIVIL WAR poems contained in *Drum-Taps* (1865) and *Sequel to Drum-Taps* (1865–66), which include Whitman's famous elegies on the death of Abraham LINCOLN, "When Lilacs Last in the Dooryard Bloom'd" and "O Captain! My Captain!" The final order of poems was established in the 1881 edition of *Leaves of Grass.* A "Death-Bed Edition," printed while the poet was mortally ill, included two final annexations, "Good-Bye, My Fancy" and "A Backward Glance o'er Travel'd Roads."

Sources

Crawley, Thomas E. *The Structure of Leaves of Grass.* Austin: University of Texas Press, 1970.

Nathanson, Tenney. *Whitman's Presence: Body, Voice, and Writing in Leaves of Grass.* New York: New York University Press, 1992.

Warren, James P. *Walt Whitman's Language Experiment.* University Park: Pennsylvania State University Press, 1990.

"Legend of Sleepy Hollow, The"

See CRANE, ICHABOD, and IRVING, WASHINGON.

Legree, Simon *character*

In Harriet Beecher STOWE's landmark novel about the prewar South, *UNCLE TOM'S CABIN* (1852), the planter Simon Legree is an arch-villain. Raised in New England, Legree went to sea and returned home only once during his years as a sailor. Nearly persuaded by his mother that he had chosen the wrong line of work, he cursed her and threw her to the floor. Some years later, leading a dissolute life, Legree learns by letter of his mother's death. He responds by throwing the blond lock of his mother's hair enclosed in the letter into the fire. Even as he does so, however, the memory of his mother's selfless love for him returns to haunt him.

Years later Legree becomes a prosperous plantation owner and slave master. He is unremittingly brutal to his human property, especially to his slave concubine, Cassy. At a New Orleans auction Legree buys Uncle Tom, a strong and intelligent black man whom Legree believes will be extremely productive. Although Tom does work hard and well, he refuses to submit his soul to his master. Legree, enraged, beats Tom harder. One day, when he is shown a lock of hair Tom had worn in a sack around his neck (belonging to the daughter of Tom's former owner), Legree is unpleasantly reminded of his mother's love and of her death, and the reminder makes him hate Tom all the more. When Tom refuses to reveal the whereabouts of Cassy and another female slave, both of whom are attempting to escape, Legree flogs the man to death. Afterwards Legree is haunted by all the evil he has perpetrated, and he sinks into drunkenness, madness, and finally death.

In later years, "Simon Legree" became a kind of shorthand for all the cruelties and inequities of the institution of slavery.

Sources

Gossett, Thomas F. *Uncle Tom's Cabin and American Culture.* Dallas: Southern Methodist University Press, 1985.

Hovet, Theodore R. *The Master Narrative: Harriet Beecher Stowe's Subversive Story of Master and Slave in Uncle Tom's Cabin and Dred.* Lanham, Md.: University Press of America, 1989.

Leland, Charles Godfrey (Hans Breitmann) (1824–1903) *poet, editor*

Charles Godfrey Leland was born in Philadelphia and educated at the College of New Jersey (now Princeton University) before going abroad to study in Heidelberg, Munich, and Paris. While working as editor of *GRAHAM'S MAGAZINE* in 1857, he wrote and published a German-American dialect poem, "Hans Breitmann's Barty." The poem proved so popular that Leland published several volumes of the humorous Breitmann verse. Leland's editing career continued at *VANITY FAIR* (1860–61) and *The Knickerbocker Magazine* (1861) (see KNICKERBOCKER SCHOOL). During the CIVIL WAR, Leland founded and edited *The Continental Monthly* (1862–63) in BOSTON to promote the Union cause. After the war he resumed his travels and the study of languages and folklore. He wrote more than 50 books devoted to such diverse topics as Gypsies and their language, Indian legends, and Roman history.

Sources

Parkhill, Thomas. *Weaving Ourselves into the Land: Charles Godfrey Leland, "Indians," and the Study of Native American Religions.* Albany: State University of New York Press, 1997.

Lewis, Alfred Henry (Dan Quinn) (c. 1858–1914) *journalist, short story writer*

Born in Cleveland, Ohio, Alfred Henry Lewis trained as a lawyer and even served as Cleveland's city attorney until

1881, when he went west to become a cowboy. He wrote for the Las Vegas *Optic* and wandered through the Southwest. Returning to the Midwest in 1885, he settled for a time in Kansas City, where in 1890 he submitted a piece to the Kansas City *Times* that he billed as an interview with an old cattleman. The "Old Cattleman" proved to be a popular character, and under the pen name Dan Quinn, Lewis wrote many more humorous stories taken from the "Old Cattleman's" reminiscences. Altogether there were six volumes of these so-called "Wolfville stories," which together present an accurate picture of what Lewis had experienced as a cowboy in the Southwest. In addition to continuing his editorial work, now for the HEARST chain, Lewis also published a number of fictionalized biographies as well as novels about the underworld and politics.

Sources

Ravitz, Abe C. *Alfred Henry Lewis.* Boise, Idaho: Boise State University, 1978.

Liberator, The *periodical*

This name has been used by two unrelated journals. Between 1831 and 1865, it was the name of an abolitionist journal (see ABOLITIONISM) founded in BOSTON by William Lloyd GARRISON. This version of *The Liberator* was so divisive that although it generated enthusiastic support among northern opponents of slavery, it was banned in many southern states. The name was also used by a magazine that superseded the leftist journal *THE MASSES* in 1918 and was finally absorbed into the *Labor Herald* in 1924.

Liberty Bell, The *periodical*

This annual GIFT BOOK—devoted to antislavery literature—was published from 1839 to 1858 in Boston under the sponsorship of abolitionist Maria Chapman (1806–85). It published works by Ralph Waldo EMERSON, Henry Wadsworth LONGFELLOW, and Bayard TAYLOR as well as English contributors like Elizabeth Barrett Browning (1806–61) and Harriet Martineau (1802–76).

Sources

Thompson, Ralph. *American Literary Annuals & Gift Books, 1825–1865.* New York: H. W. Wilson, 1936.

Life *periodical*

The name *Life* has been carried by two unrelated periodicals. It was first given in 1883 to a humor magazine founded by two Harvard University graduates, John Ames Mitchell and Edward Sanford Martin, who wanted to start a satirical weekly that would compete with and best the magazines *PUCK* and *Judge.* Mitchell had come into a $10,000 legacy, which he put toward a new zinc process for reproducing black-and-white drawings. Indeed, *Life* managed to attract the talents of Charles Dana GIBSON, who contributed his famous "Gibson girl" drawings as well as other artwork. Other well-known artists also contributed work, as did such literary lights as Brander MATTHEWS, John Kendrick BANGS, and James Whitcomb RILEY. *Life* succeeded in its aim of becoming the outstanding humor magazine of its day. It also published notable book and theater reviews and vivid editorials that condemned such varied matters as vivisection, hobble skirts (an early 1900s fashion where skirts were gathered at the ankles), and the practices of power brokers like John D. Rockefeller (1839–1937), J. P. Morgan (1837–1913), and William Randolph HEARST.

After World War I (which the magazine opposed), *Life* began to falter and was purchased by Charles Dana GIBSON, who made Robert Sherwood (1896–1955) editor from 1924 to 1928, a period during which the magazine revived its dual focus on humor and public affairs. After 1931, however, circulation declined, and in 1936 the magazine was sold to *Time,* which later reused the name for a pictorial weekly that focused largely on current affairs. That version of *Life* was published between 1936 and 1972 and was revived as a monthly magazine in 1978.

Lincoln, Abraham (1809–1865) *sixteenth president of the United States*

Born in a log cabin in Kentucky, Abraham Lincoln had a typical frontier upbringing, which meant little formal education and a good deal of hard manual labor connected with farming. Independent of mind and an avid reader, the young Lincoln shied away from churches. In 1830 his family moved to Illinois, where Lincoln split rails to build the family home. From 1831 to 1837 he studied law, cultivated friends in the legal profession, and served as a volunteer Indian fighter in the Black Hawk War (1832). From 1834 to 1841 he served in the state legislature.

Lincoln belonged to the Whig party, which meant that he opposed both the party of Andrew Jackson (1767–1845) and abolitionists, whom the Whigs believed only made tensions over slavery worse. He practiced law beginning in 1836 and later served one term in Congress (1847–49). His opposition to the MEXICAN WAR made Lincoln unpopular in his own state. At this point his political career seemed at an end, and he became a circuit-riding attorney trying cases all over the state. He had a hardy constitution and honed his grasp of the popular will. A good speaker—even a wit—he ran into trouble only when he got excited and let his voice rise.

Lincoln failed in his efforts to be elected to the U.S. Senate in 1855 and again in 1858, although his later race attracted extraordinary attention when he proved himself a worthy debater against the renowned Stephen Douglas (1813–61). Indeed, Lincoln exposed the hollowness in Douglas's concept of "popular sovereignty," which Douglas believed allowed each state to determine its own position on slavery and other matters. In effect, this position made the U.S. Constitution unenforceable, but as a temporary political expedient Douglas's position secured him victory.

In the debates Lincoln stated a position on slavery that would eventually make him a viable candidate for the presidency. He opposed slavery in principle and proposed to stop its spread in the territories. But he also promised not to work for its abolition in the slave states (he felt that slavery would prove impractical and die out in time). Thus Lincoln was able to secure support from northerners who wished to preserve the union and not make slavery the issue on which the country divided.

Lincoln cinched his hold on the national attention in his brilliant Cooper Union speech (February 27, 1860) in New York City. He presented himself with dignity, stating his moral objection to slavery but also his firm desire to mitigate its evil in a gradual, moderate way. In a convention deadlocked between several powerful contenders, Lincoln became the popular choice: he shrewdly cultivated behind-the-scenes political friends, and he did nothing to alienate the different factions in the Republican Party.

Once in office, Lincoln found the southern states obdurate in their desire to secede. They distrusted his conciliatory statements and believed he intended to destroy slavery. More important, southern patriots felt that the principles on which the nation had been established had been corrupted. They believed power resided in the states, and they viewed Lincoln as a centralizer who would usurp power by increasing the functions and the reach of the federal government. Lincoln also faced opposition in his own Cabinet and in the press, who tended to view him as a weak compromiser and incompetent—a country lawyer out of his depth in Washington. In the early stages of the war, when general after general failed to deliver victories for Lincoln, it was generally thought that either a peace would be negotiated or, after Lincoln's defeat, a new order would be established.

But Lincoln, one of the most underestimated presidents during his time in office, held on until he found the right commander in General Ulysses S. GRANT. Union victories at Vicksburg and Chattanooga under Grant sealed the South's fate. That Lincoln was aware of the gravity of his responsibility, and that he was quite consciously steering a course between the extremes of ABOLITIONISM and factions like the Copperheads (who sympathized with the South and were willing to settle for a truce) is evident in the way he carefully crafted and released not only the Emancipation Proclamation (1862) and the GETTYSBURG ADDRESS (1863) but also in his second inaugural speech.

Even during Lincoln's lifetime, certain politicians and members of the press slowly began to realize that they were dealing with a master politician and great statesman. Lincoln chose his words eloquently. His careful revisions of the Gettysburg address reveal a writer aware of how even the smallest phrase could be sharpened, often made even smaller and more effective. The growing awareness that Lincoln spoke on behalf of the people was made shockingly palpable when he was assassinated on April 14, 1865. Suddenly the grief of a nation acknowledged him as their representative.

Lincoln quickly became the very symbol of American democracy, a mythic figure born in humble surroundings but also a noble, tragic figure. Ridiculed in his lifetime, he became a symbolic figure in Walt WHITMAN's great poem "WHEN LILACS LAST IN THE DOORYARD BLOOM'D." Other commemorative poems include James Russell LOWELL's "Commemoration Ode," Edwin Markham's (1852–1940) "Lincoln," Edwin Arlington Robinson's (1869–1935) "The Master," and Vachel Lindsay's (1879–1931) "Abraham Lincoln Walks at Midnight." Gore Vidal produced a masterly novel evoking the shrewd politician as great man in *Lincoln* (1984), and Robert Sherwood (1896–1955) wrote the enormously popular play *Abe Lincoln in Illinois* (1938).

Lincoln's *Complete Works* appeared in 12 volumes in 1905, *New Letters and Papers of Lincoln* in 1930, *The Lincoln Papers* in 1948, and *Collected Works* in nine volumes in 1953.

Sources

Donald, David. *Lincoln.* New York: Simon & Schuster, 1995.

Thomas, Benjamin. *Abraham Lincoln: A Biography.* New York: Alfred A. Knopf, 1952.

Williams, Frank J. and William D. Pederson, eds. *Abraham Lincoln, Contemporary: An American Legacy: Collection of Essays.* Campbell, Calif.: Savas Woodbury, 1995.

Lippincott's Magazine *periodical*

This monthly was founded in Philadelphia by the publisher J. B. Lippincott & Co. in 1868 as competition for the preeminent periodical of the day, *The Atlantic.* Although like *The Atlantic* it published works by distinguished American writers, *Lippincott's* cast a wider net, printing works by southerners such as Sidney LANIER and William Gilmore SIMMS. It also distinguished itself as the first American publisher of Oscar Wilde's (1854–1900) only novel, *The Picture of Dorian Gray* (1890), and the first American outlet for Arthur Conan Doyle's (1859–1930) Sherlock Holmes stories. In 1914 *Lippincott's* was sold and moved to New York, where it was published as *McBride's Magazine* until 1916, when it merged with *SCRIBNER'S MAGAZINE.*

Literary Digest *periodical*

Founded in 1890 in New York City by I. K. Funk, this weekly was also edited by Funk until 1905. The periodical's emphasis was always on current events, which it covered largely by reprinting excerpts from newspapers and magazines. *Literary Digest* reached the 2 million circulation mark during the

1920s under the editorship (1905–33) of William Seaver Woods, when the digest frequently took straw polls to gauge public opinion. This strategy backfired badly when the *Literary Digest* miscalled the 1936 presidential election, which Franklin D. Roosevelt (1882–1945) won by a landslide; the miscalculation cost the *Digest* greatly, causing the public to lose confidence in it. By that time, too, competing news magazines like *Time* were making inroads on the *Digest's* subscription list. In 1937 it merged with the *Review of Reviews* and was published as *The Digest;* the next year it was absorbed by its rival, *Time.*

little magazines

This term applies to literary magazines that publish experimental works of literature or subject matter not found in mainstream, popular periodicals. Little magazines have small subscription lists—sometimes no more than a few hundred or a few thousand, as compared with large-circulation magazines with hundreds of thousands or even millions of subscribers. The little magazine may be produced by a single individual or a group of writers; it may be attached to an institution of higher learning or private organization devoted to promoting the arts.

In the United States, the little magazine did not become an important factor until the turn of the century, during the period leading up to World War I. It was the product of artists reacting against the provincial atmosphere of popular magazines, which did not take notice of the new literary developments in Europe. The little magazine rejected both the sentimentality of the 19th century and the conventions of a commercial culture, which demanded that literature teach a moral message or endorse the values of industry and capitalism. Creators of little magazines therefore saw themselves as radicals and protestors against the status quo.

Two little magazines typified the period: *Poetry: A Magazine of Verse,* established in 1912; and *The Little Review,* begun in 1914. The former, based in Chicago, published the work of writers such as Carl Sandburg (1878–1967) and T. S. Eliot (1888–1965), who would define the nature of 20th-century American literature. *The Little Review,* which was devoted to "art and good talk about art," is best remembered for its serialization of James Joyce's (1882–1941) *Ulysses* in 1918.

Sources

Anderson, Eliot and Mary Kinzie, eds. *The Little Magazine in America: A Modern Documentary History.* Yonkers, N. Y.: Pushcart, 1978.

little theater movement *literary movement*

The free-theater movement that started in Europe at the turn of the 19th century and included such theaters as the Théâtre Libre in France, the Freie Buhne in Berlin, and the Abbey Theatre in Ireland inspired American playmakers to create their own regional theaters to combat what was seen as the commercialism of BROADWAY shows and their derivative road companies. These American theater people wanted to produce new plays by American playwrights, but they also wanted to produce noncommercial drama by such exciting European talents as the Norwegian Henrik Ibsen (1828–1906) and the Anglo-Irish George Bernard Shaw (1856–1950).

The little theater movement in America began in BOSTON and spread across the nation. Two of the most significant early theatrical companies were the Washington Square Players in New York City and the Provincetown Players in Massachusetts, both of which started up in 1915. The Chicago Little Theatre was begun in a small space on the fourth floor of an office building in 1912 by Maurice Brown, who is said to have coined the term "little theater." The Neighborhood Playhouse, established in New York City in 1915, by Alice and Irene Lewisohn, was the one truly feminist participant in the movement. Sam Hume (1885–?), who founded the Arts and Crafts Theatre in Detroit in 1915, also helped launch *Theatre Arts* magazine, the voice of the new theater, on the West Coast in 1916. The Carolina Playmakers were established in Chapel Hill, North Carolina, in 1918 by George Pierce Baker (1866–1935), a Harvard English professor who also helped launch the careers of such students as Eugene O'Neill (1888–1953), Philip Barry, (1896–1949), John Dos Passos (1896–1970), and Thomas Wolfe (1900–38).

The Carolina Playmakers—an organization that has survived into the 21st century, albeit in a somewhat different form—exemplified many of the characteristics that made little theaters unique: instead of producing plays with proven track records, it featured new, often experimental plays such as the folk dramas created by Paul Green. The people associated with the group, from the playwright on down, were usually theatrical professionals, even if they worked for little or no pay. Although the movement largely died out with the coming of motion pictures, the idealism that fueled it helped create countless community theaters; college drama programs; and, in New York itself, repertory companies like the Group Theater, the off-Broadway alternative theater, and even the off-off-Broadway movement.

Sources

Gard, Robert E. *Community Theatre: Idea and Achievement.* New York: Duell, Sloan and Pearce, 1959.

———. *Grassroots Theater: A Search for Regional Arts in America.* Madison: University of Wisconsin Press, 1955.

Littleton, Mark

See PENDLETON, JOHN KENNEDY.

Little Women *Louisa May Alcott* (1868–1869) *novel*

Louisa May ALCOTT's novel, based on her own youthful experiences, has been a classic of juvenile literature ever since its initial two-part publication. The novel, subtitled *Meg, Jo, Beth, and Amy,* grew out of the publisher Thomas Niles's suggestion that Alcott write an account of her own childhood. In the novel, the March family is an idealized version of the Alcott family and its four female children: Anna (Meg), Louisa (Jo), Elizabeth (Beth), and May (Amy). Set during the CIVIL WAR, the novel virtually ignores the absent March patriarch, concentrating instead on the almost wholly female world inhabited by Marmee and her girls. Each girl has a markedly different disposition: Meg is pretty and ladylike; Jo (see MARCH, JOSEPHINE), Alcott's alter ego, is an unconventional, tomboyish sort who aspires to be a writer; Beth is fragile and musical; and Amy is an artistic prima donna. The drama in the girls' lives—just as in Jane Austen's *Pride and Prejudice* (1813)—revolves around their attempts to increase the family's income and, for all but Beth (who dies from the aftereffects of scarlet fever), to find a mate.

The only constant male presences in the March girls' lives are Laurie, the boy next door, and his tutor, John Brooke. John marries the eldest March daughter, Meg; Laurie, who loves Jo, eventually marries Amy after Jo rejects him to pursue her dreams of the literary life. Jo becomes a writer of melodramas, but she does not find her true place until she marries a middle-aged professor, Dr. Bhaer.

The immensely popular *Little Women* spawned a number of sequels: *Good Wives* (1869), *Little Men* (1871), and *Jo's Boys* (1886).

Sources

Alberghene, Janice M., and Beverly Lyon Clark, eds. *Little Women and the Feminist Imagination: Criticism, Controversy, Personal Essays.* New York: Garland, 1999.

Colins, Carolyn Strom, and Christina Wyss Eriksson. *The Little Women Treasury.* New York: Viking, 1996.

Keyser, Elizabeth Lennox. *Little Women: A Family Romance.* New York: Twayne, 1999.

local color *literary movement*

An offshoot of REALISM, the local color movement came into being in the wake of the CIVIL WAR. As the country expanded westward, particularly after completion of the transcontinental railroad in 1869, Americans gained a new sense of the vastness and the regional disparities of their land. Writers began to appreciate—and to emphasize—the customs, dialect, costumes, and landscape of their immediate locations. To be sure, such techniques had been used earlier by writers of Down East humor and frontier TALL TALES. What distinguished local color writers was their combination of closely observed particulars with exotic scenes or customs in a formula that was at once realistic and romantic. By common consent, Bret HARTE's "The Luck of Roaring Camp" (1868), a story about the spiritual transformation of a frontier gold-mining settlement under the spell of an orphaned child, is the first true piece of local color literature. Perhaps because the movement began with a short story, its most noted achievements are also in that form and include stories by such writers as Hamlin GARLAND, Joel Chandler HARRIS, Sarah Orne JEWETT, and Harriet Beecher STOWE. In the 20th century local color gave way to regionalism, which placed less emphasis on externals and more on the philosophical and sociological variations that distinguish different areas of the country.

Sources

Campbell, Donna M. *Resisting Regionalism: Gender and Naturalism in American Fiction, 1885–1915.* Athens: Ohio University Press, 1997.

Jones, Gavin R. *Strange Talk: The Politics of Dialect Literature in Gilded Age America.* Berkeley: University of California Press, 1999.

Kazin, Alfred. *A Writer's America: Landscape in Literature.* New York: Alfred A. Knopf, 1988.

Mallory, William, and Paul Simpson-Housley, eds. *Geography and Literature: A Meeting of the Disciplines.* Syracuse, N. Y.: Syracuse University Press, 1987.

Locke, David Ross (Petroleum Vesuvius Nasby) (1833–1888) *journalist, editor*

Born in Vestal, New York, David Ross Locke began his newspaper career at an early age. At age 10 he went to work as a printer's devil (printing apprentice) for the *Cortland Democrat* in his home state and became an itinerant printer a few years later. He ended up in Ohio where, at the age of 19, he founded the *Plymouth Advertiser* with a friend. Shortly thereafter he took a job as editor of the Findlay, Ohio, *Jeffersonian* which, on March 21, 1861, printed the first letter of Petroleum V. Nasby, Locke's alter ego. Enraged by what he saw as the provincial attitudes toward African Americans among some of his fellow northerners, Locke posed as a corrupt and ignorant Copperhead, the term for a northern supporter of the Confederacy. Employing a style made popular by the humorist Artemus Ward (Charles Farrar BROWNE), Locke employed tortured grammar and twisted logic to make a pointed comment on society.

When Locke became the editor of the Toledo *Blade* in 1865, he published the Nasby letters there, a practice he kept up even after he became the newspaper's owner. Nasby proved to be immensely popular, both with the common reader and with Abraham LINCOLN, who read some of Nasby's commentary to his cabinet officers before presenting them with his Emancipation Proclamation, which freed southern slaves. Eventually Lincoln's Treasury secretary, George S. Boutwell, would attribute the North's victory in the CIVIL WAR to "the Army and Navy, the Republican Party, and the *Letters of Petroleum V. Nasby.*" *The Nasby Papers* (1864) was the first of several Nasby collections. Locke also published a novel, *The Demagogue* (1891), and numerous other political works.

Sources

Austin, James C. *Petroleum V. Nasby (David Ross Locke).* New York: Twayne, 1965.
Harrison, John M. *The Man Who Made Nasby: David Ross Locke.* Chapel Hill: University of North Carolina Press, 1969.

London, Jack (1876–1916) *novelist*

Jack London was born in San Francisco, California, and spent his early life around the Oakland, California, docks and the San Francisco waterfront. His family was poor, and life was a grim struggle—facts he later used in autobiographical novels such as *Martin Eden* (1909), the story of how a young, poorly educated man teaches himself to become a writer through dogged persistence and ruthless ambition. Born illegitimate, London identified with the downtrodden and the outcasts of society. His father, William Henry Chaney, was a traveling astrologer. When his mother, Flora Wellman, a spiritualist, married his stepfather, John London, a farmer, he took his stepfather's name.

John London's farm failed, and the family faced a constant financial struggle. His stepson, bright and energetic—later photographs reveal a vigorous, ruggedly handsome man—had an intermittent education, which ceased with grammar school at the age of 14 (except for a few months at the University of California, Berkeley, in 1897). At age 10, Jack London was already selling newspapers and laboring as a pin boy in a bowling alley. At 14 he found a job in a cannery, and at 16, like his fictional heroes, he showed independence and pluck, pitching in with his pals to buy an oyster boat and becoming known as an "oyster pirate." At 17 he became a sailor employed on a sealing boat that took him to Japan. At 18 he turned hobo and toured America and Canada.

By 1895 London had embarked on a fierce program of self-education, reading Charles Darwin (1809–82), Karl Marx (1818–83), and Friedrich Nietzsche (1844–1900). These writers imbued London with a vision of society as a struggle in which the fittest survived. London's works, however, show that even the very strong could be crushed, given the political structure of society, and that the true nature of a human being might not be revealed except in the struggle against nature.

At 21, London followed the gold rush to the Klondike; two years later he sold his first story, "To the Man on the Trail." Soon he was producing a flood of stories and novels about the individual's quest not only for survival but also for triumph over both the elements of nature and the structures of society.

Jack London's name will forever be associated with the classic novel THE CALL OF THE WILD (1903). Never out of print, it has been translated into 68 languages. The book made London's career as a bestselling author and secured his place in American literary NATURALISM. The story is about a dog, Buck, half St. Bernard and half Scottish sheepdog. He is stolen from a comfortable California home and is brutalized as a sled dog. Nevertheless, his spirit overcomes adversity—including the challenge of a vicious dog, Spitz—and Buck earns the love of a kind master, Thornton, to whom Buck remains loyal even after his master's death.

The key to London's success was to make his adventure stories embody his philosophical and political ideas rather than have those ideas explicitly drive the stories. Readers could easily imbibe London's message while apparently reading only a gripping story. For London, plot itself, the structure of the story, made his political point.

London followed up his initial success with two more short adventure novels: *The Sea Wolf* (1904) and *White Fang* (1905). In the former a wealthy literary critic, Humphrey Van Weyden, is shipwrecked and has to contend with the ruthless Wolf Larsen, captain of the *Ghost,* a sealing schooner. Just as *The Call of the Wild* drew on London's own Klondike experience to present an authentic portrayal of a cold frontier world, so did *The Sea Wolf* capitalize on London's memories of rough sea voyages. In each case the author confronts readers with rugged and life-threatening environments in which the individual has to rely on his own inner resources in a way that sedate society never requires. In giving the main character in *The Sea Wolf* a Dutch name, London points to the intrepid spirit that settled America but which had, in the course of several generations, become weak. In his conflict with the Viking-like Larsen, Van Weyden builds himself up physically and mentally, returning to society a stronger and more self-aware man.

At 29 Jack London was the most famous, most widely read, and wealthiest author in America. He would write increasingly for money to maintain his lavish existence of luxury homes and yachts, although he did not forsake his withering view of a harsh world. Indeed, in *Martin Eden,* the hero as writer explicitly confronts the complacency of bourgeois society, finding himself at a middle-class dinner table arguing for his interpretation of existence with the pillars of society: the judges and politicians who hold power and look upon the powerless as unworthy.

Other books, including *The Iron Heel* (1907), the story of a fascist dictatorship destroyed by socialist revolution, and *War of the Classes* (1904), a collection of lectures and essays, demonstrate that London retained his commitment to social criticism. As a journalist he wrote about the Russo-Japanese War (1904) for the HEARST newspapers and about Mexico for *COLLIER*'s magazine. In 1902 he posed as a sailor and investigated the lives of East End slum dwellers in London, producing an exposé the next year, *The People of the*

Abyss. His novel *Smoke Bellew* (1912) covers the career of a journalist in the Yukon.

Such novels as *The Valley of the Moon* (1913) drew on the author's nostalgia for an agrarian life and his dislike of dehumanizing cities. It unrealistically proposed a return to the land. But increasingly London's work became the prisoner of the very commercial and cutthroat civilization he deplored. His personal deterioration—abetted by drug use and dipsomania—is evident in his autobiographical pro-temperance novel, *John Barleycorn* (1913). *The Cruise of the Snark*, London's account of his effort to cruise the world in his schooner, is an apt example of his overreaching; this ambitious enterprise also ruined him financially. Nevertheless, his evocations of the writer as hero remain a signal achievement, and his broad and intense engagement with society still attracts generations of readers.

Sources

Auerbach, Jonathan. *Male Call: Becoming Jack London*. Durham, N.C.: Duke University Press, 1996.

Cassuto, Leonard, and Jeanne Campbell Reesman, eds. *Rereading Jack London*. Stanford: Stanford University Press, 1996.

Kershaw, Alex. *Jack London: A Life*. New York: St. Martin's Press, 1997.

Labor, Earle, and Jeanne Campbell Reesman. *Jack London*. Rev. ed. New York: Twayne, 1994.

Watson, Charles N. *The Novels of Jack London: A Reappraisal*. Madison: University of Wisconsin Press, 1982.

Longfellow, Henry Wadsworth (1807–1882)

poet

Born in Portland, Maine, Henry Wadsworth Longfellow descended from a colonial family. He attended private school and in 1825 graduated from Bowdoin College, where he was a classmate of Nathaniel HAWTHORNE. Longfellow taught modern languages at Bowdoin, and then from 1826 to 1829 he traveled in France, Spain, Italy, and Germany. In 1829 he resumed his professorship at Bowdoin and wrote essays and sketches for magazines. A superb teacher, he was invited to become a professor at Harvard, where he began work in 1836.

Although Longfellow had published his first book of poetry in 1820, his important work does not emerge until *Voices of the Night* (1839), which contains "Hymn to the Night," "A Psalm of Life," and other poems. *Ballads and Other Poems* (1841) is an even stronger volume, with trademark Longfellow poems such as "The Village Blacksmith," "The Wreck of the Hesperus," "The Skeleton in Armor," and "Excelsior"—the last an especially good example of the uplifting rousing verse that made Longfellow such a cheering and popular poet. Like other writers in Cambridge and Concord, Longfellow was staunchly abolitionist (see ABOLITIONISM), and he published *Poems on Slavery* in 1842.

By the 1840s Longfellow had become one of the most important literary figures in the United States. In 1843 he married Frances Appleton, the daughter of a wealthy cotton-mill manufacturer. Thus Longfellow took his place as both a distinguished poet and prominent citizen.

The Belfry of Bruges and Other Poems (1845) contains classics such as "The Arsenal at Springfield," "The Bridge," "That Arrow and the Song," and "The Belfry of Bruges." Then the poet turned to immensely popular narrative poems such as *Evangeline* (1847), which evokes the pastoral life of the Acadians; and *The Golden Legend* (1851), set in medieval Germany. In this long narrative, almost novelistic poem, he was able to blend elements of ROMANTICISM with a rather genteel, even cosy domestic sensibility, which is given full flavor in *Seaside and Fireside* (1849). *Hiawatha* (1855) combined all of Longfellow's strengths in retelling an American legend in a singsong, fairy-tale style that appealed to all ages of readers.

Longfellow's success as a poet was unprecedented. When he drew on another American legend in *The Courtship of Miles Standish* (1858), the work sold more than 15,000 copies on its first day in Boston and London bookshops. Another mark of his transatlantic success is that he is the only American poet to be given a place in the Poet's Corner of Westminster Abbey, the final resting place of Great Britain's most significant literary figures.

By 1855 Longfellow had resigned his professorship, and although his happiness was shattered when his wife died in a fire in 1861, he recovered to publish *Tales of a Wayside Inn* (1863), which included perhaps his most famous poem, "Paul Revere's Ride." By the 1860s he had turned to the study of Dante Alighieri (1265–1321), translating the Italian poet's works between 1865 and 1867 and writing a sequence of "Divina Commedia" sonnets that are considered some of his best work. His later, less significant work is collected in volumes such as *The Masque of Pandora* (1975), *Ultima Thule* (1880), and *In the Harbor* (1882).

Gentle, sweet, pure—these are words often used to describe Longfellow's poetry. He lacked the modern temper—the robustness of Walt WHITMAN, the metaphysical complexity of Emily DICKINSON. The optimism of Longfellow's American poems seemed excessive after World War I, and his romanticism seems too tepid compared to that of Ralph Waldo EMERSON or Henry David THOREAU. Despite his popularity in his own lifetime, by the mid-20th century Longfellow was studied mostly as an example of a national poet, a conserver of the American myth, but not as a great poet.

A small core of Longfellow's poems, however, are great precisely because of their simplicity and accurate depiction of American manners and folkways. As a children's poet, Longfellow remains incomparable. An edition of Longfellow's *Letters* was published in six volumes between 1966 and 1982.

Sources

Wagenknecht, Edward. *Henry Wadsworth Longfellow: His Poetry and Prose.* New York: Ungar, 1986.

Williams, Cecil B. *Henry Wadsworth Longfellow.* New York: Twayne, 1964.

Longstreet, Augustus Baldwin (1790–1870) *short story writer*

A native of Augusta, Georgia, Augustus Baldwin Longstreet attended Yale University and the country's first law school in Litchfield, Connecticut. Back in Georgia, he worked as a lawyer, a clergyman, and a journalist before becoming president of Emory College (1839–48), Centenary College (1849), the University of Mississippi (1849–56), and the University of South Carolina (1857–65). The work that made Longstreet's name was *Georgia Scenes, Characters, and Incidents* (1835), a series of humorous but realistic sketches about life in the OLD SOUTHWEST that became a classic work of regionalism whose style would influence successors like George Washington HARRIS and Mark Twain (Samuel Langhorne CLEMENS). Devoted to his native state, Longstreet was an ardent supporter during the CIVIL WAR of the doctrine of nullification, which held that states need not enforce federal laws. His semiautobiographical novel about his Georgia boyhood, *Master William Mitten* (1864), proved unpopular, and subsequent stories written in the style of *Georgia Scenes* were less successful than his original work.

Sources

King, Kimball. *Augustus Baldwin Longstreet.* Boston: Twayne, 1984.

Romine, Scott. *The Narrative Forms of Southern Community.* Baton Rouge: Louisiana State University Press, 1999.

Wade, John D. *Augustus Baldwin Longstreet: A Study of the Development of Culture in the South.* Athens: University of Georgia Press, 1969.

Louisville Courier-Journal

See *LOUISVILLE DAILY JOURNAL*.

Louisville *Daily Journal* *periodical*

Founded in 1830 by Connecticut native George Dennison Prentice (1802–70) as a vehicle for combating the political philosophy and machinations of Andrew Jackson (1767–1845), this newspaper became known for Prentice's own lively style. During the CIVIL WAR the paper supported the Union cause and was widely credited with keeping Kentucky loyal to the North. During RECONSTRUCTION Prentice vacillated between Democratic and Republican loyalties. In 1868, when he retired, the paper merged with the rival—and Democratic—*Louisville Courier* to become the Louisville *Courier-Journal.* Initially edited by "Marse" Henry Watterson, the *Courier-Journal,* although its style was distinctly "Old South," held progressive views about free trade, relations with the North, and the bad influence of the Ku Klux Klan. After World War I it became a typical city newspaper, albeit one of consistently high quality that won numerous Pulitzer Prizes.

Lovingood, Sut

See HARRIS, GEORGE WASHINGTON.

Lowell, James Russell (1819–1891) *poet, critic*

A member of a distinguished colonial family, James Russell Lowell was born in Cambridge, Massachusetts, and graduated from Harvard as the class poet in 1838. He earned an M.A. in 1841 and studied law but soon turned to poetry. He abandoned his early conservatism after he married Maria White in 1843. The next year he published *Poems,* which demonstrated an active engagement with liberalism and ABOLITIONISM. He also wrote and edited the NATIONAL ANTI-SLAVERY STANDARD (1848–52) and contributed to the *Pennsylvania Freeman.*

Lowell's most important poetic work in his early career was *A Fable for Critics* (1848), which commented satirically on many of his literary contemporaries. More than any other work, this book combined Lowell's talents as critic and creator. Although he adopted a light tone, his perceptions were incisive and penetrated to the core of his subjects' styles. *The Biglow Papers* (1848), written in Yankee dialect, were comic in style but also serious attacks on the doctrine of manifest destiny and the war in Mexico.

The middle period of Lowell's career coincided with the death of his wife in 1853. He became a professor at Harvard and published little of note until *Fireside Travels* (1864), literary essays that initiated his role as man of letters. There followed a series of books of literary criticism: *Among My Books* (1870), *My Study Windows* (1871), a second *Among My Books* (1876), *Latest Literary Essays and Addresses* (1891), and *The Old English Dramatists* (1891).

Except for *The Cathedral* (1869), Lowell wrote little significant poetry after 1840s. Instead, as the first editor of the *ATLANTIC MONTHLY* (1857–61) and of *THE NORTH AMERICAN REVIEW,* he became a kind of cultural arbiter who also exercised considerable political influence as an essayist. His *Political Essays* appeared in 1888. Even more important was his second edition of *The Biglow Papers* (1876), which explored Northern attitudes toward the Civil War and solidified support for the Union cause.

Like Washington IRVING, Lowell became one of the few American writers to exert political and diplomatic influence and to take government office. He was minister to Spain (1877–80) and minister to England (1880–85).

In these later years he gradually reverted to his family's conservatism.

The *Letters of James Russell Lowell* appeared in 1894 and *New Letters of James Russell Lowell* in 1932.

Sources

Beatty, Richmond Croom. *James Russell Lowell.* Nashville: Vanderbilt University Press, 1942.

Duberman, Martin. *James Russell Lowell.* Boston: Houghton Mifflin, 1966.

McGlinchee, Claire. *James Russell Lowell.* New York: Twayne, 1967.

Luska, Sidney

See HARLAND, HENRY.

lyceum movement *literary and social movement*

This system of adult education in science and the arts was initiated by an 1826 article in the *Journal of Education* in which the educator and reformer Josiah Holbrook (1788–1854) sketched out his plan for some informal lecture series that would educate and entertain the American populace. Holbrook founded the first "American Lyceum" in Millbury, Massachusetts, in 1826, and within two years his American Lyceum group had spawned nearly 100 other lyceums. Lyceums initially concentrated on natural history but gradually widened their curriculum to include such topics as travel, art appreciation, temperance, phrenology, and spiritual uplift. Among the most popular and well-paid speakers on the lyceum circuit were Ralph Waldo EMERSON, Henry David THOREAU, Oliver Wendell HOLMES, Lucy STONE, and Elizabeth Cady STANTON. By the time of the 1839 American Lyceum Union national convention, the movement included more than 3,000 member lyceums scattered around the country. Their presence sparked interest in teacher training and schools as well as in the founding of new museums and libraries.

The CIVIL WAR interrupted the movement's momentum, and in 1870 Bayard TAYLOR, himself once a popular lyceum speaker, remarked that what had once been an educational experience had degenerated into a "nonintellectual diversion." Not long afterward, the lyceum movement would make way for the outdoor entertainments of CHAUTAUQUA.

Sources

Bode, Carl. *The American Lyceum: Town Meeting of the Mind.* New York: Oxford University Press, 1956.

Tapia, John E. *Circuit Chautauqua: From Rural Education to Popular Entertainment in Early Twentieth Century America.* Jefferson, N.C.: McFarland, 1997.

McClure's Magazine *periodical*

Published and edited by S. S. McClure (1857–1949), who had founded the first newspaper syndicate in the United States, *McClure's* was founded in 1893 and had as its original mission the publication of the best contemporary British and American literature at an affordable price. Between 1901 and 1912, however, the magazine became a major proponent of the MUCKRAKING MOVEMENT, publishing such important pieces as Ida TARBELL's "The History of Standard Oil," about the abuses of a monopoly; and Lincoln STEFFENS's "The Shame of Minneapolis," concerning metropolitan corruption. After the trust-busting movement spearheaded by Theodore ROOSEVELT and the era of progressive social and political reform waned, so did *McClure's* popularity.

MacDowell Colony *organization*

After the New York-born composer Edward MacDowell (1861–1908) died, his widow deeded their home in Peterborough, New Hampshire, to the MacDowell Memorial Association. A fund to honor the composer had been started in 1906 by such prominent individuals as Grover Cleveland (1837–1908) and Andrew Carnegie (1835–1919), and Marian Nevins MacDowell (1857–1956) used these monies to found the MacDowell Colony at the Peterborough farm in 1907. Her aim was to provide other creative artists with a retreat where they could concentrate on their art. Since then composers such as Aaron Copland (1900–90) and writers such as Thornton Wilder (1897–1975) have created important works in the tranquility of the colony.

Sources

McKee, Nancy. *Valiant Woman.* San Antonio, Tex.: Naylor Co., 1962.

McGuffey, William Holmes (1800–1873) *publisher*

Born near Claysville, Pennsylvania, William McGuffey taught in rural schools before he graduated from Washington and Jefferson College in 1826. He went on to become a professor of languages and philosophy at Miami University of Ohio (1826–36) and president of Cincinnati College (1839–43) before taking up teaching posts at Woodward College in Cincinnati (1843–45) and the University of Virginia (1845–73). He is remembered chiefly for the *Eclectic Readers,* which combined moral lessons with literary extracts, that he compiled while at Miami. The six readers he published between 1836 and 1857 sold well over 100 million copies and have been said to have taught America to read. While this claim may overstate the case, there can be no doubt about the schoolbooks' influence on the American mind. New editions of McGuffey's "Readers" appeared well into the 20th century.

Sources

Westerhoff, John H. *McGuffey and His Readers.* Nashville: Abingdon, 1978.

McLean, Sarah Pratt (Sarah Pratt McLean Greene) (1856–1935) *novelist*

Born in Simsbury, Connecticut, McLean was educated at Mount Holyoke College in Massachusetts before she began teaching school on Cape Cod in 1874. Village life on the Cape furnished her with material for her best-known work, *Cape Cod Folks* (1881), a LOCAL COLOR romance that used real people—some of whom subsequently sued the author—as characters. Several of her later novels, most set in New England and employing regional dialect, were published under her married name, Greene, after she married Franklin Lynde Greene in 1887.

McTeague Frank Norris (1899) novel

One of Frank NORRIS's best works, *McTeague* is also one of the finest examples of American literary NATURALISM. The novel is named for its main character, a brutal giant of a man named Mac McTeague. A miner turned (unlicensed) dentist, McTeague practices in a poor section of San Francisco, where he falls in love with one of his patients, the pretty young Trina Sieppe. She is the cousin of McTeague's friend Marcus Schouler, who had hoped to marry her. Immediately smitten with Trina, McTeague clumsily proposes to her while working on her teeth, and Trina accepts.

Just before the two wed, Trina wins $5,000 in a lottery, which heightens Schouler's jealousy. When Schouler leaves town to work on a ranch, the couple learn that he has instructed his political cronies to expose McTeague's illegal dental practice. Deprived of his line of work, McTeague turns to drink and begins to torture Trina, whose increasing miserliness (she has managed through thrift, investment, and deception to increase her initial $5,000 stake) enrages her husband. Finally, McTeague murders her and robs her of the $5,000 she has refused to spend to alleviate their poverty.

In flight from the law, McTeague leaves the city and returns to gold prospecting. Ultimately he and a partner strike it rich, but McTeague is forced to flee before he can claim his share of the riches. Crossing Death Valley, he encounters his nemesis, Schouler. The two men fight, and the giant McTeague beats his onetime friend to the brink of death. Before he expires, however, Schouler handcuffs himself to McTeague, who is now doomed to die of thirst shackled to the corpse of his mortal enemy.

The greed that powers the main plot of *McTeague* is mirrored in a subplot involving a mad charwoman, Maria Macapa, and a junk dealer named Zerkow. Zerkow marries Maria for no better reason than her obsession with a set of gold plate, then himself goes mad and commits suicide after murdering her. The book's emphasis on man's baser instincts and its realistic depiction of life in the lower depths have helped to make its reputation as a classic of naturalism.

Sources

Guest, David. *Sentenced to Death: The American Novel and Capital Punishment.* Jackson: University Press of Mississippi, 1997.

Norris, Frank. *McTeague: A Story of San Francisco: Authoritative Text, Contexts, Criticism.* Edited by Donald Pizer. New York: W. W. Norton, 1997.

Madame Blavatsky

See BLAVATSKY, HELENA PETROVNA HAHN.

Maggie: A Girl of the Streets Stephen Crane (1893) novel

Stephen CRANE's naturalistic masterpiece was published privately in 1893 under the name Johnston Smith, but the book was not published commercially until 1896. At the time Crane paid for his first novel to appear, he was a 22-year-old journalist living in poverty in New York City, and he knew firsthand something of the tenement life of the BOWERY that was his subject. His eponymous heroine, Maggie Johnson, is born into poverty there, the daughter of a brutal workingman and his abusive, alcoholic wife. Despite the squalor of her surroundings, Maggie retains a core of innocence. Her two brothers succumb to their environment, one dying in childhood and the other becoming a street tough. Maggie, pretty and shy, goes to work in a sweatshop, and in time she falls in love with Pete, one of her brother's friends. Pete is a bartender who takes Maggie out to beer halls, freak shows, and cheap museums. Maggie believes him to be elegant and noble, and in her innocence she allows him to seduce her.

When her mother realizes what has happened, she disowns Maggie, making her dependent on the undependable Pete. In short order, Pete throws her over for another woman. When Maggie attempts to return home, her mother jeers at her; when she appeals to Pete, he dismisses her. Maggie has only one choice left: she must become a prostitute in order to survive. By temperament, however, she is unsuited to this, and in despair she drowns herself in the East River.

Crane's bold novel was rejected by Richard Watson Gilder's *THE CENTURY ILLUSTRATED MONTHLY MAGAZINE*, but in 1896 William Dean HOWELLS recognized the importance of *Maggie* and persuaded D. Appleton and Company to publish it. Crane's first novel in fact proved to be a landmark work of American literary NATURALISM, ironic in tone and unforgiving in its condemnation of the corruption that haunted many institutions at the time. Failed by her family and her workplace and deluded by notions about romance and heroism derived from popular culture, Maggie was unfit for the world into which she was born.

Sources

Gandal, Keith. *The Virtues of the Vicious: Jacob Riis, Stephen Crane, and the Spectacle of the Slum.* New York: Oxford University Press, 1997.

Sedycias, João. *The Naturalistic Novel of the New World: A Comparative Study of Stephen Crane, Aluísio Azevedo, and Federico Gamboa.* Lanham, Md.: University Press of America, 1993.

Wertheim, Stanley, comp. *The Merrill Studies in Maggie and George's Mother.* Columbus, Ohio: C. E. Merrill, 1970.

Mann, Horace (1796–1859) *educator, orator*

Born in Franklin, Massachusetts, Horace Mann received only a spotty education as a youngster, but he nonetheless managed to graduate from Brown University, pass the Massachusetts bar exam, and practice as a lawyer. He also served as a state representative and state senator before becoming secretary of the newly created state board of education in 1837. During his 12-year tenure in that position, he greatly improved the educational standards and physical condition of the public schools and improved teacher training and remuneration. His influence as an educational reformer spread across the country. In 1848, running on an antislavery Whig Party ticket, Mann was elected to the U.S. House of Representatives. In 1853 he became the first president of Antioch College in Ohio. His *Lectures on Education* were published in 1845.

Sources

Messerli, Jonathan. *Horace Mann: A Biography.* New York: Alfred A. Knopf, 1972.

March, Josephine *character*

The central character of Louisa May ALCOTT's *LITTLE WOMEN* (1868–69), Jo March was a stand-in for her creator, whose writing became the sole support of the Alcott clan. Ungainly, tomboyish, tall, and dark-haired, Jo finds herself torn between her desire to pursue a writing career and her profound sense of loyalty to her family. With her father serving as a volunteer chaplain with the Union army during the CIVIL WAR, Jo—more than any of her three sisters—feels it is her responsibility to keep the family intact. Despite her best efforts, her oldest sister marries and her beloved sister Beth contracts scarlet fever, which eventually kills her.

Jo, unable to accept the changes time brings to the Marches and eager to try her wings, spends a winter in New York City, where she works as a governess, tries her hand at melodramatic fiction, and falls in love with a German professor, Friedrich Bhaer. Still torn between her own desires and her family ties, she returns home, only to lose her friend Laurie to heartbreak when she rejects his marriage proposal. Jo then accepts Friedrich Bhaer's suit, and after they are married, they set up a school for boys and have two boys of their own. Once again surrounded by family, Jo feels no further need to express herself and abandons her former lust for glory.

Generations of young female readers have compared themselves with the four March girls, invariably finding they wished to be like the generous, impulsive, amusing Jo.

Sources

Collins, Carolyn Strom, and Christina Wyss Eriksson. *The Little Women Treasury.* New York: Viking, 1996.

Keyser, Elizabeth Lennox. *Little Women: A Family Romance.* New York: Twayne, 1999.

Showalter, Elaine. *Sister's Choice: Tradition and Change in American Women's Writing.* New York: Oxford University Press, 1991.

Massachusetts Quarterly Review, The periodical

This Boston literary, philosophical, and humanitarian review (1847–50) was edited by Ralph Waldo EMERSON, Theodore PARKER, and J. E. Cabot. The editors—referring to a famed transcendentalist periodical—intended their review to be "the *DIAL* with a beard,"a more assertive, authoritative magazine than its predecessor. Despite contributions from such important writers as James Russell LOWELL and Julia Ward HOWE, the review was short-lived. As Thomas Wentworth HIGGINSON wryly remarked, *The Massachusetts Quarterly Review* was more like "the beard without the *Dial.*"

Masses, The periodical

Although founded in 1911 in New York City by restaurant manager Piet Vlag as "an outgrowth of the cooperative side of Socialist activity," under the leadership of its first editor, Thomas Seltzer (1875–1934), *The Masses* evinced no particular political orientation, although it tended to publish literature written by liberal European authors. Between 1912 and December 1918, when the magazine was suppressed by the federal government, *The Masses* was edited by Max Eastman (1883–1969) and showed a marked Socialist Party editorial policy. Contributions came from such prominent left-leaning Americans as Floyd Dell (1887–1969) and John Reed (1887–1920), but with U.S. involvement in World War I, the Postal Service refused to deliver the magazine, effectively shutting it down.

Three months after the government's action, the editors began another weekly devoted to leftist social criticism. *THE LIBERATOR* was, if anything, more radical than its predecessor, in 1922 affiliating itself with the Communist Party. Two years later this magazine merged with two other communist publications to become *The Workers' Monthly.*

In 1926, *The Masses* was revived as the weekly *New Masses,* a title it retained until 1948. It then merged with yet another Marxist periodical to become the monthly magazine *Masses & Mainstream,* which over the next five years published such authors as Howard Fast (1914–), W. E. B. DU BOIS, and Paul Robeson (1898–1976).

Sources

Cautor, Milton. *Max Eastman.* New York: Twayne, 1970.

Matthews, James Brander (1852–1929) *essayist, critic*

A native of New Orleans, Brander Matthews was educated at Columbia College and Columbia Law School. Instead of practicing law, however, he turned to writing, becoming a prominent member of New York and London literary circles and helping found such organizations as the Authors' Club and The Players. In addition to producing a two-volume work on the French theater in 1880–81, he coedited (with H. D. Brunner) the five-volume *Actors and Actresses of Great Britain and the United States* (1886). In the 1880s Matthews also produced a volume of short stories and several plays.

After lecturing at Columbia University during the academic year 1891–92, Matthews became a professor of English there, and between 1900 and 1924, also at Columbia, he became the first professor of dramatic literature in the United States. He kept up a steady stream of essays, compilations, and analyses on plays and playwrights, such as *The Principles of Playmaking* (1919) and *Shakspere as a Playwright* (1913), which influenced playwrights and public alike. His 1896 history of the development of American literature, *An Introduction to the Study of American Literature,* created a new field of literary scholarship.

Matthews lectured widely, both at home and abroad, and also managed to produce a series of fictional works about New York. A founding member of the National Institute of Arts and Letters, he has been called "perhaps the last of the gentlemanly school of critics and essayists."

Sources

Oliver, Lawrence J. *Brander Matthews, Theodore Roosevelt, and the Politics of American Literature, 1880–1920.* Knoxville: University of Tennessee Press, 1992.

Mauve Decade, The

See BEER, THOMAS.

Melville, Herman (1819–1891) *novelist, short story writer, poet*

Herman Melville was born in New York City on August 1, 1819, the third child and second son of Allan Melvill and his wife, Maria. At the time, Allan Melvill, the son of an old Boston family, was a fairly prosperous importer of luxury items, and the Melvills lived well. In 1830, however, Allan's business collapsed, and the family moved to Albany, New York, to seek sanctuary among Maria's relatives. Allan made another attempt at business in Albany, but in 1832 he died, bankrupt and insane, and shortly afterward Maria added the final *e* to the family name.

After working as a bank clerk and a farmhand, Herman Melville enrolled in the Albany Classical School in order to prepare for a business career. There he discovered his gift for writing and resolved to become a teacher. But he found teaching in a country school unappealing, and in 1838 he enrolled in the Lansingburgh Academy, located only a few blocks from the Melvilles' new home in Lansingburgh, New York. That November he was certified as a surveyor and engineer.

Failing to find paid employment, Melville wrote short pieces for the local newspapers while courting some of the town's young ladies and pining for adventure. In June 1839 he commenced his seagoing adventures by signing on as a cabin boy on the *St. Lawrence,* a merchant ship bound for Liverpool, England. He would later transform the experiences of this trip into fiction in *Redburn.*

Returning to Lansingburgh in September 1839, Melville found his mother and sisters in dire financial straits. Desperate for extra income, he once again took a teaching job, only to lose it a few months later when his school declared bankruptcy. After a stint of substitute teaching, Melville decided to look elsewhere for work while on a trip west. However, the American West proved not to be the land of opportunity, so Melville went back east. Failing to find a job in New York City, he determined to go back to sea, and in January 1841, he shipped aboard the whaler *Acushnet.*

Melville had signed up for the customary four-year tour, but he grew restless under the harsh conditions at sea. In June 1842, accompanied by a shipmate, Melville jumped ship. The two escaped into the jungle of the Polynesian Marquesas, where they were taken up by members of the Taipi tribe. His friend escaped almost immediately, but Melville lived among the Marquesan natives for four weeks before escaping and boarding an Australian whaler.

While the Australian ship was anchored at Papeete, Tahiti's largest port, the crew rioted. The next day most of the men, including Melville, were arrested and handed over to the British authorities, who locked them up in a makeshift outdoor jail. Melville and a friend escaped, and after touring the Society Islands briefly, they signed up on yet another whaler, the *Charles & Henry.*

Melville left the ship on May 2, 1843, in Maui, Hawaii. He traveled to Honolulu, where he went to work as a bookkeeper and angered the American colonial authorities by publicly supporting a British takeover of the islands. He left Hawaii on August 17, joining the crew of the U.S.S. *United States* as an ordinary seaman but retaining the option of quitting the navy when the ship returned to port. When the *United States* docked in Boston 14 months later, Melville was discharged, full of dark memories that would later make their way into his novel *White-Jacket.*

Melville then returned to Lansingburgh, where his tales of the South Pacific made him a minor celebrity. After friends and family encouraged him to write about his experiences, he transformed his time among the "cannibals" of the Marquesas into *Typee* and his Tahitian idyll into its sequel, *Omoo.* With the help of his brother Gansevoort, Melville published *Typee* in 1846, and *Omoo* appeared the following year. Herman Melville had finally found his calling.

Around this same time Melville began courting Elizabeth Shaw, a family friend who lived in Boston. They married in August 1847 and set up housekeeping with Melville's family, first in Lansingburgh, then in New York City.

When the veracity of his first two novels was widely questioned, Melville responded with *Mardi,* a highly ambitious allegorical romance in which he turned his exposure to the exotica of Polynesia into material for philosophical speculation. While *Mardi,* which appeared in 1849, proved to be a failure, the more conventional *Redburn,* published the same year, was received more warmly. The popularity of the latter earned Melville an advance on his next book, *White-Jacket,* large enough to permit him to travel to Europe, where he presented his latest novel to his English publishers. In 1850 *White-Jacket* appeared; Melville bought a farm he named Arrowhead near Pittsfield, Massachusetts; and he published "Hawthorne and His Mosses," an important review of *Mosses from an Old Manse,* a collection of tales and sketches recently published by his new friend and near neighbor, Nathaniel HAWTHORNE.

Melville's friendship with Hawthorne would be a tortured one, but the conversations between the two about literature that took place over the next two years were seminal for Melville and his masterpiece, MOBY-DICK (1851). Like *Mardi, Moby-Dick* failed to find an audience, so Melville, attempting still to live by his wits, wrote *Pierre* (1852), a metaphysical novel that made use of then-popular gothic conventions (see GOTHICISM).

When *Pierre* likewise failed in the marketplace, Melville tried unsuccessfully to obtain a consular appointment. Out of financial desperation he turned to writing shorter pieces that could be serialized in magazines and republished later in bound volumes. This period saw the publication of Melville's historical romance *Israel Potter* (1855); short stories such as "BARTLEBY, THE SCRIVENER," "The Bell-Tower," "BENITO CERENO," "The Encantadas," and "The Lightening-Rod Man," which he later collected in *The Piazza Tales* (1856); and other pieces that were not republished during his lifetime. In 1856–57, he once again went abroad, this time to Glasgow, Liverpool, the Holy Land, Greece, and Italy. The critical and popular failure of his satirical novel *The Confidence Man* (1857) essentially ended Melville's career as a professional writer.

In 1863 Melville worked on a series of poems about the CIVIL WAR that would appear in 1866 as *Battle-Pieces.* That same year he became a civil servant, taking a job as a customs inspector, a position he would hold for the next 19 years. By this point Melville was devoting his writing talents almost exclusively to poetry, publishing *Clarel,* his epic poem set in the Holy Land, in 1876; and privately printing his collection of sea poetry, *John Marr,* in 1888 and another collection of poetry, *Timoleon,* in 1891. Melville seemed reconciled to his obscurity (many of his early readers did not even know he was still alive) as well as to his marriage. When he died on September 28, 1891, however, he left behind an unpublished collection of love poems, *Weeds and Wildings,* that was dedicated to his wife.

Melville left behind one other important unpublished work, BILLY BUDD, a novella he had been working on since 1888. The incomplete manuscript stayed in the tin breadbox where his wife put it for safekeeping until 1924, when Melville's granddaughters, Eleanor Metcalf and Frances Osborne, saw to its publication. The appearance of this ambiguous and richly allusive tale of good and evil sparked a revival of interest in Melville that elevated him to the highest rung of the American literary pantheon.

Sources

Jehlen, Myra, ed. *Herman Melville: A Collection of Critical Essays.* Englewood Cliffs, N.J.: Prentice Hall, 1994.

Levine, Robert S. *The Cambridge Companion to Herman Melville.* New York: Cambridge University Press, 1998.

Parker, Hershel, ed. *The Recognition of Herman Melville: Selected Criticism Since 1846.* Ann Arbor: University of Michigan Press, 1967.

Robertson-Lorant, Laurie. *Melville: A Biography.* New York: Clarkson Potter, 1996.

Rollyson, Carl, and Lisa Paddock. *Herman Melville A to Z: The Essential Reference to His Life and Work.* New York: Facts On File, 2001.

Mexican War (1846–1848) *historical event*

The war started over the disputed territory of Texas. When President James K. Polk (1795–1849) deemed that American forces had been threatened on the Rio Grande, he sent the American army to attack the Mexicans. This was the first war in American history to provoke significant internal opposition. Congressman Abraham LINCOLN attacked President Polk's war, and many in the Northeast saw the conflict as contrary to American democratic ideals and more befitting an imperialistic power. In this view, the war was little more than a land grab of the Southwest. Writers such as Herman MELVILLE were also critical, regarding the war as the first signs of empire building that a republic should avoid: "Lord, the day is at hand, when we will be able to talk of our killed & wounded like some of the old Eastern conquerors reckoning them up by thousands . . . the Constitution's timbers [will] be thought no more of than bamboos." Melville's criticisms would later be echoed in Mark Twain's (Samuel CLEMENS) condemnation of the SPANISH-AMERICAN WAR. Henry David THOREAU also opposed the war, preferring to go to jail rather than pay the poll tax that supported such military adventures.

Sources

Johannsen, Robert W. *To the Halls of the Montezumas: The Mexican War in the American Imagination.* New York: Oxford University Press, 1985.

Montaigne, Sanford H. *Blood over Texas.* New Rochelle, N.Y.: Arlington House, 1976.

Miller, Joaquin (Cincinnatus Hiner [or Heine] Miller) (1837–1913) *poet*

Joaquin Miller is said to have taken his pen name from the subject of his earliest literary work, a defense of the Mexican bandit Joaquin Murietta. But even his given name of Cincinnatus is uncertain, as much of his early life remains unclear, or at least exaggerated. He was born in Liberty, Indiana, and moved at an early age with his family—ostensibly by covered wagon—to the Willamette Valley of Oregon. In early manhood he is said to have lived among the Digger and Modoc Indian nations of northern California and to have worked as, variously, a horse thief; Pony Express rider; Indian fighter; lawyer; and editor of the Eugene, Oregon, *Democratic Register.*

Although Miller began publishing poetry in 1868, he did not find an audience until he traveled to London in 1870–71, where he was feted as a frontier bard for the verse privately printed as *Pacific Poems* (1870) and *Songs of the Sierras* (1871). Returning to America, Miller continued to produce poetry, although he was unable to maintain his earlier fame. He wrote a number of plays, the most popular of which was *The Danites of the Sierras* (1877), concerning the Mormons; and published an exaggerated autobiography, *Life Among the Modocs* (1873), as well as the autobiographical *Memorie and Rime* (1884).

Sources

Frost, O. W. *Joaquin Miller.* New York: Twayne, 1967.

Lawson, Benjamin S. *Joaquin Miller.* Boise, Idaho: Boise State University, 1980.

Millerites *organization*

William Miller (1782–1849), a farmer who became a Baptist minister, believed that the world would come to an end in 1843. He was a convincing speaker, and he traveled about the country preaching his millennialist gospel, which he eventually published as *Evidence from Scripture and History of the Second Coming of Christ, about the Year 1843* (1836). A sect, called Millerites, formed around him, and periodicals such as *The Midnight Cry* and *Signs of the Times* spread his word. When the day of judgment failed to materialize in 1843, a definite date was set: October 22, 1844. When that date, too, passed uneventfully, many still continued to believe, giving rise to another group, the Seventh-Day Adventists, led by Hiram Edson (1806–82). Edward EGGLESTON's *The End of the World* (1872) deals with Millerites, as do Jane March Parker's novels (1836–1913) *Barley Wood* (1860) and *The Midnight Cry* (1886).

Sources

Numbers, Ronald L., and Jonathan M. Butler, eds. *The Disappointed: Millerism and Millenarianism in the Nineteenth Century.* Knoxville: University of Tennessee Press, 1993.

Mitchell, Silas Weir (1829–1914) *physician, novelist, poet*

Born in Philadelphia, S. Weir Mitchell obtained a medical degree from Jefferson College before traveling to Paris to do graduate work in neurology. His writing career began with specialized papers on such medical subjects as toxicology, neurology, and clinical medicine, topics he also addressed in a variety of books that proved popular with lay readers.

During the CIVIL WAR Mitchell served as a surgeon with the Union Army, and this experience turned him into a writer. His first story, "The Case of George Dedlow," appeared in the July 1866 issue of the ATLANTIC MONTHLY and concerned the psychological effects of the war on an army surgeon forced to undergo quadruple amputation. Mitchell's first two novels, *In War Time* (1885) and *Roland Blake* (1886), also grew out of his searing war experience, with the first focusing on a New England physician's cowardice during the Civil War and the second on a wartime romance. Mitchell's most significant historical novel, *Hugh Wynne, Free Quaker* (1886), concerns a Philadelphia Quaker's attempt to live up to his ideals during the Revolutionary War.

Later in his literary career Mitchell examined the psychology of women in novels such as *Circumstance* (1901), concerning an adventuress; and *Constance Trescot* (1905), about a woman possessed by vengeance. He also wrote several volumes of verse, including *The Hill of Stones* (1882), *The Masque and Other Poems* (1889), and *The Wager* (1900).

Sources

Earnest, Ernest P. *S. Weir Mitchell, Novelist and Physician.* Philadelphia: University of Pennsylvania Press, 1950.

Rein, David. *S. Weir Mitchell as a Psychiatric Novelist.* New York: International Universities Press, 1952.

Walter, Richard D. *S. Weir Mitchell, M.D., Neurologist: A Medical Biography.* Springfield, Ill.: Thomas, 1970.

Moby-Dick; or, The Whale Herman Melville (1851) *novel*

Herman MELVILLE's greatest work is a classic of American literature, combining a realistic account of a whale hunt with a symbolic exploration of human destiny and the nature of the universe. The story is told by ISHMAEL, the sole survivor of the *Pequod,* the whale ship that the whale Moby-Dick wrecks. The ship is commanded by AHAB, the monomaniacal captain who is bent on avenging himself against the whale for having taken his leg in a previous encounter.

Ahab is a tyrant who binds his men together in the hunt by the force of his will. He is magnificent in his effort to brave the elements and to do battle with the leviathan of the deep. He is also tragic in that he will not observe the limitations that nature seems to have put on human striving. As a tragic hero, Ahab has often been compared to Shakespeare's characters.

Ishmael, on the other hand, is the observer-participant, mesmerized by Ahab but also aware of his captain's fanaticism. Like Ahab and many of the other crew members, Ishmael is aboard ship because he is an outcast: He is questing for the meaning of existence as well as relief from the tedium he experiences on land.

That Melville's aim was to write a novel about the plight of humanity itself is clear in the multicultural crew that is assembled for the whale hunt. Ishmael's roommate is QUEEQUEG, a Polynesian prince, and the other sailors come from various classes and backgrounds. These include the scrupulous Starbuck, the chief mate, who opposes Ahab; and Stubb, the second mate, who takes life as it comes and throws himself into the hunt for the whale. Each crew member is carefully depicted in order to display the wide range of human temperaments as they interact with nature and carry out the mission Ahab sets for them. Other crew members include Tashtego, an American Indian; Pip, an African-American cabin boy; Daggoo, an African; and Fedallah, a mysterious Asian.

The *Pequod* meets many other whalers on its search for Moby-Dick, and each new ship reveals another side of human nature—captains and crews who exchange their views of life even as they report news of the whale. Ahab only has ears for men who share his outrage that any whale should thwart human purposes. Only Ahab believes it is his mission to avenge himself because his power and pride have been affronted.

The novel climaxes in the chase after Moby-Dick, in which Ahab is entangled in his harpoon line and the *Pequod* itself is rammed and sunk by Moby-Dick. Only Ishmael pops to the surface and is rescued by another whaler, the *Rachel.*

Sources

Gilmore, Michael T., ed. *Twentieth Century Interpretations of Moby-Dick: A Collection of Critical Essays.* Englewood Cliffs, N.J.: Prentice Hall, 1977.

Hayes, Kevin J., ed. *The Critical Response to Herman Melville's Moby Dick.* Westport, Conn.: Greenwood Press, 1994.

Higgins, Brian and Hershel Parker, eds. *Critical Essays on Herman Melville's Moby-Dick.* New York: G. K. Hall, 1992.

Moody, William Vaughn (1869–1910) *poet, playwright*

Born in Indiana, William Vaughn Moody attended Harvard University, where he taught English for a year before leaving in 1895 to teach at the University of Chicago; he remained in Chicago for the rest of his teaching career. Moody achieved widespread recognition in his lifetime for his poetry and verse dramas. His first collection of lyric *Poems* was published in 1901. Some of his most highly regarded works concerned matters of the day: "On a Soldier Fallen in the Philippines," for example, addressed turn-of-the-century notions about American manifest destiny.

Moody's verse dramas were likewise successful. Most of these, in contrast to his shorter works, concerned spiritual matters. His first, *The Masque of Judgment* (1900), addresses man's relationship to God. The 1904 verse drama *The Fire Bringer* continues this theme, and was to be rounded out by a third play, *The Death of Eve* (1912), which Moody left uncompleted at his death. In contrast to this trilogy, no part of which was ever produced, Moody's *A Sabine Woman,* a play contrasting the Puritanical East with the freewheeling West, did make it to the stage and was later published under the title *The Great Divide* (1906). *The Faith Healer,* produced in 1909, was less successful, perhaps because Moody—by then suffering the effects of the illness that would cause his early death—was unable to make the revisions that could have rescued it from what many critics regarded as an excess of idealism.

Sources

Brown, Maurice F. *Estranging Dawn: The Life and Works of William Vaughn Moody.* Carbondale: Southern Illinois University Press, 1973.

Halpern, Martin. *William Vaughn Moody.* New York: Twayne, 1964.

Moore, Julia A. (1847–1930) *poet*

Called the "Sweet Singer of Michigan"—after the title of her first collection of verse, *The Sweet Singer of Michigan Salutes the Public* (1876)—Julia A. Moore is a curious figure in literary history. Her sobriquet was often applied ironically, for she wrote bad sentimental verse on subjects like choking on roast beef and a meeting of the local cricket club. Moore employed childish grammar and elemental rhythms so obvious that many readers thought her poetic tin ear a deliberate effect. One such was Mark Twain (Samuel Langhorne CLEMENS), who remarked that she had "the touch that makes an intentionally humorous episode pathetic and an intentionally pathetic one funny." He would go on to parody her work brilliantly in *HUCKLEBERRY FINN.* Moore quickly followed her first collection with one called *A Few Words to the Public with New and Original Poems by Julia A. Moore* (1878), but she waited many years before publishing her third effort, a romance set during the American Revolution called *Sunshine and Shadow* (1915).

Sources

Riedlinger, Thomas J., ed. *Mortal Refrains: The Complete Collected Poetry, Prose, and Songs of Julia A. Moore, the Sweet Singer of Michigan.* East Lansing: Michigan State University Press, 1998.

Morgan, Lewis Henry (1818–1881) *anthropologist, nonfiction writer*

Lewis Henry Morgan was born near Aurora, New York, and educated at Union College in that state. He began his professional career as a lawyer, but soon changed his orientation to writing. As a member of a New York City secret society called the Gordian Knot, later known as The Grand Order of the Iroquois and meant to mimic the group of American Indian nations known as the Iroquois Confederacy, he became deeply interested in Native Americans. His *League of the Ho-dé-no-sau-nee, or Iroquois* (1851) was the first truly rigorous study of an Indian nation. Morgan's discovery of Iroquois kinship systems led to an exhaustive study of such systems worldwide, entitled *Systems of Consanguinity and Affinity of the Human Family* (1877). Subsequently, in the controversial *Ancient Society; or Researches in the Lines of Human Progress* (1877), he would elaborate his discoveries into a theory of social evolution based on the proposition that human family groups evolved through stages of promiscuity, group marriage, polygamy, and monogamy.

Despite the contentious nature of some of his work, Morgan pursued his research under the auspices of the Smithsonian Institution and the U.S. government. Known as "the Father of American Anthropology," Morgan also produced important work on the psychology of lower mammals in *The American Beaver and His Works* (1868).

Sources

Resek, Carl. *Lewis Henry Morgan, American Scholar.* Chicago: University of Chicago Press, 1960.

Stern, Bernhard J. *Lewis Henry Morgan, Social Evolutionist.* New York: Russell & Russell, 1967.

Tooker, Elisabeth. *Lewis H. Morgan on Iroquois Material Culture.* Tucson: University of Arizona Press, 1994.

Mormonism *religious movement*

Also known as the Church of Jesus Christ of Latter-Day Saints, Mormonism, a Christian sect, was founded in 1830 in Fayette, New York, by Joseph SMITH. Smith's claim that *The Book of Mormon,* published in 1829, was transcribed from golden tablets whose location had been revealed to him in a vision engendered considerable hostility, and in 1831 he moved his organization to Kirtland, Ohio. Here, too, the Mormons encountered persecution for their communal way of life and unconventional beliefs, and in 1838–39, after they were expelled from the state, they sought a new Zion in Nauvoo, Illinois. The Mormons prospered there, so much so that jealous neighbors murdered Smith in 1844. A schism ensued, with one group following Brigham Young (1801–77) to Salt Lake City, Utah, and another forming the Reorganized Church under the leadership of the younger Joseph Smith in Independence, Missouri.

After their 1,100-mile exodus to the valley of the Great Salt Lake, the Brigham Young group finally found a home. When Utah became a U.S. territory in 1849, Young was named as governor, but the state's admission to the Union encountered serious resistance owing to the Mormon doctrine of plural marriage. Statehood was granted only in 1890 when, after Young's death, the new church leader Wilford Woodruff (1807–98) withdrew the church's sanction of polygamy.

In addition to *The Book of Mormon,* church belief is based on the Bible and other of Joseph Smith's revelations, such as two other works translated from the golden tablets: *Doctrine and Covenants* (1835) and *The Pearl of Great Price* (1851).

Sources

Alexander, Thomas. *Mormonism in Transition: A History of the Latter-Day Saints, 1890–1930.* Urbana: University of Illinois Press, 1986.

Coates, James. *In Mormon Circles: Gentiles, Jack Mormons, and Latter-Day Saints.* Reading, Mass.: Addison-Wesley, 1991.

Motley, John Lothrop (1814–1877) *historian*

The scion of an old Boston family, John Lothrop Motley entered Harvard when he was 13 years old. After graduating in 1831, he received a doctoral degree from Göttingen University in Germany, toured the Continent, and returned to BOSTON, where he married Park BENJAMIN's sister and began reading law. Motley's true interest, however, was literature, and in short order he produced two novels, the semiautobiographical *Morton's Hope: or, The Memoirs of a Young Provincial* (1839) and *Merry-Mount: A Romance of the Massachusetts Colony* (1849). During the same period he served for a few months as secretary to the U.S. legation at St. Petersburg. He then returned home to write a historical essay on the Russian czar Peter the Great (1672–1725) and commence a career in politics that led to his appointment as minister to Austria (1861–67) and Great Britain (1869–70).

In 1847 Motley finally found his true métier when he began a lifelong study of the Netherlands. In the course of 10 concentrated years he traveled to Germany and Holland to research the work that made his reputation, the three-volume *Rise of the Dutch Republic* (1856). This dramatic, highly readable work was organized around the contrast between the Protestant William of Orange (1650–1702), the hero of the piece, and Philip II (1527–1598), the Catholic ruler whom Motley portrayed as an autocrat. Motley followed up with a four-volume *History of the United Netherlands* (1856) and *The Life and Death of John Barneveld, Advocate of Holland* (1874). Motley did not live long enough to complete what he projected as a four-work series, detailing the history of the Netherlands up to 1648.

Sources

Guberman, Joseph. *The Life of John Lothrop Motley.* The Hague, Netherlands: Martinus Nijhoff, 1973.

Mowatt, Anna Cora (1819–1870) *poet, novelist, playwright*

The daughter of a New York merchant, Anna Cora Mowatt was born in France and came to America when she was seven. She married at 15 and, often sickly, she spent much of her time indoors, writing poetry, novels, and plays. Her first produced drama, "Fashion, or, Life in New York," proved to be a success when it was staged in 1845. Her triumph seems to have reinvigorated Mowatt, who took to the stage herself in 1845. Mowatt made a success of acting as well, and although the return of ill health forced her retirement in 1854, she gained from the stage enough material for her *Autobiography of an Actress* (1854) as well as two romantic narratives about life on the stage: *Mimic Life* (1856) and *Twin Roses* (1857). After 1861 she spent her life abroad, continuing to write romantic novels and historical sketches.

Sources

Barnes, Eric Wollencott. *The Lady of Fashion: The Life and the Theatre of Anna Cora Mowatt.* New York: Scribner, 1954.

muckraking movement (1902–1917) *reform movement*

The term *muckraking* was taken from John Bunyan's *Pilgrim's Progress* (1678), which featured one character who was so busy raking the muck beneath his feet that he could not see the celestial crown above him. In a speech given in 1906, Theodore ROOSEVELT was the first to apply the term to journalists who specialized in exposing corruption in business and government. Roosevelt, who had made a name for himself as a trustbuster who broke up large industrial monopolies, agreed with the aims of reporters like Ida TARBELL, although he did not approve of some of their methods. Thus, the term *muckraker* was initially used at least ambiguously if not pejoratively. Over time, however, as the movement spread across the country, muckrakers would be widely regarded as crusaders for reform.

The advent of mass circulation periodicals like *MCCLURE'S*, *COLLIER'S*, and *EVERYBODY'S*, with their deep pockets, made it possible for Ida Tarbell and Lincoln STEFFENS to perform in-depth investigations of, respectively, Standard Oil and the Minneapolis city government. Such work attracted attention and increased circulation rolls for the magazines, which in turn made it possible for Tarbell and Steffens to publish entire monographs about their research: *History of the Standard Oil Company* (1904) and *The Shame of the Cities* (1904), respectively. Such works also influenced such fiction writers as Upton Sinclair (1878–1968), whose exposé of the meat packing industry, *The Jungle* (1906), profoundly influenced public opinion and resulted in federal pure food legislation in 1906. Sinclair, a socialist, said that although he had aimed at the public's heart, he hit people in the stomach. Other popular novels written by prominent muckrakers include David Graham PHILLIPS's tale of a modern prostitute's adventures, *Susan Lenox: Her Fall and Rise* (1917), which packaged the reform movement in a more palatable form. Even novelists not customarily associated with the movement wrote works with a reformist bias, such as Theodore DREISER's trilogy *The Financier* (1912), *The Titan* (1914), and *The Stoic* (1947). By the time the United States entered World War I, the movement was largely spent, but without it the progressive movement, spearheaded by Roosevelt himself, would not have achieved the popular support it needed to implement reforms in the early years of the 20th century.

Sources

Brasch, Walter M. *Forerunners of Revolution: Muckrakers and the American Social Conscience.* Lanham, Md.: University Press of America, 1990.

Harrison, John M., and Harry H. Stein, eds. *Muckraking: Past, Present, and Future.* University Park: Pennsylvania State University Press, 1973.

Miraldi, Robert. *Muckraking and Objectivity: Journalism's Colliding Traditions.* New York: Greenwood Press, 1990.

Muir, John (1838–1914) *essayist*

Born in Scotland, John Muir came to the United States as a boy in 1849, when his father immigrated to a Wisconsin farm. As his autobiographical *Story of My Boyhood and Youth* (1913) later made clear, it was on the family farm that Muir's interests in books and nature developed simultaneously. After studying chemistry, geology, and botany, Muir graduated from the University of Wisconsin in 1863 and spent the next five years traveling through the Midwest and Canada. He also journeyed by foot from Indiana to Mexico, an adventure he would later recount in *A Thousand Mile Walk to the Gulf* (1916).

In 1868 Muir made California his home, first spending five years in the Yosemite Valley, then roving abroad to explore glaciers, forests, mountains, and seas as far afield as Alaska, Russia, India, and Australia. His passion, however, was conservation of the natural wonders of the western states, and he became both a leader of the forest preservation movement and, with the aid of his friend President Theodore ROOSEVELT, one of the motivating forces behind the establishment of the U.S. national parks system. Muir Glacier in Alaska, which he discovered, and Muir Woods National Monument in California are named for him. Muir's success cannot be separated from the grace with which he wrote about the nation's national wonders in works such as *The Mountains of California* (1894) and *My First Summer in the Sierra* (1911).

Sources

Cohen, Michael P. *The Pathless Way: John Muir and American Wilderness.* Madison: University of Wisconsin Press, 1984.

Northwest Passages: From the Pen of John Muir in California, Oregon, Washington, and Alaska. Palo Alto, Calif.: Tioga Publishing Co., 1988.

Turner, Frederick W. *Rediscovering America: John Muir in His Time and Ours.* New York: Viking, 1985.

Wilkins, Thurman. *John Muir: Apostle of Nature.* Norman: University of Oklahoma Press, 1995.

Murfree, Mary Noailles (Charles Egbert Craddock) (1850–1922) *short story writer, novelist*

Born in Murfreesboro, Tennessee, a town named for her great-grandfather, Mary Noailles Murfree spent most of her life in her native state writing stories and novels that reflected her surroundings. After an illness left her lame in early childhood, Murfree traveled little, although she attended boarding school in Philadelphia during the CIVIL WAR and, more significantly, spent summers with her family in the Cumberland Mountains in central Tennessee. The language of the mountaineers she met there would later inform her fiction with a regional flavor, making Murfree a distinctive voice in the LOCAL COLOR movement.

Murfree began writing in the 1870s, publishing her first stories under the pen name R. Emmet Denbry and later adopting the name of one of her characters, Charles Egbert Craddock. Murfree managed to keep up a male facade until 1885, a year after publication of her acclaimed story collection *In the Tennessee Mountains,* which presented one of the first realistic portraits of life among Southern mountaineers. In 1885 Murfree revealed her true identity to the editor of the *Atlantic,* and the revelation created a stir nationwide. Readers of the acclaimed collection found it difficult to believe that the detailed specificity of the stories had come from a woman.

Murfree published several other story collections as well as two novels about Tennessee mountaineers, *The Prophet of the Great Smoky Mountains* (1885) and *The "Stranger People's" Country* (1891). She also wrote historical fiction set during the colonial period in the OLD SOUTHWEST and the Civil War. She continued to publish until 1914, with the income from her writing contributing substantially to the support of her family, which had fallen on hard times after the Civil War.

Sources

Cary, Richard. *Mary N. Murfree.* New York: Twayne, 1967.

Murray, Lieutenant

See BALLOU, MATURIN MURRAY.

Nasby, Petroleum Vesuvius

See LOCKE, DAVID ROSS.

Nast, Thomas (1840–1902) *journalist, illustrator*

Born in Germany, Nast came to the United States when he was six years old and began his career as an illustrator when he was just 15, working for *Frank Leslie's Illustrated Newspaper.* After providing sketches for European newspapers on Giuseppe Garibaldi's 1860 campaign for Italian unification, in 1862 Nast joined the staff of *HARPER'S WEEKLY,* where he drew cartoons lampooning Northern defeatists to help the Union effort during the CIVIL WAR. In 1863 he drew his first political caricature, a genre he would perfect, making him and *Harper's* the most powerful media voices in the land. Nast was the first to employ the donkey and the elephant as symbols of the Democratic and Republican parties, and he used the tiger in the greatest political fight of his life, against the corrupt politicians who made up the Tweed Ring, which controlled NEW YORK CITY government in the 1870s.

After Nast left *Harper's* in 1886, he tried to use one newspaper outlet after another for his caricatures—even starting his own short-lived *Nast's Weekly*—but all these efforts failed. In 1902, when THEODORE ROOSEVELT's administration offered him a consulship in Guayaquil, Ecuador, Nast accepted, only to die there the same year of yellow fever.

Sources

Keller, Morton. *The Art and Politics of Thomas Nast.* New York: Oxford University Press, 1968.

Visnon, Chal. *Thomas Nast, Political Cartoonist.* Athens: University of Georgia Press, 1967.

Nation, The *periodical*

Since its founding in 1815, this New York weekly journal has published reports on current affairs, book reviews, and other articles about politics and culture. Devoted to democratic principles and progressive politics, *The Nation* was proabolitionist (see ABOLITIONISM) and a strong advocate of public education. E. L. Godkin, its first editor, published the work of America's foremost writers, including William Dean HOWELLS, Henry JAMES Sr. and his two sons William and Henry, Francis PARKMAN, and Charles Francis ADAMS.

The Nation also conducted campaigns against corrupt city political machines, such as the Tweed Ring, and for civil service reform. At the same time, the journal was known for its well-informed and exacting reviews of the literature of the day.

The Nation was sold to the *New York Post* in 1881, and Godkin retired. Under the editorship (1881–1906) of W. P. Garrison, the journal remained the same in its format and outlook but suffered some loss of influence because it was viewed as the organ of a tabloid newspaper. Nevertheless, Garrison continued to publish outstanding articles by the country's major authors.

When Paul Elmer Moore (1864–1937) became editor in 1909, he rejuvenated *The Nation,* especially its coverage of the arts, and he continued the magazine's tradition of hiring the very best writers.

In 1918, O. G. Villard (1872–1949) became editor, severing the magazine's connection with the *Post,* but maintaining its liberal orientation, which later in the century turned decidedly more left-wing.

Sources

Humes, Dollena J. *Oswald Garrison Villard: Liberal of the 1920s.* Syracuse, N.Y.: Syracuse University Press, 1960.

National Anti-Slavery Standard *periodical*

Published in New York from 1840 to 1872 by the American Anti-Slavery Society, this periodical called for the immediate and complete emancipation of slaves and their subsequent education. Strongly pro-Union, it was edited from 1848 to 1849 by James Russell LOWELL, who remained affiliated with the magazine until 1852, publishing in it many of the pieces that were collected later as *The Biglow Papers* (1902). After 1870 the magazine variously changed its title, publication schedule, and causes, taking on temperance and women's rights before expiring.

National Era, The *periodical*

This Washington, D.C., antislavery journal (1847–60) was edited by Gamaliel Bailey (1807–59) and known for its literary contributions, including Nathaniel HAWTHORNE's short story "The Great Stone Face"; most of the work John Greenleaf WHITTIER produced during the years of its publication; and, most significantly, the serialization of Harriet Beecher STOWE's *UNCLE TOM'S CABIN* in 1851–52.

Sources

Harrold, Stanley. *Gamaliel Bailey and Antislavery Union.* Kent, Ohio: Kent State University Press, 1986.

National Police Gazette, The *periodical*

This New York weekly, founded in 1845 and known as the "barber shop Bible," concentrated less on reporting crime than on sensationalism, both in its reporting and in the fiction it published. Over time its shocking pink cover was given over to pictures that might have been called pinups but for the subject matter. The gazette also featured theatrical and sporting news. In 1932 it went bankrupt. Revived as a monthly, it retained its old format while changing hands several times, only to expire in 1937.

Sources

Gabor, Mark. *The Illustrated History of Girlie Magazines from National Police Gazette to the Present.* New York: Harmony Books, 1983.

Native American literature *genre*

With the exception of a few pictographic recordings such as the Delaware *WALAM OLUM*, Native American literature was largely within the oral tradition until the 19th century. Tribal histories—often including myths and legends—were a staple of the period. But personal narratives incorporating elements of oral storytelling were among the first examples of Native American literature to take the form of written narratives. The first of these to be published was *A Son of the Forest* (1829), written in English by the Pequot William Apes (1798–?) and reflecting the type of spiritual confessions popular during the period. Other significant personal narratives combining autobiography with ethnography include *The Life, History, and Travels of Kah-ge-ga-gah-bowh* (1847) by the Ojibway George Copway (1818–63), and *Life Among the Piutes* (1883) by the Piute Sarah Winnemucca Hopkins (1844–91). One of the most widely read books of this type was *Indian Boyhood,* by the Sioux Charles Eastman (1858–1939), which described the author's life up to the age of 15; and its sequel, *From the Deep Woods to Civilization* (1916), describing his life in the white man's world.

Many Native Americans, of course, did not enter the white world—at least not enough to learn English—but some of them narrated their life stories to others. The first—and to many readers the most impressive of these—was the Sauk chief BLACK HAWK's *Black Hawk, an Autobiography* (1833), translated by Antoine Le Claire and edited by John B. Patterson. An interesting comparison is afforded by the narrated autobiography of Governor Blacksnake (c. 1753–1859), which was recorded around the same time as Black Hawk's but set down in Seneca-style English by Benjamin Williams (1803–61); it was edited and released much later under the title *Chainbreaker* (1989).

Important "firsts" of Native American literature include the first Native American author to publish in English: the Mohegan Samson Occom (1723–92), whose *A Sermon Preached at the Execution of Moses Paul, an Indian* (1772), the first Indian best-seller, reflected Occom's calling as a missionary to the Indians. The first novel to be published by a Native American writer was the Cherokee John Rollin Ridge's (1827–67) *The Life and Adventures of Joaquin Murieta* (1854), which features the real-life mixed-blood bandit as a romantic figure. Ridge was also the only Native American writer to publish a volume of poetry in the 19th century, his posthumous *Poems* (1868).

The first novel to be published by a Native American woman was the Creek Sophia Alice Callahan's (1868–93) *Wynema, a Child of the Forest* (1891), which concerns the interaction between a Creek girl and her missionary teacher. The first Native American woman to be celebrated for her poetry and performance art was the Mohawk Emily Pauline Johnson (1861–1913), whose collected poems were published as *Flint and Feather* in 1912. Johnson was also the first Native American woman to publish short stories, many of which were collected in *Moccasin Maker* (1913). A major talent in the dramatic field did not emerge until the middle of the next century, when the Cherokee playwright Lynn Riggs (1899–1954) wrote a folk drama, *Green Grow the Lilacs*

(1931), which was adapted for Broadway as the seminal American musical *Oklahoma!* in 1954.

Sources

Jaskoski, Helen, ed. *Early Native American Writing: New Critical Essays.* New York: Cambridge University Press, 1996.

Krupat, Arnold. *The Voice in the Margin: Native American Literature and the Canon.* Berkeley: University of California Press, 1989.

Walker, Cheryl. *Indian Nation: Native American Literature and Nineteenth-Century Nationalisms.* Durham, N.C.: Duke University Press, 1997.

naturalism *literary movement*

A movement emphasizing scientific objectivity in fiction that developed in the late 19th century, naturalism has been viewed as an outgrowth of American literary REALISM in the sense that naturalists like Frank NORRIS, Stephen CRANE, Theodore DREISER, and Jack LONDON dealt with "common people," characters who, as in realistic novels, came from the lower and middle classes and were not great heroes. Unlike the realists, however, the naturalists did not dwell only on the concrete details of their characters' lives; instead, naturalism evolved out of a deterministic view of society. Naturalist writers believed that individuals were shaped by society and that their particular actions had to be understood in terms of how their society and their biology formed them. Characters behaved according to their social standing or class, an aspect of naturalism that would influence the proletarian fiction of the 1930s. The writings of Charles Darwin (1809–82) and Karl Marx (1818–83) had an enormous impact on such naturalists as Dreiser, Richard Wright (1908–60), James T. Farrell (1904–79), and John Steinbeck (1902–68), all of whom to varying degrees attributed their characters' actions to their psychology (determined from childhood) and their environment (the family and neighborhood which dictated, to a large extent, the range of their actions). Naturalism thus challenges the concept of free will and shows how the material conditions of the past and present largely control the behavior of individuals.

Sources

Pizer, Donald and Earl N. Harbert, eds. *American Realists and Naturalists.* Detroit: Gale, 1982.

Walcott, Charles Child. *American Literary Naturalism: A Divided Stream.* Minneapolis: University of Minnesota Press, 1956.

"Nature" *Ralph Waldo Emerson* (1836) *essay*

Ralph Waldo EMERSON's most important essay, "Nature" laid the foundation of TRANSCENDENTALISM. Emerson urges his readers to establish an "original relation to the universe" instead of relying on the ideas of others; people should concentrate on harmonizing their internal and external sense of the world, consulting their own intuition and observations. Emerson urges readers to look for evidence of the spirit in the material world by observing nature precisely, learning to appreciate its beauty, cultivating knowledge of "natural facts," and studying the processes of nature. In this way a person can discipline his or her mind—his understanding, reason, and imagination. This proximity to nature also brings one closer to the "Over-Soul," or universal mind of existence. By performing this faithful dedication to nature, Emerson says, man will restore and perpetuate a sense of unity, a unity that derives from nature itself.

Sources

Cameron, Kenneth Walter. *Young Emerson's Transcendental Vision: An Exposition of his World View with an Analysis of the Structure, Backgrounds, and Meaning of Nature (1836).* Hartford, Conn.: Transcendental Books, 1971.

Hodder, Alan D. *Emerson's Rhetoric of Revelation: Nature, The Reader, and the Apocalypse Within.* University Park: Pennsylvania State University Press, 1989.

Neal, John (1793–1876) *poet, dramatist, novelist, critic*

Born in Portland, Maine, John Neal came from a Quaker family. He was immersed in a literary career by the time he was in his mid-20s. He tried his hand at virtually every genre—a narrative poem, "Battle of Niagara" (1818); a blank verse tragedy, *Otho* (1819); and novels, including *Logan, A Family History* (1822), the story of an Indian chief. The best of Neal's early work is thought to be *Seventy-Six* (1823), a novel about the Revolutionary War.

Randolph (1823), an epistolary novel that contains attacks on English and America authors, resulted in a challenge to a duel, issued by Edward Pinkney (1802–28), the son of one of Neal's literary targets, the Baltimore editor William Pinkney (1764–1822). Neal had published *Keep Cool* (1817), a novel against dueling, and left the country rather than answer his adversary.

In England Neal wrote for *Blackwood's Magazine,* attempting the first serious studies of American authors (collected and published in 1937 as *American Writers*). Neal also continued to write novels, including *Brother Jonathan* (1825), another tale of the American Revolution; and *Rachel Dyer* (1828), an account of the Salem witchcraft trials. A prolific writer, he published many other popular novels about New England and the West.

Neal's work was important because he was often the first American writer to address subjects such as American Literary History, but his writing is riddled with errors. Neal preferred to be flamboyant rather than accurate. His lively memoirs, *Wandering Recollections of a Somewhat Busy Life* (1869), are also unreliable.

Sources

Fleischmann, Fritz. *A Right View of the Subject: Feminism in the Works of Charles Brockden Brown and John Neal.* Erlangen: Palm & Enke, 1983.

Sears, Donald A. *John Neal.* Boston: Twayne, 1978.

New Eclectic *periodical*

An offshoot of the *Richmond Eclectic,* this monthly periodical founded in 1868 was noted for its contributions by William Gilmore SIMMS and Sidney LANIER. In 1871 it became the official publication of the Southern Historical Society and was renamed the *Southern Magazine.*

New-England Magazine, The *periodical*

This Boston monthly, published from 1831 to 1835 and edited by Joseph T. Buckingham, was considered the nation's premier magazine until the advent of *ATLANTIC MONTHLY* in 1857. Notable contributors included Nathaniel HAWTHORNE, Noah WEBSTER, and Oliver Wendell HOLMES. Politically conservative, it opposed the presidential candidacy of Martin Van Buren (1782–1862). Eventually it was taken over by *THE AMERICAN MONTHLY MAGAZINE.*

New England Renaissance *See* BOSTON, MASSACHUSETTS; TRANSCENDENTALISM.

New Orleans, Louisiana *geographical location*

The largest city in Louisiana, situated on the eastern bank of the Mississippi River, New Orleans came into U.S. possession as a result of the Louisiana Purchase (1803). New Orleans has often been called the most European of American cities because of its Spanish and French heritage, derived from periods when these countries owned the city. The mixing of races—European and African (Creole) and French Canadian (Cajun)—as well as the French quarter, the music (opera and later jazz), theater, and party-like atmosphere, especially during Mardi Gras, gave the city a mystique like no other in the United States. The semitropical climate enhanced its exoticism; the trade in slaves and cotton, when the city became the destination of riverboat gamblers, also made it seem peculiarly lawless and evil. It was a strategic part of the Confederate defense during the CIVIL WAR, and its loss in 1862 was a major blow to the secessionists. During RECONSTRUCTION New Orleans suffered greatly from corruption and from the changing economic and industrial structure of the country, which made river trade less important and the city even more decadent.

Mark Twain (Samuel CLEMENS) presents vivid pictures of the city in *Life on the Mississippi,* and LOCAL COLOR writers—notably George Washington CABLE and Kate CHOPIN—explored the city's intricate integument of family, race, and culture. William Faulkner (1897–1962) provides a vivid portrayal of 19th-century New Orleans in his novel *Absalom, Absalom!* (1936).

Sources

Long, Judy, ed. *Literary New Orleans.* Athens, Ga.: Hill Street Press, 1999.

Miller, John and Genevieve Anderson, eds. *New Orleans Stories: Great Writers on the City.* San Francisco: Chronicle Books, 1992.

New Orleans Picayune *periodical*

Named for its initial price per copy, a Spanish coin used in the South prior to the CIVIL WAR, the *Picayune* was an independent newspaper that first distinguished itself with its field coverage of the MEXICAN WAR—reports on which the U.S. government itself relied for information. The leading NEW ORLEANS paper, it has published continuously since its founding in 1837, except for a two-month break during the Civil War; during RECONSTRUCTION the paper had to issue its own currency in order to continue publishing. In 1914 it merged with the *Times-Democrat* to become the *Times-Picayune.*

Sources

Dabney, Thomas E. *One Hundred Great Years: The Story of the Times-Picayune from its Founding to 1940.* New York: Greenwood Press, 1968.

Newton, Alfred Edward (1863–1940) *book collector, publisher*

Born in Philadelphia, A. Edward Newton became a wealthy man in the electrical equipment business who subsequently devoted himself to his avocation: books. Most of his writings are devoted to his bibliomania, bearing titles like *The Amenities of Book-Collecting and Kindred Affections* (1918). Newton also wrote two plays, *Doctor Johnson* (1923) and *Mr. Stahan's Dinner Party* (1930), both of them evidence of his interest in the 18th-century English literary figure Samuel Johnson (1709–84). It was therefore entirely fitting when Newton was elected as the first American president of the Johnson Club in London. His wish that his extensive collection of books, drawings, and manuscripts "not be consigned to the cold tomb of a museum" led to the sale of his library after his death.

New York American *periodical*

Founded by Gulian C. Verplanck, this daily newspaper was from its inception in 1819 Whig and National Republican in orientation. Highly influential among New York aristocrats, it was absorbed in 1845 by another Whig paper, the *New York Courier and Enquirer.*

New York City *geographical location*

This, the largest city in the United States, with a population approaching 20 million in the year 2000, is situated at the southeastern corner of New York State. The city consists of five boroughs, four of which (Manhattan, Brooklyn, Queens, and Staten Island) are located on three islands (Manhattan, Long Island, and Staten Island), with the fifth, the Bronx, located north of Manhattan Island on the mainland. First occupied by white Europeans early in the 17th century, Manhattan was purchased by the Dutch West India Company from the Canarsie Indians for a minuscule price in 1626. What followed was a long Dutch occupation of what was called New Amsterdam, a period satirized in Washington IRVING's *History of New York . . by Deidrich Knickerbocker* (1809). But in 1664 the Dutch surrendered their colony to the English, which renamed the capital New York.

The city thrived under English rule, but during the years before the Revolutionary War it became a center of disaffection with the British. Afterward, New York served briefly as the capital of the new United States (1784–90). By the middle of the next century it was not only the largest city in the nation, but also one of the largest in the world, becoming a center for immigration from all parts of the country and around the globe. In addition to attracting commercial and financial talent, it became a capital for the arts, attracting artists to Greenwich Village and playwrights to Broadway. Groups or schools of writers with like interests formed. In the 19th century these included the KNICKERBOCKER SCHOOL (Washington Irving, William Cullen BRYANT, Lydia Maria CHILD, and others) and the PFAFF'S CELLAR group (Walt WHITMAN, Bayard TAYLOR, Henry CLAPP, and others). New York also served as headquarters for many of the country's most influential newspapers and magazines, such as the *NEW YORK TIMES,* which would in the next century become the de facto national newspaper. Native sons and daughters such as Herman MELVILLE and Edith WHARTON turned their attention to grimmer aspects of city life in such works as "BARTLEBY, THE SCRIVENER" and *THE HOUSE OF MIRTH,* as did immigrants like Jacob RIIS in *How the Other Half Lives* (1890). Contrastingly, in his 1930 masterpiece, the long mystical poem *The Bridge,* the Ohio born poet Hart Crane (1899–1932) would use that architectural wonder, the Brooklyn Bridge, as a symbol of the creative power that unites past and present, seeing in New York City the same possibilities Whitman saw nearly 80 years earlier in "Crossing Brooklyn Ferry" (1856).

Sources

Jackson, Kenneth T., ed. *The Encyclopedia of New York City.* New Haven, Conn.: Yale University Press, 1995.

Mushabac, Jane, and Angela Wigan. *A Short and Remarkable History of New York City.* New York: Fordham University Press, 1999.

New York Ledger, The periodical

In 1851 the publisher Robert Bonner (1824–99) purchased *The Merchants' Ledger,* an illustrated weekly, at 1855 changing its name to *The New York Ledger.* Bonner served as editor until 1887, using his skill as a marketer to make it the most successful magazine of its day. *The New York Ledger* was both magazine and newspaper and appealed to both popular and sophisticated tastes, publishing Fanny Fern (Sara Payson Willis PARTON) beside the English poet Alfred, Lord Tennyson (1809–92). Bonner also solicited requests for advice from readers, which he would in turn farm out to various experts for answers. Bonner retired in 1887, and the publication continued for another decade largely as he created it. In 1898 it became a monthly, and in 1903 it ceased publication altogether.

New-York Mirror periodical

This arts and public-affairs weekly was founded by Samuel Woolworth in 1823. In 1831 it absorbed the *American Monthly Magazine;* in 1842 it became the *New Mirror;* and in 1844 it was rechristened once again as the *Evening Mirror.* From 1844 to 1845 Edgar Allan POE served as literary critic for the newspaper, which attracted celebrated contributors like Washington IRVING and James Fenimore COOPER. The *Mirror* ceased publication in 1860.

New York Sun periodical

Founded by Benjamin H. Day (1810–89) in 1833 as a four-page newspaper featuring human interest stories, the *Sun* was the first penny daily, pitched at the common man, to achieve genuine success. It did so in part by increasing its size while maintaining its low price until the CIVIL WAR. The *Sun* first gained wide recognition in 1835 with its sensational "Moon Hoax," an article contributed by reporter Adams Locke (1800–71) purporting to reveal the discovery by the English astronomer Sir William Herschel (1738–1822) of men living on the moon. The details of the hoax were so cleverly written that it not only fooled many readers but also added to their numbers. In 1838 the newspaper was sold and went through various incarnations as a partisan Democratic mouthpiece and an organ of evangelical religion until 1868, when Charles A. DANA became its managing editor. Dana's motto for the paper was "Be interesting," and he wrote entertaining editorials. He also was one of the first newspapermen to tackle the corruption that infiltrated the administration of President Ulysses S. GRANT. After Dana's death, his son edited the paper, and Edward P. Mitchell held the position from 1903 to 1920. In 1916 the *Sun* merged with the *Herald,* then was made into a separate evening paper, which in turn purchased the *New York Globe.* Merged in 1950 with the *World-Telegram,* the paper was closed in April 1966 following a series of labor disputes.

Sources

Steele, Janet E. *The Sun Shines for All: Journalism and Ideology in the Life of Charles A. Dana.* Syracuse, N.Y.: Syracuse University Press, 1993.

New York Times, The *periodical*

Founded in 1851 by Henry J. Raymond (1820–69) to be a bulwark of truth against what Raymond regarded as the sensational journalism of the day, the *New York Times* was initially a penny newspaper that reflected the Whig views of its financial backers. After 1856, however, it favored the newly reformed Republican Party. Following Raymond's premature death at age 49, George Jones (1811–91), one of the paper's financiers, took over the editorial chair. Under Jones's leadership the paper assumed a somewhat more sensational tone as it went after the corrupt Tammany Hall political machine that had a stranglehold on NEW YORK CITY. After Jones died in 1891, the quality of journalism at the *Times* declined further as it engaged in a losing battle for readership with the "yellow journalism" practiced at the papers owned by William Randolph HEARST and Joseph PULITZER.

By 1896, when it was purchased by Adolph Ochs (1858–1935), the *Times* reportedly was losing $1,000 a day. Within two years Ochs managed to turn the newspaper around, in part by meeting the penny price of its competitors and in part by returning the paper to its original high standards of accuracy epitomized by the slogan "All the News That's Fit to Print." World War I proved the paper's mettle: coverage by a large number of correspondents raised circulation to nearly a million readers. When Ochs died in 1935 he was succeeded by his son-in-law, Arthur Hays Sulzberger (1891–1968); and the *Times,* which continued to be controlled by Ochs's family, became a national newspaper in all but name.

Sources

Davis, Elmer H. *History of the New York Times, 1851–1921.* New York: Greenwood Press, 1969.

Salisbury, Harrison E. *Without Fear or Favor: The New York Times and Its Times.* New York: Times Books, 1980.

Tifft, Susan E. *The Trust: The Private and Powerful Family Behind the New York Times.* Boston: Little, Brown, 1999.

New-York Tribune *periodical*

Founded and edited by Horace GREELEY in 1841, the *Tribune* became known for its biting editorials and superior journalism, including the literary criticism of George RIPLEY, who wrote the first daily book review in the nation. Also on Greeley's staff were H. J. Raymond (1820–69), who would go on to found the *New York Times;* and Charles Anderson DANA, later part owner of the *NEW YORK SUN.* Before the CIVIL WAR Greeley opposed slavery and was instrumental in the election of Abraham LINCOLN to the presidency. After the war, Greeley's liberal editorials embraced suffrage for former slaves and opposed punitive RECONSTRUCTION measures. After Greeley's death in 1872, Whitelaw Reid (1837–1912) held the editorial post, turning the *Tribune* into the nation's most prominent Republican newspaper. Whitelaw was succeeded by his son Ogden Reid (1925–), under whose leadership the paper lost circulation until it merged in 1924 with the *New York Herald,* becoming the *Herald Tribune.* The *Herald Tribune* ceased publication in 1966.

Sources

Isely, Jeter Allen. *Horace Greeley and the Republican Party, 1853–1861.* New York: Octagon Books, 1965.

New York World *periodical*

The *World* started out in 1866 as a daily religious paper, but its owners found that morality did not sell, and in the 1870s the paper switched its emphasis to politics. In 1883 the *World* underwent another transformation after it was purchased by Joseph PULITZER, becoming a sensational but crusading newspaper. With the publication, starting in 1894, of the colored comic strip "Hogan's Alley," the *World* became known for its splashy "yellow journalism," named for the strip's hero, the Yellow Kid. Soon the *World* was the biggest newspaper in the country and had the largest circulation and the greatest number of advertisers. Pulitzer's *World* vied with William Randolph HEARST's New York *Journal* to provide jingoistic coverage of American exploits during the SPANISH-AMERICAN WAR; some said the competition between the two papers actually started the war.

After Pulitzer's son took over as editor, the *World* raised its standards and became a Democratic newspaper that featured such celebrated columnists as Walter Lippman (1889–1974) and Heywood Broun (1888–1939). In 1931, after merging with the *New York Telegram,* the paper was known as the *World-Telegram.* It changed its name again in 1950 when it absorbed the NEW YORK *SUN* and became the *New York World Telegram* and *The Sun.*

Sources

Juergens, George. *Joseph Pulitzer and the New York World.* Princeton, N.J.: Princeton University Press, 1966.

Norris, Frank (1870–1902) *novelist*

Born in Chicago, Frank Norris moved with his parents to San Francisco in 1884. A year later he was sent to Paris to study art. He returned to California in 1890 and graduated from the University of California in 1894. He had written medieval romances in Paris, and in his college years he contributed poems, stories, and sketches to local magazines. His writing did not mature, however, until he gave up his youthful ROMANTICISM for a much more vigorous NATURALISM inspired by the French writer Emile Zola (1840–1902). During a year at Harvard, he completed a naturalistic novel, *MCTEAGUE,* and began work on what would become *Vandover and the Brute* (1914).

From 1895 to 1896 Norris tried a career as a journalist, reporting on the Boer War in South Africa for COLLIER'S and the *San Francisco Chronicle.* Expelled from South Africa after his capture by the Boers, he returned to California and wrote short stories eventually collected in *A Deal of Wheat* (1903) and *The Third Circle* (1909). Like his contemporary Stephen CRANE, Norris covered the SPANISH-AMERICAN WAR in Cuba.

Norris wrote one of his finest works, *The Octopus* (1901), as part of a projected trilogy—to be entitled "The Epic of Wheat"—about the social and economic forces that had shaped California. The author's awareness of the struggle for control over land, the conflicts between ranchers and the railroad, and the transformation of America by corporations make him an especially prophetic figure, a precursor of John Dos Passos (1896–1970), John Steinbeck (1902–68), and other naturalistic and proletarian writers of the 1920s and 1930s. The other two parts of the trilogy, *The Wolf* and *The Pit,* both published in 1903, explored the role of wheat in the world economy, concentrating on the speculative market in Chicago that led to scarcity and overproduction in settings as far away as Europe.

Norris died after an operation on his appendix and did not live to fulfill his tremendous promise. His posthumous collection of essays, *The Responsibilities of the Novelist* (1903), shows a sophisticated sense of how modern fiction would have to grapple with the tremendous pressures coming to bear on individuals and on traditional agrarian societies. Norris, like Theodore DREISER, was also acutely aware of the biological causes of human behavior and did not shrink from portraying the more brutal aspects of human nature, especially in the concluding scene of *McTeague,* where the protagonist/murderer is handcuffed to his pursuer and remains stranded in Death Valley.

Norris's *Collected Letters* appeared in 1986.

Sources

Boyd, Jennifer. *Frank Norris: Spatial Form and Narrative Time.* New York: Peter Lang, 1993.

McElrath, Joseph R. *Frank Norris Revisited.* New York: Twayne, 1992.

Pizer, Donald. *The Novels of Frank Norris.* Bloomington: Indiana University Press, 1966.

North American Phalanx (1843–1854)

organization

Founded in Red Bank, New Jersey, by Albert BRISBANE, the North American Phalanx was one of the most successful of 19th-century Utopian communities. Based on the principles of FOURIERISM, the community consisted largely of cultured, educated individuals who spent their days in agricultural pursuits and ate communally. Part of the Phalanx's success, however, was due to the separate living quarters maintained by each family. The community disbanded after a fire destroyed its gristmill. Before its demise, such important cultural figures as W. H. CHANNING and Horace GREELEY had helped guide its formation and regulation.

Sources

Mandelker, Ira L. *Religion, Society, and Utopia in Nineteenth-Century America.* Amherst: University of Massachusetts Press, 1984.

North American Review, The *periodical*

Founded in Boston in 1815, this review grew out of a magazine called the *Monthly Anthology, or Magazine of Polite Literature,* which was started in 1803 by a group of "gentlemen of literary interests" who in 1805 organized themselves into the Anthology Club (also known as the Anthology Society). The club, whose members included George TICKNOR, William Cullen BRYANT, and Joseph STORY, subscribed to the sole mission of financing their magazine and filling its pages with material. After the *Monthly Anthology,* as well as the club, expired in 1811, the same group of individuals began *The North American Review,* which would become the most influential review in the country.

The periodical's first editor was William Tudor (1779–1830), who, with the aid of such important literary figures as Richard Henry DANA Sr., helped create a literary, critical, and historical review of unprecedented scope. The *Review* emulated its British counterparts, but it also strove to promote American literature and culture. Markedly scholarly, the *Review* never had a large circulation, but its pages were a repository for some of the most important American art and philosophy articulated over the next 125 years. Among its most significant early contributions were Bryant's poems "THANATOPSIS" (1817) and "To a Waterfowl" (1818), which appeared anonymously, like everything else the magazine published during its early years. The list of early contributors to the *Review* reads like a Who's Who of 19th-century American thought. Some of these contributors were Alexander and Edward EVERETT, John Adams (1735–1826), Daniel WEBSTER, Henry Wadsworth LONGFELLOW, and Francis PARKMAN. Several of these individuals also served as editors of the magazine, as did James Russell LOWELL and Henry ADAMS.

By the time Lowell and Adams came to occupy the magazine's editorial chair (Lowell, 1863–72; Adams, 1872–76), the *Review* was badly in need of reformation, having become notoriously dull. But Lowell was able to recruit new writing talent, and Adams helped the magazine enlarge its focus to include politics, science, and philology. In 1878 the *Review* moved to New York City, where it became yet more contemporary, focusing on the latest, most controversial social, religious, and political movements. Literature was not neglected, however, as the magazine published works by Ralph Waldo EMERSON and Walt WHITMAN. By the turn of the century, the *Review* was also publishing foreign authors such as the Russian novelist Leo Tolstoy (1828–1910) and the Italian poet Gabriel D'Annunzio (1863–1938). After World War I, however, the magazine's then-owner and editor, George Harvey (1857–1931), served as U.S. ambassador to Great Britain, and circulation declined. Finally, unable to compete with the newer illustrated reviews, the *North American Review* ceased publication in 1939. A quarterly bearing the same name appeared in 1963 at the University of Northern Iowa.

North Star, The *periodical*

An antislavery weekly founded by Frederick DOUGLASS in 1847, *The North Star* was published in Rochester, New York, and financed by a mortgage on Douglass's home. Adhering to Douglass's philosophy of peaceful political change, the newspaper featured articles concerning not only ABOLITIONISM but also temperance (see TEMPERANCE MOVEMENT), peace, education, and capital punishment. In 1851, after copublisher William C. Nell resigned over political differences, the newspaper merged with the *Liberty Party Paper* to become *Frederick Douglass's Paper.*

Sources

Levine, Robert S. *Martin Delany, Frederick Douglass, and the Politics of Representative Identity.* Chapel Hill: University of North Carolina Press, 1977.

Norton, Charles Eliot (1827–1908) *editor*

The son of the Massachusetts Bible scholar Andrews Norton, Charles Eliot Norton made a name for himself as an art historian and man of letters. A professor of fine art at Harvard University from 1873 to 1898, Norton also was a frequent contributor to *THE ATLANTIC MONTHLY*, a coeditor of *THE NORTH AMERICAN REVIEW* (1864–68), and one of the founders of *THE NATION*. Although he was an academic, his interests were broad-ranging, and his publications included a bibliography of Michelangelo, a biography of Rudyard Kipling, a prose translation of Dante's *Divine Comedy,* and editions of poems by John Donne and Anne Bradstreet as well as of Thomas Carlyle's letters. Norton's own letters, published in 1913, are famous in themselves, demonstrating not only his wit and erudition but also the diversity of his many friendships.

Sources

Turner, James. *The Liberal Education of Charles Eliot Norton.* Baltimore, Md.: Johns Hopkins University Press, 1999.

Nye, Edgar Wilson (Bill Nye) (1850–1896) *journalist*

Born in Maine, Bill Nye grew up on what was then the Wisconsin frontier. Reaching adulthood, he moved further west to Laramie, Wyoming, where he was admitted to the practice of law and where, in 1881, he founded the Laramie *Boomerang.* This local newspaper proved to be an excellent outlet for Nye's humorous sketches, which were frequently reprinted elsewhere. In 1886 Nye went to work for the New York *World,* where he continued to publish his broad humor, laced with malapropisms and mangled syntax. New York proved to be his springboard to the greater world, and he soon embarked on the successful lecture tours that made his name a household word. Starting with *Bill Nye and Boomerang* (1881), Nye published numerous collections of his newspaper pieces, as well as longer works like his comic *History of the United States* (1894) and two plays.

Sources

Kesterson, David B. *Bill Nye.* Boston: Twayne, 1981.
———. *Bill Nye: The Western Writings.* Boise, Idaho: Boise State University, 1976.

Octopus, The *Frank Norris* (1901) *novel*

This is the first volume of Frank NORRIS's uncompleted "The Epic of Wheat" trilogy. Magnus Derrick, the owner of the Rancho de Los Muertos in the San Joaquin Valley, leads his fellow farmers in a battle against the Pacific and Southwestern Railroad, an aggressive concern that has coopted the state legislature and the press and is taking over other industries. The railroad monopoly charges heavy freight rates. Even when the farmers, through Derrick, manage to get their man on a state commission to lower the rates, he accepts a bribe and betrays the farmers. The farmers, including Magnus, are now put in a desperate position, and the novel ends with one of their representatives, Presley, confronting Shelgrim, president of the railroad. Much to Presley's surprise, Shelgrim does not behave like a monster; instead he points out that his corporation's actions are the result of circumstances and economic laws.

The Octopus is a good example of the naturalistic novel that sought to show how the forces of modern society were destroying the American belief in individualism and self-reliance. Business relationships were "fixed," often as a result of the typical businessman's response to market conditions. His behavior had little to do with the traditional categories of right and wrong; instead, he acted to protect his business and maximize profit. The American agrarian tradition that taught reverence for the land and for the values of hard work and fair play simply do not apply to the economy Norris portrays in this novel.

Sources

Graham, Don, ed. *Critical Essays on Frank Norris.* Boston: G. K. Hall, 1980.

McElrath, Joseph R. *Frank Norris Revisited.* New York: Twayne, 1992.

Old Southwest *geographical area*

This area, bounded by the Savannah River in the east and the Mississippi River in the west, constituted the southern frontier of the United States in the early 19th century. Included in the area were the present-day states of Georgia, Alabama, Louisiana, Mississippi, Arkansas, Kansas, and Tennessee. Settlers in this area became known for their distinctive form of FOLKLORE characterized by humorous exaggeration and dialect. Practitioners of this species of the TALL TALE genre included Augustus Baldwin LONGSTREET and Thomas Bangs THORPE. Old Southwestern humor would also, somewhat later, influence the writing of Mark Twain (Samuel Langhorne CLEMENS).

Sources

Dick, Everett N. *The Dixie Frontier: A Social History of the Southern Frontier from the First Transmontane Beginnings to the Civil War.* Norman: University of Oklahoma Press, 1993.

Guilds, John Caldwell, and Caroline Collins, eds. *William Gilmore Simms and the American Frontier.* Athens: University of Georgia Press, 1997.

Watson, Ritchie D. *Yeoman Versus Cavalier: The Old Southwest's Fictional Road to Rebellion.* Baton Rouge: Louisiana State University Press, 1993.

Olmsted, Frederick Law (1822–1903) *landscape architect, travel writer*

Born in Connecticut, Frederick Law Olmsted is remembered today primarily for his landscape designs of such areas as Central Park in New York City; the Capitol grounds in Washington, D.C.; and the BOSTON park system. But before he became known for these works and for his interest in conserving areas like Niagara Falls and Yosemite as public lands, Olmsted was famous for his travel writing. Three popular books that grew out of his travels through the slaveholding South in 1850—*A Journey in the Seaboard Slave States* (1856), *A Journey through Texas* (1857), and *A Journey in the Back Country* (1860)—were later combined into *The Cotton Kingdom* (1861). He was also known for his *Walks and Talks of an American Farmer in England* (1852).

Sources

Mitchell, Broadus. *Frederick Law Olmsted: A Critic of the Old South.* New York: Russell & Russell, 1968.

Rybczynski, Witold. *A Clearing in the Distance: Frederick Law Olmsted and America in the Nineteenth Century.* New York: Scribner, 1999.

Todd, John E. *Frederick Law Olmsted.* Boston: Twayne, 1982.

Oneida Community (1848–1881) *Utopian community*

This Utopian living experiment was established by the Society of Perfectionists (see PERFECTIONISM), led by John Humphrey Noyes (1811–86) in central New York state with a mere 40 people. Eventually some 300 members of the community grew prosperous from the manufacture of steel traps and silverware. They held all property in common, conducted weekly sessions of group therapy called Mutual Criticism, and—until 1879, when they bowed to public pressure—engaged in a form of sexual freedom known as Complex Marriage. Branches were formed in Wallingford, Connecticut, and elsewhere on the east coast. The Oneida Community published several newspapers, including the weekly *Circular* (1864–76), and encouraged participation in education and the arts. By the 1870s, however, a new generation of the community had lost its core belief in the tenets of perfectionism, and the outside world had grown increasingly critical of the community's unorthodox way of life. In 1879 Noyes left the country and established a new group on the Canadian side of Niagara Falls. Two years later the community was reorganized as a business venture, and the experiment in communal living ended. Former members, granted financial settlements, moved away to other parts of the country.

Sources

Carden, Maren Lockwood. *Oneida: Utopian Community to Modern Corporation.* Baltimore: Johns Hopkins University Press, 1969.

Thomas, Robert D. *The Man Who Would Be Perfect: John Humphrey Noyes and the Utopian Impulse.* Philadelphia: University of Pennsylvania Press, 1977.

Whitworth, John M. *God's Blueprints: A Sociological Study of Three Utopian Sects.* Boston: Routledge and Kegan Paul, 1975.

"Open Boat, The" *Stephen Crane* (1898) *short story*

Stephen CRANE wrote this story based on his experiences as a reporter during the SPANISH-AMERICAN WAR. Four men escape from a wrecked steamer, the *Commodore,* near the Florida shore. With land in sight, the men are thwarted because of the rough waters and have to spend a night in the boat before attempting, the next day, a desperate swim to the beach. The captain, the cook, and the newspaper correspondent survive the exhausting swim, but the oiler does not.

"The Open Boat" is a model of terse storytelling. Although the narrative is focused entirely on the efforts of these men to stay alive, the author evokes a universe that is indifferent, if not hostile, to man's fate. Crane's story, like much of his other work, as affinities with NATURALISM. Although most of the men survive, their narrow escape is a chilling reminder of the tenuous hold humankind has on its existence.

Sources

Schaefer, Michael. *A Reader's Guide to the Short Stories of Stephen Crane.* New York: G. K. Hall, 1996.

Wolford, Chester L. *Stephen Crane: A Study of the Short Fiction.* Boston: Twayne, 1989.

Optic, Oliver

See ADAMS, WILLIAM TAYLOR.

Oregon Trail *migratory route*

This overland trail from Missouri to what was then the Oregon country was created in the early years of the 19th century largely through the efforts of fur trappers known as "mountain men" traveling to Astoria, a trading post near the mouth of the Columbia River. Immigrants first attempted the trip in 1832, but the first group to actually reach Oregon did so in 1842. The trail was used by Mormons migrating to Utah and was the preferred route of the "great emigration" to the West that began in 1843. Use of the trail declined with the coming of the railroads, but it lived on in American popular culture thanks in part to works like Francis PARKMAN's *The Oregon Trail* (1849).

Sources

Levine, Robert S. *Martin Delany, Frederick Douglass, and the Politics of Representative Identity.* Chapel Hill: University of North Carolina Press, 1997.

Overland Monthly *periodical*

Published in San Francisco from 1868 to 1875 and originally edited by Bret HARTE, the *Overland Monthly* was a regional magazine that published works by Harte and other California writers, such as the poet Charles Warren STODDARD and the humorist Prentice Mulford (1834–91). When the magazine was revived in 1883, it published works by such prominent writers as Jack LONDON, but for the most part its contents were undistinguished, prompting Ambrose BIERCE to dub the periodical the "warmed-Overland Monthly."

Overland Trail *migratory route*

The term "overland trail" was applied to a number of the routes followed by migrants on their journey westward. Most commonly, however, it referred to a trail that started at Independence, Missouri, eventually joining—then deviating from—the OREGON TRAIL. This southern alternative to the Oregon Trail was taken by the ill-fated Donner Party in 1846–47, when winter storms left them snowbound and so bereft of resources that they turned to cannibalism. In 1849 the Overland Trail became the principal route during the California gold rush. The legendary route west was definitively explored in George R. Stewart's *The California Trail* (1963).

Sources

Eaton, Herbert. *The Overland Trail to California in 1852.* New York: Putnam, 1974.

Monaghan, Jay. *The Overland Trail.* Indianapolis: Bobbs-Merill Co., 1947.

Watson, William J. *Journal of an Overland Journy to Oregon Made in the Year 1849.* Fairfield, Wash.: Ye Galleon Press, 1985.

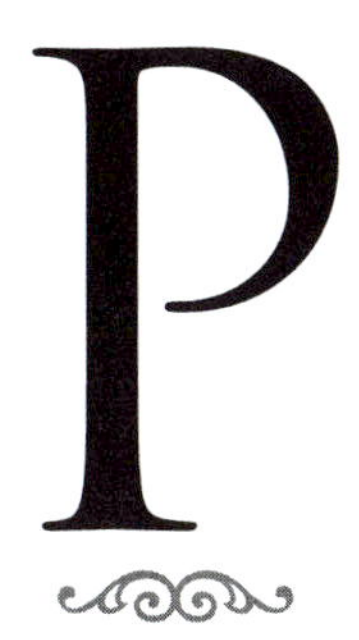

Page, Stanton

See FULLER, HENRY BLAKE.

Page, Thomas Nelson (1853–1922) *short story writer, novelist*

A leader of the LOCAL COLOR movement, Thomas Nelson Page was born on a Virginia plantation, a relative to many of the state's first families. Trained as a lawyer, Page gave up this career in 1893 for that of a writer. His first volume of short stories, *In Ole Virginia* (1887), reflected traditional Southern notions of romantic chivalry. His sentimental narratives, often laced with black dialect and aristocratic notions of gentility, proved highly popular. *Red Rock* (1898), concerning the revolt against RECONSTRUCTION that gave rise to the Ku Klux Klan, was a best-seller. Page also wrote dialect verse and quasi-historical works, including a hagiographic biography, *Robert E. Lee, Man and Soldier* (1911). From 1913 to 1919, Page served as U.S. ambassador to Italy, an experience recounted in his *Italy and the World War* (1920).

Sources

Gross, Theodore L. *Thomas Nelson Page.* New York: Twayne, 1967.

Romine, Scott. *The Narrative Forms of Southern Community.* Baton Rouge: Louisiana State University Press, 1999.

Parker, Theodore (1810–1860) *theologian, essayist*

Born in Lexington, Kentucky, Theodore Parker was a prodigious intellect who came from a family too poor to pay for his education. From the age of 17 to 21 he worked as a schoolteacher until he passed the entrance examination for Harvard. He could not pay his tuition, but he was granted a special dispensation that permitted him to graduate from Harvard Divinity School in 1836. The next year Parker took the pulpit of a Unitarian church (see UNITARIANISM) in Roxbury, Massachusetts, where he became friends with Ralph Waldo EMERSON, Bronson ALCOTT, and other transcendentalists (see TRANSCENDENTALISM). As his faith in miraculous revelation gave way to dependence on a direct intuition of God, Parker's philosophy became increasingly unorthodox. Eventually he developed his own system of religious belief, which he explicated in *The . . . Question Between Mr. Andrews Norton and His Alumni . . .*, which he published in 1839 under the pen name Levi Blodgett; and in the sermon "The Transient and Permanent in Christianity" (1841).

Having joined the TRANSCENDENTAL CLUB and turned his back on traditional church doctrine, Parker was ostracized by his fellow clergy. He was able to deliver the lectures later collected in *A Discourse of Matters Pertaining to Religion* (1842) only in nonchurch venues. Parker stubbornly refused to resign from the church, however, and he retained a loyal following that in 1845 installed him as minister of the new Twenty-eighth Congregational Society of Boston. There the 7,000 members of his congregation heard Parker preach not just about religion per se but also about such pressing contemporary concerns as war, slavery, women's rights, and temperance. Outside the church, he campaigned aggressively against slavery, not only delivering passionate speeches and publishing his *Letter to the People of the United States Touching the Matter of Slavery* (1848) but also rescuing fugitive slaves and aiding John BROWN. All this activity finally robbed Parker of his vitality, and he died in Italy during a trip meant to restore his health.

The character Mr. Power, an inspired preacher in Louisa May ALCOTT's novel *Work* (1873), is based on Parker, who also appears in a 1952 novel by Truman John Nelson, *The Sin of the Prophet.*

Sources

Albrecht, Robert C. *Theodore Parker.* New York: Twayne, 1971.

Chesebrough, David B. *Theodore Parker: Orator of Superior Ideas.* Westport, Conn.: Greenwood Press, 1999.

Collins, Robert E., ed. *Theodore Parker: American Transcendentalist: A Critical Essay and a Collection of His Writings.* Metuchen, N.J.: Scarecrow Press, 1973.

Parkman, Francis (1823–1893) *historian*

Born in Boston to a prominent family, Francis Parkman graduated from Harvard in 1844, already having developed an interest in studying the frontier experience and Indian life. He graduated from Harvard Law School in 1846 but never practiced law. Instead he journeyed west to Wyoming, intent on exploring the land and restoring his fragile health. Although the journey stimulated his imaginative powers, it also worsened his health. Nearly blind, he had to dictate his first book, *The Oregon Trail* (1849), which immediately established him as America's first great historian of the frontier experience.

Although illness continued to make him weak and dependent on the help of others, Parkman undertook an epic historical project about the conflict of the French and English in North America, beginning with *History of the Conspiracy of Pontiac* (1851). The journeys of exploration; military and political strategies; encounters with indigenous people; and the fate of the French Huguenots (Protestants), Spanish Catholics, the Indians, and the European religious mission in North America are all explored in his magisterial volumes: *Pioneers of France in the New World* (1865), *The Jesuits in North America in the Seventeenth Century* (1867), *La Salle and the Discovery of the Great West* (1869), *The Old Regime in Canada* (1874), and *Count Frontenac and New France under Louis XIV* (1877). *Montcalm and Wolfe* (1884), detailing the Seven Years' War—or the French and Indian War, as the American colonists called it—dramatized the final confrontation between the British and the French, in which the fate of much of North America was decided.

Although Parkman was a partisan—the English represented the forces of an emerging democracy and the French the despotism of Europe—his conservative side prevented him from ignoring the excesses of democratic rule and prompted him to see the virtue of constitutional monarchies. His style has often been deemed romantic, although he shaped his dramatic narratives in accordance with a strict sense of scholarship and the quest for accuracy. Like the romantics (see ROMANTICISM), Parkman had a tremendous feeling for nature, which resulted in the publication of *The Book of Roses* (1866) and his appointment at Harvard as professor of horticulture (1871).

Parkman wrote one novel, *Vasall Morton* (1856). His *Journals* were published in 1948 and his *Letters* in 1960.

Sources

Gale, Robert L. *Francis Parkman.* New York: Twayne, 1973.

Jacobs, Wilbur R. *Francis Parkman, Historian as Hero: The Formative Years.* Austin: University of Texas Press, 1991.

Levin, David. *History as Romantic Art: Bancroft, Prescott, Motley, and Parkman.* Stanford, Calif.: Stanford University Press, 1959.

Pease, Otis A. *Parkman's History: The Historian as Literary Artist.* New Haven, Conn.: Yale University Press, 1953.

Park Theatre (1798–1848)

The actor and theater manager Lewis Hallam Jr. (1740–1808) opened this playhouse at the New Theatre with theater manager John Hodgkinson (1767–1805) to replace the John Street Theatre, New York City's first permanent playhouse. Over the next quarter of a century, the Park served as the city's only venue for drama, and even after other theaters were opened, the Park remained a prestigious playhouse. The theater's original, highly regarded repertory stock company gradually gave way, under the management of Stephen Price (1783–1840), to a star system featuring foreign actors and popular productions. The Park staged Dion BOUCICAULT's celebrated *London Assurance* in 1841, giving New York its first long-running play and securing the city's new position as the theater capital of America. After the Park burned to the ground in 1848 it was not rebuilt, since the theater district had moved elsewhere in the city.

Sources

Picton, Thomas. *Old Gotham Theatricals: Selections from a Series, "Reminiscences of a Man about Town."* San Bernardino, Calif.: Borgo Press, 1995.

Parley, Peter

See GOODRICH, SAMUEL GRISWOLD.

Parton, Sara Payson Willis (Fanny Fern) (1811–1872) *novelist, journalist*

Sara Payson Willis Parton—a once-widowed, then divorced mother of two—began her writing career when sewing failed to bring in enough money to support her family. In 1852 she joined the staff of the *New York Musical World and Times,* where she published articles under the pen name Fanny Fern. A collection of these pieces, *Fern Leaves from*

Fanny's Portfolio (1853), was a best-seller. When she joined the staff of the Philadelphia *Saturday Evening Post* the same year, she became the first female newspaper columnist in America. Two years later, when she was paid $100 per column by the *NEW YORK LEDGER*, she was the most highly paid newspaper writer of her day. The author of two novels, the autobiographical *Ruth Hall* (1855) and *Rose Clark* (1856), Parton also produced six collections of essays as well as books for children and is remembered for her championship of feminist issues as well as her informal style. She is the originator of the aphorism "The way to a man's heart is through his stomach."

Sources

Walker, Nancy A., ed. *Fanny Fern.* New York: Twayne, 1993.

Warren, Joyce W. *Fanny Fern: An Independent Woman.* New Brunswick, N.J.: Rutgers University Press, 1992.

Pattie, James Ohio (1804–1850?) *explorer, memoirist*

Born in Kentucky, fur trapper James Ohio Pattie undertook several hazardous expeditions to Santa Fe, in what is now New Mexico, as well as to Baja California and Mexico. These journeys, taken between 1824 and 1830, resulted in a book, *The Personal Narrative of James O. Pattie, of Kentucky, During an Expedition from St. Louis, through the vast regions Between That Place and the Pacific Ocean* (1831). Blending fact and fiction, the memoir was edited—and probably largely ghostwritten—by the missionary and novelist Timothy Flint (1780–1840). It was later plagiarized in *The Hunters of Kentucky, or, The Trails and Toils of Trappers and Traders* (1847), a book purporting to tell of the adventures of a B. Bilson. Pattie's work proved to have lasting popularity and was included in Reuben G. Thwaites's (1853–1913) *Early Western Travels* (1905) and reissued 25 years later in a new edition put together by Milo M. Quaife (1880–1959). Little is known of Pattie beyond what is revealed in his book. When last seen he was a participant in the California gold rush of 1849.

Sources

Hafen, LeRoy R. *Fur Trappers and Traders of the Far Southwest: Twenty Biographical Sketches.* Logan: Utah State University Press, 1997.

Paulding, James Kirke (Launcelot Langstaff) (1778–1860) *novelist, historian*

Born in New York state and raised in Tarrytown, James Kirke Paulding was 18 when he and his brother met Washington IRVING and Irving's brother William. The four became fast friends (William Irving eventually married Paulding's sister) and formed the nucleus of an informal literary group that called itself The Nine Worthies of Cockloft Hall. In 1807 and 1808, Paulding and Irving collaborated on a humorous periodical called *Salmagundi; or, The Whim-Whams and Opinions of Launcelot Langstaff, Esq.*, which published essays modeled on the witty English *Spectator* and which was the first magazine of its kind in America. Later Paulding alone published a second series, *Tellers from the South; A Sketch of Old England, Salmagundi; Second Series* (1819–20).

Paulding took another page from Irving's book when he published a comic account of the settling and revolt of the American colonies, *The Diverting History of John Bull and Brother Jonathan* (1812), inspired by his friend's *History of New York* (1809). This work, too, was later followed by a sequel, *The History of Uncle Sam and His Boys* (1835). Paulding clearly excelled at burlesque, which he combined with his distaste for the ROMANTICISM of the novelist Sir Walter Scott (1771–1832) in the long poem *The Lay of the Scottish Fiddle* (1813). On the other hand, Paulding would laud his ideal of rugged American individualism in the poem *The Backwoodsman* (1818). Between 1815 and 1825 he published a series of histories, some serious, others not, upholding American values while lampooning Old World, conservative British Toryism. Works such as the wholly serious *The United States and England* (1815); *Letters from the South* (1817), a defense of the agrarian Southern states; and *John Bull in America; or, the New Munchausen* (1825) earned Paulding a popular following as well as an appointment to the Board of Navy Commissioners (1815–23).

Paulding's first truly important work of long fiction, *Konigsmarke, The Long Finn: A Story of the New World* (1823), is a historical romance concerning Swedish settlement of Delaware in the 17th century. It was followed by a drama about the western frontier, *The Lion of the West* (1831), which proved to be a popular success on stage. Other works of historical fiction followed: *The Dutchman's Fireplace* (1831), an account of life in upper New York State during the French and Indian War, which is thought to be Paulding's best novel; *Westward Ho!* (1832), which follows a Virginia family's pioneering adventures in Kentucky; and *The Puritan and His Daughter* (1849), a tale of 17th-century Virginia.

Paulding's prodigious output of novels and dramas based on American history and continuing interest in naval affairs won his appointment by President Martin Van Buren (1782–1862) as secretary of the navy from 1838 to 1841. After returning to private life he continued to publish until 1849, when he retired to his estate in Hyde Park, New York.

Sources

Aderman, Ralph M., ed. *Letters of James Kirke Paulding.* Madison: University of Wisconsin Press, 1962.

Ratner, Lorman. *James Kirke Paulding: The Last Republican.* New York: Greenwood Press, 1992.

Reynolds, Larry J. *James Kirke Paulding.* Boston: Twayne, 1984.

Payne, John Howard (1791–1852) *playwright*

A native New Yorker, John Howard Payne began his dramatic career early, first publishing his own theater review, *Thespian Mirror* (1805–06), at the age of 14. The paper attracted the attention of established theater people—not only because of Payne's precocity—who encouraged the boy in his literary ambitions. The next year, at age 15, Payne had his first play, a melodrama called *Julia; or, The Wanderer* (1806), produced on the New York stage. That milestone was succeeded by another newspaper, *The Pastime* (1807–08), which was in turn followed by Payne's acting debut in 1809. Payne followed up with more successes: an adaptation of the German playwright August Friedrich Ferdinand von Kotzebue's (1761–1819) *Das Kind der Liebe,* produced in 1809 as *Lovers' Vows;* and a series of acting roles. Soon, however, Payne's youthful success faded, and he found it harder and harder to get work. In 1813 friends took up a collection to send Payne to England, where it was thought he could reestablish himself.

In England Payne met with some initial success, but the constant threat of bankruptcy forced him to do theatrical hackwork. In 1818 the actor Edmund Kean (1787?–1833) mounted a production of Payne's *Brutus; or, the Fall of Tarquin,* which proved to be a triumph. Payne was an inept businessman, however, and was sent to debtors' prison. After his release he fled to Paris to escape his creditors. From there he sent plays back to London for production. Among these was perhaps his best known work, *Clari; or, The Maid of Milan* (1823), which, mounted as an opera, included Payne's song "Home, Sweet Home." Unfortunately, as he had sold the play outright, Payne realized no royalties from its popularity. Penniless again—and having been spurned by Mary Shelley (1797–1851), the author of *Frankenstein* and widow of the poet Percy Bysshe Shelley—Payne returned to the United States in 1832. The popularity of the American productions of his plays that had been staged in his absence enabled friends to raise $10,000 for him through a series of benefit performances. Finally, in 1842, Daniel WEBSTER secured Payne's appointment as U.S. ambassador to Tunis, Tunisia, where he died, still debt-ridden and planning another theatrical comeback.

Sources

Overmyer, Grace. *America's First Hamlet.* New York: New York University Press, 1957.

Peabody, Elizabeth Palmer (1804–1894) *memoirist, essayist*

Elizabeth Peabody began her remarkable career teaching at her mother's school in Billerica, Massachusetts, which was also her birthplace. The future sister-in-law of Nathaniel HAWTHORNE (who married Sophia Peabody) and the educator Horace MANN (who married Mary Peabody), Elizabeth was herself associated with the transcendentalists (see TRANSCENDENTALISM) through Ralph Waldo EMERSON, who tutored her in Greek when she was 18; through William Ellery CHANNING (1), whom she served as secretary during the 1820s and 1830s; and through Bronson ALCOTT, whom she served as assistant at Alcott's Temple School from 1834 to 1836 (she would recall the latter experience in her *Record of a School* [1835]). In 1839 Peabody opened a BOSTON bookstore that became a meeting place for the local intelligentsia, including the TRANSCENDENTAL CLUB, and her house was the site of Margaret FULLER's "conversation classes." Her bookstore was also the birthplace of BROOK FARM and a home for *THE DIAL,* which was published in the back of the store between 1842 and 1843. An ardent abolitionist and reformer, Peabody published a number of essays in the periodical, which were later reprinted, together with some of her memoirs, in *A Last Evening with Allston* (1886).

When the bookstore burned down in 1844, Peabody began a series of lecture tours and returned to teaching, which brought her into the orbit of Horace Mann, with whom she maintained a close but platonic relationship all her life. In Boston in 1860, Peabody opened one of the first kindergartens in the nation; her study of the philosophy of the German educator Friedrich Froebel (1782–1852) led to publication of her and her sister Mary's *Moral Culture of Infancy and Kindergarten Guide* (1866) as well as a magazine *Kindergarten Messenger* (1873–75). In 1861 Peabody also opened the first kindergarten training center in the United States.

Sources

Ronda, Bruce A. *Elizabeth Palmer Peabody: A Reformer on Her Own Terms.* Cambridge, Mass.: Harvard University Press, 1999.

Tharp, Louise Hall. *The Peabody Sisters of Salem.* Boston: Little, Brown and Company, 1950.

Percival, James Gates (1795–1856) *poet*

Born in Connecticut and trained as a physician, James Gates Percival held a number of professions in addition to being a literary man. After practicing medicine briefly, he worked as a journalist for the Connecticut *Herald* and the *American Athenaeum.* In addition to teaching chemistry at West Point, he also served as state geologist for Connecticut (1835–42) and Wisconsin (1854–56) and contributed valuable new knowledge to the latter field. His great interest, however, was poetry, and he believed himself to be a great romantic poet. He gained much public recognition with such works as the epic *Prometheus* (1821) and the experimental *The Dream of a Day* (1843). His reputation was hampered, however, by a lifelong struggle with mental illness that caused him to commit himself to the state hospital in New Haven, Connecticut, for a decade.

Percy, Florence

See ALLEN, ELIZABETH ANNE CHASE AKERS.

perfectionism *religious movement*

This radical doctrine is closely associated with John Humphrey Noyes (1811–86), a failed theologian who advocated a belief that man was perfectible through direct communion with God. The doctrine appealed to the mid-19th-century temperament that embraced such other liberal religious and social beliefs as FOURIERISM, Millerism (see MILLERITES), and TRANSCENDENTALISM. Like some of these other sects, the so-called perfectionists established Utopian communities. The first of these was a community of Bible communists in Putney, Vermont, but the most successful and long-lived was the ONEIDA COMMUNITY in New York, which lasted from 1848 to 1879 and established a branch in Wallingford, Connecticut. The prosperity of the Oneida Community aroused the jealousy of its neighbors, who also took a dim view of the commune's policy of "complex marriage," which encouraged sexual freedom and practiced eugenics (attempts to improve the human species by selective breeding). Noyes was eventually forced to flee the country, and the sect dissolved.

Sources

DeMaria, Richard. *Communal Love at Oneida: A Perfectionist Vision of Authority, Property, and Sexual Order.* New York: E. Mellen Press, 1978.

Haksar, Vinit. *Equality, Liberty, and Perfectionism.* New York: Oxford University Press, 1979.

Thomas, Robert D. *The Man Who Would Be Perfect: John Humphrey Noyes and the Utopian Impulse.* Philadelphia: University of Pennsylvania Press, 1977.

Pfaff's Cellar *location*

This tavern, located at 653 Broadway in Lower Manhattan, was a meeting place for literary bohemians during the 1850s, when it was frequented by such writers as Walt WHITMAN, Fitz-James O'Brien (c. 1828–62), Bayard TAYLOR, George ARNOLD, William Winter (1836–1917), Adah Menken (1835?–68), Henry CLAPP, and Ada Clare (1836–74). The group broke up with the onset of the CIVIL WAR, but their numerous magazine pieces about the tavern made it a tourist attraction.

Sources

Parry, Albert. *Garrets and Pretenders: A History of Bohemianism in America.* New York: Covici, Friede, 1933.

Phillips, David Graham (1867–1911) *journalist, novelist*

Born in Indiana, David Graham Phillips began his journalistic career with the Cincinnati *Times-Star* in 1887, then moved in 1890 to New York City, where he wrote for the *NEW-YORK TRIBUNE,* the NEW YORK *SUN,* and the NEW YORK *WORLD.* Between 1901 and 1911 Phillips devoted himself to MUCKRAKING: He published a series called *The Treason of the Senate* in *Cosmopolitan* in 1906, as well as a play and a succession of 23 "problem" novels dealing with contemporary social ills. Most of the latter—with titles like *The Great God Success* (1901), *Golden Fleece* (1903), *Light-Fingered Gentry* (1907), and *The Fashionable Adventures of Joshua Craig* (1909)—concern greed and corruption in the private and public lives of the privileged.

Beginning in 1908, when he published his play *The Worth of a Woman,* Phillips turned increasingly to the subject of the "new woman" and society's changing attitudes towards her. His most important work, the novel *Susan Lenox: Her Fall and Rise* (1917), combines his muckraking background with the story of a country girl who achieves success as an urban prostitute. The strength of *Susan Lenox* led some to compare Phillips with the great French naturalist Honoré de Balzac (1799–1850), but Phillips was never able to wear Balzac's mantle. Shortly after completing *Susan Lenox,* which was published posthumously, Phillips was murdered in New York by a madman who believed that the novelist had maligned his sister in *Joshua Craig.*

Sources

Filler, Louis. *Voice of the Democracy: A Critical Biography of David Graham Phillips, Journalist, Novelist, Progressive.* University Park: Pennsylvania State University Press, 1978.

Ravitz, Abe C. *David Graham Phillips.* New York: Twayne, 1966.

Pike *character*

A standard character type prominent in western American literature of the mid-19th century, Pike, an immigrant to the West, was by tradition a native of Pike County, which could be a location in Missouri, Arkansas, Illinois, Texas, or any other frontier area. Pike first appeared in American literature in the humorous sketches of George Horatio Derby (1823–61), but he was not widely known until after 1870, when he was popularized by Bret HARTE and in particular by the dialect poems of John Hay (1838–1905), *Pike County Ballads* (1871). Usually presented as an ignorant backwoodsman, Pike was crude, greedy, bibulous, and suspicious of strangers. In his *At Home and Abroad* (1860), Bayard TAYLOR pictured Pike as

> the Anglo Saxon relapsed into semi-barbarism. He is long, lithe, and sallow; he expectorates vehemently; he takes naturally to whisky; he has the "shakes" his life long at home, though he generally manages to get rid of them in California; he has little respect for the rights of others; he distrusts men in "store clothes," but venerates the memory of Andrew Jackson.

The Pike dialect perpetuated by Harte and Hay would later influence Samuel CLEMENS (Mark Twain), who elevated the use of American regional dialect into something far richer than the creation of stock characters.

Sources

Garner, Claud W. *Cornbread Aristocrat.* New York: New American Library, 1952.

Poe, Edgar Allan (1809–1849) *short story writer, poet, critic*

Edgar Allan Poe was born in BOSTON in 1809. His father died a year later, and his destitute mother moved the family to Richmond, Virginia, where she died the following year. John Allan, a Richmond merchant, took charge of Poe, although he never legally adopted the child. Poe accompanied the Allans to England, where he was educated between 1815 and 1820. He later portrayed this period in his short story "William Wilson." Tensions between foster father and son developed, and Poe could count on little support from Allan when he attended the University of Virginia in 1826. After he got into trouble over gambling debts, he dropped out of school and quarreled with Allan, refusing to pursue the legal career Allan urged on him.

Poe went off on his own to Boston, there publishing anonymously his first book of poetry, *Tamerlane* (1827). He enlisted in the army, and after a brief reconciliation with Allan was able to secure a place at the United States Military Academy (West Point) in 1830 (he was expelled the same year). Poe continued to write, publishing another book of verse, *Al Aaraaf* (1829). By 1831 he had been dismissed from West Point for neglect of duty and continued to pursue his literary career with *Poems by Edgar A. Poe* in 1831. This collection included Poe's famous poem "To Helen," about Helen of Troy, and the mysterious and suggestive poem "The City in the Sea."

Poe's early poetry was derivative, drawing on romantic conventions (see ROMANTICISM), but it also had a symbolic heft and ethereal quality quite unlike the poetry made popular at the time by Henry Wadsworth LONGFELLOW, John Greenleaf WHITTIER, and William Cullen BRYANT. As his later critical essays would demonstrate, Poe scorned didactic poetry that expressed conventional sentiments. He strove to create poems complete in themselves to be admired as poems, not as aids to understanding the world or inculcating moral values. His notion of art as autonomous was quite modern and would influence 20th-century poets and writers as various as Allen Tate (1899–1979), Hart Crane (1899–1932), Richard Wilbur (1921–), and Susan Sontag (1933–).

In the mid-1830s Poe began to establish a reputation as a short-story writer. This led to an editorial position at the *SOUTHERN LITERARY MESSENGER,* in which he published incisive reviews that articulated a well-thought-out aesthetic position. Poe favored American writers like Nathaniel HAWTHORNE who did not imitate European models. He believed in American originals who created their own forms of literature and relied on their own imaginations instead of copying fashion or catering to readers.

In 1838 Poe published *The Narrative of Arthur Gordon Pym,* his one relatively long piece of fiction. The novella's symbolic narrative, especially its emphasis on the "meaning" of whiteness and its exploration of extreme states of mind, was a precursor to the later novels of Herman MELVILLE, especially *MOBY-DICK.* Poe rejected REALISM in favor of highly subjective, metaphysical fantasies.

By the late 1830s and early 1840s Poe was publishing in magazines his most celebrated short stories, including "The Fall of the House of Usher," "William Wilson," and "Morella." In *TALES OF THE GROTESQUE AND ARABESQUE* (1839) he included "Berenice," "Ligeia," "The Conqueror Worm," and "The Assignation," some of the most powerful short fiction ever written by an American author. His subject was often the brooding human consciousness of death and yearning for immortality, a morbid yet thrilling exploration of characters in various states of extremity. This remarkable work challenged much of the optimism of popular American literature during this period.

Poe confronted the human compulsion to repeat self-destructive acts in such tales as "The Imp of the Perverse" and "A Descent into the Maelstrom," both published in *GRAHAM'S MAGAZINE,* which he edited. His essay "The Philosophy of Composition" (1846), one of his major statements on literature, emphasizes the importance of form over content. Poe sought to enforce the idea of writing as a craft carefully thought-out instead of as an expression of emotion. His attention to the details of a work of art presaged the 20th-century critical writing of T. S. Eliot (1888–1965) and the New Critics, a school of literary criticism that would not emerge until the middle of the next century.

An innovator in literary form, Poe has often been called the originator of DETECTIVE FICTION because of "The Murders in the Rue Morgue" (1841) and "The Mystery of Marie Roget" (1842–43), which introduced his detective C. Auguste DUPIN. Poe then achieved tremendous popular success with his poem "The Raven," which demonstrated his dedication to form as a series of repetitions of a single idea or conceit: the inescapability of mortality.

Writing for the *BROADWAY JOURNAL* in the 1840s, Poe produced several of his most popular tales, including "The Pit and the Pendulum," "Eleonora," "The Premature Burial," and "THE TELL-TALE HEART" as well as his best detective tale, "The Purloined Letter."

Both Poe's grotesque, supernatural tales, and his tales of ratiocination—his romanticism and his rationalism—were leading him to a metaphysical and poetical statement, which became the book *Eureka* (1848). An intricately argued essay, *Eureka* posited a contracting universe that impinged on the individual consciousness and made forebodings of doom and disintegration inevitable. Poe's entire corpus read in the light of *Eureka* makes him not the psychologist of extreme states of mind but instead the philosopher of a universe gradually pulling itself apart. The plots of Poe's stories and poems, in other words, become the unraveling plot of the universe itself. Yet as with all great art, Poe's works can be read on many different levels and certainly enjoyed without any knowledge of *Eureka.*

Poe's own frail health, apparently abetted by his weakness for alcohol (although the true extent of his addiction has never been determined), made his last few years miserable. He was found in a delirious state shortly before he died, having wandered the streets of Baltimore for several days.

Poe's body of work is uneven, yet the core of his short stories, a handful of poems, and certain essays like "The Poetic Principle" and "The Rationale of Verse" put him in the front rank of writers. Unquestionably he has had an extraordinary influence on American literature, especially due to his insistence that a work of art must have unity and contain no extraneous elements. He argued that works of literature are autonomous, complete in themselves, and insofar as they achieve this ideal they are perfect emblems of immortality.

Sources

Bloom, Harold, ed. *Edgar Allan Poe.* New York: Chelsea House, 1985.

Kennedy, J. Gerald, ed. *A Historical Guide to Edgar Allan Poe.* New York: Oxford University Press, 2001.

Silverman, Kenneth. *Edgar A. Poe: Mournful and Never-Ending Remembrance.* New York: HarperCollins, 1991.

Sova, Dawn. *Edgar Allan Poe A to Z: The Essential Reference to His Life and Work.* New York: Facts On File, 2001.

Szumski, Bonnie. *Readings on Edgar Allan Poe.* San Diego, Calif.: Greenhaven Press, 1998.

Poetry Society of America *organization*

Founded in 1910 to encourage a national poetry renaissance, the Poetry Society of America counted among its original members some of the most distinguished poets in the country, poets such as W.H. Auden, Robert Frost, Langston Hughes, Edna St. Vincent Millay, Marianne Moore, and Wallace Stevens. Today the society sponsors numerous regional groups and conferences and suggests candidates for the annual Pulitzer Prize in poetry.

Sources

Davidson, Gustav, ed. *In Fealty to Apollo: Poetry Society of America, 1910–1950.* New York: Fine Editions Press, 1950.

Porter, William Sydney (O. Henry) (1862–1910)

short story writer

Raised in Greensboro, North Carolina, the man who became O. Henry had an inauspicious beginning. After working in Greensboro in his uncle's drugstore, William Sydney (or Sidney) Porter drifted to Texas, where for the following decade he worked as a clerk, a draftsman in a state land office, and a teller in an Austin bank. In Texas he eloped with his sweetheart, wrote humorous anecdotes for a Houston paper, and began his own humorous weekly, *The Rolling Stone* (1894–95). In 1896 his life changed forever when he was indicted for embezzlement of funds from the Texas bank where he worked.

Porter fled to Honduras, where he met other fugitives and where he later set his first book, *Cabbages and Kings* (1904), a series of sketches about Latin American revolution loosely linked by recurring characters. Learning that his wife was mortally ill, Porter returned to Austin and stayed with her until she died; he then surrendered to police. He was convicted and sentenced to five years in the federal penitentiary in Columbus, Ohio. With time off for good behavior, Porter spent three years behind bars, during which he worked as the prison pharmacist and, in order to support his young daughter, wrote a series of short stories based on his life in Texas and Central America.

The first of Porter's stories to be signed O. Henry was "Whistling Dick's Christmas Stocking," which appeared in MCCLURE'S MAGAZINE in 1899. He also employed other pen names, including Oliver Henry and S. J. Peters, for the stories he wrote in prison, but the one that stayed with him was most likely taken from the *U.S. Dispensatory,* to which he must have referred while working in the pharmacy. The name of the famous French pharmacist, Etienne-Ossian Henry, appears in this volume in the abbreviated form of O. Henry.

After his release from prison Porter went to New York City, where he had already established a reputation with his stories, some of them inspired by tales he had heard in prison. Porter soon became America's top short-story writer as well as one of its most prolific ones. He wrote so much that volumes of his stories continued to appear for years after his death. Many of his tales continued to draw on his life in Texas and Central America, but Porter made Manhattan and the lives of ordinary New Yorkers, "the four million," his special subject. For Porter New York was, as he said in several of his stories, "Bagdad-on-the-Subway." He specialized in plots that relied heavily on coincidence, and he wrote to a formula so distinctive as to be instantly recognizable. The surprise ending of such stories as "The Gift of the Magi" and "The Furnished Room" are prime examples of the irony and twists of fate synonymous with the name O. Henry. In 1918 the O. Henry Memorial Awards were established to recognize the best short stories published each year.

Sources

Blansfield, Karen C. *Cheap Rooms and Restless Hearts: A Study of Formula in the Urban Tales of William Sydney Porter.* Bowling Green, Ohio: Bowling Green State University Popular Press, 1988.

Current-García, Eugene. *O. Henry: A Study of the Short Fiction.* New York: Twayne, 1993.

O'Quinn, Trueman E., and Jenny Lind Porter. *Time to Write: How William Sidney Porter Became O. Henry.* Austin, Tex.: Eakin Press, 1986.

Portrait of a Lady, The Henry James (1881) *novel*

This work is often cited as Henry's JAMES's first undisputably great novel. The highly intelligent and attractive heroine, Isabel Archer, is brought to England by her aunt Mrs. Touchett. She befriends her invalid cousin Ralph, Mrs. Touchett's son, and she is wooed by Lord Warburton. She rejects Warburton's proposal of marriage primarily because she does not want to relinquish her independence; this only makes her more valuable in Warburton's eyes and more admirable in Ralph's. Isabel also rejects the suit of Caspar Goodwood, an earnest businessman who comes to England hoping to make her change her mind about him. He is so persistent that she finally agrees to wait two years before giving her final answer. The ailing Ralph, also in love with Isabel but realizing the futility of proposing to her, persuades his father to make the penniless Isabel his heir.

When Mr. Touchett dies, Isabel, now an heiress, travels to Florence with Mrs. Touchett. There she meets an elegant American expatriate, Madame Merle, who introduces Isabel to the charming Gilbert Osmond, a widower with a young daughter. Captivated by Osmond's refinement and self-assurance, Isabel falls in love with him, ignoring warnings from Caspar and others that Osmond desires only her fortune. Charmed by Florence and a way of life that seems unfettered by the commercial world, which Caspar Goodwood represents, and by the declining English aristocracy, which Warburton embodies, Isabel marries Osmond, thinking he will cherish her choice and honor her independence. In fact, Osmond is selfish and cold-hearted. The proud Isabel struggles to adjust to this but is horrified when she observes Madame Merle trying to facilitate a match between Warburton and Osmond's daughter, Pansy. Almost at the same time, Isabel is called to England to say goodbye to the dying Ralph, whereupon she learns that Pansy is Madame Merle's daughter. Isabel finally realizes that Madame Merle and Osmond have conspired to acquire her to ensure their own future. Isabel confesses her grave error and has a kind of reconciliation with Goodwood, but she returns to Florence, evidently set on coping with a disastrous situation her own pride has helped to create.

The Portrait of a Lady is James's earliest foray into a fully developed psychological novel. Every detail of the plot is intricately connected to Isabel's psychology and the way others respond to her. James has been justly praised for his ability to portray a young woman's thoughts and ambitions.

Sources

Bamberg, Robert D., ed. *The Portrait of a Lady: An Authoritative Text, Henry James and the Novel, Reviews and Criticism.* New York: W. W. Norton, 1995.

Buitenhuis, Peter, ed. *Twentieth Century Interpretations of The Portrait of a Lady: A Collection of Critical Essays.* Englewood Cliffs, N.J.: Prentice Hall, 1968.

Porte, Joel, ed. *New Essays on The Portrait of a Lady.* New York: Cambridge University Press, 1990.

Powell, John Wesley (1834–1902) *geologist, ethnologist, nonfiction writer*

Born in Mt. Morris, now a part of New York City, John Wesley Powell was raised in Illinois, where he first exhibited an interest in geology by serving as secretary of the Natural History Society. Powell served in the CIVIL WAR, rising to the rank of major and losing an arm at the battle of Shiloh. Afterward he joined the staff of Illinois Wesleyan College as a professor of geology, a post he held while leading geological expeditions into Colorado and Utah before beginning, in 1869, a geographical and geological survey of the Colorado River under the auspices of the Smithsonian Institution. He memorialized his observations and experiences on this and a second trip three years later in *Exploration of the Colorado River of the West and Its Tributaries* (1875), later revised and republished as the scientific but vividly written *Canyons of the Colorado* (1895). His reconciliation of conflicting surveys of the American West helped bring about the formation of the U.S. Geological Survey, where Powell served as director from 1881 to 1894. Powell's scientific rigor and organizational powers shaped government policies towards reclamation and conservation in a process that has come to be known as the "second opening of the west."

Sources

Aton, James M. *John Wesley Powell.* Boise, Idaho: Boise State University, 1994.

Stegner, Wallace. *Beyond the Hundredth Meridian.* 1954. Reprint, Lincoln: University of Nebraska Press, 1962.

Worster, Donald. *A River Running West: The Life of John Wesley Powell.* New York: Oxford University Press, 2001.

pragmatism *philosophy*

William JAMES defined pragmatism as a mode of thought that arose from the inadequacies of rationalism and empiricism. Instead of putting faith in ideas per se or in a priori concepts, the pragmatist, James argued, discovered ideas in action and thus exercised a kind of power over reality. His notion that truth was instrumental—that is, derived from experience—became a driving tenet of John DEWEY's educational philosophy.

The term *pragmatic* is often used to describe a distinctively American brand of thought that prefers concrete outcomes to abstract arguments or theories. Learning by doing is another way of describing pragmatism. Much of American literature reflects a pragmatic bias, with characters developing their ideas from their experience in society. Tradition—that is, a habit of thinking in certain patterns—generally has been rejected in a country which, after all, is part of what has been called the "New World."

By the same token, American authors who have sought to ground themselves in European values and to live on the European continent have revealed the limits of pragmatism. The novels of Henry JAMES, for example, might be said to refute his older brother's pragmatism: Characters like Isabel Archer in *PORTRAIT OF A LADY* rely too heavily on their ability to learn from experience, reject the counsels of those steeped in European traditions, and suffer the consequences.

Sources

Cormier, Harvey. *The Truth Is What Works: William James, Pragmatism, and the Seed of Death.* Lanham, Md.: Rowman & Littlefield, 2001.

Levin, Jonathan. *The Poetics of Transition: Emerson, Pragmatism, & American Literary Modernism.* Durham, N.C.: Duke University Press, 1999.

Prairie, The *James Fenimore Cooper* (1827) *novel*

This is the third of James Fenimore COOPER's five *LEATHER-STOCKING TALES* and chronologically the last installment of the saga of his hero, Natty BUMPPO. Writing in Paris and drawing on such sources as reports of the Lewis and Clark expedition of 1803–06 and the explorer Edwin James's (1797–1861) *Account of an Expedition from Pittsburgh to the Rocky Mountains* (1822–23), Cooper set his story in a land he had himself never seen, western Nebraska and Wyoming. On these western plains, Natty Bumppo, now almost 90, encounters a wagon train led by the antisocial frontiersman Ishmael Bush and his brother-in-law, Abiram White. In their company is a naturalist; a beekeeper; a mysterious woman hidden in a covered wagon; and her companion, Ellen Wade. After fending off an Indian raid on the wagon train, Bumppo is joined by Duncan Heyward Middleton, a young soldier searching for his kidnapped betrothed, Doña Inez de Certavallos. When Middleton discovers that the mystery woman in the covered wagon is in fact his beloved, he manages to rescue her with Bumppo's aid, and together with Ellen Wade and the beekeeper, Paul Hover, they escape. Numerous adventures follow, including capture by hostile Sioux, a prairie fire, a buffalo stampede, and recapture by Ishmael Bush. In the end, after his friends have been saved by Middleton's army troops, Natty Bumppo retires to the quiet of the prairie and a hospitable Pawnee camp, where he breathes his last.

Although the novel features the same sorts of good and bad Indians and dark and light women that appear in Cooper's other *Leather-Stocking Tales, The Prairie* is notable for its evocation of the vast western prairie lands and the elegiac tone that accompanies Bumppo's—and the frontier's—inevitable demise.

Sources

Øverland, Orm. *James Fenimore Cooper's The Prairie: The Making and Meaning of an American Classic.* New York: Humanities Press, 1973.

Peck, H. Daniel. *A World by Itself: The Pastoral Moment in Cooper's Fiction.* New Haven: Yale University Press, 1977.

Rans, Geoffrey. *Cooper's Leather-Stocking Novels: A Secular Reading.* Chapel Hill: University of North Carolina Press, 1991.

Prescott, William Hickling (1796–1859) *historian*

William Hickling Prescott was born in Salem, Massachusetts, into an important family. He received his B.A. and M.A. degrees from Harvard in 1814 and 1817. A childhood accident left him nearly blind, but he was determined to pursue a literary career and set off for Europe as a kind of seasoning for historical works he wished to write. He steeped himself in Spanish history while writing articles and reviews, later collected in *Biographical and Critical Miscellanies* (1845).

Prescott's three-volume *History of Ferdinand and Isabella* appeared in 1838. Like Francis PARKMAN, Prescott wrote in a grand romantic style that included picturesque scenes and a novel-like narrative. In 1843 he published another three-volume history, *The Conquest of Mexico,* an epic work critics have compared to the novels of Sir Walter Scott (1771–1832). Prescott was particularly admired for his character portraits, especially of Cortes and Montezuma. Later historians faulted him for not paying closer attention to the material conditions of society and to the social and economic circumstances in which these characters functioned.

Prescott nearly equaled his earlier triumphs with a two-volume *History of the Conquest of Peru* (1847), this time centering his narrative on Pizarro. Despite failing health that made it difficult for him to command all the primary sources required for his histories, Prescott managed to publish the three-volume *History of the Reign of Philip the Second* (1849, 1855, 1858).

Sources

Darnell, Donald G. *William Hickling Prescott.* Boston: Twayne, 1975.

Gardiner, C. Harvey. *William Hickling Prescott: A Biography.* Austin: University of Texas Press, 1969.
Levin, David. *History as Romantic Art: Bancroft, Prescott, Motley, and Parkman.* Stanford, Calif.: Stanford University Press, 1959.

progressivism

See MUCKRAKING MOVEMENT; SUFFRAGISM; ROOSEVELT, THEODORE.

Prynne, Hester *character*

The heroine of Nathaniel HAWTHORNE's *THE SCARLET LETTER* is an attractive young English woman married to a much older man who has sent her to Boston alone to make a home for them in the New World. The novel opens with Hester on a town scaffold, holding her infant daughter Pearl and wearing a scarlet A on her dress—which signifies, as clearly as her child, that she is an adulterer. Although she refuses to reveal the identity of her lover, Hester accepts her fate, living on the outskirts of the Puritan settlement and caring for its sick and disabled members. In time, the community comes to believe that the A is a sign that Hester is "able" and not merely an adulteress.

In contrast, Hester's lover, the minister Arthur Dimmesdale, bears his shame internally, tormented also by the supposed assistance provided by Roger Chillingworth, the name adopted by Hester's husband. Chillingworth, who arrives in Boston in time to see Hester's public shaming, has made Hester promise not to reveal his true identity. Determined to discover the man who has wronged him, Chillingworth poses as a doctor and attaches himself to Dimmesdale, whom he correctly believes to be that man.

Hester, perceiving that her husband has found her lover, proposes to Dimmesdale that they leave for Europe with the child. Declaring that their passion has a consecration of its own, Hester flings off the scarlet letter, only to be forced to retrieve it when Pearl does not recognize her mother without the characteristic marking. Just before the threesome is about to depart for a new beginning elsewhere, Dimmesdale confesses his sin before the community, then collapses and dies in Hester's arms.

After some time Hester returns to her life on the outskirts of the community and to the penance that has become her reason for being. When she dies, she is buried alongside Dimmesdale under a tombstone that serves for both: "On a field, sable, the letter A, gules [scarlet]."

Generations of Hawthorne scholars have seen Hester as something of a martyr, but in recent years she has undergone a rehabilitation largely at the hands of feminist critics, who see her as an embodiment of strength. Modern readers are likely to view Hester Prynne as an independent woman who, despite the toll exacted by her rebellion against social mores, manages to endure.

Sources

Barlowe, Jamie. *The Scarlet Mob of Scribblers: Rereading Hester Prynne.* Carbondale: Southern Illinois University Press, 2000.
Bloom, Harold, ed. *Hester Prynne.* New York: Chelsea House, 1990.

Puck (1871–1918) *periodical*

Founded in St. Louis, Missouri, by the Austrian cartoonist Joseph Keppler (1838–94), *Puck* was originally published in German as a humorous weekly. Five years later Keppler moved his weekly to NEW YORK CITY. *Puck* continued as a German-language publication until 1877, when an English edition appeared. With the arrival of H. C. Bunner (1855–96) as editor in 1878, the weekly became known, not only for its cartoons, but also for its witty satirical sketches and sharp attacks on the corrupt political machine known as Tammany Hall that controlled Manhattan. Starting in the 1890s, however, the magazine's tone became lighter, and *Puck*'s influence began to wane. In 1917, it was sold to William Randolph HEARST, who extinguished the magazine's wit altogether. It ceased publication the following year.

Sources

West, Richard S. *Satire on Stone: The Political Cartoons of Joseph Keppler.* Urbana: University of Illinois Press, 1988.

Pudd'nhead Wilson, The Tragedy of Mark Twain (1894) *novel*

In this, the last of his novels about the antebellum South, Twain (Samuel Langhorne CLEMENS) creates a parable that addresses the evils of slavery, avarice, and conformity. Set in the mythical town of Dawson's Landing, on the Mississippi River south of St. Louis, *Pudd'nhead Wilson,* like Twain's *The Prince and the Pauper* (1882), concerns both twinship and two people whose identities have been confused because they were switched at birth. In Dawson's Landing on the same day, the wife of Percy Driscoll, a wealthy slaveholder, and Roxy, one of Driscoll's slaves, give birth to male children. Roxy, whose infant son Chambers was fathered by a member of the white Virginia aristocracy, is naturally concerned about her child's future in a slaveholding state. Her solution to this dilemma is to switch her child with her master's son Tom. The two boys, who so resemble one another as to be twins, are both then raised by Roxy.

Percy Driscoll's wife dies not long after giving birth to Tom, and when Driscoll himself later dies, his brother adopts Chambers, believing him to be Tom. Chambers grows up to be a selfish, cowardly young man, and when he gets into trouble after incurring massive gambling debts, he sells Roxy to raise money, even though she tells him she is actually his mother. Roxy manages to escape, and when she blackmails Chambers, he robs his stepfather and then murders him with a knife he has stolen from Luigi, one of a pair of Italian twins. Suspicion of murder then falls on the twins, who are defended by the title character, a lawyer named David Wilson, whom the locals call "Pudd'nhead" because of his interest in palmistry and fingerprints. Wilson's "tragedy" is that he is an outsider and the butt of the town's ridicule, but in court he is able to demonstrate through fingerprint evidence that those other outsiders, the Italians, are innocent. Through similar means Wilson is able to discover that Chambers is not only the real culprit, but also not who he seems. Chambers is then sold down the river, just as his mother always feared he would be.

Sources

Gilman, Susan, and Forrest G. Robinson, eds. *Mark Twain's Pudd'nhead Wilson: Race, Conflict, and Culture.* Durham, N.C.: Duke University Press, 1990.

Hoffman, Andrew Jay. *Twain's Heroes, Twain's Worlds: Mark Twain's Adventures of Huckleberry Finn, A Connecticut Yankee in King Arthur's Court, and Pudd'nhead Wilson.* Philadelphia: University of Pennsylvania Press, 1988.

Rowe, Katherine. *Dead Hands: Fictions of Agency, Renaissance to Modern.* Stanford, Calif.: Stanford University Press, 1999.

Pulitzer, Joseph (1847–1911) *journalist, editor*

Born in Hungary, Joseph Pulitzer came to the United States in 1864, when he served in the Union army for a year during the CIVIL WAR. Afterward he became a reporter for a German-language newspaper, the *Westliche Post,* in St. Louis, of which he later became part owner. In 1869 Pulitzer was elected to the Missouri legislature, where he earned a reputation as a liberal reformer. In 1878 he purchased the St. Louis *Dispatch,* transforming it into one of the most profitable newspapers in what was then the West. In 1883, after an editorial campaign against corruption resulted in a shooting in the newspaper offices, Pulitzer left for New York City. Once there, he bought the NEW YORK *WORLD* and in seven years' time increased the paper's circulation tenfold through such means as illustrations, aggressive news coverage, and publicity stunts.

After 1895, when William Randolph HEARST established his New York *Journal,* Pulitzer resorted to more drastic measures to outdo this rival, engaging in the kind of sensationalism and emotional exploitation that came to be known as "yellow journalism." Following the SPANISH-AMERICAN WAR, during which the rivalry reached fever pitch, the *World* turned subdued, ultimately becoming the premier Democratic paper in the country. Elected to the U.S. House of Representatives in 1885, Pulitzer served only briefly. He retired from public life in 1890 because of partial blindness and failing health. Upon his death, he left a $2 million bequest to the Columbia University School of Journalism for the establishment of the Pulitzer Prizes, annual awards for journalism and literature.

Sources

Juergens, George. *Joseph Pulitzer and The New York World.* Princeton, N.J.: Princeton University Press, 1966.

Rammelkamp, Julian S. *Pulitzer's Post-Dispatch, 1878–1883.* Princeton, N.J.: Princeton University Press, 1967.

Swanberg, W. A. *Pulitzer.* New York: Scribner, 1967.

Putnam's Monthly Magazine (1853–1910) *periodical*

Founded in New York City in 1853 by the publishing house of the same name, *Putnam's Monthly* was exclusively American in focus, publishing such authors as Herman MELVILLE, Henry Wadsworth LONGFELLOW, James Russell LOWELL, Henry David THOREAU, James Fenimore COOPER, and William Cullen BRYANT. After it ceased publication in 1868, the magazine was revived in 1868 as *Putnam's Magazine* and published such writers as Frank R. STOCKTON, William Dean HOWELLS, and John BURROUGHS. After merging in 1870 with *SCRIBNER'S,* in 1906 a third version of the original journal, now titled *Putnam's Monthly and The Critic,* provided a venue for humorists such as Don Marquis (1878–1937) and Gelett Burgess (1866–1951). In 1910 *Putnam's* finally merged with the *ATLANTIC MONTHLY.*

Queequeg *character*

This memorable character in Herman MELVILLE's *MOBY-DICK* is both the narrator *ISHMAEL*'s boon companion and harpooner for Starbuck, the first mate of the whaler *Pequod.* A native of a Pacific island called Kokovoko, Queequeg might have been based loosely on a description of the New Zealand chief Ko-towatowa provided by Charles Wilkes (1798–1877) in his *Narrative of the U.S. Exploring Expedition During the Years 1838, 1839, 1840, 1841, 1842 (1845),* who was, like Queequeg, tall, brawny, and heavily tattooed. After Ishmael and Queequeg are obliged to share a bed in an overcrowded New Bedford inn—and after Ishmael overcomes his initial fear of this "savage," who proves to be the gentlest, politest of men—the two swear allegiance to one another, and Queequeg insists on sailing with Ishmael in order to share his fate.

The two do, in fact, share nearly the same fate. When Queequeg falls ill with a fever, he has a coffin custom made, its exterior covered with mysterious markings that mimic his body tattoos. The harpooner recovers from his fever, only to go down with *Pequod* and most of her crew when the ship is stove in by the malicious force that is the white whale Moby-Dick. The only exception is Ishmael, who is saved from drowning in the sinking ship's maelstrom by Queequeg's coffin—now become a lifebuoy.

Sources

Higgins, Brian, and Hershel Parker, eds. *Critical Essays on Herman Melville's Moby-Dick.* New York: G.K. Hall, 1992.

Martin, Robert K. *Hero, Captain, and Stranger: Male Friendship, Social, and Literary Form in the Sea Novels of Herman Melville.* Chapel Hill: University of North Carolina Press, 1986.

Reno, Janet. *Ishmael Alone Survived.* Lewisburg, Pa.: Bucknell University Press, 1990.

Quincy, Josiah (1772–1864) *historian*

After a distinguished career as a Federalist congressional representative (1805–12), Josiah Quincy was elected mayor of Boston (1823–28) and then named president of Harvard University (1829–45). While serving in this last position, Quincy published a two-volume *History of Harvard University* (1840) that became a standard work. He continued writing in retirement, publishing *A Municipal History of Boston* in 1852 and an 1858 biography of John Quincy ADAMS (1767–1848) as well as an 1825 memoir of his own father, the prominent patriot Josiah Quincy (1744–75).

Sources

McCaughey, Robert A. *Josiah Quincy, 1772–1864: The Last Federalist.* Cambridge, Mass.: Harvard University Press, 1974.

Quinn, Dan

See LEWIS, ALFRED HENRY.

Rabinowitz, Solomon J. (Sholem Aleichem) (1859–1916) *short story writer*

Born in Ukraine, Solomon J. Rabinowitz became a rabbi when he was only 17 years old. Forced to leave the country because of anti-Semitic pogroms, in 1906 he came to the United States. He settled briefly in New York City where, under the pen name of Sholem Aleichem ("Peace be with you" in Hebrew), he contributed many short stories about Jewish village life to periodicals published in the city's Lower East Side, a primarily Jewish immigrant neighborhood at the time. During this year of residence, he also had two of his plays produced in New York's thriving Yiddish theater. When these endeavors failed financially, he returned to Europe in 1907 and remained there until the outbreak of World War I forced him to flee once more to America. He spent the last two years of his life in New York City, working on his unfinished autobiographical fiction. This work was published posthumously as *The Old Country* (1946), *Tevye's Daughters* (1949), and *The Great Fair* (1955).

Aleichem wrote in Hebrew, Russian, and Yiddish, but he favored the last as a literary medium. His collected works in Yiddish ultimately filled 23 volumes. They did not, however, become popular in the United States until the 1950s and 1960s, when the success of such Jewish-American writers as Saul Bellow (1915–) helped bring attention to other Jewish writers who had been largely forgotten. When one of Aleichem's sketches was adapted as the Broadway musical *Fiddler on the Roof* in 1964, it played for 3,242 performances, setting a record at the time for Broadway's longest-running musical production.

Sources

Frieden, Ken. *Classic Yiddish Fiction: Abramovitsh, Sholem Aleichem, and Peretz.* Albany: State University of New York Press, 1995.

Gittleman, Sol. *Sholom Aleichem: A Non-Critical Introduction.* The Hague, Netherlands: Mouton, 1974.

Roshwald, Miriam. *Ghetto, Shtetl, or Polis?: The Jewish Community in the Writings of Karl Emil Franzos, Sholom Aleichem, and Shemuel Yosef Agnon.* San Bernardino, Calif.: Borgo Press, 1997.

Radical Club *organization*

This informal association of New England Unitarian and transcendentalist ministers and laymen had as its goal the abolition of superstition and the introduction of liberty to Christianity. To that end, the group published a journal, *The Radical,* that appeared from 1865 to 1872 and included the work of such contributors as Thomas Wentworth HIGGINSON, Bronson ALCOTT, and the elder Henry JAMES.

Ragged Dick *character*

The protagonist of Horatio ALGER Jr.'s 1868 novel of the same name, Dick is the archetype of the Alger hero: a poor boy who, through pluck and luck, rises to riches and other success. Ragged Dick is an orphaned bootblack who lives rough—and tough—on the streets of New York City. But as Alger portrays him, "our hero" is not bereft of natural advantages: he is honest, intelligent, handsome, and—above all—very, very lucky.

Dick comes into his luck one day when plying his trade on the shoes of a Mr. Greyson, who likes the boy so much that he invites Dick to attend Sunday school at a prosperous church on Fifth Avenue. There Dick meets an affluent young visitor to New York to whom he shows the sights. In return for his helpfulness, Dick is rewarded with five dollars, a new suit of clothes, and his first real friend, who inspires him to save his money and educate himself. Dick moves into a rented room, which he shares with another bootblack named Fosdick, who trades reading lessons for rent. Nine months later Dick is entirely transformed into a handsome young man named Richard Hunter, who flirts with Mr. Greyson's daughter after church on Sundays.

Dick's luck increases when he bravely saves a boy from drowning in the East River. In gratitude, the boy's father offers Dick a job in his trading company. With the American dream now within his reach, Dick moves into more spacious quarters, sharing his wealth with young Fosdick.

Ragged Dick was Alger's first successful novel, appearing first in *Student and Schoolmate* by Oliver Optic (William Taylor ADAMS). The book would spawn two popular series and numerous clones of its hero, whose rags-to-riches story seemed nearly irresistible to youthful readers of the day.

Sources

Scharnhorst, Gary. *Horatio Alger, Jr.* Boston: Twayne, 1980.

———. *The Lost Life of Horatio Alger, Jr.* Bloomington: Indiana University Press, 1985.

Tebbel, John W. *From Rags to Riches: Horatio Alger, Jr. and the American Dream.* New York: Macmillan, 1963.

realism *literary movement*

As a movement in American literature, realism is associated with the 1870s and with the rise of novelist such as Mark Twain (Samuel Langhorne CLEMENS), Henry JAMES, and William Dean HOWELLS.

In novels like *TOM SAWYER* and *HUCKLEBERRY FINN*, Twain used colloquial American language to capture the rhythms of American speech that accurately reflected regional differences. In Huckleberry Finn he also created a narrator different from the literary, formal first- or third-person narrators of earlier American fiction. Huck's style is informal and critical. He sizes up the mores and manners of his society from his adolescent perspective. In other words, he is a social critic without knowing it and "realistic" in the sense that he reports phenomena as he sees them. Thus Twain creates the illusion that his novel is not shaped by a literary sensibility but rather by a fresh, unaffected sensibility.

James developed a realism that probed both the manners of his society and his characters' states of mind. James's famous later style, convoluted and allusive, was meant to capture the complexities and meanderings of his characters' consciousness. James dramatized the way the mind perceives reality, and consequently he has often been called a psychological realist. He took realism into new areas in his short stories of the supernatural. Ghosts appear, or seem to appear, in such tales as "The Jolly Corner" and "THE TURN OF THE SCREW" in vivid, haunting scenes; yet James leaves open the possibility that this "reality" is only what his characters imagine or project onto their environment.

William Dean Howells wrote novels that were almost sociological in their emphasis on everyday details, on how people dressed, spoke, ate, and so on. He strove to avoid melodrama and sought a plain style aimed at recording, rather than heightening, reality. Like Twain, he was interested in notating regional differences with quirky humor. Howells thought of himself as writing what was true, not for entertainment or moral uplift.

The limitations of Howells's methods were apparent to writers of the naturalistic school (see NATURALISM). Howells tended to avoid the dark side of life, the intense impulses that led to violence and alienation from society. Even James and Twain, who had a more complex and ambiguous view of society, did not go as far as naturalists like Theodore DREISER and Frank NORRIS, whose characters often were crushed under the weight of economic, social, and psychological forces. Realism tended to uphold the virtues of individualism, no matter how flawed human beings might be. Naturalism questioned the American confidence and pride in self-reliance.

Sources

Pizer, Donald and Harbert, Earl N., eds. *American Realists and Naturalists.* Detroit: Gale, 1982.

Smith, Christopher, ed. *American Realism.* San Diego, Calif.: Greenhaven Press, 2000.

Sundquist, Eric J., ed. *American Realism: New Essays.* Baltimore, Md.: Johns Hopkins University Press, 1982.

Reconstruction (1865–1877) *historical period*

At the end of the CIVIL WAR, Congress was controlled by a group calling itself the Radical Republicans, who advocated the imposition of harsh measures on the former Confederate states. This group was opposed by President Andrew Johnson (1808–75), a southerner who took his oath of office after Abraham LINCOLN's assassination and who proposed to follow Lincoln's more lenient plan for reorganizing the governments of southern states and reuniting the country.

In June 1866 both houses of Congress adopted the 14th Amendment to the Constitution, which theoretically codified racial equality throughout the nation but was used during Reconstruction to justify suppression of state control over private enterprise. (The Amendment prohibits states from depriving citizens of due process of law, which was construed so as to protect business from regulation.) The effect was such that when Republican officials were sent south to enforce Reconstruction laws, they were seen as "carpetbaggers" who exploited their privileged positions for personal economic gain. In 1868, after Johnson's impeachment trial resulted in a vote of 35–19, one vote short of the number needed to remove him from office, the president was effectively stripped of his powers, and the Radical Republicans imposed military rule on 10 of the former Confederate states, which were regarded as conquered provinces.

There was, inevitably, a southern backlash. The Ku Klux Klan, a secret society that was the subject of Thomas DIXON's *THE CLANSMAN* (1905), terrorized newly enfranchised African Americans and helped create a new solidarity among southern whites. The resentment that fueled the "Solid South" grew stronger during the two administrations of Ulysses S. GRANT, when political corruption at the top gave the northern carpetbaggers and their southern counterparts, the "scalawags," more latitude to pillage the defeated members of the former Confederacy. Reconstruction finally came to an end with the disputed election of 1876, when Democrats permitted the Republican Rutherford B. Hayes (1822–93) to assume the presidency in return for a Republican promise to withdraw federal troops from the South.

Numerous writers have taken Reconstruction as subject matter for their work. Nonfiction works dating from the late 19th and early 20th centuries include George Washington CABLE's *Silent South* (1885) and W. A. Dunning's (1857–1922) *Reconstruction, Political and Economic* (1907). Many novelists also took up Reconstruction. In addition to Thomas Dixon's *The Clansman,* these include Albion W. TOURGÉE's *Bricks Without Straw* (1880), John W. DE FOREST's *Kate Beaumont* (1872), and Mary Noaille MURFREE's *Where the Battle Was Fought* (1884).

Sources

Diffley, Kathleen, ed. *Where My Heart Is Turning Ever: Civil War Stories and Constitutional Reform, 1861–1875.* Athens: University of Georgia Press, 1992.

Eiselein, Gregory. *Literature and Humanitarian Reform in the Civil War Era.* Bloomington: Indiana University Press, 1996.

Foner, Eric, and Olivia Mahoney. *America's Reconstruction: People and Politics after the Civil War.* New York: HarperPerennial, 1995.

Red Badge of Courage, The *Stephen Crane* (1895) *novel*

Subtitled *An Episode of the American Civil War, The Red Badge of Courage* is one of the most celebrated works of war fiction ever published, even though the author, Stephen CRANE, who was only 24 at the time, had not seen a single battle. Instead of firsthand experience, Crane drew on a popular anthology, *Battles and Leaders of the Civil War* (1884–88) and on his precocious understanding of human nature in writing this compelling psychological study of a soldier's response to war.

Crane's protagonist is Henry Fleming, an infantry private with the Union army. Filled with patriotic zeal and romantic notions of heroism, Henry begins his war experience marching for days on end with the Army of the Potomac. When his unit finally comes under fire, Henry at first reacts mechanically, loading, shooting, and reloading his rifle. The enemy retreats, and Henry is temporarily elated, but when the Confederates counterattack, Henry flees, convinced that his army is in retreat. When he learns that the Union line held, he is filled with shame over his cowardice. Wandering away from the front lines, he joins a column of wounded, where he finds himself longing for an injury, a "red badge of courage." When one of the marching wounded queries him about his injuries, Henry demurs, and even though he realizes that the other man is badly hurt and in need of help, Henry's shame causes him to desert this fellow too.

While he struggles over whether or not to return to the fighting, he accidentally receives the injury he has coveted when a retreating soldier pushes him aside with his rifle butt, leaving Henry with a head wound. Henry is led back to his regiment, where he declines to respond to inquiries from his fellow soldiers about how he was wounded. Soon, however, Henry is given a second chance to prove himself when his brigade is placed in the front line of what seems a hopeless defensive action. When their standard-bearer falls, Henry instinctively seizes the flag and rallies the men to victory. Praised by his commander afterward, he basks in a sense of "quiet manhood," having at last confronted death and survived.

Crane's lack of battlefield experience led him to adopt an impressionistic technique for relating Henry's wartime perceptions and emotions. This technique has made the novel last, influencing such 20th-century war novelists as John Dos Passos (1896–1970), Ernest Hemingway (1899–1961), and James Jones (1921–77).

Sources

Mitchell, Lee Clark, ed. *New Essays on The Red Badge of Courage.* New York: Cambridge University Press, 1986.

Pizer, Donald, ed. *Critical Essays on Stephen Crane's The Red Badge of Courage.* Boston: G. K. Hall, 1990.

Red Score

See WALAM OLUM.

Review of Reviews (1890–1938) *periodical*

Modeling itself on an English magazine of the same name, this monthly of politics and the arts published editorials and book reviews, along with reprints of articles that had originally appeared in other magazines. The *Review* had a decidedly European bias, thanks in large part to the shaping hand of Albert Shaw, who served as editor from 1894 until competition from other news magazines such as *Time* caused *The Digest,* as it was then called, to fold in 1938.

Sources

Graybar, Lloyd J. *Albert Shaw of the Review of Reviews: An Intellectual Biography.* Lexington: University Press of Kentucky, 1974.

Riis, Jacob August (1849–1914) *journalist, reformer*

Born in Denmark, Jacob Riis came to the United States in 1870 and settled in New York City, where he took a job as a police reporter. His experiences while covering this beat for various newspapers led him to become one of the most outspoken—not to say eloquent—crusaders for social reform of his day. His reporting on slum dwellers and the conditions of lower-class urban life resulted in *How the Other Half Lives* (1890), which attracted the attention and support of Theodore ROOSEVELT, then head of the New York police board, and probably influenced Stephen CRANE's novel *MAGGIE: A GIRL OF THE STREETS.* Other books tackled such problems as child labor (*The Children of the Poor* [1892]) and the evils of tenements (*The Battle with the Slum* [1902]). Perhaps Riis's most lasting book is his own autobiography, *The Making of an American* (1901). In addition to writing about the underclass, he took concrete action to improve their living conditions, establishing a pioneer settlement house and agitating for public parks and playgrounds. In 1901 the settlement house was named for him, and his work on behalf of the park and playground movement was commemorated with the establishment of Jacob Riis Park on Long Island.

Sources

Fried, Lewis. *Makers of the City.* Amherst: University of Massachusetts Press, 1990.

Gandal, Keith. *The Virtues of the Vicious: Jacob Riis, Stephen Crane, and the Spectacle of the Slum.* New York: Oxford University Press, 1997.

Lane, James B. *Jacob A. Riis and the American City.* Port Washington, N.Y.: Kennikat Press, 1974.

Riley, James Whitcomb (1849–1916) *journalist, poet*

Indiana Hoosier poet James Whitcomb Riley took some time finding his true métier. After working at such jobs as selling patent medicines and painting houses, he finally landed a job with the Anderson (Indiana) *Democrat,* a job he promptly lost after perpetrating a hoax by publishing a poem he attributed to Edgar Allan POE that was actually an imitation he had himself written. He next went to work for the *Indianapolis Journal* where, in 1877, he contributed a series of Hoosier dialect poems under the pen name "Benjamin F. Johnson, of Boone." The series, subsequently published as *"The Old Swimmin'-Hole" and 'Leven More Poems* (1883), included such sentimental works as "When the Frost Is on the Pumpkin" and launched his career as a popular bard. Numerous other collections followed, repeating Riley's formula combining quaintness, cheerfulness, and simplicity, and making him the most highly paid poet American had yet seen. He was also a successful reader of his own work, often appearing with the humorist Bill NYE on a bill that catered to the then contemporary taste for sentimentality.

Sources

Revell, Peter. *James Whitcomb Riley.* New York: Twayne, 1970.

Van Allen, Elizabeth J. *James Whitcomb Riley: A Life.* Bloomington: Indiana University Press, 1999.

Ripley, George (1802–1880) *reformer, literary critic*

Born in Massachusetts, George Ripley was educated in theology at Harvard Divinity School before becoming a Unitarian (see UNITARIANISM) minister in Boston in 1826. He would remain in the post for the next 15 years, studying the German transcendentalist thinkers (see TRANSCENDENTALISM) and editing the *Christian Register,* a liberal Unitarian periodical. He also coedited, with F. H. Hedge (1805–90), *Specimens of Foreign Standard Literature* (1838–42), a 14-volume work that had considerable influence on the American transcendentalist movement. After defending his own *Discourses on the Philosophy of Religion* (1836) and Ralph Waldo EMERSON's *Harvard Divinity School Address* (1838) from attacks by more conservative Unitarians, Ripley retired from the ministry.

In 1841, together with other members of the TRANSCENDENTAL CLUB, Ripley helped found BROOK FARM in Roxbury, Massachusetts. Ripley became president of the community and helped start *THE DIAL,* which he edited. He worked on the farm and helped it make the transition into FOURIERISM, which he also employed in the foundation of the NORTH AMERICAN PHALANX. After a fire destroyed much of Brook Farm in 1846, Ripley moved to BROOKLYN, New York, where he edited the Fourierist newspaper *THE HARBINGER* until, in 1849, he became literary critic of the NEW-YORK *TRIBUNE,* where he instituted the first daily book reviews in the nation. Over the next 30 years Ripley would exert enormous influence over American letters, promoting such worthy books as Nathaniel HAWTHORNE's *THE SCARLET LETTER* and helping to found several important periodicals, among them *HARPER'S New Monthly Magazine.* His ambitious *History of Literature and the Fine Arts* (1852), which he prepared with Bayard TAYLOR, was followed in 1858 by his work on volume one of the 16-volume *New American Cyclopedia* (1858–63).

Sources

Golemba, Henry L. *George Ripley.* Boston: Twayne, 1977.

"Rip Van Winkle" *Washington Irving* (1819–1820) *short story*

Published as part of Washington IRVING's *SKETCH BOOK*, this tale concerns a layabout Dutch-American man who lives with his shrewish wife in a Hudson River village before the time of the Revolutionary War. In the story, which is based on an ancient folk tale, the eponymous hero one day escapes his wife's nagging by wandering into the Catskills with his dog, Wolf. There they encounter a stranger who leads them deeper into the woods, where a group of dwarfish fellows are engaged in a game of ninepins in a clearing. Rip, who has helped the stranger carry a keg to this place, takes a drink or two of its liquor and then falls into a deep sleep.

Rip Van Winkle's slumber proves so profound that—unbeknownst to himself—he sleeps for 20 years. When he wakes, he is confused by what he sees. Hurrying back home to avoid exacerbating his wife's anger about his absence, he finds her dead—soon to be followed by old Wolf—and his own beard grown white and grizzled. In fact, the whole village has changed, with George Washington's portrait replacing that of George III on the inn's signboard and the once quiet streets now bustling with traffic. All alone in this new world, Rip reassesses matters, on the whole concluding that while he misses the guiding hand of the British monarch, he is not unhappy to be free of Dame Van Winkle's domestic tyranny.

Herman MELVILLE's poem "Rip Van Winkle's Lilac" (1924), a tribute to Irving, relates a later episode from the character's life. Other writers were taken with Irving's tale as well: Dramatized on numerous occasions, the standard play about Rip Van Winkle was written by Dion BOUCICAULT in 1865, commissioned by the actor Joseph Jefferson (1829–1905), who used the play as his major vehicle for the next 40 years. In addition, "Rip Van Winkle" has been transformed into opera on at least three occasions.

Sources

Bowden, Mary Weatherspoon. *Washington Irving.* Boston: Twayne, 1981.

Roth, Martin. *Comedy and America: The Lost World of Washington Irving.* Port Washington, N.Y.: Kennikat Press, 1976.

Rise of Silas Lapham, The *William Dean Howells* (1885) *novel*

In what is probably his best-known work, William Dean HOWELLS paints a memorable portrait of an American type: the upwardly mobile, self-made businessman. Raised on an unproductive Vermont farm, Silas has as an adult exploited the mineral wealth discovered there just before his father died. He formulates the mineral into a paint, which sells so successfully that it makes Silas Lapham one of the richest men in Boston. Vigorous and energetic, he and his family set about conquering Boston's Brahmin society, only to find themselves subtly rejected. When Tom Corey, the scion of an old but only moderately wealthy Boston family, seeks employment at the Lapham paint factory, Silas senses an opening—and this impression intensifies when Tom seems to fall in love with the youngest Lapham daughter, Irene.

But when Silas's moment arrives, and the Laphams are invited to a dinner party at the Coreys' house, Silas reveals his true colors by first getting roaring drunk, then spending the evening bragging about his wealth. Tom declares his love for Irene's older sister, Penelope, who, unwilling to hurt Irene, sends him packing. The Corey connection ends abruptly.

Meanwhile, Silas has begun to experience financial troubles. When a former business partner, Milton Rogers, asks him for a loan, Silas gives it, in part because he feels some residual guilt about having treated Rogers unfairly in the past. When Rogers invites him to get involved in various risky real estate and stock deals, Silas acquiesces, to his detriment. Adding to his woes, an upstart company has begun manufacturing a paint comparable to Silas's—but at a much cheaper price.

Silas considers various plans to save himself and his family. He rejects Tom Corey's generous offer of financial assistance owing to the unresolved nature of Tom's relationship with Penelope. Silas considers selling the lavish new house he is building, but when he carelessly leaves some embers burning in a fireplace, it burns down, uninsured. An effort to buy out his competitors is unsuccessful, although they hold out the promise of partnership if Silas can raise the money. Turning to his last available resource, Silas asks Rogers for help, and Rogers produces some Englishmen who are willing to buy one of the worthless properties Rogers previously sold Silas. While Silas wrestles with the dubious morality of this proposition, both he and Rogers are ruined when the railroad claims the land in question for itself.

Having lost his money but gained some valuable insight into himself as well as reinforcement of his fundamental integrity, Silas returns to Vermont, where he resumes the small-scale manufacture of only the highest quality paint. The subplot is resolved when Tom and Penelope marry and escape to Mexico, where they can be free of the social restraints imposed on them in their old milieu. Howells does not, however, inform his novel with sentiment or simplicity. Silas Lapham's "fall" is only in some senses a "rise." For Howells, the Horatio ALGER version of the American dream, in which virtue is always rewarded, is a fairly empty promise.

Sources

Alexander, William Raymond Hall. *William Dean Howells, The Realist as Humanist.* New York: B. Franklin, 1981.

Nettels, Elsa. *Language, Race, and Social Class in Howells's America.* Lexington: University Press of Kentucky, 1988.

Pease, Donald E., ed. *New Essays on The Rise of Silas Lapham.* New York: Cambridge University Press, 1991.

Robinson, Rowland Evans (1833–1900)

short story writer

A native Vermonter, Robinson's work as a wood carver and cartoonist rendered him totally blind in 1893. By that time, however, he had already established himself as a prolific writer of sketches based on the simple rural existence he had known as a farmer. His first collection of short fiction, *Forest and Stream Fables* (1886), was followed quickly by several others featuring a character named Uncle Lisha, a shoemaker who served as the community leader of a small rural Vermont community. Robinson's apt renderings of Down East humor and good ear for Vermont dialect made him an important figure in the LOCAL COLOR movement. He also wrote with great skill about other aspects of his native region in such works as *Vermont: A Study of Independence* (1892), *In New England's Fields and Woods* (1896), and *Hunting Without a Gun and Other Papers* (1905).

Sources

Baker, Ronald L. *Folklore in the Writings of Rowland E. Robinson.* Bowling Green, Ohio: Bowling Green University Popular Press, 1973.

romance *genre*

Many of the novels written in the first half of the 19th century were billed as romances. The term arose in Europe during the Middle Ages, when lengthy compositions—in prose or verse—delivered in one of the Romance languages were commonly referred to as romances. Later the term applied to works of fiction dealing with knights, chivalry, and courtly love. The first American writer to borrow heavily from this tradition was James Fenimore COOPER, who explicitly referred to his novels—filled with adventure and set in remote lands—as romances. Cooper had many followers, but none who advanced the genre. Of those who succeeded and surpassed him, two writers stand out as having created a specifically American form of the romance: Nathaniel HAWTHORNE and Herman MELVILLE.

In his famous "The Custom House" preface to *THE SCARLET LETTER*, Hawthorne helped to define the romance form, which because it concerns "the truth of the human heart" presents "that truth under circumstances . . . of the writer's own choosing or creation." The writer of such a romance may, Hawthorne declares, "so manage his atmospherical medium as to bring out or mellow the lights and deepen and enrich the shadows of the picture." Hawthorne would follow this prescription in four distinguished longer works—*The Scarlet Letter* (1850), *THE HOUSE OF THE SEVEN GABLES* (1851), *The Blithedale Romance* (1852), and *The Marble Faun* (1860)—as well as in numerous works of short fiction. His onetime friend, Melville, added new dimensions to the romance by increasing the quotient of supernatural and allegorical elements in his novels, reaching a pinnacle of sorts with *MOBY-DICK* (1851).

In the latter half of the century, romance fell out of favor as many writers and critics—spurred perhaps, by the horrors of the Civil War—called for a more realistic fiction. Thus a trend that began with the LOCAL COLOR movement and resulted in REALISM and NATURALISM displaced the romance until it was revived and refashioned in the 1930s by the dark symbolism of William Faulkner (1897–1962).

Sources

Bell, Michael D. *The Development of American Romance: The Sacrifice of Relation.* Chicago: University of Chicago Press, 1980.

Budick, E. Miller. *Fiction and Historical Consciousness: The American Romance Tradition.* New Haven, Conn.: Yale University Press, 1989.

Greenwald, Elissa. *Realism and the Romance: Nathaniel Hawthorne, Henry James, and American Fiction.* Ann Arbor, Mich.: UMI Research Press, 1989.

Hurley, Jennifer A., ed. *American Romanticism.* San Diego, Calif.: Greenhaven Press, 2000.

romanticism *literary movement*

This is a term usually defined by contrasting it with classicism. Romanticism favors the imagination and the originality of the artist; art springs from deep feelings and intuitions. Classicism emphasizes reason and the limitation of ancient models of art. The classicist has examples of literary forms to imitate; the romantic creates new forms or changes traditional genres.

Romanticism is associated with the late 18th and early 19th centuries, when artists thought of art as revolutionary, unique, and iconoclastic. Literature was based on the concept of the individual and of individual freedom. The source of authority and inspiration for the romantic was often nature. The poet's perceptions of nature led him, like Walt WHITMAN, to understand the nature of the universe by meditating on a leaf of grass.

Puritans and other Protestant denominations in America emphasized the role of the individual and the individual's conscience. For the romantic writer, the individual soul or imagination became paramount, even in circumstances where the individual stood against the community and the community censured the individual, as in Nathaniel HAWTHORNE's *THE SCARLET LETTER*.

In America, romanticism became connected to Utopian ideas about the idea of community—a collection of thinking, self-governing individuals—and to efforts to establish ideal societies, as in BROOK FARM and FRUITLANDS. Out of the romantic spirit of reform also rose ABOLITIONISM and FEMINISM. The TRANSCENDENTALISM that emerged in Concord, Massachusetts, offered a secular version of religious belief, proposing that the individual is capable of apprehending universal truths.

EMERSON's emphasis on man's ability to learn from nature and his charge that the American scholar not rely so heavily on the teachings of Europe also led to an exuberant confidence in the common man and in public education as promulgated by such transcendentalists as Bronson ALCOTT. Experience became a kind of school in itself, and book learning—the province of the classicists—was balanced against the concept of a native wit that could be developed by communing with its sources in nature. Man's power of observation, Emerson implied, was enhanced as he began to react to his place in nature. Henry David THOREAU gave this Emersonian doctrine of self-reliance a practical turn when he emphasized that the individual could set himself apart from society and learn by doing for himself virtually everything that civilization could teach him.

Quite another side of romanticism was revealed in the histories of Francis PARKMAN and William Hickling PRESCOTT. Like the great romantic novelists, these historians were attracted to the past as the repository of great human dramas and picturesque scenes that stimulated the imagination. They evoked the past not as a model for the present but instead as a way to identify with heroic individuals of the past who transcended their times and created—like the heroes of gothic novels (see GOTHICISM)—new worlds by the force of their will. Writers like Hawthorne and Herman MELVILLE also pointed out, however, the dangers of the romantic hero's titanic will, which could result in the self-destructiveness of an AHAB or the human isolation of a Hester PRYNNE.

Romanticism gradually gave way to REALISM in the mid- to late 19th century, for it had become too sentimental and too oblivious to the material conditions of daily life. American novelists such as William Dean HOWELLS and Mark Twain (Samuel Langhorne CLEMENS) injected a much-needed sense of satire and social criticism into American literature. By the end of the century such naturalists as Frank NORRIS and Theodore DREISER were questioning the extent to which individuals could prevail in a modern industrial and capitalist economy.

Sources

Andrews, William L., ed. *Literary Romanticism in America.* Baton Rouge: Louisiana University Press, 1981.

Bickman, Martin. *American Romantic Psychology: Emerson, Poe, Whitman, Dickinson, Melville.* Dallas, Tex.: Spring Publications, 1988.

Hurley, Jennifer A., ed. *American Romanticism.* San Diego, Calif.: Greenhaven Press, 2000.

Lieber, Todd M., ed. *Endless Experiments: Essays on the Heroic Experience in American Romanticism.* Columbus: Ohio State University Press, 1973.

Roosevelt, Theodore (1858–1919) *twenty-sixth president of the United States, biographer, historian*

Theodore Roosevelt was born in New York City and sent by his distinguished family to Harvard University. He graduated in 1880 and two years later published *The Naval Operations of the War Between Great Britain and the United States—1812–1815.* Entering politics, Roosevelt served in the New York legislature between 1882 and 1884. Already known as a reformer, he challenged party leaders but then left to explore the West, publishing biographies of Thomas Hart Benton (1886) and Gouverneur Morris (1888) as well as his history of the Northwest Territory, *The Winning of the West* (1889–96).

Roosevelt returned to politics in 1886, running unsuccessfully for major of New York City. After working on President Benjamin Harrison's (1833–1901) Civil Service Commission (1889–95), he was put in charge of the New York City Police Board (1895–97). There he resumed his attack on corrupt politicians and made efforts to reform the police force.

Roosevelt established his national reputation during the SPANISH-AMERICAN WAR with his troupe of cavalry Rough Riders who charged San Juan Hill. Elected governor of New York in 1898, Roosevelt continued his progressive programs. In 1900 he was put on the Republican ticket and became vice president and then president after William McKinley was assassinated.

As president, Roosevelt continued his campaigns against big business and political machines, introducing government regulations and institutions that ensured better food and drugs and more competition between corporations. His legacy in foreign policy was balanced between peacemaking—he won a Nobel Prize for mediating the end of the Russo-Japanese War of 1905—and military buildup. He initiated construction of the Panama Canal and increased the size of the U.S. fleet.

Roosevelt retired from the presidency in 1908, but he ran again for the office in 1912 when his successor, William Howard Taft (1857–1930), proved more conservative than Roosevelt could tolerate. His run split the Republican Party and led to the election of Democrat Woodrow WILSON.

Roosevelt was a prolific writer. He completed his masterpiece, the four-volume *The Winning of the West,* in 1896. His other books include *American Ideals and Other Essays* (1897), *The Rough Riders* (1899), *The Strenuous Life* (1900), *African Game Trails* (1910), *African and European Addresses* (1910), and *History as Literature and Other Essays* (1913). He published *An Autobiography* in 1913 and expressed his views on World War I in *The Great Adventure* (1918).

Roosevelt's legacy to American ideas and to its literature consisted of his belief in American dynamism and integrity. He believed in the individual's ability to surmount both physical and mental problems, and he held that the "strenuous life" produced its own rewards and gratifications. Roosevelt himself suffered from weak eyesight and had to build up his health for his trips West. His strong feeling for the American land made him the first president to take steps to conserve national resources, build national parks, and protect the environment.

Sources

Collins, Michael L. *That Damned Cowboy: Theodore Roosevelt and the American West, 1883–1898.* New York: Peter Lang, 1989.

McCullough, David. *Mornings on Horseback.* New York: Simon & Schuster, 1981.

Morris, Edmund. *The Rise of Theodore Roosevelt.* New York: Coward, McCann & Geoghegan, 1979.

Norton, Aloysius A. *Theodore Roosevelt.* Boston: Twayne, 1980.

Oliver, Lawrence J. *Brander Matthews, Theodore Roosevelt, and the Politics of American Literature, 1880–1920.* Knoxville: University of Tennessee Press, 1992.

Rouquette, Adrien Emmanuel (1813–1887) *poet*

Born in New Orleans of a French father and a Creole mother, Adrien Emmanuel Rouquette was enamored of American Indian life. As a youth he frequently ran away from his parents' summer home to live among the local Choctaw tribe. His love of nature and the Indian way of life first found expression in a collection of verse, *Les Savanes* (1841). After becoming a priest, he continued to publish poetry; *Wild Flowers: Sacred Poetry* appeared in 1848. He also spoke out fervently against slavery, and his abolitionist sentiments drove him out of New Orleans and into the company of his beloved Choctaw, whom he served as a priest. When he died he was working on a dictionary of the Choctaw language. He also continued to produce poetry: a romance titled *La Nouvelle Atala* (1879); and—under the pen name E. Junius—*Critical Dialogue between Aboo and Caboo* (1880), a denunciation of George Washington CABLE's depiction of Creoles.

Sources

Le Breton, Dagmar Renshaw. *Chahta-Ima: The Life of Adrien-Emmanuel Rouquette.* Baton Rouge: Louisiana State University Press, 1947.

Royall, Anne Newport (1769–1854) *travel writer*

Born in Maryland and raised on what was then the Pennsylvania frontier, Anne Newport moved back to the South after her father died; she was then 13. In Virginia, she and her mother kept house for a Captain William Royall, who educated Anne and who, in 1797, married her. When he died 16 years later, however, he left his money to another heir, forcing Anne to rely on her own resources once more. From 1824 to 1831 she made her way in the world by traveling continuously throughout the United States and recording her impressions. Royall's observations of virtually every significant settlement in the country were published in 10 separate volumes, including the three-volume *Sketches of History, Life, and Manners in the United States* (1828–29) and *Letters from Alabama* (1830). Settling in Washington, D.C., she published two newspapers, *Paul Pry* (1831–36) and its successor, *The Huntress* (1836–54). A frequent critic of government corruption and social decadence, she was herself a frequent target of retaliatory ridicule in the press.

Sources

James, Bessie Rowland. *Anne Royall's U.S.A.* New Brunswick, N.J.: Rutgers University Press, 1972.

Maxwell, Alice S., and Marion B. Dunlevy. *Virago!: The Story of Anne Newport Royall (1769–1854).* Jefferson, N.C.: McFarland, 1985.

Royall, Anne Newport. *Letters from Alabama, 1817–1822.* Biographical introduction and notes by Lucille Griffith. Tuscaloosa: University of Alabama Press, 1969.

Royce, Josiah (1855–1916) *philosopher, essayist*

Josiah Royce was born in California, where he attended the newly established University of California before pursuing advanced studies in Germany and at Johns Hopkins University in Baltimore. In 1878, after receiving a Ph.D. from Johns Hopkins, Royce returned to the University of California to take a position as a professor of English. He stayed for four years, after which he was brought to Harvard by William JAMES to act as James's replacement. Royce would remain at Harvard for the rest of his life.

Royce and James were initially of one mind in their approach to philosophy, but before long the two had ideological differences. Whereas James was a pluralist, believing that no one system could account for all aspects of existence, Royce came to believe wholeheartedly in the oneness of existence. *The Religious Aspect of Philosophy* (1885) established Royce as a leading idealist, postulating a fundamental goodness at the heart of existence that "satisfies the highest moral needs." Royce wrote of the Absolute, an all-knowing mind or Universal Thought capable of transcending human limitations. He extended this theory in *The Conception of God* (1897) by positing that human beings retain their identities in the face of the Absolute because the will of the Absolute is available to all for independent use. In *The World and the Individual* (1900–01), Royce goes on to argue that reality is the life of the Absolute, all-encompassing mind.

After 1900 Royce began to apply his philosophy to specific contemporary moral problems. The result was *The Philosophy of Loyalty* (1908), in which he contends that humankind has an ethical obligation to the moral order that can be fulfilled through loyalty to the human community. Royce applied this theory to the dilemma of the Great War (World War I) in *The Hope of the Great Community* (1916).

Sources

Buranelli, Vincent. *Josiah Royce.* New York: Twayne, 1964.

Clendenning, John. *The Life and Thought of Josiah Royce.* Madison: University of Wisconsin Press, 1985.

Kuklick, Bruce. *Josiah Royce: An Intellectual Biography.* Indianapolis, Ind.: Bobbs-Merrill, 1972.

Russell's Bookstore Group *literary group*

This informal literary association met during the 1850s at the Charleston, South Carolina, bookstore operated by John Russell. The group included the writers Henry TIMROD, William Gilmore SIMMS, William John Grayson (1788–1863), S. H. Dickson (1798–1872), and Paul Hamilton HAYNE. Hayne acted as editor of *Russell's Magazine,* which appeared from 1857 to 1860 and reflected the contributors' decidedly regional perspective.

S

Sabin's Dictionary (1868–1936) *bibliography*

This comprehensive listing of Americana—formally titled *A Dictionary of Books Relating to America, from Its Discovery to the Present Time,* or *Bibliotheca Americana*—derives its popular name from its maker, the English-born New York City rare-book dealer Joseph Sabin (1821–81). Beginning in 1856, Sabin endeavored to list alphabetically every monograph, whether book or pamphlet, written in any language that related to the United States. Before his death he completed 14 volumes of this ambitious work, which provides both bibliographical and content information on its entries. Sabin was succeeded in this endeavor by the bibliographer of the New York Public Library, Wilberforce Eames (1855–1937), who completed volumes 15 through 20 of *Sabin's.* The last nine volumes of the work were produced by a staff supervised by R. W. G. Vaill, with volume 29 appearing in 1936. In 1974 a three-volume *Author-Title Index,* the work of John E. Molnar, was published, and that same year Lawrence S. Thompson began publishing *The New Sabin,* a revised and updated version of the original.

Sources

Goff, Frederick R. *Joseph Sabin, Bibliographer, 1821–1881.* Amsterdam: N. Israel, 1963.

Molnar, John E. *Author-Title Index to Joseph Sabin's Dictionary of Books Relating to America.* Metuchen, N.J.: Scarecrow Press, 1974.

St. Nicholas (1873–1940) *periodical*

This children's magazine was founded in New York City by Roswell Smith. Known for the high quality of its fiction, *St. Nicholas* was edited from 1873 to 1905 by Mary Mapes DODGE, who was also a contributor. Most prominent authors of juvenile fiction published here, including Americans such as Mark Twain (Samuel Langhorne CLEMENS), Frank STOCKTON, and Louisa May ALCOTT, as well as such English authors as Rudyard Kipling (1865–1936) and Robert Louis Stevenson (1850–94). Juvenile authors were also encouraged to send in contributions, and 20th-century writers like F. Scott Fitzgerald (1896–1940) and E. B. White (1899–1985) first published here. After 1930 the magazine began to lose readership and changed hands several times, finally ending as a picture magazine for young children put out by the Woolworth store chain. After its demise a decade later, however, two volumes of the *St. Nicholas Anthology* (1948 and 1950) found large readerships.

Sources

Shaw, John Mackay, comp. *The Poems, Poets & Illustrators of St. Nicholas Magazine 1873–1943: An Index.* Tallahassee: Strozier Library, Florida State University, 1965.

Saltus, Edgar Evertson (1855–1921) *essayist, novelist*

Born in New York City, Edgar Saltus studied at Yale University and abroad in Germany and Paris before returning to New York and obtaining a law degree from Columbia University in 1880. His literary career began with an 1884 biography of the French novelist Honoré de Balzac (1799–1850), which he followed with *The Philosophy of Disenchantment* (1885), a book that helped to popularize the pessimistic perspectives laid out in the works of such philosophers as the

German Arthur Schopenhauer (1788–1860). Yet another European thinker, the antitheistic Dutch philosopher Baruch Spinoza (1632–1677), was the subject of *The Anatomy of Negation* (1886).

Saltus had long been immersed in a hedonistic, decadent way of life, and this environment, together with an amoral philosophical outlook, lent him the material for his so-called "diabolical novels" about New York society, works such as *Mr. Incoul's Misadventure* (1887), *The Truth About Tristrem Varick* (1888), *The Pace That Kills* (1889), *Enthralled* (1894), *The Pomps of Satan* (1904), *The Perfume of Eros* (1905), and *Vanity Square* (1906). Characterized by decadent *fin de siècle* ROMANTICISM and lush, unusual language, these works reflected his motto: "In fiction as in history it is the shudder that tells."

In treating historical subjects, Saltus managed to maintain his focus on the exotic and the erotic. *Mary Magdalene* (1891) deals with a story taken from biblical apocrypha; *The Imperial Purple* (1892) is a history of the Roman emperors; *Historia Amoris* (1906) is a history of love; *The Lords of Ghostland* (1907) is a history of religions; and the even more provocatively titled *The Imperial Orgy* (1920) concerns the Russian imperial dynasty, the Romanoffs.

A member of a group dubbed the "Erotic School," which also included the novelists Gertrude ATHERTON and Princess Amélie Rives Troubetzkoy (1863–1945), Saltus was heavily influenced by the British art-for-art's-sake movement spearheaded by Oscar Wilde (1854–1900), whom Saltus met in London and memorialized in *Oscar Wilde: An Idler's Impression* (1919). Saltus's exoticism won him a large following, but he was also attacked by the more conventional critics of his day. After his reputation declined, writers like H. L. Mencken (1880–1956) and Carl Van Vechten (1880–1964) tried to resurrect it, and James Huneker (1860–1921) made Saltus a character in his daring novel, *Painted Veils* (1920). Saltus's third wife, Marie Saltus, was influential later in his life in shifting his orientation toward the unorthodox philosophy-cum-religion known as theosophy. She published his biography, *Edgar Saltus the Man*, in 1925.

Sources

Sprague, Claire. *Edgar Saltus.* New York: Twayne, 1968.

San Francisco, California *geographical location*

The first Westerner to see San Francisco Bay was probably the English explorer Sir Francis Drake (c. 1545–96), who sailed along the northern coast of what is now California in 1579. In 1770 an expedition led by the Spaniard Gaspar de Portolá (c. 1734–84) reached the city's current site and was followed in 1776 by Juan Bautista de Anza (1735–88), founder of the mission and presidio of Yerba Buena, San Francisco's precursor. In 1821 the entire region came under Mexican rule and remained so until the Bear Flag Revolt of 1846 established California as a U.S. territory.

The California gold rush of 1849 caused San Francisco to mushroom into a bustling frontier town and simultaneously gave rise to a flowering of literary talent that lasted for the next two decades. Among the many writers to make a vital connection with the Bay Area in those years was Richard Henry DANA Jr., whose book *TWO YEARS BEFORE THE MAST* describes the era of the Mexican occupation of California. Writers as diverse as Bret HARTE, Samuel CLEMENS (Mark Twain), Ambrose BIERCE, Joaquin MILLER, and John MUIR were also associated with San Francisco—and with local periodicals like *OVERLAND MONTHLY* and *The Golden Era*—during this period. Later in the 19th century, Frank NORRIS, Jack LONDON, Gertrude ATHERTON, and George STERLING would take up residence in the city, as would Evan Connell (1924–), Herbert Gold (1924–), and William Saroyan (1908–81) in the next century. In the 1950s San Francisco became the backdrop to the San Francisco Renaissance and the western center of the Beat movement, which included poets like Kenneth Rexroth (1905–82) and Allen Ginsberg (1926–97) and novelists like Jack Kerouac (1922–69). The literary ferment of this era was in a sense merely a continuation of the liberal, bohemian atmosphere established during the gold rush and extended in the 1890s by the literary aesthetes known as Les Jeunes, a group led by poet Gelett Burgess (1866–1951) that published the iconoclastic "little magazine" *The Lark* between 1895 and 1897.

Sources

Barker, Malcolm E., ed. *San Francisco Memoirs, 1835–1851: Eyewitness Accounts of the Birth of a City.* San Francisco: Londonborn Publications, 1994.

Benemann, William, ed. *A Year of Mud and Gold: San Francisco in Letters and Diaries, 1849–1850.* Lincoln: University of Nebraska Press, 1999.

Robbins, Millie. *Tales of Love and Hate in Old San Francisco.* San Francisco: Chronicle Books, 1971.

Santa Fe Trail *geographical location*

This 780-mile trail from Independence, Missouri, to Santa Fe, New Mexico, was the main overland route to the West for much of the 19th century. "Opened" by a trader named William Becknell in 1821–22, after Mexico opened the outpost of Santa Fe (then under its control) to trade, the trail traced a route that first went southwest from Independence to Council Grove, Kansas, which was the chief wagon train organization point, and across the Kansas plains to the Arkansas River. The trail then followed the river to a fork near Dodge City, Kansas, where the path divided into two routes. The Mountain Division continued to hug the river until it turned southward, crossing from Colorado into New Mexico over the 7,834-foot Raton Pass. A more direct route, called the Cimarron or Cutoff Division, crossed the Great Plains to Fort Union, New Mexico. After 1822 a wagon train made the journey annually, taking up to five months for a round trip. The amount of goods being transported to Santa Fe steadily increased, and in 1850 a stagecoach began taking the northern route monthly. In 1880, when the Santa Fe Railroad finally reached Santa Fe, the trail became defunct.

Numerous literary works have explored the significance of the trail, from histories such as Josiah Gregg's (1806–50) two-volume *Commerce of the Prairies* (1941) and autobiographical narratives like Lewis H. Garrard's (1829–87) *Wah-tó-yah, and the Taos Trail* (1850) to Harvey Fergusson's (1890–1971) fiction trilogy, *Followers of the Sun* (1921–29), and Vachel Lindsay's (1879–1931) 1914 poem, "The Santa Fe Trail: A Humoresque."

Sources

Chalfant, William Y. *Dangerous Passage: The Santa Fe Trail and the Mexican War.* Norman: University of Oklahoma Press, 1994.

Connor, Seymour V., and Jimmy M. Skaggs. *Broadcloth and Britches: The Santa Fe Trade.* College Station: Texas A&M University Press, 1977.

Taylor, Morris F. *First Mail West: Stagecoach Lines on the Santa Fe Trail.* Albuquerque: University of New Mexico Press, 1971.

Saturday Club, The *organization*

Begun in BOSTON in 1855 as a literary dinner club, the formation of The Saturday Club was inspired by earlier symposia organized by Ralph Waldo EMERSON and Bronson ALCOTT. The moving force behind founding of the club, however, was the lawyer and publishing agent Horatio Woodman, who combined a purely social organization with a literary one known as the Magazine Club or the Atlantic Club. The group met monthly at the Parker House, and after the founding of the *ATLANTIC MONTHLY* in 1857, The Saturday Club hosted banquets for magazine contributors. Such literary lights as Emerson, Nathaniel HAWTHORNE, and Louis AGASSIZ were members of the club, but Oliver Wendell HOLMES was its leader. In 1884 Holmes published a poetic tribute to the club, "At the Saturday Club."

Sources

Emerson, Edward W. *The Early Years of the Saturday Club, 1855–1879.* Boston: Houghton Mifflin, 1918.

Howe, M. A. DeWolfe, ed. *The Later Years of the Saturday Club.* Boston: Houghton Mifflin, 1927.

Saturday Evening Post, The *periodical*

Two young printers, Charles Alexander and Samuel C. Atkinson, brought out the first issue of their weekend miscellany on August 18, 1821. Alexander's primary contribution was the subscription list of an earlier failed publication, while Atkinson held an interest in the Philadelphia printing plant that had once produced the defunct *Pennsylvania Gazette,* edited by Benjamin Franklin. The pair capitalized on the latter asset in 1827 by carrying a legend on the masthead indicating that the *Post* had been founded by Benjamin Franklin in 1728, a tenuous connection.

The *Post* flourished, despite its hodgepodge of reviews, serials, news, and household hints. After 1826, when Alexander and Atkinson began publishing the literary monthly *Casket* (later *GRAHAM'S MAGAZINE*), the *Post* had access to contributors such as James Fenimore COOPER, Edgar Allan POE, and N. P. WILLIS. In 1832 the *Post* absorbed the *Saturday Bulletin,* becoming one of the nation's leading weekend miscellanies. When the poet, novelist, and book publisher Henry Peterson (1818–91) took over as editor, the magazine entered its first golden age, publishing such popular authors as Fanny Fern (Sara Payson Willis PARTON) and the serial fiction writer E.D.E.N. Southworth. After the CIVIL WAR, however, the magazine went into a decline.

The *Post* was rescued from bankruptcy in 1897 by Cyrus H. K. Curtis, publisher of the fantastically successful *LADIES' HOME JOURNAL.* Two years later Curtis installed George Horace Lorimer (1867–1937) as editor, and the magazine entered a second golden age characterized by a boosterism that conformed to the expansive American mood. Curtis would head the *Post* for the next 40 years, boosting circulation as high as 3 million by emphasizing coverage of business, public affairs, and romance while serializing fiction by such distinguished contributors as Stephen CRANE, Frank NORRIS, and Ring Lardner (1885–1933). Illustrations were copious, as were advertisements.

The *Post* maintained more or less the same format until 1942 when, under Ben Hibbs, the editorial policy began to favor nonfiction. By 1960 circulation had risen to 6 million, but soon thereafter the *Post*'s rather lowbrow tone began to hurt it, as did expensive litigation resulting from investigative reporting. In 1969 it ceased publication. When it was revived in 1971, it was a glossy magazine that appeared nine times yearly, then bimonthly.

Sources

Cohn, Jan. *Creating America: George Horace Lorimer and The Saturday Evening Post.* Pittsburgh, Pa.: University of Pittsburgh Press, 1989.

Friedrich, Otto. *Decline and Fall.* New York: Harper & Row, 1970.

Saturday Press *periodical*

Founded in 1858 in New York City by Henry CLAPP, this weekly drew its contributors from among members of the PFAFF'S CELLAR group. Known as a haven for experimental works, the *Saturday Press* attained a high reputation. Some of its noteworthy publications include works by Walt WHITMAN and "The Celebrated Jumping Frog of Calaveras County" by Mark Twain (Samuel Langhorne CLEMENS), which appeared in one of the magazine's last issues.

Scarlet Letter, The *Nathaniel Hawthorne* (1850) *novel*

Nathaniel HAWTHORNE opens his most famous ROMANCE with the equally famous "Custom House essay," in which he describes his experiences as an official at the Salem, Massachusetts, Custom House, where he claims to have discovered the scarlet letter and an accompanying manuscript, the text of which is the novel itself. Set in 17th-century Salem, where a Hawthorne ancestor had been a judge during the infamous witchcraft trials, the novel reflects Hawthorne's lifelong interest in his Puritan heritage.

Carefully structured around three scaffold scenes, *The Scarlet Letter* opens on Hester PRYNNE in the town pillory, holding her infant daughter Pearl in her arms. As the village elders exhort Hester to confess the name of her illegitimate baby's father, this scene is observed by Hester's much older husband, a scholar who has just arrived from England, having sent his wife to Boston two years earlier to establish a home. When Hester refuses to reveal her lover's name, she is forced to wear the scarlet A, a symbol of her adultery. Meanwhile, her husband, disguising himself as a doctor and adopting the name Roger Chillingworth, attaches himself to the town's upright young minister, Arthur Dimmesdale, whom he suspects to be his wife's lover.

As numerous critics of the novel have noted, *The Scarlet Letter* is not about sin but instead about its aftereffects. Sin, Hawthorne clearly saw, is the lot of all humankind, and the strength of a person's character can be measured by how he or she deals with it. Hester, for her part, accepts her sin, both literally and symbolically. She bears her punishment well, wearing what she turns into an embroidered scarlet A. Devoting herself to her child and to other less fortunate members of the community, she is gradually accepted, even respected—if not forgiven—by those who originally condemned her to a life apart. Dimmesdale, for his part, keeps his secret hidden, and his inner guilt ruins his spirit and his health. In secret, he mutilates his own flesh by way of exorcizing his weakness. Rejecting Hester's plea that he run away with her to Europe, the Old World, Dimmesdale—driven to despair by Chillingworth's spiritual and physical "ministrations"—opts instead to make a public confession. In a second scaffold scene, he stands upon the village pillory—together with Hester and Pearl—at midnight, but that act is insufficiently punishing. In the end he can escape Chillingworth's pursuit only by standing before his congregation and admitting his sin. By this time the burden of his secret guilt has become so heavy that he collapses and dies in Hester's arms.

Hawthorne reserves the worst outcome for Chillingworth, who has sinned not out of love but out of hate. Having invaded Dimmesdale's heart in order to exact his revenge, the old man has become a succubus, the only member of the trilogy of sinners left truly alone and—now that he has destroyed his host—without purpose. Dimmesdale in death achieves a kind of martyrdom, and Hester lives on with Pearl, the child who is both the symbol and fruit of her lost love. But Chillingworth is left with nothing; there is not a single person left on whom he can project his hatred and perform his perverse experimentations. For Hawthorne, no fate is more fearful.

A masterwork of symbolism, *The Scarlet Letter* embodies Hawthorne's romanticism as well as his profound skepticism about both God and man. What might be seen as a reflection of the pessimism of his time is tempered with an open-ended inquiry into the mysteries of existence, giving the novel both the depth and the ambiguity required of literary classics.

Sources

Barlowe, Jamie. *The Scarlet Mob of Scribblers: Rereading Hester Prynne.* Carbondale: Southern Illinois University Press, 2000.
Bercovitch, Sacvan. *The Office of The Scarlet Letter.* Baltimore: Johns Hopkins University Press, 1991.
Colacurcio, Michael, ed. *New Essays on The Scarlet Letter.* New York: Cambridge University Press, 1985.

Schoolcraft, Henry Rowe (1793–1864) *ethnologist, nonfiction writer*

Born in Watervliet, New York, Henry Rowe Schoolcraft is regarded as a pioneer of modern Native American studies. In 1818 he defected from the family glassmaking business and traveled down the Ohio River to Missouri in order to make a geographical, geological, and mineralogical survey, which he published in 1819 as *A View of the Lead Mines of Missouri.* These findings led to his inclusion as a geologist in the 1820 expedition to northern Michigan and Lake Superior led by Lewis Cass, a journey Schoolcraft described in *A Narrative Journal of the Travels . . . from Detroit Through the Great Chain of the American Lakes to the Sources of the Mississippi River* (1821).

In 1822 Schoolcraft was appointed as Indian agent for northern Michigan, where he married the granddaughter of a Chippewa chieftain and began his research in indigenous culture. He was the first white person to translate Indian poetry and among the first to relate Indian legends and religious beliefs. His investigations led to the publication of many influential books, including *Algic Researches* (1839), concerning the Indians of the Allegheny region. This book in particular had a profound influence on Henry Wadsworth LONGFELLOW, whose poem *The Song of Hiawatha* (1855) repeated Schoolcraft's confusion of the Iroquois Hiawatha with a Chippewa woman. He thus mistakenly set his work on the southern shores of Lake Michigan, when it should have been set in central New York state.

In 1841, when the Whig party came to dominate federal government, Schoolcraft lost his post as Indian agent and moved back east, where he continued his prolific output of works on American Indians, culminating in his six-volume *Historical and Statistical Information Respecting . . . the Indian Tribes of the United States* (1851–57).

Sources

Bremer, Richard G. *Indian Agent and Wilderness Scholar: The Life of Henry Rowe Schoolcraft.* Mount Pleasant: Clarke Historical Library, Central Michigan University, 1987.

Schurz, Carl (1829–1906) *journalist, statesman*

Born in Germany, Carl Schurz was forced to leave his homeland when the revolutionary movement he belonged to failed in 1849. Three years later he made his way to the United States, finally settling in Watertown, Wisconsin, where he studied law and was admitted to practice. He soon became interested in ABOLITIONISM and affiliated with the new Republican Party. His work on behalf of Abraham LINCOLN, primarily speechmaking in the campaign of 1860, resulted in his appointment as minister to Spain the next year. In 1862, however, Schurz resigned his post in order to serve in the Union army during the CIVIL WAR. As a brigadier general he commanded a division that failed to perform bravely. Accused of cowardice, Schurz was later exonerated and even commended by a military court of inquiry.

After the war Schurz toured the South and made a report of his findings for the administration. Schurz's report recommended extension of the voting franchise to African Americans in the former Confederate states as one of the conditions for the states' readmission to the Union. When the administration of Andrew Johnson (1808–75) suppressed the report because the president feared it would impede RECONSTRUCTION, the radical Republicans who controlled Congress nevertheless managed to make Schurz's report public.

Schurz next went into journalism, serving as Washington correspondent for the *NEW-YORK TRIBUNE* and editing both the Detroit *Post* and the German-language St. Louis *Westliche Post.* In 1868 he returned to politics, first acting as temporary chairman and keynote speaker for the Republican National Convention that year and then serving as a U.S. senator from Missouri. An outspoken opponent of political corruption, Schurz was appointed secretary of the interior in 1877 by President Rutherford B. Hayes (1822–93). In this position Schurz distinguished himself with his support for native peoples, his concern for conservation of natural resources, and his installation of a merit-promotion system within his department.

At the end of his cabinet term in 1881, Schurz became coeditor of the New York *Evening Post,* helping to burnish the newspaper's reputation for liberal independence. When he had a falling-out with his coeditors about editorial policy, Schurz wrote editorials for *HARPER'S WEEKLY* (1892–98), but he left that periodical because he did not agree with its support for America's war with Spain.

From 1891 to 1901 Schurz served as president of the National Civil Reform League, where he continued his efforts to reshape government. He was the author of a biography of statesman Henry Clay (1887); an insightful essay on Abraham Lincoln (1891); and his own memoirs, published as *The Reminiscences of Carl Schurz* (1907–08). His greatest literary achievement, however, was his speechwriting, the products of which appeared as *Speeches of Carl Schurz* (1865) and *Speeches, Correspondence, and Political Papers of Carl Schurz* (1913).

Sources

Terzian, James P. *Defender of Human Rights: Carl Schurz.* New York: J. Messner, 1965.

Trefousse, Hans Louis. *Carl Schurz: A Biography.* Knoxville: University of Tennessee Press, 1982.

Scribner's Magazine periodical

In 1881, when *SCRIBNER'S MONTHLY* was sold and transformed into *CENTURY ILLUSTRATED MONTHLY MAGAZINE,* part of the bargain was that the publisher, Charles Scribner's Sons, would not reenter the magazine business for a minimum of five years. After observing this hiatus, the younger Charles Scribner (1854–1930) came out with his competing magazine in January 1887. Concentrating on fiction, travel, biography, and criticism, *Scribner's Magazine* was immediately recognized as a superior production. Edited by Edward L. Burlingame (1848–1922), it boasted as regular contributors such illustrious names as Henry JAMES, Theodore ROOSEVELT, and Jacob RIIS. It was also copiously and beautifully illustrated, first with woodcuts, then with halftones supplied by such celebrated illustrators as Charles Dana GIBSON and Maxfield Parrish (1870–1966), and after 1900, with full-color illustrations by the likes of Frederic Remington (1861–1909) and N. C. Wyeth (1882–1945).

Scribner's devoted a great deal of space to World War I, and it continued to cover public affairs extensively after the war. It also continued to publish outstanding fiction and featured works by such exciting new talents as Ernest Hemingway (1898–1961) and the mystery writer S. S. Van Dine (1888–1939). Circulation began to decline in the 1930s, however, and in 1939 the magazine's subscription list was sold to *Esquire* and its name to the *Commentator.* In 1942, after the United States had entered World War II, the publisher of *Scribner's Commentator* was convicted of taking money from the Japanese government in return for publishing Japanese propaganda.

Sources

Woodress, James Leslie. *Essays Mostly on Periodical Publishing in America.* Durham, N.C.: Duke University Press, 1973.

Scribner's Monthly *periodical*

Founded by the elder Charles Scribner (1821–71) in 1870 as an adjunct to his publishing business, *Scribner's Monthly* was distinguished by its many departments and its publications of serial fiction, such as Bret HARTE's *Gabriel Conroy* (1875–76) and George Washington CABLE's *The Grandissimes* (1880). Graced by well-executed engravings and fine typography, the magazine's superior quality was maintained after 1881, when some of its founders took it over and renamed it the *CENTURY ILLUSTRATED MONTHLY MAGAZINE*.

Sources

John, Arthur. *The Best Years of the Century: Richard Watson Silder, Scribner's Monthly, and the Century Magazine, 1870–1909.* Urbana: University of Illinois Press, 1981.

Seaman, Elizabeth Cochran (Nellie Bly) (1867–1922) *journalist*

Born in Pennsylvania, Elizabeth Cochran Seaman began in childhood to exhibit a talent for writing the kinds of extravagant stories she would specialize in later in life. After she sold her first article to the Pittsburgh *Dispatch,* she took the name of a character from a Stephen Foster song as her pseudonym and set about pursuing the sorts of sensational exposés that would make her reputation. She interested Joseph PULITZER's NEW YORK *WORLD* in a series about conditions in the city mental hospital and, feigning madness, had herself committed. She published her observations in *Ten Days in a Mad House* (1887), which led to the city appropriation of $3 million for institutional improvements.

Bly also took on prisons, factories, nursing homes, politics, and domestic employment as subjects for investigation before the advent of the MUCKRAKING MOVEMENT. Perhaps Bly's most renowned exploit was her besting, in 1889, of the fictitious record set by Phineas Fogg in Jules Verne's *Around the World in Eighty Days* (1873), a feat she recollected in *Nellie Bly's Book: Around the World in Seventy-Two Days* (1890).

Sources

Davidson, Sue. *Getting the Real Story: Nellie Bly and Ida B. Wells.* Seattle, Wash.: Seal Press, 1992.

Ehrlich, Elizabeth. *Nellie Bly.* New York: Chelsea House Publishers, 1989.

Kroeger, Brooke. *Nellie Bly: Daredevil, Reporter, Feminist.* New York: Times Books, 1994.

Sedgwick, Catharine Maria (1789–1867) *novelist*

Born into a prominent family in the Berkshire Hills region of western Massachusetts, Catharine Maria Sedgwick distinguished herself as one of the leading figures of the emerging American literary culture of the early 19th century. Her fiction, admired in Europe as well as America, often drew on the Berkshire scenes she knew best and concentrated on the domestic and local customs she considered the bedrock of the republic. Early novels such as *A New England Tale* (1822) and *Redwood* (1824) had a Unitarian flavor (see UNITARIANISM) that appealed strongly to liberal Protestants of the era—among them many of the prominent writers of her day—and her Stockbridge home became a gathering place for writers from all over the country. She was liberal politically, too, using her novel *Clarence* (1830) to mock the kind of Federalism espoused by her family, embracing Jacksonian democracy instead. A feminist, Sedgwick would explore female identity in her most famous work, the historical romance *Hope Leslie* (1827); and in her last novel, *Married or Single?* (1857), which contrasts the lifestyles of a variety of women.

Sources

Foster, Edward H. *Catharine Maria Sedgwick.* New York: Twayne, 1973.

Gould, Philip. *Covenant and Republic: Historical Romance and the Politics of Puritanism.* New York: Cambridge University Press, 1996.

The Power of Her Sympathy: The Autobiography and Journal of Catharine Maria Sedgwick. Boston: Massachusetts Historical Society; Distributed by Northeastern University Press, 1993.

Seeger, Alan (1888–1916) *poet*

This New York City–born poet graduated from Harvard University before enlisting with the French Foreign Legion at the start of World War I. Before he was killed at the Battle of the Somme, Seeger wrote a number of memorable war poems, the most famous of which is "I Have a Rendezvous with Death" (1916), which haunted readers with its prescience.

Sources

Werstein, Irving. *Sound No Trumpet: The Life and Death of Alan Seeger.* New York: Crowell, 1967.

"Self-Reliance" *Ralph Waldo Emerson* (1841) *essay*

This lengthy essay by Ralph Waldo EMERSON was first published in his *Essays, First Series.* Emerson used it to preach the gospel of independence and individualism in terms that have echoed through the years. The two greatest enemies of creativity, he writes, are fear of public opinion ("Whoso would be a man must be a nonconformist") and undue concern for consistency ("A foolish consistency is the hobgoblin of little minds"). According to Emerson, in order to realize one's own potential, each must disregard received wisdom and authority ("An institution is the lengthened shadow of a man") and obey intuition, for in the end "Nothing is at last sacred but the integrity of your own mind." It was these sorts of sentiments that prompted his fellow transcendentalist Bronson ALCOTT to observe wryly that "Emerson's church consists of one member—himself. He waits for the world to agree with him."

Sources

Cayton, Mary Kupiec. *Emerson's Emergence: Self and Society in the Transformation of New England, 1800–1845.* Chapel Hill: University of North Carolina Press, 1989.

Kateb, George. *Emerson and Self-Reliance.* Thousand Oaks, Calif.: Sage Publications, 1995.

Newfield, Christopher. *The Emerson Effect: Individualism and Submission in America.* Chicago: University of Chicago Press, 1996.

Sewanee Review, The *periodical*

Founded in 1892 by English professor William Peterfield Trent at the University of the South in Sewanee, Tennessee, this literary quarterly is now the oldest U.S. periodical devoted to literary criticism. Its focus has always been on the South, but in the 1940s, '50s, and '60s, under the editorship of such writers as Allen Tate (1899–1979) and Andrew Lytle (1902–95) it became the focal point of the New Criticism, an approach to literature emphasizing the elements of a work rather than its context.

Shaw, Henry Wheeler (Josh Billings) (1818–1885) *humorist*

Born in Massachusetts, Henry Wheeler Shaw pursued a wide range of occupations—explorer, farmer, riverboat captain, real estate agent, auctioneer—until, in middle age, he settled into a literary life. Writing for small newspapers, he adopted many of the idiosyncrasies of his contemporary, Artemus Ward (Charles Farrar BROWNE)—wild misspellings, malapropisms, crazy syntax—in executing his humorous sketches, ostensibly written by his alter ego, Josh Billings. He finally attracted the attention of Artemus Ward himself, who arranged for the publication of Shaw's first book, *Josh Billings, His Savings* (1865). Other Josh Billings books, together with the humorous annual *Allminix* (1869–80), made Shaw a much-quoted—and misquoted—CRACKER-BARREL philosopher and enabled him to have a successful second career as a popular lecturer.

Sources

Kesterson, David B. *Josh Billings (Henry Wheeler Shaw).* New York: Twayne, 1973.

Sholem Aleichem

See RABINOWITZ, SOLOMON J.

showboats *entertainment venues*

These traveling theaters first appeared early in the 19th century in frontier settlements along the nation's western rivers, particularly the Mississippi and the Ohio. At first the companies merely traveled by boat and performed on land, bringing entertainment to the hinterlands. When the companies began to perform on board, at first it was on rather inelegant boats such as keelboats, canalboats, and flatboats. Later, elegant paddleboats and steamboats plied the waters and staged melodramas and variety shows. Other showboats carried circuses and minstrel shows, and many served in daylight hours as museums. With the coming of the CIVIL WAR, however, the popularity of the showboats dwindled. Several writers have depicted life aboard these floating theaters. The best known is perhaps Edna Ferber's (1887–1968) 1926 novel, *Show Boat,* which was adapted in 1927 as an operetta by the librettist Oscar Hammerstein (1895–1960) and the composer Jerome Kern (1885–1945). Two novels, Graham PHILLIPS's *Susan Lenox* (1917) and John Barth's (1930–) *The Floating Opera* (1956), also address the subject.

Sources

Bryant, Betty. *Here Comes the Showboat!* Lexington: University Press of Kentucky, 1994.

Gillespie, C. Richard. *The James Adams Floating Theatre.* Centreville, Md.: Tidewater Publishers, 1991.

Graham, Philip. *Showboats: The History of an American Institution.* Austin: University of Texas Press, 1951.

Sigourney, Lydia Howard Huntley (1791–1865) *poet, novelist*

Lydia Sigourney, a Connecticut writer of sentimental verse, most often took her inspiration from the newspapers, particularly the death notices of prominent individuals—a habit that caused her work to be known as "death's second terror." She published 60 books. Most were collections of her poetical works, but she also wrote novels, a memoir of her dead son, and an autobiography.

Sources

Haight, Gordon. *Mrs. Sigourney, The Sweet Singer of Hartford.* New Haven, Conn.: Yale University Press, 1930.

Sill, Edward Rowland (1841–1887) *poet, essayist*

Born in Connecticut, Edward Rowland Sill was orphaned when young and subsequently reared by an uncle in Ohio. Frail in health, Sill attempted to fortify himself by emulating

Richard Henry DANA Jr. and sailing around Cape Horn to California. He tried his hand at several occupations, among them law and medicine, before returning east to study at the Harvard Divinity School. He then went on to work in New York City as a journalist and in Ohio and California as a teacher. All the while he was writing poetry, some of which appeared in *The Hermitage and Other Poems* (1868), the only volume of his verse to be published in his lifetime. In 1874 he took a position as professor of English at the University of California, where he remained for the next eight years. His last years were spent in Ohio where, under the name Andrew Hedbrooke, he contributed essays and verse to magazines. In 1883 he privately printed *The Venus of Milo and Other Poems.* The posthumously published collected *Poems* (1902) and *Prose* (1900) reveal Rowland to have been a highly cultured individual filled with profound religious skepticism and a classical sense of form.

Sources

Ferguson, Alfred Riggs. *Edward Rowland Sill: The Twilight Poet.* The Hague, Netherlands: Nijhoff, 1955.

The Poetry of Edward Sill. Cleveland: A. Romanoff, 1965.

Simms, William Gilmore (1806–1870) *novelist*

Born in Charleston, South Carolina, the son of a poor storekeeper, William Gilmore Simms aspired to reach the top of the social and literary hierarchy of his native state. Although he was never fully accepted as a member of the aristocratic class to which he aspired, Simms's major achievement was to bring the conventions of the historical ROMANCE, as developed by Sir Walter Scott, to the storytelling of the SOUTH.

Guy Rivers (1834), the story of Georgia outlaws, was the first Simms novel to blend LOCAL COLOR with the historical romance's evocation of the past and of a culture's manners. Simms extended this formula to what is regarded as his masterpiece, *The Yemassee* (1835), the stirring account of Indian warfare in South Carolina. That same year he also published *The Partisan,* set during the American Revolution. He had now found his basic story: the clash between white settlers and Indians, between the settlers and their Colonial master, and the often lawless life of the frontier. These three subjects became the focus of his "Border Romances," which stretched from the colonial period to the mid-19th century.

Among Simms's most important titles are *Mellichampe* (1836); *Richard Hurdis* (1838); *Border Beagles* (1840); *The Kinsman* (1841); *Beauchampe* (1842); *Helen Halsey; or, The Swamp State of Conelachita* (1845); *Katherine Walton* (1851); *The Sword and the Distaff* (1853); *The Forayers* (1855); *Charlemont* (1856); and *The Cassique of Kiawah* (1859). His work helped shaped the bedrock belief in the "Old South," a time of gracious manners and conservative order that southern planters and other patriots evoked when criticized by northerners for the institution of slavery. Simms's novels celebrated an ideal and did not examine closely the realities of the South. They presented stereotyped characters and melodramatic plots. Even so, as the poet and historian of his region he has been compared to James Fenimore COOPER. If Simms did not create memorable characters or evoke the land as graphically as Cooper, he has been praised for being more accurate than Cooper in observing social manners and customs.

Simms perpetuated the legend of the South by editing magazines such as *The Southern and Western Monthly Magazine* (1845) and *The Southern Quarterly Review* (1856–57) and writing essays and biographies that championed slavery. He wrote both a *History of South Carolina* (1840) and a *Geography of South Carolina* (1843). A five-volume edition of Simms's *Letters* appeared between 1952 and 1956.

Sources

Guilds, John Caldwell and Caroline Collins, eds. *William Gilmore Simms and the American Frontier.* Athens: University of Georgia Press, 1997.

Guilds, John Caldwell. *Long Years of Neglect: The Work and Reputation of William Gilmore Simms.* Fayetteville: University of Arkansas Press, 1988.

Ridgely, J. V. *William Gilmore Simms.* New York: Twayne, 1962.

Wimsatt, Mary Ann. *The Major Fiction of William Gilmore Simms.* Baton Rouge: Louisiana State University Press, 1989.

Sister Carrie *Theodore Dreiser* (1900) *novel*

Theodore DREISER's first novel contrasts the fates of its two main characters: Carrie Meeber, a poor country girl; and George Hurstwood, the prosperous manager of a Chicago bar. The novel follows the rise of Carrie's fortunes and the fall of Hurstwood's as the lives of the two intersect.

Carrie, who has come from the country to the big city in order to seek her fortune, is "full of the illusions of ignorance and hope." After spending some time living with her sister and brother-in-law and working at a dull, demoralizing job, she takes up with Charles Drouet, a traveling salesman whose seeming worldliness impresses her. Unemployed, she eventually becomes Drouet's mistress and moves in with him. While he is away on business, however, Carrie becomes more familiar with Drouet's friend, Hurstwood, who is older, more polished, and more intelligent. He is also married. But Hurstwood falls in love with Carrie, sacrificing his family, his reputation, and even his self-respect when he steals $10,000 from his employer and lures Carrie away, first to Montreal and then to New York City. Once there, he uses the last of his funds to set up his own saloon.

Uprooted from his familiar environment, however, Hurstwood starts a long, inexorable slide downward. The bar fails, and he and Carrie are forced to move to smaller, meaner quarters, where they are soon sleeping in separate rooms. Dissatisfied with her lot, Carrie decides to pursue her dreams of a career on the stage. She finds work as a chorus girl, but her meager wages are not enough, she feels, to support herself and Hurstwood, who is by now completely dependent upon her. Even after Carrie's star begins to rise, she resents having to give the morose and moribund Hurstwood money, and one day she departs for good, leaving Hurstwood only $20 and a farewell note.

Hurstwood has lost his way in the world. Unable to find work, he resorts to begging. Alone one night in a BOWERY flophouse, he commits suicide by turning on the gas. Carrie does not learn of his death until three years later, in a chance encounter with Drouet. By this time Carrie has become a star, and while she pities Hurstwood, she wants no part of him or Drouet or what they represent. Alone in her splendid rooms at the Waldorf Astoria Hotel, however, happiness still eludes her. As the novel ends, the narrator asks rhetorically, "Oh, Carrie, Carrie! . . . In your rocking chair, by your window, shall you dream such happiness as you may never feel."

A masterpiece of NATURALISM, *Sister Carrie* presents city life in documentary detail. Dreiser did not shirk from presenting such controversial matters as seduction, adultery, and suicide in a clear-sighted manner, eschewing the melodrama and ROMANTICISM that would have surrounded them in literary works of an earlier period. Owing to its "immorality," the publisher withheld *Sister Carrie* from circulation, and it was not released to the public until 1907, when the novel was reissued by another publisher. Contemporary critics were largely hostile to what they considered a decadent and depressing book, but later novelists such as Sherwood Anderson (1876–1941), James T. Farrell (1904–79), and John Dos Passos (1896–1970) applauded Dreiser's rejection of convention. The strong plot of *Sister Carrie* made it easy to translate into film as "A Star is Born," the first version of which was released in 1937.

Sources

Pizer, Donald, ed. *New Essays on Sister Carrie.* New York: Cambridge University Press, 1991.

Sister Carrie: An Authoritative Text, Backgrounds, and Sources Criticism. Edited by Donald Pizer. New York: W. W. Norton, 1991.

Sketch Book, The *Washington Irving* (1819–1820) *story and essay collection*

Also known as *The Sketch Book of Geoffrey Crayon, Gent.*, this collection by Washington IRVING is often cited as the first appearance of the American short story. Highly successful both in America and abroad, the volume includes a number of sketches in which Irving presents his observations as an American in England, but the most influential pieces in the book feature American scenes. "RIP VAN WINKLE" and "The Legend of Sleepy Hollow" (see CRANE, ICHABOD) draw heavily on German folktales, but Irving also made use of American FOLKLORE in these pieces. Essays such as "English Writers of America" and "Traits of Indian Character" are decidedly nationalistic in tone. While Irving's previous works had had an 18th-century flavor, here he moved into the romantic realm carved out by Sir Walter Scott (1771–1832), marking a path that would be followed by later American romantics such as Nathaniel HAWTHORNE and Herman MELVILLE.

Sources

Roth, Martin. *Comedy and America: The Lost World of Washington Irving.* Port Washington, N.Y.: Kennikat Press, 1976.

Rubin-Dorsky, Jeffrey. *Adrift in the Old World: The Psychological Pilgrimage of Washington Irving.* Chicago: University of Chicago Press, 1988.

slave narratives *genre*

The first published slave narrative—*The Interesting Narrative of the Life of Olaudah Equiano, or Gustavus Vassa, the African, Written by Himself* (1789)—begins with Vassa's childhood in Africa and emphasizes his dual identity (represented in his African and American names). That an ex-slave could write the story of his own life was in itself a refutation of the slave owner's claim that Africans and their descendants were an inferior people. As Frederick DOUGLASS would pointedly observe in his own slave narrative, the literature of African Americans was a direct threat to the slavemaster's code. Overhearing his master say that teaching a slave to read and write would only cause trouble confirmed Douglass's belief in his own worth. Why should a master fear educating a slave if slaves could not be educated? To Douglass, the hypocrisy and contradictions of a slave society were thus exposed.

Whereas *Narrative of the Life of Frederick Douglass, An American Slave* (1845) told the triumphant story of a man's liberation of himself, Harriet Ann JACOBS's *Incidents in the Life of a Slave Girl* (1861) told a grim story of the sexual abuse of female slaves. Jacobs wrote sensitively and frankly about the master whose children she bore. She was not without tender feeling for this man, although she knew he exploited her and she had no way to refuse him or to change her lot in life. Jacobs's narrative is of the utmost importance because of the moral responsibility she takes for her own actions and because of the candid way she writes about her dilemma. Her literary ability, especially the power to describe human character and to portray dramatic scenes, invites comparison with 19th-century novels such as Charlotte Brontë's *Jane Eyre.* Indeed, in Jacobs's hands the slave narrative becomes a feminist story as well, since Jacobs, like Jane Eyre, finds herself in the service of men and of households that have the power to determine her future and to treat her as inferior because she is a woman.

Abolitionists (see ABOLITIONISM) often published introductions to slave narratives and used the stories to promote their campaigns against slaveholders and to put pressure on the federal government to outlaw slavery. Douglass's book, for example, was endorsed by William Lloyd GARRISON. After the CIVIL WAR, the slave narrative became a powerful tool to argue for the enfranchisement of freed slaves and for their full rights as citizens.

Other published slave narratives include *Narrative of Henry Watson, a Fugitive Slave* (1849); *Experience and Personal Narrative of Uncle Tom Jones, Who Was for Forty Years a Slave. Also The Surprising Adventures of Wild Tom, of the Island Retreat, a Fugitive Negro from South Carolina* (1858); *Narrative of the Life of J.D. Green, A Runaway Slave, from Kentucky: Containing an Account of His Three Escapes, in 1839, 1846, and 1848* (1864); *Life of James Mars, A Slave Born and Sold in Connecticut, Written by Himself* (1866); and *Wonderful Eventful Life of Rev. Thomas James by Himself* (1887). *Slave Narratives* (2000) is a compilation published by The Library of America. *Slave Narratives: The Journey to Freedom* (2001) is a similar collection published by Franklin Watts.

Sources

Starling, Marion Wilson. *The Slave Narrative: Its Place in American Literary History.* 2nd ed. Washington, D.C.: Howard University Press, 1988.

Tackach, James, ed. *Slave Narratives.* San Diego, Calif.: Greenhaven Press, 2001.

Smart Set, The periodical

Founded in NEW YORK CITY in 1890 by William D'Alton, who went by the name Colonel Mann, this monthly was pitched to New York society, which also supplied its contributors. It was not a financial success, but it did have the distinction of publishing the first short story written by O. Henry (William Sydney PORTER). In 1900 it was purchased by John A. Thayer (1861–1936), who attracted such distinguished writers as Gertrude ATHERTON, James Branch Cabell (1879–1958), H. L. Mencken (1880–1956), and George Jean Nathan (1882–1958) as contributors. Willard Huntington Wright (1888–1939), known later as the mystery writer S.S. Van Dine, became the magazine's editor in 1912 and aimed to provide "lively entertainment for minds that are not primitive." Wright succeeded in making *The Smart Set* a kind of LITTLE MAGAZINE with a large circulation. It was at once lively and intellectually serious, publishing magazine contributions from such foreign authors as James Joyce (1882–1941), D. H. Lawrence (1885–1930), and Gabriele D'Annunzio (1863–1938) for the first time in the United States. In December 1914, however, Thayer replaced Wright with Mencken and Nathan, and *The Smart Set* assumed a more satiric tone, especially in its "Americana" department, with its war on gentility and what Mencken called the "booboisie." The coeditors continued Wright's policy of publishing new writers, however, and the early work of authors such as Eugene O'Neill (1888–1953), F. Scott Fitzgerald (1896–1940), and Joseph Wood Krutch (1893–1970) appeared in *The Smart Set.* After the magazine was sold in 1923 to William Randolph HEARST, it adopted a more conventional editorial policy, and the magazine finally ceased publication in 1930.

Sources

Dolmetsch, Carl R. *The Smart Set: A History and Anthology.* New York: Dial Press, 1966.

Douglas, George H. *The Smart Magazines: 50 Years of Literary Revelry and High Jinks at Vanity Fair, the New Yorker, Life, Esquire, and The Smart Set.* Hamden, Conn.: Archon Books, 1991.

Smith, Charles Henry (Bill Arp) (1826–1903)

journalist, humorist

Born in Georgia, Charles H. Smith practiced law before joining the Confederate Army during the CIVIL WAR. He began his writing career during the first year of the war, contributing to a Georgia newspaper humorous letters addressed to "Mr. Abe Linkhorn" and signed with what would become his pseudonym, Bill Arp. These letters, which satirized the North through Smith's adoption of a deliberately unschooled, uncouth persona, proved highly popular with readers. After the war, Smith kept on writing Bill Arp letters to the Atlanta *Constitution* for the next 25 years. Over time, however, Arp evolved into a shrewd CRACKERBARREL philosopher, holding forth on such diverse topics as women's suffrage, income tax, and equal rights. Although in 1866 Smith dropped the use of comic misspellings, he often employed the dialect of the Georgia "cracker" and the African American in a style said to have influenced Joel Chandler HARRIS. Smith's books, including *Bill Arp So Called* (1866) and *Bill Arp: From the Uncivil War to Date* (1903), were collections of his newspaper pieces.

Sources

Austin, James C. *Bill Arp.* New York: Twayne, 1969.

Parker, David B. *Alias Bill Arp: Charles Henry Smith and the South's "Goodly Heritage."* Athens: University of Georgia Press, 1991.

Smith, Francis Hopkinson (1838–1915)

short story writer, novelist, illustrator

Born in Baltimore, F. Hopkinson Smith worked in his brother's iron foundry until after the CIVIL WAR. He moved to New York City and worked as an engineer in the construction of many important buildings in the area, including the base for the Statue of Liberty. Painting had long been his avocation, however, and when, at age 50, he turned to a writing career, he was able to combine his pictorial and literary gifts. He wrote and illustrated two popular books of travel sketches: *Well-Worn Roads of Spain, Holland, and Italy* (1887) and *A White Umbrella in Mexico* (1889). His next work, a LOCAL COLOR novella based on his own after-dinner stories, *Colonel Carter of Cartersville* (1891), sold so well that Smith was able to retire from engineering altogether. Over the next twenty-three years he published numerous collections of stories and novels, as well as an autobiographical story concerning the life of a young painter in Baltimore and New York, *The Fortunes of Oliver Horn* (1902), and two volumes of charcoal drawings, *In Thackeray's London* (1913) and *In Dickens's London* (1914).

Smith, Joseph (1805–1844) *religious leader*

Born in Vermont, Joseph Smith was raised in Palmyra, New York, in an area that had seen many revivalist religious sects come and go. Smith himself began to experience visions when he was young, and in 1823 he had a vision of the angel Maroni, who told him of the existence of a sacred text written on golden tablets. According to Smith's account, the location of these tablets was not revealed to him until four years later. That year Smith moved to Pennsylvania and, with the aid of a magical device, translated the tablets into a text that was published in 1830 as *The Book of Mormon.* That year, on the basis of this sacred text, Smith founded the Church of Jesus Christ of Latter-Day Saints, also known as the Mormons (see MORMONISM), in New York State. After the seer and his followers encountered hostility there, in 1831 they began an exodus that took them first to Ohio, then to Missouri, and finally to Nauvoo, Illinois, where in 1840 the Mormons founded a colony that prospered for several years.

The Mormons were regarded with envy and suspicion by some of their neighbors, especially after Smith proclaimed the doctrine of plural marriage in 1843. Church members also rebelled against Smith's autocratic rule, and dissenters founded their own newspaper, the *Expositor,* with the express purpose of criticizing Smith. When he announced his candidacy for president of the United States in 1844, the criticism became vehement; and when Smith's supporters destroyed the presses at the *Expositor,* lapsed Mormons and other critics of Smith attacked him.

Incarcerated in Carthage, Illinois, on charges of treason and conspiracy, Joseph Smith and his brother Hyrum were murdered in jail by a mob on June 27, 1844. Smith's martyrdom had the effect of stabilizing the church, and when the Mormons were once again subjected to discrimination, in 1847, they moved westward en masse, led by Smith's successor, Brigham YOUNG, to the site of what would later become Salt Lake City, Utah.

Sources

Brodie, Fawn M. *No Man Knows My History: The Life of Joseph Smith, the Mormon Prophet.* 2d ed., rev. New York: Alfred A. Knopf, 1971.
Bushman, Richard L. *Joseph Smith and the Beginnings of Mormonism.* Urbana: University of Illinois Press, 1984.
Draper, Maurice L. *The Founding Prophet: An Administrative Biography of Joseph Smith, Jr.* Independence, Mo.: Herald Pub. House, 1991.
Persuitte, David. *Joseph Smith and the Origins of the Book of Mormon.* Jefferson, N.C.: McFarland, 2000.

Smith, Richard Penn (1799–1854) *playwright, novelist*

Richard Penn Smith was a Philadelphia lawyer who also edited his hometown newspaper, *The Aurora,* from 1822 to 1827. In 1825 he began to act on his love of the theater, and over the next decade he produced some 20 plays. He introduced the romantic tragedy and historical themes to American drama. Of his works that are based on American history, *William Penn; or, The Elm Tree* (1829) and *The Triumph at Plattsburg* (1830), set during the War of 1812, are truly original creations. However, *The Eighth of January* (1829), concerning Andrew Jackson's victory at the Battle of New Orleans during that same war, borrows heavily from French melodrama. Most of Smith's other plays were adaptations of foreign works. Among his best-known works of this type is *The Actress of Padua* (1836), which is based on a tragedy by the French literary master Victor Hugo (1802–85).

The Actress of Padua, like a number of Smith's other plays, no longer exists in manuscript. Today it is known only from the narrative version Smith published in 1836, *The Actress of Padua and Other Tales.* In addition to adapting others' work, Smith frequently reused his own material. He reworked his first romantic comedy, for example, the never-produced *The Divorce,* into the verse drama *The Deformed* (1830).

In addition to his collection of tales and a novel set during the Revolutionary War, *The Forsaken* (1831), Smith's prose works probably include the ghost-written autobiography of the frontiersman and politician Davy CROCKETT, *Col. Crockett's Exploits and Adventures in Texas* (1836), also known as *Davy Crockett and His Adventures in Texas, Told Mostly by Himself.*

Sources

McCullough, Bruce C. *The Life and Writings of Richard Penn Smith.* Menasha, Wis.: George Banta, 1917.

Smith, Seba (1792–1868) *humorist*

Seba Smith came from Maine and graduated from Bowdoin College in 1818. He founded the *Portland Courier* (1829) and won popularity for his creation of the fictional Major Jack Downing, a rustic Yankee who dispensed down-to-earth advice in a comic, unpretentious style. Major Jack commented on politics—local and national—and became a confidant of Andrew Jackson (1767–1845) and a satirical authority on Jacksonian democracy.

Smith wrote, however, as an unaffiliated pundit, speaking simply in home truths that cut through partisan politics. He resembles James Russell LOWELL's Hosea Biglow and Finley Peter DUNNE's Mr. Dooley as well as later 20th-century homespun political philosophers such as Will Rogers (1879–1935).

Smith collected his newspaper sketches in *Letters Written During the President's Tour "Down East," By Myself, Major Jack Downing, of Downingville* (1833); *Jack Downing's Letters* (1845); and *'Way Down East, or Portraitures of Yankee Life* (1854). These books not only comment on contemporary affairs but also provide vivid LOCAL COLOR portraits of New England characters and scenes.

Sources

Rickels, Milton and Patricia. *Seba Smith.* Boston: Twayne, 1977.

Wyman, Mary Alice. *Two American Pioneers, Seba Smith and Elizabeth Oakes Smith.* New York: Columbia University Press, 1927.

"Song of Myself" *Walt Whitman* (1855) *poem*

Originally published as the untitled introduction to the first edition of Walt WHITMAN's *Leaves of Grass,* "Song of Myself" was not given a title until the sixth edition, published in 1881, of Whitman's ever-evolving masterwork. Just over 1,300 lines of free verse, "Song of Myself" is a revolutionary manifesto in which the poet, who declares himself "a kosmos," embodies the democracy itself ("I am large, I contain multitudes"). As such, the poet is at once universal ("of every hue and caste am I, of every rank and religion") and egalitarian ("I am the poet of the Body and . . . of the Soul . . . not the poet of goodness only . . . I believe a leaf of grass is no less than the journey-work of the stars").

The poem's structure underscores its theme, spelling out its inclusiveness with catalogues of people and things and reconciling all creation by alternating assertion with illustration, man with nature, good with evil to form a mystical whole that is the poem, the poet, and, finally, all creation. "I bequeath myself to the dirt, to grow from the grass I love," Whitman declares, "If you want me again look for me under your boot-soles."

Sources

Aspiz, Harold. *Walt Whitman and the Body Beautiful.* Urbana: University of Illinois Press, 1980.

Miller, Edwin H. *Walt Whitman's "Song of Myself": A Mosaic of Interpretations.* Iowa City: University of Iowa Press, 1989.

Updike, John. *Ego and Art in Walt Whitman.* New York: Targ Editions, 1980.

Souls of Black Folk, The *W. E. B. Du Bois* (1903) *essays and sketches*

W. E. B. DU BOIS had published nine of the 14 pieces in this collection earlier, most in *The ATLANTIC MONTHLY.* With the addition of five new pieces, he intended the volume to trace the history of African Americans from slavery to segregation, and to outline their dilemma:

> It is a peculiar sensation, this double-consciousness, this sense of always looking at one's self through the eyes of others, of measuring one's soul by the tape of a world that looks on in amused contempt and pity. One ever feels his twoness,—an American, a Negro; two souls, two thoughts, two unreconciled strivings; two warring ideals in one dark body. . . .

Du Bois states forthrightly that "the problem of the Twentieth Century is the problem of the color line" and finds fault with the most powerful black man of his day, Booker T. WASHINGTON, whom Du Bois finds too accommodating of white society. *The Souls of Black Folk,* with its sympathetic studies of black sharecroppers and appreciation of African-American religious music, nonetheless split black Americans into two camps—one that sought peaceful coexistence with the whites and one which, like Du Bois himself, could not reconcile itself to life amidst a hostile majority. Thirty years later the novelist and critic James Weldon Johnson (1871–1938) would still declare that *The Souls of Black Folk* "had a greater effect upon and within the Negro race in America" than any book after UNCLE TOM'S CABIN.

Sources

Andrews, William L., ed. *Critical Essays on W. E. B. Du Bois.* Boston: G.K. Hall, 1985.

Aptheker, Herbert. *The Literary Legacy of W. E. B. Du Bois.* White Plains, N.Y.: Kraus International Publications, 1989.

Rampersad, Arnold. *The Art and Imagination of W. E. B. Du Bois.* Cambridge, Mass.: Harvard University Press, 1976.

South, the *geographical region*

The South in 19th-century American literature has always been a well-defined region based on its agrarian character and the persistence of slavery. Historians such as W. J. Cash (1900–41) have attributed the South's unique character to an aristocratic or cavalier mythology, with the great planters and their plantations serving as the focal point of the region's economy and way of life. Although most southerners did not own slaves, they nevertheless defined themselves in relation to the slave, the lowest order of society, Cash argued. Later historians have disputed what they consider to be Cash's simplistic account of the southern caste and class system. Yet his evocation of the myth of the South is powerful and certainly applies to the way its 19th-century writers, such as William Gilmore SIMMS and Thomas Nelson PAGE, portrayed the planter class and the society organized around the cotton kingdom.

Mark Twain (Samuel Langhorne CLEMENS) pointed out the romantic streak in the South and how its people had grown up on the historical romances of Sir Walter Scott (1771–1832). During the CIVIL WAR, poets such as Henry TIMROD and Sidney LANIER idealized the Southern cause and consoled the Confederacy.

After the Civil War, the LOCAL COLOR writers tended to sentimentalize southern life, portraying happy "darkies" on plantations, although certain writers such as Kate CHOPIN and George W. CABLE provided more complex portraits of the region's rigid social and political structure. Near the end of the century, African-American writers such as W. E. B. DU BOIS and Paul Laurence DUNBAR broke through the sentimental veneer of local color to treat candidly the oppression of former slaves and the tyranny of the "color line" meant to keep a whole people in subjection.

Sources

Cash, W. J. *The Mind of the South.* New York: Knopf, 1941.

Genovese, Eugene. *The Southern Tradition: The Achievement and Limitations of an American Conservatism.* Cambridge, Mass.: Harvard University Press, 1994.

Morrison, Joseph L. *W. J. Cash, Southern Prophet: A Biography and Reader.* New York: Alfred A. Knopf, 1967.

Phillips, Ulrich Bonnell. *Life and Labor in the Old South.* Boston: Little Brown, 1929; Baton Rouge: Louisiana State University Press, 1968.

South Atlantic Quarterly, The *periodical*

Founded in 1902 by John S. Bassett, a professor of history at what was then Trinity College (now Duke University) in Durham, North Carolina, the focus of *The South Atlantic Quarterly* was—and continues to be—the South and its history, culture, and economy. The journal has, however, also has published special issues devoted to such diverse topics as 18th-century literature and Soviet foreign policy.

Sources

Hamilton, William B., comp. *Fifty Years of the South Atlantic Quarterly.* Durham, N.C.: Duke University Press, 1952.

Southern Literary Messenger, The *periodical*

Founded in Richmond, Virginia, in 1834 by Thomas W. White, *The Southern Literary Messenger* is best remembered for its association with Edgar Allan POE, whose first contribution, the story "Berenice," appeared in March 1835. That December Poe became the magazine's editor, and although he continued to use the *Southern Literary Messenger* as an outlet for his own work, he also succeeded in increasing its circulation from 500 to more than 3,500 subscribers in a year. Poe's ruthless reviews of others' literary works brought the magazine into conflict with numerous authors, and in January 1837, when his drinking problems began to interfere with his work, he was fired. White then took over the editorship, which he held until his death in 1843. Afterward, the magazine lost its literary bent, concentrating instead on military matters until it expired toward the end of the CIVIL WAR. During its brief revival (1939–44), the magazine merely reprinted material that had appeared between its covers during its earlier incarnation.

Sources

Jackson, David K. *Poe and the Southern Literary Messenger.* Richmond, Va.: Press of the Dietz Printing Co., 1934.

Southern Review, The *periodical*

The first of three magazines bearing this title was founded in Charleston, South Carolina, in 1828. Edited by Hugh S. Legaré (1797–1843), it concentrated on southern culture and lasted until 1832. A second periodical of the same name and with the same focus was published in Baltimore between 1867 and 1879, edited by the critic Paul Hamilton HAYNE. A third quarterly named *The Southern Review* appeared in Baton Rouge, Louisiana, in 1935, published by Louisiana State University. Under such editors as Cleanth Brooks (1906–94) and Robert Penn Warren (1905–89), it became a locus for the New Criticism, publishing works by such critics as John Crowe Ransom (1888–1974) and Yvor Winters (1900–68) and fiction by writers like Caroline Gordon (1895–1981) and Eudora Welty (1909–2001).

Spanish-American War *historical event*

This 1898 war was the result of years of tension over Cuba. The Monroe Doctrine had warned European powers to stay out of those parts of the western hemisphere that seemed a natural area of U.S. interests, in keeping with the doctrine of "manifest destiny," which sanctioned the spread of American civilization across the North American continent and to neighboring lands. U.S. business and military interests viewed Spain as a particularly corrupt, decadent, and despotic nation intent on crushing Cuba—a strategic site worth developing for its industrial and agricultural potential. Newspaper chains, especially the one owned by William Randolph HEARST, were also eager to report on a war that would portray the United States as both a mighty power and a liberator.

The war began after the U.S. ship *Maine* sank mysteriously and the publication of an offensive letter from the Spanish ambassador to President William McKinley

(1843–1901). The United States destroyed the Spanish fleet at Santiago and conducted a highly publicized invasion of Cuba. Theodore ROOSEVELT made his national reputation by organizing his own group of "Rough Riders" and taking San Juan Hill in Cuba with much exuberance and publicity. No match for U.S. firepower, the Spanish made peace and relinquished Cuba, Puerto Rico, Guam, and the Philippines to the United States for $20 million.

The Spanish-American War marked the entry of the United States into world politics as a major power. American writers such as Richard Harding DAVIS and Stephen CRANE enhanced their literary reputations by reporting on the war. Other writers such as Mark Twain (Samuel CLEMENS) and later John Dos Passos (1896–1970) in his *U.S.A.* trilogy bitterly opposed the war and saw it as a sign that the country was changing from a democratic republic to a menacing imperial nation. Writers such as Carl Sandburg (1878–1967) and Sherwood Anderson (1876–1941) fought in the war.

Theodore Roosevelt wrote his account of the war in *The Rough Riders* (1899). Finley Peter DUNNE satirized the war in *Mr. Dooley in Peace and War,* and Joseph Hergesheimer (1880–1954) dramatized it in a novel, *The Bright Shawl* (1922).

Sources

Brands, H. W. *The Reckless Decade: America in the 1890s.* New York: St. Martin's Press, 1995.

Keller, Gary D. and Cordelia Candelaria, eds. *The Legacy of the Mexican and Spanish-American Wars: Legal, Literary, and Historical Perspectives.* Tempe, Ariz.: Bilingual Review/Press, 2000.

Traxel, David. *1898: The Birth of the American Century.* New York: Knopf, 1998.

Spirit of the Age, The *periodical*

This NEW YORK CITY weekly (1849–50) was edited by reformer William Henry CHANNING with the goal of achieving "the Peaceful Transformation of human society from isolated to associated interests." It included contributions from writers such as Henry JAMES Sr. and Parke GODWIN and advocated for such controversial causes as ABOLITIONISM and an end to capital punishment.

Spirit of the Times *periodical*

Founded in 1831 by the humorist and newspaperman William Porter (1809–58), this magazine was devoted to sports and humor. Achieving a circulation of more than 40,000, it became highly influential throughout the country owing to contributions from such accomplished humorists and sports writers as J. J. Hooper (1815–62) and George Washington HARRIS. T. B. THORPE's classic tall tale "THE BIG BEAR OF ARKANSAS" was first published in 1841 in *Spirit of the Times,* which also featured the first appearance of some of Harris's "Sut Lovingood" sketches.

Sources

Yates, Norris W. *William T. Porter and the Spirit of the Times: A Study of the Big Bear School of Humor.* Baton Rouge: Louisiana State University Press, 1957.

spiritualism (c. 1848–1888) *superstitious belief and social phenomenon.*

In the 19th century, communications from the dead—particularly from deceased loved ones—were thought to manifest themselves as auras and vibrations available only to clairvoyants and mediums as well as to ordinary persons through such means as table rapping and spirit photography. The American vogue for spiritualism began in 1848 when the Fox sisters of Arcadia, New York, claimed that they heard mysterious rappings in their house that were communications from the spirit world. Soon they began to organize séances for which they charged admission. The popularity of spiritualism reached its zenith in the wake of the CIVIL WAR, which claimed so many lives and produced countless bereaved families. In 1888 Margaret Fox put an end to her career, if not to spiritualism's vogue, by admitting that the effects she and her sister "interpreted" were fraudulent.

For decades, however, spiritualism was a constant of American life. Notables such as William JAMES, Walt WHITMAN, the "Poughkeepsie Seer" Andrew Jackson Davis (1826–1910), and even Abraham LINCOLN took an interest in the subject. Many found it wanting: writers as diverse as Herman MELVILLE (in "The Apple-Tree Table," 1856) and Louisa May ALCOTT (in *Little Women,* 1868–69) pointed to some of the absurdities of this "faith."

Sources

Brandon, Ruth. *The Spiritualists: The Passion for the Occult in the Nineteenth and Twentieth Centuries.* New York: Alfred A. Knopf, 1983.

Goldtarb, Russell N. *Spiritualism and Nineteenth-Century Letters.* Rutherford, N.J.: Fairleigh Dickinson University Press, 1978.

Jackson, Herbert G. *The Spirit Rappers.* Garden City, N.Y.: Doubleday, 1972.

Kerr, Howard, and Charles L. Crow, eds. *The Occult in America: New Historical Perspectives.* Urbana: University of Illinois Press, 1983.

Spofford, Harriet Elizabeth Prescott (1835–1921) *short story writer, novelist, poet*

Born in Calais, Maine, into a family of modest means, Harriet Prescott began her writing career out of financial necessity. She published in Boston newspapers but failed to raise either much money or her profile until, in 1858, she submitted "In the Cellar," a story about jewels and international diplomacy, to the ATLANTIC MONTHLY, where it was published the following year to great acclaim. Over the next 60 years she would publish hundreds of stories, novels, poems, and essays, most of which clung to romantic and GOTHIC conventions even after these genres went out of style. "The Amber Gods," the title story of her first collection, published in 1863, remains her best-known work and, with its vain, untrustworthy narrator, perhaps her most "modern." In 1865 Harriet Prescott married Richard S. Spofford; they lived in Washington, D.C., whose LOCAL COLOR she captured in *Old Washington* (1906).

Sources

Halbeisen, Elizabeth Kobus. *Harriet Prescott Spofford: A Romantic Survival.* Philadelphia: University of Pennsylvania Press, 1935.

Springfield Republican, The *periodical*

This New England newspaper gained a national reputation for independence under the editorship of the Bowles family. Begun as a weekly in 1824 by the elder Samuel Bowles (1797–1851), under the younger Samuel Bowles (1826–78) the paper began to publish daily and departed from its conservative Whig editorial policy to oppose slavery and the MEXICAN WAR. During the CIVIL WAR it supported Abraham LINCOLN, but afterward the paper was harshly critical of the corrupt administration of Ulysses S. GRANT. In 1926 the Bowles family bought out the three other Springfield, Massachusetts, newspapers and continued to maintain them as separate, independent entities with individual editorial policies. Around the same time the *Republican* ceased daily publication and became a Sunday newspaper.

Sources

Weisner, Stephen G. *Embattled Editor: The Life of Samuel Bowles.* Lanham, Md.: University Press of America, 1986.

Stanley, Sir Henry Morton (John Rowlands) (1841–1904) *journalist, explorer*

Born in Wales, John Rowlands came to the United States as a youth, working as a cabin boy for his passage. He landed in New Orleans and was hired by a man named Stanley, whose name Rowlands appropriated. After stints in the U.S. Navy and the Confederate army, he went to work as a reporter for the New York *Herald,* which sent him to Africa in search of the Scottish missionary and explorer David Livingstone (1813–73). When Stanley located the lost man, he is said to have greeted him with the memorable phrase "Dr. Livingstone, I presume?" The following year, Stanley published *How I Found Livingstone,* but he stayed on in Africa, continuing Livingstone's explorations and working to establish the Congo Free State. He described his further adventures in *Through the Dark Continent* (1878) and *In Darkest Africa* (1890). In 1895 he gave up his American citizenship and became, once again, a British subject. Four years later he was knighted.

Sources

Bierman, John. *Dark Safari: The Life behind the Legend of Henry Morton Stanley.* London: Hodder & Stoughton, 1990.

Jackson, Peggy H. *Meteor Out of Africa: Henry Morton Stanley's Journey to Find Livingstone, 1871.* London: Cassell, 1962.

Stanton, Elizabeth Cady (1815–1902) *suffragist, editor, autobiographer*

A native of Johnstown, New York, Elizabeth Cady was an intelligent, ambitious young woman whose gender would have prohibited her from attending the local school except that her brother's death had left a vacancy there. After attending the Troy Female Academy in Troy, New York, she found that no college would accept her because of her sex, so she determinedly read law in her father's office. Afterward, she was not permitted to take the bar examination or to practice law.

In 1840 Elizabeth Cady married the journalist and abolitionist Henry Stanton, and her career as a radical activist began. Attending a World Anti-Slavery Convention in London, where Henry Stanton was a delegate, Elizabeth Cady Stanton met the Philadelphia abolitionist Lucretia Mott (1793–1880) in the visitors' gallery. Women delegates were not permitted to take the floor, a fact that bonded the two in their belief that a women's rights movement was badly needed. Eight years later they organized the first Women's Rights Convention in Seneca Falls, New York, where Stanton wrote a Declaration of Sentiments calling for higher education and professional opportunities for women, property rights for married women, the right of women to divorce, and—most radically of all—a woman's right to vote (see SUFFRAGISM).

Over the next decade, Stanton reared eight children while continuing to attend women's rights conventions, at one of which, in 1852, she met her lifelong friend and collaborator, Susan B. ANTHONY. Both women made a radical gesture by taking up the liberating costume popularized by Amelia BLOOMER, and together they produced and delivered the lectures that helped win converts to their cause. Although Stanton said that she "forged the thunderbolts" and Anthony "fired them," Stanton was in truth both a fine writer and a brilliant orator. Her statement may have referred to the difference in the two women's temperaments, which frequently tested, but never dissolved, their working relationship.

During the CIVIL WAR Stanton and Anthony worked for the Women's Loyal League, which raised money for the Union army. When the war was over they assumed that they, together with African Americans, had been granted the voting franchise by the 14th and 15th Constitutional amendments. Bitterly disappointed by the antebellum defeat of the movement for women's suffrage, Stanton and Anthony split off from Lucy STONE's American Woman Suffrage Association, which worked for black male suffrage, and founded the National Woman Suffrage Association. Between 1868 and 1870, the NWSA published the radical periodical *Revolution,* edited by Stanton and Anthony. Stanton's bid for a seat in the U.S. Congress failed in 1868, but the next year she was elected president of the NWSA. In 1890, when the NWSA reunited with the American Woman Suffrage Association to become the National American Woman Suffrage Association, Stanton become the new group's first president.

In her later years Stanton became increasingly radical. Together with fellow suffragists Anthony and Mathilda Gage (1826–98), she wrote the first three volumes of *History of Woman Suffrage* (1881–86). But her 1895 publication of *The Woman's Bible,* which included feminist (see FEMINISM) reinterpretations of the canon, proved incendiary, causing Stanton to be censured not only by organized religion but also by her own National American Woman Suffrage Association. Stanton recorded her thoughts on her full life in her 1898 autobiography, *Eighty Years and More.*

Sources

Banner, Lois W. *Elizabeth Cady Stanton: A Radical for Woman's Rights.* Boston: Little, Brown, 1980.

DuBois, Ellen Carol, ed. *The Elizabeth Cady Stanton–Susan B. Anthony Reader: Correspondence, Writings, Speeches.* Boston: Northeastern University Press, 1992.

Griffith, Elisabeth. *In Her Own Right: The Life of Elizabeth Cady Stanton.* New York: Oxford University Press, 1984.

Stedman, Edmund Clarence (1833–1908) *poet, critic*

Born in Connecticut, Edmund Clarence Stedman studied at Yale University for two years before moving to New York City, where he worked as a journalist and a stockbroker. The influence of the latter experience can be readily seen in his most famous work, the poem "Pan in Wall Street" (1869). An influential critic, Stedman was a supporter of Edgar Allan POE, whose work he edited with critic George E. Woodberry (1855–1930) and published in 10 volumes in 1894–95. Stedman also was among the first to recognize the genius of Walt WHITMAN. Although Stedman published numerous volumes of poetry, collected in *Poetical Works* (1873), his criticism—particularly that in *Victorian Poets* (1875) and *Poets of America* (1885)—is considered his major achievement. His editions of *A Library of American Literature* (11 volumes, 1888–90) and *An American Anthology* (1900) helped promote an appreciation of American literature.

Sources

Scholnick, Robert J. *Edmund Clarence Stedman.* Boston: Twayne Publishers, 1977.

Steffens, Joseph Lincoln (1866–1936) *journalist*

Born in SAN FRANCISCO, Lincoln Steffens migrated to New York, where he wrote for the *Evening Post* and the *Commercial Advertiser* and worked as managing editor of *MCCLURE'S MAGAZINE* (1902–06) and associate editor of the *American* and *EVERYBODY'S* (1906–11). In his editorial positions he wielded tremendous influence, and his 1902 article in *McClure's* about corruption in the St. Louis city government is said to have launched the MUCKRAKING MOVEMENT. Steffens's articles were later collected in several books, most notably *The Shame of the Cities* (1904) and *The Struggle for Self-Government* (1909). His 1931 *Autobiography* describes how his writing evolved from sensational exposés to a deeper analysis of the common underpinnings of official corruption.

Sources

Horton, Russell M. *Lincoln Steffens.* New York: Twayne, 1974.

Kaplan, Justin. *Lincoln Steffens: A Biography.* New York: Simon & Schuster, 1974.

Sterling, George (1869–1926) *poet, playwright, critic*

Born in New York and educated by the poet-priest John B. Tabb in Maryland, Sterling migrated to California, where he became a member of a group of writers who called themselves the "Bohemian Club." Although he wrote plays for the club's shows at the Bohemian Grove, he was most prolific as a poet. His mentor and greatest influence was Ambrose BIERCE, but Sterling's sonnets, with their lush ROMANTICISM and musicality, were greatly influenced by the English poet John Keats (1795–1821). Best remembered for his poem "A Wine of Wizardry" (1907), Sterling committed suicide in 1926 at the Bohemian Club. Reportedly Jack LONDON made Sterling the model for the socialist poet Russ Brissenden in *Martin Eden* (1909).

Sources

Benediktsson, Thomas E. *George Sterling.* Boston: Twayne, 1980.

Longtin, Ray C. *Three Writers of the Far West: A Reference Guide.* Boston: G. K. Hall, 1980.

Stockton, Francis Richard (1834–1902) *short story writer, novelist*

Born in Philadelphia, Frank R. Stockton was by training an engraver and draftsman. He began his literary career writing children's stories, many of which appeared in *ST. NICHOLAS* magazine, which he also edited from 1873 to 1881. Early in his career Stockton also worked for various Philadelphia and New York newspapers, contributing humor pieces to magazines like *VANITY FAIR* and joining the staff at *SCRIBNER'S MAGAZINE*. His first novel, *Rudder Grange* (1879), about a pair of newlyweds who set up housekeeping aboard a canal boat, made him a celebrity. Bowing to popular demand, Stockton produced two sequels: *The Rudder Granges Abroad* (1891) and *Pomona's Travels* (1894).

The sensational success of his story "The Lady or the Tiger?" (1882) made it possible for Stockton to devote himself to writing adult fiction. His mature fiction did not, however, throw over the love of the fanciful and the absurd that had made his children's fiction so popular. In what is generally considered his best novel, *The Casting Away of Mrs. Lecks and Mrs. Aleshine* (1886), for example, Stockton used realistic details to underscore the absurdity of a plot involving two widows, an overpopulated desert island, and a series of marriages. As with some of his other successful fiction, he wrote a sequel to this novel: *The Dusantes* (1888). Stockton also wrote one of the first science-fiction stories, "A Tale of Gravity," which appeared in the December 1884 issue of *CENTURY ILLUSTRATED MONTHLY MAGAZINE*, which had also published "The Lady or the Tiger?" Many of his later works, such as *The Great War Syndicate* (1889), *The Great Stone of Sardis* (1898), and *A Vizier of the Two Horned Alexander* (1899), are concerned with pseudo-scientific matters.

Stockton spent the last three years of his life in West Virginia, territory he had explored in the novels *The Late Mrs. Null* (1886) and *Ardis Claverden* (1890). He continued writing almost to the end: *Kate Bonnet*, a sendup of romantic pirate tales, appeared in 1902.

Sources

Golemba, Henry L. *Frank R. Stockton.* Boston: Twayne, 1981.

Griffin, Martin J. *Frank R. Stockton: A Critical Biography.* Philadelphia: University of Pennsylvania Press, 1939.

Stoddard, Charles Warren (1843–1909) *poet, travel writer*

Born in Rochester, New York, Charles Warren Stoddard was educated in Oakland, California, and it was in the Golden State that he made the acquaintance of Bret HARTE. Stoddard contributed to Harte's magazine, *Golden Era*, and when Stoddard's first book of verse, simply titled *Poems*, was published in 1867, Harte served as editor. Stoddard then commenced a prolonged period of foreign travel, searching for good health. Two trips to Hawaii and one to Tahiti resulted in *South-Sea Idyls* (1873), which attracted many readers—Robert Louis Stevenson among them—and started a literary vogue for things Polynesian. Journeys to Egypt and the Levant resulted in the travel accounts *Mashallah!* (1880) and *A Cruise Under the Crescent* (1898).

During a prolonged stay in Hawaii (1881–84) Stoddard wrote *The Lepers of Molokai* (1885), which attracted public attention to the priest who ministered to the Hawaiian leper colony and prompted Stevenson to write a defense of the priest when he was slandered. During this three-year Hawaiian sojourn, Stoddard also wrote an account of his conversion to Roman Catholicism, *A Troubled Heart* (1885). When he returned to the mainland, Stoddard took a position as professor of English at the University of Notre Dame (1885–86), then at the Catholic University of America (1889–1902).

Sources

Austen, Roger. *Genteel Pagan: The Double Life of Charles Warren Stoddard.* Amherst: University of Massachusetts Press, 1991.

Gale, Robert L. *Charles Warren Stoddard.* Boise, Idaho: Boise State University, 1977.

Stoddard, Richard Henry (1825–1903) *poet, editor*

Born in Massachusetts, Richard Henry Stoddard was raised in poverty in New York City, where he managed to educate himself while working as an iron molder. He wrote verse influenced by the English Romantic and Victorian poets, and in 1852 he published a collection, *Poems*. Like other poets of his or any other day, he found it impossible to support his family with his verse, and in 1853 he prevailed upon his friend Nathaniel HAWTHORNE to help him obtain a position as an inspector at the New York Custom House, a favor he would himself later perform for Herman MELVILLE. After working at the Custom House as well as at other political appointments, in 1880, on the basis of reviews he had written during the previous two decades for the *NEW YORK WORLD*, Stoddard became literary editor of the New York *Mail and Express.*

Stoddard had continued to publish collections of his poetry through the years, and volumes such as *Songs of Summer* (1857), *Abraham Lincoln: An Horatian Ode* (1865), and *The Lion's Cub, and Other Poems* (1890) were greatly admired in their day. Starting in 1870, Stoddard and his wife, the novelist and poet Elizabeth Drew Stoddard (1823–1902), hosted a literary salon that was considered the center of New York literary life and included well-known figures such as Bayard TAYLOR as well as relative unknowns such as Melville. Stoddard's position as a book reviewer gave him enormous power, which he used to introduce new authors to the reading public and to dictate literary fashions. His later work included an 1894 edition of Edgar Allan POE, whom he had known when young; and *Recollections Personal and Literary* (1903), a complacent memoir in which he attacked his former acquaintance. In later times Stoddard went completely out of fashion; critics dismissed his verse as too mannered, too sentimental, and too derivative.

Stone, Lucy (1818–1893) *reformer, journalist*

Born in Massachusetts and educated at Oberlin College, Lucy Stone devoted her life to the causes of ABOLITIONISM and SUFFRAGISM. Retaining her own name after she married in 1855, she founded the *Women's Journal* in 1870, and for the next 50 years it would serve as the official publication of the National Woman Suffrage Association.

Sources

Hays, Elinor Rice. *Morning Star.* New York: Harcourt & World, 1961.

Kerr, Andrea Moore. *Lucy Stone: Speaking Out for Equality.* New Brunswick, N.J.: Rutgers University Press, 1992.

Wheeler, Leslie, ed. *Loving Warriors: Selected Letters of Lucy Stone and Henry B. Blackwell, 1853 to 1893.* New York: Dial Press, 1981.

Story, Joseph (1779–1845) *jurist, legal writer*

Born in Massachusetts, Joseph Story was active in state and federal politics before being appointed to the U.S. Supreme Court in 1811. Although he published a collection of verse, *The Power of Solitude* (1804)—which he later tried to suppress—Story's literary skills were best deployed in legal writing in works such as the three-volume *Commentaries on the Constitution of the United States* (1833) and the two-volume *On Equity Jurisprudence* (1835–36). While serving on the Supreme Court, Story also held an appointment at Harvard Law School, where he helped to modernize legal pedagogy by helping to develop the standard, institutional approach that has characterized legal education ever since.

Sources

Schwartz, Mortimer D., and John C. Hogan, eds. *Joseph Story: A Collection of Writings by and about an Eminent American Jurist.* New York: Oceana Publications, 1959.

Story, William Wetmore (1819–1895) *artist, travel writer, poet, essayist*

The son of U.S. Supreme Court Justice Joseph STORY, William Wetmore Story was born in Massachusetts and educated at Harvard. Following in his father's footsteps, he practiced law from 1838 to 1847, but he then turned his avocations, literature and art, into his vocation. He moved to Italy, where he became acquainted with many of the literary expatriates of the day and also came under the sway of artistic sentimental classicism. One of his sculptures, *Cleopatra,* would make an appearance in Nathaniel HAWTHORNE's novel *The Marble Faun* (1860). Story's first verse collection, *Poems,* appeared in 1845; a second, *Graffiti d'Italia,* much influenced by the work of Story's friend Robert Browning (1812–89), was published in 1868. Story also published popular collections of essays and travel pieces, such as *Excursions in Art and Literature* (1891), and a play, *Nero* (1875). Henry JAMES's *William Wetmore Story and His Friends* (1903) explores the interests and interactions of the circle that formed around Story during his years in Rome.

Sources

Earnest, Ernest P. *Expatriates and Patriots: American Artists, Scholars, and Writers in Europe.* Durham, N.C.: Duke University Press, 1968.

Excursions in Art and Letters. Freeport, N.Y.: Books for Libraries Press, 1891; reprint, 1972.

James, Henry. *William Wetmore Story and His Friends: From Letters, Diaries, and Recollections.* 1903. Reprint, New York: Kennedy Galleries, 1969.

Stowe, Harriet Elizabeth Beecher (1811–1896) *novelist*

Harriet Beecher Stowe was the daughter of the Reverend Lyman BEECHER, a prominent clergyman known for his Calvinist convictions. She was brought up in Connecticut and learned to temper her father's pessimistic view of human nature with her uncle Samuel Foote's liberalism and the romances of Sir Walter Scott (1771–1832). Thus, at a very early age Stowe found a way to meld the moral earnestness of her ancestors with a more outgoing, genial, and even entertaining democratic sensibility.

In 1832 the Beecher family moved to Cincinnati, where Harriet taught at a girl's school and began to write her impressions of New England. In 1836 she married C. E. Stowe, a colleague of her father's. She visited nearby Kentucky, observed the behavior of slaveholders, and fortified her outrage with abolitionist sentiments.

The Stowes moved to Maine in 1850. Aroused again by the antislavery cause, Harriet wrote her immensely popular and influential novel, *UNCLE TOM'S CABIN* (1852). The novel's power derived not merely from her moral outrage but also from her skillful employment of melodrama and her ability to create a Christian saint in the figure of the slave Uncle Tom. Tom, a suffering black man, was also a symbol of a humble yet noble turn-the-other-cheek hero. Much later Uncle Tom would become a shameful symbol to militant African Americans who rejected both his passivity and his brand of Christianity, but in the context of Stowe's time, Uncle Tom invigorated everyone who supported the abolition of slavery (see ABOLITIONISM).

Perhaps even more important than the novel itself were the countless dramatizations of it that moved audiences across the country, many of them illiterate and thus only able to experience the missionary momentum of the novel through stage performances. The dramatizations, as much as the novel, made Stowe a public figure. The facts of her work were attacked by proslavery forces, and the controversy over her account of a slave society became so intense that in 1853 she published *A Key to Uncle Tom's Cabin,* a record of the data she had drawn from laws, court documents, newspapers, and correspondence.

Stowe's fame went well beyond the borders of her own country. She was cheered in England, honored by Queen Victoria, and wrote about her visit in *Sunny Memories of Foreign Lands* (1854). She wrote a kind of sequel to *Uncle Tom's Cabin,* entitled *Dred: A Tale of the Dismal Swamp* (1856), which shifted the focus from the suffering of slaves to the corrupting consequences of being a slaveholder. She modeled her rugged black protagonist on Nat Turner (1800–31), leader of the only successful slave revolt in American history.

Much of Stowe's other writing concentrated on New England culture. *The Minister's Wooing* (1859) is a ROMANCE that contains an attack on Calvinism. *The Pearl of Orr's Island* (1862) and especially *Oldtown Folks* (1869) are charming examples of LOCAL COLOR writing. Her later books in a similar vein include *Sam Lawson's Oldtown Fireside Stories* (1872) and *Poganuc People* (1872), which draws on memories of her childhood.

In a different mode, Stowe wrote *Agnes of Sorrention* (1862), a historical romance set in Italy, and two novels promoting the right of women to have careers: *My Wife and I* (1871) and *We and Our Neighbors* (1875). She published her *Religious Poems* in 1867.

After the CIVIL WAR the Stowes moved to Florida; Stowe described her life there in *Palmetto-Leaves* (1873). *The Life and Letters of Harriet Beecher Stowe* appeared in 1897.

Sources

Adams, John R. *Harriet Beecher Stowe.* Boston: Twayne, 1989.

Davison, Moira. *Uncle Tom's Cabin and Mid-Nineteenth Century United States.* Jefferson, N.C.: McFarland, 1985.

Hedrick, Joan. *Harriet Beecher Stowe: A Life.* New York: Oxford University Press, 1994.

Holmes, Edward M. *Harriet Beecher Stowe: Woman and Artist.* Orono, Me.: Northern Lights, 1991.

Kimball, Gayle. *The Religious Ideas of Harriet Beecher Stowe: Her Gospel of Womanhood.* New York: Mellen Press, 1982.

Stratemeyer, Edward (1863–1930) *writer of children's literature, editor*

A native of New Jersey, Edward Stratemeyer used a number of different pen names to produce numerous popular series of fiction for young readers. Under the name Arthur M. Winfield he published 20 volumes of Rover Boys adventures, his most popular series, between 1899 and 1916. A 10-volume sequel that appeared between 1917 and 1936—also under the Winfield pseudonym—concerned the second generation of Rover Boys. Beginning in 1910 Stratemeyer used the same pen name to produce 40 volumes about the boy inventor Tom Swift. When he turned to writing books for girls, he used the name Laura Lee Hope for books about the Bobbsey Twins, and books about the girl detective Nancy Drew were written under the name Carolyn Keene. Stratemeyer's formula for juvenile fiction was so popular that in 1914 he organized a Stratemeyer Literary Syndicate to produce novels from his outlines. Stratemeyer's daughter, Harriet Stratemeyer Adams (1894–1982), continued the Nancy Drew series as Carolyn Keene, and as Franklin W. Dixon she also wrote the Hardy Boys mystery stories, which the Syndicate had begun in 1927. The Syndicate continued to produce works even after Stratemeyer's death.

Sources

Billman, Carol. *The Secret of the Stratemeyer Syndicate: Nancy Drew, the Hardy Boys, and the Million Dollar Fiction Factory.* New York: Ungar, 1986.

Dizer, John T. *Tom Swift & Company: "Boys' Books" by Stratemeyer and Others.* Jefferson, N.C.: McFarland & Co., 1982.

Johnson, Deidre. *Edward Stratemeyer and the Stratemeyer Syndicate.* New York: Twayne, 1993.

suffragism (c. 1848–1920) *social movement*

The struggle for the right to vote primarily concerned two groups of Americans: blacks and women. Inevitably, the abolitionist movement (see ABOLITIONISM) and the suffragist movement were bound together for much of the second half of the 19th century. The beginning of the suffragist movement can be traced to July 1848, when Elizabeth Cady STANTON and Lucretia Mott (1793–1880), both active in the antislavery campaign, called for a Woman's Rights Convention. The two had met eight years earlier at a World Anti-Slavery Convention where women delegates were denied the floor because of their sex. Realizing that women could not fight slavery if they themselves were denied the voting franchise, Stanton and Mott drafted a Declaration of Sentiments, modeled on the Declaration of Independence, in which the most radical demand was for what came to be known as "woman suffrage."

During the CIVIL WAR most suffragists turned their attention to the war effort, but immediately afterward many found their hopes dashed when the 14th Amendment, ratified in 1866, granted the full rights of citizenship to African-American men alone. The 15th Amendment, ultimately ratified in 1870 and specifically granting African-American men the right to vote, split the suffragist movement in two. While some feminist leaders like Lucy STONE and Julia Ward HOWE urged women to set their aspirations aside in order to work for black suffrage, another camp, led by Stanton and Susan B. ANTHONY, opposed the 15th Amendment because it excluded women. In the women's rights magazine *Revolution,* Stanton used racist and nativist rhetoric to urge support for women's voting rights.

Stanton began to lobby for a woman suffrage amendment to the Constitution in 1869. It would take half a century and another war for suffragists to realize this dream. The movement for a Constitutional amendment gained momentum during the Progressive Era, which lasted from roughly 1890 to 1920 and included other reform movements such as MUCKRAKING and trustbusting. During this period the suffragists healed their rift and linked the need for a women's ballot to such causes as labor reform, peace, and temperance. Reformers like Jane ADDAMS, Ida B. WELLS-BARNETT, and the feminist author Charlotte Perkins GILMAN all spoke out in favor of woman suffrage.

Inevitably, the suffragists' momentum inspired a backlash. Perhaps not surprisingly, the liquor industry, which feared prohibition, was among the movement's most powerful critics. With the onset of World War I, however, the nation needed grain more for food than for intoxicating beverages, and passage of the 1917 Lever Act, prohibiting the use of grain for the manufacture of alcohol, led inexorably to the 18th Amendment, which was ratified in 1919 and instituted nationwide prohibition. World War I freed women not only from the stranglehold of the liquor lobby but also from many traditional social constraints. With so many men fighting a war in Europe, women flooded into the workplace. President Woodrow WILSON, who had previously opposed woman suffrage, now bowed to necessity and, citing the need for national unity in time of war, endorsed the 19th Amendment. When it was ratified in 1920, women were finally granted full citizenship, including the right to vote.

Sources

Kugler, Israel. *From Ladies to Women: The Organized Struggle for Woman's Rights in the Reconstruction Era.* New York: Greenwood Press, 1987.

Terborg-Penn, Rosalyn. *African American Women in the Struggle for the Vote, 1850–1920.* Bloomington: Indiana University Press, 1998.

Wang, Xi. *The Trial of Democracy: Black Suffrage and Northern Republicans, 1860–1910.* Athens: University of Georgia Press, 1997.

Sumner, William Graham (1840–1910) *economist, sociologist, biographer*

Born in New Jersey and educated at Yale University, William Graham Sumner served as a professor of social science at his alma mater from 1872 to 1909. From this pulpit he preached the gospel of free trade and laissez-faire, arguing that government interference in the marketplace was too political to be rational in treatises such as *What Social Classes Mean to Each Other* (1883) and *Protectionism* (1885). His theories about the organization of society emphasized the interrelationships among organizations, and in *Folkways* (1907) Sumner attempted to trace the evolution of social institutions. Sumner also wrote biographies of President Andrew Jackson (1882) and founding fathers Alexander Hamilton (1890) and Robert Morris (1892). When Sumner died, he left unfinished four volumes of essays, including his four-volume *Science in Society,* edited by A. G. Keller and published in 1929.

Sources

Curtis, Bruce. *William Graham Sumner.* Boston: Twayne, 1981.

Davie, Maurice R. *William Graham Sumner.* New York: Crowell, 1963.

McCloskey, Robert G. *American Conservatism in the Age of Enterprise: A Study of William Graham Sumner, Stephen J. Field, and Andrew Carnegie.* Cambridge, Mass.: Harvard University Press, 1951.

Survey Graphic, The *periodical*

This journal first saw life as *Charities,* the official publication of the New York Charity Organization Society. In 1897 it was renamed *The Survey.* In 1912, after the magazine endorsed Theodore ROOSEVELT for president, the Society withdrew its support and the magazine was rechristened *The Survey Graphic,* becoming a liberal journal whose concentration on American social problems attracted an audience of social workers. In its period of greatest influence, it published pieces by such important reformers as Lincoln STEFFENS, Jacob RIIS, and Ida TARBELL. The magazine folded in 1952 when the illness of its long-time editor, Paul Kellogg, forced his resignation.

Swedenborgianism *religious movement*

Based on the philosophy of the Swedish theologian Emanuel Swedenborg (1688–1772), Swedenborgianism is a system of largely mystical religious beliefs. For Swedenborg, nature itself, not only the Bible, was a text to be read for spiritual meaning. According to him, God is one being and the Trinity merely a division of essences, whereby the Father is love, the Son is the Word sent to redeem mankind, and the Holy Spirit a proceeding whereby love and life are combined as act. Man, Swedenborg declared, could aspire to a state of infinite perfectibility by working with the spirit of Jesus in love and obedience.

Originally a scientist, Swedenborg claimed to have received a divine vision in April 1744 in which the true sense of the scriptures was revealed to him. Thereafter he devoted himself to expounding his vision in works such as *Heaven and Hell* (1758) and *The Apocalypse Revealed* (1758). Believing that any Christian church could incorporate his teaching, Swedenborg established no church of his own, but in London in 1788, members of his sect organized The Church of the New Jerusalem, which created its first American affiliate in Baltimore in 1792. One of its early leaders in the United States was Sampson Reed (1800–80), whose writings greatly influenced Ralph Waldo EMERSON, and through Emerson and others, the transcendentalist movement (see TRANSCEN-

DENTALISM). Numerous other figures important to American literary history, ranging from the legendary Johnny Appleseed (John CHAPMAN) to the philosopher Henry JAMES Sr., were strongly impressed with the doctrines espoused by the small but widespread sect fostered by the 17th-century Swedish mystic.

Sources

Myers, Mary Ann. *A New World Jerusalem: The Swedenborgian Experience in Community Construction.* Westport, Conn.: Greenwood Press, 1983.

Tales of the Grotesque and Arabesque Edgar Allan Poe (1839) *short-story collection*

Edgar Allan POE's first collection of tales appeared in two volumes published in December 1839. Poe took his title from an essay by Sir Walter Scott, and included in this collection of 25 pieces some of his most memorable fiction. Highlights include "MS. Found in a Bottle," a tale about a ghost ship that may have influenced Herman MELVILLE's story "The Ghost Ship" (1839). In "The Assignation," which includes Poe's poem "To One in Paradise," an unsuspecting narrator witnesses the fulfillment of a suicide pact between adulterous lovers. "Berenice" concerns an unhealthy young man's grotesque obsession with his epileptic cousin's white teeth. "Morella" is a tale of revenge in which an unloved wife dies but comes back to haunt her husband in the form of their beloved child. In "Ligeia," another tale about reincarnation, a beloved first wife dies, only to return in the form of a second wife's corpse. "The Fall of the House of Usher," perhaps Poe's most masterful work, is a symbolist work that tells a story about an incestuously close brother and sister indirectly by focusing on the disintegration of their ancient family seat. In "William Wilson," when the hero succeeds in killing the döppleganger who has haunted his life, he also kills himself. Reviewers recognized Poe's originality and skill, but his collection failed to sell widely and was largely accounted a failure at the time.

Sources

May, Charles E. *Edgar Allan Poe: A Study of the Short Fiction.* Boston: Twayne, 1991.

Silverman, Kenneth, ed. *New Essays on Poe's Major Tales.* New York: Cambridge University Press, 1993.

Smith, Andrew. *Gothic Radicalism: Literature, Philosophy, and Psychoanalysis in the Nineteenth Century.* New York: St. Martin's Press, 2000.

tall tale *genre*

This type of satirical fiction, characterized by either exaggeration or gross understatement, made its first published appearance in the early days of the republic in the Rev. Samuel A. Peters's *General History of Connecticut* (1781). The form was further refined by Washington IRVING in his *History of New York by Deidrich Knickerbocker* (1809). In part because the effectiveness of the tall tale often depended upon the device of having an outsider as the audience for the tale, the tall tale genre is usually associated with the frontier, or with the West, about which easterners knew little but were willing to believe much.

Frontier tall tales were originally strictly oral rather than written, and it was in this mode that such mythic—or mythologized—characters as Paul BUNYAN, JOHN HENRY, and Mike FINK were invented. The reported exploits of such historic figures as Daniel BOONE (1734–1820) and Davy CROCKETT were only one step removed from purest invention: the Crockett *Almanacs,* some 50 of which appeared between 1835 and 1856 and were attributed to Crockett or his heirs, were filled with aggrandizing stories about the author and various real and imaginary characters.

Soon the tall tale became a literary genre in its own right, with mock oral tales written by frontier journalists "reprinted" in such newspapers as *The Spirit of the Times.* Amateur writers contributed their own send-ups as well, but soon professional writers of fiction were making a mark in the form. Among the best known and best loved of these literary products are Augustus Baldwin LONGSTREET's *Georgia Scenes* (1835), T. B. THORPE's "THE BIG BEAR OF ARKANSAS" (1839), and George Washington HARRIS's "Sut Lovingood" yarns (1867). This "western" approach to the tall tale reached it apogee with Mark Twain's (Samuel Langhorne CLEMENS) autobiographical travel book, *Life on the Mississippi* (1883), recounting his apprenticeship as a steamboat captain.

"Down East" Yankee tall tales were of a somewhat different order, often featuring a dim-witted individual who is not party to the jokes he tells. The folk hero Captain Stormalong, giant hero of the sea, is about as close as eastern tall tales came to their more farfetched western counterparts.

Sources

Brown, Carolyn S. *The Tall Tale in American Folklore and Literature.* Knoxville: University of Tennessee Press, 1987.

Dorson, Richard M. *Man and Beast in American Comic Legend.* Bloomington: Indiana University Press, 1982.

Wonham, Henry B. *Mark Twain and the Art of the Tall Tale.* New York: Oxford University Press, 1993.

Tarbell, Ida Minerva (1857–1944) *journalist, historian, biographer*

Born in Erie County, Pennsylvania, Ida Tarbell first made a name for herself in 1901 as the biographer of Napoleon Bonaparte. This work was serialized in *MCCLURE'S MAGAZINE*, where she went on to publish a number of muckraking articles exposing corruption and waste in American business and politics. Tarbell's belief that her father, who had worked in Pennsylvania oil fields, had been victimized by Standard Oil culminated in her exposé of the company in *The History of the Standard Oil Company* (1902). This work made her one of the most celebrated journalists in the country and a leading light of the MUCKRAKING MOVEMENT in the American press. Among other works, Tarbell also wrote a life of Abraham LINCOLN (1900) and an autobiography, *All in a Day's Work* (1939).

Sources

Brady, Kathleen. *Ida Tarbell: Portrait of a Muckraker.* New York: Seaview/Putnam, 1984.

Kochersberger, Robert C., ed. *More Than a Muckraker: Ida Tarbell's Lifetime in Journalism.* Knoxville: University of Tennessee Press, 1994.

Taylor, James Bayard (1825–1878) *poet, travel writer, novelist*

A Quaker from Pennsylvania, Bayard Taylor began to write poetry early, expressing a lifelong yearning to travel. He published his first book of romantic poetry, *Ximena,* in 1844 and then embarked on travels to Europe, collecting his impressions in letters sent to the *NEW-YORK TRIBUNE* in *Views A-foot* (1846). Taylor's forte was finding exotic detail. When the newspaper sent him to California to report on the 1849 gold rush, he took the opportunity to portray himself as an adventurer in his two-volume *Eldorado* (1850).

By 1851 Taylor was off to Egypt, Abyssinia (Ethiopia), Turkey, India, and China—trips that resulted in the publication of *A Journey to Central Africa* (1854), *The Lands of the Saracen* (1855), and *A Visit to India, China, and Japan, in the Year 1853* (1855). These books put Taylor in enormous demand as a public lecturer in the United States. Indeed, he was one of the key figures in inventing the author tour and the role of author as public celebrity catering to public demand.

To his public image of a gallivanting journalist Taylor added the figure of romantic poet, publishing *Rhymes of Travel, Ballads and Poems* (1849), *A Book of Romances, Lyrics, and Songs* (1852), and *Poems of the Orient* (1855). He then initiated another cycle of travel and writing and lecturing in the late 1850s, documented in *Northern Travel* (1858), *Travels in Greece and Russia* (1859), and *At Home and Abroad* (1860).

In the 1860s Taylor turned to the novel, writing a love story, *Hannah Turston* (1863), set in upstate New York, and *John Godfrey,* a vivid portrait of New York literary life. He wrote about small-town and rural life in *The Story of Kennett* (1866) and *Joseph and His Friend* (1870), both set in Pennsylvania where he grew up.

Taylor collected his stories of America and the world of his travels in *Beauty and the Beast and Tales of Home* (1872). He complemented his prose with *Home Pastorals, Ballads, and Lyrics* (1875) and *The Echo Club and Other Literary Diversions* (1876), which contained lampoons of Whitman and other poets of the day.

The versatile and learned Taylor became a professor of German at Cornell (1870–77) and published a translation of Goethe's *Faust* in two volumes (1870–71). Of all his work, critics consider this the most important—a serious achievement that towers over his rather superficial fictions and verses.

The Life and Letters of Bayard Taylor appeared in 1885 and *Selected Letters of Bayard Taylor* in 1997.

Sources

Cary, Richard. *The Genteel Circle: Bayard Taylor and his New York Friends.* Ithaca, N.Y.: Cornell University Press, 1952.

Croom, Richmond Beatty. *Bayard Taylor: Laureate of the Gilded Age.* Norman: University of Oklahoma Press, 1936.

Teasdale, Sara (1884–1933) *poet*

Born in St. Louis, Missouri, Sara Teasdale became associated with Harriet Monroe's "LITTLE MAGAZINE," *Poetry,* which was based in Chicago. The author of eight volumes of poetry, Teasdale is best remembered for short, spare verses that were meant to conjure up a mood rather than to explore ideas. She knew considerable popularity during her lifetime, and her volume *Love Songs* (1917) won the Columbia University Poetry Society Prize (later the Pulitzer Prize for poetry) and the Poetry Society of America Prize.

Sources

Schoen, Carol. *Sara Teasdale.* Boston: Twayne, 1986.

Teasdale, Sara. *The Collected Poems of Sara Teasdale.* New York: Macmillan, 1937.

"Tell-Tale Heart, The" *Edgar Allan Poe* (1843) *short story*

The plot of Edgar Allan POE's tale of murder and madness, first published in a BOSTON magazine called *The Pioneer,* is fairly straightforward: A disturbed boarder kills his landlord, dismembers the old man's body, and then confesses his crime when the police come to investigate. What is most arresting about the story is its technique, said to be a forerunner of modern fictional treatments of the subconscious. Poe's protagonist is also his narrator, and thus readers are privy to the madman's thoughts as his nervous disorder, which makes him unnaturally sensitive, drives him to murder. His landlord, he declares, has one filmed blue eye that casts a pall over his own existence. In order to rid himself of this manifestation of what he believes is the "evil eye," the narrator resolves to kill the old man. After keeping vigil in his landlord's bedroom for a week, he wakens his frightened victim, whose accelerated heartbeat so infuriates the madman that he crushes the old man beneath his heavy bed and—so the narrator thinks—silences his heartbeat forever.

The narrator next dismembers his victim's body and hides it under some floorboards, citing the care with which he performs these tasks as evidence of his sanity. He has, however, forgotten to remove the old man's watch from the body. When police come to investigate a neighbor's report of screams coming from the house, the narrator explains that the scream was his, induced by a nightmare. His landlord, he says, is temporarily out of town. So sure is he of the perfection of his crime that the narrator invites the police into the house. But as the narrator stands chatting with the officers, he suddenly hears a rhythmic sound he believes to be the beating of the old man's heart. Convinced that the police cannot help but hear the "tell-tale heart" beneath the boards, the narrator hysterically confesses his crime.

Sources

Burduck, Michael L. *Grim Phantasms: Fear in Poe's Short Fiction.* New York: Garland, 1992.

Smith, Andrew. *Gothic Radicalism: Literature, Philosophy, and Psychoanalysis in the Nineteenth Century.* New York: St. Martin's Press, 2000.

temperance movement (c.1808–1919) *reform movement*

Although efforts to ban production and consumption of alcoholic beverages existed in the United States even before the Revolutionary War, the movement gained momentum in the later decades of the 19th century, when it was taken up by groups also agitating for women's suffrage (see SUFFRAGISM). In 1808 a group in Saratoga, New York, took a public pledge not to drink intoxicating beverages. Other formal organizations—many of them church-sponsored—sprang up, inspired by the success of such tracts as Timothy Shay ARTHUR's *Ten Nights in a Barroom and What I Saw There* (1854). Many of these groups, however, refused to admit women and African Americans. The World Temperance Convention held in New York in 1853 was the first to admit women, although no blacks were permitted to attend.

During the CIVIL WAR the temperance movement took a back seat, in both the North and the South, to the war effort. Afterward, however, the movement was reborn, this time trading its religious orientation for more direct political action. The movement maintained the air of a moral crusade, but its leaders began to appeal to voters in an effort to legislate morality. Women, still secondary players in the movement, took matters into their own hands, abandoning their auxiliary missionary societies in favor of on-site agitation in beer halls and saloons. Perhaps the best known—and certainly one of the most colorful—of these activists was Carry Nation, who made her name wielding a hatchet amidst liquor barrels. In 1874, the Woman's Christian Temperance Union (WCTU) was founded in Cleveland, Ohio, and under its second president, Frances Willard (1839–98), became the largest and most influential women's organization in the nation. The WCTU took on other causes, such as prison reform and world peace, but they were most successful at linking temperance with woman suffrage, which leaders such as Susan B. ANTHONY pitched less as a right than as a means to protect the family and improve society.

The temperance movement gained considerable political power, culminating in the ratification, in 1919, of the Eighteenth Amendment to the Constitution, which made Prohibition the law of the land. The Eighteenth Amendment would be repealed in 1933, but in the meantime, women's suffrage, which had been delayed by liquor industry lobbying, became a reality with the ratification of the Twenty-first Amendment in 1920.

Sources

Bordin, Ruth Birgitta Anderson. *Woman and Temperance: The Quest for Power and Liberty, 1873–1900.* Philadelphia: Temple University Press, 1981.

Epstein, Barbara L. *The Politics of Domesticity: Women, Evangelism, and Temperance in Nineteenth-Century America.* Middletown, Conn.: Wesleyan University Press, 1981.

"Thanatopsis" *William Cullen Bryant* (1817) *poem*

William Cullen BRYANT first wrote this blank-verse poem—whose title translates from the Greek as "view of death"—when he was 17 years old and under the influence of such meditations on mortality as Robert Blair's *The Grave* (1743) and William Cowper's *The Task* (1785). The poem was further revised before it first appeared in the September 1817 issue of the *NORTH AMERICAN REVIEW*, and by the time "Thanatopsis" was published in Bryant's first collection of poems in 1821, it had new opening and concluding stanzas. These stanzas entirely recast the poem, removing it from the philosophical influence of the melancholy English "graveyard" school of poets. Instead of having the poet's "better genius" serve as the narrative voice, a personified Nature counters "thoughts of the last bitter hour" with a pantheistic faith in the unity of life. This change made Bryant's poem into a kind of pagan celebration of death, in which visions of the Christian afterlife are replaced by a vision of final "communion with the visible forms of nature."

Sources

Brown, Charles H. *William Cullen Bryant.* New York: Scribner, 1971.

McLean, Albert F. *William Cullen Bryant.* Boston: Twayne, 1989.

Theory of the Leisure Class, The Thorstein Veblen (1899) *treatise*

Subtitled "An Economic Study of Institutions," Thorstein VEBLEN's early examination of the concept of status in America proved to be immediately popular, making its author, an economics and social sciences professor, an unlikely celebrity. The book also proved enormously influential in the field of economics.

Veblen theorized that turn-of-the-century social structures were remnants of feudal times, "atavistic cultural survivals" that perpetuated social classes that arose in conjunction with the institution of ownership. While the lower classes struggle at industrial pursuits in order to support the whole of society, the aristocratic leisure class occupies itself with "conspicuous leisure and conspicuous consumption." This consumption itself determines who will be admitted to the leisure class, so that, in Veblen's view, waste—that is, any activity not contributing to material productivity—begets waste. The lack of balance in American society's social structure was, he argued, inherently regressive.

Veblen was reacting to the society he saw around him, the aftermath of the GILDED AGE, in which industrial robber barons seemed to govern an economy to which the government had adopted a laissez faire attitude. *The Theory of the Leisure Class* profoundly affected ordinary citizens'—as well as politicians'—views about the structure of American society and almost certainly contributed to the trust-busting, labor organizing, and other progressive reforms that greeted the new century. Veblen certainly had his detractors, however. Academics objected to his methods, and such defenders of cultural and aristocratic values as H. L. Mencken (1880–1956) derided Veblen's lack of discrimination. Mencken's attack, "Professor Veblen and the Cow," which first appeared in the May 1919 issue of *THE SMART SET*, was almost as unrelenting as *The Theory of the Leisure Class* itself.

Sources

Diggins, John P. *Bard of Savagery: Thorstein Veblen, Theorist of the Leisure Class.* Princeton, N.J.: Princeton University Press, 1999.

Dorfman, Joseph. *Thorstein Veblen and His America.* 1961. Reprint, New York: A.M. Kelley, 1966.

Jorgensen, Elizabeth Watkins, and Henry Irvin Jorgensen. *Thorstein Veblen: Victorian Firebrand.* Armonk, N.Y.: M.E. Sharpe, 1999.

Thomas, Augustus (1857–1934) *playwright*

Born in St. Louis, Missouri, and largely self-educated, Augustus Thomas worked as a cartoonist for the *Post-Dispatch*, as a theatrical agent, and as a mind reader in his native city, where his first two plays were produced by amateur companies. In the late 1880s Thomas left for New York, where he expanded his first produced play, an adaptation of Frances Hodgson BURNETT's *Editha's Burglar* (1888), into a four-act play titled *The Burglar* which, starting in 1889, ran for 10 years on BROADWAY. On the basis of this success, Thomas succeeded Dion BOUCICAULT as script doctor for the Madison Square Theatre. He also began writing original dramas, many of which were based on American themes, such as *In Mizzoura* (1893), concerning the love of a western sheriff for a young girl; and *Arizona* (1900), centering on a group of soldiers in the Arizona Territory. Thomas also wrote popular comedies and produced some 60 plays. Criticized for working too quickly and unevenly, he was also praised for his determination to bring a decidedly American idiom to Broadway.

Sources

Davis, Ronald J. *Augustus Thomas.* Boston: Twayne, 1984.

Thompson, Daniel Pierce (1795–1868) *novelist, historian*

Reared in rural Vermont and educated at Middlebury College, Daniel Pierce Thompson first distinguished himself as a lawyer and jurist, compiling the state code, *Laws of Vermont*, in 1835. His literary career began in 1835 with publication of *The Adventures of Timothy Peacock, Esq.*, a satire of the mysterious practices of Masonry in his state. His *The Green Mountain Boys* (1839), a historical novel about Ethan Allen (1738–89) and New Hampshire land grants, proved to be highly popular, setting the course for the remainder of his writing life. Aside from the abolitionist journal *Green Mountain Freeman,* which Thompson published from 1849 until after the CIVIL WAR, he wrote fictional works based on the history and customs of his native region. He also wrote a *History of Vermont and the Northern Campaign of 1777* (1851) and a *History of the Town of Montpelier* (1860).

Sources

Flitcroft, John E. *The Novelist of Vermont: A Biographical and Critical Study of Daniel Pierce Thompson.* Cambridge, Mass.: Harvard University Press, 1929.

Thomson, Mortimer Neal (Q.K. Philander Doesticks) (1831–1875) *journalist, humorist*

One of America's first professional humorists, Mortimer Neal Thomson (or Thompson) also wrote serious journalism, serving as a Southern correspondent for the *NEW-YORK TRIBUNE* during the CIVIL WAR. In 1854, however, he adopted the pen name "Q.K." (for "Queer Kritter") Philander Doesticks, P. B., and began publishing parodies in periodicals like *SPIRIT OF THE TIMES.* His first collection of sketches was published as *Doesticks, What He Says* (1855); he went on to publish *Plu-ri-bus-tah, A Song That's By No Author* (1856), a lengthy parody of Henry Wadsworth LONGFELLOW's "Hiawatha" that covered feminism, P. T. BARNUM, the civil war over Kansas's slaveholding status, the Know-Nothing political movement, SPIRITUALISM, free love, and greed. In addition to parodying other writers such as the satirical poet William Allen Butler (1825–1902), Thomson also published his *Tribune* pieces on criminals as *The History and Records of the Elephant Club* (1856) and on fortune tellers as *The Witches, Prophets, and Planet Readers of New York* (1859).

Thoreau, Henry David (1817–1862) *autobiographer, poet*

Henry David Thoreau was born in Concord, Massachusetts. Unlike many of his fellow transcendentalists who came primarily from Puritan and colonial stock, Thoreau's French, Quaker, and Scottish ancestry—added to a Puritan strain—produced a sensibility that made him stand out. Although Ralph Waldo EMERSON became famous for his essay "Nature," it was Thoreau who more directly lived the experience of the wood and described himself as a naturalist.

Thoreau graduated from Harvard in 1837 and came under Emerson's spell, taking to heart the older writer's belief that men must immerse themselves in the natural environment and thereby come to grips with universal principles. Thoreau did so by traveling on the Concord and Merrimack rivers and then writing about it in *A Week on the Concord and Merrimack Rivers* (1849). It is revealing as well that when Thoreau lived with Emerson for two years (1841–43) he worked as a handyman, using his hands and performing physical labor that put him into direct contact with his world.

Thoreau's great adventure was his stay at Walden Pond, which he transformed into his classic book *WALDEN* (1854). Thoreau's time at Walden was relatively short—a little more than a year. But his stay was symbolic, a statement about a man's desire to confront his own talents and come to an understanding of his convictions. Unlike other transcendentalists, Thoreau was not attracted to Utopian communities like FRUITLANDS and BROOK FARM. Instead he wished to study nature and human nature on his own. He made it plain that he was not setting himself up as a representative man or recommending a particular way of life. On the contrary, Walden was only his way of finding out about himself and the world around him.

During his stay at Walden, Thoreau was imprisoned for refusing to pay the poll tax that supported the MEXICAN WAR. To him the war masked the desire for territory and the greed of Southern slaveholders who wanted to expand their economy in the West. Like other transcendentalists, Thoreau was a staunch abolitionist (see ABOLITIONISM). He later welcomed John BROWN's assault on Harper's Ferry and expressed his approval in three public lectures. Out of his jail stay came one of his classic essays, "CIVIL DISOBEDIENCE" (1849), in which he argued for the primacy of the individual conscience over government dictates.

Thoreau viewed nature through both scientific and mystical sensibilities; indeed this dualism is what makes his prose so intriguing as both a record of precise observation and an evocation of values that transcend the material world. His friend, William Ellery CHANNING (2), called him a "poet-naturalist."

Thoreau traveled extensively in New England and wrote about his experiences in manuscripts that were published after his death as *Excursions* (1863), *The Maine Woods* (1864), *Cape Cod* (1865), and *A Yankee in Canada* (1866). He continued his travels and his abolitionist activities in spite of the tuberculosis that finally killed him. Before his death Thoreau had planned to write an extensive study of the Indians. He gathered material on a trip South in 1861, but he could not recover his health and realized that he would soon die. He spent his remaining days putting his journals in order.

Thoreau's complete *Journals* were published in 14 volumes in 1906. A lost journal appeared in 1958, the same year as his *Correspondence.* His *Collected Poems* were published in 1943. Notes and fragments that Thoreau did not prepare for publication appeared in 1993 as *Faith in a Seed: "The Dispersion of Seeds" and Other Late Natural History Writings.* They are a remarkable record of his observations and thoughts about nature.

Sources

Harding, Walter. *The Days of Henry Thoreau: A Biography.* New York: Dover Publications, 1982.

Myerson, Joel, ed. *The Cambridge Companion to Henry David Thoreau.* New York: Cambridge University Press, 1995.

Paul, Sherman, ed. *Thoreau: A Collection of Critical Essays.* Englewood Cliffs, N.J.: Prentice Hall, 1962.

Thorpe, Thomas Bangs (1815–1878) *short story writer, editor*

This humorist of the OLD SOUTHWEST was in fact born in Massachusetts. T. B. Thorpe did, however, live in Louisiana from 1833 to 1853, during which time he owned and edited several newspapers and wrote his most famous work, "THE BIG BEAR OF ARKANSAS," often called the most famous tall tale of the Southwest. This tale was published in 1841 in the New York journal *SPIRIT OF THE TIMES,* which Thorpe would also edit. Thorpe's other regionalist sketches were collected in *The Mysteries of the Back Woods* (1846), *The Hive of the Bee Hunter* (1854), and *Colonel Thorpe's Scenes of Arkansas* (1858). Thorpe served in the MEXICAN WAR and turned this experience into literature in *Our Army on the Rio Grande* (1846), *Our Army at Monterey* (1847), and *The Taylor Anecdote Book* (1848), based on General Zachary Taylor's exploits. Thorpe served as a colonel during the CIVIL WAR, and from 1869 until his death he held a civil service position in the New York Custom House.

Sources

Estes, David C., ed. *A New Collection of Thomas Bangs Thorpe's Sketches of the Old Southwest.* Baton Rouge: Louisiana State University Press, 1989.

Rickels, Milton. *Thomas Bangs Thorpe: Humorist of the Old Southwest.* Baton Rouge: Louisiana State University Press, 1962.

Ticknor, George (1791–1871) *biographer, literary historian*

Born in BOSTON, George Ticknor entered Dartmouth College when he was 14 years old. After a grand tour of the Atlantic States (1814–15) and travel abroad (1815–19) with his friend Edward EVERETT, Ticknor undertook graduate studies in Göttingen, Germany, and traveled through Latin America before becoming, at age 25, the first Abiel Smith Professor of the French and Spanish Languages and Literatures and Professor of Belles Lettres at Harvard. After systematizing course materials and stimulating the interest of aspiring poets in romantic literature, in 1835 Ticknor resigned his post to tour Europe once again in preparation for writing his influential three-volume *History of Spanish Literature* (1849). In addition to writing biographies of his friend the historian William Hickling PRESCOTT (*Life of William Hickling Prescott,* 1863) and a *Life of Lafayette* (1824), Ticknor devoted himself to improving the Boston Public Library, which upon his death inherited his matchless collection of Spanish literature.

Sources

Earnest, Ernest P. *Expatriates and Patriots: American Artists, Scholars, and Writers in Europe.* Durham, N.C.: Duke University Press, 1968.

Tyack, David B. *George Ticknor and the Boston Brahmins.* Cambridge, Mass.: Harvard University Press, 1967.

Ticknor, William Davis (1810–1864) *publisher*

In 1832 William Davis Ticknor founded the BOSTON publishing firm that was known after 1854 as Ticknor & Fields. In addition to publishing such literary lights as Nathaniel HAWTHORNE, Ralph Waldo EMERSON, and Oliver Wendell HOLMES, Ticknor & Fields published the *ATLANTIC MONTHLY* and *THE NORTH AMERICAN REVIEW.* The firm also owned the Old Corner Bookstore, a Boston institution.

Sources

Ticknor, Caroline. *Hawthorne and His Publisher.* Boston: Houghton Mifflin, 1913.

Timrod, Henry (1828–1867) *poet, essayist, journalist*

Born in Charleston, South Carolina, Henry Timrod was educated at what is now the University of Georgia, but when illness and financial strain forced him to leave school, he returned to his native city, where he became a member of the RUSSELL'S BOOKSTORE GROUP and studied the classics on his own. Before the CIVIL WAR he eked out a living as a private tutor on several Carolina plantations. During the decade leading up to the war Timrod published several important essays, including "Literature in the South" and "A Theory of Poetry," in the Charleston periodical *Russell's Magazine.* In 1859 he published the only volume of his poetry that would appear during his lifetime.

Timrod's reputation, however, arose primarily from the poems he wrote during the war, works like "The Cotton Boll" and "Ethnogenesis." The tubercular poet known as the "laureate of the Confederacy" even managed to serve for 10 months in 1862 as a regimental clerk in the Confederate Army, afterward reporting on the war for the Charleston *Mercury.* In 1864 Timrod was made editor of the Columbia *South Carolinian,* and one of the benefits of a steady income was his ability to support a wife. He married Kate S. Goodwin, for whom he wrote the long, posthumously published love poem *Katie* (1884). When Union general William Tecumseh Sherman destroyed Columbia in 1865, however, he also ruined

Timrod's prospects. The last two years of Timrod's life were consumed by poverty, malnutrition, and illness.

Sources

Parks, Edd Winfield, and Aileen Wells Parks, eds. *Collected Poems.* Athens: University of Georgia Press, 1965.
Parks, Edd Winfield. *Henry Timrod.* New York: Twayne, 1964.

Todd, Mabel Loomis (1856–1932) *editor*

A native of Massachusetts, Mabel Loomis Todd came to Amherst in 1879 when her husband was appointed as a professor at Amherst College. A writer herself, Todd came to know Emily DICKINSON, and after the poet's death the Dickinson family asked Todd to prepare some of the poet's nearly 2,000 manuscript works for publication. Together with Dickinson's mentor, Thomas Wentworth HIGGINSON, Todd edited two series of Dickinson's poems, which were published in 1890 and 1891. A third series, which appeared in 1894, was edited solely by Todd, who also edited *Letters of Emily Dickinson* (1894). Todd's daughter, Millicent Todd Bingham, used her mother's transcriptions of other Dickinson poems to publish *Bolts of Melody: New Poems by Emily Dickinson* in 1945, after Todd's death.

Sources

Walsh, John Evangelist. *This Brief Tragedy: Unraveling the Todd-Dickinson Affair.* New York: George Weidenfeld, 1991.

Tom Sawyer, The Adventures of Mark Twain (1876) *novel*

Although less significant to American literature than its sequel, *HUCKLEBERRY FINN*, *Tom Sawyer*, Mark Twain's (Samuel Langhorne CLEMENS) first important solo work of long fiction, is unquestionably a classic. Immensely popular with children, it is a thoroughgoing boys' book, an episodic record of its hero's adventures. But as Twain himself observed, "it [is] read only by adults"—that is, the essence of childhood the novel strove to capture is available only via nostalgia, by looking backward.

Set in the mid-19th century in the drowsy river town of St. Petersburg, Missouri (a stand-in for Twain's own hometown, Hannibal), *Tom Sawyer* is an idyll of childhood in which the hero, like America itself, is an innocent hovering on the edge of a new frontier. Tom's adventures, trivial as some of them seem, together constitute a kind of moral education that fits him for adulthood and entry into society. Tom and his older brother Sid live with their Aunt Polly, who serves as a foil for the mischievous Tom. When Aunt Polly catches Tom in a lie, his punishment is whitewashing a fence. But clever Tom makes light work of this chore, convincing his friends that it is a privilege to paint fences—a privilege they should pay for.

Aunt Polly's antithesis is the social outcast Huckleberry Finn, who brings out Tom's imaginative instead of his practical side. But oddly, most of the adventures the two boys share involve death in some way. When the two boys, together with another friend, decide to run away to Jackson's Island to become pirates, their absence for more than a day sends St. Petersburg into mourning in the belief that they have drowned. Their funeral is interrupted by the discovery of the lost boys in the church gallery, where they have been listening to the eulogy.

A continuous thread in the novel involves a murder that Tom and Huck witness one night in a graveyard. Having gone there to test the efficacy of a superstition involving warts and a dead cat, they witness first an argument among three men and then a murder. Although the actual murderer, Injun Joe, convinces the drunken Muff Potter that he did the deed, Tom and Huck know better—and they know better than to say so. At the murder trial a few days later, Tom proves unable to keep his secret. Unfortunately, Injun Joe escapes from the courthouse shortly thereafter. Later, when Tom and Huck visit a haunted house in search of buried treasure, they overhear Injun Joe planning future murders with a crony; and when Tom and his sweetheart, Becky Thatcher, get lost for several days in a cave after a picnic, it is the cave where Injun Joe has come to hide the buried treasure he has dug up.

Tom, of course, finds a way out eventually. But when Injun Joe is found dead inside the cave, Tom and Huck go back to retrieve the treasure. Civilization, respectability, and adulthood utterly triumph over anarchy when the Widow Douglas announces her intention to adopt the orphaned Huck. Huck's only hope of happiness is being admitted to Tom's robber gang on account of his new social status.

Sources

Evans, John D. *A Tom Sawyer Companion: An Autobiographical Guided Tour with Mark Twain.* Lanham, Md.: University Press of America, 1993.
Norton, Charles A. *Writing Tom Sawyer: The Adventures of a Classic.* Jefferson, N.C.: McFarland, 1983.
Scharnhorst, Gary, ed. *Critical Essays on The Adventures of Tom Sawyer.* New York: G. K. Hall, 1993.

Tourgée, Albion Winegar (1838–1905) *novelist*

Born in Williamsfield, Ohio, Albion W. Tourgée attended the University of Rochester before he left school to join the Union Army as an officer during the CIVIL WAR. He was seriously wounded in the war, and after it was over, in 1865, he moved with his family to North Carolina in order to be part of the North's efforts at reforming the South's political and social institutions. Working first as a lawyer, then as a judge, Tourgée made himself unpopular with the locals because of his conspicuously hostile attitude. He did, however, make himself rich through corrupt administration of the courts. Unquestionably a carpetbagger, he was nonetheless committed to RECONSTRUCTION, founding and editing several journals that advocated the imposition of radical measures on the citizens of the former Confederacy.

In 1878, tired of the hostile atmosphere in North Carolina, Tourgée returned north, settling in New York, where he wrote novels. His books, mostly ROMANCES tempered by realistic detail, dealt almost exclusively with the post–Civil War South. *A Fool's Errand* (1879), considered his best work, drew heavily on his own biography to tell a romantic tale that was nevertheless filled with propaganda about mistreatment of northerners in the South during Reconstruction. A sequel, *Bricks Without Straw* (1880), addresses the difficulty of making former slaves truly free without providing a proper social and economic base for their development. From 1882 to 1884 Tourgée edited and published *The Continent,* a literary weekly that serialized his own work and demonstrated a marked Republican editorial policy, supporting African Americans and damning the Ku Klux Klan.

Tourgée is credited with having reintroduced southern life as a suitable theme for popular fiction in the North. Writing in *THE FORUM* in December 1888, he said that he found American literature to have become "distinctly Confederate in sympathy," having forgotten the root causes of the CIVIL WAR. Plainly he felt it was his mission to correct such misguidedness. In 1897 he was rewarded for his stalwart Republicanism with an appointment as the U.S. consul in Bordeaux, France, by the administration of William McKinley (1843–1901).

Sources

Gross, Theodore L. *Albion W. Tourgée.* New York: Twayne, 1963.

Olsen, Otto H. *Carpetbagger's Crusade: The Life of Albion Winegar Tourgée.* Baltimore: Johns Hopkins Press, 1965.

Transcendental Club (1836–c. 1843) *organization*

Founded in the BOSTON home of George RIPLEY, this loosely organized club was dedicated to the "exchange of thought among those interested in the new views in philosophy, theology, and literature." The group grew out of the transcendentalist movement (see TRANSCENDENTALISM) inspired by the writings of Ralph Waldo EMERSON and initially included Emerson, Bronson ALCOTT, and the Unitarian theologian James Freeman CLARKE. Another charter member was the clergyman Henry Hedge (1805–90), who provided the club with an alternative moniker, the Hedge Club, so called because it met only when Hedge had traveled to Boston from his home in Bangor, Maine. Later the group attracted such luminaries as Margaret FULLER, Orestes BROWNSON, Jones VERY, and Elizabeth Palmer PEABODY and her sister Sophia, who would become the wife of another member, Nathaniel HAWTHORNE. Two important endeavors were direct outgrowths of the club's discussion: the literary journal called *THE DIAL,* and the experiment in communal living known as BROOK FARM.

Sources

James, Laurie. *Men, Women, and Margaret Fuller: The Truth That Existed between Margaret Fuller and Ralph Waldo Emerson and Their Circle of Transcendental Friends.* New York: Golden Heritage Press, 1990.

Myerson, Joel. *The New England Transcendentalists and the Dial: A History of the Magazine and Its Contributors.* Rutherford, N.J.: Fairleigh Dickinson University Press, 1980.

Simon, Myron, ed. *Transcendentalism and Its Legacy.* Ann Arbor: University of Michigan Press, 1966.

transcendentalism *literary movement*

This is a term associated with New England writers such as Bronson ALCOTT, Ralph Waldo EMERSON, and Henry David THOREAU. A literary and philosophical concept, transcendentalism reacted against both the Puritanism and the rationalism of the 17th and 18th centuries. Transcendentalists adopted neither religious faith nor radical skepticism but instead explored the spiritual and immaterial side of humanity through the imagination and contact with nature. In this respect transcendentalism is a variant of ROMANTICISM, which also exults in human intuition and creativity that goes well beyond mere observation of the world.

There is a kind of God in transcendentalism—that is, a belief in a divine principle inherent in men that binds them to the creation—but transcendentalists rejected specific creeds. Thus Emerson left the Unitarian church because he did not wish to be bound by an institution's principles, no matter how liberal.

The term *transcendentalism* derives from the German philosopher Immanuel Kant (1724–1804), who argued that human knowledge arose not out of the material conditions of life but out of the nature of being human. In other words, the ability to know was not generated by experience but was inherent in human beings and transcended matter. Through the English Romantics, especially Samuel Taylor Coleridge (1772–1834), the thinking of Kant and other German philosophers informed American thinking and pushed it toward mysticism and idealism—as in Plato's notion that truth was found in ideal forms that human beings could only dimly perceive with their senses but which they could intuit with their minds. American transcendentalists were also greatly influenced by Eastern thought—Confucianism and Buddhism—which also emphasized the human need to go beyond the evidence of the senses.

The American version of German and Eastern thought located a core of meaning in the individual, who in his or her person contained all the elements of the universe. The unity between the individual and the world, the one and the many, was called the "Oversoul." Awareness of the oversoul gave transcendentalists a remarkable air of authority, because they were, in a sense, speaking for the world. In political terms, this doctrine allowed writers such as Thoreau to stand firmly on what their conscience told them. The writer might be a "minority of one," but he felt himself in tune with the truths of nature, which claimed a deeper allegiance than the laws of any particular society.

The key works of transcendentalism include Thoreau's *WALDEN* and Emerson's "NATURE." Some other key transcendentalists are Alcott, Margaret FULLER, Theodore PARKER, Jones VERY, and Orestes BROWNSON. They composed an informal TRANSCENDENTAL CLUB and established the Utopian communities of FRUITLANDS and BROOK FARM. But the teachings of transcendentalism were never codified as a school of thought or enforced as a discipline among believers. Consequently, there was considerable variation in the way transcendentalism was interpreted, and various members of this informal group broke away at different times to express their distinctive points of view. Other writers, such as Nathaniel HAWTHORNE, were influenced by transcendentalism but also treated it with considerable reserve. While Walt WHITMAN clearly found inspiration in Emerson and other transcendentalists, Herman MELVILLE was skeptical of a philosophical and literary orientation that seemed insufficiently rooted in reality.

Sources

Barbour, Brian M., ed. *American Transcendentalism: An Anthology of Criticism.* Notre Dame, Ind.: University of Notre Dame Press, 1973.

Gura, Philip E., and Joel Myerson, eds. *Critical Essays on American Transcendentalism.* Boston: G. K. Hall, 1982.

Mott, Wesley T., ed. *Biographical Dictionary of Transcendentalism.* Westport, Conn.: Greenwood Press, 1996.

Myerson, Joel. *The New England Transcendentalists and The Dial: A History of the Magazine and its Contributors.* Rutherford, N.J.: Fairleigh Dickinson University Press, 1980.

Tuckerman, Frederick Goddard (1821–1873) *poet*

Born to a family of BOSTON Brahmins, Frederick Goddard Tuckerman was little known as a poet during his lifetime. After graduating from Harvard and practicing law briefly, he retired to Greenfield, Massachusetts, where he spent the remainder of his life as a recluse. In Greenfield Tuckerman closely observed nature and turned his observations into some of the most finely honed poetry of his time. Few knew his work, however, because he published only one volume of poetry, consisting entirely of sonnets, while he was alive. Tuckerman sent copies of his 1860 *Poems* to some of the most highly regarded writers of the time, and many responded with enthusiasm. New editions of *Poems* were issued in 1864 and 1869, but after that Tuckerman was forgotten until 1913, when the poet Witter Bynner (1881–1968) resuscitated the late poet's work, publishing a new edition of *The Sonnets of Frederick Goddard Tuckerman* with a highly appreciative introduction. The volume brought Tuckerman to the attention of modernist critics like Yvor Winters (1900–1968), who compared Tuckerman's ability to write about the natural world with that of the great English Romantic, William Wordsworth (1770–1850).

Sources

England, Eugene. *Beyond Romanticism: Tuckerman's Life and Poetry.* Provo, Utah: Brigham Young University Press, 1991.

Golden, Samuel A. *Frederick Goddard Tuckerman.* New York: Twayne, 1966.

"Turn of the Screw, The" *Henry James* (1898) *short story*

This ghostly mystery by Henry JAMES achieves its richness from his masterful use of an unreliable narrator, a suggestible young woman who undertakes a position as governess for two young children at an isolated English country estate. She is more than half in love with her employer, the children's uncle, whom she meets just once in London. The uncle remains in the city and insists that she contact him no further. When the governess arrives at the estate, Bly, she finds her charges, Flora and Miles, to be marvelously attractive and precocious, and she is especially drawn to the boy. Soon, however, she discovers that she has rivals for the children's affections and that the rivals are both dead. She believes Flora and Miles to be under the evil influence of her predecessor, Miss Jessel, and Miss Jessel's dead lover, Peter Quint, who was once a valet at Bly. With only the simpleminded housekeeper—who does not see the ghosts—as her ally, the governess decides that she must wrest the not-so-innocent children from the malicious hold of Miss Jessel and Peter Quint. But in her struggle for what she convinces herself is the children's souls, she terrorizes Flora and kills Miles, who dies in her arms.

While one school of criticism has taken James's tale at face value, figuring it a ghost story of the first order, another interprets "The Turn of the Screw" in psychological terms, with Miss Jessel and Peter Quint as projections of the lovesick governess's overactive imagination. Postmodern readings of the tale see its ambiguity as an allegory, or "ghost effect," of the events of the story itself: both are indeterminate. The richness of the story has generated derivative works as well, including William Archibald's 1950 dramatization, *The Innocents;* and Benjamin Britten's 1954 opera, also titled *The Turn of the Screw.*

Sources

Beidler, Peter G. *Ghosts, Demons, and Henry James: The Turn of the Screw at the Turn of the Century.* Columbia: University of Missouri Press, 1989.

Cranfill, Thomas M., and Robert Lanier Clark. *An Anatomy of The Turn of the Screw.* New York: Gordian Press, 1971.

Willen, George, ed. *A Casebook on Henry James's The Turn of the Screw.* New York: Crowell, 1960.

Twain, Mark

See CLEMENS, SAMUEL LANGHORNE.

Twice-Told Tales *Nathaniel Hawthorne* (1837) *short story collection*

Some of the 39 stories that make up Nathaniel HAWTHORNE's collection first appeared in magazines and GIFT BOOKS. In all likelihood the author took his title from William Shakespeare's play *King John* (c. 1591–98): "Life is as tedious as a twice-told tale." Many of the stories in the volume concern New England history, and some are rendered with a touch of the supernatural.

Among the best-known stories in the collection is "The Ambitious Guest," in which a stranger stops for the night at a lonely cottage in the White Mountains. The young man speaks of his hopes for fame and fortune, and the members of his host family are moved to do the same. Later that night, a landslide buries them all.

In "The Minister's Black Veil," the title character dons a black veil on the eve of his marriage. When he refuses ever to remove it, his fiancée abandons him and his congregation grow to fear him. He goes to his grave wearing his veil, declaring it a symbol of the barrier that separates every person from his fellows, his loved ones, and even his God.

"The Maypole of Merrymount" is based on the history of Merrymount—now Quincy, Massachusetts—established in the early 17th century by English anti-Puritan immigrants. When Thomas Morton and the other settlers of Merrymount set up a maypole, it was cut down by neighboring Puritans. In the story, the maypole revelers include a couple who are about to be married by an Anglican priest. During the marriage ceremony, the Puritans stage a raid. The newly married couple plead each other's case, and they are both spared punishment for their "paganism." Soon thereafter they become sober citizens of the Puritan colony.

"The Gentle Boy" concerns the fate of a Quaker child at the hands of the Puritans. The innocent Ilbrahim, shunned and mistreated, inevitably dies from the ill effects of his harsh social environment.

"Twice-Told Tales" also includes four tales classified as "Legends of the Province House." Among these are "Lady Eleanore's Mantle," an allegorical story about the cold beauty, Lady Eleanore Rochcliffe, who comes to live at the Boston Province House. Her unusual cloak comes to symbolize her pride, which at first protects her from the smallpox epidemic that destroys many of those around her. Eventually she too succumbs, confessing on her deathbed, "I wrapped myself in Pride as in a Mantle, and scorned the sympathies of nature; and therefore has nature made this wretched body the medium of a dreadful sympathy." After her death, the mantle is destroyed, and the epidemic subsides.

Hawthorne came into his own with the publication of *Twice-Told Tales.* The stories in the volume, in their preoccupation with Puritan New England, reflect themes that he would continue to explore for the remainder of his literary career.

Sources

Cameron, Sharon. *The Corporeal Self: Allegories of the Body in Melville and Hawthorne.* Baltimore: Johns Hopkins University Press, 1981.

Swisher, Clarence, ed. *Readings on Nathaniel Hawthorne.* San Diego, Calif.: Greenhaven Press, 1996.

Thompson, Gary R. *The Art of Authorial Presence: Hawthorne's Provincial Tales.* Durham: Duke University Press, 1993.

Two Years Before the Mast *Richard Henry Dana Jr.* (1840) *travel journal*

When Richard Henry DANA Jr.'s sight was impaired by a bout of measles, he took an unusual route to recuperation. Leaving Harvard, the undergraduate shipped out of Boston on August 14, 1834, as an ordinary seaman aboard the brig *Pilgrim.* On a hide-trading expedition, the *Pilgrim* sailed around Cape Horn to San Francisco, its voyage recorded in a journal by Dana who, as a lowly member of the crew, lived his life below decks "before the mast." These journal entries would later be transformed into something like a novel, but Dana never lost sight of his intent to present "the life of a common sailor at sea as it really is,—the light and the dark together."

Following a diary format, the book describes in detail the 150-day voyage, recording both the routines essential to shipboard life and what the sailors speak of and how they occupy themselves during their off hours. Dana also describes the harsh treatment sailors had to endure at the hands of the captain—including flogging—without access to avenues of legal redress. Dana's 16-month sojourn (January 13, 1835–May 8, 1836) along the California coast is also a part of his narrative. During this period the *Pilgrim* called at such California ports as San Diego, Santa Barbara, Monterey, and San Francisco, stopping to cure and collect hides. Dana also describes some of his shipmates, such as the self-educated Tom Harris and the irascible John the Swede, as well as his ship's sadistic Captain Thompson.

Dana's book continues with the trip back around the Horn from May 8 to September 20, 1836, aboard the *Alert.* As eagerly as he has looked forward to his homecoming, once back on land, he finds himself recollecting his seagoing experience with something like nostalgia: "[T]he emotions which I had so long anticipated feeling I did not find, and in their place was a state of very nearly apathy." *Two Years Before the Mast* proved to be a popular book and went through many editions, which after 1859 carried an additional chapter Dana wrote after he made a return trip to California. In this chapter he follows up on the fates of some of the men and ships that appear in the original narrative.

The public was nearly as outraged as Dana had been to discover the cruelties perpetrated on seamen. Dana's book suggests numerous ways to improve their lot, and as a result of his analysis, *Two Years before the Mast* was distributed by the British Board of Admiralty to the entire British Navy. In America its most important aftereffect was its influence on Herman MELVILLE, whose book about life aboard a man-of-war, *White-Jacket* (1850), was heavily influenced by Dana's narrative and helped advance the cause of those opposed to corporal punishment in the U.S. Navy.

Sources

Gale, Robert L. *Richard Henry Dana, Jr.* New York: Twayne, 1969.

Shapiro, Samuel. *Richard Henry Dana, Jr., 1815–1882.* East Lansing: Michigan State University Press, 1961.

Uncle Sam *symbolic figure*

The first recorded instance of this moniker being applied to the United States government is on September 7, 1813, in the *Troy* (New York) *Post,* which reported that the nickname derived from the "U.S." signage on government wagons. The name might, however, have been inspired by a Troy resident, Samuel Wilson, who was a government inspector. The name appeared frequently thereafter in upstate New York newspapers, and during the War of 1812 it was used derisively by opponents of the war.

Uncle Sam made his first literary appearance in *The Adventures of Uncle Sam: In Search of His Lost Honor* (1816), by "Frederick Augustus Fidfaddy, Esq." The English writer William Faux was the first foreigner to refer extensively to Uncle Sam in his book *Memorable Days in America* (1832). In that same year a caricature form of Uncle Sam, decked out in stars and stripes, began to appear in political cartoons. This costume seems to have been borrowed from Major Jack Downing, a shrewd but comic Down East Yankee who was the alter ego of the humorist Seba SMITH. Uncle Sam quickly replaced Jack Downing as a national symbol, and by 1860 the term "Uncle Sam" appeared in dictionaries without negative connotations. In 1961 the U.S. Congress officially adopted Uncle Sam as a national symbol.

Sources

Gerson, Thomas I., and Flora M. Hood. *Uncle Sam.* Indianapolis, Ind.: Bobbs-Merrill, 1963.

Ketchum, Alton. *Uncle Sam: The Man and the Legend.* New York: Hill and Wang, 1959.

Uncle Tom's Cabin, or, Life Among the Lowly

Harriet Beecher Stowe (1851–1852) *novel*

Abraham LINCOLN is said to have called Harriet Beecher STOWE the woman who started the CIVIL WAR with her novel *Uncle Tom's Cabin,* which was first serially published in the *NATIONAL ERA.* Although the allegation certainly is not true—and the anecdote might not be, either—Stowe did manage to reach an enormous popular audience. The novel sold 300,000 copies during its first year after publication, making it the bestselling American novel to date. Eventually it would sell in the millions, reaching not only those already converted to the abolitionist cause (see ABOLITIONISM) but also the larger American public which had, up to that time, been largely indifferent to the controversy over slavery. After reading *Uncle Tom's Cabin,* a great many more people took the problem to heart.

The main plot of the novel revolves around two slave protagonists: the noble, devoutly Christian slave, "Uncle Tom" Shelby; and a young mulatto woman, Eliza Harris. Both ultimately triumph over slavery, albeit in radically different ways. Tom and Eliza are both slaves on the Shelby plantation in Kentucky, but when the Shelbys experience financial difficulties that require them to sell their slaves, Tom and Eliza have very different reactions. Eliza, whose child is to be taken away from her and sold to a slave trader, flees northward, a journey that requires her to cross the broken ice of the Ohio River barefoot in order to escape slave catchers empowered by the Fugitive Slave Law to capture her and return her to slavery. With the help of the Underground Railroad and others opposed to the law, Eliza and her son manage to escape to Canada, where they are reunited with

Eliza's husband George. The family then leaves to make a new life in Liberia.

Uncle Tom takes a different course. Realizing that his sale will help the Shelbys clear their debts, he allows himself to be removed in chains from his wife and children and sent downriver for sale. While aboard a ship bound for Louisiana, he befriends a young white child, little Evangeline, or "Eva," St. Clare. After Tom saves Eva from drowning when she falls overboard, her father buys Tom, taking him to their St. Clare, Louisiana, home to work as a household servant and companion to little Eva. Eva and Tom grow close, and the religious feeling they share increases even as Eva falls ill with a mysterious illness. Eva blames her sickness on slavery, which she claims hurts her heart, and when she dies, her father resolves to free his slaves.

St. Clare, however, dies before he can carry out his resolution, with the result that Tom is sold further downriver, becoming the property of a cruel new master, Simon LEGREE. Legree beats his slaves in order to make them submit to his will, and when Tom offers no resistance, he receives especially harsh treatment. Legree grows to fear Uncle Tom, whose Christian forbearance the slave master cannot comprehend. When Tom refuses to betray the hiding place of two female slaves attempting to escape Legree's plantation, the slave master has Tom savagely beaten. As Tom lies dying, George Shelby, his original master, arrives on the scene. Tom ultimately endures a martyr's death, and George Shelby vows to devote his life to the cause of abolition.

After publication of *Uncle Tom's Cabin,* Stowe was attacked not for the sentimentality of her novel but instead for its lack of authenticity. Numerous anti-Tom novels appeared, purporting to show the true, happy conditions under which their authors believed most slaves lived. This forced Stowe in turn to publish *A Key to Uncle Tom's Cabin* (1853), which documents some of the abuses her novel replicated. Other authors simply took advantage of the popularity of *Uncle Tom's Cabin:* In 1852 the playwright George Aiken dramatized the novel without Stowe's consent, and his successful melodramatic version helped to create the stereotypes so many future generations found objectionable in Uncle Tom's story.

Sources

Ammons, Elizabeth, ed. *Uncle Tom's Cabin: Authoritative Text, Backgrounds and Contexts, Criticism.* New York: W. W. Norton, 1994.

Gossett, Thomas. *Uncle Tom's Cabin and American Culture.* Dallas, Tex.: Southern Methodist University Press, 1985.

Kirkham, Edwin B. *The Building of Uncle Tom's Cabin.* Knoxville: University of Tennessee Press, 1977.

Moers, Ellen. *Harriet Beecher Stowe and American Literature.* Hartford, Conn.: Stowe-Day Foundation, 1978.

Reynolds, Moira Davison. *Uncle Tom's Cabin and Mid-Nineteenth Century United States.* Jefferson, N.C.: McFarland & Co., 1985.

Union Magazine, The *periodical*

First edited by the novelist Caroline Stansbury KIRKLAND who also contributed stories, this monthly magazine was published from 1847 to 1852. It was taken over after 18 months by John Sartain (1808–97) who renamed it *Sartain's Union Magazine.* Known for its superior mezzotint reproductions, the magazine also published Edgar's Allan POE's poems "To Helen" and "The Bells" as well as his critical essay "The Poetic Principle." Other important contributors were Henry Wadsworth LONGFELLOW, James Russell LOWELL, and Henry David THOREAU, who contributed the first part of his autobiographical narrative, *The Maine Woods.*

Unitarianism *religious movement*

The central tenet of Unitarianism—that there is no Holy Trinity, but only a single God—dates back to early movements within Christianity, such as Arianism, which thrived in Palestine in the fourth century. Unitarianism was introduced to America in the mid-18th century, and in 1785 the first Unitarian church on American soil was founded at King's Chapel, Boston, when trinitarian doctrines were removed from the liturgy. Joseph Priestley (1733–1804), who fled England to escape persecution for what were regarded as heretical beliefs, spread the word farther afield, establishing a Unitarian church in Philadelphia in 1796.

In approximately 1815, a liberal wing of the established New England Congregationalist Church (founded on a belief that each congregation was autonomous) formed a separate entity that was denominated Unitarian by their opponents, and a final split from Congregationalism was generated by the choice of liberal preacher Henry Ware (1764–1845) as professor of divinity at Harvard in 1805 and by William Ellery CHANNING's (1) 1819 ordination speech at Baltimore. Channing's speech became the basis for the formation in 1825 of the American Unitarian Association, which requires neither ministers nor members that espouse any creed.

As professed by Channing and other members such as Ralph Waldo EMERSON, Unitarianism was a religion of reason, characterized by tolerance and an innate belief in human goodness, beliefs that contributed greatly to the transcendentalist movement (see TRANSCENDENTALISM).

Sources

Ahlstrom, Sydney E., and Jonathan S. Carey, eds. *An American Reformation: A Documentary History of Unitarian Christianity.* Middletown, Conn.: Wesleyan University Press, 1985.

Robinson, David. *The Unitarians and the Universalists.* Westport, Conn.: Greenwood Press, 1985.

United States Literary Gazette *periodical*

This Boston review of literary news and criticism was published twice monthly from 1824 to 1826 and edited by the Harvard law professor Theophilus Parsons (1797–1882). It published contributions by William Cullen BRYANT, Richard Henry DANA Sr., and Henry Wadsworth LONGFELLOW, among others. In 1826 it merged with *The New York Review and Athenaeum Magazine* to appear for one more year as *The United States Review and Literary Gazette,* edited by Charles Folsom and Bryant.

United States Magazine and Democratic Review *periodical*

A monthly literary and political review published in Washington, D.C., from 1837 until 1841, when it was moved to New York City, the *United States Magazine and Democratic Review* published Nathaniel HAWTHORNE's "Legends of the Province House" and John Greenleaf WHITTIER's "Songs of Labor." In 1841, after a merger with the *BOSTON QUARTERLY REVIEW,* the magazine became more overtly political, in large part because of the nationalism of its founder and editor John L. O'Sullivan (1813–95). It was in this magazine that O'Sullivan's coinage for American imperialism, "manifest destiny," first appeared. After another merger, this time with *United States Review* in 1846, the magazine declined.

Universalism (c. 1779–1961) *religious movement*

Universalism is an almost entirely American phenomenon, although it originated with an English cleric, John Murray (1741–1815), who emigrated to the United States in 1770. In 1779 Murray became pastor of the first Universalist church, located in Gloucester, Massachusetts, where he preached a doctrine holding that it is God's intention that each individual be saved through divine grace as revealed through Jesus Christ. The movement spread, and its doctrine was codified in the 1803 Winchester Profession. The church did not become truly organized until the middle of the 19th century, however, when Hosea Ballou (1771–1852) helped separate the Universalists from their Calvinist origins. Ballou's doctrine of "Christ's subordination to the Father" was close to that espoused by the Unitarian church (see UNITARIANISM), with which it eventually merged in 1961 to form the Unitarian Universalist Association. While still a separate entity, however, the Universalist church established Tufts University in Boston in 1852 and the Tufts Divinity School in 1861.

Sources

Cassara, Ernest, ed. *Universalism in America: A Documentary History.* Boston: Beacon Press, 1971.

Robinson, David. *The Unitarians and the Universalists.* Westport, Conn.: Greenwood Press, 1985.

Up From Slavery *Booker T. Washington* (1901) *autobiography*

Although Booker T. WASHINGTON was born a slave, by the time he wrote his autobiography, he was, as president of Tuskegee Institute, arguably the most powerful black person in the country. Far from a conventional SLAVE NARRATIVE, *Up From Slavery* is both a personal and an institutional history that marks the beginning of African-American literary modernism. The book is unquestionably an all-American rags-to-riches story, but it concentrates more on the symbolism of Washington's accomplishments and the power of his philosophy of racial conciliation than on his personal life. *Up From Slavery* traces his origins as a slave on a Virginia plantation and his struggle for an education, but the moment when his custodial services at the Hampton Institute earn him a place as a student there is fraught with symbolic import.

For Washington, deprivation affords blacks an opportunity for advancement, not an excuse for disillusionment. Filled with the need to provide uplift for his people, to make himself an exception that proves the rule, Washington leads his readers to believe that they can—because of the very existence of institutions like Tuskegee—attain self-sufficiency despite segregation. *Up From Slavery* ends with a picture of Washington as a confidante of presidents and business magnates, a conduit for the hopes of a people, and an instrument for the betterment of the nation.

Washington's autobiography grew out of a series of articles he had published in the periodical *Outlook.* Although he was heavily criticized by other black leaders—W. E. B. DU BOIS, in particular—for his endorsement of a kind of second-class vocational education for African Americans and for his accommodation of segregation, Washington did leave readers of *Up From Slavery* with hope for a better day. The book concludes with Washington delivering a speech before an enthusiastic and racially mixed audience in Richmond, Virginia, the former capital of the Confederacy.

Sources

Andrews, William L., ed. *Up From Slavery: Authoritative Text, Contexts, and Composition History, Criticism.* New York: Norton, 1996.

Harris, Thomas E. *Analysis of the Clash over the Issues between Booker T. Washington and W. E. B. Du Bois.* New York: Garland, 1993.

Weisberger, Bernard A. *Booker T. Washington.* New York: New American Library, 1972.

Vanity Fair *periodical*

Founded in New York as a weekly by brothers Louis, William, and Henry Stephens, the original *Vanity Fair* (1859–63) was a humor magazine that lampooned national, social, and political affairs as well as literary lions. Edited from 1860 to 1861 by Charles Godfrey LELAND and from 1862 until its demise the following year by Charles Farrar BROWNE, the magazine enjoyed contributions from members of the PFAFF'S CELLAR crowd. A second magazine bearing the same name was begun in New York in 1868. Edited from 1907 to 1911 by Frank HARRIS, it did not become a success until it was purchased in 1913 by the media magnate Condé Nast, who in 1935 merged it with another of his holdings, the women's fashion magazine *Vogue.* From 1914 to 1935 *Vanity Fair* was edited by Frank Crowninshield, who made it one of the most polished and sophisticated reviews of society and the arts of its time. After its merger with *Vogue, Vanity Fair* was revived in 1983, emerging in 1990 as a monthly devoted to a miscellany of topics, including celebrity profiles, style, and finance.

Varieties of Religious Experience, The *William James* (1902) *philosophical study*

This psychological and philosophical study grew out of two lectures William JAMES delivered at the University of Edinburgh in 1901 and 1902. Written from a psychologist's perspective, *The Varieties of Religious Experience,* subtitled *A Study in Human Nature,* concerns individual rather than institutional experiences of religious awareness. For James, institutional religion is characterized by external, ritual acts, as opposed to the "neurally conditioned" states of mind that interest him.

James's "arbitrary" definition of religion reflects his bias: it is "the feelings, acts, and experiences of individual men in their solitude, so far as they apprehend themselves to stand in relation to whatever they may consider the divine." His approach is pragmatic (see PRAGMATISM), attempting to discover the function of religion and what difference it makes to an individual's existence. The significance of religious experiences, he writes, "must be tested not by their origin but by the value of their fruits."

Starting, then, from the premise that religion is a "way of accepting the universe," James proceeds to examine the lives of individuals who have testified to a subjective, but nevertheless real, experience of an "unseen order." Individual case histories presenting "the religion of healthy-mindedness," "the sick soul," "the divided self, and the process of its unification," religious conversion, and saintliness are all examined, with James ultimately concluding that some individuals have the capacity for mysticism, or in any event the ability to transcend the limits of normal human experience. When the effects of this facility are positive, the individual has a right to exercise belief, although not to impose it on others.

James, who presents himself as "piecemeal supernaturalism," makes a powerful argument for religion as a unique aspect of human experience. By presenting a multifaceted examination of the phenomenon of belief and a qualified endorsement not only of its existence but its potential practicality, he succeeds at once in codifying religion and acknowledging its mystery.

Sources

Capps, Donald, and Janet L. Jacobs, eds. *The Struggle for Life: A Companion to William James's The Varieties of Religious*

Experience. West Lafayette, Ind.: Society for the Scientific Study of Religion, 1995.
Croce, Paul J. *Science and Religion in the Era of William James.* Chapel Hill: University of North Carolina Press, 1995.
Ramsey, Bennett. *Submitting to Freedom: The Religious Vision of William James.* New York: Oxford University Press, 1993.

Variety *periodical*

Founded and edited in 1905 in New York City by Sime Silverman (1873–1933), *Variety* has always been a theatrical trade journal. Initially devoted to vaudeville, the magazine expanded to cover all the theatrical arts as well as business, and in 1933 began to publish a separate daily edition in Hollywood. Known from the start for its racy language, *Variety* introduced numerous slang expressions into the American argot. Perhaps the most famous of its staff neologists was Jack Conway, who invented such terms as "high-hat," "belly laugh," and "pushover."

Sources

Besas, Peter. *Inside "Variety": The Story of the Bible of Show Business, 1905–1987.* New York: Ars Millenii, 2000.
Green, Abel, ed. *The Spice of Variety.* New York: Holt, 1952.

Veblen, Thorstein Bunde (1857–1929) *economist, social scientist*

Born to Norwegian immigrant parents in Cato Township, Wisconsin, Thorstein Veblen spent his first 17 years there and in the clannish Norwegian-American farming communities of Minnesota. Although something of a misfit, he nevertheless absorbed his society's mores and shared the anger that erupted in the 1870s and 1880s over the abuses local farmers endured at the hands of railroad monopolies and Eastern capitalists who controlled them. The Populist philosophy born of this revolt would later inform much of Veblen's most important works.

After studying at Carleton College, Johns Hopkins, and Yale University, where he received a Ph.D. in philosophy, Veblen returned to Minnesota, where he spent seven years reading and translating works written in the Norse languages. In 1891 he left to pursue further studies at Cornell University, after which he accepted a post teaching economics at the University of Chicago. Teaching positions followed at Stanford, the University of Missouri, and the New School for Social Research in New York City.

In New York in 1918, Veblen became an editor of *THE DIAL.* By then he was something of a celebrity, despite his acerbic wit and aloofness from mainstream society. His attack on materialism and the monied elite in *The Theory of the Leisure Class* (1899) struck a chord with many Americans, although Veblen's satiric style and coinage of such catchy phrases as "conspicuous consumption" did not go over well with academics. In 1925, when he was offered the presidency of the American Economic Association, Veblen turned it down, remarking dryly, "They didn't offer it to me when I needed it."

Veblen went on to publish many more books that influenced economics by emphasizing industry over business and helped to create a trend toward social control. *The Instinct for Workmanship* (1914) argued that man's inherent will to work had been thwarted by predatory greed. His attack on the dominant financial order in *The Vested Interests and the State of the Industrial Arts* (1919) was expanded into a revolutionary proposal for the reorganization of labor into self-governing bodies in *The Engineers and the Price System* (1921). Despite the radical cast of his critique of capitalism, however, Veblen remained a theoretician of liberal sentiments, true to his Midwestern agricultural roots. He would figure in John Dos Passos's (1896–1970) trilogy *U.S.A.* (1938) as a hero of the working class.

Sources

Diggins, John P. *Bard of Savagery: Thorstein Veblen, Theorist of the Leisure Class.* Princeton, N.J.: Princeton University Press, 1999.
Tilman, Rick. *The Intellectual Legacy of Thorstein Veblen: Unresolved Issues.* Westport, Conn.: Greenwood Press, 1996.
———, ed. *A Veblen Treasury: From Leisure Class to War, Peace, and Capitalism.* Armonk, N.Y.: M. E. Sharpe, 1993.

Very, Jones (1813–1880) *poet, critic*

Born in Salem, Massachusetts, Jones Very worked as a tutor in Greek at the Fiske Latin School in order to earn money to attend Harvard Divinity School after graduating from Harvard College in 1836. A Unitarian by training and affiliation, Very nonetheless became a mystic who claimed that the poetry he wrote during this period came to him from the Holy Ghost during religious ecstasies. The Harvard faculty feared for his sanity, and in 1838 Very allowed himself to be committed to McLean Asylum in Somerville, Massachusetts. Very's friend Ralph Waldo EMERSON continued to promote Very's religious sonnets, however, declaring that the poet was "profoundly sane." J. F. Clarke, assistant editor at *THE WESTERN MESSENGER,* which published some of Very's verse, countered charges that the poet suffered from monomania with the claim that Very had "monosania."

Very's stay in the asylum was brief, and after he was released he put together, with Emerson's help, a collection of poetry and literary criticism, *Essays and Poems* (1839), Very's only publication to appear during his lifetime. Although he had left Harvard without a divinity degree, he took temporary pastorates in Maine and Massachusetts, but shyness prevented him from preaching well, and he retired to Salem. Living a reclusive life with his sister Lydia, Very published occasionally in the Salem *Gazette* and the *Christ-*

ian Register, but produced little more work during the last 40 years of his life.

Very's metaphysical verse and mystical approach to literature attracted such contemporary admirers as William Cullen BRYANT and the elder William Ellery CHANNING. Two posthumous collections—*Poems* (1883) and the complete *Poems and Essays* (1886), which contained more than 600 verses—attracted more admirers. In the 20th century his reputation rose once again with the publication in 1938 of a study by the influential critic Yvor Winters.

Sources

Deese, Helen R., ed. *Jones Very: The Complete Poems.* Athens: University of Georgia Press, 1993.

Gittleman, Edwin. *Jones Very: The Effective Years, 1833–1840.* New York: Columbia University Press, 1967.

Winters, Yvor. *Maule's Curse: Seven Studies in the History of American Obscurantism: Hawthorne, Cooper, Melville, Poe, Emerson, Jones Very, Emily Dickinson, Henry James.* Norfolk, Conn.: New Directions, 1938.

Villard, Henry (Ferdinand Heinrich Gustav Hilgard) (1835–1900) *journalist, financier*

Born in Bavaria, Henry Villard immigrated to the United States in 1853. He settled first in Illinois, where he studied law and got to know Abraham LINCOLN, whose election to the presidency in 1861 Villard covered in a series of newspaper dispatches. A participant in the Pike's Peak gold rush in Colorado in 1859, he wrote about his experience in *The Past and Present of the Pike's Peak Gold Regions* (1860). Later in his career he became a financier, controlling a number of western railways, founding the General Electric Company, and editing the New York *Evening Post.* Married to the only daughter of William Lloyd GARRISON, he fathered Henry Oswald Villard, a liberal journalist.

Sources

Memoirs of Henry Villard: Journalist and Financier, 1835–1900. 1904. Reprint, New York: Da Capo Press, 1969.

Virginian, The: A Horseman of the Plains Owen Wister (1902) *novel*

This novel by Owen WISTER is often considered the first WESTERN, which set the pattern for the genre. Set in Wyoming cattle country in the 1870s and 1880s, the novel features a hero known only as "the Virginian." When the Virginian faces off in a poker game against the villain Trampas, the hero utters what has become a deathless phrase: "When you call me that, smile." After the Virginian marries a New England schoolmistress whom he has saved from peril, the novel reaches its climax during a confrontation between the Virginian and Trampas that features the first known "walkdown" in American literature. When the two draw their guns, Trampas is vanquished. The novel was first dramatized in 1903. Several remakes followed, making the Virginian the prototype of the American cowboy.

Sources

Fifty Years of The Virginian, 1902–1952. Laramie: University of Wyoming Library Associates, 1952.

Walam Olum (*Red Score*) *poem*

This tribal chronicle of the Lenni Lenape (Delaware) Indians consists of five books of 183 verses that recount the tribal history from creation myth through a prehistoric migration from the Northwest to the Atlantic coast, where the tribe ultimately encountered white men. The original *Red Score,* or "painted record," was inscribed in pictographs on birch bark and is now lost. In 1833, however, the European naturalist Constantine Rafinesque (1783–1840) made a manuscript copy of the work as an addendum to his translation of Lenni Lenape songs, published in his book *The American Nations* (1836). Later translations of the *Walam Olum* were made by the archaeologist Ephraim Squier (1821–88) and by the anthropologist Daniel G. Brinton (1837–99), who published his version in *The Lenape and Their Legends, With the Complete Text of the Walam Olum* (1885). The *Walam Olum* is not only an important anthropological artifact, but a great epic poem.

Sources

Weslager, C. A. *The Delaware Indians: A History.* New Brunswick, N.J.: Rutgers University Press, 1972.

Walden *Henry David Thoreau* (1854) *nonfiction narrative*

Determined to test the transcendentalist doctrines of self-reliance, individualism, and the necessity of sublimating the material to the spiritual, Henry David THOREAU submitted himself to an experiment in living between the years 1845 and 1847. Starting in March 1845, he built a cabin on the banks of Walden Pond outside Concord, Massachusetts. The following July 4, Independence Day, he began his occupation, living alone and meeting his earthly needs through his own labor. Thoreau states his purpose thus: "I went to the woods because I wished to live deliberately, to front only the essential facts of life." The 18 essays that constitute *Walden* are the intellectual fruit of his 2 $^1/_2$-year journey into the soul, written in the epigrammatic, meditative style suggested by the passage above.

Thoreau's situation was as spare as his prose. His one-room cabin was furnished with only the bare essentials. He wore the least expensive clothes he could find, and for the most part he ate what he could gather wild or cultivate on his own. The business of living was kept to a minimum so that he could concentrate on reading, writing, and above all, nature. Thoreau believed, like his transcendentalist fellows, that concentration on the natural world would reveal hidden truths too often hidden by humankind's concentration on materialism. "Shams and delusions are esteemed for soundest truths," he writes, "while reality is fabulous." "To live deep and suck out all the marrow of life" one must "simplify, simplify."

Thoreau's ascetic exile resulted in some extraordinary observations about such diverse matters as the moles in his cellar, the changing seasonal features of the woods around him, and his imprisonment for refusing to pay a poll tax. Thoreau's sojourn at Walden Pond reinforced not only the American archetype of the self-sufficient individual but also the national mythology that there is always a new frontier, a fresh, unsullied place to make a new beginning. In September 1847, Thoreau came back home to Concord.

Sources

Boudreau, Gordon V. *The Roots of Walden and the Tree of Life.* Nashville: Vanderbilt University Press, 1990.

Dillman, Richard. *Essays on Henry David Thoreau: Rhetoric, Style, and Audience.* West Cornwall, Conn.: Locust Hill Press, 1993.

Johnson, William C. *What Thoreau Said: Walden and the Unsayable.* Moscow: University of Idaho Press, 1991.

Wall Street *location*

Named for the stockade, or wall, that Dutch colonizers put up in 1653 to protect their small enclave at the tip of Manhattan island, this narrow thoroughfare in New York City has become the most important financial center in the United States. In the post-Revolutionary period, when New York was the nation's capital, Federal Hall on Wall Street was the site both of George Washington's 1789 inauguration and of the first convention of the U.S. Congress. Later, Federal Hall would serve as the birthplace of the stock market, when auctioneers sold stocks and bonds on this site. Not long afterward, stockbrokers set up a separate trading floor at 40 Wall Street, and the New York Stock Exchange was created.

During the 19th century, financiers like J. P. Morgan (1837–1913) and Cornelius Vanderbilt (1794–1877) controlled their vast empires from offices on Wall Street, which by then had already come to stand for an entire district extending several blocks north and south of the street itself. By this time Wall Street was also becoming a literary metaphor, used by Herman MELVILLE as a symbol of social alienation in "BARTLEBY THE SCRIVENER: A Story of Wall Street" and by Charles Dudley WARNER for satirical purposes in his trilogy—*A Little Journey in the World* (1889), *The Golden House* (1895), and *That Fortune* (1899)—about the era of excess he had dubbed, in a previous novel, "the GILDED AGE."

Sources

Gordon, John Steele. *The Scarlet Woman of Wall Street: Jay Gould, Jim Fisk, Cornelius Vanderbilt, the Erie Railway Wars, and the Birth of Wall Street.* New York: Weidenfeld & Nicholson, 1988.

Westbrook, Wayne W. *Wall Street in the American Novel.* New York: New York University Press, 1980.

Ward, Artemus

See BROWNE, CHARLES FARRAR.

Ward, Elizabeth Stuart Phelps (Mary Adams) (1844–1911) *novelist, poet*

Born in Boston and christened Mary Gray, Elizabeth Ward was the daughter of the religious novelist Elizabeth Stuart Phelps (1815–52). After her mother's death, Ward carried on not only her mother's name but also her calling. Success came early with the religious fiction *The Gates Ajar* (1868), in which the young female protagonist finds faith and, in so doing, comes to believe that she will be reunited with her dead soldier brother in the afterlife. The emotional message of the work found an equally fervent audience among female readers who had recently lost loved ones in the CIVIL WAR. The spectacular success of *The Gates Ajar* led almost inexorably to a series of sequels, none of them as successful as the original.

Ward knew her audience, however, and for them she wrote a succession of novels and short stories pointing to women's plight in society. The first of these, *Hedged In* (1870), is a novel about the ostracism of morally unconventional women from polite society. Influenced by Rebecca Harding DAVIS's *Life in the Iron Mills,* Ward wrote "The Tenth of January," a story about the 1860 Pemberton Mills fire in Lawrence, Massachusetts. The story appeared in the *ATLANTIC MONTHLY* in 1868 and garnered Ward's first critical success. She followed with a novel about the lives of New England "spinster" mill girls, *The Silent Partner* (1871). Tracing a similar pattern, *The Story of Avis* (1877), a fictionalized treatment of Ward's mother's struggle to balance motherhood and a literary career, and *Doctor Zay* (1882), an account of a fictional female doctor probably based on the life of Ward's friend Dr. Mary Briggs Harris, followed a series of essays on women's rights that Ward published in the *Independent* and *Women's Journal* between 1871 and 1874. Two realistic novels about the lives of Gloucester fishermen, *The Madonna of the Tubs* (1886) and *Jack, the Fisherman* (1887), were something of a departure.

A Singular Life (1895), a novel about an unorthodox clergyman, returned Ward to familiar territory and memorialized her recently deceased father, a minister. Ward had married a younger man, a journalist named Herbert Dickinson Ward (1861–1932), and together they wrote several novels concerning figures from the Bible. The union was not a good one, but with the novel *Confessions of a Wife* (1902), published under the pen name Mary Adams, Ward managed to write a sensational book about the institution of marriage. She next turned to the cause of antivivisection, condemning the scientific practice of dissecting live animals in such works as the novel *Trixy* (1904). In all, Ward wrote more than 50 works, including several volumes of religious verse, and the autobiographical *Chapters from a Life* (1896).

Sources

Coultrap-McQuin, Susan. *Doing Literary Business: American Women Writers in the Nineteenth Century.* Chapel Hill: University of North Carolina Press, 1990.

Kelly, Lori Duin. *The Life and Works of Elizabeth Stuart Phelps, Victorian Feminist Writer.* Troy, N.Y.: Whitston Publishing Co., 1983.

Kessler, Carol Farley. *Elizabeth Stuart Phelps.* Boston: Twayne, 1982.

Warner, Charles Dudley (1829–1900) *essayist, editor, novelist*

Born in Massachusetts and reared in western New York state, where he graduated from Hamilton College in 1851, Charles Dudley Warner first took a job far from home, working as a railroad surveyor in Missouri. In the mid-1850s he came back east to attend law school at the University of Pennsylvania, then practiced law in Chicago from 1858 to 1860. His first love, however, was literature, and in 1861 he settled in Hartford, Connecticut, where he edited first the Hartford *Evening Post,* and then the *Courant.*

Warner had published his first monograph, a version of his Hamilton College commencement address titled *The Book of Eloquence,* in 1851. His first mature work was a graceful collection of essays and sketches about his farm, which he published in 1870 as *My Summer in a Garden.* Praised for its stylistic likeness to the works of Washington IRVING, the book went through 44 editions by 1895. Other equally successful essay collections followed: *Backlog Studies* (1873), *Baddeck* (1874), *Being a Boy* (1878), *On Horseback* (1888), *As We Were Saying* (1891), *The Relation of Literature to Life* (1896), and *Fashions in Literature* (1902). Warner also traveled a good deal, and he put these experiences to good use in such travel literature as *Saunterings* (1872), *My Winter on the Nile* (1876), *In the Levant* (1877), *In the Wilderness* (1878), *A Roundabout Journey* (1883), and *Our Italy* (1891). He also wrote biographies of Washington IRVING (1881) and Captain John Smith (1881).

The prolific Warner was also a novelist, producing a trilogy that satirized the GILDED AGE and included *A Little Journey in the World* (1889), *The Golden House* (1895), and *That Fortune* (1899). But Warner is best remembered for an earlier work of fiction, his collaboration with Mark Twain (Samuel CLEMENS) that gave the post–Civil War period its name, *The Gilded Age* (1873). Warner was a close friend of many of the important literary figures of his day, including Twain and William Dean HOWELLS, whom Warner replaced as author of the "Editor's Study" department at HARPER'S in 1892. Warner also edited Houghton Mifflin's American Men of Letters series of biographies and served as president of the American Social Science Association and the National Institute of Arts and Letters.

Sources

Condon, Garrett. "Charles Dudley Warner, 1829–1900," in "His World: Mark Twain in Hartford." Available on-line; URL: http://www.courantclassifieds.com/projects/twain/warner.htm. Downloaded October 25, 2001.

Washington, Booker Taliaferro (1856–1915) *educator, autobiographer*

Booker T. Washington was born into bondage in rural Virginia, the offspring of a black slave mother and a white father he never knew—although, as his autobiography *UP FROM SLAVERY* reveals, Washington suspected that his father was also his master. Later freed, Washington worked in the West Virginia coal mines while struggling to get an education. He began by teaching himself to read, then walked most of the 500 miles to the Hampton Normal and Agricultural Institute in Virginia, where he parlayed a janitorial job into a vocational education. After he successfully established a program for Native Americans at Hampton in 1881, the 25-year-old Washington was named to head a new normal school for African American students at Tuskegee, Alabama.

Washington served as principal of the Tuskegee Institute until his death in 1915, transforming it from a vocational school into a college that also offered professional education. The success of this endeavor, combined with his compelling personal story and his oratorical gifts, made him the most influential black person of his age. He hobnobbed with presidents and industrialists, and in 1895 he delivered an address to the Cotton States and International Exposition in Atlanta that transformed him—at least for white Americans—into the spokesperson for an entire race.

Washington's "Atlanta Exposition Address" did not go over so well with some other African-American leaders. W. E. B. DUBOIS, in particular, objected to Washington's acceptance of the status quo that perpetuated segregation and unequal rights. In the end Washington proved to be a divisive figure: It was reaction to his 1895 address that galvanized African-American activists into forming the National Association for the Advancement of Colored People in 1909.

Sources

Harlan, Louis R. *Booker T. Washington in Perspective: Essays of Louis R. Harlan.* Edited by Raymond W. Smock. Jackson: University Press of Mississippi, 1988.

———. *Booker T. Washington: The Making of a Black Leader, 1856–1901.* New York: Oxford University Press, 1972.

———. *Booker T. Washington: The Wizard of Tuskegee, 1901–1915.* New York: Oxford University Press, 1983.

Washington Square Henry James (1881) *novel*

In writing this novel, Henry JAMES might have had in mind the Washington Square of his childhood, when he lived with his family in what was then NEW YORK CITY's most fashionable residential district. The novel centers on Catherine Sloper, an unremarkable young woman whose only distinguishing characteristic, as her father says, is that she is an heiress. Although the action of the story involves Catherine's romance with a young man, Morris Townsend, its central relationship is that between the stolid daughter and her sardonic father, Dr. Austin Sloper.

Embittered by the loss of his wife and son, Dr. Sloper is profoundly disappointed in his plain, unimaginative daughter, now his only family. For her part, Catherine is only too conscious of her father's disapproval, in spite of which—or because of which—she adores him. For his sake she has turned away a number of potential suitors, choosing instead to remain her father's companion. All this changes overnight, however, when she meets Morris Townsend at a party. Catherine, who finds him the most beautiful man she has ever known, is instantly smitten. Townsend seemingly returns her regard, and within two months they are engaged to be married.

When Catherine dutifully informs her father that she has accepted Townsend's proposal, Dr. Sloper is immediately on guard. He has heard that Townsend is a penniless bounder who lives off his widowed sister, and he tells his daughter as much. When Catherine confronts her fiancé with her father's suspicions, Townsend assures her that he is marrying her for love, not money. Nevertheless, he declines to ask Dr. Sloper for Catherine's hand, asking her to intercede on his behalf.

At age 20, Catherine is already a wealthy woman, owing to a bequest from her late mother. Upon Dr. Sloper's death, Catherine stands to inherit a great deal more. Convinced that Townsend is after his daughter's inheritance, Dr. Sloper refuses to give his consent, telling Catherine that he will disinherit her if she goes ahead with the marriage. Catherine decides to go ahead with her plans anyway, but when Townsend encourages her to accompany her father on a six-month trip to Europe, she agrees to go.

When after six months Catherine gives no sign that she has forgotten Townsend, Dr. Sloper suggests they stay on for another six months. But even after a full year away from the man she loves, she still has not changed her mind about marrying him, and her father reacts with disgust and a cruel coldness. Finally fathoming the depth of her father's dislike—not just of Townsend, but of herself—Catherine's own heart freezes. She will never again bend to her father's will.

Upon her return, Catherine intends to carry out the plans she and Townsend made a year earlier. To her surprise, however, Townsend reacts with little enthusiasm, saying he may have to go away. Townsend's true plans dawn slowly on Catherine, but after he leaves, promising to return in a week, she collapses. She understands that her father has been right all along: Because she has failed to change her father's attitude toward her intended and thus ensure her full inheritance, Townsend is no longer interested.

Life goes on, seemingly unchanged, in the Washington Square household. But some years later, as Dr. Sloper lays dying, Catherine refuses to promise that she will never marry Townsend. Not realizing that she is long past caring for his money—or for him—Dr. Sloper disinherits his daughter. But Catherine has no intention of marrying Townsend. When she sees him again after a 20-year hiatus, she responds to his renewed suit by asking him to leave. Now a spinster "maiden-aunt to the younger portion of society," Cather Sloper is left with her tapestry work, her $10,000 per year, and a diminished—but intact—sense of her own worth.

Washington Square was first dramatized as *The Heiress* in 1947 and made into a film two years later. In the 1990s it enjoyed a triumphant revival on BROADWAY.

Sources

Boren, Lynda S. *Eurydice Reclaimed: Language, Gender, and Voice in Henry James.* Ann Arbor, Mich.: UMI Research Press, 1989.

Fowler, Virginia C. *Henry James's American Girl: The Embroidery on the Canvas.* Madison: University of Wisconsin Press, 1984.

Walton, Priscilla L. *The Disruption of the Feminine in Henry James.* Toronto: University of Toronto Press, 1992.

Webster, Daniel (1782–1852) *orator, attorney, U.S. senator*

A native of New Hampshire, Daniel Webster graduated from Dartmouth College and was admitted to the bar in 1805. He was first elected to Congress in 1813 and quickly established his reputation as a dynamic public speaker and successful lawyer. Elected to the U.S. Senate in 1827, Webster became the arch opponent of John C. Calhoun (1782–1850), the South Carolina senator who championed states' rights and believed in the rights of the states to nullify federal laws. Often touted as a likely president, Webster was never nominated for the nation's highest office, although he served as secretary of state (1841–43) and then returned to the Senate in 1845.

Webster opposed slavery but he also sought to protect the constitutional rights of slaveholders. This divided stand cost him political support and doomed his presidential ambitions. New England abolitionists treated Webster as a traitor when he supported the Compromise of 1850, which sanctioned slavery while retarding its advance into the western territories. John Greenleaf WHITTIER attacked Webster in a poem, "Ichabod," and Ralph Waldo EMERSON treated Webster like a fallen great man.

Because of the power of his oratory and his ability to rise to important occasions—notably his speeches at Bunker Hill (1825, 1843), one of the sacred sites of the American Revolution—Webster became identified with the spirit of American patriotism itself and the desire to preserve the union, epitomized in his *Discourse in Commemoration of Jefferson and Adams* (1826). Even his fiercest critics later relented and recognized his greatness—as did Whittier in his poem "The Lost Occasion" (1880), in which he regretted and apologized for his attacks on Webster.

Webster's oratory was published in 18 volumes in 1903. His style has often been called "Ciceronian" in recognition of the Roman-like majesty of his rhetoric. His legend lasted well beyond his own lifetime and indeed was enhanced in

Stephen Vincent Benét's (1889–1943) libretto, *The Devil and Daniel Webster* (1939). *The Daniel Webster Reader* was published in 1956, and *Speak For Yourself, Daniel: A Life of Webster in His Own Words* in 1969.

Sources

Bartlett, Irving H. *Daniel Webster.* New York: W. W. Norton, 1978.

Erickson, Paul D. *The Poetry of Events: Daniel Webster's Rhetoric of the Constitution and Union.* New York: New York University Press, 1986.

Shewmaker, Kenneth E., ed. *Daniel Webster: "The Completest Man."* Hanover: University Press of New England, 1990.

Webster, Noah (1758–1843) *lexicographer*

Connecticut native Noah Webster joined the Continental Army with his father and fought in the Revolutionary War. Afterward, he obtained a degree from Yale University and began a series of teaching jobs that continued even after he was admitted to the bar in 1781. Strongly committed to federalism, he wrote numerous pamphlets supporting a strong central government, including *Sketches of American Policy* (1785), and from 1793 to 1798 he worked as a journalist supporting the policies of Presidents George Washington (1732–1799) and John Adams (1735–1826).

Webster's support for the republic eventually translated into an interest in the American language. In his *Dissertation upon the English Language* (1789), he wrote: "As an independent nation, our honor requires us to have a system of our own, in language as well as government." His *Grammatical Institute of the English Language,* which appeared in three parts—spelling in 1783, grammar in 1784, and reading and rhetoric in 1785—attempted to provide that system. The first part, published separately and known as the "blue-back Speller," became a best-seller in the course of standardizing and thereby unifying the American idiom. It is worth noting that the difficulty of copyrighting his work separately in every state added to his Federalist ardor and spurred him to work for a federal copyright law.

All the while, Webster was hard at work on his *Dictionary,* which would reflect not only his Americanist bias but also his wide-ranging interests in such matters as literature, economics, science, and gardening. In 1806 Webster published his *Compendious Dictionary of the English Language,* which was but a forerunner of his highly influential two-volume *American Dictionary of the English Language* (1828). The latter went toe-to-toe with Joseph WORCESTER's *Comprehensive Pronouncing and Explanatory Dictionary of the English Language* (1830) in what came to be known as the "War of the Dictionaries." But while the literary elite favored Worcester's purist approach to the language, Webster's emphasis on American usage—and his inclusion of some 5,000 words new to any English-language dictionary—won the day.

In 1840 Webster published a revised version of his dictionary, nearly doubling the number of entries. This work, in its many subsequent editions, set the standard for American English. This status was assured when George and Charles Merriam, who purchased the rights to Webster's dictionary after his death, issued a revised one-volume edition that sold for only $6. Immediately, both Massachusetts and New York purchased a copy for every schoolhouse in each state, and the U.S. Congress made it a standard reference.

Webster pursued other interests while creating his master work, serving his city, his state, and his nation in a variety of political and judicial roles, helping to found Amherst College, and writing a revised version of the Bible. All of these experiences contributed to, but could not surpass, his achievement of helping to unify the entire country by recording and organizing its language.

Sources

Micklethwait, David. *Noah Webster and the American Dictionary.* Jefferson, N.C.: McFarland, 2000.

Snyder, K. Alan. *Defining Noah Webster: Mind and Morals in the Early Republic.* Lanham, Md.: University Press of America, 1990.

Unger, Harlow G. *Noah Webster: The Life and Times of an American Patriot.* New York: John Wiley & Sons, 1998.

Wells-Barnett, Ida Bell (1862–1931) *journalist, pamphleteer, autobiographer, reformer*

The daughter of slaves, Ida B. Wells was born in Holly Springs, Mississippi. The eldest of eight children, she took responsibility for her younger siblings when her parents and their youngest child died in a yellow fever epidemic in 1878. She had been attending Shaw University, but at 18 she was forced to drop out and go to work as a country schoolteacher, a position she kept until 1884, when she moved to Memphis to take a position in that city's public school system.

That same year saw the advent of Wells's social activism. After being forcibly removed from a first-class ladies' coach because of her race, she sued the Chesapeake, Ohio and Southwestern Railroad and won, only to have the trial verdict reversed on appeal. This experience prompted Wells to write a series of letters concerning racial and gender issues to local, then national periodicals. Her public criticism of the poor-quality black-only schools in Memphis caused her dismissal in 1891, after which she devoted herself full time to journalism.

Already part-owner of the Memphis *Free Speech and Headlight,* Wells stepped up the militancy of her editorials. After the lynching of three Memphis African-American grocers in 1892, Wells urged her fellow citizens to leave the city, alleging that lynching was a racist strategy to destroy the hard-won economic independence of the black middle class. When some outraged white Memphians responded by destroying her offices, Wells remained undaunted: She kept a loaded gun at home and advised other African-Americans to follow her example. She broadened her antilynching crusade, buying an interest in the *New York Age,* where she published two weekly columns under the byline "Iola." She published numerous antilynching pamphlets over the next few years and, in 1893, took her lecture tour to England in an effort to bring international pressure to bear on the cause.

By the time Wells married lawyer Ferdinand L. Barnett, she was living in Chicago, which would remain her base of operations. She gave birth to four children, and she would often take them with her on the lecture circuit, which had widened to include her interest in women's suffrage (see SUFFRAGISM). Active in the civic-minded women's club movement of the late 19th century, she founded the Ida B. Wells Club of Chicago in 1893. Later she would found the Alpha Suffrage Club and cofound the Cook County League of Women's Clubs. As secretary of the National Afro-American Council she helped initiate the formation of the NAACP. In 1910 she formed the Negro Fellowship League, which helped find employment for Southern blacks who had migrated north. To fund the project Wells contributed the salary she earned as a probation officer working with young black men in Chicago.

Wells continued to work as a journalist into her fifties, covering the 1918 race riot in East St. Louis, Illinois, for the *Chicago Defender* and the indictment of 12 innocent farmers for murder in Arkansas in 1921. In 1928 she started an autobiography, and two years later she resumed work on the diaries she had kept intermittently throughout her hectic life. After her death in 1931 following a sudden illness, her daughter, Alfreda Duster (1904–), edited and published these works.

Sources

McMurry, Linda O. *To Keep the Waters Troubled: The Life of Ida B. Wells.* New York: Oxford University Press, 1998.

Miller, Ericka M. *The Other Reconstruction: Where Violence and Womanhood Meet in the Writings of Wells-Barnett, Grimke, and Larsen.* New York: Garland, 2000.

Thompson, Mildred I. *Ida B. Wells-Barnett: An Exploratory Study of an American Black Woman, 1893–1930.* Brooklyn, N.Y.: Carlson Pub., 1990.

western *genre*

Type of popular fiction focused on adventures set in the American West. First built around historical figures such as Daniel BOONE and on various anonymous trappers and Indian scouts, westerns changed their focus after the CIVIL WAR, when the West was opened for cattle ranchers. Cowboys then became the heroes of the genre, which also took up the Indian wars that accompanied settlement of the West in the later part of the 19th century. The first practitioners of the western were such DIME NOVEL writers as E. Z. C. JUDSON, but Owen WISTER's 1902 *THE VIRGINIAN* (1902) changed the genre forever. Formulaic westerns were still alive and well—often published in such pulp magazines as *Smith's Magazine* (1905) and *Western Story Magazine* (1919)—but the formula had changed. Gone was the emphasis on "real" persons and exaggerated accounts of "genuine" events. Instead one had (at least in Wister's case) a nameless stranger obliged to make his way in a hostile environment, with the narrator taking careful note of the stranger's dress, speech, and manner. The new formula did not do away with ROMANCE—far from it—but the archetypal attachment of the stranger and the schoolmarm gained validity from the realistic detail with which it was conveyed and the violent effects with which it was contrasted.

Many worthy successors elaborated the singular narrative form that Wister had created. Perhaps the most significant of these was Zane GREY, who became one of the most prolific and widely read authors of his—or any other—time. Although Grey probed less into his characters' emotions, he gave his books a philosophical bent that was lacking in most other popular westerns. Other late 19th- and early 20th-century writers of westerns included the artist Frederick Remington (1816–89); Clarence E. Mulford (1883–1956), the creator of the cowboy hero Hopalong Cassidy; and Frederick Faust (1892–1944), who wrote an astonishing 600 western novels and stories under a variety of pseudonyms, the most famous of which is "Max Brand." Female writers of westerns were rare, but Bertha M. Bower (1871–1940) created a notably unglamorous cowboy protagonist in *Chip, of the Flying U* (1906).

Sources

Lawlor, Mary. *Recalling the Wild: Naturalism and the Closing of the American West.* New Brunswick, N.J.: Rutgers University Press, 2000.

Milton, John R. *The Novel of the American West.* Lincoln: University of Nebraska Press, 1980.

Walle, Alf H. *The Cowboy Hero and Its Audience: Popular Culture as Market Derived Art.* Bowling Green, Ohio: Bowling Green State University Popular Press, 2000.

Western Messenger, The (1835–1841) *periodical*

This monthly was founded in Cincinnati, Ohio, by a group of Unitarian ministers and served as an outlet for transcendentalist and Unitarian articles as well as for the exploration of German and Asian literature. William Henry CHANNING was the magazine's editor as well as a contributor. Others contributors included Margaret FULLER, Ralph Waldo EMERSON, and Elizabeth PEABODY.

Sources

Habich, Robert D. *Transcendentalism and the Western Messenger: A History of the Magazine and its Contributors, 1835–1841.* Rutherford, N.J.: Fairleigh Dickinson University Press, 1985.

"When Lilacs Last in the Dooryard Bloom'd"
Walt Whitman (1865–1866) *poem*

Walt WHITMAN's elegy to the assassinated president Abraham LINCOLN ranks among the most celebrated works in this genre. First published in Whitman's second volume of CIVIL WAR poetry, *Sequel to Drum Taps,* and later incorporated into *Leaves of Grass* (1867), the poem is written in 16 sections that constitute four cycles. The symbolic lilac, with its flowers and heart-shaped leaves representing love and rebirth, is introduced in the first cycle, in which the speaker laments the death of Lincoln. The second cycle traces the journey of Lincoln's coffin, which becomes symbolic of all coffins, all deaths. The third cycle juxtaposes grief with the regenerative power of the cycle of death. Cycle four resolves this tension and celebrates the mystery of death, in which the lilac, the western star (Lincoln, the beloved comrade), and the hermit thrush (the soul) are twined with the chant of the poet's soul.

Sources

Bauerlein, Mark. *Whitman and the American Idiom.* Baton Rouge: Louisiana State University Press, 1991.

Beach, Christopher. *The Politics of Distinction: Whitman and the Discourses of Nineteenth-Century America.* Athens: University of Georgia Press, 1996.

Erkkila, Betsy. *Whitman the Political Poet.* New York: Oxford University Press, 1989.

Whig Party

See AMERICAN WHIG REVIEW.

White, Andrew Dickson (1832–1918) *educator, historian*

A national leader in the field of higher education, Andrew D. White began his academic career as a professor of history at the University of Michigan, a post he held from 1857 to 1863. A native of New York state, he was elected in 1864 to the state legislature, where he joined with his fellow senator, Ezra Cornell (1807–74), to found Cornell University in Ithaca, New York. White served as the university's first president (1867–85), and he is credited with creating a nonsectarian, coeducational institution with a modern, liberal curriculum emphasizing agriculture, engineering, and the natural sciences. White succeeded in attracting such prominent scholars as James Russell LOWELL and Bayard TAYLOR to Cornell, while at the same time responding to attacks on what some called his "godless institution" with *The Warfare of Science* (1876), the *History of the Warfare of Science with Theology in Christendom* (1896), and *Seven Great Statesmen in the Warfare of Humanity with Unreason* (1910).

In 1884 White helped found the AMERICAN HISTORICAL ASSOCIATION and served as its first president. He also served the federal government, first as minister to Germany (1878–81), then as minister to Russia (1892–94) and ambassador to Germany (1896–1902), and finally as head of the American delegation to the 1899 Hague Conference on the creation of an international court of arbitration.

Sources

Altschuler, Glenn C. *Andrew D. White, Educator, Historian, Diplomat.* Ithaca, N.Y.: Cornell University Press, 1979.

White Fang *Jack London* (1906) *novel*

Jack LONDON intended this book to be a sequel to *THE CALL OF THE WILD* (1903), which traces a tame dog's reversion to wildness. In *White Fang,* a wild wolf-dog gradually becomes domesticated after he is rescued from a life in professional dogfights. Weedon Scott, a mining engineer, gradually wins White Fang over with gentleness, and the dog reciprocates by sacrificing his life to save Weedon's family from an assault by an escaped convict. In later days a classic of children's literature, *White Fang* proved enormously popular when published, helping to make London's reputation as a naturalist.

Sources

Watson, Charles N. *The Novels of Jack London: A Reappraisal.* Madison: University of Wisconsin Press, 1983.

Whitman, Walter (1819–1892) *poet*

Walt Whitman was born on Long Island and lived in BROOKLYN, New York, with his family from 1823 to 1833. He went to schools there, and his early jobs were in printing shops and journalism. A voracious and comprehensive reader, he absorbed Shakespeare, the Bible, Sir Walter Scott, Homer, Dante, and some of the writings of Eastern religion and philosophy—all of which would show in his prodigious vocabulary and poetic ideas that ranged freely among the world's philosophies and religions.

Whitman's early poetry appeared in newspapers in the 1840s. He was a conventional poet and exhibited none of the brash experimentalism of his major work. He also wrote sad stories and other articles later arranged in two volumes as *The Uncollected Poetry and Prose of Walt Whitman* (1921) and *The Half-Breed and Other Stories* (1927). His most important journalistic job during this apprentice period as a writer then as the editor of *The BROOKLYN EAGLE* (1846), a newspaper that supported the Democratic Party and attack the abolitionists (see ABOLITIONISM). Whitman's own belief in free soil (the policy of admitting to statehood only those territories disavowing slavery) and antislavery politics cost him his job in 1848. His pieces in *The Brooklyn Eagle* were later assembled in two volumes in *The Gathering of Forces* (1920).

In 1848 Whitman traveled to New Orleans, where he worked briefly, and also traveled in the Midwest before returning to Brooklyn to work on several local papers, including the Brooklyn *Times;* his pieces are collected in *I Sit and Look Out* (1932). By the late 1840s Whitman was making a study of New York City, spending a good deal of time at the opera, riding the ferryboats, talking to the drivers of horse-drawn cabs, and in modern parlance just "hanging out" and soaking up the atmosphere. The long catalogues of *Leaves of Grass* would demonstrate his encyclopedic knowledge of the city and would include vivid pictures of other parts of the country he had visited.

Exactly how Whitman transformed himself from a journeyman journalist and uninspired poet into a major writer who has influenced American and world literature is a mystery. Something in his makeup, however, decided him on a startling openness to experience, a lack of reservation that put him well beyond the ken of any other writer in America of his time. Certainly his reading influenced him—above all Thomas Carlyle's (1795–1881) concept of the hero who transforms history. Whitman selected himself as just such a man. He was also inspired by Ralph Waldo EMERSON's essay "The Poet," which became virtually a blueprint for Whitman, sanctioning his prophetic power and releasing his inhibitions. Emerson might write about such a poet/prophet, but Whitman decided to become the very thing.

When Whitman burst into American literature with *Leaves of Grass* (1855), he had completely revolutionized himself and his concept of poetry. Even calling himself "Walt" and putting an engraving of himself in his book in casual dress, striking a jaunty stance with his hat cocked to the side, announced a new poetic sensibility. Until then American poets presented themselves as august, establishment figures, often with three names—for example, Henry Wadsworth LONGFELLOW, William Cullen BRYANT, and John Greenleaf WHITTIER. Whitman brushed aside all formalities. He was rough and ready like the city he lived in; he was all energy; he did not stand on his dignity. His verse was not shackled by the meters or the rhymes of the past; it flowed in long lines but also compacted itself into vivid images.

Whitman's poems were sensual, erotic, and, for his time, scandalous. They were also the product of an enormous ego. Whitman claimed he had the vision to speak for a whole country because the United States was essentially one great poem. Whitman promoted himself, using a letter of Emerson's (without the writer's permission) as a blurb for *Leaves of Grass.* Whitman even wrote his own reviews of *Leaves of Grass.*

Leaves of Grass became Whitman's lifework. He continued to revise and add to it, incorporating his extraordinary experiences as a nurse during the CIVIL WAR—first issued as *Drum-Taps* in 1865. He also wrote prose about the war in *Specimen Days* (1882). Often misunderstood, he was fired from his job in the Department of the Interior because his books were thought to be immoral. But he had already begun to attract an international audience, with many visitors making pilgrimages to see him during his last 19 years of retirement in Camden, New Jersey, a wreck of a man who had suffered a paralyzing stroke in 1873.

It is doubtful that Whitman actually had all the erotic experiences and other adventures described in his poetry. His work was imaginative, and he endowed people with the inspiration to see themselves as great souls partaking of a universal fellowship, much as the transcendentalists advocated (see TRANSCENDENTALISM).

It is not an exaggeration to name Whitman as the father of modern American poetry. Twentieth-century poets as different as Allen Ginsberg (1926–97), William Carlos Williams (1883–1963), and Ezra Pound (1885–1972) have accorded him that title, realizing that their own bold experimentation with poetry owed a huge debt to Whitman. His work has its faults—including a tendency to treat every subject in the same ecstatic tones so as to risk trivializing and leveling all differences among experiences. At his greatest, however, Whitman perceives the unity in diversity and celebrates a world that is many and yet one. Much of his Civil War verse, such as "Cavalry Crossing a Ford," prefigures the precision of the early 20th-century imagists, and his open discussion of sexuality inspired the work of many Beat poets in the 1950s.

Sources

Bloom, Harold, ed. *Walt Whitman.* New York: Chelsea House, 1985.

Greenspan, Ezra, ed. *The Cambridge Companion to Walt Whitman.* New York: Cambridge University Press, 1995.

Kaplan, Justin. *Walt Whitman: A Life.* New York: Simon & Schuster, 1980.

Pearce, Roy Harvey, ed. *Whitman: A Collection of Critical Essays.* Englewood Cliffs, N.J.: Prentice Hall, 1962.

Reynolds, David. *Walt Whitman's America: A Cultural Biography.* New York: Alfred A. Knopf, 1995.

Whittier, John Greenleaf (1807–1892) *poet*

John Greenleaf Whittier was born into a Massachusetts Quaker family. His basic values remained those of his family, although early on he became attracted to poetry, reading the verse of Scottish poet Robert Burns (1759–96) and taking perceptive delight in rural England. He was employed as an editor and mentored by William Lloyd GARRISON, the journalist and New England abolitionist who printed some of Whittier's earliest poems.

Whittier published his first book, *Legends of New-England in Prose and Verse,* a work of LOCAL COLOR and history, in

1831. He pursued New England themes and characters in *Moll Pitcher* (1832) and *Mogg Megone* (1836), the story of Indian life during the colonial period. These works also reflected his abiding concern with social justice. He spoke at many antislavery meetings, served in the state legislature in 1835, and published *Poems Written During the Progress of the Abolition Question* (1838) and *Voices of Freedom* (1846).

While he continued a full engagement with social and political causes, Whittier also continued to probe New England history, producing *Leaves from Margaret Smith's Journal in the Province of Massachusetts Bay, 1678–79* (1849), his only sustained work of fiction. The novel has been compared to Nathaniel HAWTHORNE's fiction because Whittier pursues a deeply romantic view of Puritan behavior that attempts to do justice to the rebelliousness of individuals and the Puritan sense of community. Whittier's other prose includes *Old Portraits and Modern Sketches* (1850) and *Literary Recreations and Miscellanies* (1854).

Whittier's pastoral poetry includes some of his best work. *The Chapel of the Hermit* (1853); *The Panorama and Other Poems* (1856); and *Home Ballads, Poems and Lyrics* (1860) include the poems on which his poetic reputation is based: "Maud Muller," "The Barefoot Boy," "Skipper Ireson's Ride," and "Telling the Bees." But *Snow-Bound* (1866), an idyl based on his memory of being snowed in on his father's Massachusetts farm, is considered his masterwork. Other volumes of verse about rural life and Colonial/Quaker history followed: *Among the Hills* (1869), *Miriam and Other Poems* (1871), *Hazel-Blossoms* (1875), *The Vision of Echard* (1878), *St. Gregory's Guest* (1886), and *At Sundown* (1890).

Whittier also edited John Woolman's *Journal* (1871), the work of a Quaker ancestor who greatly influenced Whittier's world view. The poet's *Letters* were published in three volumes in 1975. *John Greenleaf Whittier's Poetry: An Appraisal and a Selection,* by Robert Penn Warren (1905–89), appeared in 1971.

Whittier retains his high place in American literature as a poet of nature, rural life, and the New England past. He is a precursor of such poets as Robert Frost (1874–1963) and Robert Penn Warren, the latter writing sympathetically about Whittier as an agrarian ancestor. Whittier's faults are plain: the forced effort to state a moral message, the forcing of lines to fit ill-conceived metrical patterns, and a sentimentality that makes the emotion of his poems seem contrived. Even his honest abolitionist poems have an abstract quality—a desire to express his outrage rather than a concrete coming-to-grips with the plight of the slaves. Nevertheless, his best work has a purity that seems to arise out of the natural scenes he evokes. He has been called a "pure poet" because his finest work is unadorned, plain, even homespun and heartfelt.

Sources

Kribbs, Jayne K., ed. *Critical Essays on John Greenleaf Whittier.* Boston: G. K. Hall, 1980.

Leary, Lewis. *John Greenleaf Whittier.* New York: Twayne, 1962.

Pickard, John B. *John Greenleaf Whittier: An Introduction and Interpretation.* New York: Barnes & Noble, 1961.

Willis, Nathaniel Parker (1806–1867) *editor, literary gadfly*

In modern times N. P. Willis is remembered primarily for who he knew and for one poem, a moralistic piece called "Unseen Spirits," but in his day he cut a wide swath through the literary world. Born in Maine, Willis was educated at Yale, where he quickly made a name for himself as a poet and prose stylist. He then founded *THE AMERICAN MONTHLY MAGAZINE* (1829–31), which, although it lasted only two years, served as an outlet for his own stories—later frequently reprinted—and a brilliant bit of self-promotion: Only 25 years old, he was already regarded as one of the most sophisticated editors in the nation. Some, however, regarded his pose as an aesthete with skepticism. With reference to the early 19th-century French dandy and tastemaker, Count D'Orsay (1801–57), and the late-century scandal-ridden Irish playwright, Oscar Wilde (1854–1900), Oliver Wendell HOLMES remarked that Willis was "something between a remembrance of Count D'Orsay and an anticipation of Oscar Wilde."

Willis continued his colorful career by publishing two more volumes of poetry, then becoming a foreign correspondent for the *NEW-YORK MIRROR.* His beat was social affairs, and after traveling on the Continent, in England, and through Turkey from 1832 to 1836, he recorded his impressions of the personages he had encountered in *Pencillings by the Way* (1835) and *Loiterings of Travel* (1840). While still in England, where he attracted both attention and opprobrium, Willis published *Melanie and Other Poems* (1835) and, under the pseudonym Philip Slingsby, a series of sketches collected as *Inklings of Adventure* (1836). He also engaged in a pistol duel with the editor of the London *Metropolitan Magazine,* whom Willis felt had slandered him in a negative review of *Pencillings.*

Back in the United States, Willis turned to drama, writing such romantic tragedies as the blank verse play *Tortesa, or the Usurer* (1839), which garnered the support of Edgar Allan POE. Willis returned the favor by hiring Poe as literary critic for the *Mirror,* which he was then editing. The *Mirror* also served as an outlet for Willis's American sketches, later collected as *Al'Abri; or, The Tent Pitch'd* (1839) and *American Scenery* (1840). His other literary efforts from that time—some society verse and a volumes of stories with surprise endings titled *Dashes at Life with a Free Pencil* (1845)—exhibited the same sort of casualness. His one novel, *Paul Fane* (1857), was a semiautobiographical account of a young painter who is at once a celebrity and a social pariah.

Willis continued to make good use—and reuse—of his life and works. In addition to publishing accounts of trips to

Europe and the West Indies in magazines and as collections of letters, he reissued earlier works under new titles. Celebrated for the lavish hospitality displayed at his country residence on the Hudson River, Willis was also unflatteringly portrayed in *Ruth Hall* (1855), a novel written by his sister, Sarah Payson Willis PARTON.

Sources

Auser, Courtland P. *Nathaniel P. Willis.* New York: Twayne, 1969.

Baker, Thomas N. *Sentiment & Celebrity: Nathaniel Parker Willis and the Trials of Literary Fame.* New York: Oxford University Press, 1999.

Wilson, Harriet E. Adams (1825/28–1870?)

novelist

The first published African-American novelist, Harriet Wilson—and her one novel, *Our Nig* (1859)—were mere footnotes to American literary history until 1984, when the scholars Henry Louis Gates Jr. and Davis Ames Curtis revealed that the novelist, long believed to be a white woman, was in fact black. Born in Milford, New Hampshire, sometime between 1825 and 1828, Harriet Adams was left at age six at the home of the Haywards, a wealthy old Milford family who apparently subjected Adams to severe mistreatment. When she was 18 she left the Haywards, and in 1850—the year that passage of the Fugitive Slave Act endangered African Americans in the North—lived in the household of a carpenter named Samuel Boyle. On October 6, 1851, in Milford, Adams married Thomas Wilson, a free man posing as a fugitive slave in order to earn money lecturing about the evils of slavery. In June of the next year, deserted by her husband, Harriet Wilson gave birth to a son, George Mason Wilson, in a pauper's "country house."

Alone, ill, and impoverished, Harriet Wilson was compelled to write *Our Nig,* subtitled *Sketches from the Life of a Free Black, in a Two-Story White House, North, Showing That Slavery's Shadows Fall Even There.* The book recounted the story of Frado, a mixed-race servant who is abandoned as a child by her white mother and abused by the white family for whom she works. Wilson registered the book's copyright and published it in September 1859. Her son, who had been placed in foster care, died five months later. It was his death certificate, rediscovered by Gates and Curtis, that would reveal the true racial identity of the author of *Our Nig,* a "Northern" SLAVE NARRATIVE Wilson based on her own biography but transformed into fiction.

Sources

Andrews, William L. *To Tell a Free Story: The First Century of Afro-American Autobiography, 1760–1865.* Urbana: University of Illinois Press, 1986.

Curtis, David Ames, and Henry Louis Gates Jr. "Establishing the Identity of the Author of *Our Nig.*" In *"Wild Women in the Whirlwind: Afro-American Culture and the Contemporary Literary Renaissance,"* edited by Joanne Braxton and Andree McLaughlin. New Brunswick, N.J.: Rutgers University Press, 1990, pp. 48–69.

Wilson, Thomas Woodrow (1856–1924)

historian, essayist, public official, 27th president of the United States

Born in Staunton, Virginia, Woodrow Wilson graduated from Princeton University in 1879 and went on to study law at the University of Virginia. He practiced law only briefly before returning to school to obtain a Ph.D. in history and political science from Johns Hopkins University. He then began an academic career that took him from teaching positions at Johns Hopkins, Bryn Mawr College, and Wesleyan University back to Princeton, where he served first as a professor of jurisprudence and political economy, and then, from 1902 to 1910, as president.

In 1910, after losing a bitter struggle to democratize the social climate at Princeton, Wilson entered the New Jersey gubernatorial race as the Democratic nominee and won, largely on the strength of his oratorical abilities, his knowledge of American history and politics, and his genuinely democratic leanings. Two years later, campaigning on his record as a reformer and a platform he called the New Freedom, Wilson won the White House.

Wilson was by nature a progressive, and his banking and tariff reforms were considered radical. He was unable, however, to pursue his domestic agenda owing to the outbreak of war in Europe. Even though he won reelection in 1916 by proclaiming that he had kept America out of war, in 1917, after the Germans sank several American merchant ships and the United States discovered that Germany had proposed a military alliance with Mexico, Wilson was forced to go to war. Within 15 months, the nation had deployed a million troops to eastern France, where they helped bring the war to an end. On November 11, 1918, World War I ended with an armistice, and Wilson began a diplomatic crusade that was intended to bring "peace without victory" through a proposal he called the Fourteen Points. This proposal, which was essentially a master plan for world peace, stalled in the U.S. Senate over the issue of the League of Nations, the precursor of the United Nations that many senators—angry with Wilson's proposals and tactics—opposed out of spite rather than principle. A frustrated Wilson took to the road in a personal crusade to drum up support for his project, only to collapse in Pueblo, Colorado, and then return to Washington, where he suffered a debilitating stroke. He never entirely recovered, although he served out his term.

Wilson was not only a noted orator but also a fine writer whose works include both historical writings, such as the five-volume *History of the American People* (1902); and polished literary criticism, such as that found in *Mere Literature and Other Essays* (1893).

Sources

Clements, Kendrick A. *The Presidency of Woodrow Wilson.* Lawrence: University Press of Kansas, 1992.

Link, Arthur S., comp. *Woodrow Wilson: A Profile.* New York: Hill and Wang, 1968.

Thorsen, Niels. *The Political Thought of Woodrow Wilson, 1875–1910.* Princeton, N.J.: Princeton University Press, 1988.

Wister, Owen (1860–1938) *novelist, short story writer, biographer*

The grandson of Fanny KEMBLE, Owen Wister was born in Philadelphia to a long-established Pennsylvania family. After attending St. Paul's School in New Hampshire, he went to Harvard, where he studied music and law and met a man who would become his lifelong friend, Theodore ROOSEVELT. Like Roosevelt, when Wister grew ill he went west, and it was there that he discovered his true métier. On the ranches of Wyoming where he spent his summers, Wister gathered the material that would make up short-story collections like *Red Men and White* (1896), tales of the Western cattle country; and especially the work for which he is best remembered, *The VIRGINIAN* (1902). Dedicated to his friend Roosevelt (whose request for the excision of an especially gory passage Wister granted), *The Virginian* set the pattern for an entire genre. The later stages of Wister's literary career focused on other venues, however. In addition to *Philosophy 4* (1903), a novel about undergraduate life at Harvard, and *Lady Baltimore* (1906), a romance set in Charleston, Wister published biographies of Ulysses S. GRANT (1900) and George Washington (1907), as well as a memoir about his relationship with Roosevelt (*Roosevelt: The Story of a Friendship, 1880–1919* [1930]).

Sources

Cobbs, John L. *Owen Wister.* Boston: Twayne, 1984.

Estleman, Loren D. *The Wister Trace: Classic Novels of the American Frontier.* Ottawa, Ill.: Jameson Books, 1987.

Payne, Darwin. *Owen Wister: Chronicler of the West, Gentleman of the East.* Dallas, Tex.: Southern Methodist University Press, 1985.

Woman's Home Companion *periodical*

This fortnightly was founded in 1873 in Cleveland, Ohio, as the *Ladies' Home Companion* and was originally a children's magazine. In 1884 it was bought by *Farm & Fireside* and moved to Springfield, Ohio. Then part of the Crowell-Collier magazine chain, it was edited from New York and published both articles of domestic interest and popular fiction written by such authors as Willa Cather (1873–1947), Zona Gale (1874–1938), and Edna Ferber (1887–1968). After a circulation high point of 4 million, it declined in popularity until it folded in 1956.

Woodberry, George Edward (1855–1930) *poet, biographer, critic*

Born in Beverly, Massachusetts, George Edward Woodberry studied at Harvard under such eminent teachers as Henry ADAMS and James Russell LOWELL before becoming a professor of English at the University of Nebraska. In 1891 he took a position teaching comparative literature at Columbia University in New York City, a post he held until 1904. Woodberry gained the attention of the academy with his 1885 biography of Edgar Allan POE, which was expanded into a new edition that appeared in 1909 after he had edited a 10-volume edition of *The Works of Edgar Allan Poe* (1894–95). His 1902 life of Nathaniel HAWTHORNE was considered to be an even better work. Around this time Woodberry was also working on two collections of essays, published as *Heart of Man* (1899) and *Makers of Literature* (1900), that are precursors of the New Humanism, a philosophical and critical movement of the 1920s that stressed the ethical nature of human experience. His literary history, *America in Literature* (1900), underscored his antipathy to REALISM by failing to address the significance of Walt WHITMAN and Mark Twain (Samuel CLEMENS).

After resigning from Columbia, Woodberry retired to Massachusetts but continued his prodigious literary output. He had published his first collection of poetry, *The North Shore Watch,* in 1890. In 1917 he published *Ideal Passion,* a sonnet sequence dedicated to his aestheticism; and *The Roamer,* a lengthy narrative poem that constituted a kind of spiritual autobiography, appeared in 1920. These publications were preceded by two collections of his lectures, *The Torch* (1905) and *The Appreciation of Literature* (1907), a biography of Ralph Waldo EMERSON (1907), and a book charting some of his wide-ranging travels, *North Africa and the Desert* (1914).

Sources

Woodberry, George Edward. *Selected Poems of George Edward Woodberry.* Boston: Houghton Mifflin, 1933.

Woodhull, Victoria Claflin (1838–1927) *reformer, pamphleteer*

Born in Ohio, Victoria Woodhull first made a name for herself with the spiritualist performances, fortune telling, and patent-medicine peddling she engaged in with her mother and sister, Tennessee Celeste Claflin (1846–1923). Victoria married twice before moving with her sister to New York City, where they so charmed the transportation magnate Cornelius

Vanderbilt (1794–1877) that he helped set them up as Wall Street brokers. Then, with the help of Stephen P. Andrews, they started the radical periodical, *Woodhull and Claflin's Weekly* (1870–76) which, in addition to advocating socialism, free love, birth control, and women's suffrage (see SUFFRAGISM), was also the first periodical to publish news of the sexual scandal surrounding Henry Ward BEECHER, in addition to an English translation of Karl Marx's *Communist Manifesto.*

In 1872 Woodhull was nominated for president by the Equal Rights Party, with Frederick DOUGLASS as her running mate. Five years later the Claflin sisters moved to England, where Victoria married into a wealthy banking family and Tennessee married a baronet.

From 1892 to 1901 Woodhull published a periodical called *Humanitarian* with her daughter, Zulu Maud Woodhull. With her sister she also published the pamphlet *The Human Body as the Temple of God* (1890). Woodhull's own significant publications include the pamphlets *Origin, Tendencies and Principles of Government* (1871), the eugenics tracts *Stirpiculture* (1888) and *The Alchemy of Maternity* (1889), and *And the Truth Shall Make You Free: A Speech on the Principles of Social Freedom* (1894).

Sources

Gabriel, Mary. *Notorious Victoria: The Life of Victoria Woodhull, Uncensored.* Chapel Hill, N.C.: Algonquin Books, 1998.

Goldsmith, Barbara. *Other Powers: The Age of Suffrage, Spiritualism, and the Scandalous Victoria Woodhull.* New York: Alfred A. Knopf, 1998.

Johnston, Johanna. *Mrs. Satan: The Incredible Saga of Victoria C. Woodhull.* New York: Putnam, 1967.

Worcester, Joseph Emerson (1784–1865) *lexicographer, geographer, historian*

Born in New Hampshire and educated at Yale, Joseph Emerson Worcester taught school in Salem, Massachusetts, where Nathaniel HAWTHORNE was one of his pupils. While still teaching in Salem, Worcester published three geographical works, starting with the ambitious *A Geographical Dictionary, or Universal Gazetteer, Ancient and Modern* (1817). After moving to Cambridge, Massachusetts, in 1819, he published two comprehensive historical works, including *Elements of History Ancient and Modern* (1826), before embarking on a long series of dictionaries.

Worcester first produced a new edition of *Johnson's English Dictionary* in 1828 before publishing his own *Comprehensive Pronouncing and Explanatory Dictionary of the English Language* in 1830. The latter resulted in a bitter rivalry with Noah WEBSTER, who accused Worcester of plagiarism. Worcester responded with *A Gross Literary Fraud Exposed* (1853) and another edition of his dictionary. The "War of the Dictionaries" was protracted and remained unresolved until scholars working on Webster's behalf had the last word after both men had died. During his lifetime, though, Worcester's conservative approach to the English language was preferred by the literati, and his *Dictionary of the English Language* (1860), the first illustrated dictionary, was considered a masterwork.

Sources

Micklethwait, David. *Noah Webster and the American Dictionary.* Jefferson, N.C.: McFarland, 2000.

Wright, Frances (1795–1852) *reformer, editor*

Born in Scotland, Fanny Wright toured the United States several times before settling there in 1829. From 1818 to 1820 she toured the country with a production of her play, *Altorf* (1819), about Swiss freedom fighters, and carried out the fact-gathering missions that resulted in *Views of Society and Manners in America* (1821). In 1824 she accompanied the Marquis de Lafayette (1757–1834) on his triumphal tour of America, in the course of which Wright met both Thomas Jefferson (1743–1826) and James Madison (1751–1836). The two former presidents encouraged Wright's efforts to gradually emancipate slaves through the foundation in 1825 of the Tennessee Nashoba Community, an experiment in communal living that lasted for three years, until Wright grew ill and had to leave. From 1828 to 1829, Wright coedited the liberal periodicals *New Harmony Gazette* and *Free Enquirer* with the social reformer Robert Dale Owen (1801–77). Even after she permanently settled in the United States, she continued to tour, giving public lectures on the redistribution of wealth, the errors of orthodox religion, the need for free public education, ABOLITIONISM, and women's rights.

Sources

Bartlett, Elizabeth Ann. *Liberty, Equality, Sorority: The Origins and Interpretation of American Feminist Thought: Frances Wright, Sarah Grimke, and Margaret Fuller.* Brooklyn, N.Y.: Carlson Pub., 1994.

Kissel, Susan S. *In Common Cause: The "Conservative" Frances Trollope and the "Radical" Frances Wright.* Bowling Green, Ohio: Bowling Green State University Popular Press, 1993.

Morris, Celia. *Fanny Wright, Rebel in America.* Cambridge, Mass.: Harvard University Press, 1984.

Young, Brigham (1801–1877) *religious leader*

Born in Vermont like his predecessor, the Mormon founding father Joseph SMITH, Brigham Young spent his early adulthood working as a carpenter and painter in Mendon, New York, near the town of Palmyra, where Smith would publish *The Book of Mormon* in 1830. Two years later Young was baptized into the faith, becoming a preacher and leader of the growing church membership both in the United States and in England. When Smith was assassinated in 1844, Young took over as president of the church, leading its persecuted and fugitive members on a great migration to the valley of the Great Salt Lake in 1846–47. An effective leader, Young was constantly at loggerheads with the federal government over Mormon practices, but in 1850 President Millard Fillmore nonetheless made Young governor of the Utah Territory. Two years later Young announced the doctrine of polygamy and in 1871 was himself indicted for—although never convicted of—this offense; he is said to have had between 19 and 27 wives. Ultimately Young's efforts preserved Mormonism from suppression by the federal government and helped make his church into a thriving, prosperous community.

A colorful as well as a powerful figure, Young has figured in numerous literary works, among them Mark Twain's (Samuel CLEMENS) autobiographical narrative *Roughing It* (1872) and Samuel Bowles's travel diary *Across the Continent* (1868). In addition, Young's legend has been put to use in such fictional narratives as Harry Leon Wilson's (1867–1939) *The Lions of the Lord* (1903) and Vardis Fisher's (1895–1968) *Children of God* (1939).

Sources

Arrington, Leonard J. *Brigham Young: American Moses.* New York: Alfred A. Knopf, 1985.

Bringhurst, Newell G. *Brigham Young and the Expanding American Frontier.* Boston: Little, Brown, 1986.

Nibley, Hugh. *Tinkling Cymbals and Sounding Brass: The Art of Telling Tales about Joseph Smith and Brigham Young.* Salt Lake City, Utah: Deseret Book Co., 1991.

Youth's Companion, The periodical

This Boston weekly was founded in 1827 by Nathaniel Willis (1780–1870) and Asa Rand (1783–1871) as a secular magazine for children. In 1899 Daniel Ford Sharp purchased the magazine and, targeting adults as well as children, raised circulation from 4,000 to 500,000. Contributors ranged from Jack LONDON to Alfred Lord Tennyson (1809–1892). In 1929 *The Youth's Companion* merged with *The American Boy,* and in 1941, publication ceased altogether. In 1954, however, an anthology from *Youth's Companion* appeared.

Selected Bibliography

Bercovich, Sacvan, ed. *The Cambridge History of American Literature.* 2 vols. New York: Cambridge University Press, 1994.

Berthoff, Warner. *The Ferment of Realism: American Literature, 1884–1919.* New York: Cambridge University Press, 1981.

Buell, Lawrence. *Literary Transcendentalism: Style and Vision in the American Renaissance.* Ithaca, N.Y.: Cornell University Press, 1973.

———. *New England Literary Culture from Revolution through Renaissance.* New York: Cambridge University Press, 1986.

Coultrap-McQuin, Susan M. *Doing Literary Business: American Women Writers in the Nineteenth Century.* Chapel Hill: University of North Carolina Press, 1990.

Dauber, Kenneth. *The Idea of Authorship in America: Democratic Poetics from Franklin to Melville.* Madison: University of Wisconsin Press, 1990.

Davidson, Cathy. *Revolution and the Word: The Rise of the Novel in America.* New York: Oxford University Press, 1986.

Elliott, Emory. *The Columbia History of the American Novel: New Views.* New York: Columbia University Press, 1991.

Fryer, Judith. *The Faces of Eve: Women in the Nineteenth-Century American Novel.* New York: Oxford University Press, 1976.

Fussell, Edwin. *Frontier: American Literature and the American West.* Princeton, N.J.: Princeton University Press, 1965.

Gura, Philip F. *The Crossroads of American History and Literature.* University Park: Pennsylvania State University Press, 1996.

Hurley, Jennifer A., ed. *American Romanticism.* San Diego, Calif.: Greenhaven Press, 2000.

Loving, Jerome. *Lost in the Customhouse: Authorship in the American Renaissance.* Iowa City: University of Iowa Press, 1993.

McDowell, Deborah E., and Arnold Rampersad, eds. *Slavery and the Literary Imagination.* Baltimore: Johns Hopkins University Press, 1989.

Mordden, Ethan. *The American Theatre.* New York: Oxford University Press, 1981.

Ostrander, Gilman M. *Republic of Letters: The American Intellectual Community, 1776–1865.* Madison, Wis.: Madison House, 1999.

Parini, Jay, ed. *The Columbia History of American Poetry.* New York: Columbia University Press, 1993.

Powell, Timothy B., ed. *Beyond the Binary: Reconstructing Cultural Identity in a Multicultural Context.* New Brunswick, N.J.: Rutgers University Press, 1999.

Price, Kenneth M., and Susan Belasco Smith, eds. *Periodical Literature in Nineteenth-Century America.* Charlottesville: University Press of Virginia, 1995.

Rubin, Louis D. *The Edge of the Swamp: A Study in the Literature and Society of the Old South.* Baton Rouge: Louisiana State University Press, 1989.

Ruoff, Lavonne Brown, and Jerry W. Ward, eds. *Redefining American Literary History.* New York: Modern Language Association of America, 1990.

Samuels, Shirley, ed. *The Culture of Sentiment: Race, Gender, and Sentimentality in Nineteenth-Century America.* New York: Oxford University Press, 1992.

Sundquist, Eric. *To Wake the Nations: Race and the Making of American Literature.* Cambridge, Mass.: Harvard University Press, 1993.

Tallack, Douglas. *The Nineteenth-Century American Short Story: Language, Form, and Ideology.* New York: Routledge, 1993.

Tompkins, Jane. *Sensational Designs: The Cultural Work of American Fiction, 1790–1860.* New York: Oxford University Press, 1985.

Walker, Cheryl. *Indian Nation: Native American Literature and Nineteenth-Century Nationalisms.* Durham, N.C.: Duke University Press, 1997.

Weber, Ronald. *Hired Pens: Professional Writers in America's Golden Age of Print.* Athens: Ohio University Press, 1997.

INDEX

Page numbers in **boldface** indicate main articles.

A

B

D

E

F

G

H

I

J

K

L

M

N

Q

R

S

X

Y

List of Entries

Numbers indicate the volume in which an entry appears.

B

C

G

H

I

J

K

N

O

S

T

U

V

W

Y

Z